T0192864

Lecture Notes in Computer Science 13342

More information about this series at https://link.springer.com/bookseries/558

Klaus Miesenberger ·
Georgios Kouroupetroglou · Katerina Mavrou ·
Roberto Manduchi ·
Mario Covarrubias Rodriguez · Petr Penáz (Eds.)

Computers Helping People with Special Needs

18th International Conference, ICCHP-AAATE 2022
Lecco, Italy, July 11–15, 2022
Proceedings, Part II

Springer

Editors
Klaus Miesenberger
Johannes Kepler University
Linz, Austria

Katerina Mavrou
European University Cyprus
Engomi, Cyprus

Mario Covarrubias Rodriguez
Politecnico di Milano
Milan, Italy

Georgios Kouroupetroglou
National and Kapodistrian University of Athens
Athens, Greece

Roberto Manduchi
University of California at Santa Cruz
Santa Cruz, CA, USA

Petr Penáz
Masaryk University
Brno, Czech Republic

ISSN 0302-9743 ISSN 1611-3349 (electronic)
Lecture Notes in Computer Science
ISBN 978-3-031-08644-1 ISBN 978-3-031-08645-8 (eBook)
https://doi.org/10.1007/978-3-031-08645-8

This Springer imprint is published by the registered company Springer Nature Switzerland AG
The registered company address is: Gewerbestrasse 11, 6330 Cham, Switzerland

Preface

Welcome to the proceedings of ICCHP-AAATE 2022! We are delighted to present to you the proceedings of the Joint International Conference on Digital Inclusion, Assistive Technology, and Accessibility, a conference jointly organized by the International Conference on Computers Helping People with Special Needs (ICCHP) and the Association for the Advancement of Assistive Technology in Europe (AAATE).

Rapid technological deployments are showing the way to a world with no barriers and more flexibility, with personalized and adaptable technologies that will allow full participation of people with disabilities of all ages. We are in a position to hold high-level discussions on the topics of eHealth and eCare, eLearning and eInclusion, eDemocracy and eGovernment, eServices and social innovation, ambient and assisted active living, accessible traveling and tourism, user centered design for all, and many others.

Within this framework, and after the COVID-19 pandemic forced us to cancel AAATE 2021 and move ICCHP 2020 online, we decided to join efforts and propose a new venue for researchers and practitioners in assistive and access technologies, to showcase their work and mingle together. By merging our bi-annual meetings into a single event, we endeavored to provide a single platform for exchanging ideas, stimulating conversation, and facilitating networking. The result is a success in terms of the number of answers to the Call for Contributions and the broader and richer thematic scope: we received a total of 37 proposals for Special Thematic Sessions (STS). A total of 285 abstracts were submitted from which 112 were accepted for publication in these proceedings. More than 25 proposals for workshops, tutorials, seminars, posters, policy sessions, and a product/demonstrator presentation framed a rich and interesting program for discussion and exchange.

The ICCHP-AAATE joint conference was hosted during July 11–15, 2022, by the Politecnico di Milano at its campus in Lecco, by the picturesque Lake Como. Following the tradition of the ICCHP and AAATE biannual meetings, it was an event open to everyone and anyone interested in new and original ways to put technology at the service of people living with a disability. ICCHP-AAATE 2022 hosted presentations, panels, and forums devoted to the creation of tools, systems, and services that are accessible by design and that can level the playing field for a world where everyone can enjoy equal opportunities. By bringing the AAATE and ICCHP communities together, this joint conference explored the common threads linking policy, practice, research, and advocacy for people living with disabilities, working together towards a more equitable, just, and participatory future.

Participants contributed to the conference in multiple ways. The scientific contributions, which underwent a rigorous peer review process, are now available in two different publications:

- these Springer Lecture Notes in Computer Science (LNCS) volumes, which focus more on the development, engineering, and computer science perspective of assistive technology and accessibility, and

- the open access compendium Assistive Technology, Accessibility and (e)Inclusion, which focuses more on the policy, education, implementation, and social services perspective of the field.

Both publications are structured into 22 Special Thematic Sessions. The review process involved 137 experts from around the globe. Three to five independent reviews of each submitted abstract were assessed by one of the program chairs to allow a fair final decision on acceptance during a two-day decision meeting and to provide professional advice for the submissions of the camera-ready versions of papers for publication.

This three step review process sought to guarantee the high-quality of the ICCHP-AAATE publications. Additionally, ICCHP-AAATE invited selected sessions on topics of high interest to publish new and extended work in their domain in a Special Issue of AAATE's Technology and Disability Journal.

Contributions to the Inclusion Forum, which provided a space for discussion, collaborations, and participation of multiple stakeholders, were reviewed by the Program Committee and presented in the conference in different programs including workshops, tutorials, seminars, poster sessions, and policy sessions with panel discussions. It also included a space where participants showcased projects, products, and services. Inclusion Forum contributions are published in the Book of Abstracts, which collects short descriptions and abstracts of all contributions to the conference. In addition, students presented their ongoing research in the Young Researchers' Consortium.

We would like to thank all the members of the Scientific Committee, the Young Researchers Committee, the Inclusion Forum Committee, the Organization Committee, the additional paper reviewers, and the student volunteers who dedicated precious time and effort to the organization of this event.

Moreover, we want to thank all of the participants at the conference for furthering the mission of AAATE and ICCHP, based on the belief that technology can contribute to breaking barriers, empowering people, and enhancing equity and inclusion for people with all abilities.

July 2022

Klaus Miesenberger
Georgios Kouroupetroglou
Katerina Mavrou
Roberto Manduchi
Mario Covarrubias Rodriguez
Petr Penáz

Organization

Conference Chair

Mavrou, K.	European University Cyprus, Cyprus

Scientific Chair

Manduchi, R.	University of California, Santa Cruz, USA

Publication Committee

Covarrubias Rodriguez, M.	Politecnico di Milano, Italy
Kouroupetroglou, G.	University of Athens, Greece
Miesenberger, K.	University of Linz, Austria
Penáz, P.	University of Brno, Czech Republic

Scientific Committee Chairs

Archambault, D.	University of Paris 8, France
Buehler, C.	TU Dortmund, Germany
Coughlan. J.	Smith-Kettlewell Eye Research Institute, USA
Debevc, M.	University of Maribor, Slovenia
Fels, D.	Ryerson University, Canada
Graziosi, S	Politecnico di Milano, Italy
Kobayashi, M.	Tsukuba University of Technology, Japan
Suzuki, M.	Kyushu University, Japan
Weber, G.	TU Dresden, Germany
Zagler, W.	TETRAGON Braille Systems GmbH, Austria

Young Researchers Committee

Archambault, D.	University of Paris 8, France
Chen, W.	University of Bergen, Norway
Caruso, G.	Politecnico di Milano, Italy
Fels, D.	Ryerson University, Canada
Fitzpatrick, D.	National Disability Authority, Ireland
Kobayashi, M.	Tsukuba University of Technology, Japan
Morandell, M.	Smart In Life and Health University of Applied Sciences Tyrol, Austria

Pontelli, E.	New Mexico State University, USA
Prazak-Aram, B.	University of Vienna, Austria
Ruh, D.	Ruh Global IMPACT, USA
Weber, G.	TU Dresden, Germany
Zimmermann, G.	Stuttgart Media University, Germany

Inclusion Forum Committee

Ferrise, F.	Politecnico di Milano, Italy
Hoogerwerf, E. J.	AIAS Bologna Onlus, Italy
Puehretmair, F.	KI-I, Austria
Petz, A.	University of Linz, Austria
Tarabini M.	Politecnico di Milano, Italy

Scientific Committee

Abascal, J.	University of the Basque Country, Spain
Abbott, C.	King's College London, UK
Abu Doush, I.	American University of Kuwait, Kuwait
Andrich, R.	The Global Assistive Technology Information Network (EASTIN), Italy
Atkinson, M. T.	TPGi, USA
Augstein, M.	University of Applied Sciences Upper Austria, Austria
Azevedo, L.	Instituto Superior Tecnico, Portugal
Banes, D.	Dave Banes Access, UK
Bernareggi, C.	Universita degli Studi di Milano, Italy
Besio, S.	Università degli Studi di Bergamo, Italy
Boland, S.	Saint John of God Liffey Services, Ireland
Bonarini, A.	Politecnico di Milano, Italy
Bosse, I.	Technische Universitaet Dortmund, Germany
Bu, J.	Zhejiang University, China
Burger, D.	Inserm, France
Chamberlain, H.	Helen Chamberlain Consulting, USA
Chen, W.	Oslo Metropolitan University, Norway
Christensen, L. B.	Sensus, Denmark
Chutimaskul, W.	King Mongkut's University of Technology Thonburi, Thailand
Craddock, G.	Centre for Excellence in Universal Design, Ireland
Crombie, D.	Utrecht School of the Arts, The Netherlands
Dantas, P.	Universidade Federal do Rio Grande do Norte, Brazil
Darvishy, A.	ZHAW Zurich, Switzerland

Debeljak, M.	University of Ljubljana, Slovenia
DeRuyter, F.	Duke University Medical Centre, USA
Desideri, L.	AIAS Bologna Onlus, Italy
De Witte, L.	University of Sheffield, UK
Diaz del Campo, R.	Antarq Tecnosoluciones, Mexico
Draffan, E. A.	University of Southampton, UK
Dupire, J.	Cnam, France
Ebling, S.	University of Zurich, Switzerland
Encarnação, P.	Catolica Lisbon School of Business & Economics, Portugal
Engelen, J.	Katholieke Universiteit Leuven, Belgium
Fanucci, L.	University of Pisa, Italy
Ferrando, M.	K-veloce I+D+i, Spain
Gherardini, A	AIAS Bologna Onlus, Italy
Galinski, Ch.	InfoTerm, Austria
Gardner, J.	Oregon State University, USA
Gowran, R. J.	University of Limerick, Ireland
Hakkinen, M. T.	Educational Testing Service, USA
Haselwandter, T.	University of Applied Sciences Upper Austria, Austria
Hemmingsson, H.	Stockholm University, Sweden
Hill, K.	University of Pittsburgh, USA
Hocckner, K.	Hilfgemeinschaft der Blinden und Sehschwachen, Austria
Holloway, C.	University College London, UK
Inoue, T.	National Rehabilitation Center for Persons with Disabilities, Japan
Iversen, C. M.	U.S. Department of State (retired), USA
Jaskova, L.	Comenius University of Bratislava, Slovak Republic
Jitngernmadan, P.	Burapha University, Thailand
Kacorri, H.	University of Maryland, USA
Kanto-Ronkanen, A.	Kuopio University Hospital, Finland
Kiswarday, V.	University of Primorska, Slovenia
Koumpis, A.	University of Passau, Germany
Kozuh, I.	University of Maribor, Slovenia
Kueng, J.	Johannes Kepler University Linz, Austria
Kunz, A.	ETH Zurich, Switzerland
Layton, N.	ARATA, Australia
Leader, G.	National University of Ireland Galway, Ireland
Leblois, A.	G3ict, USA
Lee, S.	W3C WAI, UK

Leporini, B.	Italian National Research Council (CNR), Italy
Lewis, C.	University of Colorado at Boulder, USA
Lhotska, L.	Czech Technical University in Prague, Czech Republic
Malavasi, M.	AIAS Bologna Onlus, Italy
Mattia, D.	Fondazione Santa Lucia, Italy
McDonald, J.	DePaul University, USA
Mirri, S.	University of Bologna, Italy
Mohamad, Y.	Fraunhofer Institute for Applied Information Technology, Germany
Mrochen, I.	University of Silesia in Katowice, Poland
Muratet, M.	INSHEA, France
Nussbaum, G.	KI-I, Austria
Ono, T.	Tsukuba University of Technology, Japan
Oswal, S.	University of Washington, USA
Paciello, M.	WebAble, USA
Panek, P.	Vienna University of Technology, Austria
Paredes, H.	University of Tras-os-Montes e Alto Douro, Portugal
Petrie, H.	University of York, UK
Pissaloux, E.	University of Rouen Normandy, France
Rassmus-Groehn, K.	Lund University, Sweden
Raynal, M.	University of Toulouse, France
Rea, F.	Italian Institute of Technology, Italy
Scherer, M.	The Institute for Matching Person & Technology, Inc., USA
Seeman, L.	Athena ICT, Israel
Sik Lányi, C.	University of Pannonia, Hungary
Simsik, D.	University of Kosice, Slovakia
Slavik, P.	Czech Technical University in Prague, Czech Republic
Sloan, D.	TPGi, UK
Starcic, A.	University of Ljubljana, Slovenia
Stephanidis, C.	University of Crete and FORTH-ICS, Greece
Stiefelhagen, R.	Karlsruhe Institute of Technology, Germany
Stoeger, B.	University of Linz, Austria
Takahashi, Y.	Toyo University, Japan
Teixeira, A.	Universidade de Aveiro, Portugal
Teshima, Y.	Chiba Institute of Technology, Japan
Tjoa, A. M.	Technical University of Vienna, Austria
Truck, I.	University of Paris 8, France
Velleman, E.	The Accessibility Foundation, The Netherlands

Vigo, M.	University of Manchester, UK
Vigouroux, N.	IRIT Toulouse, France
Wagner, G.	University of Applied Sciences Upper Austria, Austria
Wada, C.	Kyushu Institute of Technology, Japan
Waszkielwicz, A.	Foundation for Persons with Disabilities (FRONia), Poland
Watanabe, T.	University of Niigata, Japan
Weber, H.	University of Kaiserslautern, Germany
White, Jason J.	Educational Testing Service, USA
Wolfe, R.	DePaul University, USA
Yamaguchi, K.	Nihon University, Japan
Yeliz, Y.	Middle East Technical University, Cyprus
Zapf, S.	Rocky Mountain University, USA

Organization Committee

Ayala Castillo, C.	Politecnico di Milano, Campo Territoriale di Lecco, Italy
Bieber, R.	Austrian Computer Society, Austria
Brunetti, V.	Politecnico di Milano, Campo Territoriale di Lecco, Italy
Bukovský, T.	Masaryk University, Czech Republic
Caruso, G.	Politecnico di Milano, Campo Territoriale di Lecco, Italy
Cincibus, Z.	Masaryk University, Czech Republic
Covarrubias Rodriguez, M.	Politecnico di Milano, Campo Territoriale di Lecco, Italy
Feichtenschlager, P.	Johannes Kepler University Linz, Austria
Ferrise, F.	Politecnico di Milano, Campo Territoriale di Lecco, Italy
Graziosi, S.	Politecnico di Milano, Campo Territoriale di Lecco, Italy
Hoogerwerf, E.	AAATE, Italy
Letocha, J.	Masaryk University, Czech Republic
Lobnig, S.	AAATE, Italy
Miesenberger, K.	Johannes Kepler University Linz, Austria
Murillo Morales, T.	Johannes Kepler University Linz, Austria
Ondra, S.	Masaryk University, Czech Republic
Pavlíček, R.	Masaryk University, Czech Republic
Peňáz, P.	Masaryk University, Czech Republic
Perego, P.	Politecnico di Milano, Campo Territoriale di Lecco, Italy

ICCHP Roland Wagner Award Committee

Acknowledgements. Once again we thank all those who helped in putting ICCHP-AAATE in place and thereby supporting the AT field and a better quality of life for people with disabilities. Special thanks go to all our supporters and sponsors, displayed at https://www.icchp.org/sponsors-22.

Contents – Part II

Internet of Things: Services and Applications for People with Disabilities and Elderly Persons

Technologies for Inclusion and Participation at Work and in Everyday Activities

ICT to Support Inclusive Education - Universal Learning Design (ULD)

Design for Assistive Technologies and Rehabilitation

Contents – Part I

Art Karshmer Lectures in Access to Mathematics, Science and Engineering

Haptic and Digital Access to Art and Artefacts

Accessibility of Co-located Meetings

Interactions for Text Input and Alternative Pointing

Cognitive Disabilities and Accessibility

Digital Accessibility: Readability and Understandability

Digital Accessibility: Readability and Understandability

Introduction to the Special Thematic Session

Helen Petrie[1(✉)], Klaus Höckner[2], and Werner Rosenberger[2]

[1] University of York, York YO10 5GH, UK
helen.petrie@york.ac.uk

[2] Hilfsgemeinschaft der Blinden und Sehschwachen Österreichs, 1200 Vienna, Austria
{hoeckner,rosenberger}@hilfsgemeinschaft.at

Digital accessibility is now a very diverse topic, covering many user groups and many differing devices and situations, as can be seen from the nine papers presented in this Special Thematic Session (STS). Twenty years ago, this session would probably have been called "Web accessibility" and would have been largely concentrated on issues around the accessibility of websites. The Web Accessibility Initiative (WAI) [10] and the Web Content Accessibility Guidelines [11] were then relatively new and researchers and practitioners were grappling with the complex issues of making the Web accessible and usable by the widest possible range of people.

Sadly, twenty years later we are still grappling with issues of web accessibility, although great improvements have been made. The WAI and many other organizations, both public and private, have done much to publicise the important issues around the accessibility of website. In particular, we now have the European Accessibility Act [3] which covers all kinds of digital systems, not only computers, but also electronic kiosk systems (Automatic Teller Machines, ticketing and check-in systems), smartphones and e-books.

Our STS reflects that new diversity, in that we start with two papers which address broad website accessibility issues [2, 12] (although these could also be applied to other digital systems as well) and we then move on to a number of more specific aspects of web and digital accessibility, and finally look at two particular technologies providing new digital access for people who are blind and visually disabled.

Egger et al. [2] investigate the effectiveness of overlay tools as a method for making websites accessible. This is a very important topic to research, as many people are promoting overlay tools as a quick and easy route to website accessibility. But do they really work? Egger et al. investigate a number of tools and find that although they do solve some problems, an understanding of web accessibility issues is still needed to make a website accessible, so they may not be worth the effort of using.

Yoldi [12] investigates the effect of the layout of a page or screen on accessibility. This is a very interesting and important aspect of accessibility, which thus far has received very little investigation. It reminds us that accessibility should not just be conceptualized at the level of individual components of a digital system, but how those components are put together to create a holistic experience for users. This can affect both usability and accessibility.

K. Miesenberger et al. (Eds.): ICCHP-AAATE 2022, LNCS 13342, pp. 3–5, 2022.
https://doi.org/10.1007/978-3-031-08645-8_1

McCall and Chagnon [5] consider one specific element of web and digital accessibility which clearly needs more work, that of providing descriptions of graphics, colloquially known as "alt text" after the attribute of the HTML image element which provides the description. Currently only some screen readers pick up the descriptions provided in the alt text attribute. But as McCall and Chagnon note, such descriptions could be useful to many more users. There are also many limitations of the current alt text implementation, and the authors set out an excellent set of proposals for its revision. On a similar theme, Schneider et al. [9] consider audio description of video material, which is becoming more and more common on websites, on dedicated channels such as YouTube and TikTok, and on individuals' social media streams. They propose a very useful three level classification of the level of detail in audio description to guide those who produce these descriptions.

A series of papers investigates another specific aspect of digital accessibility, that of authentication, proving who you are in order to access your online accounts. People now have many accounts and consequently many passwords to remember (or not) and other authentication systems to use. So not only should password systems be fully accessible, but also other authentication and associated systems such as CAPTCHAs (Completely Automated Public Turing Test to Tell Computers and Humans Apart), password managers, QR (Quick Response) codes, and biometric authentication systems such as fingerprint, and face recognition. All of these types of systems are becoming more commonly used. Schmeelk and Petrie [8] investigate the problems that visually disabled people have in this area, Kelly and Petrie [4] investigate problems that people with dyslexia have, and Petrie, Merdenyan and Xie [6] investigate problems that older people in both China and the United Kingdom have. All three papers highlight the fact that there are numerous issues to be solved on this topic. This is in spite of considerable research, particularly on CAPTCHAs for visually disabled people, which are still causing problems.

Ramôa [7] considers the emerging technology of two-dimensional tactile displays which are able to present graphics to visually disabled people. This technology has been discussed for a long time, but is now maturing into commercial products. The paper compares a number of products in terms of the user interface and highlights strengths and weaknesses. In particular, the paper highlights the next challenge for this technology, which is to integrate audio information with the tactile information. Tactile information alone is often hard for visually disabled people to interpret, so an effective audio-tactile device for graphics would be a great innovation for this user group.

Finally, Desvergnes [1] considers a very innovative technology, that of visual neuroprostheses to restore, or at least partially restore, vision to people with severe visual disabilities. Currently, one of the problems is the limited resolution of the systems. This paper proposes that providing different renderings of the information and allowing a user to switch between them significantly increases their understanding of the environment.

References

1. Desvergnes, J.: Does switching between different renderings allow blind people with visual neuroprostheses to better perceive the environment?. In: Petz, A., Hoogerwerf, E.-J., Mavrou, K. (eds.) Assistive Technology, Accessibility and (e)Inclusion, ICCHP-AAATE 2022 Open Access Compendium, accepted for publication; online: https://www.icchp-aaate.org. Johannes Kepler University Linz, Austria
2. Egger, N., Zimmermann, G., Strobbe, C.: Overlay tools as a support for accessible websites – possibilities and limitations, In: Miesenberger, K., Kouroupetroglou, G., Mavrou, K., Manduchi, R., Covarrubias Rodriguez, M., Penaz, P. (eds.) Computers Helping People with Special Needs, LNCS 0000, p, 000, Springer International Publishing, Cham (2022)
3. European Union: European Accessibility Act. https://eur-lex.europa.eu/legal-content/EN/TXT/?uri=CELEX%3A32019L0882
4. Kelly, N., Petrie, H.: Digital authentication and dyslexia: a survey of the problems and needs of dyslexic people. In: Miesenberger, K., Kouroupetroglu, G., Mavrou, K., Manduchi, R., Covarrubias Rodriguez, M., Penaz, P. (eds.) Computers Helping People with Special Needs, LNCS 0000, p. 000. Springer International Publishing, Cham (2022)
5. McCall, K., Chagnon, B.: Rethinking Alt text to improve its effectiveness. In: Miesenberger, K., Kouroupetroglou, G., Mavrou, K., Manduchi, R., Covarrubias Rodriguez, M., Penaz, P. (eds.) Computers Helping People with Special Needs, LNCS 0000, p. 000. Springer International Publishing, Cham (2022)
6. Petrie, H., Merdenyan, B., Xie, C.: Password challenges for older people in China and the United Kingdom. In: Miesenberger, K., Kouroupetroglou, G., Mavrou, K., Manduchi, R., Covarrubias Rodriguez, M., Penaz, P. (eds) Computers Helping People with Special Needs, LNCS 0000, p. 000. Springer International Publishing, Cham (2022)
7. Ramôa, G.: Classification of 2D refreshable tactile user interfaces. In: Petz, A., Hoogerwerf, E.-J., Mavrou, K. (eds.) Assistive Technology, Accessibility and (e)Inclusion, ICCHP-AAATE 2022 Open Access Compendium, accepted for publication; online: https://www.icchp-aaate.org. Johannes Kepler University Linz, Austria
8. Schmeelk, S., Petrie, H.: Digital authentication and security for visually disabled people: initial results of an online survey. In: Miesenberger, K., Kouroupetroglou, G., Mavrou, K., Manduchi, R., Covarrubias Rodriguez, M., Penaz, P. (eds.) Computers Helping People with Special Needs, LNCS 0000, p 000. Springer International Publishing, Cham (2022)
9. Schneider, R., Ableitner, T., Zimmermann, G.: Layered audio descriptions for videos, In: Miesenberger, K., Kouroupetroglou, G., Mavrou, K., Manduchi, R., Covarrubias Rodriguez, M., Penaz, P. (eds.) Computers Helping People with Special Needs, LNCS 0000, p. 000. Springer International Publishing, Cham (2022)
10. World Wide Web Consortium: Web Accessibility Initiative. https://www.w3.org/WAI/
11. World Wide Web Consortium: Web Content Accessibility Guidelines. https://www.w3.org/WAI/standards-guidelines/wcag/
12. Yoldi, B.: Impact of the layout on web comprehension. In: Petz, A., Hoogerwerf, E.-J., Mavrou, K. (eds.) Assistive Technology, Accessibility and (e)Inclusion, ICCHP-AAATE 2022 Open Access Compendium, accepted for publication; online: https://www.icchp-aaate.org. Johannes Kepler University Linz, Austria

Overlay Tools as a Support for Accessible Websites – Possibilities and Limitations

Niklas Egger(✉), Gottfried Zimmermann, and Christophe Strobbe

Hochschule der Medien, Stuttgart, Germany
egger@hdm-stuttgart.de

Abstract. Current laws and directives such as the Americans with Disabilities Act and the European Union's Directive 2016/2102 aim to support people with disabilities. At the same time, they also represent a challenge for many website owners who have to comply with these legal requirements. Providers of so-called overlay tools offer, among other things, fully automated solutions which, according to their own statements, can be installed within a few minutes and subsequently improve the website in such a way that it is accessible and compliant with the laws and standards. This raises two questions. First, to what extent overlay tools provide real accessibility improvements? And second, is it possible to identify possibilities and limitations and therefore suggest potential improvements. Based on a comparison of the features of nine existing tools, three were selected for closer examination (accessiBe, EqualWeb and UserWay). In addition, a comparative study of these providers was conducted. For this purpose, a total of seven metrics were defined, which are based on the information and promises of the providers as well as on the requirements of the Web Content Accessibility Guidelines 2.1. To validate the changes made by the overlay tools, the adaptations were evaluated using 29 of the 92 test steps of the BIK BITV-Test. Moreover, the site owner's perspective was taken into account and the corresponding features and functions were analyzed and evaluated within four metrics. However, user tests are not part of this work. Significant differences between the overlay tools can be seen primarily in the adjustments to the actual website. In comparison, accessiBe corrects more failures and barriers for blind users and users who use the keyboard navigation and thus also achieves the best result in the overall score. Despite these improvements, full compliance is clearly not possible. However, both theoretical and concrete opportunities for improvement were identified.

Keywords: Accessibility (for disabled) · Overlay tool · Comparative study

1 Introduction

Accessibility and the inclusion of people with disabilities is becoming more important, both for demographic and for legal reasons. For one, the number of people in Germany aged 67+ will increase by up to 22% by 2035, and for another, severe disabilities due to illness are becoming more prevalent, especially in old age [1, 2]. Legislative pressure has also been increasing. The European Union's Web Accessibility Directive (Directive

K. Miesenberger et al. (Eds.): ICCHP-AAATE 2022, LNCS 13342, pp. 6–17, 2022.
https://doi.org/10.1007/978-3-031-08645-8_2

2016/2102) required all member states to enact legislation to ensure the accessibility of websites and mobile applications of public sector bodies [3]. In addition, the European Accessibility Act is intended to ensure more accessibility for information and communication technologies (ICT) in the near future [4]. That litigation can occur is demonstrated by the increasing number of Americans with Disabilities Act (ADA) Title III lawsuits which increased from 2722 in 2013 to 11053 in 2019 [5].

While these legal requirements are intended to support people with disabilities, they present new challenges for businesses. With regard to websites and mobile apps, there are a variety of possible reasons why businesses do not make them accessible. A lack of personnel with the necessary knowledge, the cost factor, and a lack of time in development can be listed as potential examples. However, there are providers, such as accessiBe [6], which offer fully automated solutions that, according to their own statements, can be installed quickly and easily and then improve the customer's website or even make it fully compliant with these legal requirements.

Within the accessibility community, these solutions are referred to as overlay tools and are highly criticized. For example, over 600 accessibility experts, lawyers, and contributors to accessible web content guidelines have signed the statement that these overlay tools should be removed [7]. Research such as that by Groves [8] and Faulkner [9] already demonstrates limitations of these technologies. Nonetheless, no detailed analysis of overlay tools has been conducted within a scientific framework up to this point. Due to this fact, the goal of this work is to examine whether and to what extent overlay tools improve the accessibility of a website. For this purpose, a selection of current providers is presented and a more detailed analysis of accessiBe, EqualWeb and UserWay is performed. While within a quantitative comparison these overlay tools are evaluated and therefore ranked, the primary goal is to show limitations and possibilities of these technologies and to derive possible improvements based on these findings.

2 Methods

Both quantitative and qualitative methods are used to answer the research question. In the following, these are explained as well as the basic procedure.

As already described in the introduction, no scientific publications on overlay tools could be identified during the literature search. For this reason, the information regarding overlay tools is generally based on various articles, blog entries and other Internet sources. Based on these findings, a search was conducted using the Google search engine, whereby the essential aspects of an overlay tool were selected as search terms in order to elicit further providers that are not listed in the articles.

As a result of this research, accessiBe, EqualWeb and UserWay were selected for a detailed analysis and comparison as they meet the requirements that will be explained in the course of the paper. To test the overlay tools, the website of the Unithekle student bar (https://www.unithekle.de/) was cloned and a test environment was created based on this replication for each overlay tool. This website was chosen because it has multiple as well as different failures[1] and barriers. The Barrierefreie-Informationstechnik-Verordnung

[1] For the purposes of this paper, a "failure" is an accessibility issue that does not meet the requirements of WCAG 2.1 and EN 301 549.

(BITV) test of the 'barrierefrei informieren und kommunizieren' (BIK) project was applied for testing. The BIK BITV-Test was used, as it is the established test procedure for this purpose in Germany. In addition, more failures were added manually to obtain a broader range of findings through further testing steps. In total, 29 of 92 test steps could be taken into account.

Seven metrics were defined for the evaluation and comparison of the overlay tools, which take the user's and the site owner's point of view into account. The basis for the evaluation metrics were the promises of the providers regarding the compliance of their solutions as well as the requirements of the Web Content Accessibility Guidelines (WCAG) 2.1. Furthermore, they were weighted in a survey of 17 participants.

With regard to the failures and barriers of the test website, the changes made by the overlay tools, if any, are evaluated using the BIK-BITV-Test. A five-stage evaluation scheme is also used for the aspects of the site owner metrics in order to highlight deficiencies more clearly than is possible in the context of a binary evaluation.

3 BIK BITV-Test

With the directive 2016/2102, the European Parliament and the European Council obligate the member states to comply with EN 301 549 for public bodies [3]. In the case of Germany, this directive is realized by the Barrierefreie-Informationstechnik-Verordnung (BITV) 2.0 [10]. The BIK BITV-Test is based on BITV 2.0 and thus the EN 301 549 requirements [11]. These requirements are divided up into 92 test steps within the test procedure [12]. In contrast to WCAG, the BIK BITV-Test does not evaluate in a binary way. A five-step evaluation scheme is used [13]. For this work, no testing agency is commissioned to apply the procedure, but the BITV self-assessment [14] is used, since the essential information is publicly available. The BIK BITV-Test can therefore be performed independently.

4 Overlay Tools

This chapter includes a definition of what exactly overlay tools are in the context of accessibility for websites and introduces nine different providers of them.

4.1 Definition

On the Overlay Fact Sheet website [7], Groves [15] defines overlay tools as a collective term for technologies that have the basic goal of improving the accessibility of a website. According to him, in most cases, third-party JavaScript code is implemented on the website for this purpose. Beyond this implementation, the source code does not need to be changed, since the overlay with the changes can be seen as an additional layer between the user and the source code [16]. However, as Kornmeier [17] notes, it is important to distinguish between customer- and website-specific overlays and overlays that work on any page according to the provider's claims. The paper and the following providers refer to the latter.

4.2 Current Providers

To ensure an accurate and up-to-date selection of overlay tool providers, an Internet search was conducted. For this purpose, a search was performed with the Google search engine and the results of the first ten pages were compared with the knowledge and definition of the previous chapters. Search terms such as "wcag automatische Lösung" (in English: wcag automatic solution), "overlay tools" or "website automatic accessible" were used. In addition, the providers named on the Overlay Fact Sheet website are taken into account [7]. The following selection is not intended as an exhaustive list of providers. Moreover, only a few essential features are mentioned. Furthermore, this information is based exclusively on the providers' own statements:

- accessiBe offers a fully automated solution for, among other things, ADA and WCAG 2.1 compliance [6].
- AudioEye automatically fixes up to 80% of all failures on the website [18].
- DIGIaccess is a provider from Germany and offers a fully automated solution as well [19].
- EqualWeb promises up to 95 percent compliance with its automated solution. In addition, the site owner can subsequently adjust the alternative texts of images [20].
- FACIL'iti states that it improves compliance and offers cross-website profiles, which are automatically adopted on every website with the tool installed [21].
- MaxAccess offers a fully automated solution as well as WCAG training videos and reports [22].
- Purple-Lens is a plugin for WordPress that scans the site for failures and afterwards supports the site owner with further tools to fix them [23].
- UserWay offers an automated solution. In addition, several changes can be adjusted manually by the site owner afterwards. According to its own statements, it is installed on over 1.4 million websites [24].
- User1st offers among other solutions also "uRemediate", which is supposed to automatically improve the accessibility of a page [25].

5 Parameters of the Comparative Study and Analysis

Within the scope of this chapter, all important aspects and factors are mentioned, which serve as the basis for the comparison and analysis of the selected overlay tools.

5.1 Overlay Tools Selection

Decisive for the selection of accessiBe, EqualWeb and UserWay for the study are the following criteria, all of which the overlay tools must meet:

- Provider promises EN 301 549 and thus also WCAG 2.1 (AA) compliance. Consequently, the BIK BITV-Test can be applied.
- The overlay tool supports the German language, since it is tested on a German website.

- The tool is not limited to a Content Mangamenet System (CMS) and can therefore be implemented on a plain HTML, CSS and JavaScript website. This ensures that it is possible to continue to incorporate failures without restrictions.
- The overlay tool is compatible with a password-protected website.

The three overlay tools meet these requirements. Therefore, for testing, the "Small Business Website" option of UserWay, "Standard" option of accessiBe and the "Small" option of EqualWeb's "Auto Accessibility Plan" were subscribed.

5.2 Test Environment

Three replicas of the Unithekle student bar website, i.e., one per overlay tool, were used as a test environment. An examination of the original Unithekle website using the BIK BITV-Test revealed several failures and barriers that can be used to test the overlay tools. Additional failures were added to the website to enable testing on a wider range of accessibility requirements. In order not to infringe the copyright of the website, the hosted copies are protected with a password. For hosting, the Netlify (https://www.netlify.com/) platform is used. The conditions of the BIK BITV-Test are also taken into account during the examination of the overlay tools on the test environment [26]. These include: operating system (Windows 10), browser (latest Mozilla Firefox version), cookies are accepted and popups and auto-playing audio are allowed. JavaScript is activated. In the case of accessiBe and UserWay, the tools are updated automatically. This is not the case with EqualWeb, so the version used is the one that was current at the start of this study, 3.0.3.

5.3 Evaluation Metrics

The different metrics used to evaluate the three overlay tools are based on both the promises of the providers and the requirements of WCAG 2.1. Likewise, the point of view of the site owner is taken into account within four metrics. The evaluation metrics are: compliance (cumulative), compliance (holistic), showstopper, implementation, feedback, configurability of the toolbar[2], and training. The metrics are explained in more detail in the corresponding results chapters. Generally, the evaluation scheme of the BIK BITV-Test is applied for the evaluation of the compliance and the showstopper metric, which can be seen in Table 1. A score is assigned for each level, which can also be found in the table. Thus, the evaluation is always in a value range from 0% to 100%, the latter being the best possible result. This type of evaluation is also used for the aspects of the other metrics, insofar as they do not have countable values. If the latter is the case, then the highest value is assigned a 100% and the numbers of the other overlay tools are normalized in this respect. The result of a metric is the average of all evaluations of the examined aspects or test steps.

[2] All three overlay tools (accessiBe, EqualWeb and UserWay) offer a toolbar, which can be opened on the client's page by a button. There, options can be activated, for example to adjust the appearance of the page.

Table 1. BIK BITV-Test evaluation scheme and corresponding scoring.

BIK BITV-Test[3]	Non-conforming	Rather non-conforming	Partially conforming	Rather conforming	Conforming
Score	0%	25%	50%	75%	100%

To check whether and to what extent the individual metrics are significant, they were additionally weighted. For this purpose, a public webinar was held on the topic of overlay tools, in which accessiBe, EqualWeb and UserWay were also presented both theoretically and in practice. Following this, the individual metrics were presented with examples and explanations so that a better understanding could be ensured. 18 people participated in the subsequent survey, in which they could assign their personal weighting. As this was a public webinar, it cannot be guaranteed that only experts in this field weighted the metrics. The data from 17 participants were however considered valid and were normalized and averaged accordingly. The individual weightings are included in Table 2.

6 Results

Both EqualWeb and UserWay offer features to the site owner that allow them to make manual changes to the site. To take this into account, two results are given for the overall result and the metrics compliance (cumulative)/(holistic). Consequently, Table 2 includes the overall result for the automatic changes and Table 3 takes into account the potential manual adjustments. In summary, accessiBe achieves the best overall score of 43% for the automatic updates, and UserWay achieves the best overall score of 44%

Table 2. Results of the individual metrics as well as the overall result for all overlay tools.

Metric	Weighting	accessiBe	EqualWeb	UserWay
Compliance (cumulative)	15.78%	45%	33%	27%
Compliance (holistic)	19.22%	45%	30%	27%
Showstopper	17.94%	31%	0%	19%
Implementation	12.28%	100%	75%	86%
Feedback	10.05%	0%	38%	25%
Configurability of the toolbar	12.78%	74%	79%	83%
Training	11.91%	0%	25%	0%
Overall result		**≈43%**	**≈37%**	**≈37%**

[3] These are own translations, the original German terms are: "nicht erfüllt", "eher nicht erfüllt", "teilweise erfüllt", "eher erfüllt" and „erfüllt". In addition, the "eher erfüllt" (rather conforming) level also meets the requirements of WCAG 2.1 and EN 301 549.

Table 3. Overall results for all overlay tools taking into account the potential manual adjustments of the site owner for the metrics compliance (cumulative) and compliance (holistic).

Overlay tool	accessiBe	EqualWeb	UserWay
Overall result	≈43%	≈39%	≈44%

when the manual adjustments are taken into account. Table 3 also shows that EqualWeb achieves a better overall score of 39% with the manual adjustments. However, in this case they only make a difference of 2% to the overall score with the automatic changes. For the overall result of an overlay tool, the results of all metrics are multiplied by their respective weights and then summed.

The following subsections provide more information on the individual metrics and results.

6.1 Compliance (Cumulative)

Improving accessibility or complying with standards and guidelines is the basic goal of an overlay tool and the promise of the providers. Consequently, this is examined and tested in this work. The sub-division of compliance on two metrics is explained in the following chapter. In general, for this metric, the individual test steps are considered separately from each other. Within the scope of this metric, the overlay tools were examined on the basis of a total of 25 different test steps of the BIK BITV-Test and evaluated accordingly. It should be noted that for 'cumulative compliance', the failures, i.e., the code changes made by the overlay tools, are examined separately from the rest of the page. Thus, the second conformance requirement of WCAG 2.1 is not met [27]. Since the failures are scattered over several pages and the overlay tools offer multiple options in their toolbars it was not possible to take this into account within the scope of this study. Figure 1 shows that accessiBe automatically fixes the most failures. This is due to the fact that it detects more nonconforming components that were missing a matching ARIA attribute. For example, a table heading that did not use the appropriate HTML element will be supplemented with the correct role attribute. One problem that all three overlay tools have in common are the automatically added alternative texts for images. These are not accurate and mostly do not contain the core aspect of the image. UserWay and EqualWeb offer features for site owners to adjust these. However, in both cases guidance on writing appropriate text alternatives is not provided. The Aria Editor from UserWay can also be mentioned at this point, which can be used to subsequently give an element a role attribute, among other things. It is also taken into account in the manual adjustments in Fig. 1.

6.2 Compliance (Holistic)

According to the Web Content Accessibility Guidelines 2.1, alternative versions of a website that are more targeted to specific user groups are allowed. However, a fully compliant version of the site must be offered as well. [27].

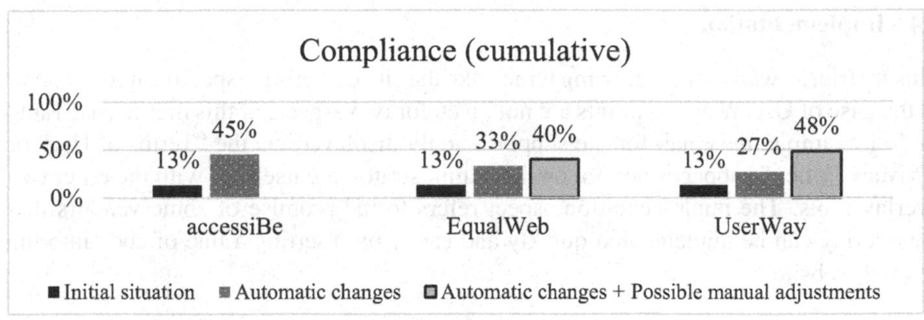

Fig. 1. Compliance (cumulative) results.

Based on this requirement, the test steps and therefore also the toolbar options of the overlay tools are considered holistically in this metric. All toolbar options with which the accessibility issues in compliance (cumulative) are fixed must be simultaneously activatable. In the case of accessiBe and UserWay, this is possible under the conditions of this work, which is why the result is identical to the compliance (cumulative) metric. EqualWeb cannot activate a feature simultaneously with the other options, which is why the corresponding test step is rated as "not conforming". EqualWeb's result for this metric is 30% with the automatic changes and 36% considering the manual adjustments.

6.3 Showstopper

Under the fifth conformance requirement, WCAG 2.1 [27] highlights the four success criteria from Table 4. Failure to meet these criteria can affect the overall use of the site and, in the worst case, lead to an epileptic seizure for certain users [28]. In the case of "Three Flashes or Below Threshold", all three overlay tools offer an option to stop flashing content. However, after loading the page, the flashing is not automatically stopped immediately without activating the option. Thus, they do not meet the WCAG requirement [28].

Table 4. Showstopper metric summary and result.

WCAG 2.1 success criteria	Initial situation	accessiBe	EqualWeb	UserWay
Audio Control	0%	25%	0%	75%
No Keyboard Trap	0%	100%	0%	0%
Three Flashes or Below Threshold	0%	0%	0%	0%
Pause, Stop, Hide	0%	0%	0%	0%
Result	0%	**≈31%**	**=0%**	**≈19%**

6.4 Implementation

This metric, as well as the following three, take the site owner's perspective into account. In the case of UserWay, full points are not given for two aspects of this metric (see Table 5). For example, the email for the support is only displayed via the "Terms of Use" or "Privacy Policy" subpages but not on the administrator site itself, as with the other two overlay tools. The implementation aspect refers to the promise of some vendors that the overlay can be implemented quickly and easily by inserting a line of code into the desired website.

Table 5. Implementation metric summary and result.

Aspect	accessiBe	EqualWeb	UserWay
One code line implementation	100%	100%	100%
Installation guides	100%	100%	75%
Automatic updates	100%	0%	100%
Support contact options	100%	100%	75%
Result	**=100%**	**=75%**	**≈86%**

6.5 Feedback

The aspects presented in Table 6 are the only information offered by the overlay tools. Further feedback or the like could not be identified.

Table 6. Feedback metric summary and result.

Aspect	accessiBe	EqualWeb	UserWay
Information about automatic changes	0%	0%	50%
Usage statistics	0%	75%	0%
Result	**=0%**	**≈38%**	**=25%**

6.6 Configurability of the Toolbar

Within this metric, UserWay achieves the best result with 83% , which is due to the fact that it is the only overlay tool that automatically applies the adjustments (Table 7).

Table 7. Configurability of the toolbar metric summary and result. The number before the equal sign refers to the actual number of options while the number after the equal sign represents the normalized number in percent.

Aspect	accessiBe	EqualWeb	UserWay
Color customizable	100%	100%	100%
Adjustable language	100%	100%	100%
Changes automatically applied	0%	0%	100%
Button icons	$10 \approx 71\%$	$14 = 100\%$	$4 \approx 29\%$
Button sizes	$3 = 100\%$	$3 = 100\%$	$2 \approx 67\%$
Button positions	$6 = 75\%$	$6 = 75\%$	$8 = 100\%$
Result	**≈74%**	**≈79%**	**≈83%**

6.7 Training

EqualWeb offers a document that explains how to create accessible videos, PDF and Word files. This 20-page document lists information about accessible websites in bullet points on one page. Moreover, some information is incorrect and no more specific details about WCAG 2.1 requirements are described. Based on these factors, EqualWeb is given a score of 25%.

7 Discussion

Taking potential manual adjustments into account, UserWay achieves the best overall rating of 44%. However, several assumptions are made for this rating. First, it is assumed that the site owner knows where the failure is and why it is one, because in many cases UserWay itself does not recognize the issues. Furthermore, he needs to know how to fix this failure, which requires in-depth WCAG 2.1 knowledge. Consequently, it can be questioned why a site owner with such knowledge would use an overlay tool instead of fixing the errors directly in the source code. As the feedback and training metrics show, the site owner does not have access to essential information or learning support. For these reasons, the overall score for automatic changes is chosen as the final score, which is why accessiBe achieves the best result with 43%. All three tools score primarily by the fact that they are easy to implement and offer several options for configuring the toolbar. From the provider's point of view, it is understandable that no feedback or training is offered in order not to lose customers in the long term. However, EqualWeb and UserWay miss out on potentially better results in terms of WCAG 2.1 and EN 301 549 compliance.

8 Limitations and Possible Future Work

The results have shown, among other things, that overlay tools are limited in their ability to generate appropriate text alternatives for images. At the same time, this shows the potential of manual adjustments. This requires that site owners are taught how to do so in a correct way. Another concrete suggestion for improvement is to automatically stop flashing content.

There are several limitations to this study itself. First, only one website was used for testing. As a consequence, less than one third of all BIK BITV-Test steps were covered. In addition, mobile view was not addressed. Moreover, these results are based on a snapshot of the current state of overlay tools. Since these technologies are continuously being developed further, it is possible that the findings of this study will no longer be valid in the future. At the same time, the results may differ in the context of other sites and initial situations.

Nevertheless, this work has laid a first foundation for further research on this topic. Thus, the limitations of this work and other aspects such as user tests can be used for future work. Compatibility between overlay tools and assistive technologies can also be mentioned as an example in this regard. In general, these studies do not have to be limited to accessiBe, EqualWeb and UserWay. As shown in this paper, there are other providers with different approaches. Furthermore, the evaluation metrics of this work can be used for this purpose or replaced by others.

9 Conclusion

In summary, overlay tools can only be used as support for accessible websites to a limited extent. In particular, accessiBe has shown several improvements on the actual website in the context of this study, but full compliance with WCAG 2.1 (AA) and EN 301 549 could definitely not be achieved. The overlay tool currently still has too many limitations for this. If the statements of the providers are correct, their overlay tool solutions are already being used on thousands of websites. It is possible that this will make them a permanent part of web content accessibility in the future. In this case, however, providers should continue to develop their technologies with current WCAG and legal requirements in mind, as well as involve and teach the site owner to fix errors that are not covered by the automated solutions. Specifically, providers should be more open in communicating the limitations of their technologies.

References

1. Statistisches Bundesamt: 7,9 Millionen schwerbehinderte Menschen leben in Deutschland (2020). https://www.destatis.de/DE/Presse/Pressemitteilungen/2020/06/PD20_230_227.html. Accessed 30 Oct 2021
2. Statistisches Bundesamt: Bis 2035 wird die Zahl der Menschen ab 67 Jahre um 22% steigen (2021). https://www.destatis.de/DE/Presse/Pressemitteilungen/2021/09/PD21_459_12411.html. Accessed 30 Oct 2021
3. The European Parliament and the Council of the European Union: Directive (EU) 2016/2102 of the European Parliament and of the Council of 26 October 2016 on the accessibility of the websites and mobile applications of public sector bodies (Text with EEA relevance) (2016)
4. The European Parliament and the Council of the European Union: Directive (EU) 2019/882 of the European Parliament and of the Council of 17 April 2019 on the accessibility requirements for products and services (Text with EEA relevance) (2019)

5. Seyfarth Shaw LLP: 2019 Was Another Record-Breaking Year for Federal ADA Title III Lawsuits (2020). https://www.adatitleiii.com/2020/02/2019-was-another-record-breaking-year-for-federal-ada-title-iii-lawsuits/. Accessed 30 Oct 2021
6. accessible: https://accessibe.com/. Accessed 30 Oct 2021
7. Overlay Fact Sheet: Overlay Fact Sheet (2021). https://overlayfactsheet.com. Accessed 30 Oct 2021
8. Groves, K.: Sole reliance on accessiBe will not be sufficient in ensuring full and equal access to a website (2020). https://de.scribd.com/document/490740167/Exhibit-A-for-21-cv-00017. Accessed 30 Oct 2021
9. Faulkner, S.: Bolt-on Accessibility – 5 gears in reverse (2020). https://www.tpgi.com/bolt-on-accessibility-5-gears-in-reverse/. Accessed 30 Oct 2021
10. German federal ministry of labour and social affairs: Verordnung zur Schaffung barrierefreier Informationstechnik nach dem Behindertengleichstellungsgesetz (Barrierefreie¬Informationstechnik-Verordnung -BITV 2.0) (2019)
11. DIAS GmbH: Die BITV 2.0 – Was prüft der BITV-Test, was prüft er nicht?. https://www.bitvtest.de/bitv_test/das_testverfahren_im_detail/vertiefend/die_bitv_20_was_prueft_der_bitv_test_was_prueft_er_nicht.html. Accessed 30 Oct 2021
12. DIAS GmbH: Überarbeitung von Prüfschritten im Jahr 2021. https://www.bitvtest.de/bitv_test/das_testverfahren_im_detail/vertiefend/ueberarbeitung/2021.html. Accessed 30 Oct 2021
13. DIAS GmbH: Beschreibung des Prüfverfahrens. https://www.bitvtest.de/bitv_test/das_testverfahren_im_detail/verfahren.html. Accessed 30 Oct 2021
14. DIAS GmbH: BITV-Selbstbewertung. https://www.bitvtest.de/bitv_test/bitv_test_selbst_anwenden/selbstbewertung.html. Accessed 30 Oct 2021
15. Groves, K.: overlay factsheet. https://github.com/karlgroves/overlayfactsheet (2021). Accessed 30 Oct 2021
16. Henry, B.: Accessibility Overlays in Digital Content. https://www.tpgi.com/accessibility-overlays-in-digital-content/ (2020). Accessed 30 Oct 2021
17. Kornmeier, T.: Not All Accessibility Overlays Are Created Equal. https://www.deque.com/blog/not-all-accessibility-overlays-are-created-equal/ (2020). Accessed 30 Oct 2021
18. AudioEye: https://www.audioeye.com/. Accessed 30 Oct 2021
19. DIGIaccess: https://digiaccess.org/. Accessed 30 Oct 2021
20. EqualWeb: https://www.equalweb.com/. Accessed 30 Oct 2021
21. FACIL'iti: https://www.facil-iti.com/. Accessed 30 Oct 2021
22. MaxAccess: https://maxaccess.io/. Accessed 30 Oct 2021
23. Purple-Lens: https://purple-lens.com/. Accessed 30 Oct 2021
24. UserWay. https://userway.org/. Last accessed 2021/10/30
25. User1st: https://www.user1st.com/. Accessed 30 Oct 2021
26. DIAS GmbH: Werkzeugliste. https://www.bitvtest.de/bitv_test/das_testverfahren_im_detail/werkzeugliste.html. Accessed 30 Oct 2021
27. W3C: Web Content Accessibility Guidelines (WCAG) 2.1. https://www.w3.org/TR/WCAG21/ (2018). Accessed 30 Oct 2021
28. W3C: Understanding Success Criterion 2.3.1: Three Flashes or Below Threshold. https://www.w3.org/WAI/WCAG21/Understanding/three-flashes-or-below-threshold.html. Accessed 30 Oct 2021

Digital Authentication and Dyslexia: A Survey of the Problems and Needs of Dyslexia People

Nicole Kelly and Helen Petrie(✉)

University of York, York YO10 5GH, UK
helen.petrie@york.ac.uk

Abstract. It might be expected that people with dyslexia would have difficulties with password creation and maintenance, given their difficulties with language, often with spelling and correctly ordering elements. However, very little research has investigated this issue. Therefore, an online survey was conducted with 69 individuals with dyslexia and a matched sample of 90 non-dyslexic individuals. The survey found that the dyslexic individuals reported significantly more difficulty in creating and remembering passwords than the non-dyslexic individuals, and significantly more difficulties with CAPTCHAs and pattern authentication systems, but not with biometric authentication, including face recognition. The results show there is a great need to address the problems which individuals with dyslexia face with passwords and other authentication systems.

Keywords: Passwords · Digital authentication · People with dyslexia

1 Introduction

In spite of many technological advances, passwords remain a very widespread form of authentication for digital systems. Passwords are sometimes replaced or augmented by other authentication processes such as CAPTCHAs, two factor authentication (often using a string of digits), pattern recognition systems (for example a hand drawn shape) and biometric systems using fingerprint, iris or face recognition. Nonetheless, password only authentication is still very common, in spite of the problems it creates for human users. It is well established that people find it difficult to remember long complex passwords and resort to potentially risky behaviours such as re-using the same or similar passwords for different systems, writing them down and sharing them with others [see 9 for an overview].

Password authentication systems also create particular difficulties for people with a number of different disabilities. For example, visual CAPTCHAs are impossible for people who are blind and may be extremely difficult for people who are visually impaired. Considerable research efforts have been invested in creating accessible alternatives to visual CAPTCHAs, usually auditory CAPTCHAs [4, 6, 10, 13, 16]. Research has also investigated the authentication problems for people with intellectual disabilities [2, 7], for those with dexterity and other relevant disabilities [3]. However, surprisingly little research has investigated the problems which people with dyslexia might have with

K. Miesenberger et al. (Eds.): ICCHP-AAATE 2022, LNCS 13342, pp. 18–25, 2022.
https://doi.org/10.1007/978-3-031-08645-8_3

passwords and other authentication processes. Dyslexia is a language processing disorder which results in problems with spelling, reading, and putting linguistic elements at every level (i.e. letters, syllables, words) in the correct order [14]. All these problems could have severe consequences for using passwords or other authentication systems.

Marne and colleagues [8] used a cued graphical password system, CuedR [1], with dyslexic users. 14 dyslexic participants found the system helpful, but this does not throw much light on the problems that dyslexic users have with the wide range of authentication systems they encounter in day to day life. Renaud and colleagues [11] noted the lack of research in this area and highlighted six areas with need addressing: real-world coping strategies and behaviours; password managers and their adoption; multi-factor authentication; alternative authentication mechanisms for individuals with dyslexia; understanding dyslexia in the security context; and carrying out studies with individuals with dyslexia.

The current research addresses a number of this areas by conducting an online survey with individuals with dyslexia and a matched sample of non-dyslexic individuals to investigate whether dyslexic individuals have more difficulties in creating and managing passwords and other authentication processes for digital systems compared to individuals who are not dyslexic.

2 Method

2.1 Design

Two groups of respondents were asked to complete an online survey about their experiences with passwords and other authentication systems, a dyslexic group and a non-dyslexic control group. All respondents were asked to complete the Adult Reading Questionnaire (ARQ) [15] which comprises 15 questions about abilities and problems with reading and writing. While this does not provide a definitive diagnosis of dyslexia, it does provide a good indication of whether someone is dyslexia. So, scores on the ARQ, as well as whether they had ever had a diagnosis of dyslexia were used to ensure they were in the appropriate group.

In a key set of questions, respondents were asked to rating and comment on difficulties of creating and remembering passwords for online accounts which were important or unimportant in value to them (they were asked to self-select two such accounts). This allowed us to investigate whether the pressure of creating and remembering passwords for high value accounts put particular pressure on dyslexic respondents.

In general, comparing results on the online survey between the two groups allows us to investigate whether respondents with dyslexia are more likely to have problems with passwords and other authentication systems, and answers from the dyslexia group on a number of open-ended questions gives us greater insight into the nature of their problems.

2.2 Participants

The dyslexic group was recruited first, using a variety of channels. This included personal contacts, students registered with the disability service at the University of York, a Facebook support group for adults with dyslexia, as well as two online research participant recruitment sites (callforparticipants.com and prolific.co). The dyslexic group consisted of 69 respondents (see Table 1 for demographic details).

The non-dyslexic group was then recruited, with the aim to match the demographic characteristics of the dyslexic group as closely as possible. Similar recruitment channels were used including personal contacts, messages on university email lists, and the two online research participant sites. The non-dyslexic group consisted of 90 respondents (see Table 1 for demographic details). The matching of the two groups was considered successful. The largest difference between the two groups was in educational level, although this was not great, with more respondents in the dyslexic group having lower qualifications. However, as people with dyslexia often do not achieve as well as they might educationally [5, 12], this was deemed acceptable.

Table 1. Demographic details for the dyslexic and non-dyslexic groups.

Demographic characteristic	Dyslexic group (N = 69)	Non-dyslexic group (N = 90)
Gender		
Women	39 (56.5%)	54 (60.0%)
Men	24 (34.8%)	35 (38.9%)
Other	6 (8.6%)	1 (1.1%)
Age		
Median	29.0 (9.5)	31.5 (10.0)
Range	18 – 69	18 – 69
18 – 19	7 (10.1%)	5 (5.6%)
20 – 29	27 (39.1%)	37 (41.1%)
30 – 39	15 (21.7%)	21 (23.3%)
40 – 49	8 (11.6%)	13 (14.4%)
50 – 59	6 (8.7%)	10 (11.1%)
60 – 69	5 (6.2%)	4 (4.4%)
Education		
No qualification	4 (5.8%)	0 (0.0%)
High school qualification	28 (40.8%)	30 (33.3%)
Bachelors degree	19 (27.5%)	31 (34.4%)
Professional qualification	6 (7.2%)	6 (6.7%)
Higher degree	12 (17.4%)	23 (25.6%)

2.3 Online Questionnaire

The questionnaire for the survey comprised 70 questions divided into five sections. First, participants completed the Adult Reading Questionnaire (ARQ) [15] which comprises 15 questions about abilities and problems with reading and writing. There is no particular cut-off score in the ARQ for indicating a diagnosis of dyslexia. However, there are two groups of questions which relate particularly to dyslexia (as opposed to other reading and writing problems) - Reading/Spelling (scores range from 0 to 13) and Wordfinding/Labelling (scores range from 0 to 12). The ARQ also asks whether the participant has ever had a diagnosis of dyslexia. Therefore, participants were included in the dyslexia group if they had had a diagnosis or scores on both these groups of over 5 (approximately the midpoint on each group).

The next section was about password usage and creation for important and unimportant systems. There were 11 questions on each type of system, respondents were asked to think of an important, high value system and an unimportant, low value system, and answer the questions for each of these systems. This section included 7-point Likert items, open-ended and multiple-choice questions. The order of the questions on important and unimportant systems was alternated between respondents to ensure there were no fatigue or practice effects in the responses.

The next section asked about coping strategies around password usage (11 questions) again using Likert items, open-ended and multiple-choice questions. The next section asked about CAPTCHAs, biometric and face recognition authentication systems and pattern passwords (16 questions). The final section asked for demographic information (6 questions).

3 Results

Table 2 summarizes the ratings for the dyslexic and non-dyslexic groups on the difficulty of a number of aspects of password creation and use for important and unimportant accounts. For both important and unimportant digital accounts, dyslexic participants reported that creating and remembering passwords was significantly more difficult than non-dyslexic participants did. However, the dyslexic participants did not report significantly more re-use of the same or a similar password than the non-dyslexic participants (although this approached significance for re-using the same password for unimportant accounts).

Dyslexic participants reported difficulties in creating passwords because there are "so many rules about upper case, lower case, symbols and numbers" and because "each app/ website has different requirements". Combining all of the mandatory criteria often proves to be difficult to form a password, but even harder to remember due to the "different numbers, symbols and capitals". Often dyslexic participants expressed the idea that they find it difficult to recall the order these occur in or even what password they used in general. Some participants mentioned that they use a password manager to try to overcome this problem. Remembering passwords was particularly difficult for dyslexic participants when they have multiple passwords to remember for different systems. This becomes increasingly more difficult if they "do not use it frequently" or do not "write it down". Many find that "remembering which order they go in" is the most difficult element of password recall.

In commenting on creating and remembering passwords for important accounts dyslexic participants expressed their concerns with making a secure password for an important system, which often has "restrictive requirements". They found that there is a greater stress when making this password as they want it to be secure as it is an important account, so they feel more at pressure when forming the password. When remembering such passwords, dyslexic participants found that as it is an important system, this requires "a longer and more complicated password" which has more requirements. Dyslexic participants mentioned how they might use different variations of one password so that they can remember the main part and try different versions. However, even coping strategies such as writing down passwords could be unsuccessful as they acknowledge they can forget where they wrote it down.

Table 2. Difficulty of password creation and use for important and unimportant digital accounts (Rating from 1 = not at all difficult to 7 = very difficult)

Activity/ Account type	Dyslexic group median (SIQR)	Non-dyslexic group median (SIQR)	Mann Whitney test (z)	Probability
Important account				
Creating passwords	3.0 (1.5)	2.0 (1.0)	4.39	<0.000
Remembering passwords	4.0 (2.0)	2.0 (2.0)	4.43	<0.000
Re-using same password	5.0 (2.0)	4.0 (2.0)	1.91	0.057
Re-using similar password	5.0 (2.0)	5.0 (2.0)	0.26	n.s.
Unimportant account				
Creating passwords	3.0 (1.5)	2.0 (1.0)	3.89	<0.000
Remembering passwords	6.0 (2.0)	3.0 (2.0)	5.00	<0.000
Re-using same password	5.0 (2.0)	5.0 (2.0)	0.02	n.s.
Re-using similar password	6.0 (1.5)	5.5 (1.5)	0.19	n.s.

Table 3 summarizes the ratings of difficulty with a number of other authentication systems for the dyslexic and non-dyslexic groups. Dyslexic participants reported significantly more difficulty with CAPTCHAs and pattern authentication systems, but not with biometric systems in general, nor face recognition systems specifically.

Table 3. Difficulty with other authentication processes (Rating from 1 = not at all difficult to 7 = very difficult)

Authentication process	Dyslexic group median (SIQR)	Non-dyslexic group median (SIQR)	Mann Whitney U (z)	Probability
CAPTCHAs	5.0 (1.5)	3.0 (1.5)	4.33	<0.000
Biometric	1.0 (0.5)	1.0 (0.0)	0.32	n.s.
Face recognition	1.5 (1.0)	1.0 (0.5)	1.36	n.s.
Patterns	2.0 (1.0)	1.0 (0.5)	2.87	0.004

Dyslexic participants reported finding it difficult to use CAPTCHAs which contain letter or numbers because they are "distorted" or "warped", creating a "blurry effect". Overall, 34.0% of dyslexic participants mentioned problems reading letters and numbers in CAPTCHAs because "the warped letters and numbers are very hard to read" and "it can be hard to see the letters clearly enough". Dyslexic participants noted that they "find it hard to read regular text", so CAPTCHAs are even more difficult. That being said, a minority of the dyslexic participants (20.0%) said they did not struggle with CAPTCHAs and found them "simple" and "a majority of the time the letters/numbers are easy to read". It is known that many people with dyslexia find that when they read, letters appear to move about and slide down the page [14], so the distorted appearance of letters and numbers in CAPTCHAs would exacerbate these effects. This is supported by comments from several participants who noted that how the letters ''swim in front of my eyes" and they can also "disappear" and "move". Some dyslexic participants also noted that they "cannot always see what the letters or numbers are", meaning it is "easy to misrepresent a letter for me … a 'b' could be a 'd', 'p', 'q', or '9' depending on how it is deformed … A '3' into an '8' …the deformity makes me take extra long to determine it". Some dyslexic participants also noted that CAPTCHAs take a lot of time for them to work out and that they often have to complete them "more than once" before they are successful. One participant remarked that they "regularly take over 5 CAPTCHAs to get in" and sometimes "can't at all and give up." Finally, several participants noted that the presentation of letters in different fonts can make the CAPTCHA look "animated", thus it is "hard to read and distorted".

In commenting on systems which require using a non-linguistic pattern, dyslexic participants on average reported significantly more difficulties with these than non dyslexic respondents. However, one third of dyslexic participants (33%) found patterns easy to use, for example, stating that using "patterns and shapes [are] much easier than words and keyboard symbols". One participant also noted that "patterns don't have the same effect on me as a sequence of independent letters". A further 21% of dyslexic participants commented that it was easier to recall a pattern, for example as "remembering the path is easier". Many dyslexic participants felt it was also easy to recall a pattern as it became "muscle memory" and they note that they have better "spatial reasoning" compared to the difficulties they face with letters and words. As a result, working with shapes and paths is easier, which is why patterns work well for many dyslexic participants. A small proportion of the dyslexic group did note if they forget the pattern it was substantial harder to remember it because there are "no prompts". One dyslexic participant recalled that patterns "do not have any easy ways to remember them", they "can remember text passwords by shortening them and using hints but patterns don't have an easy way to remember".

4 Discussion and Conclusions

This online survey is to the best of our knowledge is the first large scale study of the problems individuals with dyslexia have with passwords and other authentication systems. By recruiting matching groups of dyslexic and non-dyslexic respondents we were able to quantify the magnitude of differences in levels of difficulty with authentication for these two groups. It should also be noted that individuals with severe dyslexia would probably not volunteer to complete an online survey, so these results may actually under-estimate the magnitude of the problems. Yet in many cases, our results show considerable levels of difficulty for individuals with dyslexia, particularly with passwords, CAPTCHAs and even pattern authentication systems. It is therefore important to understand more about the nature of the problems faced by dyslexic individuals and develop methods to support them better in using authentication systems.

Acknowledgements. We would like to thank all our participants, both dyslexic and non-dyslexic, who took the time to respond to the online survey, and provided much insight into the issues around online authentication systems.

References

1. Al-Ameen, M.N., Wright, M., Scielzo, S.: Towards making random passwords memorable: leveraging users' cognitive ability through multiple cues. In: Proceedings of the 33rd Annual ACM Conference on Human Factors in Computing Systems (CHI '15). ACM Press, New York (2015)
2. Hayes, J., Li, X., Wang, Y.: "I always have to think about it first": Authentication experiences of people with cognitive impairments. In: Proceedings of the 19th International ACM SIGACCESS Conference on Computers and Accessibility. ACM Press, New York (2017)
3. Helkala, K.: Disabilities and authentication methods: usability and security. In: 2012 Seventh International Conference on Availability, Reliability and Security. IEEE (2012)
4. Holman, J., Lazar, J., Feng, J.H., D'Arcy, J.: Developing usable CAPTCHAs for blind users. In: Proceedings of the 9th international ACM SIGACCESS conference on Computers and accessibility (ASSETS '07). ACM Press, New York (2007)
5. Knight, C.: The impact of the dyslexia label on academic outlook and aspirations: an analysis using propensity score matching. Br. J. Educ. Psychol. **91**(4), 1110–1126 (2021)
6. Lazar, J., et al.: The SoundsRight CAPTCHA: an improved approach to audio human interaction proofs for blind users. In: Proceedings of the SIGCHI Conference on Human Factors in Computing Systems (CHI '12). ACM Press, New York (2012)
7. Ma, Y., Feng, J., Kumin, L., Lazar, J.: Investigating user behavior for authentication methods: a comparison between individuals with Down Syndrome and neurotypical users. ACM Transactions on Accessible Computing **4**(4) (2013). Article 15

8. Marne, S.T., Al-Ameen, M.N., Wright, M.: Learning system-assigned passwords: a preliminary study on the people with learning disabilities. In: Proceedings of the Thirteenth Symposium on Usable Privacy and Security (SOUPS 2017). USENIX Association (2017). https://www.usenix.org/conference/soups2017/workshop-program/wips2017/marne
9. Merdenyan, B., Petrie, H.: Generational differences in password management behaviour. In: Bond, R., Mulvenna, M., Wallace, J. Black, M. (eds.) Proceedings of the 32nd International BCS Human Computer Interaction Conference (HCI 2018). British Computer Society (2018)
10. Olalere, A., Feng, J.H., Lazar, J., Brooks, T.: Investigating the effects of sound masking on the use of audio CAPTCHAs. Behav. Info. Technol. **33**(9), 919–928 (2014)
11. Renaud, K., Johnson, G., Ophoff, J.: Dyslexia and password usage: accessibility in authentication design. In: Clarke, N., Furnell, S. (eds.) Human Aspects of Information Security and Assurance: 14th IFIP WG 11.12 International Symposium, (HAISA 2020). Springer, Cham (2020)
12. Richardson, J.T.E., Wydell, T.N.: The representation and attainment of students with dyslexia in UK higher education. Read. Writ. **16**, 475–503 (2003)
13. Sauer, G., Holman, J., Lazar, J., Hochheiser, H., Feng, J.H.: Accessible privacy and security: a universally usable human-interaction proof tool. Univ. Acce. Info. Soc. **9**(3), 239–248 (2010)
14. Snowling, M.: Dyslexia: a very short introduction. Oxford University Press (2019)
15. Snowling, M., Dawes, P., Nash, H., Hulme, C.: Validity of a protocol for adult self-report of dyslexia and related difficulties. Dyslexia **18**, 1–15 (2012)
16. Tariq, N., Khan, F.A.: Match-the-Sound CAPTCHA. In: Latifi, S. (ed.) Information Technology – New Generations. AISC, vol. 558, pp. 803–808. Springer, Cham (2018). https://doi.org/10.1007/978-3-319-54978-1_99

Rethinking Alt Text to Improve Its Effectiveness

Karen McCall[1(✉)] and Beverly Chagnon[2(✉)]

[1] Karlen Communications, Paris, ON, Canada
info@karlencommunications.com
[2] PubCom.com, Takoma Park, MD, USA
chagnon@pubcom.com

Abstract. Traditional Alt Text on a simple graphic can be an effective way to describe the graphic, but Alt Text often fails when used on complex diagrams, maps, infographics and charts. One key reason that might cause the limitations is that Alt Text is only an attribute on an <img> or <Figure> tag, rather than a full, standardized tag that contains semantic information. This paper identifies barriers created by Alt Text as an attribute on tags in HTML, PDF, and EPUB and explores the need to develop better, innovative solutions that can provide more accessible and usable information for those who use adaptive technologies to understand the communication represented by complex graphics.

Keywords: Inclusion · Writing content · Usability · Accessibility · Alt Text · Alternative text · Graphics

1 Introduction

The primary technique used by content authors and content remediation professionals to provide information about graphics in digital content has been the "Alt attribute," also known as Alt Text or alternative text.

When digital content was an immature technology in the early 1990s, it became common practice to use an Alt Text attribute on a visual element, such as a <Figure> tag in PDF or a <img> tag in HTML.

When simple Alt Text wasn't enough for more complex graphics, the "LongDesc" attribute was implemented. However, this solution was ineffective because the reader was taken away from the article being read to another webpage and would have to find their way back to where they left the original document to continue reading.

2 User Survey

In an initial informal survey conducted in 2021, screen-reader users were asked what worked and what didn't work in terms of their access to Alt Text (McCall 2022). They were also asked to offer ideas to improve Alt Text. The survey, privately funded by Karlen Communications, is part of an ongoing series of research surveys on end user access to digital content and remediator access to stable, consistent and usable remediation tools. This research dates back to 2015 (McCall, PDF and the User Experience, 2022).

K. Miesenberger et al. (Eds.): ICCHP-AAATE 2022, LNCS 13342, pp. 26–33, 2022.
https://doi.org/10.1007/978-3-031-08645-8_4

Excerpts of the responses from the Alt Text Survey include:

- "Meaningless verbiage that is simply there to check a box for some minimal level of compliance that may be considered accessible but is not at all usable or functional in my efforts for gathering information or needed to navigate a digital platform."
- "Alt Text descriptions that are so generic that they don't relate to the content and context."
- "The limitations are that it relies on the designers to use it appropriately to add information to the content produced."
- "If Alt Text is too long and wordy, I find it hard to understand and want to repeat it multiple times. For example, an image that has too much description or a diagram that has too much data read out for me to understand."

The results suggest that it's time for the industry to rethink alt text as it relates to complex graphics. Alt Text either has to be adjusted to eliminate short comings or "we" have to invent a different/better method to present information about complex graphics.

We can use blindness as a baseline, but we also need to consider learning, cognitive, and information processing disorders, as well as end-users who require screen magnification without speech support.

3 Shortcomings with the Current Alt Text Method

As a preface to this topic, the skills of visually interacting with graphics must be identified. When learning to read text, there is simultaneous learning of concepts associated with graphics such as "the concepts of action, extension, importance, intentionality, partiality, permanence, relevance, and representation" (Roberts et al. 2022). As students progress through elementary school, they begin to understand that there is a relationship between text and graphics and that not all graphics are associated with text (Roberts et al. 2022).

Even among students/people who are blind or visually disabled, the skills to understand graphics vary depending on literacy skills (Zebehazy and Wilton 2021). For example, a different set of skills are used if someone primarily accesses print graphics versus someone who primarily accesses Braille tactile graphics.

As we develop better techniques and technologies for describing graphics in digital content, we must consider all users, especially those with disabilities. We must consider how people use graphics, how graphics are accessed by people with different types of disabilities, and what the users' expectations are.

Upon investigation, research and an initial survey, the authors have found that shortcomings of dependence on Alt Text as the primary means of describing complex graphics fall into one of three general categories:

1. **Limited functionality** of the Alt Text attribute. Because it's an attribute on a <Figure> or <img> tag, Alt Text is metadata about the tag. Therefore, it can provide only limited functionality to all users. The majority of technologies, both adaptive and traditional technologies, can access the attribute, but the attribute's functionality itself is limited.

2. **Poorly defined tags** among the standards (WCAG, PDF/UA, EPUB) often conflict with each other or duplicate the purpose. Should the content author use Alt Text? Actual text? Caption? Body Text? Summary?
3. **Limited advice for content creators** on how to provide accessibility of their graphics. They might not be skilled writers and not know what to write to adequately, but succinctly, describe a graphic. Standards leave out this guidance, and current guidelines and best practices conflict with each other.

4 Functional Limitations of Alt Text

Within the general categories of functional limitations of Alt Text, more granular accessibility barriers emerge:

- There isn't a way for an end-user not using screen readers or Text-to-Speech tools to access the Alt Text.
- Alt Text can't contain multiple languages.
- Alt Text can't recognize many Unicode characters.
- Most adaptive technologies can't search inside Alt Text.
- The end-user experience is inconsistent between different media and adaptive technologies. Access differs from one media to the next, such as websites, PDFs, and desktop applications. The same user will have a different experience when using JAWS or NVDA screen readers, and Read&Write Text-to-Speech provides access to all or none of the Alt Text in all environments.
- Alt Text doesn't transfer when content is sent to a Braille embosser or Braille translation software. Captions and live body text do.
- There isn't an indication when Alt Text ends and body text resumes. Users are told they've encountered a "graphic," but not told when they have left the graphic's Alt Text.
- Content authors commonly use more complex graphics in documents and websites.
- If a graphic shows a process or workflow, Alt Text fails to show the relationship and order of the process. "If then" decision trees are in this category.
- The graphic design and publishing industries are moving toward more use of infographics to convey a concept or statistical information. Alt Text is not adequate to convey the complex relationships within most infographics.
- The use of statistical software such as MS Visio, Tableau, and ArcGIS has increased dramatically over the past decade. Alt Text isn't sufficient to describe the detailed data within the graphic (Fig. 1).

All the items in this list can be mapped back to the concepts of graphics that we are supposed to learn in elementary school previously cited in this article. However, information on how to craft Alt Text seldom makes the link to those concepts.

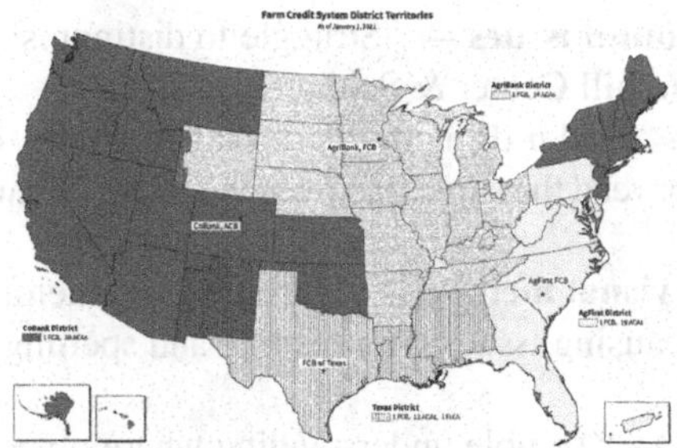

Fig. 1. A sample map from ArcGIS shows banking districts by state in the US.

4.1 Content Creators don't Know How to Best Provide Accessibility of Their Graphics

There are no standards or formal guidelines about how to make graphics fully accessible to all users: there are only opinions and interpretations by various individuals and organizations. They mean well, but when reviewed as a whole, there is no consistency between experts, government agencies, standards, best practices, COPs, and guidelines. The guidance often conflicts from one source to another.

The industry lacks suggestions as to what an author should do when the <Caption> or body text contains all the necessary information about the graphic and Alt Text isn't needed. For example, a National Geographic two-page spread shows multiple images on one topic with one caption for the collage. The <Caption> can describe the visual details of the group, but it is not Alt Text and, therefore, fails automated accessibility checkers.

5 Broadening the Base of Alt Text Users and Their Needs

Today, in 2022, the field of accessible digital content acknowledges that the need for Alt Text has expanded from a baseline of end-users who are blind to one that includes everyone, especially those with other disabilities and impairments such as learning disabilities and information processing disorders (Churchill Center & School 2022a).

Generally, information processing disorders are not considered learning disabilities, although some people may have both. Whether information processing disorders are segregated from learning disabilities depends on the research examined and the organization cited.

A visual processing disorder "can cause issues with the way the brain processes visual information. There are many different types of processing disorders and many different symptoms, which can include trouble drawing or copying, the inability to detect differences in shapes or letters, and letter reversals. … There are eight different types of visual processing difficulties." (Churchill Center & School 2022b).

For this paper, the following information processing disorders were considered for appropriate use of Alt Text.

- **Visual discrimination issues** — "Trouble seeing the difference between similar letters, shapes, or objects." (Churchill Center & School 2022a)

- **Visual figure/background issues** — "Struggle to distinguish a shape or letter from its background." (Churchill Center & School 2022a)
- **Visual sequencing** — "Find it difficult to see shapes, letters, or words in the correct order; may skip lines or read the same line over and over." (Churchill Center & School 2022a)
- **Long- or short-term visual memory** — "Struggle to remember shapes, symbols, or objects they've seen, causing issues with reading and spelling." (Churchill Center & School 2022a)
- **Visual-spatial issues** — "Trouble understanding where objects are in space; unsure how close objects are to one another." (Churchill Center & School 2022a)
- **Visual Closure** — "Difficulty identifying an object when only parts of it are showing." (Churchill Center & School 2022a)
- **Letter and symbol reversal** — "Switch numbers or letters when writing, or may mistake "b" for "d" or "w" for "m"." (Churchill Center & School 2022a)
- **Colour blindness** — "Color blindness — or more accurately, poor or deficient color vision — is an inability to see the difference between certain colors." (Mayo Clinic 2022)

6 Current Techniques to Describe Graphics

Although the Alt Text attribute is not the only technique that can be used to provide information about complex images, diagrams and charts in digital content, it is the one that is most often used, and it is required to pass automated accessibility checking software.

A brief description of the techniques currently available to describe graphics:

- **Regular body text content** — Ideally, a document author will provide enough detail in the body text of digital content that the image supports information in the document and isn't what can be considered stand-alone content. Without context for images that are complex, the end-user may have difficulty understanding the relationship between the image and the text.
- **Matching data tables for charts** — The inclusion of matching data tables in the body of the content can support complex diagrams and charts, and provide an alternative, accessible view of the data.
- **Alt Text attribute** — Once the content author has included detailed information in the body of the document about the data or flow chart, the Alt Text attribute is used to provide a summary of the information as an alternate format to the data. Typically, Alt Text is only available to those using screen readers or Text-to-Speech tools.
- **Captions** (Prefatory Text) — Typically appear above or below images and can provide more details about the graphic. Captions are available to everyone. This means that if someone is having difficulty seeing or visually decoding an image, they have access to the caption text. Captions can be created in most word processors and desktop publishing software and some e-mail clients.

7 Lack of Industry-Wide Standardized Guidelines

There are no formal standards or guidelines for writing Alt Text. Neither WCAG, PDF, PDF/UA, or EPUB standards address how to write Alt Text; they define only the mechanics of how it must be built into the file.

What's available are merely **opinions** of what content authors should do, and these recommendations vary depending on the author of the policy or the organization that publishes the guidelines. Some samples of various guidelines about how long Alt Text should be:

- "There's no one-size-fits-all, cookie-cutter method for writing Alt-text. Writing Alt-text is both an art and craft." (Chagnon 2020)
- "The Alt Text shouldn't be longer than a sentence or two—most of the time a few thoughtfully selected words will do. Consider what is important about an image. For example, important context may be the setting, the emotions on people's faces, the colours, or the relative sizes." ((Microsoft 2022)
- "Alt Text is short, about 10–15 words or 140 characters or so." (Hogle and Elliott 2020)
- "Be no longer than 10 words." (Province of British Columbia 2022)
- "Limit the text to around 140 characters (including spaces)." (Government of Canada 2022)
- WebAIM.org, one of the leading independent resources for accessibility, does not say anything about the length of Alt Text in their online tutorial (WebAIM.org 2022).
- This is a common question on industry forums: "Is there a character limit on the Alt Text for images in PDFs? If not, then how long is too long?" In this particular post on WebAIM, several readers gave their suggestions that varied widely. (WebAIM.org online discussion list 2013)
- "All images, form image buttons, and image map hot spots have appropriate, concise alternative text." (HHS 2022)

8 Conclusion

The goal of our future research is to explore various ways to provide information about graphics to all users, and to ensure that all types of graphics can be conveyed across different adaptive technologies and media.

Future study will include:

1. More research from end users with cognitive, learning, and comprehension disorders regarding what they need for a description of different types of graphics. Our aim is to make Alt Text more inclusive.
2. Develop more robust use of the Alt Text attribute already available.
3. Develop more advanced ways to convey complex graphical information.
4. Consult with adaptive technology manufacturers about what is possible from their software.

5. Consider brand-new methods to convey graphics that include semantics (such as semantic tags), granular detail (such as census data per tract), and relationships (such as infographics, organization charts, and flow charts). Allow users to choose how much detail they want about the graphic and its parts.

Participants in the initial Alt Text survey were asked to "think out of the box" to address their needs in accessing graphics (McCall, Alt Text Survey 2021, 2022). Contributions seem to indicate that the people affected by complex graphics are willing to take their seat at the table and contribute to accessible digital design.

- "Have a way of adding audio to Alt Text content. It could bring a completely different dynamic to the experience. For example, if it's a picture of a beach, when the screen read user hits the alt text area, there could be some text describing the beach. But you could also hear the sounds of waves crashing on the beach. You did say to think out of the box. :)"
- "Alt Text needs structure and needs to be visible to low vision users."
- "Hmmm... ask that the industry consider establishing better-streamlined standards for what is enough and what is too much and what is proper for a proctor or gold standard to work from? I suppose this is purely subjective but if we could come to some consensus in this regard it would help corporations better provide clear descriptive tags that are meaningful and useful for all."
- "I would probably want a sound to tell me that there is an image there and if I don't get enough context from the printed material and it's important to me, then I could go back to that mark and say describe the image. I believe JAWS will almost do this now."

In the meantime, there must be a concerted effort to educate content authors on the importance of supporting complex graphics in text that surrounds the complex graphic.

Subject Matter Experts (SME) must be in contact with the content author to determine the data or information the complex graphic is intended to convey.

Alternatives to providing detailed information on surrounding content must be implemented while we explore new technologies. These can include a detailed description as an appendix to a document or digital content. Using an appendix to a publication could provide additional tools to structure the description, such as the use of headings, lists and tables.

References

Chagnon, B.: A Simple Guide to Writing Alt Text (20 July 2020). Retrieved from PubCom.com: https://www.pubcom.com/blog/2020_07-20/alt-text_part-1.shtml

Churchill Center & School.: Learning Disability Resources (Jan 2022a). Retrieved from Churchill Center & School: National Leader in Learning Disabilities: https://www.churchillstl.org/learning-disability-resources/

Churchill Center & School.: What is Visual Processing Disorder? (Jan 2022b). Retrieved from Churchill Center & School: National Leader in Learning Disabilities: https://www.churchillstl.org/learning-disability-resources/visual-processing-disorder/

Government of Canada: Government of Canada Style Guide (Nov 01 2022). Retrieved from Treasury Board Secretariat: https://www.canada.ca/en/treasury-board-secretariat/services/government-communications/canada-content-style-guide.html

HHS: Accessibility Compliance Checklists (2022). Retrieved from US Dept. of Health and Human Services: https://www.hhs.gov/web/section-508/accessibility-checklists/index.html

Hogle, P.S., Elliott, D.: How to write great alt text — And why it matters (01 May 2020). Retrieved from aces The Society for Editing: https://aceseditors.org/news/2020/how-to-write-great-alt-text-and-why-it-matters

Mayo Clinic: Color blindness (Jan 2022). Retrieved from Mayo Clinic: Patient Care & Health Information, Diseases & Conditions: https://www.mayoclinic.org/diseases-conditions/poor-color-vision/symptoms-causes/syc-20354988

McCall, K.: Alt Text Survey 2021. Karen McCall, Paris Ontario Canada (2022). Retrieved from: https://www.karlencommunications.com/adobe/AltTextSurveyResults2021.pdf

Microsoft: Everything You Need to Know to Write Effective Alt Text (11 Jan 2022). Retrieved from Microsoft Support: https://support.microsoft.com/en-us/topic/everything-you-need-to-know-to-write-effective-alt-text-df98f884-ca3d-456c-807b-1a1fa82f5dc2

Province of British Columbia: Using graphics and alt text (11 Jan 2022). Retrieved from Accessibility and Inclusion Toolkit: https://www2.gov.bc.ca/gov/content/home/accessible-government/toolkit/accessible-digital-content/graphics

Roberts, K., Norman, R., Duke, N., Morsink, P., Martin, N.: Diagrams, Timelines, and Tables (01 April 2022). Retrieved from Reading Rockets: https://www.readingrockets.org/article/diagrams-timelines-and-tables

WebAIM.org: Alternative Text (Jan 2022). Retrieved from WebAim: https://webaim.org/techniques/alttext/

WebAIM.org online discussion list: Thread: Character limit on alt-text in PDF? (28 June 2013). Retrieved from WebAIM E-mail List Archives: https://webaim.org/discussion/mail_thread?thread=6017

Zebehazy, K.T., Wilton, A.P.: Graphic reading performance of students with visual impairments and its implication for instruction and assessment. Journal of Visual Impairment and Blindness **115**(3), 215–227 (2021). Retrieved from https://doi.org/10.1177/0145482X211016918

Password Challenges for Older People in China and the United Kingdom

Helen Petrie[✉], Burak Merdenyan, and Chen Xie

University of York, York YO10 5GH, UK

{helen.petrie,burak.merdenyan,cx849}@york.ac.uk

Abstract. As vital services are moving increasingly online, it is important that everyone, including older people, can access them. Both high risk and many low risk online services require password authentication. Although there has been some research proposing easier to use and remember password systems, there is surprisingly little research on what problems older people have with real world authentication systems. This research conducted an online survey with 61 Chinese older people and 75 British older people about what problems they have in creating and managing passwords. There were differences between the samples of older people in the two countries in creating passwords, but few differences between the two samples in managing passwords. There were many problems in creating passwords, but not as many in terms of managing them. In particular, remembering passwords was not a particular concern, which may surprise many researchers who assume older people would have memory problems. The results have implications for where future research on password authentication for older users should be focussed.

Keywords: Password creation · Password management · Older people · China · United Kingdom

1 Introduction

Increasingly vital services such as healthcare, banking and shopping are moving online, and this trend has increased since the coronavirus pandemic. Online services with important personal information such as medical and financial information require good security and therefore authentication of accounts. However, even relatively low risk services also often require users to set up an account and create authentication. For older people, who are generally less used and expert with online services, creating and maintaining numerous accounts with the associated authentication mechanisms may be problematic. Most online services currently use textual passwords for authentication, although two factor authentication, biometric authentication and other security mechanisms such as CAPTCHAs are becoming increasingly common.

The population of older people is growing rapidly in nearly all countries throughout the world and although their use of digital devices and online services lags behind that of younger people, it is also growing. For example, in the United Kingdom, in 2019

K. Miesenberger et al. (Eds.): ICCHP-AAATE 2022, LNCS 13342, pp. 34–40, 2022.
https://doi.org/10.1007/978-3-031-08645-8_5

there were 16.2 million people over the age of 65, 18.5% of the population. By 2039 that figure is expected to rise to 21.9 million people, 23.9% of the population [8]. In China the situation is even more dramatic. In 2020, there were 190.64 million people over the age of 65 in China, 13.5% of the population. By 2050 it is expected that the number of people in this age group will increase to over 400 million, approximately 34% of the population [5]. This is due not only to the very large total population of China (1.4 billion people in 2020) but also to the one child policy introduced in the 1970s [2].

A small body of research has investigated the authentication problems encountered by older people and proposed a number of solutions. Pilar et al. [9] conducted face-to-face interviews with 263 Brazilians in three age groups: 18 – 39 years, 40 – 64 years, and 66 to 93 years. Interviews concerned password usage and particularly problems of remembering passwords. Contrary to expectations, differences due to aging were not found in remembering passwords. On the other hand, Hartnett et al. [3] conducted a study with 27 UK participants over the age of 65 using a range of methods including workshops, and group and individual interviews. They describe the "main obstacle" as forgetting passwords, which encouraged older people to write their passwords down.

In spite of the lack of empirical evidence that older people have particular difficulty remembering their passwords, much of the research on authentication innovations has been based on the assumption that this is their main problem. For example, Renaud and Ramsay [10] developed an interesting authentication system for older people based on the recognition of doodles or handwriting rather than the recall of a password (recognition being a much easier memory task than recall). Nicholson et al. [6, 7] investigated a face-based graphical authentication system for older people and found it was more effective with age-appropriate faces. Again, this was designed to avoid the need to remember passwords. A number of other researchers have also investigated graphical password systems for older users [1, 4, 12].

While the research on easier to use and remember password authentication for older people is interesting and useful, it is also important to understand what problems older people are actually having with passwords in the real world. Solutions need to be targeted at those problems. Therefore we conducted a study to investigate what problems older people are having in creating and managing passwords in two different countries, both concerned with their ageing populations.

2 Method

An online questionnaire was distributed to older people in China and the UK to develop an understanding of their current habits and challenges with password creation and management.

2.1 Participants

A number of online channels were used to recruit participants. In China, messages were posted on the WeChat social media channel. In addition, the third author distributed an announcement about the questionnaire in a number of community centres for older citizens. In the UK, participants were recruited via the Prolific research participant website (prolific.co). UK respondents were offered £1.25 for completing the survey, Chinese participants were not offered any compensation, as it was not deemed necessary.

Table 1. Demographic characteristics of the Chinese and UK older participants.

	China (N = 61)	UK (N = 75)
Gender	Women: 29 (47.5%) Men: 31 (50.8%) Prefer not to say: 1 (1.6%)	Women: 42 (56.0%) Men: 33 (44.0%)
Age	Range: 60 – 81 years Median: 66.0 years In their 60s: 49 (80.3%) In their 70s: 10 (16.4%) In their 80s: 2 (3.3%)	Range: 65 – 89 years Median: 68.0 years In their 60s: 52 (69.3%) In their 70s: 19 (25.4%) In their 80s: 4 (5.3%)
Status	Retired: 47 (77.0%) Working full-time: 3 (4.9%) Working part-time: 8 (13.1%) Other/prefer not to say: 3 (4.9%)	Retired: 60 (80.0%) Working full-time: 7 (9.3%) Working part-time: 7 (9.3%) Other/prefer not to say: 1 (1.3%)
Living arrangements	Live alone: 13 (21.3%) With spouse/partner: 44 (72.1%) With other family: 3 (4.9%) Prefer not to say: 1 (1.6%)	Live alone: 27 (36.0%) With spouse/partner: 41 (54.7%) With other family: 7 (9.3%)
Physical difficulties affecting password use	Yes: 21 (34.4%) Poor eyesight: 11 (52.4%) Dexterity issues: 6 (28.6%) Mental issues: 3 (14.3%)	Yes: 1 (1.3%)
Level of online security knowledge	Median: 3.0 Semi-interquartile range: 1.0	Median: 5.0 Semi-interquartile range: 0.5

The demographics of the participant groups from the two countries are summarized in Table 1. Both groups are reasonably balanced for gender. The UK group is a little older, in particular with a higher percentage of participants in their 70s compared to the Chinese group. However, the difference in distribution across the three decades was not significant (chi-square = 2.13, df = 2, n.s.). The majority of participants were retired and most had worked in white collar occupations before retirement. Another difference between the groups was that a higher percentage of the Chinese group were living with a spouse or partner, again this difference was not significant (chi-square = 4.42, df = 2, n.s.).

Participants were asked whether they had any physical difficulties that affected their use of passwords. We did not want to ask whether they had "disabilities", as older people often do not recognise declining perceptual and physical capabilities as "disabilities". Interestingly far more Chinese participants acknowledged these (despite being slightly younger), with typical difficulties associated with ageing of poor eyesight and dexterity.

Why this was more commonly reported by Chinese participants is not clear. Finally, participants were asked to rate how knowledgeable they felt about computer and online security issues on a 7-point Likert scale. Here the UK participants rated themselves as significantly above the midpoint of the scale (Wilcoxon = 3.37, $p < 0.001$), whereas the Chinese participants rated themselves significantly below the midpoint (Wilcoxon = -3.52, $p < 0.001$).

2.2 Online Questionnaire

The online questionnaire comprised 41 questions, divided into four parts. The first part asked about general use of passwords, such as what kinds of accounts the participants have passwords for, what devices they access these accounts from. The second part asked about password creation processes and strategies, including what aspects of password creation participant have problems with, what kinds of components they use in passwords and what strategies if any they have for creating passwords. The third part asked about password management, including the difficulty of remembering passwords, whether passwords are written down, shared with others. The final section asked the demographic questions. Questions consisted of a mixture of 7-point rating items, multiple choice and open-ended questions.

The questionnaire was developed in English and then translated into Chinese with a second native Chinese speaker conducting a backtranslation to ensure the translation was accurate (several small discrepancies were resolved between the two translators).

3 Results

Data on the 7-point rating items was often quite skewed, so non-parametric statistics were used in the inferential analysis.

Table 2 summarizes participants' ratings of three questions participants answered about how often they have different potential problems in creating passwords. On the problem of choosing the right character combinations for passwords, Chinese participants rated the frequency of problems as significantly above the midpoint of the rating item, whereas UK participants rated it as significantly below the midpoint. The same pattern of results was repeated for problems of understanding the steps in the password creation process and problems of creating passwords of the right length.

A follow-up open-ended question asking about what other problems participants encountered in password creation yielded a range of answers from both Chinese and UK participants. These included:

- Difficulty of understanding the requirements for a password
- Needing to have different passwords for different online accounts
- Need to enter a password twice to confirm it
- Distinguishing between upper and lower case characters
- Difficulty of understanding what a strong password consists of

Table 2. Ratings of password creation problems by Chinese and UK participants (ratings: 1 = never, to 7 = very often)

	Chinese participants	UK participants
Problems choosing the right character combinations for passwords	Median: 5.0 SIQR: 1.5 W = 1.78, n.s	Median: 3.0 SIQR: 1.5 W = −3.08, $p < 0.005$
Understanding the steps in the password creation process	Median: 5.0 SIQR: 1.5 W = 2.99, $p < 0.005$	Median: 2.0 SIQR: 1.0 W = −7.26, $p < 0.001$
Problems creating passwords of the right length	Median: 5.0 SIQR: 1.5 W = 1.98, $p < 0.05$	Median: 2.0 SIQR: 1.5 W = −5.53, $p < 0.001$

N.B. SIQR = semi-interquartile range; W = One-sample Wilcoxon Signed Rank Test.

Table 3. Number and percentage of participants using different password creation strategies.

Strategy	Chinese participants	UK participants
User familiar dates or numbers (e.g. birthdays, house numbers)	42 (68.6%)	31 (41.3%)
Use familiar names (e.g. family members, famous people)	31 (50.2%)	22 (29.3%)
Re-use passwords exactly	20 (32.8%)	20 (26.7%)
Use common words	18 (29.5%)	15 (20.0%)
Re-use passwords with small changes	12 (19.7%)	49 (65.3%)
Use cryptic sequences (e.g. nonsense words, random sequences of letters)	9 (14.8%)	29 (38.7%)

Table 3 summarizes the strategies that Chinese and UK participants said they used in creating passwords, chosen from a list provided of common and in most cases poor, strategies. The results show that both Chinese and UK participants used poor strategies. Over half the Chinese participants reported using familiar dates or numbers, although only about a third re-use passwords exactly and fewer re-use passwords with small changes. Whereas over half the UK participants re-use passwords with small changes and are less likely to use the other poor strategies. Only approximately 15% of Chinese participants and 40% of UK participants use the good strategy of cryptic sequences.

Table 4 summarizes participants' ratings of four questions about password management. For the difficulty of remembering passwords, both Chinese and UK participants rated this as not significantly different from the midpoint of the scale, so neither particularly difficult or easy. This aligns with the research by Pilar et al. [9] and suggests that researchers have been concentrating too much on this area. Participants was also neutral about whether they write down passwords to remember them, and do not report

Table 4. Ratings of password management problems by Chinese and UK participants (Remembering: 1 = very easy, 7 = very difficult; Writing down/sharing: 1 = never, 7 = always; Changing: 1 = never, 7 = very often)

	Chinese participants	UK participants
Remembering passwords	Median: 4.0 SIQR: 2.5 W = −0.49, n.s	Median: 4.0 SIQR: 1.0 W = 1.47, n.s
Writing down passwords	Median: 3.0 SIQR: 3.0 W = −0.60, n.s	Median: 4.0 SIQR: 2.5 W = −0.23, n.s
Sharing passwords with others	Median: 3.0 SIQR: 1.5 W = −3.09, $p < 0.005$	Median: 1.0 SIQR: 0.5 W = −7.66, $p < 0.000$
Changing passwords without being asked	Median: 1.0 SIQR: 5.5 W = −2.29, $p < 0.005$	Median: 2.0 SIQR: 1.0 W = −6.08, $p < 0.000$

doing this with high frequency. They definitely do not share passwords with others as a strategy, but neither are they good at changing their passwords. Participants were also asked in a follow-up question about what other problems they have with password management. A full content analysis of these problems will be presented in the final paper. It is interesting that on the password management issues, the pattern of responses for Chinese and UK participants was very similar.

4 Discussion and Conclusions

This research conducted an online survey with 61 Chinese people and 75 British people about what problems they have in creating and managing passwords. There were differences between the samples in the two countries in creating passwords, but few differences between them in managing passwords. There were many problems in creating passwords, but not as many in terms of managing them. In particular, remembering passwords was not a particular concern.

A limitation of this study is that not all older people in either China or the UK may not be comfortable completing an online questionnaire, even if they do use online accounts which require authentication. Those older people may have even greater problems than those reported here. Further research could interview older people face-to-face about their online security issues, to reach a wider and potentially more representative sample of older people. Interviews may also elicit more detail about the problems that older people encounter in this area.

The results suggest that research needs to address how to support older people more in creating strong passwords. Given that so many online systems require passwords, older people cannot avoid them. However, if the designers of authentication systems had information about how to guide older people through strong password creation better, they would be able to deal with these systems more easier. In addition, it is not just older people who have difficulties creating strong passwords, this is a widespread problem, with many people making weak passwords [11]. Thus, creating systems that clearly and simply help people make stronger passwords would be a beneficial exercise in universal design.

Acknowledgements. We would like to thank all the older people in China and the United Kingdom who took the time to complete the online questionnaire.

References

1. Carter, N., et al.: Graphical passwords for older computer users. In: Proceedings of HotWeb '17. ACM Press, New York (2017)
2. Chen, K., Chan, A.H.: The ageing population of China and a review of gerontechnology. Gerontechnology **10**(2), 63–71 (2011)
3. Hartnett, E., et al.: Older people and online social interactions: an empirical investigation. In: Proceedings of the UKAIS International Conference on Information Systems. University of Oxford (2013)
4. Jittibumrungrak, P., Hongwarittorrn, N.: A preliminary study to evaluate graphical passwords for older adults. In: Proceedings of the 5th ACM in Cooperation International Conference in UX and HCI (CHIuXiD 2019). ACM Press, New York (2019)
5. National Bureau of Statistics (China): Annual data 2020 (2020). https://data.stats.gov.cn/easyquery.htm?cn=C01&zb=A0301&sj=2020
6. Nicholson, J., Coventry, L., Briggs, P.: Age-related performance issues for PIN and face-based authentication systems. In: 31st[d] ACM Conference on Human Factors in Computing Systems (CHI '15). ACM Press, New York (2013a)
7. Nicholson, J., Coventry, L., Briggs, P.: Faces and pictures: understanding age differences in two types of graphical authentications. Int. J. Hum Comput Stud. **71**, 958–966 (2013)
8. Office for National Statistics (UK): Overview of the UK population: January 2021 (2021). https://www.ons.gov.uk/peoplepopulationandcommunity/populationandmigration/populationestimates/articles/overviewoftheukpopulation/january2021#the-uks-population-is-ageing
9. Pilar, D.R., Jaeger, A., Gomes, C.F.A., Stein, L.M.: Passwords usage and human memory limitations: a survey across age and educational background. PlosOne **7**(12), e51067 (2012)
10. Renaud, K., Ramsay, J.: Now what was that password again? A more flexible way of identifying and authenticating our seniors. Behav. Info. Technol. **256**(4), 309–322 (2007)
11. Renaud, K., Zimmermann, V.: Nudging folks towards stronger password choices: providing certainty is the key. Behavioural Public Policy **3**(20), 228 – 258 (2018)
12. Vu, K.-P.L., Hill, M.M.: The influence of password restrictions and mnemonics on the memory for passwords of older adults. In: Yamamoto, S. (ed.) HIMI/HCII 2013, Part I. LNCS 8016, pp. 660 – 668. Springer, Las Vegas, NV, USA (2013)

Digital Authentication for Visually Disabled People: Initial Results of an Online Survey

Suzanna Schmeelk[1,2] and Helen Petrie[1](✉)

[1] University of York, Deramore Lane, York YO10 5GH, UK
[2] St Johns University, 8000 Utopia Parkway, Queens, New York 11439, USA
{ss3134,helen.petrie}@york.ac.uk

Abstract. Digital authentication is becoming essential to use a wide range of online services. A considerable amount of research has proposed accessible alternatives for visual CAPTCHAs for visually disabled people, which are often part of the authentication process, but surprisingly little research has investigated other aspects of the accessibility of digital authentication for this user group. We are conducting an online survey of visually disabled people in the UK and USA. In this paper we present preliminary results of the survey from the UK. These indicate a wide range of accessibility problems, particularly with CAPTCHAs and face recognition systems.

Keywords: Digital authentication · QR codes · Visually impaired people

1 Introduction

As more and more services move online, people who need or want to interact with these services need to establish accounts, handle transactions, automate pandemic mitigations, and build their personal profiles. Account interactions related to authentication include creating accounts, creating, entering and changing passwords, establishing authentication tokens, and navigating through the authentication process. However, applications, including the authentication processes to access applications, have generally that have not been developed with the needs of people with disabilities, particularly people with visual disabilities, in mind.

It is clear that there are a range of possible accessibility challenges in authentication for people with visual disabilities. Yet most of the research in this area has concentrated on one issue, the accessibility of CAPTCHAs (Completely Automated Public Turing test to tell Computers and Humans Apart), which are also known as Human Interaction Proofs (HIPs). Of course, this is a very important issue, as CAPTCHAs have generally been very visual and need to be made accessible to users who cannot see them. However, it is clear that there are a number of other challenges in authentication which may need addressing for this user group. In addition, since the coronavirus pandemic, the use of QR (Quick Response) codes has become very widespread for personal authentication of vaccine status and other critical functions. This technology also poses potential challenges for users with visual disabilities.

K. Miesenberger et al. (Eds.): ICCHP-AAATE 2022, LNCS 13342, pp. 41–50, 2022.
https://doi.org/10.1007/978-3-031-08645-8_6

Our programme of research has started with a review of previous research on the different aspects of accessibility of authentication for people with visual disabilities. Given the status of current research, we are now conducting a survey of people with visual disabilities to investigate their needs and challenges in relation to digital authentication and online security.

2 Related Work

The first step in addressing the needs of a group of people with disabilities is to understand thoroughly what challenges they face and what their needs are. A number of small but interesting studies has been conducted on the needs and challenges of visually disabled people in relation to digital authentication and online security. One of the earliest studies was conducted by Lazar and colleagues [12, 19] using a focus group of blind screen reader users. An interesting "top 10" list of security related concerns for blind users on the web was elicited (see Table 1). Some of these issues have been solved since the work was conducted. For example, Issue 3, relates to dynamic content, which potentially screen readers can now address. Some issues do not really seem to be security concerns. For example, Issue 10, relates to spam emails, which are not necessarily security problems, although they are time-consuming and annoying. None the less, this is an interesting first list of authentication and security problems for visually disabled users.

Azenhot et al. [5] interviewed 13 legally blind iPhone users (users of the VoiceOver screen reader) about their use of passwords and screen occlusion techniques to ensure their privacy and security. All the participants accessed private information via their iPhones and six used online banking. None of the participants used optional authentication procedures to protect their information, although all but one was aware of the iPhone's lock mechanism. Passwords were only used when required, and usually stored in the application, so they did not require repeated entry. Only one participant expressed concern about auditory "shoulder surfing" (i.e. people hearing the output of VoiceOver which might give access to private information). However, 10 of the 13 participants used the iPhone screen occlusion feature (Screen Curtain), which would provide protection from visual shoulder surfing. These interviews showed that visually disabled users were clearly exposing themselves to security risks. This led the research group to develop a touch-based authentication system, PassChords [5] and a gesture-based digit input system for entering personal identification numbers (PINs) which avoids auditory feedback, DigiTaps [4].

Desono et al. [9] conducted a contextual inquiry with 12 blind and partially sighted people, mainly screen reader users and also undertook a hierarchical task analysis of the authentication tasks which the participants performed in the contextual inquiry. This work revealed a number of important problems associated with online authentication, such as the inability to locate or identify the elements of the authentication process, knowing whether authentication has been successful, issues with accessing error messages in the authentication process, issues with mechanisms to prevent auditory shoulder surfing, problems with case sensitive passwords, and difficulties with password recovery processes.

Ahmed et al. [1] conducted interviews with 14 visually impaired individuals about a range of privacy and security issues, including password management, use of password

Table 1. "Top 10" security related concerns for blind users on the web [12, 19].

1	Web sites with forms using visual HIP tools that do not include audio output are inaccessible to blind users. To use these sites, blind users must either ask a colleague for assistance or phone technical support
2	Many web sites have secure login sessions that time-out if the user does not complete the login within the allotted amount of time. Unfortunately, some users, especially users of assistive technologies, can sometimes take longer to fill out the login forms. If timeouts are too short, users may be required to start the forms over, once again running the risk of a timeout
3	Some web sites occasionally automatically refresh/reload the page's content. An example of this type of page is yahoo sports, which reloads a page every 30 s for constantly updating sports scores. While there may or may not be valid security-related reasons for these refreshes, screen readers may respond by re-reading the entire page. This may lead to confusion, as the user may not be aware of what is going on and why, because they did not request for the page to be reloaded. Web pages should only reload per the user's request
4	Many PDFs are inaccessible, often in ways that imply security issues. When creating an Adobe PDF file the option is provided to allow changes or "lock it" and not allow changes. If changes are allowed, any user can copy and paste and make modifications to the document. If the document is locked so that changes are not allowed, it must be specifically noted that the text has to be accessible to users with assistive technology. If this accessibility option is not selected and the document is locked, then the PDF file may be inaccessible to screen reader users. In addition, the use of the term "lock" to prevent writes conflicts with most users perception of "lock" being used for security purposes
5	Some antivirus packages are inaccessible. Participants observed that Norton 2007 is apparently inaccessible, although 2006 was perceived to be very good. They also noted that some versions of McAfee are inaccessible. This is a security concern, as blind users want to protect themselves from viruses, but are unable to do so using some of the most current antivirus versions. This presents another trade-off: should users keep older virus software, which is accessible, or upgrade to newer virus software, which is more secure but less accessible?
6	Many times when a user loads a web page, some sort of software tries to automatically install. Such packages are often spyware that should not be installed. However, blind users may not be presented with enough information about what is trying to install to allow them to make an informed decision about installation. Improvements must be made to provide the users with more information about what piece of code is attempting to be installed, and to allow users to respond appropriately
7	Operating system and application updates can sometimes make some software packages inaccessible. This is another security compromise for users: if they update they could lose accessibility, but if they don't upgrade they could compromise security. This concern has led many blind users to disable automatic updating of software applications
8	SecureID is a handheld device that displays a frequently changing number that must be provided, along with a PIN, in order to authenticate to a VPN (virtual private network). Blind users cannot read the number displayed on the SecureID devices, so whatever system is being secured by this means is inaccessible to them

(continued)

Table 1. (*continued*)

9	Key loggers are malicious software packages that log every key that the user presses. These logs can later be reviewed to disclose user's passwords, credit card info, or other private information. These pieces of malicious software could be even more of a threat to blind users due to their dependency on the keyboard (and non-use of pointing devices). Key logging software is typically installed as spyware and is hard to identify on a computer
10	Spam is very annoying and inconvenient to all users, including blind users. Since blind users need to listen to the text of their e-mails, it may take more time to discern the true nature of the e-mails when compared with a quick visual scan. SPAM can also cause users—especially those who are underage—to be caught off guard by the content of some of these unsolicited junk messages

managers and CAPTCHAs and concerns about shoulder surfing. Participants reported problems in entering passwords accurately due to lack of feedback. Only one participant used a password manager, and other participants reported that they were not accessible and expressed concerns about their security. Two participants experienced difficulties with CAPTCHAs and similar mechanisms to deter bots on websites. Several participants felt they were more vulnerable to phishing and hacking attacks than sighted people.

Hayes and colleagues [11] conducted interviews with 12 visually disabled individuals about their experiences with password creation and management. They reported problems with creating strong passwords (although there is no mention of problems with password strength indicators) and password recovery systems. The researchers concluded that the issues of concern for visually disabled individuals are largely similar for those of sighted individuals, although their causes can be very different.

A considerable body of research has addressed the authentication problems of visually disabled individuals. However, it is interesting that it has been concentrated very heavily on a small subset of the problems identified, and not addressed all the areas which need attention. So, by far the greatest body of research has been on creating alternatives to visual CAPTCHAs, certainly an important issue. CAPTCHA was proposed in 2003 [3], and by 2007 [13] researchers were publishing audio alternative. A review of this research [a partial list of relevant research: 7, 13, 15, 16, 18–21, 23, 28] is beyond the scope of this paper, but we will address it elsewhere.

A smaller body of research has investigated more accessible alternatives to password authentication systems, for example PassTones [8], the tactile systems such as PassChords [5] and Kuber and Sharma's [14], a gesture-based system [22] and a very novel gesture plus token password system, BendyPass [10]. However, we could find no research which investigated the accessibility of password creation and use systems within the context of the Web Content Accessibility Guidelines [27], to investigate how accessible systems are and whether these guidelines can be used to assist developers in improving the accessibility of their systems. Nor could we find any research investigating the accessibility of password strength indicators and accessible forms for these, in spite of the fact that many of these use colour and graphics to indicate strength. Finally, one proposal for an accessible password manager [6] could be found.

Given the enormous growth in the use of QR codes since the coronavirus pandemic, this is another potential accessibility issue for visually disabled people. These codes are now used in many parts of the world to establish one's vaccination status when entering many locations (e.g. restaurants, shops, public transport), to trace whether individuals have been in contact with others who have or may have the coronavirus and for many other uses such as access to restaurant menus, information about goods in shops and exhibits in museums and art galleries. A priori, there seem to be two fundamental issues for using QR codes for visually disabled people – finding where a code or code reader is located to be able to interact with it, and then orienting one's device appropriately to interact with the code (neither of these issues is always straightforward for sighted individuals). A recent small survey of 38 visually disabled people [26] found that 35% had used QR codes independently, 26% had used them with sighted assistance and 39% have heard of them but never used them. Of those who had used them independently, 60% reported them difficult or very difficult to use. Vision Australia [25] have developed an app to help make QR codes accessible, and the NaviLens app (navilens.com) also addresses some of these problems. Research on their effectiveness and usability would be welcome.

Given the rapidly changing state of the digital world and assistive technologies, we decided to start our research with an online survey of visually disabled people in the United Kingdom and USA, to investigate what problems they are currently have with digital authentication and QR codes. This paper reports on the initial results from the United Kingdom.

3 Method

3.1 Participants

11 participants in the UK thus far have responded to the online survey. They are all male, aged between 40 and 71 years (mean 55.9 years). All are legally blind with no useful vision. They use a range of digital technologies including desktop computers, laptop computers, and smartphones (all used by 10 of the 11 participants, although different participants for each technology), although only 5 use tablet computers. All participants use the Windows operating system (OS), with 9 using iOS, 3 using Android and one using Linux as an OS. All participants use a screen reader, with 10 using NVDA 9 using JAWS, one using VoiceOver and one using Narrator when necessary.

3.2 Online Survey

An online survey was deployed using the Qualtrics survey software. A preliminary version of an online questionnaire for the survey was tested by an experienced blind screen reader user, to ensure it was accessible. One small problem was found which affected the "next page" button if the questionnaire was accessed via some versions of the Chrome browser. A work-around was indicated in the recruitment email and on the introductory screen of the questionnaire in Qualtrics and participants were also offered a Word version of the questionnaire to complete if they preferred. None of the participants asked for the Word version and all completed the questionnaire through Qualtrics successfully.

The questionnaire aimed to be short and simple and collect some initial data about the types and frequency of problems visually disabled people encounter with digital authentication and QR codes. It was divided into three sections:

Passwords: it was assumed that all participants would use passwords at least occasionally, so questions asked whether they ever have problems with systems for creating/entering/changing passwords and CAPTCHAs on a scale from "never" through "sometimes", "about half the time", "most of the time" to "always". If they answered more than "never", they were asked a follow-up open-ended question about the kind of problems they encounter. This section ended with an open-ended question asking about any other problems they have with password systems.

Other authentication systems: this section asked about password management systems, two factor authentication, fingerprint and facial recognition authentication systems and QR codes (for any purpose). The first question for each of these types was always "Have you used, or ever tried to use, [system]?", with a brief explanation of what each type of system involves, in case participants were not familiar with them. This was followed by an open-ended question to all participants: "Please describe whether you had success or not with [system] and any problems you have encountered".

Demographics: this section asked for basic demographic information of age, gender, nature of visual disability, use of mainstream and assistive technologies to access the internet.

4 Results

Table 2 shows the frequency of encountering problems with the different aspects of password use and CAPTCHAs. The majority of participants encounter problems with all aspects of passwords at least sometimes. CAPTCHAs cause problems most frequently (median of 4.0, corresponding to "most of the time"), with all participants encountering problems. This is followed in frequency of problems by creating, entering, and changing passwords, all with the same median frequency (corresponding to "sometimes"). The answers to the open-ended questions revealed a wide range of problems. In relation to CAPTCHAs, problems included no alternative to a visual CAPTCHA; but more importantly, difficulties with hearing and understanding audio CAPTCHAs which includes the ratio of deliberate background noise to signal being too high; and difficulties with remembering the items heard, due to the need to navigate to text field where it needs to be entered. One participant summed the situation up well with the comment: "the audio CAPTCHA, even if it was an acceptable alternative, which it is not, is usually hard to use" (P9). In relation to creating, entering and changing passwords, problems encountered included unlabeled edit fields; instructions, requirements for password composition and error messages that are difficult to find; and difficulty with using systems which require entering password characters in individual boxes.

Table 3 summarizes participants' use of password management systems, different digital authentication methods, and QR codes. Participants have had a range of experiences with password management systems. One participant tried three different systems, but none of them worked with his screen reader, so he gave up. Another participant has found one that is reasonable accessible (1Password), although he would like more short-cut keys and notes that the app version is easier to use than the website version. A further participant used a password manager happily for some time, but now finds it "way too complicated and not as nice and straight-forward as I'd [originally] found it" (P8).

Table 2. Frequency of encountering problems with passwords and CAPTCHAs

Creating passwords	5 participants never have problems, 5 participants sometimes, 1 participant about half the time (Median frequency: 2.0)
Entering passwords	2 participants never have problems, 8 participants sometimes, 1 participant most of the time (Median frequency: 2.0)
Changing passwords	4 participants never have problems, 7 participants sometimes (Median frequency: 2.0)
CAPTCHAs	0 participants never have problems, 2 participants sometimes, 1 participant about half the time, 4 participants most of the time, 4 participants always (Median frequency: 4.0)

Note. Ratings scored as Never = 1, Sometimes = 2, About half the time = 3, Most of the time = 4, Always = 5.

Table 3. Participants use of password management systems, different methods of digital authentication, and QR codes

Password management Systems	3 participants currently use, 2 used in the past but no longer use, 5 participants have never used
Two factor authentication	11 participants have used or tried to use
Fingerprint authentication	6 participants have used or tried to use, 5 have never used
Face recognition authentication	6 participants have used or tried to use, 5 have never used
QR codes	5 participants have used or tried to use, 6 have never used

All participants have used or tried to use two factor authentication, generally with success, although there are some problems. As with CAPTCHAs, codes are sometimes difficult to hear and understand. Screen readers can interpret the code incorrectly for example one participant noted that a three letter code was interpreted as "an abbreviations for a currency such as Kenyan Shillings. As I'm not familiar with such abbreviations, this can make it impossible" (P2) (Note: the abbreviation for the Kenyan Shilling is KES). Screen readers also have difficulty with codes which are a mixture of letters and digits. Several participants noted that they preferred the code to come in a text message, rather than a voice message, as with CAPTCHAs, the voice messages are sometimes difficult to hear and understand and do not create problems for screen readers.

All six participants who had used fingerprint recognition had been successful and reported no particular problems. On the other hand, of the six participants who had tried to use face recognition, five were not successful and needed sighted help to progress, although the other participant reported having no problems. As one participant noted "I once tried to use such a system without assistance, but there was no way I could line my face up in the position they wanted … the second time when I needed to use the NHS COVID app, I had sighted assistance" (P7).

On QR codes, only five participants had used them or tried to use them. All five reported some success, with the main problem being locating the code itself. As one participant concluded " … locating the QR code can be a challenge. When they work though they are extremely useful" (P9).

5 Discussion and Conclusions

This paper reported initial findings of an online survey to develop an understanding of the problems visually disabled people encounter with digital authentication methods, particularly passwords, and also with QR codes, which have become very widespread since the coronavirus pandemic. Thus far we only have a small sample of responses, from 11 totally blind people, and an all male sample and all people in the UK. We continue to collect data, in both the UK and the USA, to obtain a large and more diverse sample of visually disabled people. However, even with this small sample, some interesting results are suggested.

Perhaps most striking is the fact that although CAPTCHAs is the topic which has received the most research attention in the literature, it is also the aspect of digital authentication with which this sample of blind people encountered problems most frequently. All participants have encountered CAPTCHAs, and on average have problems with them "most of the time". There are clearly problems with the audio in audio alternatives to visual CAPTCHAs, and problems with the overall design of the interaction for someone using an audio CAPTCHA. Further work on the design of usable audio CAPTCHAs is still needed.

Password creation, entry and change systems, as well as password management systems, all suffer from a typical range of accessibility problems, although participants could generally use them. Developers of such systems would probably benefit from a guide to the common accessibility problems in their systems, which could be extracted from the Web Content Accessibility Guidelines (WCAG) [27]; this could potentially decrease the number of accessibility problems substantially. It is also interesting to note that password management systems seem to suffer from the common problem "feature creep" (the incremental addition of features, which users often find makes a system or product too complex to use) [24] and system updates, which often render a system less accessible than formerly.

In relation to other authentication systems, participants had few problems with two factor authentication, apart from some issues with audio messages, similar to the problems encountered with CAPTCHAs. Fingerprint recognition was also perhaps surprisingly successful, given that the feedback of how much of the fingerprint has been mapped is visual. However, there is usually an auditory tone to indicate successful recognition of the fingerprint, which would be helpful to blind and partially sighted users. On the other hand, it was not surprising that participants had little success with face recognition authentication. This is a problem that we have already highlighted as an accessibility issues [17]. As yet, the participants have have had little experience with QR codes, but have already identified that they can be hard to find in the environment without vision. So, if QR codes continue to be widely used in the post pandemic period, their accessibility will need to be addressed in more detail.

Overall, this small sample of blind participants had a wide range of accessibility problems with digital authentication and related issues. We will continue to collect data from a wider sample of participants and consider how we can address some of the problems raised by the research thus far.

References

1. Ahmed, T., Hoyle, R., Connelly, K., Crandall, D., Kapadia, A.: Privacy concerns and behaviors of people with visual impairments. 33rd ACM Conference on Human Factors in Computing Systems (CHI '15). New York: ACM Press (2015)
2. von Ahn, L., Blum, M., Hopper, N.J., Langford, J.: CAPTCHA: Using Hard AI Problems for Security. In: Biham, E. (ed.) EUROCRYPT 2003. LNCS, vol. 2656, pp. 294–311. Springer, Heidelberg (2003). https://doi.org/10.1007/3-540-39200-9_18
3. Alnfiai, M.: A novel design of audio CAPTCHA for visually impaired users. Int. J. Comm. Netw. Info. Sec. **12**(2), 168–179 (2020)
4. Azenkot, S., Bennett, C.L., Ladner, R.E.: DigiTaps: eyes-free number entry on touchscreens with minimal audio feedback. In: 26th Annual Symposium on User Interface Software and Technology (UIST '13). ACM Press, New York (2013)
5. Azenkot, S., Rector, K., Ladner, R., Wobbrock, J.: PassChords: secure multi-touch authentication for blind people. 14th International ACM SIGACCESS Conference on Computers and Accessibility (ASSETS '12). ACM Press, New York (2012)
6. Barbosa, S., Hayes, J., Wang, Y.: UniPass: design and evaluation of a smart device-based password manager for visually impaired users. In: 2016 ACM International Joint Conference on Pervasive and Ubiquitous Computing (UbiComp '16). ACM Press, New York (2016)
7. Bigham, J.P., Cavender, A.C.: Evaluating existing audio CAPTCHAs and an interface optimized for non-visual use. In: 27th ACM Conference on Human Factors in Computing Systems (CHI '09). ACM Press, New York (2009)
8. Brown, M., Doswell, F.R.: Using passtones instead of passwords. In: 48th Annual Southeast Regional Conference (ACM SE '10). ACM Press, New York (2010)
9. Dosono, B., Hayes, J., Wang, Y.: "I'm stuck!": a contextual inquiry of people with visual impairments in authentication. In: 11th Symposium on Usable Privacy and Security (SOUPS 2015). USENIX (2015)
10. Faustino, D.B., Girouard, A.: Bend passwords on BendyPass: A user authentication method for people with vision impairment. In: 20th International ACM SIGACCESS Conference on Computers and Accessibility (ASSETS '18). ACM Press, New York (2018)
11. Hayes, J., Dosono, B., Wang, Y.: They should be convenient and strong: password perceptions and practices of visually impaired users. In: Proceedings of iConference 2017 (2017). https://doi.org/10.9776/17215
12. Holman J., Lazar J., Feng J.: Investigating the security-related challenges of blind users on the Web. In: Langdon, P., Clarkson, J., Robinson, P. (eds.), Designing Inclusive Futures. Springer, London (2008). https://doi.org/10.1007/978-1-84800-211-1_13

13. Holman, J., Lazar, J., Feng, J.H., D'Arcy, J.: Developing usable CAPTCHAs for blind users. In: 9th International ACM SIGACCESS Conference on Computers and Accessibility (ASSETS '07). ACM Press, New York (2007)
14. Kuber, R., Sharma, S., Toward tactile authentication for blind users. In: 12th International ACM SIGACCESS Conference on Computers and Accessibility (ASSETS '10). ACM Press, New York (2010)
15. Lazar, J., et al.: The SoundsRight CAPTCHA: an improved approach to audio human interaction proofs for blind users. In: SIGCHI Conference on Human Factors in Computing Systems (CHI '12). ACM Press, New York (2012)
16. Olalere, A., Feng, J.H., Lazar, J., Brooks, T.: Investigating the effects of sound masking on the use of audio CAPTCHAs. Behav. Info. Technol. **33**(9), 919–928 (2014)
17. Petrie, H., Wakefield, M.: Remote moderated and unmoderated evaluation by users with visual disabilities of an online registration and authentication system for health services. In: Proceedings of the 9th International Conference on Software Development and Technologies for Enhancing Accessibility and Fighting Info-exclusion (DSAI 2020). ACM Press, New York (2020)
18. Sauer, G., Hochheiser, H., Feng, J., Lazar, J.: Towards a universally usable CAPTCHA. In: 4th Symposium on Usable Privacy and Security (SOUPS '08). USENIX (2008)
19. Sauer, G., Holman, J., Lazar, J., Hochheiser, H., Feng, J.: Accessible privacy and security: a universally usable human-interaction proof tool. Univers. Access Info. Soc. **9**(3), 239–248 (2010)
20. Sauer, G., Lazar, J., Hochheiser, H., Feng, J.: Towards a universally usable human interaction proof: evaluation of task completion strategies. ACM Transactions on Accessible Computing **2**(4) (2010). Article 15
21. Shirali-Shahreza, S., Penn, G., Balakrishnan, R., Ganjali, Y.: SeeSay and HearSay CAPTCHA for mobile interaction. In: SIGCHI Conference on Human Factors in Computing Systems (CHI '13). ACM Press, New York (2013)
22. Sreeramareddy, L., Miao, S., Feng, J.H.: Investigating gesture-based password: usability and vulnerability to shoulder-surfing attacks. In: Conference on Research in Adaptive and Convergent Systems (RACS '14). ACM Press, New York (2014)
23. Tariq, N., Khan, F.A.: Match-the-Sound CAPTCHA. In: Latifi, S. (ed.) Information Technology - New Generations. Advances in Intelligent Systems and Computing, vol. 558. Springer, Cham (2018). https://doi.org/10.1007/978-3-319-54978-1_99
24. Thompson, D.V., Norton, M.I.: The social utility of feature creep. J. Mark. Res. **48**(3), 555–565 (2011)
25. Vision Australia: QR code advice for people who are blind or have low vision (2021). https://www.visionaustralia.org/community/news/2021-08-24/qr-code-advice-people-who-are-blind-or-have-low-vision
26. VocalEyes: Digital accessibility: QR codes and short number SMS (n.d.). https://vocaleyes.co.uk/about/research/digital-accessibility-qr-codes-and-short-number-sms/
27. Web Accessibility Initiative: Web Content Accessibility Guidelines 2.1 (2018). www.w3.org/TR/WCAG21/
28. Yamaguchi, M., Nakata, T., Watanabe, H., Okamoto, T., Kikuchi, H.: Vulnerability of the conventional accessible CAPTCHA used by the White House and an alternative approach for visually impaired people. In: IEEE International Conference on Systems, Man, and Cybernetics (SMC). IEEE (2014)

Layered Audio Descriptions for Videos

Remo Schneider(✉), Tobias Ableitner(✉), and Gottfried Zimmermann(✉)

Stuttgart Media University, Nobelstraße 10, 70569 Stuttgart, Germany
remo.schneider@gmx.de, {ableitner,zimmermanng}@hdm-stuttgart.de

Abstract. The increasing availability of online video content, partially fueled by the Covid-19 pandemic and the growing presence of social media, adds to the importance of providing audio descriptions as a media alternative to video content for blind and visually impaired persons. To address concerns as to what can be sufficiently described, we developed a concept providing audio descriptions in three levels of detail. We included an additional feature for providing optional explanations to terms and abbreviations, helping users without specific knowledge or persons with neurodiversity in comprehending complex video content. We implemented these features in a prototype based on the open-source Able Player, using an XML-based data structure to store information for all layers of audio descriptions. A qualitative user test focused on the benefits of multi-layered audio descriptions and optional explanatory content. Findings suggest that the choice on several levels of detail is received positively by users. They also appreciated the concept of optional explanations and came up with further use cases for such a practice. Participants preferred a higher level of detail for a high-paced action video and a lower level for informative content.

Keywords: Audio description · HTML5 · Layered audio description · User test · XML · Text-to-speech (TTS) · Web accessibility · Blind users · Visually impaired users · Users with cognitive impairments

1 Introduction

The Covid-19 pandemic and associated stay-at-home orders imposed by multiple governments worldwide have set forth a dramatic increase in the overall consumption of online video content. Combined with the constant growth of social media platforms that focus primarily on visuals, audiovisual content plays an increasingly important role in our everyday lives. In this context, the ability to see is often taken for granted.

However, blind or vision impaired people might encounter difficulties consuming video content without media alternatives and proper aid from assistive technologies. The European Blind Union estimates that an average of 1 in 30 Europeans experience sight loss, and, according to the WHO, at least 1.2 million people in Germany are visually impaired (EBU 2010). These figures are proportionally similar in other European countries such as Belgium, Italy, Poland, Portugal, Spain, and the UK. Additionally, the age factor bends these statistics. People aged 65 and older constitute the most extensive

K. Miesenberger et al. (Eds.): ICCHP-AAATE 2022, LNCS 13342, pp. 51–63, 2022.
https://doi.org/10.1007/978-3-031-08645-8_7

and growing group of blind and visually impaired people in all participating countries, which is projected to rise in coming years (ADLAB 2012).

Legislation by the European Union (EU) demands that the Member States take appropriate measures to ensure equal access for all people, regardless of disabilities, to fully participate in society, and interact with public institutions without obstruction. The European Web Accessibility Directive (European Commission 2016) demands basic accessibility requirements to be applied based on the four basic principles of W3C's Web Content Accessibility Guidelines (WCAG) version 2.1 (W3C 2018). The technical European Standard (EN) 301 549 specifies requirements for ICT products and services and is recognized by the EU as the de-facto reference for the accessibility of electronic media.

One of the primary adaptation strategies for blind and visually impaired audiences is the practice of audio description, narrations describing visuals spoken into existing gaps or pauses in video content. As it may occur that the existing pauses do not suffice to provide enough capacity for standard audio description, another practice referred to as extended audio description may be employed in such cases. Extended audio descriptions provide extensive detail by pausing a video for the duration of the descriptions. Modern web technology has increased developers' availability to use synthesized voices in browsers, potentially enabling authors to provide audio descriptions more easily by merely embedding a text-based description script.

This study explores an approach to extend the existing practices of arranging audio descriptions by a concept that consolidates description information in multiple levels, or layers, of detail. We developed an XML-based data structure that incorporates three layers of audio description into one single source file. Further, a novel feature provides supplementary content in the form of explanations to accompany visual content, aiding people without specific knowledge about a portrayed subject or potential users with cognitive impairments.

2 Related Work

There is previous work related to layered audio descriptions. In this chapter, we briefly described the most important works, and how our work resembles or contrasts them. For a description of our work, refer to chapters 3 and 4.

Our structure of an XML-based audio description script resembles the language by Adams and Lemieux (2018), which does not contain the functionality to include several levels of detail but bears the potential to be extended with such.

Senina et al. (2014) generated descriptions coherently in varying levels of detail by employing automatic segmentation and extraction algorithms. While our work focuses on storing and processing descriptions in several levels of detail, their algorithm could potentially accelerate the generation of such descriptions through automatization.

The National Center for Accessible Media "NCAM" (2012) has developed a similar system providing supplementary materials to display glossary definitions and Wikipedia entries along with video content. Their idea resembles our concept of opt-in explanations but offers no user-based evaluation.

Kobayashi et al. (2009) describe the development of a platform providing audio descriptions for online videos, covering the process from authoring to the output as a text script and a synthesized audio track, which we utilize in our work as well. Their text-based script format is, however, not disclosed in detail.

Kobayashi et al. (2010) assessed the feasibility of synthesized audio descriptions by conducting a user test where vision-impaired participants watched video samples with audio descriptions from speech synthesis engines and a human voice. Their results suggest that synthesized descriptions are generally accepted, while clarity and the choice of words outweigh the emotional expression or character of voices. We assume this general acceptance of synthesized voices in our work.

Fryer and Freeman (2013) studied levels of presence between sighted and vision-impaired participants when watching a video without audio description, with a standard audio description and cinematic audio description, which includes cinematic elements such as editing techniques and camera work. Their findings suggest that visually impaired audiences experience levels of presence equal to or even exceeding those of the sighted audience. Our work focuses on incorporating several levels of detail into a data structure that could potentially include cinematic information.

Ely et al. (2006) conducted a test with fourth-grade students to examine the amount of knowledge acquired by watching curricular videos with both standard and extended audio descriptions. Their results show that students performed better on tests for content that included extended audio descriptions even though the original video is frequently interrupted. We observe a similar behavior in the results of our work.

3 Method

3.1 Development

We developed a concept where the information contributed by audio description to a video is incorporated into three layers of detail (low, medium, high). The differentiation between these layers is laid out in Table 1.

Table 1. Overview on the three levels of detail

Level	Characteristics	Example
Low	Basic information that is necessary to follow the watched content. Comparable to the amount of information available in current audio descriptions in a non-extended form. The description content fits into the natural pauses of the main content without a freeze or auditory overlap	"An avatar appears on the screen"

(continued)

Table 1. *(continued)*

Level	Characteristics	Example
Medium	Descriptions are no longer bound to fit into natural pauses. The level of details exceeds those of "low" by including additional effects that led to or result from actions that would have been described in "low"	"An avatar of a man with white hair appears on the screen"
High	Highly exceptional level of detail. Comparable to the amount of information available in common extended audio descriptions. Description content is unbound to natural pauses and includes details regarding the appearance, color, and other visual details that may be subtle but still bear meaning within the content, although not explicitly required to follow the visual content at a given position	"The speaker turns to the screen behind him, where an avatar of a man appears with white hair combed to the side. They look at each other"

Further, we developed a feature of explanations that provide additional insight into the video content. These explanations are referred to as "opt-in explanations" because users must trigger the explanation content to be displayed actively. This feature is comparable with the HTML <abbr> element, which provides a corresponding definition to an abbreviation that might be unknown to the user. The appearance of how such an element is rendered in a browser suggests visibly to a user that a definition is available. Most browsers realize this visual indication through a dotted underline, while the definition is displayed in a tooltip when hovering the mouse pointer over the abbreviated term. Following this concept, opt-in explanations aim to indicate visually to a user that additional information to a spoken term is available while watching a video. By providing background knowledge of complicated terms or contexts, this feature aims to help users that are unfamiliar with the content or with cognitive impairments to follow content more efficiently. The procedure is this: A user watches a video in which a specific term, or cue, is spoken or shown. Identified by the current playback position, the title of this cue is displayed to the user. Within a defined time frame, which is intended to last for several seconds, the user has the option to prompt the explanation content to that specific cue by pressing a defined shortcut key. The video playback is temporarily paused and can be resumed once the user is ready to continue watching (Fig. 1).

We integrated these features into Able Player, an open-source media playout software based on HTML5 and the <track> element, developed by Thompson (2018). Able Player supports all kinds of text tracks that can be provided via the track element: Subtitles, captions, metadata, and chapters. Multiple text-track sources can be embedded into a video element. They are consolidated during web page loading and made available within the user interface of Able Player.

WebVTT (Pfeiffer et al. 2019), the de-facto file format for captions in a web context, does not allow for incorporating several levels of detail; nor do other existing data structures for embedding description texts on media content. Therefore, we developed a custom structure and prototypically implemented the processing of such into the open-source Able Player. We used an XML format due to its flexibility and customizability through element attributes and schema definitions. It allows for incorporating multiple levels of detail into one single file and classifying such levels with a corresponding attribute. Additionally, translations of descriptions for other languages can be included in a single file while maintaining a status of an industry standard (XML) whose validity can be thoroughly ensured by using XML schema definitions.

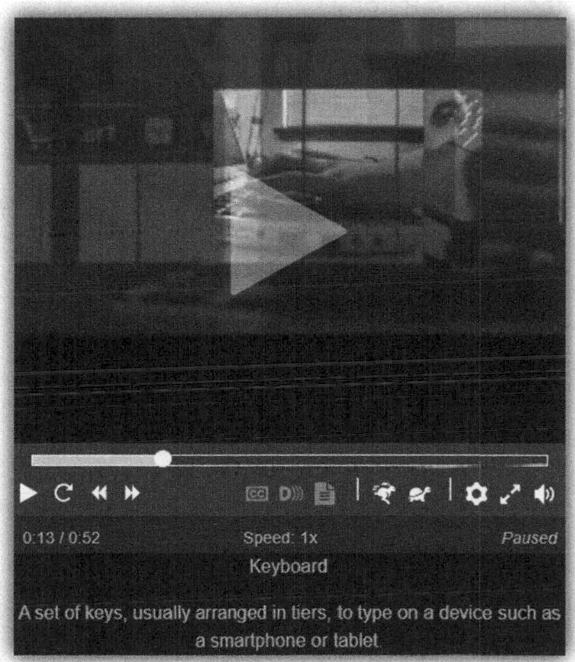

Fig. 1. Player paused while description is shown underneath the keyword.

In a prototypical implementation, we extended the Able Player to allow the XML-based script files to be embedded via HTML5 <track> elements, using the attribute-value pair "kind = ext-descriptions", building upon the existing value of "descriptions". Our prototype arranges description cues by parsing the XML data structure according to the corresponding element names (<desc> or <expl>), and their attributes level/category, start and end time. The following code demonstrates an exemplary XML code with three <desc> elements, with increasing levels of detail ("low", "medium" and "high").

```
<desc level="low" position="00:00:11.000"
end="00:00:15.000">
  <content>
    He pulls out his phone and presses a button twice.
  </content>
</desc>
<desc level="medium" position="00:00:11.000"
end="00:00:15.000">
  <content>
    He unfolds his phone and presses a center button
twice.
    Then, another button.
  </content>
</desc>
<desc level="high" position="00:00:11.000"
end="00:00:15.000">
  <content>
    He pulls out his phone and unfolds it. The inside
screen reads "Welcome".
    He presses the center button twice. Then, another
button.
  </content>
</desc>
```

3.2 Evaluation

To validate the prototypical implementation developed during this research, we conducted a user test to determine:

1. benefit and added value for a user who does not see the video visuals but instead is provided with audio descriptions in multiple levels of detail, and
2. the usefulness of opt-in explanations for unfamiliar content provided as supplementary content to the video.

We chose a mixed-method approach by conducting a qualitative user test (talk-aloud), while obtaining user satisfaction quantitatively in a survey. Due to the circumstances associated with the Covid-19 pandemic during July of 2021, the user test took place as a synchronous remote test. As the recruitment of blind and vision-impaired participants proved difficult within the available time in a remote setting, we used a convenience sample of five Bachelor students of media informatics and mobile media at Stuttgart Media University. Previous knowledge about digital accessibility, including audio description, can be presumed, since they had attended a lecture on Human Computer Interaction. We offered students a small grading bonus for their participation in the study. The requirement for all participants were a minimum of 18 years of age and consent to the terms of the study themselves. Also, for English language skills, we recommended a level of at least B2 of the Common European Framework of Reference for Languages. This was deemed necessary since the test was conducted in English and contained English video material and descriptions.

The test environment was based on the open-source video conferencing software Big Blue Button where recordings of the sessions could be produced and stored securely and in accordance with applicable privacy laws. Conducted as a synchronous test, the main author moderated and observed the session in real-time. The role of the main author being the moderator and developer of the prototype at the same time was not disclosed to the participants in order to avoid bias.

The five participants signed a consent form acknowledging that the sessions would be recorded and that they could abandon or interrupt the study at any time. Prior to the study, the supervising professor approved the consent form in an ethical review.

The session consisted of three scenarios utilizing features of multi-layered audio descriptions and opt-in explanations. With a presentation, participants were introduced to the prototype and asked demographic questions and whether they had previous knowledge about the practice of audio description.

For scenario 1A, participants followed on our prototypical player a short excerpt of about 1:30 min from a recent technology conference keynote. The video track of the sample had been concealed with a black layer to simulate a vision impairment situation, where relevant content was perceivable only through an audio channel combined with the corresponding layered audio description prepared for this scenario. Users were asked to play the scene and adjust the level of detail to their liking until they felt most comfortable with the extent of details provided for this type of video (Fig. 2). The participants were not given a time restriction on finishing this task or how often they would choose to re-play the video. The moderator's microphone was muted during this exploratory time to not disturb or distract the participants. The participants signaled when they were finished with the task. Subsequently, participants answered a set of questions regarding the perception and impression of the video content in consideration of their selection of level of detail.

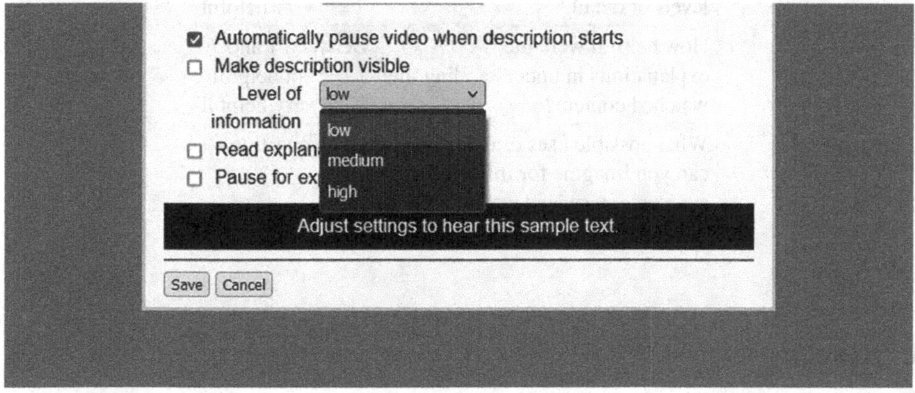

Fig. 2. Settings window where users can switch between levels of detail.

The second round, scenario 1B, contained a short excerpt about 1:30 min from an action movie that involved a car chase, shooting, and high-paced editing. Again, the video track was concealed. The purpose of this difference in character was to determine whether participants would choose different settings for this type of video and why. Participants were given the same task as before to follow the content, find their suitable setting and subsequently answer the same set of questions.

Finally, scenario 2 focused on the feature of opt-in explanations and the interaction of users with the proposed explanation content. A short scene of about 1:30 min was played (with full video and audio), depicting an interview with the director of a biological research project. The interviewee's remarks included subject-specific terms. Three of these terms were, at the appropriate positions, displayed in text form underneath the player's control panel. Participants could then choose, by pressing the key 'E' (for explanation), to display the definitions of the terms at their discretion. This time, the video was not concealed. Again, the participants were free to take their time and to re-play the video. Upon signaling the completion of the task, participants answered another set of questions regarding the usefulness of the explanations and possible applications and extensions (see Table 2).

Table 2. Catalog of questions for participants.

Question identifier	Question	Response option
1A.1 (scenario 1A) 1B.1 (scenario 1B)	Which setting did you prefer for this video and why?	Open question
1A.2 (scenario 1A) 1B.2 (scenario 1B)	How detailed can you imagine the visuals being described?	Between 1 and 7 1 = "not at all", 7 = "very detailed"
1A.3 (scenario 1A) 1B.3 (scenario 1B)	How would you rate your ability to follow the described content?	Between 1 and 7 1 = "not at all", 7 = "very easy"
1A.4 (scenario 1A) 1B.4 (scenario 1B)	How helpful did you find the option to choose from different levels of detail?	Between 1 and 7 1 = "not helpful at all", 7 = "very helpful"
2.1 (scenario 2)	How helpful were the explanations in understanding the watched content?	Between 1 and 7 1 = "not helpful", 7 = "very helpful"
2.2 (scenario 2)	What possible uses or extensions can you imagine for this kind of supplementary content?	Open question

4 Results

In the following, we present the results of the validation of our prototype. We hereby refer to the five participants as P1, P2, P3, P4 and P5.

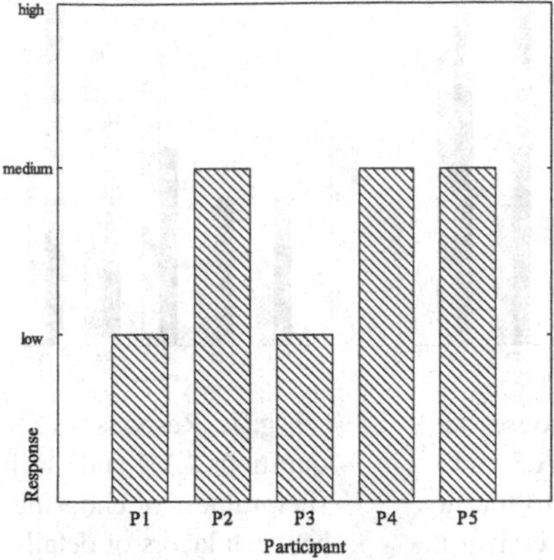

Fig. 3. Level of detail preferred by participants for scenario 1A (conference keynote).

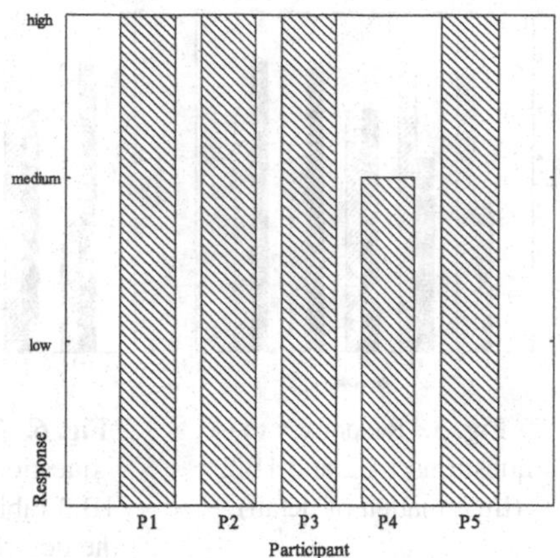

Fig. 4. Level of detail preferred by participants for scenario 1B (action movie).

4.1 Tree-Layered Audio Description

For scenario 1A (conference keynote), participants preferred audio descriptions of level low or medium (see Fig. 3). P1 stated that options other than low be distracting from the content. P3 rated information in level high as partially unnecessary, explaining that a description that provides more information than the actual presentation is distracting. In a similar fashion, P5 perceived the highest level of information as overwhelming for this kind of video.

For scenario 1B (action movie), participants preferred a more extensive level of detail (see Fig. 4). P1 regarded low and medium levels as insufficient for an action scene and stated that, to have an imaginary inner picture of the scene, a high degree of details was necessary. A similar statement was made by P2, who shuffled through different settings but settled on high without repeating the video, affirming the need for a high amount of details. P3 initially chose low but changed the settings quickly to high. P5 stated that because of the nature of an action scene, they wanted to know what was happening exactly and described the high level of detail as "very good." P4 chose medium as the only participant, arguing it was a comfortable option. Participant's ratings on their imagination and ability to follow the content with the chosen settings are shown in Figs. 5, 6 and 7 (scenario 1A presented in black, scenario 1B shaded).

Watching the conference video (scenario 1A), participants rated their ability to imagine the visual content distinctively (question 1A.2), with two participants rating 6 out of 7, while the remaining chose 3, 4, and 5, respectively (see Fig. 5). Regarding the ability to follow the content considering the interruptions caused by the descriptions (question 1A.3), all participants stated that they were able to follow the content rather well, with two participants rating the highest available option, while two others chose the second-highest available options (see Fig. 6). P2 acknowledged not being used to the generated voice, causing the consumption to be hard at first, but remarked to have

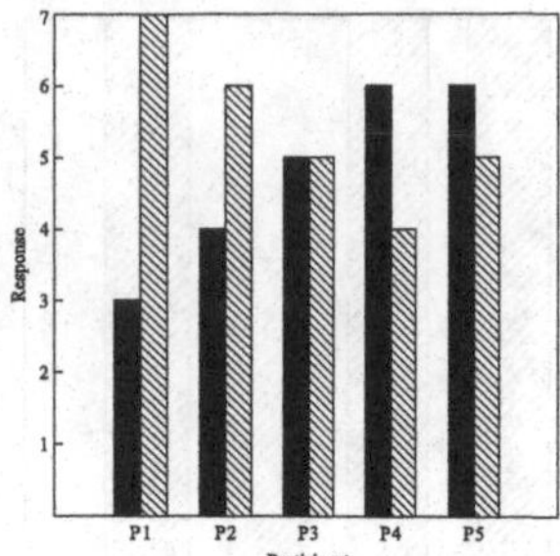

Fig. 5. Responses to questions 1A.2 and 1B.2 (imagination of detail).

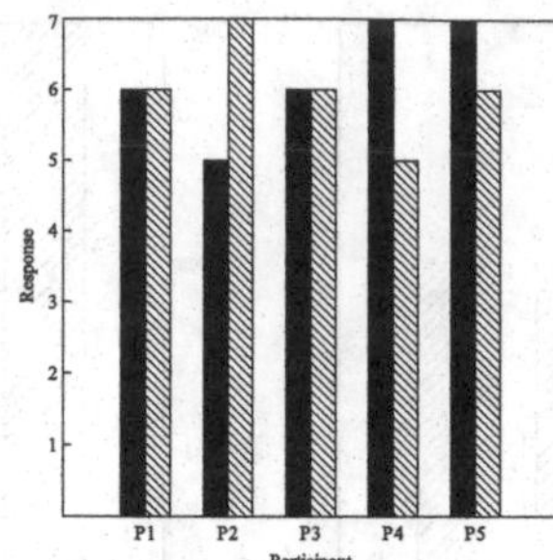

Fig. 6. Responses to questions 1A.3 and 1B.3 (ability to follow the described content).

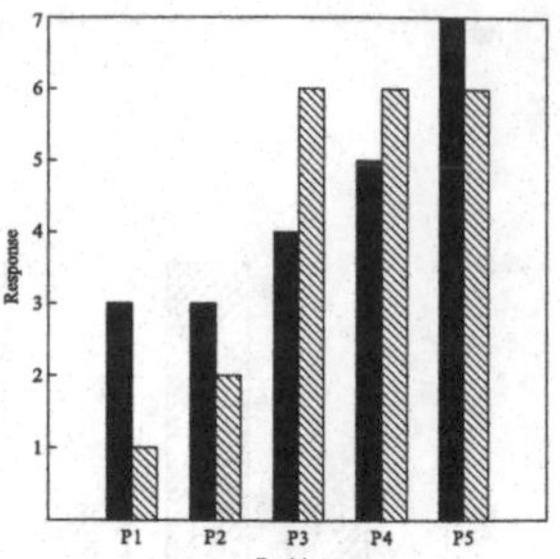

Fig. 7. Responses to questions 1A.4 and 1B.4 (helpfulness of choosing between layers of detail).

become accustomed to the voice as the video progressed. P2 ultimately rated their ability as 5, expressing a position on the upper half of the scale.

The scene from the action movie (scenario 1B) saw a minor variation in their ability to imagine the visual content (question 1B.2) (see Fig. 5). Only P4 chose to rate a value of four while being the only participant who preferred to watch the content with a "medium" level of detail setting. All participants rated their ability to follow the watched content (question 1B.3) remarkably high, with three rating second-highest, one rating highest (see Fig. 6). P4 as the only participant who preferred to set a "medium" level of detail rated five.

Finally, the usefulness of being able to choose from different levels of detail revealed a significant difference in rating (see Fig. 7). Regarding scenario 1A (question 1A.4), P2 stated that if the description content is sufficient, they would not need more or fewer details, explaining that the description should either describe the content correctly or leave something out. Scenario 1B (question 1B.4) revealed an even higher dissimilarity among participants. While P1 and P2 chose the lowest available rating of one and second-lowest rating of two, the remaining participants chose the second-highest rating of 6. Both P1 and P2 stated that they would not change the setting of a high level of detail and, therefore, would not need the option to switch between such. P2 added that while watching a movie, they would not know how much information they would be missing and would prefer to watch through the movie instead of changing the level and repeating a scene with different settings.

4.2 Opt-in Explanations

During scenario 2, participants interacted individually with the offered explanations, as they were free to choose which to display and whether to repeat the video or not. Their responses are presented in Fig. 8.

P1 chose to display all three of the explanations in one round. P2 chose only the second explanation on the first round, then watched the video again and chose the other explanations as well. P3 used the explanation only for the first one, then on a second round, after a page reload caused by a software malfunction, also chose the explanation

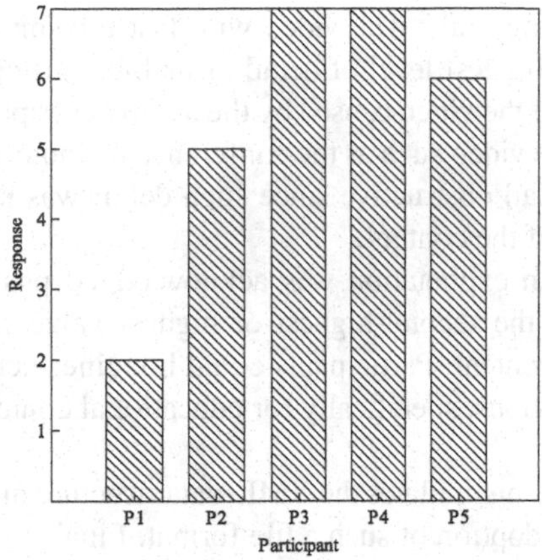

Fig. 8. Participant's rating of the helpfulness of the explanations to the watched content (question 2.1).

for the second cue. Likewise, P4 had to reload the page after choosing the first and second explanation cue on the first round, then after the reload, used the third cuc as well. P5 chose the first and third one in a single round.

Participants ultimately stated their imaginable use cases or extensions for the concept of opt-in explanations as supplementary content to audiovisual media. Four out of five participants stated the same use case as presented in scenario 2, i.e., showing a definition of unknown or complex terms. P2 appreciated that, while watching the video, it would not be necessary to abandon the page where content is played to retrieve additional information on the content actively. P3 recognized that understanding the content of the video would not have been possible without thc provided explanations. P3 and P5 both emphasized the benefit of this concept for advanced terms, especially when presented in a language that is not native to the user. Documentaries were mentioned as an additional example for this situation. P1 and P5 both indicated potential use for such a function when combined with educational content, such as teaching videos for students on platforms such as YouTube. P5 suggested a possible extension of this feature by providing several categories, ranging from general explanations, such as term definitions and abbreviations, to more detailed and advanced explanations like contextual information. At last, P2 expressed concerns regarding the expectations authors potentially have towards the audience, specifically on the question of whether an audience may be considered knowledgeable on a particular subject or not.

5 Conclusion

In this paper, we described a novel concept for audio descriptions containing three levels of detail. We developed a schema for an XML-based data structure and applied it to a prototypical implementation based on Able Player. Finally, we validated the prototype by a qualitative user test.

Generally, participants accepted the concept as presented through the three scenarios. The majority rated the usefulness of choosing between different levels of detail on the upper half of the rating scale. The video with fast transpiring content was preferably consumed with the highest level of detail available. Participants did not mind the numerous interruptions of the video caused by the audio descriptions in extensive detail. Merely for an informative video such as the conference keynote, participants considered the higher amount of detail obstructive since such detail was not perceived to aid the essential understanding of the content.

The concept of opt-in explanation was acknowledged positively, with three participants rating the cues the second-highest or highest value concerning the merit in understanding complex content. Participants could imagine such a feature being incorporated in everyday situations, specifically for educational content and subjects outside of a viewers' expertise.

An authoring tool that manipulates the XML-data structure in a simplified way would potentially increase the adoption of such a file format. Finally, to make opt-in explanations available in settings such as a lecture or a cinema where video content is presented to an audience of multiple persons with possibly varying preferences, a distributed system could enable users to individually interact with the explanation process, possibly involving devices such as smartphones and smartwatches. In order to avoid visual clutter and/or distraction, these devices could have a tactile interface to alert their users on the availability of opt-in explanations.

References

Adams, G., Lemieux, P.-A.: Timed Text Markup Language 1 (Third Edition). W3C Recommendation (2018). https://www.w3.org/TR/ttml1/

ADLAB: Report on User Needs Assessment (No. 1; ADLAB -- Audio Description: Lifelong Access to the Blind) (2012). http://www.adlabproject.eu

Kirkpatrick, A., O Connor, J., Campbell, A., Cooper, M.: Web Content Accessibility Guidelines (WCAG) 2.1 (2018). https://www.w3.org/TR/WCAG21/

EBU: About blindness and partial sight: Facts and figures [European Blind Union] (2010). http://www.euroblind.org/about-blindness-and-partial-sight/facts-and-figures

Ely, R., Emerson, R.W., Maggiore, T., Rothberg, M., O'Connell, T., Hudson, L.: Increased content knowledge of students with visual impairments as a result of extended descriptions. J. Spec. Educ. Technol. **21**(3), 31–43 (2006). https://doi.org/10.1177/016264340602100304

European Commission—Directive on making public sector websites and apps more accessible (EU) 2016/2102 (2016). http://data.europa.eu/eli/dir/2016/2102/oj

Fryer, L., Freeman, J.: Visual impairment and presence: measuring the effect of audio description. In: Proceedings of the 2013 Inputs-Outputs Conference: An Interdisciplinary Conference on Engagement in HCI and Performance, pp. 1–5 (2013). https://doi.org/10.1145/2557595.2557599

Kobayashi, M., Fukuda, K., Takagi, H., Asakawa, C.: Providing synthesized audio description for online videos. In: Proceedings of the 11th International ACM SIGACCESS Conference on Computers and Accessibility, pp. 249–250 (2009). https://doi.org/10.1145/1639642.1639699

Kobayashi, M., O'Connell, T., Gould, B., Takagi, H., Asakawa, C.: Are synthesized video descriptions acceptable? In: Proceedings of the 12th International ACM SIGACCESS Conference on Computers and Accessibility, pp. 163–170 (2010). https://doi.org/10.1145/1878803.1878833

NCAM: Using HTML5 and Javascript to Deliver Accessible Supplemental Materials [Demonstrational model and description]. National Center for Accessible Media; Readers Digest Partners for Sight Foundation (2012). http://ncamftp.wgbh.org/rd/hgp/

Pfeiffer, S., Pieters, S., Jägenstedt, P., Hickson, I.: WebVTT: The Web Video Text Tracks Format [W3C Candidate Recommendation] (2019). https://www.w3.org/TR/webvtt1/

Schneider, R.: Development and validation of a concept for layered audio descriptions. Master thesis. Hochschule der Medien Stuttgart (2021). https://nbn-resolving.org/urn:nbn:de:bsz:900-opus4-66690

Senina, A., Rohrbach, M., Qiu, W., Friedrich, A., Pinkal, M., Schiele, B.: Coherent Multi-sentence Video Description with Variable Level of Detail. In: Jiang, X., Hornegger, J., Koch, R. (eds.) GCPR 2014. LNCS, vol. 8753, pp. 184–195. Springer, Cham (2014). https://doi.org/10.1007/978-3-319-11752-2_15

Thompson, T.: Media player accessibility: summary of insights from interviews & focus groups. J. Technol. Persons Disabil. **6**, 325–336 (2018). Library of Congress

Serious and Fun Games

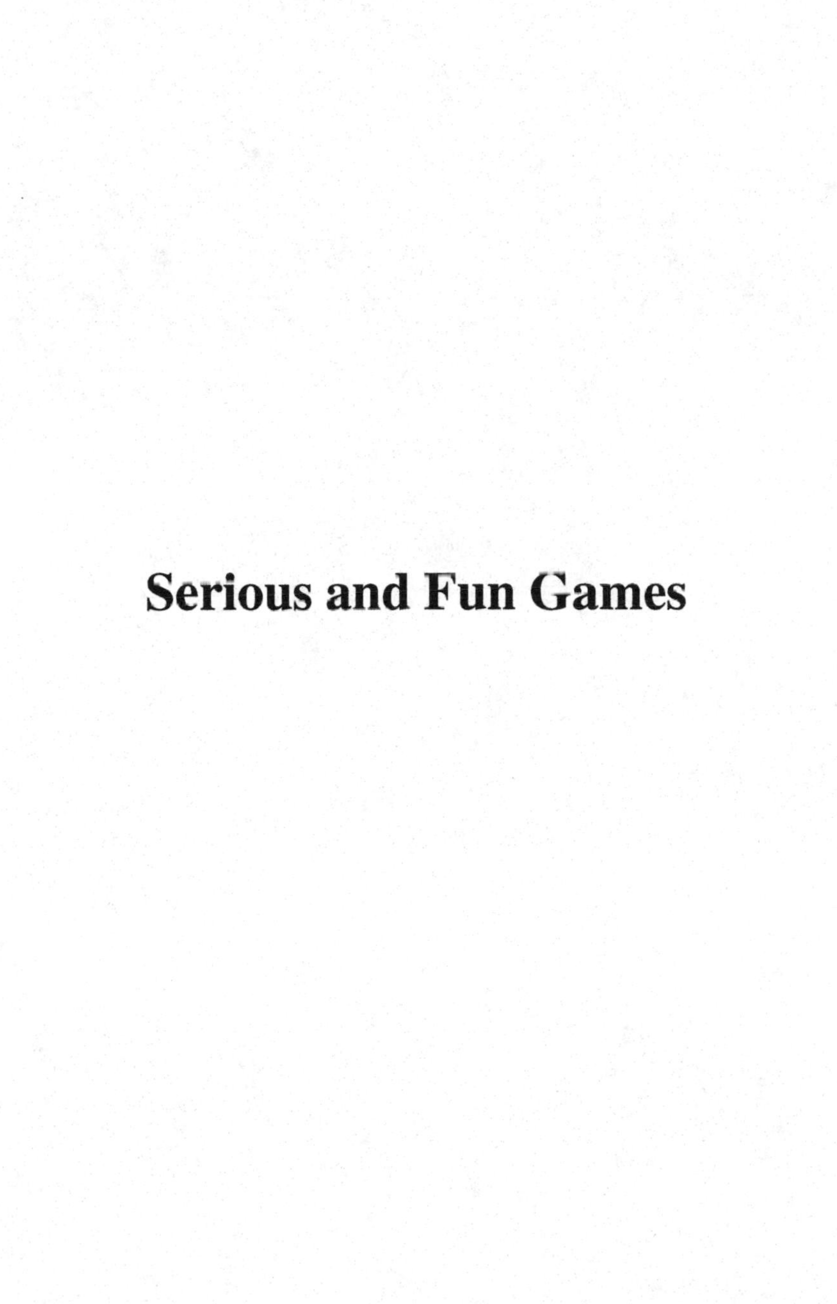

Serious and Fun Games

Introduction to the Special Thematic Session

Cecilia Sik-Lanyi(✉) and Jinat Ara

University of Pannonia, Egyetem Street 10, Veszprem 8200, Hungary
lanyi@almos.uni-pannon.hu, jinat.ara@virt.uni-pannon.hu

Abstract. The objective of game-based learning or serious game is to learn and apply in a real-life scenario. This technological learning process is not just for play, it is designed to increase knowledge and guide users toward their goals. Therefore, Serious and Fun Games Special Thematic Session aims to bring together academic scientists, researchers, Ph.D. students, and research scholars to exchange and share their experiences, opinions, and research results on all aspects of Game-Based Learning and Serious Games to help people with disabilities and people who need special technology to improve their daily activities to overcome the limitations they have. The target groups of these Serious Games are blind people or people with low vision, hearing impairment, motion challenges, learning problems, special children or autism, diabetic patient, or any sorts of physical and mental disabilities. This session also provides an interdisciplinary platform for researchers, practitioners, and educators to present and discuss the most recent innovations and trends in the focused area. High-quality research contributions describing original and unpublished results of conceptual, constructive, empirical, experimental, or theoretical work in all areas of Game-Based Learning and Serious Games were cordially invited for presentation at the Special Thematic Session (STS). This session is the continuing session of the previous conference "Serious and Fane Games" STS.

Keywords: Game-based learning · Serious game · Disabilities · Special Thematic Session

1 What We Know About Serious Games

The serious-game paradigm is related to learning with gameplay scenarios, scoring points, clearing levels, and getting badges to facilitate the acquisition of new knowledge and skills [1]. In other terms, the serious game known as "exergames" that develop for encouraging and guiding physical activity for fitness. The development of exergames includes smooth animations of avatars to play on behalf of the human factor with human-computer interaction knowledge.

According to Kapp 2012, Gamification is a buzzword that incorporates several mechanisms to engage a wide array of people to promote their thinking and learning ability to solve a specific problem [2]. A serious game is a branch of gamification with the same motivation to design for a specific group of people with a unique purpose related

K. Miesenberger et al. (Eds.): ICCHP-AAATE 2022, LNCS 13342, pp. 67–72, 2022.
https://doi.org/10.1007/978-3-031-08645-8_8

to training, learning, etc., not just for fun. The prime objective of a serious game is improving a certain situation or ability that is beyond entertainment. The unique purpose of a serious game is to achieve the predetermined. For example, training post covid patients to teach how to improve their memory to overcome memory fog that might be a potential future development conception. In other words, beyond the surface of gaming actions, serious games try to evoke learning processes or even complex experiences. For example, according to the perspective of the current refugee wave, the training is about the danger zone and how to bring them out safely.

The serious game is also known as the digital game. It performs in an electronic device by integrating microprocessors, specialized hardware sensors, controllers, game engines, and algorithms. It serves in several domains with different purposes such as education, training, healthcare, exercising, rehabilitation, prevention, etc. In education, serious games enhance the learning process of special education by supporting the teaching and learning process of typical school subjects. It also helps to improve various conceptual, social, practical, and intellectual functioning skills. In recent, serious games has developed to help and train dental students to develop their clinical reasoning skills and improve knowledge [3]. From the healthcare perspective, a serious game was developed by [4] to educate and improve nursing student attitude, knowledge, and uptake of the influenza vaccination. In the context of exercising, acute and chronic neck pain are common medical conditions. The treatment against these complications is physical therapy involving daily exercises. Sometimes, insufficient motivation hampers the exercise process that delays the recovery rate. Therefore, a Virtual Reality (VR) environment-based serious exergame was initiated by [5] to motivate people for their neck exercises which could be a great example of serious games. Following this application, [1] developed a serious game to motivate users to exercise regularly and correctly. Furthermore, in rehabilitation, serious games are used to train people with Intellectual Disability (ID) and autism spectrum disorder (ASD) to improve their adaptive and intellectual functioning, such as social interaction skills and emotion recognition. An excellent example of serious game implementations for people with cognitive disabilities is discussed by [6] to improve motor coordination ability.

In general, video games, computer games, and mobile games are major types of digital games. According to [7], the electronic or digital game can improve 40% ability to learn new skills or methods that seem useful for most users. In recent days, it has also attracted all people beyond age, such as children, youth, younger and older adults, including senior citizens over 60 years old approximately. Therefore, it seems to polarize science and society alike [8]. According to healthcare and technological scientist, serious games would be an appropriate option to enhance and improve cognitive, sensory-motor, emotional, personal, and social competencies.

Serious games are built with pedagogical principles for education and training purposes, supported by gaming techniques and entertainment [9]. Digital games, simulations, virtual environments, and mixed reality/media provide opportunities to educate or train through responsive narrative/story, gameplay, or encounters [10]. Successful serious game development is related to several technological aspects such as design and development frameworks, for instance, development technology for implementation and design prototypes for graphical user interface [9]. These components assure the quality and productivity of the developed serious game to achieve the targeted objective.

According to the world report on disability [11], 15% of the world's population lives with some form of disability, including hearing problems, visual impairment, learning disabilities, etc. Considering the statistic by [12], over 16% of the world population will be 65 years old by 2050. These large numbers of people are not a stranger to the gaming world. In fact, with the growing age, they need more useful learning aspects like serious games to overcome several obstacles by themself without asking for help from others at their older age. Furthermore, this large number of people are the most frequent mobile game engaged players, around 55+ of their age.

As such, taking all levels of disabilities, age groups, and other aspects, several potential serious games have developed in recent times. Among several positive motivation and successful implementation, Carvelho et al. [13] has focused on the population with visual disabilities, while Baker [14] and Schneider et al. [15] has focused on similar motive for people with autism and the user with dyslexia. Similarly, Brown et al. [16] focused on the effectiveness of combining serious games with mobile apps to reach a higher level of independence for persons with Down's syndrome.

Intelligent serious games are raising day by day with a wide array of implementation concerning several areas. Numerous studies have demonstrated the effectiveness and usefulness of serious games not only in education [17–19] but also in other areas. For example, the most interesting application in rehabilitation is for stroke patients [20]. As this field is continuously growing, many more applications are in their development phase to show their effectiveness in the upcoming decades.

2 The Session of Serious and Fun Games

This year, three (3) papers were selected for the session of Serious and Fun Games from different countries in Europe and Asia (one from Germany and two from Japan). The STS presentation "Serious and Fun Games" tries to achieve progress here to the future perspectives in Assistive Technology, e-Accessibility, and e-Inclusion. The target groups could be any age group and disability, including young, adults, people with disabilities, etc. Moreover, if the game is not only for entertainment, if it helps people with special needs, then these games or applications are suitable for the aim of this session. Additionally, games designed and developed considering the universal accessible design and development guidelines are highly appreciated.

One of this year's papers focused on the accessibility of leisure sports for people with vision impairment (BLV). The prime objective of this study is to improve the accessibility of Mölkky sports (Finnish leisure sport activity) involving both vision impaired and sighted people. The target group of this study is children to older adults, including challenged people. The proposed improvement framework has two approaches: the primitive approach and the AI vision approach. In the primitive approach, during playing the game, basic information (direction, position, alignment of skittles, etc.) was provided for the people with vision impairment through voice indication by the sighted people. In addition, sighted players supported the blind player by clapping against every skittles throwing to make the game accessible. In the AI vision approach, based on the observation of the primitive approach, a system was developed considering a notebook computer and an arm-shaped wireless haptic device. To show the motion of the throwing arms, they used a microprocessor with a wireless chipset (ESP32), two small servo motors (SG90), and a card-type lithium polymer battery. Google MediaPipe is used to detect the positions of a shoulder and an elbow on a throwing arm. They used ESP32 to send angle values via a Bluetooth serial port and servo motors on the device to express these angles in real-time. They evaluated the effectiveness of the system by inviting two low vision persons and one blind person. The evaluation result depicts the nobility of the developed system.

Auditory training for visually impaired people through Virtual Reality (VR) has increased and improved day by day. It is more exciting when it comes to Goalball training (a popular sport for visually impaired people). It is interesting to note that most of the VR-based Goalball training systems are designed to respond only to the left and right directions of the ball's arrival, which is difficult to understand the detailed localization information, such as the distance and height of the ball. Thus, to improve the localization abilities of visual impairment people, it is necessary to respond to height and farther directions in addition to left-right judgments for more practical localization training. One of the papers of this session focused on the localization issues during Goalball training and developed an acoustical VR system that enables users to perform comprehensive goalball training independently without going to the gym. It enables a user to train the sense of sound localization, such as the ball being thrown from various directions to various positions. The developed system consists of three phases, a questionnaire-based survey, implementation, and effectiveness evaluation. The questionnaire was answered by the five Goalball circle member and five certified athletes from the Japan Goalball Association. This application was developed by recording the throwing sound binaurally using a dummy head microphone. The application interface presents the sound randomly to receive a user reaction. The application was developed using Python on Windows 10, even able to run with or without screen reader applications. The evaluation was performed by inviting two visual impairment Goalball players. The result shows the effectiveness of the proposed system as an innovative and potential training system.

Unfortunately, without accessible design in mind, it is impossible to incorporate Augmented Reality (AR) into the daily life of people with disabilities. One of the accepted papers of this session focused on the guidelines for the accessible design of AR applications. This paper summarizes and compares the guidelines from both commercial vendors and the World Wide Web Consortium (W3C) to derive the common criteria from these guidelines. Apple Human Interface Guidelines (AHIG) and Google Augmented Reality Design Guidelines (GARDG) are selected as commercial vendor guidelines. These two guidelines are not focused on accessibility criteria. It focused on usability criteria for all users. From W3C consortium guidelines, they consider the XR Accessibility User Requirements (XAUR) guidelines to define accessibility requirements for information and communications technology, including AR technology. Also, they consider European Norm ETSI EN 301 549 for comparison that focuses on the accessibility requirements or improvement. The comparison result reveals that only a few criteria have equivalents in three of the guidelines; none in all four guidelines. Additionally, XAUR and ETSI EN 301 549 sufficiently cover aspects of several disabilities (blind user) and do not cover barriers related to the general audience, for example, handling issues relating to the comfort and security of the user in an AR environment.

3 Conclusion

Until now, this Special Thematic Session received a wide array of submissions, including the previous and the current year. Through the presentation of this year in the ICCHP conference series, this session expanded its objective and find a new opportunity to introduce several new and innovative development or application in the area of Serious Game for special needs users. Hopefully, there will be similar sessions in future conferences. The future submission from young scientists has expected to fulfill the objective of this session. We hope that the young scientists are motivated by these Special Thematic Sessions.

Acknowledgements. The authors would like to thank the support of the National Research Development and Innovation Office, project no. MEC_R 141159.

References

1. Fernandez-Cervantes, V., Neubauer, N., Hunter, B., Stroulia, E., Liu, L.: VirtualGym: a kinect-based system for seniors exercising at home. Entertainment Computing **27**, 60–72 (2018)
2. Kiryakova, G., Angelova, N., Yordanova, L.: Gamification in education. In: Proceedings of 9th International Balkan Education and Science Conference (2014)
3. Wu, J.H., Du, J.K., Lee, C.Y.: Development and questionnaire-based evaluation of virtual dental clinic: a serious game for training dental students. Med. Educ. Online **26**(1), 1983927 (2021)
4. Mitchell, G., Leonard, L., Carter, G., Santin, O., Brown Wilson, C.: Evaluation of a 'serious game'on nursing student knowledge and uptake of influenza vaccination. PLoS ONE **16**(1), e0245389 (2021)
5. Mihajlovic, Z., Popovic, S., Brkic, K., Cosic, K.: A system for head-neck rehabilitation exercises based on serious gaming and virtual reality. Multimedia Tools and Applications **77**(15), 19113–19137 (2017). https://doi.org/10.1007/s11042-017-5328-z
6. Tsikinas, S., Xinogalos, S.: Towards a serious games design framework for people with intellectual disability or autism spectrum disorder. Educ. Inf. Technol. **25**(4), 3405–3423 (2020). https://doi.org/10.1007/s10639-020-10124-4
7. Wiemeyer, J., Kliem, A.: Serious games in prevention and rehabilitation—a new panacea for elderly people? European Review of Aging and Physical Activity **9**(1), 41–50 (2011). https://doi.org/10.1007/s11556-011-0093-x
8. Giang, V.: Gamification techniques increase your employees' ability to learn by 40%. Business Insider 18 (2013)
9. Gallegos, B., Kepple, M.T., Bukaty, C.A.: Using video gameplay to measure achievement for students with disabilities: a new perspective to grading and achievement reporting. In: Handbook of Research on Gaming Trends in P-12 Education. IGI Global Publisher, pp. 326–352 (2016). https://doi.org/10.4018/978-1-4666-9629-7.ch016
10. Sik-Lanyi, C.: Colour-fidelity and barrier-free design of virtual worlds and games. The Theses Submitted for the Habilitation Procedure at the University of Pannonia, Veszprem, Hungary (2017)

11. https://www.who.int/teams/noncommunicable-diseases/sensory-functions-disability-and-rehabilitation/world-report-on-disability
12. Deutsche Welle News: (Jun 17 2019) https://www.dw.com/en/world-population-to-reach-97-billion-by-2050-un/a-49241728
13. Carvelho, T., Allison, R.S., Irving, E.L., Harriot, C.: Computer gaming for vision therapy. IEEE, Washington, D. C. (2008)
14. Baker, M.J.: Incorporating the thematic ritualistic behaviors of children with autism into games. Journal of Positive Behavior Interventions (2000). https://doi.org/10.1177/109830070000200201
15. Schneider, W., Roth, E., Ennemoser, M.: Training phonological skills and letter knowledge in children at risk for dyslexia: A comparison of three kindergarden intervention programs. J. Edu. Psychol. **92**, 284–29 (2000)
16. Brown, D.J., McHugh, D., Standen, P.J., Evett, L., Shopland, N., Battersby, S.J.: Designing location-based learning experiences for people with intellectual disabilities and additional senzory impairments. Comput. Educ. **56**(1), 11–20 (2011)
17. Sik Lanyi, C., Brown, D.J., Standen, P., Lewis, J., Butkute, V.: User Interface Evaluation of Serious Games for Students with Intellectual Disability. In: Miesenberger, K., Klaus, J., Zagler, W., Karshmer, A. (eds.) ICCHP 2010. LNCS, vol. 6179, pp. 227–234. Springer, Heidelberg (2010). https://doi.org/10.1007/978-3-642-14097-6_37
18. Sik Lanyi, C., Brown, D., Standen, P., Lewis, J., Butkute, V.: Results of user interface evaluation of serious games for students with intellectual disability. Acta Polytechnica Hungarica **9**(1), 225–245 (2012). http://www.uni-obuda.hu/journal/Issue33.htm
19. Sik-Lanyi C., Szucs V.: Play for children with disabilities: some reflections on the results on the users' needs and on the role of technologies. In: Allodi Westling, M., Zappaterra, T. (eds.) Users' Needs Report on Play for Children with Disabilities - Parents' and children's views, pp. 117–123. De Gruyter Poland Ltd, Warsaw/Berlin (2017)
20. Sik Lanyi, C., Szucs, V.: Motivating rehabilitation through competitive gaming. In: Vogiatzaki, E., Krukowski, A. (eds.) Modern Stroke Rehabilitation through e-Health-based Entertainment, pp. 137–167. Springer, Heidelberg (2016). https://doi.org/10.1007/978-3-319-21293-7_5

Accessibility Improvement of Leisure Sports "Mölkky" for Visually Impaired Players Using AI Vision

Makoto Kobayashi[1(✉)] and Takuya Suzuki[2]

[1] Department of Computer Science, Tsukuba University of Technology, Tsukuba, Japan
koba@cs.k.tsukuba-tech.ac.jp

[2] Department of Synthetic Design, Tsukuba University of Technology, Tsukuba, Japan
suzukit@a.tsukuba-tech.ac.jp

Abstract. To establish an accessible sport that blind and low vision players can easily play with sighted players, we focused on the Finnish leisure sport, Mölkky. Trying to play it with blind and low vision players revealed that primitive assisting way such as clapping hands or explaining positions by voice were useful to some extent. On the other hand, the fact is observed that the throwing form of a congenital blind player was apparently different from the forms of other players. Therefore, to show that difference to the blind player, a prototype system that consists of a computer and a handy size wireless haptic device equipped with servo motors and a model arm was developed. The system detects the positions of a shoulder, an elbow, and a wrist on the throwing arm using a Mediapipe framework provided by Google. Then, a shoulder angle and an elbow angle are calculated by these positions, and the computer send these data to the haptic device via Bluetooth. Finally, the blind player touches the device and understands the motion of the throwing arm. The system was assessed by three visually impaired people, and they reported that they could clearly recognize the difference between throwing motions.

Keywords: Mölkky · MediaPipe · Blind · Haptic device and throwing motion

1 Introduction

Many types of adapted sports for blind and low vision (BLV) players exist in the world. Some of them are listed in Paralympics events [1], some of them are listed on the web site of International Blind Sports Federation [2, 3]. In addition to these famous adapted sports, varieties of sports for BLV people are played and enjoyed everywhere [4]. Typical examples of these sports are, Blind Football, Goal Boal, Showdown, and Judo for the blind. Obviously, these sports are well considered for BLV people and allow them to play, however, it is still difficult to enjoy them with sighted people. If sighted people would like to participate them, sometimes having equal conditions like wearing an eye mask is needed and it might not be comfortable for sighted person.

K. Miesenberger et al. (Eds.): ICCHP-AAATE 2022, LNCS 13342, pp. 73–78, 2022.
https://doi.org/10.1007/978-3-031-08645-8_9

Against this background, our projects have aimed to establish accessible sports for the BLV people and to arrange them to be able to play with sighted people. Several sports such as Climbing or bouldering, and ten pin bowling are already accessible for the blind people and can be enjoyed with sighted people. In the past project, we added information technologies to these sports to allow blind players to enjoy and practice without help by sighted supporters. For example, a support system that automatically tells positions of holding stones of bouldering wall was developed [5]. Also, automatic pin counting system that tells number of pins by synthetic voice was developed [6]. Such systems might be useful in certain condition though, these sports need special large-scale equipment and environment to play. It might be a problem to enjoy them with sighted people in casual way.

Therefore, to solve it, we focused on casual leisure sports which does not need large-scale equipment to play. In the same timing, the movement of playing Mölkky was imported from Finland to our country.

2 How to Play Mölkky

Mölkky is a Finnish leisure activity. Players throw a short woody bar to the area in where twelve skittles stand and take down them. In these days, this sport is gradually spreading and being popular in Japan. It is well designed for everyone to be able to enjoy it even if they do not have physical strength or special skills. A wide range of age groups from children to older adult, including challenged people can play it together [7]. The rules are quite simple. Each number is printed on each skittle, from one to twelve, and if a player gets down only one skittle, the printed number will be added the point of the player. If the number of laid down skittles is larger than two, the number will be added the point. When acquired points reach just 50, the player will be a winner, but if it is over 50, the count of points should be back to 25. And when a player repeated three times of miss-operation and no skittles are laid down, the player will be disqualified. To enjoy it, players should know the positions of skittles and its number. Although Mölkky is such a simple and enjoyable leisure sports for everyone, it is easy to imagine that blind and severely visually impaired players have some difficulties to acquire the positions of skittles.

3 Research Framework

3.1 Overview

To make Mölkky more accessible, a framework of three different approaches is planned in our project, which is shown in Fig. 1. The first one of the three is "Primitive approach." In this section, traditional methods and/or low technology tools are used for the improvement of accessibility. We tried to play Mölkky with BLV players using such methods and tools, then, discussed their feedback. The second one is, "Artificial Intelligence (AI) vision approach 1." Based on the primitive approach, we developed a system to detect the motion of other player's arm with AI vision software and show it with haptic hardware. The third one is, "AI vision approach 2," which aims to detect and tell positions of skittles using software found by combining object recognition and number recognition, is currently in developing. In this paper, the first approach and the second approach are reported.

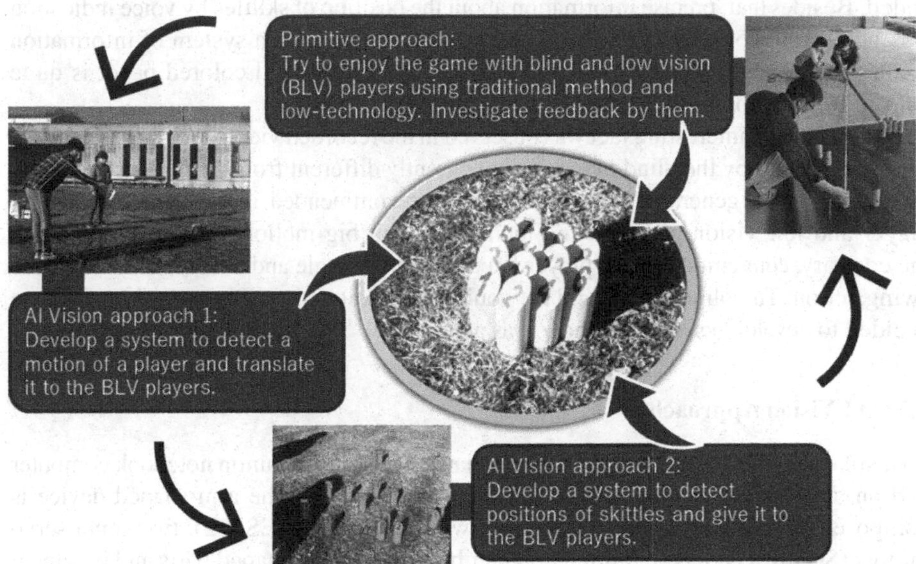

Fig. 1. Framework of approaches to improve an accessibility of Mölkky

3.2 Primitive Approach

As a primitive approach mentioned above, a game of Mölkky with BLV players was conducted using a normal set of skittles. While the game was proceeding, we tried to adapt traditional way for supporting visually impaired players in other sports and discussed how to improve its accessibility. From the beginning, basic information about skittle alignments was given by voice indications. A voice description of the position of each skittle contains a direction that is expressed by a clock position and a distance. In addition to the description, sighted players supported the blind player by clapping hands over every skittle and explain the number of the skittle like "(Clapping hands and say) Here is number eight!" Then, after several throws, a blind player requested a tactile cue to understand the direction of the skittles. We prepared a long string and sticked it with tape on the ground to indicate the center direction and prepared another long string to indicate the direction of the other skittles. These trials are shown in the right upper part of Fig. 1. Different from the requests by the blind player, A low vision player requested a black sheet on the ground for easy recognition of skittles, and we prepared it. In addition, he said that wrapping up skittles with different colored paper might be helpful to distinguish them, therefore wrapping skittles are prepared in the second game and it was clear that he could distinguish skittles with less time.

After those two times trial, our discussion concluded as follows: The string that indicates the center direction is useful. On the other hand, another long string operation that tells every skittle takes too much time and loses the rhythm of the game. It makes the blind player feel uncomfortable because other players must wait until the operation ended. Besides that, precise information about the position of skittles by voice indication was helpful. It would be better if it came automatically using a system of information technology. And to support low vision player, black sheet and colored paper is quite helpful to enjoy the game.

Furthermore, interesting fact was observed in the recorded video during these games. Throwing action by the blind player was apparently different from that of conducted by other players. In general, "under throwing" is recommended in Mölkky and sighted player and low vision player swing their arms with big motion before throwing. On the contrary, congenitally blind player fixed the elbow angle and throws with minimum swing action. The blind player said he would like to know the difference, therefore, we decided to develop a system to show it as a next step.

3.3 AI Vision Approach

To display the motion of the arm, a system that consists of a common notebook computer and an arm-shaped wireless haptic device was developed. The arm-shaped device is composed of a small microprocessor with wireless chip set (ESP32), two small servo motors (SG90), a card type lithium polymer battery, and arm shaped parts and basement made by a 3D printer. The length of the arm parts is approximately 11[cm] so that it can be hold by one hand and touched by another hand. The overview of the haptic device and its hardware components are shown in Fig. 2. The total cost of the device is less than 4,000 JPY (30 EUR).

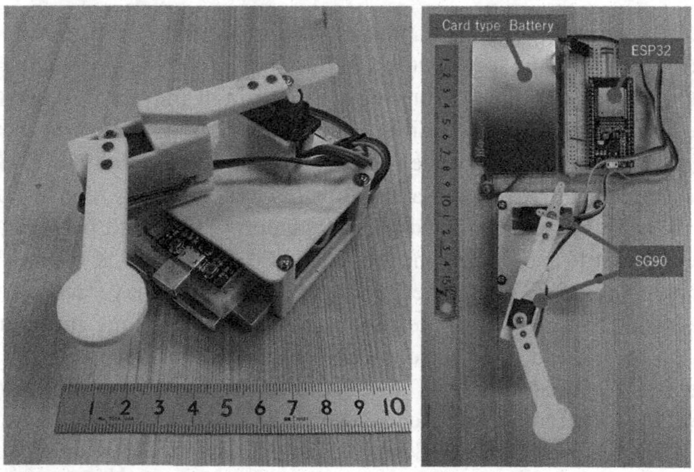

Fig. 2. An overview of the haptic device (left) and its hardware components (right).

The software to drive this device is based on Google MediaPipe framework [8]. The advantage of using MediaPipe is to be able to realize a system with low cost, because it works with common web camera, not a special hardware such as a depth camera, a stereo camera, or an infrared camera. MediaPipe automatically detects joint positions of a human by an artificial intelligence. The developed software was written in Python, and it uses three positions: a shoulder, an elbow, and a wrist on a throwing arm. From these data of positions, angles of shoulder and elbow are calculated. Although MediaPipe provides depth information, we do not use it and the system calculates angles on the screen. Therefore, the camera position must be adjusted to the throwing side of the player, to capture the swinging motion effectively. These angle values are sent to the ESP32 via a Bluetooth serial port and servo motors on the device move to express these angles in real time. The software works with both of video input by a web camera and recorded movie file. The overview and the workflow of the system is shown in Fig. 3.

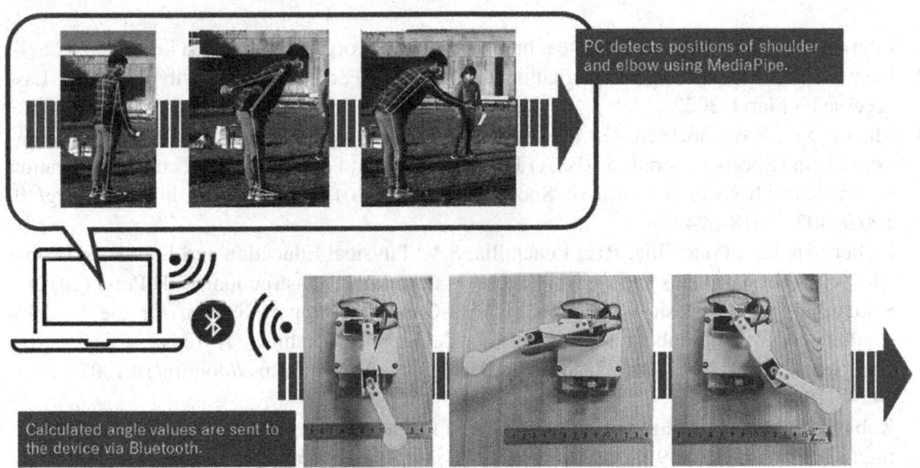

Fig. 3. An overview of throwing arm display system

To estimate this system, two of low vision persons who have severe visual impairment and one totally blind person (average age was 21.6) tried to touch the motion of the arm-shaped device using recorded movie files of throwing that is recorded in the primitive approach phase. These estimators use a braille in their daily life. While the estimation, these three visually impaired subjects held the device by an undominant hand and touched the arm parts by a dominant hand. Loaded movie file represents throwing motion by a low vision player which length is 15 s at first, then, motion by a blind player which length is 10 s afterwards. In the movie file, the low vision player swings his arm back and forth and the angle of shoulder varies wide, on the contrary, the blind player does not widely move the shoulder and the elbow was almost fixed near 90° during throwing. The estimators touched the moving arm parts that displayed these motions several times, and all of them commented that they can clearly distinguish the difference between them. After the estimation, the blind subject added a comment that it is better that the software provides slow-motion playing mode, to understand the difference more precisely.

4 Summary

To improve the accessibility of Mölkky for visually impaired players, traditional support methods with sound or voice or tactile queue are useful and effective. Addition to them, we developed a small wireless haptic device to show the arm motion to enjoy the leisure sports and estimation by three visually impaired people showed the device can present features of throwing forms. As a next step, this project plans to develop a system to show positions of skittles in the future.

Acknowledgement. This work was supported by JSPS KAKENHI Grant Number 19K11544. We would like to thank Miss Naho Ohyagi for supporting us to conduct games of Mölkky.

References

1. International Paralympic Committee: https://paralympic.org. Last accessed 4 March 2022
2. Home of Blind Sports – IBSA International Blind Sports Federation: https://ibsasport.org. Last accessed 4 March 2022
3. Mann, D.L., Ravensbergen, H.J.C.: International Paralympic Committee (IPC) and International Blind Sports Federation (IBSA) Joint position stand on the sport-specific classification of athletes with vision impairment. Sports Med. **48**(9), 2011–2023 (2018). https://doi.org/10.1007/s40279-018-0949-6
4. Lieberman, L.J., Ponchillia, P.E., Ponchillia, S.V.: Physical Education and Sports for People with Visual Impairments and Deafblindness: Foundations of Instruction. APH Press (2012)
5. Kobayashi, M.: A Basic Inspection of Wall-Climbing Support System for the Visually Challenged. In: Miesenberger, K., Klaus, J., Zagler, W., Karshmer, A. (eds.) ICCHP 2010. LNCS, vol. 6180, pp. 332–337. Springer, Heidelberg (2010). https://doi.org/10.1007/978-3-642-14100-3_49
6. Kobayashi, M.: Automatic pin counting system for the blind bowling. J. Adv. Comput. Intell. Intell. Inform. **21**(1), 119–124 (2017). https://doi.org/10.20965/jaciii.2017.p0119
7. Heinola, J.: Adapted Physical Activity in Rehabilitating Work Activity for Adults with Intellectual Disability: Case Monituote (2010)
8. Home-mediapipe: https://google.github.io/mediapipe/. Last accessed 31 May 2022

GoalBaural-II: An Acoustic Virtual Reality Training Application for Goalball Players to Recognize Various Game Conditions

Michiharu Watanabe[1], Takahiro Miura[2(✉)], Masaki Matsuo[1], Masatsugu Sakajiri[1], and Junji Onishi[1]

[1] Tsukuba University of Technology, 4-12-7 Kasuga, Tsukuba, Ibaraki 305-0821, Japan
[2] Human Augmentation Research Center (HARC), National Institute of Advanced Industrial Science and Technology (AIST), 6-2-3 Kashiwanoha, Kashiwa, Chiba 277-0882, Japan
miura-t@aist.go.jp

Abstract. Goalball is one of the most popular sports for visually impaired people worldwide. The aim of goalball is to throw a ball with bells embedded in it to the goal line of the opponents as many times as possible while the defenders try to block the thrown ball with their bodies. Since goalball players cannot rely on visual information, they must perceive the game situation using only their auditory sense. However, it is difficult, especially for beginners, to perceive the direction and distance of the thrown ball. In previous research, we developed and evaluated an application called GoalBaural (Goalball + Aural) that allowed users to improve their recognition of the direction of a thrown ball based on acoustic virtual reality. However, GoalBaural did not provide exercises to help users judge the distance of the ball. In this paper, we develop an improved acoustic virtual reality system that allows users to independently perform comprehensive goalball training without going to the gym. We conducted a questionnaire survey to determine the sounds that players used to perceive the status of a goalball game, and implemented the training application GoalBaural-II. The result of the questionnaire indicated that skilled goalball players tended to rely on sound information to predict the features of a throw by an opponent. Also, the application based on the result can help users more accurately determine the direction and distance of an approaching ball.

Keywords: Goalball · Visually impaired people · Acoustic virtual reality

1 Introduction

Parasports, which began as a therapeutic exercise for individuals with various sensory and physical disabilities and impairments, are becoming increasingly

M. Watanabe and T. Miura—Both authors contributed equally to this manuscript.

K. Miesenberger et al. (Eds.): ICCHP-AAATE 2022, LNCS 13342, pp. 79–88, 2022.
https://doi.org/10.1007/978-3-031-08645-8_10

popular and competitive worldwide through international competitions, such as the Paralympic Games [3–5]. In Japan, the public and private sectors worked together to prepare for the 2020 Tokyo Olympics and Paralympics to provide more opportunities for people with disabilities to enjoy various sports [2].

Goalball is one of the most popular sports for visually impaired people and is an official Paralympic event [1]. Goalball is played in an indoor court of the same size as a volleyball court. Two teams of three players wearing eyeshades use a specialized ball that weighs 1.25 kg and contains bells inside. The purpose of the game is to throw the ball across the goal line of the opposing team as many times as possible. The opposing team's defenders attempt to block the thrown ball with their bodies. Since goalball players cannot rely on visual information, they must perceive the game situation using their auditory sense. However, it is difficult, especially for beginners, to perceive the state of the game, such as the positions of the opponents and the direction and distance of the thrown ball. In addition, beginners tend to be afraid of a high-speed approaching ball because they may get injured due to the lack of visual information. Furthermore, the environment to practice defensive techniques is limited.

However, physical and auditory training systems for visually impaired people, such as exergames, have increased and improved over time. Morelli et al. developed VI-Tennis and VI-Bowling, which can be played by visually impaired people and can improve movement coordination using sensory information [12–14]. In addition, Rector et al. developed Eyes-free Yoga using Microsoft Kinect, which helps visually impaired people perform yoga poses [16,17]. Training environments using acoustic virtual reality (VR) have also been proposed. Seki et al. and Wersenyi proposed training systems of orientation and mobility for visually impaired trainees to enhance their localization ability without going outside [18,19,22]. In addition, Hodges et al. reported that virtual environments can effectively treat the fear of heights [6]. Other research proposed two training applications based on acoustic VR technologies. One is AcouSTTic for sound Table tennis players to train their auditory sense to instantaneously recognize the direction and distance of the ball and whether they should return the ball or not without needing to play on a real court [10]. The other application is GoalBaural, which allows goalball players to practice judging the direction of a ball thrown by opponents [11]. These systems employing acoustic VR techniques can allow players with visual impairments to enhance their sound localization abilities. However, GoalBaural was designed to respond only to the left and right directions of an approaching ball, and it was difficult for players to perform detailed localization, such as of the distance and height of the ball. Therefore, it is necessary to simulate the height and directions of the ball and make trainee respond for the height and directions other than left and right for more practical localization training.

In this paper, our goal is to develop an acoustic VR system that allows users to independently perform comprehensive goalball training without going to the gym. First, we conducted a questionnaire survey to determine the sounds that players used to perceive the status of a goalball game. Then, we implemented the training application GoalBaural-II (Goalball + Aural, version 2) and evaluated its training effectiveness. The following are our research questions:

Q1. What sounds do skilled goalball players pay attention to?
Q2. Can training with the binaural sound of goalball pitches improve the localization accuracy of both the direction and distance of the ball?

2 Questionnaire

2.1 Method

We conducted a questionnaire survey about the sounds that goalball players used as clues during a game. Ten participants completed the questionnaire: five were members of the goalball club at Tsukuba University of Technology, while the other five were certified athletes with a grade of D or higher for the Japan Goalball Association.

The questionnaire evaluated 84 items on a 5-point scale to rate the degree to which the participants relied on cues in 20 situations (see Table 1), where 1 indicated no reliance on sound cues and 5 indicated high reliance on sound cues. An F-test was used to examine the difference in the consistency of the responses between the certified and non-certified participants. Then, the two groups were compared in terms of the standard deviation and mean of the responses to evaluate the consistency of the responses and the degree of reliance on sound cues.

2.2 Results and Discussion

Table 1 presents the number of items with significant differences and trends ($p < .05$ and $p < .10$, respectively) in the responses. The responses of the certified athletes were more consistent in 19 items than those of the non-certified athletes. In the defensive phase, the degree of reliance on sound in predicting the type, direction, and power of the throw by an opponent and the height of a bouncing ball was significantly more consistent in the certified group. Moreover, the certified group had higher mean values of responses to the items concerning defense than the non-certified group. The same tendency was also observed in the offensive phase when predicting the attacker's position, the opponent's status, and the type, direction, and power of the ball thrown by a teammate.

In contrast, the non-certified group had a significantly more consistent degree of reliance on sound in predicting the position of their teammates during defense and immediately after a throw, and the mean values of the responses for these items were larger than those of the certified group. The reason for these differences may be the fact that the certified group was more skilled in formations and could better focus on predicting the movement of the ball.

Based on these results, we built a training system that presents various types of throws during defensive scenarios and instructs the user to report the detailed characteristics of the ball.

Table 1. Questionnaire items and responses by two groups.

Category	Situation	Number of significant items	Group with more consistent responses
Use of sound during defense	Searching	0/6	
	Grasping the opponent's position just before throwing the ball	0/6	
	Predicting the type of a throw by the opponent	3/4	Certified
	Predicting the direction of the throw	1/5	Certified
	Predicting the power and speed of the throw	1/4	Certified
	Predicting the height of a bouncing ball	3/5	Certified
	Predicting the position of a teammate while the ball is approaching	1/3	Non-certified
	Predicting the position of the ball after a block by a teammate	0/4	
Use of sound during offense	Predicting a teammate's position when holding the ball	0/2	
	Predicting an attacker's position when a teammate throws the ball	1/4	Certified
	Predicting an opponent's status just before one's own attack	1/3	Certified
	Predicting an opponent's status when a teammate throws the ball	1/3	Certified
	Grasping a teammate's position when the teammate throws the ball	3/4	Depending on items
	Predicting the type of a throw by a teammate	2/4	Certified
	Predicting the direction of the throw	2/5	Certified
	Predicting the power and speed of the throw	2/4	Certified
	Predicting the height of a bouncing ball	3/6	Depending on items
	Predicting the arrival position of a teammate's throw	0/5	
	Predicting the position of the ball after opponents' block	2/5	Depending on items
	Predicting the position of a teammate just after the teammate' throws the ball	1/2	Non-certified

3 Overview of Proposed Training System

Our proposed application, GoalBaural-II, allows users to train their sound localization ability for situations such as a ball being thrown from various directions to various positions. GoalBaural-II first presents the binaural sound of throwing and then instructs the user to provide the exact direction and distance for defense. We developed this application by recording the throwing sound binaurally using a dummy head microphone, and then implemented an interface to present sound randomly and determine the user's reaction.

3.1 Binaural Recording of Sounds

We used a dummy head to record moving sounds with the cooperation of three goalball players with partial visual impairments. The dummy head microphone (Southern Acoustics, SAMREC Type 2500 s s conforming to the standards IEC 60959 and IEC 60268-7) was set at the center in a university gym (background noise level: 45.6 dBA, reverberation time: 1.8 s). We used the dummy head to record the sound in various situations (48 cases in total) listed in Table 1, including throws. In the case of throws, the time-series sounds included the approach run for throwing the ball, the throw, and the ball passing horizontally. We instructed one of the participants to start running straight from a distance of 15 m in front of the dummy head and then throw the ball at the 9 m line from the dummy head. The recording application was Audacity running on Windows

10. The measured sound of the dummy head microphone was captured by an audio interface (Roland Rubix24) with a sampling frequency of 44.1 kHz and a quantization bit rate of 16 bits.

3.2 Application Implementation

We designed GoalBaural-II so that individuals with visual impairments can listen to randomized situations and learn to determine the positions of players, and the direction and distance of the ball under training conditions. GoalBaural-II was developed using Python with the Pygame package on Windows 10 and can run in a Windows environment with or without screen readers, such as NVDA, Jaws, and PC Talker. Users wear headphones to listen to the binaural sound. The user input can also be recorded by the system to determine whether the user responds correctly or incorrectly.

When the user presses the enter or space key, the recorded binaural sound is emitted by the headphones after a brief silence lasting 1–2 s. The silence simulates the experience of receivers in an actual game because they must wait for sudden pitches. Then, to defend against throws, the user must determine the direction from which the virtual ball is traveling and press the D/F or J/K key for the left or right side, respectively. The user presses the D and K keys when the ball's arrival position is virtually farther away from the user at the defensive line than when they press the F and J keys. If the user does not press a key at the end of the sound, the next session starts after a short rest period.

4 Evaluation

We evaluated the effect of training on the participants who have played goalball.

4.1 Participants

Five men in their early 20s participated in the experiment. There were two participants with partial visual impairment and three participants with total blindness. The participants all had over two years of experience with goalball and belonged to a goalball club at Tsukuba University of Technology. They could all manipulate a personal computer with screen reader functions for more than a year. All participants had hearing within normal limits (20-dB hearing level) as defined by pure-tone audiometry. The experimenter explained the evaluation procedure to the participants, and all of the participants agreed to take part in the experiment.

4.2 Procedure and Data Analysis

The experiment on the performance of GoalBaural-II was conducted in a silent room. Before the experiment, the experimenter instructed the participants to wear headphones (Logicool, G430) and adjust the volume to a comfortable level.

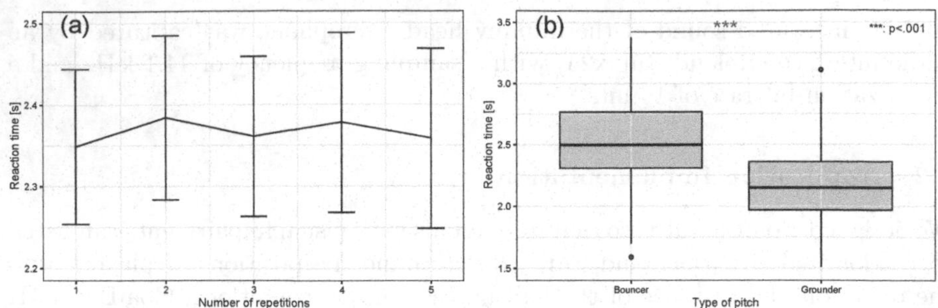

Fig. 1. Reaction time as a function of (a) the number of repetitions and (b) pitch types (bouncer and grounder).

Then, the participants pressed the trigger button, listened to the sound presented binaurally, and pressed a key corresponding to the direction from which the virtual ball traveled and the ball's distance from the participants at the defensive line. The order of the presented sounds was randomized. The participants repeated this task 125 times (25 sound conditions listed in Table 1 repeated five times). The reaction time [s] and correct response rate [%] results were summarized by aggregating the participant responses.

For data analysis, we compared the reaction time and correct response rate for pitch types (grounder and bouncer), pitch distances (far and near from the virtual participant position), pitch trajectories (straight and crossing throws), and number of repetitions (1 to 5) by analysis of variance (ANOVA) and post-hoc multiple comparison. When the distribution of the data satisfied normality, we employed two-way ANOVA as well as the Tukey–Kramer test. When it did not satisfy normality, we employed two-way ANOVA with aligned rank transform as well as the least squares mean with Tukey's multiplicity adjustment [9,23]. In addition, we determined the change in performance related to the number of repetitions by Pearson's or Spearman's correlation coefficients r.

4.3 Results and Discussion

Figure 1(a) and (b) illustrates the change in reaction time based on the number of repetitions, and the difference of reaction time in pitch types. From the ANOVA results, no significant main effect of the number of repetitions was observed on the reaction time ($p > .10$). However, there were significant main on pitch types ($p < .001$) and whether the direction that participant' answered was correct ($p = .004 < .01$). Also, significant interaction between pitch types and pitch distances ($p = .007 < .01$), pitch distances and pitch trajectories ($p < .001$), and the number of repetitions and pitch distances ($p = .03 < .05$). When the number of repetitions increases, reaction time increased with marginal significance when the pitch distance was far from the participant (Spearman's $r = 0.15, p = .086 < .10$). Thus, the reaction time did not change significantly due to the number of repetitions generally but was likely to increase when the pitch distance was far.

In other words, the training effect was not observed in the speedup of reaction with the number of repetitions.

Figure 2(a) depicts the change in the correct response rates regarding the ball direction based on the number of repetitions. An increase in the correct response rate was observed for a larger number repetitions ($r = 0.46, p = .019 < .05$). The mean correct response rate of the first trial was 93.6%, while that of the last trial was 100%. Significant main effects of the pitch trajectories and number of repetitions were also observed on the percentage of correct responses ($p = .018 < .05$ in pitch trajectories and $p = .004 < .01$ in number of repetitions). The mean correct rates were 95.6% and 98.7% in crossing and straight throws, respectively. This result is consistent with a previous study [11]. Furthermore, a significant interaction among pitch distances, pitch trajectories, and number of repetitions was also observed ($p = .006 < .01$). Thus, the percentage of correct responses regarding ball direction increased significantly with the number of repetitions, which varied with the pitch distances and trajectories. However, the observed interaction suggests that the training effect for correct response rate of each pitch type differs for each number of repetitions.

Figure 2(b) displays the correct response rates regarding the ball direction and distance based on the number of repetitions. An increase in the correct response rate was observed for a larger number of repetitions (Pearson's $r = 0.62, p < .001$). The mean correct rates of the first and last trial were 55.2% and 86.4%, respectively. For the correct response rate, significant main effects were observed for the pitch distances and number of repetitions. Significant interactions of correct response rate were also observed among pitch types, pitch distances, and pitch trajectories ($p = .004 < .01$ in pitch types and pitch trajectories, $p < .001$ in pitch types and pitch distances, $p = .007 < .01$ in three pitch conditions). Furthermore, a significant interaction between pitch distances and number of repetitions was also observed ($p = .04 < .05$). The increase of correct rates from the first and the last trials were 36% and 12% when the pitch distance was near and far from the participants, respectively. Therefore, the number of repetitions significantly affected the accuracy of judging the ball direction and distance. Notably, the correct response rate tends to improve with the number of repetitions when the pitch distance from the participant is near, while it is less likely to improve when the pitch distance is far.

The above results indicate that GoalBaural-II can be used to effectively help goalball players improve their ability to determine the direction and distance of a virtual ball. As demonstrated in a previous study [11], Honda et al. reported that sound localization training with a virtual auditory display can significantly reduce errors in vertical and horizontal localization in the real world [7]. Moreover, head motions and the movement of sound sources can improve localization ability and reduce the unnaturalness caused by the acoustic differences of users' individual listening conditions and head-related transfer functions [8,15,20,21]. Thus, GoalBaural-II can not only improve players' ability to localize balls in the real world, but also provide a virtual practice space for goalball players.

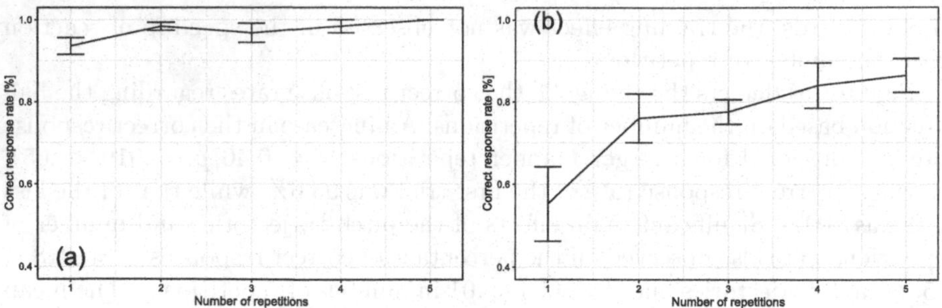

Fig. 2. Correct response rates regarding ball direction (a), and correct response rates regarding ball direction and distance (b) as a function of the number of repetitions.

5 Summary and Future Work

In this study, we analyzed the difference in sound usage by certified and non-certified goalball players by using a small-scale questionnaire survey. Based on the results, we implemented an improved application for training the goalball-related auditory sense, called GoalBaural-II, and evaluated its training effect on goalball players. Our contributions are as follows:

A1. Certified goalball players mainly relied on sound information to predict the type, direction, and power of a throw by an opponent and the height of a bouncing ball, while non-certified players mainly relied on sound to predict the position of their teammates during defense.

A2. By training repeatedly using the GoalBaural-II application, users improved the localization accuracy of not only the direction but also the distance of an approaching ball. However, no improvement in the reaction time was observed generally.

Our future work will include classifying easy-to-learn and difficult-to-learn situations and analyzing their acoustic features in detail. In addition, we plan to publicly release the developed application and analyze the effectiveness of its use by a larger number of people.

Acknowledgment. This work was supported by JSPS KAKENHI Grant Numbers JP18K18625, JP21H05347 and JP21K18485. Special thanks are due to the members of the goalball club at Tsukuba University of Technology.

References

1. Goalball - General information - Sports - IBSA. https://goalball.sport/about-goalball/overview/
2. White Paper on Sport in Japan 2017. https://www.ssf.or.jp/Portals/0/resources/outline/en/pdf/SportWhitePaperinJapan2017_c.pdf

3. DePauw, K.P., Gavron, S.J.: Disability sport. Human Kinetics (2005)
4. Gold, J.R., Gold, M.M.: Access for all: the rise of the Paralympic Games. J. R. Soc. Prom. Health **127**(3), 133–141 (2007)
5. Guttmann, L.: Textbook of Sport for the Disabled. HM&M Publishers (1976)
6. Hodges, L.F., Kooper, R., Meyer, T.C., Rothbaum, B.O., Opdyke, D., de Graaff, J.J., Williford, J.S., North, M.M.: Virtual environments for treating the fear of heights. Computer **28**(7), 27–34 (1995)
7. Honda, A., Shibata, H., Gyoba, J., Saitou, K., Iwaya, Y., Suzuki, Y.: Transfer effects on sound localization performances from playing a virtual three-dimensional auditory game. Appl. Acoust. **68**(8), 885–896 (2007)
8. Iwaya, Y., Suzuki, Y., Kimura, D.: Effects of head movement on front-back error in sound localization. Acoust. Sci. Technol. **24**(5), 322–324 (2003)
9. Lenth, R.V.: Least-Squares Means: the R package lsmeans. J. Stat. Softw. **69**(1), 1–33 (2016)
10. Miura, T., Fujito, M., Matsuo, M., Sakajiri, M., Onishi, J., Ono, T.: AcouSTTic: a training application of acoustic sense on Sound Table Tennis (STT). In: Miesenberger, K., Kouroupetroglou, G. (eds.) ICCHP 2018. LNCS, vol. 10897, pp. 3–11. Springer, Cham (2018). https://doi.org/10.1007/978-3-319-94274-2_1
11. Miura, T., Soga, S., Matsuo, M., Sakajiri, M., Onishi, J., Ono, T.: GoalBaural: a training application for goalball-related Aural Sense. In: Proceedings of the 9th Augmented Human International Conference, pp. 20. ACM (2018)
12. Morelli, T., Foley, J., Columna, L., Lieberman, L., Folmer, E.: VI-Tennis: a vibrotactile/audio exergame for players who are visually impaired. In: Proceedings of the Fifth International Conference on the Foundations of Digital Games, pp. 147–154. ACM (2010)
13. Morelli, T., Foley, J., Folmer, E.: Vi-bowling: a tactile spatial exergame for individuals with visual impairments. In: Proceedings of the 12th International ACM SIGACCESS Conference on Computers and Accessibility, pp. 179–186. ACM (2010)
14. Morelli, T., Folmer, E.: Real-time sensory substitution to enable players who are blind to play video games using whole body gestures. Entertain. Comput. **5**(1), 83–90 (2014)
15. Perrett, S., Noble, W.: The contribution of head motion cues to localization of low-pass noise. Percept. Psychophys. **59**(7), 1018–1026 (1997)
16. Rector, K., Bennett, C.L., Kientz, J.A.: Eyes-free yoga: an exergame using depth cameras for blind & low vision exercise. In: Proceedings of the 15th International ACM SIGACCESS Conference on Computers and Accessibility, pp. 12. ACM (2013)
17. Rector, K., et al.: Design and real-world evaluation of eyes-free yoga: an exergame for blind and low-vision exercise. ACM Trans. Access. Comput. (TACCESS) **9**(4), 12 (2017)
18. Seki, Y.: Wide-range auditory orientation training system for blind O&M. In: Antona, M., Stephanidis, C. (eds.) UAHCI 2015. LNCS, vol. 9178, pp. 150–159. Springer, Cham (2015). https://doi.org/10.1007/978-3-319-20687-5_15
19. Seki, Y., Sato, T.: A training system of orientation and mobility for blind people using acoustic virtual reality. IEEE Trans. Neural Syst. Rehabil. Eng. **19**(1), 95–104 (2011)
20. Thurlow, W.R., Mangels, J.W., Runge, P.S.: Head movements during sound localization. J. Acoust. Soc. Am. **42**(2), 489–493 (1967)

21. Wenzel, E.M., Arruda, M., Kistler, D.J., Wightman, F.L.: Localization using non-individualized head-related transfer functions. J. Acoust. Soc. Am. **94**(1), 111–123 (1993)
22. Wersenyi, G.: Virtual localization by blind persons. J. Audio Eng. Soc. **60**(7/8), 568–579 (2012)
23. Wobbrock, J.O., Findlater, L., Gergle, D., Higgins, J.J.: The aligned rank transform for nonparametric factorial analyses using only Anova procedures. In: Proceedings of the SIGCHI Conference on Human Factors in Computing Systems, pp. 143–146 (2011)

Comparison of Guidelines for the Accessible Design of Augmented Reality Applications

Sebastian Koch(✉), Tobias Ableitner, and Gottfried Zimmermann

Hochschule der Medien, Responsive Media Experience Research Group, Nobelstraße 10, 70569 Stuttgart, Germany
sebastian@koch.cf, gzimmermann@acm.org

Abstract. Innovative technologies, such as augmented reality, have the potential to disrupt the way people use technology today. Unfortunately, numerous people will not be able to use and derive value from augmented reality applications in their daily lives, if these are not designed with accessibility in mind.

Yet, still only few guidelines on the accessible design of augmented reality applications exist to date. This work summarizes and compares the most important guidelines devised at this point. This includes both guidelines by commercial vendors and the World Wide Web Consortium (W3C) as well as international standards. In addition, a catalog of common criteria is derived from these guidelines.

Keywords: Accessibility · Augmented reality · Guidelines · Usability

1 Introduction

Before understanding how to design accessible (AR) applications, it is important to understand what AR itself is, and how to differentiate it from similar concepts such as virtual reality (VR). A continuum can be defined [8], between reality—i.e. environments consisting only of real, actual objects—and virtuality—i.e. environments consisting only of virtual objects.

Every AR and VR application lies somewhere on this continuum and is subsumed under the label mixed reality (MR). Under this view, AR describes experiences consisting mainly of real objects, which are augmented by virtual objects. For example, a visitor in a museum is shown additional information about the exhibits, using a pair of AR glasses.

In total AR and VR is estimated to generate an annual revenue of USD 161.1 billion by 2025 [12]. This, combined with the evident interest [6,7] of large, multinational companies such as Facebook or Google strongly implies a growing number of people will use AR technologies in their daily lives—be it by choice or by necessity.

K. Miesenberger et al. (Eds.): ICCHP-AAATE 2022, LNCS 13342, pp. 89–98, 2022.
https://doi.org/10.1007/978-3-031-08645-8_11

This inevitably will create challenges for over a billion people (or around 15% of the global population) estimated to live with some sort of disability [14], if these applications were not designed with accessibility in mind. Following the social model of disability, barriers to access are not created by the existence of disabled persons, but by the environment put in place around them [10]. As such, it is important to outline clear and concise guidelines on how to implement accessible AR applications, since not everyone tasked with building these applications is themselves an expert on the needs of disabled persons. Without these guidelines numerous people may not be able to profit from AR technologies, leading to further ostracization of affected persons.

To date, few formal guidelines exist on the accessible design of AR applications exist. The two most relevant for this work are the XR Accessibility User Requirements (XAUR) [3] and the European Norm ETSI EN 301 549 [5], defining accessibility requirements for information and communications technology in general. Additionally, both commercially relevant mobile operating system vendors provide guidelines on the use of AR applications on their respective platforms (Apple Human Interface Guidelines (AHIG) and Google Augmented Reality Design Guidelines (GARDG))—albeit not focused specifically on accessibility concerns, rather usability more generally. This work summarizes and compares these guidelines and derives a catalog of common criteria from them.

2 Methodology

Four guidelines were considered for this work, which can be broadly categorized into two groups:

Accessibility The XAUR and ETSI EN 301 549 focus on aspects of accessibility for users with "classic" disabilities, such as impaired vision.

Usability The AHIG and GARDG have the focus on general aspects of usability for all users. As part of this, aspects of accessibility are also addressed, but beyond this, specific usability aspects of AR are also included.

The AHIG and GARDG were included due to being the official guidelines by both commercially relevant mobile operating system vendors. As such, these guidelines will likely affect the future of consumer-oriented AR technology the most.

In addition, the XAUR was included as the most promising work by an internationally recognized consortium—namely the W3C. Since other work by the W3C has strongly influenced national laws, such as the Web Content Accessibility Guidelines (WCAG) forming the basis of the relevant German legislature regarding the accessibility of web applications (BITV) [4], these guidelines warrant consideration.

Finally, the ETSI EN 301 549 was included as an example of the application of more general accessibility requirements on the design of information and communication technology within AR applications.

Other related standards and guidelines, such as the Game accessibility guidelines [1] were not considered for this early work, since they only tangentially mention AR applications.

3 Results

A common catalog of criteria was derived from the guidelines under consideration. This catalog contains criteria from every guideline, as well as criteria added by the authors to conform to the current understanding of barriers to access resulting from the interaction of the environment and the user—not just from the user [11] (Table 1).

Table 1. Derived catalog of common criteria for the accessibility of AR applications

§	Criterion	Description
1. Perceivable		
1.1 Visual perceivability		
1.1.1	Contrast between elements	Fore- and background colors must have a contrast of at least 4.5:1[a]
1.1.2	Contrast to background	A sufficient contrast between single elements—those without their own background—and the real world must be ensured—e.g. using text frames
1.1.3	Importance of colors	The meaning of elements must not be signaled by color differences alone
1.1.4	Font size	Fonts must be at least 16px big in screen space, even if they are placed somewhere in virtual space
1.1.5	Adaptability	The application must allow to adjust colors and contrasts, fonts up to 200% magnification[b] and the field of view
1.2 Auditive Perceivability		
1.2.1	Absolute volume	The application must allow to adjust the absolute volume in general and for specific devices like headphones
1.2.2	Relative volume	The application must allow to adjust the relative volume between different sources—such as foreground and background noise
1.2.3	Dynamic range	The dynamic range of each sound source must be adjustable
1.2.4	Monaural output	The output of all sounds on a single output device—i.e. in mono—must be possible

(*continued*)

Table 1. (*continued*)

§	Criterion	Description
1.2.5	Localization	The origin of the sounds must be recognizable non-auditively, e.g. visually or tactilely
1.2.6	Sign language	The application must support the output of sign language for pre-recorded audio and text content
1.2.7	Voice output	The application must support speech output for UI elements and texts to allow visually impaired users to use them
1.2.8	Subtitles	The application must allow the output of pre-recorded auditory content through subtitles and make them customizable by the user
1.3 Focusability		
1.3.1	Focus on the necessary	Non-critical elements, such as animations or background noise, must be able to be disabled to enable users to concentrate on the most important things
2. Operable		
2.1 Inputs		
2.1.1	Multiple input devices	The application must support the use of multiple input devices simultaneously
2.1.2	Single input device	The application must support the use of a single input device
2.1.3	Reassignment	The application must allow to configure the assignment of inputs and their sensitivity
2.1.4	Mobility-independent input	To trigger interactions, it must not be necessary to perform physical movement in space
2.1.5	Location-independent use	If the application is not designed for a specific location—such as a particular museum—it must support locations of various sizes and inform the user of the space requirements
2.1.6	Fine-motor inputs	The application must not require fine motor skills, such as simultaneous input of several gestures. This also includes defining sufficiently large interaction goals
2.1.7	Timings	If certain timings are required for input, the application must allow to extend or disable them
2.1.8	Voice input	The application must be controllable by voice such that visually impaired users can use it
2.1.9	Voice	Persistent control functions must be positioned such that the device does not need to be gripped differently to use them

(*continued*)

Table 1. (*continued*)

§	Criterion	Description
2.2 Screen magnifiers		
2.2.1	Screen magnifiers	The application must support screen magnifiers
2.2.2	Reset focus	To use screen magnifiers it must be possible to reset the focus.
2.2.3	Critical outputs	Critical issues must be communicated to the user without losing focus
2.3 Physical stimuli		
2.3.1	Avoidance	The application must allow to avoid or disable stimuli known to cause negative physical reactions—such as epileptic seizures or motion sickness
2.3.2	Warning	If it is not possible to avoid the stimuli from 2.3.1 completely, the user must be advised of this at the beginning of the application
2.4 Accessibility		
2.4.1	Documentation	The accessibility options supported by the application must be documented.
2.4.2	Independent adjustment	The de-/activation and configuration of the supported accessibility options must itself be accessible to allow users configure the app themselves
3. Understandable		
3.1 Errors		
3.1.1	Language	The application should use clear, non-technical language to communicate with the user
3.1.2	Problem solution and avoidance	The application should show the user suggestions for solving and preventing problems so that they can execute them
3.1.3	Avoiding distractions	Should the application place realistic elements in the virtual world, they must behave in a credible and understandable way so as not to distract the user. For example, realistic shadows and reflections can be used for this
3.2 Input		
3.2.1	Gestures	As far as possible, the application should use familiar gestures, such as pinch-to-zoom. Direct manipulation is preferable to indirect manipulation
3.2.2	Tutorial	The application should provide a tutorial that introduces important operating concepts and guides the user through any necessary setup tasks

(*continued*)

Table 1. (*continued*)

§	Criterion	Description
3.3 Modalities		
3.3.1	Multiple modes	If the application allows switching between AR and non-AR contests, this must be clearly indicated to the user in advance
3.3.2	Change of mode	In the case of 3.3.1, the switch should only be initiated by the user himself and not automatically
4. Miscellaneous		
4.1 Security		
4.1.1	Privacy	Accessibility adjustments must not restrict the privacy of the user. For example, speech output must not read masked text fields aloud
4.1.2	Movements	The application must not prompt the user to perform dangerous movements—such as running backwards
4.2 Comfortability		
4.2.1	Multi-user environments	As far as possible, the application should support the presence of multiple users in a shared environment, allowing for example children with autism spectrum disorder to explore the environment with their parents in a comfortable way
4.2.2	Breaks	The application must allow to be interrupted and stopped at any time. For this purpose, an input must be created that always opens a safe mode
4.2.3	Intensity	The application should remind of regular breaks or provide quieter sections
4.3 Emotional stimuli		
4.3.1	Avoidance	Content that can be disturbing to certain users—such as drug use or nudity—should be avoided or should be deactivatable[c]
4.3.2	Warning	If it is not possible to avoid the stimuli from 4.3.1 completely, the user must be advised of this at the beginning of the application
4.4 Assistive Technologies		
4.4.1	Semantic information	Elements of the virtual environment must be described semantically for assistive technologies

[a] see 1.4.3 [13].
[b] see 1.4.4 [13].
[c] A current example of such accessibility settings is the Arachnophobia Safe Mode in Grounded, in which the spiders appearing in the game can be made less spider-like in several levels [9].

4 Discussion

Table 2 compares the derived catalog of common criteria with the four guidelines under consideration. For each criterion, the closest equivalent—if any—to the respective guideline is given. Only a few criteria have equivalents in three of the guidelines; none in all four.

In general, it is shown, that these guidelines are not comprehensive by themselves. While the XAUR and ETSI EN 301 549 sufficiently cover aspects of "classic" disabilities, such as the usage of an application by a blind person, they do not cover barriers resulting from the use of a wholly new technology by a general audience. For example, they don't offer guidance on handling issues relating to the comfort and security of the user in an AR environment.

Finally, while triggers of physical conditions such as epilepsy are covered, none of the guidelines touch on emotional triggers, which may prevent access to some users.

Table 2. Comparison of the common criteria catalog derived from guidelines under consideration

Criterion	XAUR	ETSI EN	AHIG	GARDG
1.1.1 Contrast between elements	(6a)[a]	Via WCAG[b]	–	–
1.1.2 Contrast to background	–	Via WCAG	–	–
1.1.3 Importance of colors	–	4.2.3	–	–
1.1.4 Font size	–	Via WCAG	–	–
1.1.5 Adaptability	6a, 13b	4.2.2	–	–
1.2.1 Absolute volume	–	–	–	–
1.2.2 Relative volume	–	4.2.5	–	–
1.2.3 Dynamic range	–	4.2.5	–	–
1.2.4 Monaural output	–[c]	–	–	–
1.2.5 Localization	(14a)[d]	–	–	–
1.2.6 Sign language	10a	–	–	–
1.2.7 Voice output	9a	(4.2.1)[e]	–	–
1.2.8 Subtitles	18	Via WCAG	–	–
1.3.1 Focus on the necessary	3b	–	–	–
2.1.1 Multiple input devices	2c	–	–	–
2.1.2 Single input device	2b	–	–	–
2.1.3 Reassignment	1b	–	–	–
2.1.4 Mobility-independent inputs	2a	–	–	6.1

(continued)

Table 2. (*continued*)

Criterion	XAUR	ETSI EN	AHIG	GARDG
2.1.5 Location-independent usage	–	–	1.8	4.1
2.1.6 Fine-motor inputs	4a, 4b, 4c	4.2.7, 5.5.1	–	24.3
2.1.7 Timings	15b	4.2.10	–	–
2.1.8 Voice input	5a	–	–	–
2.1.9 Gripping	–	–	1.7	–
2.2.1 Screen magnifiers	7a	4.2.2	–	–
2.2.2 Reset focus	13a, 7a	–	–	–
2.2.3 Critical outputs	8a	–	–	–
2.3.1 Avoidance	16a, 16b	4.2.9	–	–
2.3.2 Warning	–	–	–	–
2.4.1 Documentation	–	12.1.1	–	–
2.4.2 Independent adjustment	–	5.2	–	–
3.1.1 Language	–	–	7.1	–
3.1.2 Problem solution and avoidance	–	4.2.10	9.2	15.2
3.1.3 Avoiding distractions	–	–	1.2, 4.7	8.1
3.2.1 Gestures	–	–	1.7, 4.2	32.1
3.2.2 Tutorial	–	–	2.1	31.1
3.3.1 Multiple modes	–	–	(11.3)[f]	26.1
3.3.2 Change of mode	–	–	–	26.1
4.1.1 Privacy	–	4.2.11	–	–
4.1.2 Movements	–	–	1.11	5.4, 7.1
4.2.1 Multi-user environments	–	–	5.1, 5.2	29.2
4.2.2 Breaks	15d/11a/12a	–	1.9	7.2
4.2.3 Intensity	15a	–	1.10	5.2
4.3.1 Avoidance	–	–	–	–
4.3.2 Warning	–	–	–	–
4.4.1 Semantic information	1a	4.2.1	–	–

[a] 6a requires only the adaptability of colors and contrasts with reference to color-blind users—no explicit contrasts are required.

[b] Criteria covered by reference to WCAG.

[c] This criterion is proposed to be added to the guidelines [2].

[d] 14a requires the ability to output ambient noise to other equipment, thus partially covering this criterion.

[e] 4.2.1 calls for a non-visual mode of interaction—but not specifically a voice output.

[f] Apple prescribes the use of special system glyphs here—but only if the application uses Apple ARKit.

5 Conclusion

Clearly, there is a strong market trend towards exploring different applications of AR and VR, due to which many more people will use AR technologies in the future. This work compared four current guidelines for the accessible design of AR applications and found that none is comprehensive by itself. As a result, the formulation of unified guidelines for the accessible design of AR applications is imperative. To this end, this work derived a catalog of common criteria containing criteria from all considered guidelines. This catalog is presented to initiate discussion about accessibility aspects not covered by the different guidelines.

Future research should expand this work to include more guidelines than the four considered for this work. In particular, it may be useful to include gaming related guidelines.

References

1. Various Contributors: Game accessibility guidelines. https://gameaccessibilityguidelines.com/full-list/
2. Accessible Platform Architectures Working Group: ACTION-2254: Draft text around the need for mono (2020). https://www.w3.org/WAI/APA/track/actions/2254
3. Accessible Platform Architectures Working Group: XR Accessibility User Requirements (2020). https://www.w3.org/TR/2020/WD-xaur-20200213/
4. Bundesministerium des Innern: Verordnung zur Schaffung barrierefreier Informationstechnik nach dem Behindertengleichstellungsgesetz (Barrierefreie Informationstechnik-Verordnung - BITV) (2002)
5. European Telecommunications Standards Institute: EN 301 549 V2.12 (2018–08) - Accessibility requirements for ICT products and services. Harmonised European Standard (2018)
6. Hong, J.: Considering privacy issues in the context of google glass. Commun. ACM **56**(11), 10–11 (2013). https://doi.org/10.1145/2524713.2524717
7. Luckerson, V.: Facebook Buying Oculus Virtual-Reality Company for $2 Billion (2014). http://time.com/37842/facebook-oculus-rift/
8. Milgram, P., Takemura, H., Utsumi, A., Kishino, F.: Augmented reality: a class of displays on the reality-virtuality continuum. Proc. SPIE **2351**(Telemanipulator and Telepresence Technologies), 282–292 (1994). 10.1.1.83.6861
9. Obsidian Entertainment Inc.: Accessibility features (2020). https://grounded.obsidian.net/news/grounded/accessibility-features
10. Shakespeare, T.: The social model of disability. In: Davis, L.J. (ed.) The Disability Studies Reader, 5th edn., chap. 16, p. 672. Routledge, New York (2006). https://lccn.loc.gov/2016013306
11. United Nations: Convention on the Rights of Persons with Disabilities. UN Convention 45, pp. 1–28, December 2008. https://treaties.un.org/Pages/ViewDetails.aspx?src=TREATY&mtdsg_no=IV-15&chapter=4&clang=_en

12. VynZ Research: Global Augmented Reality and Virtual Reality Market is expected to reach USD 161.1 billion by 2025, witnessing 48.8% CAGR during the forecast period (2020–2025) (2020). https://www.globenewswire.com/news-release/2020/05/29/2041108/0/en/Global-Augmented-Reality-and-Virtual-Reality-Market-is-expected-to-reach-USD-161-1-billion-by-2025-witnessing-48-8-CAGR-during-the-forecast-period-2020-2025-VynZ-Research.html
13. W3C: Web Content Accessibility Guidelines (WCAG) 2.0 (2008). https://www.w3.org/TR/WCAG20/
14. World Health Organization: World report on disability. World Health Organization (2011). https://www.who.int/publications/i/item/world-report-on-disability

Internet of Things: Services and Applications for People with Disabilities and Elderly Persons

Internet of Things – Services and Applications for People with Disabilities and Elderly Persons
Introduction to the Special Thematic Session

Alireza Darvishy(✉)

Zurich University of Applied Sciences, 8400 Winterthur, Switzerland
alireza.darvishy@zhaw.ch

Abstract. This short paper presents and summarizes six Special Thematic Session (STS) papers discussing accessibility and usability aspects related to the Internet of Things for elderly and disabled people. The papers include case studies, the development of new prototypes, devices and services, as well as end user-interviews and end-user questionnaires on useability. Primary target users include elderly persons, persons with mobility impairments, persons with visual impairments, persons with hearing impairments, and persons with cognitive impairments.

Keywords: Internet of Things · Assistive technology · Ambient assisted living · Smart homes

1 Introduction

The Internet of Things is ushering in a societal revolution: anything and everything can now be connected. The emergence of MicroElectro-Mechanical Systems (MEMS) – miniaturized structures, sensors, actuators and microelectronics – will allow any object to be connected, which could have substantial positive impacts for persons with disabilities as more and more products can be controlled from accessible computing platforms. The Internet of Things refers not just to devices, but also to the connections between them. For IoT applications to work, the sensors and the actuators must be able to communicate with the devices that inform their action, whether it is a smartphone or something as simple as a remote thermometer. Every day new smart devices and networks are being created for public use. Many of these, however, are not suited to be used by elderly people or people with disabilities. Meanwhile, demographics are changing worldwide and an ever-increasing number of elderly people are interested in taking advantage of smart technology. This Special Thematic Session includes papers covering various aspects of IoT applications and services for people with disabilities and elderly persons, including:

- New innovative IoT applications and services
- Successful case studies in development IoT applications and services in the area of accessibility
- IoT platforms supporting accessibility

K. Miesenberger et al. (Eds.): ICCHP-AAATE 2022, LNCS 13342, pp. 101–104, 2022.
https://doi.org/10.1007/978-3-031-08645-8_12

2 Session Papers

This section summarizes the methods and key findings of each of the STS paper contributions.

2.1 Home Automation System Controlled through Brain Activity

This paper focuses on brain-controlled smart home interactions. The authors present a new flexible domotic control system (or home automation system) that takes commands via a brain-computer interface (BCI) – with users using BCI to output written commands, and these commands then being converted into voice commands and interpreted by a voice assistant. Although the authors note that a similar project has been done before (using Alexa as a voice assistant) [1], it had some cumbersome programming issues. For this study, the authors used Google Assistant and a software called "UMA-BCI Speller". They recruited 6 healthy participants, none of whom had previous experience with BCI systems. Participants were presented with various screen menus, where participants could focus on a given word or term. This would then result in a written command, which would then be output via a speaker and interpreted by Google Assistant. (For example: Focusing on "Radio On" would output a command like "OK Google, turn the radio on"). After learning to interact with the system, participants were asked to perform 13 tasks, such as turning on a light, adjusting the air conditioning, or using WhatsApp, all through BCI. All participants completed the tasks with an average 79.73% accuracy (±13.85%), taking an average of 28.4 min (±9.52 min) for all the tasks.

2.2 BUZZBAND: A Vibrating Wristband for Hearing-Impaired Elderly People

The topic of this study is the reception of household sounds for hearing-impaired people, especially elderly persons. The authors examine existing solutions for common sounds such as the intercom, telephone, alarms, etc., and propose a solution based on a vibrating wristband. This technology would utilize sound sensors in the home, placed close to the sound source(s); the sensor would recognize the sound and send a notification to the wristband using a specific vibration. As the authors note, a similar solution has been proposed which relies on Bluetooth [2]; however, this had the disadvantage of a relatively short range. Here, the authors propose using the LoRa (Long Range), which would offer higher range and better performance. A prototype for this solution was created and tested; details will be presented in the full paper.

2.3 Hands-free Interaction Methods for Smart Home Control with Google Glass

Current augmented reality (AR) devices are largely reliant on hand gestures from the user to receive commands. This presents a challenge for users with physical limitations. This study's aim was to create and test alternative input techniques for assistive augmented reality environments that did not require the use of hands. The authors evaluated 5 potential interaction approaches for managing a smart TV using Google Glass without hands; these included head movements, head movements plus blinking, timed scanning and blinking, voice control, and scanning of labelled QR code. A user test was conducted in a smart home lab with 15 people without disabilities, ranging in age from 19 to 56 years. Users were asked to perform tasks such as changing a TV channel or changing the volume, using all of the 5 alternative input methods. Mistake rate, time required, and subjective user satisfaction were used as performance metrics. A post-test questionnaire was also used to collect qualitative input. The method of head movements plus blinking was found to have the lowest error rate, while the voice control and head movement methods were rated highest by the participants in terms of operability, usefulness, and fun. Full results will be presented in the final paper.

2.4 Ontenna: Design and Social Implementation of Auditory Information Transmission Devices Using Tactile and Visual Senses

This paper describes the product development of Ontenna, a wearable device that uses tactile feedback to allow users with hearing impairments to perceive sound through their bodies. It can be clipped to the hair, earlobe, collar, or sleeve, and conveys sound characteristics via vibrations and light. The authors present anecdotal results from case studies conducted at schools for the deaf and hard of hearing in Japan, as well as case studies conducted in recreational environments such as watching a sporting event. Users reported benefits such as being better able to perceive rhythm during a drumming class, and perceiving the crowd chanting and cheering at a football match. The authors also summarize the evolution of the Otenna prototype over the course of four years, from 2014 to 2017. Ontenna was released as a product in June 2019, and it has since been used in music and physical education classes in deaf schools across Japan. Since their release, reports have been received of pupils becoming more interested in music and better able to properly reproduce rhythms.

2.5 Usability Study of Tactile and Voice Interaction Modes by People with Disabilities for Home Automation Controls

This paper describes a comparative usability study on tactile and vocal interaction modes for home automation control, as tested by people with different disabilities within an inclusive housing context. For the study, 7 persons with disabilities (1 with a cognitive disability, 4 with motor disabilities including 2 with speech disorders, 1 with a visual impairment and 1 with a hearing impairment) were asked to perform various smart home tasks, by giving commands to Amazon Fire Cube TV intelligent personal assistant. Users interacted either through a tablet touchscreen or by voice to give various commands, such as "open the living room shutter", "turn on the bedroom light", and "call for help". Users were then asked to complete established questionnaires on the useability [3] and user experience [4] of the system, as well as completing an additional survey on the interaction modalities (preference and multimodality). The authors report that usefulness and satisfaction were rated well, while operability scored lower. Full results will be presented in the final paper.

2.6 Universal Access Panel: A Novel Approach for Accessible Smart Homes and IoT

Many modern smart home devices and appliances rely on complex touch-based interaction without haptic feedback, making them inaccessible to many people with visual impairments. This paper describes the development process of novel solution for enabling barrier-free access to home appliances and IoT devices, called the Universal Access Panel (UAP). The aim of the system is to offer a single simple multi-modal interaction concept, consisting of just a few interaction elements, for interacting with smart home devices and functions. The authors describe how various appliances, consumer electronics products and smart home devices can be integrated and controlled via the UAP, using established APIs and communication protocols like HomeConnect2 or openHab3. The authors also describe a user study performed with 5 visually impaired persons at a Living Lab in Vienna, Austria. Participants were given tasks such as operating the lights, shutters, oven and dishwasher. They were then interviewed about their experience and also asked to complete a questionnaire based around the System Usability Scale [5]; participants gave the prototype an average score of 89.5/100.

References

1. Shivappa, V.K.K., Luu, B., Solis, M., George, K.: Home automation system using brain computer interface paradigm based on auditory selection attention. In: I2MTC 2018 – 2018 IEEE Int. Instrum. Meas. Technol. Conf. Discov. New Horizons Instrum. Meas. Proc., pp. 1–6 (2018)
2. Mielke, M., Brück, R.: A home automation based environmental sound alert for people experiencing hearing loss. In: 2016 38th Annual International Conference of the IEEE Engineering in Medicine and Biology Society (EMBC), pp. 5348–5351 (2016). https://doi.org/10.1109/EMBC.2016.7591935
3. Lund, A.M.: Measuring usability with the USE questionnaire. STC Usabil. SIG Newslett. **8**, 2 (2001)
4. Schrepp, M., Hinderks, A., Thomaschewski, J.: Construction of a Benchmark for the User Experience Questionnaire (UEQ) (2017)
5. Brooke, J.: SUS—a quick and dirty usability scale. Usability Evaluation in Industry. CRC Press (June 1996). ISBN: 9780748404605

Home Automation System Controlled Through Brain Activity

Francisco Velasco-Álvarez, Álvaro Fernández-Rodríguez, and Ricardo Ron-Angevin(✉)

Departamento de Tecnología Electrónica, ETSI Telecomunicación, Universidad de Málaga, 35 Louis Pasteur Boulevard, 29071 Malaga, Spain
fvelasco@dte.uma.es, {afernandezrguez,rron}@uma.es

Abstract. Brain-computer interface (BCI) technology allows brain activity to be used as a communication channel without the need for muscle activity. Therefore, this technology could be suitable for patients with severe muscular impairments. However, BCI systems have not been easily adapted to control external devices. Therefore, the aim of the present work is to control a home automation system through a BCI that allows the construction of voice commands. Six healthy users have tested the proposed system. The controlled appliances were: WhatsApp, Spotify, Google Nest, smart light bulb, smart plug (to turn on/off a radio) and an infrared controller (to control a TV and an air conditioner). Participants controlled the system for approximately 32 min, with an accuracy of about 80%. In definitive, it has been successfully demonstrated that the use of a BCI system for home automation control could be implemented in a flexible way and could be adapted to the needs of a user.

Keywords: Brain-computer interface (BCI) · Home automation · Voice · Event-related potential (ERP)

1 Introduction

Brain-computer interfaces (BCI) are a type of technology that uses the brain signal of users to establish a communication and control channel between them and an external device [1]. Thus, this technology may be a suitable option for those people who have lost the ability to move their muscles. The neuroimaging technique most used by BCIs is the electroencephalography (EEG), possibly due to its portability, relatively low cost and high temporal resolution [2]. Therefore, the present work was focused on the use of the EEG as an input signal of a BCI system.

The most used EEG signals are the visual event-related potentials (ERP), changes in the EEG signal that are elicited as a response to a determined visual event. These BCI systems based on visual ERPs have generally offered a good performance and high number of available commands [3]. In addition, these systems have shown promising results in users with severe muscle control problems (e.g., [4, 5]). Usually, these ERPs

K. Miesenberger et al. (Eds.): ICCHP-AAATE 2022, LNCS 13342, pp. 105–112, 2022.
https://doi.org/10.1007/978-3-031-08645-8_13

are evoked through an oddball paradigm, in which a set of visual stimuli are pseudo-randomly presented while the user pays attention only to one of them, thus resulting in an ERP after the stimulation of this desired item (i.e., the target stimulus). Therefore, the objective of the BCI system is to detect the ERPs associated with the presentation of the target stimulus, which has an associated control command. The EEG-based BCI applications developed by previous works have been extensive and prepared for the control of several devices [6]. The present work will be focused on the control of a home automation system using a visual ERP-based BCI, that is, an assistive technology controlled via brain activity.

Thanks to the ERP-based BCI, different stimuli associated with certain letters or words could be selected by the user to construct written commands. Then, these written commands can be converted into voice commands by the computer and interpreted by a virtual assistant. To our knowledge, this idea of bridging communication between the BCI system and a domotic system through voice commands was previously employed by [7] using the auditory steady state response (ASSR) signal. Specifically, this work used Alexa as voice assistant, OpenBCI as BCI software, and two Arduino boards (one used for playing predetermined sound files and other equipped with a proximity sensor). The drawback of this system was that, to adapt its use to new devices, programming skills would be required to manipulate the EEG processing integrated development environment (IDE) and to be able to modify the emitted voice messages. Therefore, it would be interesting – and a novelty – to use a BCI system that can be easily configured by caregivers who, without the need for technical knowledge, can adapt the domotic devices that will be controlled by the patient. This adaptation could be provided by the UMA-BCI Speller software, an easily configurable software that uses the visual ERP signal and allows flexibility in creating the graphical user interface [8]. Therefore, the use of this software could be appropriate to generate voice commands to control a domotic system.

In short, the aim of this work is to present a flexible domotic control system (home automation system), which can be adapted to the devices and applications that the user wishes to control. To our knowledge, this is the first BCI work that proposes the domotic control of several devices and applications using voice commands and an easily configurable BCI that can be manipulated for non-technical users. Due to the novelty of the present work, it is convenient to test this system with healthy users in a controlled laboratory environment before making the leap to test it with patients in their actual context (e.g., at home). However, the advantage of the proposed system is that, after a proper configuration of the different menus in the BCI software (UMA-BCI Speller), it allows the control of all those devices and applications that have been previously configured to be controlled through voice commands by a virtual assistant (Google Assistant).

2 Method

2.1 Participants

The present study involved 6 healthy participants (aged 18–39 years, 3 males and 3 females, named D1–D6). None of them had previous experience on BCI systems. The study was approved by the Ethics Committee of the University of Malaga and met the ethical standards of the Helsinki Declaration. All participants provided written consent. According to self-reports, none of the participants had any history of psychiatric or neurological illness. They received a monetary remuneration of 5€ after completing the session.

2.2 Data Acquisition and Signal Processing

The EEG was recorded at a sample rate of 250 Hz using the electrode positions: Fz, Cz, Pz, Oz, P3, P4, PO7 and PO8, according to the 10/20 international system. All channels were referenced to the left mastoid and grounded to position AFz. Signals were amplified by an acti-CHamp amplifier (Brain Products GmbH, Munich, Germany). All aspects of the EEG data collection and processing were controlled by the BCI2000 system [9]. No artifact detection or correction techniques were applied. The ERP-based paradigm required a calibration phase in order to obtain the subject-dependent parameters for the online experimental part. These subject-dependent parameters consisted of the weights of a classifier that was applied to the EEG signal to determine which item the participants attended to. The analysis involved to obtain the weights was the stepwise linear discriminant analysis (SWLDA).

2.3 System Implementation

The aim of the BCI system was to generate voice commands that could be interpreted by Google Assistant, which would control the external devices or applications. On the one hand, a laptop ran the UMA-BCI Speller that presented the stimuli and registered and analyzed the EEG signal. On the other hand, Google Assistant running on a smartphone received and interpreted the voice commands sent by the UMA-BCI Speller, performing the corresponding action.

In this developed domotic system, different applications and devices that were controlled with the implemented BCI system has been proposed: WhatsApp, Spotify, Google Nest, smart light bulb, smart plug (to turn on/off a radio) and an infrared controller (to control a TV and an air conditioner). Google Assistant could directly control WhatsApp to send messages and Spotify to play music. It was also possible to communicate directly with the assistant to make specific requests (e.g., set an alarm at 9:00 or ask if it is going to rain tomorrow). On the other hand, Google Assistant communicated through a Wi-Fi connection with different devices: a smart light bulb, a smart plug that enabled to turn on/off a radio, the Google Nest device, and an infrared emitting controller that managed two other devices (a TV and an air conditioner). The infrared controller received the commands from Google Assistant via Wi-Fi and emulated a conventional remote control. In addition, the UMA-BCI Speller includes a text prediction function – based on the characters already written in that word and the probability of occurrence – that may help users when spelling words, for example, to write the WhatsApp's message.

To avoid the influence of ambient noise on the understanding of the command by the virtual assistant, the voice commands from UMA-BCI Speller were sent to the smartphone via a cable connection (using a mini-jack audio cable) connecting the laptop audio output with the smartphone microphone input. The output volume of the laptop was fixed throughout the whole experiment, so the assistant always received the same level of audio. The Windows 10 Narrator (a text-to-speech feature) was used, particularly the voice named "Microsoft Helena" from the Spanish voice catalogue. Since the voice commands were generated using a synthesized voice, the assistant was expected to interpret the same received commands in the same way. As the virtual assistant used in the experiment was Google Assistant, each command started with the words "Ok Google…", which is one of the wake-up keywords of the assistant. In order to present feedback to the user, the voice commands sent by the UMA-BCI Speller were played on a set of speakers. However, responses from the Google Assistant or music from Spotify were played on other set of speakers.

2.4 Control Paradigm

In order to send a control command to the virtual assistant, users had to select items (also called stimuli) from different menus. The selection of an item followed the usual procedure in an ERP row-column paradigm (RCP): users had to pay attention to the desired item (within a matrix of possible items) and mentally count the number of times an image appears overlapping that item. The duration of the stimuli was 192 ms and the interstimulus interval (ISI) was 32 ms. The timing of each selection for all the menus was the same, as all the interfaces consisted of a 7 × 7 matrix, even though in three of them there were dummy items (i.e., items that had no associated command and, therefore, had no effect when selected).

To control the domotic system, several menus were implemented. Navigating through these menus, subjects selected different items to form a sentence that would finally be converted to speech (this conversion will be denoted as "speak") to provide a specific command.

As mentioned above, for the stimuli presentation and menu navigation the UMA-BCI Speller was used. Six menus were implemented, as shown in Fig. 1.

2.5 Procedure

Participants arrived at the laboratory where the entire experimental set was already prepared. Once the task had been explained and the necessary instrumentation for the recording of EEG activity had been set up, the experiment consisted of two parts for both healthy participants: i) a calibration phase used to obtain the subject-dependent parameters of the EEG classifier, and ii) an online experimental phase. The experiment had a duration of 80–90 min.

The calibration consisted of paying attention, without feedback, to 12 predetermined items ("DOMOTICA2021") in the Spelling menu (Fig. 1e). The number of sequences (i.e., the number of times that each row and column were highlighted) was fixed at five, so each item was highlighted 10 times. After the calibration, an SWLDA analysis was performed to obtain the subject-dependent P300 classifier. According to the accuracy results obtained with such a classifier, the number of sequences was also adjusted for each subject. The criterion to choose this number of sequences was to maximize the written symbol rate (WSR), as used in [10, 11]. However, this criterion was adapted so that the minimum number of sequences was always three. The online experimental part consisted of several tasks to be performed for controlling different applications and

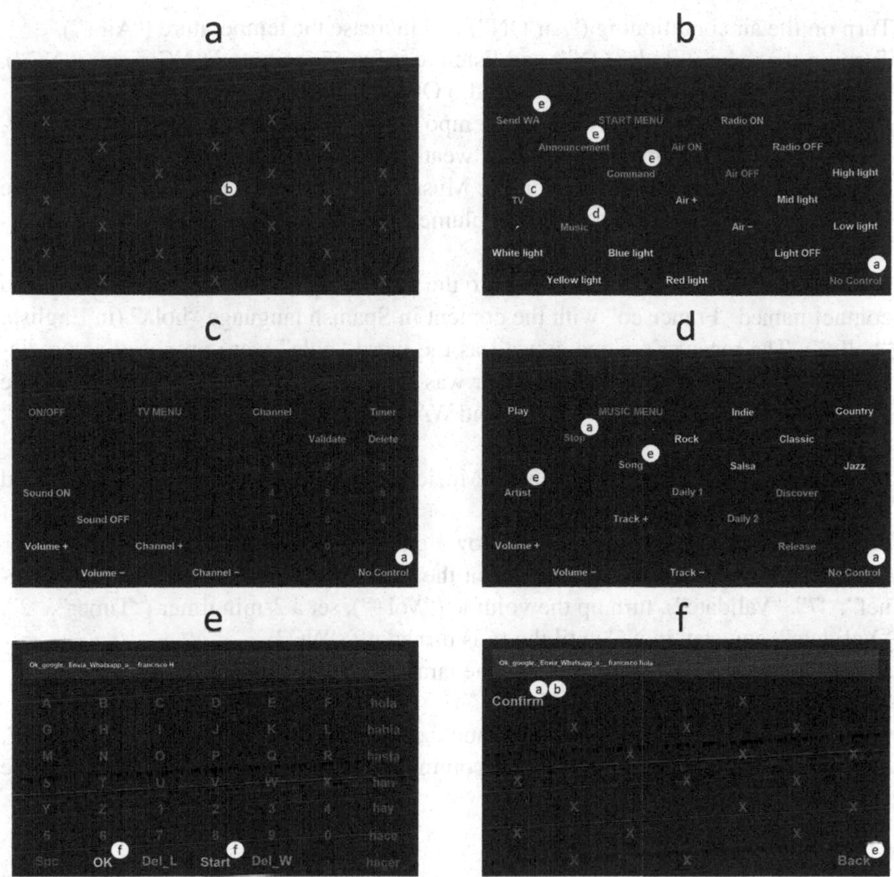

Fig. 1. Navigation scheme between the six available menus: a) no control (NC): menu of no control, b) start menu: to select a device, c) TV menu: a specific menu for TV device, d) music menu: a specific menu for spotify, e) spelling menu: specific menu to spell word, required to use Whatsapp, and f) confirmation: used to confirm a selection. The letters placed within a white circle represent a change to correspondent menu.

devices. All participants carried out the same tasks, been the objective to control all the devices proposed by the domotic system. The tasks to perform were displayed on two separate paper pages, one on each side of the screen, so the subjects could look if they forgot the details. These instructions made explicit which command had to be chosen on the interface to accomplish the given task. In case the participant made a mistake (even if that mistake completed a subsequent task), he/she had to correct the selection and continue where he/she was going. The tasks were carried out in the same order and are listed next (the specific commands required to complete each task are between parenthesis):

- The participant started in the NC menu.
- Go to the Start menu ("IC") and turn on the lamp at high intensity ("High Light").

- Turn on the air conditioning (“Air ON”) and increase the temperature (“Air+”).
- Turn on the radio (“Radio ON”) and listen to it for one minute in NC menu (“NC”). Turn it off after that minute (“IC”, “Radio OFF”).
- Access the Command menu to enter “tiempo hoy” (“Command”, “T”, “tiempo”, “H”, “hoy”, “OK”, “Confirm”), in English, “weather today”.
- Access the Start menu (“IC”), then the Music menu (“Music”), choose a free genre (e.g., “Jazz”), increase the volume (“Volume+”), select next song (“Track+”) and go to the NC menu (“No control”).
- Go to Start menu (“IC”) and, then, go to the WhatsApp menu to send a message to a contact named “Francisco” with the content in Spanish language “hola” (in English, “hello”). The receiver’s name as well as the word “hola” were proposed as predictions by the system when the first letter was selected. A minimum of 8 actions were needed to complete this task (“IC”, “Send WA”, “F”, “Francisco”, “H”, “hola”, “OK”, “Confirm”).
- Access the Start menu (“IC”), then the Music menu (“Music”) to turn off Spotify and return to NC (“Stop”).
- Turn on the light to a low intensity (“Low light”) and set to blue (“Blue light”).
- Access the TV menu (“TV”) to turn on the tv (“ON/OFF”), set channel 7 (“Channel”, “7”, “Validate”), turn up the volume (“Vol+”), set a 2-min timer (“Timer”, “2”, “Validate”) and stay in NC until the tv is turned off (“NC”).
- Go to the Start menu (“IC”) and turn the lamp off (“Light off”).
- Turn off the air conditioning (“Air OFF”).
- Access the Announcement menu (“Announcement”) to write “fin” (“F”, “fin”, “OK”, “Confirm”) – in English, “end” – and communicate via Google Nest device that the experiment was finished.

3 Results

3.1 Calibration Phase

Most of the participants (5 out of 6) reached the 100% of accuracy with only 3 sequences. Using the maximum number of sequences allowed (i.e., 5 sequences), all participants obtained their highest WSR on or before the third sequence, so all participants used 3 sequences for the online phase.

3.2 Online Phase

All participants completed the task apart from D5, who abandoned it due to the large number of errors that were occurring (she abandoned the task when she had 41.77% accuracy and was on task 5, related to manage Spotify). Therefore, this participant has not been considered for the averages reported in this section. The average accuracy obtained by participants who completed the task was 79.73 ± 13.85%. Specifically, the average number of total incorrect selections was 20 ± 18.12 (out of 83.6 ± 28.03), which included 10.4 ± 9.21 selections of dummy elements with no consequences. In addition, the average time to complete all tasks was 31.58 ± 9.63 min, including periods of optional rest in the NC menu. If these standby periods are subtracted, it took users an average of 28.4 ± 9.52 min to complete the required tasks. Regarding the two tasks related to staying in the NC menu in standby state (while listening to the radio or watching TV), two participants did not meet the required time: D1 for the one minute listening the radio, and D3 for the two minutes watching TV.

4 Discussion and Conclusions

In this work, an assistive technology to control a domotic system through brain activity was presented. It has been successfully demonstrated that the use of a BCI system for home automation control could be implemented in a flexible way and could be adapted to the needs of a user. In general, BCI systems are complex to adapt for the control of external devices and applications. However, voice control is becoming more and more common. Therefore, the idea of this proposal facilitates the work to control these devices previously adapted to voice commands, something that can be essential for the objective population of these interfaces. It is important to remember that the potential users of these systems (i.e., patients or their caregivers) may not have the technical expertise to manipulate complex systems. Also, the UMA-BCI Speller software has once again proven to be a useful tool that is highly adaptable for controlling numerous devices in the environment using voice command bypassing.

Currently, new tests are being prepared to prove this system with actual patients in their usual environment. These tests would be an important demonstration of the flexibility of the system, as it would imply adapting the system to the devices owned by the users themselves. In addition, it would be advisable to explore the long-term use of these systems by patients daily. This evaluation of daily use by patients would make it possible to test the system for real use and to continue improving it. Likewise, it would be advisable to evaluate not only the software but also the hardware, with the aim of developing low-cost portable devices that do not require technical knowledge or specialized technicians for their use.

Acknowledgements. This research was funded in part by the Spanish Ministry of Science, Innovation, and Universities (Project SICCAU, reference: RTI2018-100912-B-I00), by the European fund ERDF, and by the University of Malaga (Universidad de Málaga). Moreover, the authors would like to thank all participants for their cooperation.

References

1. Wolpaw, J.R., Birbaumer, N., McFarland, D.J., Pfurtscheller, G., Vaughan, T.M.: Brain-computer interfaces for communication and control. Clin. Neurophysiol. **113**, 767–791 (2002)
2. Nicolas-Alonso, L.F., Gomez-Gil, J.: Brain computer interfaces, a review. Sensors **12**, 1211–1279 (2012)
3. Allison, B.Z., Kübler, A., Jin, J.: 30+ years of P300 brain–computer interfaces. Psychophysiology **57**, 1–18 (2020)

4. Utsumi, K., Takano, K., Okahara, Y., Komori, T., Onodera, O., Kansaku, K.: Operation of a P300-based braincomputer interface in patients with Duchenne muscular dystrophy. Sci. Rep. **8**, 4–11 (2018)
5. Medina-Juliá, M.T., Fernández-Rodríguez, A., Velasco-Álvarez, F., Ron-Angevin, R.: P300-based brain-computer interface speller: usability evaluation of three speller sizes by severely motor-disabled patients. Front. Hum. Neurosci. **14**, 1–10 (2020)
6. Saha, S., et al.: Progress in brain computer interface: challenges and opportunities. Front. Syst. Neurosci. **15**, 1–20 (2021)
7. Shivappa, V.K.K., Luu, B., Solis, M., George, K.: Home automation system using brain computer interface paradigm based on auditory selection attention. In: I2MTC 2018 – 2018 IEEE Int. Instrum. Meas. Technol. Conf. Discov. New Horizons Instrum. Meas. Proc., pp. 1–6 (2018)
8. Velasco-Álvarez, F., Sancha-Ros, S., García-Garaluz, E., Fernández-Rodríguez, Á., Medina-Juliá, M.T.T., Ron-Angevin, R.: UMA-BCI speller: an easily configurable P300 speller tool for end users. Comput. Methods Programs Biomed. **172**, 127–138 (2019)
9. Schalk, G., McFarland, D.J., Hinterberger, T., Birbaumer, N., Wolpaw, J.R.: BCI2000: A General-Purpose Brain-Computer Interface (BCI) System (2004)
10. Townsend, G., et al.: A novel P300-based brain-computer interface stimulus presentation paradigm: moving beyond rows and columns. Clin. Neurophysiol. **121**, 1109–1120 (2010)
11. Velasco-Álvarez, F., Fernández-Rodríguez, Á., Vizcaíno-Martín, F.-J., Díaz-Estrella, A., Ron-Angevin, R.: Brain–computer interface (BCI) control of a virtual assistant in a smartphone to manage messaging applications. Sensors **21** (2021)

BUZZBAND: A Vibrating Wristband for Hearing-Impaired Elderly People

Elisabetta Romoli, Jacopo Pollastri, Andrea Masciadri, Sara Comai(✉), and Fabio Salice

Department of Electronics Information and Bioengineering, Politecnico di Milano, Milan, Italy

{andrea.masciadri,sara.comai,fabio.salice}@polimi.it

Abstract. In this paper, we focus on the problem of getting notifications about sounds for hearing-impaired people in home environments. After analyzing available solutions for typical sounds like, e.g., the intercom, the telephone, various alarms, etc., we propose a solution based on a wearable device that vibrates as soon as a sound is detected. The goal is to maintain already existing devices that emit sounds and provide a simple, low-cost, accessible, and versatile solution that can be used with any device. The paper describes the main functionalities of the proposed solution and the first technical experimental results obtained with our prototype.

Keywords: Assistive technology · Ageing · Sound sensors · Lora · Ambient assistive living

1 Introduction

According to data from "World Population Prospects: the 2019 Revision" by United Nations [2], in recent years, the number of persons aged 65 years or over has increased substantially in most countries and regions, and the growth is projected to accelerate in the coming decades, doubling and reaching nearly 1.5 billion people by 2050.

In this work, we focus on hearing impairment, one of the physical disabilities typical of the elderly population. Hearing cell degeneration starts already at 18 years old, leading initially to a loss of high frequency perception, but with age there is an increase in the loss of the capacity to hear and distinguish spoken words. The hearing ability and the severity of the hearing loss is measured in dBHL (decibels Hearing Level). Normal hearing is defined as 0 dBHL, whereas the threshold for a moderate hearing impairment is typically 40 dBHL.

A study on the number of hearing-impaired people in England and Wales [1] shows that 7.4 million people have average hearing thresholds at mid frequencies of 25+ dBHL, for an adult population of 38.7 million (aged 18+ years). Eighty percent are 60+. Given the growth of the elderly population and no change in prevalence rates over the next 20 years, the number of hearing-impaired is expected to increase by approximately 20% [1].

K. Miesenberger et al. (Eds.): ICCHP-AAATE 2022, LNCS 13342, pp. 113–120, 2022.
https://doi.org/10.1007/978-3-031-08645-8_14

In the following, we will first analyze available solutions that support hearing-impaired people in being notified about sounds at home (e.g., the intercom, the telephone, a kitchen timer) (Sect. 2). We discuss their possible issues and propose a solution for the elderly based on a vibrating wristband connected through a LoRa network (Sect. 3). The solution exploits a sound sensor positioned in the proximity of the sound source, recognizes the sound, and sends a notification to the wristband so that a specific vibration can be perceived by the person. Finally, we report our first technical experimental results obtained with our prototype using different kinds of ringtones (Sect. 4).

2 State of the Art

Several assistive technologies are available or have been proposed in the literature for deaf people.

Considering smart home environments, the authors in [8] propose a Home Automation solution based on a Bluetooth-based mesh network to notify deaf people about sounds in the house. In their experiments, the mesh node is integrated either into a ceiling lamp or into a power plug. The focus is on the architecture of the system. One of its disadvantages is that the short range of Bluetooth Low Energy requires equipping the house with several nodes to guarantee a good coverage.

Other solutions exploit mobile applications to notify the user about particular sounds (like, e.g., the Sound Alert app): the signal from the sound source is first recorded on the smartphone (some predefined sounds like those of smoke alarms are already pre-installed in the application), then the app constantly listens to the environment and when a sound is recognized, the user is alerted. Such kinds of solutions allow a great personalization of notification alerts, but they can only be applicable for those people who always carry their smart devices with them. The KitMe solution (https://www.intendime.com/kitme/) allows to position a sensor close to the sound source and when this rings, an alert is sent to a smartwatch that vibrates, lights up and shows the name of the activated sensor on the display.

Wearable devices could be a valid alternative for the elderly. Neosensory Buzz (https://neosensory.com/) is a haptic wristband that exploits haptic technology to communicate the sounds to the brain by sending vibrations via the nervous system for any noise or sound, including voices and music. These devices are meant for deaf people, and they have outstanding performances. However, such kinds of solutions can be expensive and hard to use for older people.

A simpler solution on the market is represented by sound amplification devices. They can be intercoms or telephones with the possibility of regulation in the ringtone volume. An example is the Panasonic Amplified Cordless phone. The ringtone can be set to very high decibel values, far above the hearing-impaired threshold of 40+ dBHL. However, these solutions require replacing the already present telephone or intercom, are available only for specific devices, and the very loud sound can be annoying for the people who live next to the elderly.

Some devices use light indications, possibly combined with sound amplification. When they ring, the object starts to emit a light signal. However, the usefulness of the solution is strongly related to the user position with respect to the light indication object.

Considering the vibrating devices available on the market for deaf people, most of them are alarm clocks. This solution consists of a vibrating object that can be put under the pillow or very close to the sleeping person, connected to an alarm clock via wire (some examples are Sonic Bomb, Sleek Bedside Buddy, etc.). These devices are cheap and extremely easy to use and to integrate into the environment, therefore suitable for the hearing-impaired elderly. However, this is just a partial solution for a single type of device, not applicable to any kind of ringing device.

An interesting concept is represented by Vibering [9], a wrist watch that associated with a pair or rings to be worn on both hands that act as the "ears" of the person, identifies the sound captured by the rings and presents the information to the user in a display. The watch is programmed to capture key words or phrases (e.g., the name of the person, car noises etc.). However, no further studies are available.

Considering the elderly or people with hear impairments, even when they wear hearing aids or cochlear implants they have difficulties in localizing the origin of the sound [4]. If haptic stimulation is provided on their wrists, the studies in [5] show that locating sounds can improve.

Current reviews on wrist-wearable devices do not include solutions thought for the hearing impaired people. They tipically focus on problems like fall, movement activities, or bio-signal detection [6,7]. On the other side, reviews on tools of assistive technology for hearing impaired people do not include vibrating wearable devices [3].

3 Proposed Solution

In this paper, we propose a solution based on a wearable device that aims at being simple, low cost and flexible to be applied to any device that emits a sound at home. Its main architecture consists of two separate objects: a transmitter that must be placed in the proximity of the sound source and a wristband worn by the user that vibrates as soon as a sound is detected. Figure 1 shows the basic architecture of the solution. The transmitter must be able to identify a specific sequence of sounds for the selected device. To do that, a computing platform in the transmitter must be configured to analyse the modes of the sound waves and recognize them when the same sounds are played again. The sequence of sounds can be detected by a microphone connected to the computing platform.

The information about the recognized sound is then transmitted to the wristband. Since the hearing problem is strongly related to distance, the wristband must be able to receive the command in the whole house, including the outside area, therefore the range network must me higher than 100 m. In addition, the power consumption must be as low as possible that guarantees a clear communication between the transmitter and the receiver. By comparing Bluetooth,

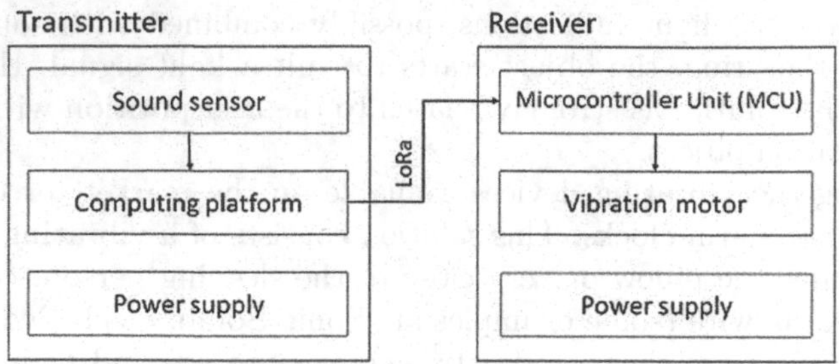

Fig. 1. Architecture of the proposed solution

Wi-Fi, Zigbee, and LoRa networks, we chose the LoRa (Long Range) network for its range of communication and its great consumption performance ratio. When the signal is received by the LoRa receiver in the wristband, a microcontroller unit connected to the LoRa receiver will make a vibration motor buzz. The user will then feel a mild vibration on his/her wrist.

The operation of the system is based on the ability of the device to recognize specific sounds and, in particular, the characteristic tones and the time sequence of these tones. Generally, each element of the house (intercom, telephone, washing machine, dishwasher, oven) has its own specific sound. In simplified form, the process is as follows. The device is initially calibrated to recognize a specific element of the house. During this phase, a sound spectrum analysis of the sound produced by the element is performed using the Fast Fourier Transform (FFT). Frequencies whose peak exceeds a threshold are considered characterizing. The characterizing frequencies are stored and used to recognize the sound in the future. Recognition is done by correlating the stored characterizing frequencies with the characterizing frequencies detected in a moving window. If the correlation exceeds 0.75, a vibration trigger signal is sent.

Also the LoRa network needs to be calibrated for the correct transmission of the data. Even if the network range could reach dozens of kilometres, for our purpose a local network must be set up. Since every LoRa module has to be configured individually it has to be done for both the transmitter one and the receiver one in the same way. The first thing to set is the transmission mode. The transparent transmission is the most suitable to Buzzband purpose, since in the system only two LoRa modules are present there is no necessity in managing or filtering the data transport. Hence, in this mode, the transmitter will send all the data to the receiver. Therefore, no address is required to identify the modules but they both need to be set in the same channel otherwise they will not be able to communicate to each other.

4 Prototype and Experimental Results

In our prototype, we implemented the basic functionalities of the proposed solution: the ability to analyse simple sequences of sounds and the data transmission to the wristband.

The transmitter prototype is composed of a controller board Elegoo UNO R3, connected to the GY -MAX4466 microphone with fixable gain and to the LoRa transmitter module Ra01 SX1278 (433 Hz). The connection between the Elegoo UNO R3 and the microphone is made via a breadboard. The Buzzband prototype is composed by a second controller board Elegoo UNO R3 connected to the LoRa receiver module Ra01 SX1278 (433 Hz) and to a 01 vibrating motor module. The power supply of both devices is obtained via a 9 V battery.

The developed prototype can be seen in Fig. 2.

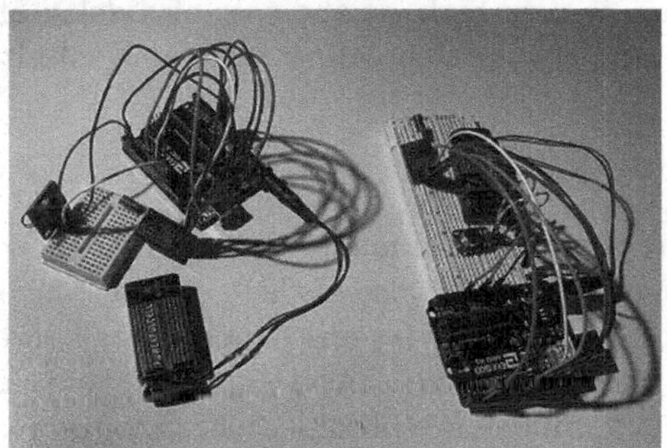

Fig. 2. Prototype

The following sections describe the different experiments have been carried out to test the main functionalities.

4.1 Monotone Ringtone

The first functionality that has been tested is the capability to recognize and to respond to a simple monotone ringtone in a neutral environment (without any other loud noises). We used a very common bell ringtone used by old fashioned telephones. Due to the lack of computational power the number of samples to be processed using the FFT technique is set to 128. During the experiments the sound frequencies detected never passed 1000 Hz so we decided to set the sample frequency to 2000 Hz in order to have a more precise spectrum without violating the Nyquist-Shannon sampling theorem. Hence all of the measures were made with a sampling period of 500 μs.

A typical frequency spectrum of few samplings of the selected ringtone is shown in Fig. 3.

In this experiment, the dominant frequence was 840 Hz. To be robust to noise, the signal is sent to Buzzband only if the matching dominant frequency is

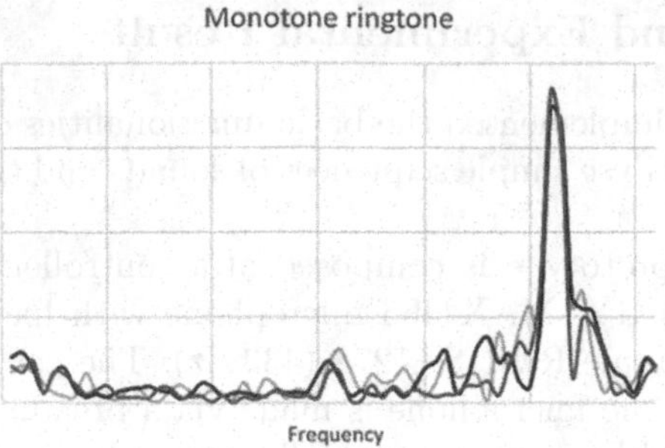

Fig. 3. Monotone ringtone frequency spectrum

returned three times in a row, by adding a delay of 0.4 s between two consecutive samples. The accuracy is very high, at the cost of a delay of 1–2 s between the start of the ringtone and the corresponding Buzzband vibration.

4.2 Bitonal Ringtone

Since nowadays many ringtones are made by two different notes, we decided to upgrade Buzzband in order to work also in these circumstances. We did not manage to find a good test audio track for our experiments so we created one using two notes alternating in rapid succession. Using the same sampling parameters as in the monotone experiment, we obtained the frequency spectrum shown in Fig. 4.

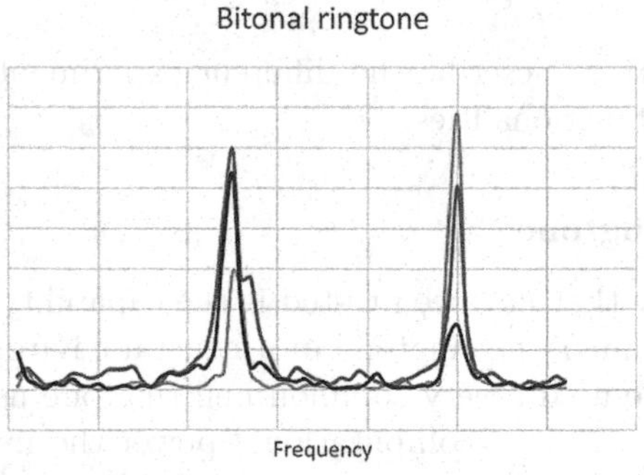

Fig. 4. Bitonal ringtone frequency spectrum

Two peaks are present around the frequencies 405 Hz and 800 Hz. Sometimes the major peak was the former sometimes the latter, so for both peaks the intensity of the minor peak is considered as a threshold to detect the peak.

4.3 Steady Operation and Additional Considerations

After testing the prototype in a controlled environment, we checked its performances in normal conditions. We simulated all the external noises that can occur in a daytime.

We performed 10 samplings with the monotone ringtone and 10 ten samplings using the bitonal ringtone without any other noise in the environment. In these conditions we did not obtain any false negative results. We also performed 10 samplings with both ringtones in presence of various noises that could be present in a home: people talking in the background, noises and music from the TV, strong noises such as people shouting and objects falling. We observed that, with the transmitter placed at a distance of less than 15 cm from the sound source playing the ringtone, there were no interferences of such noises: 0 false negatives were obtained. The analysis of false positives was done by playing only the noises described above and in addition we introduced different ringtones from the ones that the device is taught to detect. No false positives were observed, therefore we obtained complete accuracy of the device.

As far as data transmission is concerned, we tested its operation in a house of 75 m^2. The communication between the LoRa modules occurred without any impediment even if some obstacles, such as doors and walls, were present.

Finally, we tried to make Buzzband work with a more complicated ringtone, for example a song. Unfortunately the high numbers of different sounds coming out of several instruments and the low performances of our microphone made it impossible for us to recognize a pattern or at least something characteristic in the frequency spectrum for consecutive samples. Every measure showed something completely different every time. This result helped us to set a limit in our project capabilities due to the low budget threshold and the low computational power.

5 Conclusions

The proposed solution is a simple and cheap solution to detect monotone and bitonal ringtones. The solution has been designed to be applicable in home environments and to be suited for the elderly: the LoRa network has been selected and a simple wristband needs to be worn by the user. The analysis of the sounds is based on the Fast-Fourier Transform (FFT) technique to find the dominant frequencies and characterize each sound. For monotone and bitonal ringtones the approach is reliable. Future work includes further experiments will be aimed both at the analysis of different sources of warning sounds (for example, the oven) and at the usability of the proposed solution. The prototype can be extended with a module to "memorize" the user own ringtones and sound alarms in the house (the current prototype does not have a memory). In this way, the solution would become customizable and it could work with every sound source without any restrictions. Finally, also wearability aspects should be considered: finding the correct size components, the perfect power supply and the most efficient connections would make it possible to design a bracelet with the desired functionalities.

References

1. Davis, A.: Epidemiological profile of hearing impairments: the scale and nature of the problem with special reference to the elderly. Acta Otolaryngol. **111**(sup476), 23–31 (1991)
2. DESA, U.: World population prospects 2019. United Nations. Department of Economic and Social Affairs. World Population Prospects 2019 (2019)
3. Dhanjal, A.S., Singh, W.: Tools and techniques of assistive technology for hearing impaired people. In: 2019 International Conference on Machine Learning, Big Data, Cloud and Parallel Computing (COMITCon), pp. 205–210 (2019). https://doi.org/10.1109/COMITCon.2019.8862454
4. Dorman MF, Loiselle, L.H., Cook, S.J., Yost, W.A., Gifford, R.H.: Sound source localization by normal-hearing listeners, hearing-impaired listeners and cochlear implant listeners. Audiol. Neurootol. **21**(3), 127–131 (2016). https://doi.org/10.1159/000444740
5. Fletcher, M.D., Zgheib, J., Perry, S.W.: Sensitivity to haptic sound-localization cues at different body locations. Sensors **21**(11) (2021). https://doi.org/10.3390/s21113770
6. Jaegeol, C.: Current status and prospects of health-related sensing technology in wearable devices. J. Healthc. Eng. **2019** (2019). https://doi.org/10.1155/2019/3924508
7. Kamišalió, A., Fister, I., Turkanović, M., Karakatič, S.: Sensors and functionalities of non-invasive wrist-wearable devices: a review. Sensors **18**(6) (2018). https://doi.org/10.3390/s18061714
8. Mielke, M., Brück, R.: A home automation based environmental sound alert for people experiencing hearing loss. In: 2016 38th Annual International Conference of the IEEE Engineering in Medicine and Biology Society (EMBC), pp. 5348–5351 (2016). https://doi.org/10.1109/EMBC.2016.7591935
9. Tiwari, A.S.: Vibering jewelry senses danger to help deaf (2008). http://inventorspot.com/articles/vibering_senses_danger_to_help_deaf_16776

Hands-Free Interaction Methods for Smart Home Control with Google Glass

Tobias Ableitner[1(✉)], Fiona Heilemann[1], Andreas Schilling[2], Surjo Soekadar[3], and Gottfried Zimmermann[1]

[1] Stuttgart Media University, Responsive Media Experience Research Group, 70569 Stuttgart, Germany
tobias.ableitner@googlemail.com, gzimmermann@acm.org
[2] University of Tübingen, 72074 Tübingen, Germany
andreas.schilling@uni-tuebingen.de
[3] Charité – Universitätsmedizin Berlin, 10117 Berlin, Germany
surjo.soekadar@charite.de

Abstract. Augmented reality glasses (AR glasses) provide their users with visual and sometimes also acoustic information without requiring their hands. This fact allows users to consume the information provided by AR glasses even in situations where they need their hands to perform an activity. However, if interaction with the AR glasses is also required, users will still need to use their hands most of the time.

In order to prevent hindering the user in his or her actual activity, a well designed human-machine interaction concept that does not involve the hands is desirable. One solution could be to develop interaction methods for AR glasses that do not involve the user's hands and to use the AR glasses not only as an output device but also as an input device. From those methods also people with physical limitation who rely on assistance systems, like a hand exoskeleton, could benefit.

Therefore, we developed and evaluated alternative input methods without hands in assistive augmented reality (AR) contexts, in terms of accessibility. With 15 subjects we investigated 5 alternative interaction concepts for operating a smart TV without hands via a Google Glass. The results show that it is possible to develop hands-free input methods for the Google Glass that work quickly and reliably and achieve high user satisfaction. Thus, our user study also shows that it seems to be possible to use the Google Glass to control smart home and assistance systems, such as a hand exoskeleton.

Keywords: Augmented reality glasses (AR glasses) · Hands-free input methods · Smart home

1 Introduction and Methodology

Augmented reality glasses (AR glasses) provide their users with visual and sometimes also acoustic information without requiring their hands. This fact allows users to consume the information provided by AR glasses even in situations (e.g., logistics [1, 2]) where

K. Miesenberger et al. (Eds.): ICCHP-AAATE 2022, LNCS 13342, pp. 121–129, 2022.
https://doi.org/10.1007/978-3-031-08645-8_15

they need their hands to perform an activity. However, if interaction (pointing gestures, menus, etc.) with the AR glasses is also required, users will still need to use their hands most of the time.

For people with physical limitations who rely on assistance systems, AR glasses also offer interesting solutions. For example, AR glasses can be used as a feedback device when controlling prosthesis [3]. Hand exoskeletons, for example, give people with hand paralysis, such as can occur as a result of a stroke or paraplegia, parts of their former motor ability back [4]. However, in order for a hand exoskeleton to actually provide added value in everyday life and for its operation not to hinder the user in his or her actual activity, a well-designed human-machine interaction concept that does not involve the hands is desirable and, in the case of bilateral paralyzed persons, mandatory. One solution could be to develop interaction methods for AR glasses that do not involve the user's hands and to use the AR glasses not only as an output device but also as an input device when controlling the hand exoskeleton.

The user study described below took place in preparation for the development of a neurally controlled hand exoskeleton. The goal of the study was to develop and evaluate alternative input methods without hands in assistive augmented reality (AR) contexts in terms of accessibility and for hand exoskeleton control. In a user test with 15 subjects without disabilities aged 19–56 years, we investigated 5 alternative interaction concepts for operating a smart TV usable without hands via a Google Glass. We used error rate, time required, and subjective user satisfaction as metrics. We also collected qualitative feedback via a post-test questionnaire. A prototype app was used in the experimental setup, which provided us with qualitative and quantitative results for each interaction method.

2 Hands-Free Input Methods

In the following, we look at 5 different interaction methods for input via Google Glass that do not require hands.

2.1 Head Movements

With this input method, the user controls the smart TV using head movements. To do this, he tilts his head to the left, right, up or down. The app detects the head movement with the help of the gyroscope built into Google Glass. In action level 8, two actions are mapped to each direction of head movement due to the 8 possible control commands. To allow the user to choose between them, our app additionally differentiates between a short-term and a long-term tilt of the head in action level 8. To prevent the next input from being detected immediately after an input because the user does not move his head back to its starting position fast enough, the app ignores all data from the gyroscope for the following 2 s after an input.

2.2 Head Movements and Blinking

This form of input is also based on head movements, but only distinguishes whether the user tilts his head to the left or right. Each control command has its own card. The cards are located in a fixed list. By tilting his head, the user scrolls horizontally through the list. Using the Google Glass' built-in blink detection, he confirms the selected control command with a double blink and sends it to the smart TV. This form of control is comparable to 2-button scanning.

2.3 Timed Scanning and Blinking

The user interface has the same structure as that of the input method head movements and blinking. However, it is based on the principle of 1-button scanning. The app shows the user each card for 2.5 s in an endless loop. Selecting a control command is also done by double blinking. In addition, the app still shows a progress bar in the user interface so that the user can better estimate how long the current card will still be visible and selectable.

2.4 Voice Control

The voice recognition of Google Glass is used for this input method. A voice input can be started via the start command "ok glass". Google Glass then displays all available voice commands or control commands in a list. If a voice command is recognized, the list closes again. Due to the small display, it is not possible to display all control commands in a sufficiently large font in the list in action level 8. Therefore, the direct selection of the TV channels has been moved to a sub menu.

2.5 QR Code Scan

The input method for controlling the smart TV via QR codes uses the Google Glass camera. The app starts the scanning process with a double blink. During this process, the app shows the camera preview. There is a QR code for each control command. We labeled the QR codes with the respective control command so that the test subjects know which QR code they have to scan. As soon as the app has successfully recognized a QR code, it sends the control command encoded in it to the smart TV and closes the camera preview. If the app does not detect a QR code for 8 s, it cancels the input.

3 Prototype App

The prototypical app for Google Glass envisions that the users can use it to control devices in their smart home without having to use their hands. We chose a smart TV in the form of the VLC player as the smart home device because this setup requires little smart home infrastructure, is transportable, and a smart TV or VLC player has extensive functionality compared to other devices (e.g., lamps). This allowed for more diverse use cases to be defined for the user study and more further development opportunities for the input methods app (Fig. 1).

The app sends HTTP GET requests to the VLC's built-in HTTP server to control it. The individual control commands are sent along as URL parameters. On the display

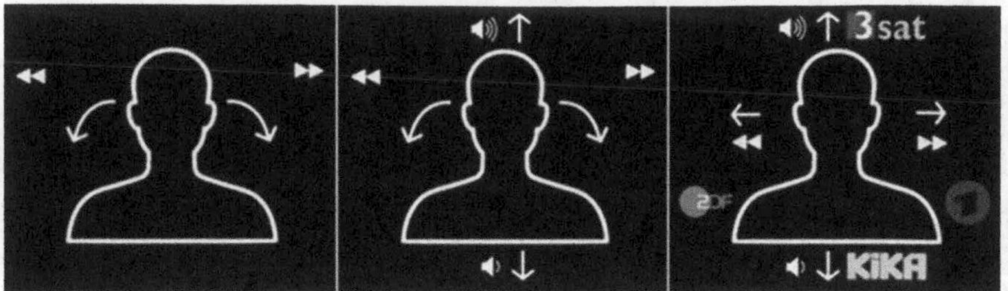

Fig. 1. Screenshots of the app user interface for the head movement input method in all 3 action levels. From left to right: A2, A4 and A8.

of the Google Glass, the app visualizes the available control commands (e.g., 4 TV channels) for the user as well as help for using the selected input method.

The user selects the hands-free input method in advance via the main menu. This displays the input methods on so-called cards. The user can navigate between the cards via swipe gestures on the touch pad of the right frame and select the desired hands-free input method via a touch gesture. How many control commands are available for selection depends on a configured action level. We used them to investigate whether the input methods perform differently depending on the control commands available for selection. We implemented 3 different action levels:

- **Action level 2 (A2):** In this action level, the next and previous TV station or the next and previous playlist item can be selected via the app.
- **Action level 4 (A4):** In addition to the control commands from A2, the user can increase and decrease the volume.
- **Action level 8 (A8):** In addition to the control commands from A2 and A4, there are 4 TV stations for direct selection.

4 Experimental Setup

We conducted the user study in our smart home lab. The lab has typical pieces of furniture from a living room and smart home devices. This also includes a television. We used this as a smart TV for the user study by connecting a computer to the TV and running the VLC player on it. In the VLC player, a playlist with the recordings of 5 TV channels was open. The recordings prevented interference in the transmission of the TV signal or different program content between subjects from influencing the study results. The Google Glass was connected to a notebook via USB cable during the user study. Through this, we were able to launch the app and to track the subjects' activities via the log outputs and better support them during the familiarization phase. The Google Glass and the computer connected to the TV were in the same WLAN network so that the app could send the HTTP GET requests to the VLC player. We placed the QR codes needed for the QR code scan input method in the area of the TV. They had a size of 9×9 cm. During the user study, the subjects were allowed to sit in an armchair. The subjects sat on it between 0.5 m and 1 m away from the TV and the QR codes (Fig. 2).

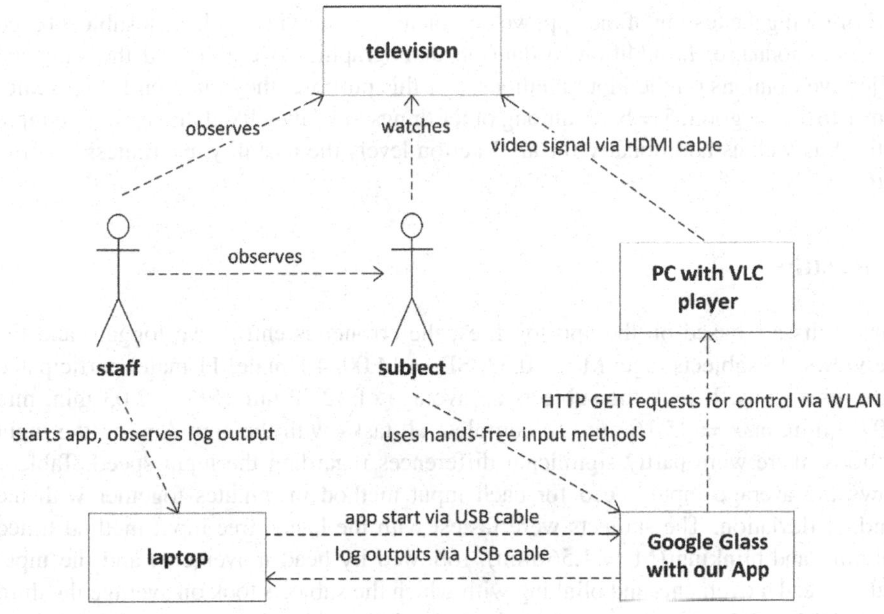

Fig. 2. User study setup in our smart home lab.

5 Study Process

The user study involved a total of 15 subjects who had no discernible limitations. The user study lasted approximately 45 min per participant. At the beginning, each subject received a briefing on the operation of the Google Glass and our app. After that, testing of the input methods began. All subjects were asked to use the 5 input methods to control the smart TV. To counteract learning effects as well as fatigue effects in the study results, we randomized the order of the input methods between subjects. Action levels A2, A4, and A8 were tested for each of the 5 input methods in ascending order. For this purpose, we had implemented a study mode in the app. The start of the next test section or action level (and hands-free input method after A8) was performed by the subjects themselves using a tap gesture on the right temple of the Google Glass. This did not require switching hands-free input methods via the app's main menu. The subjects performed tasks that were defined in advance in a test plan, such as changing a TV channel or changing the volume. The order of the tasks differed between subjects. In contrast, the number of tasks per hands-free input method and action level was the same. In A2 there were 2 tasks and in A4 and A8 3 tasks per hands-free input method. When defining the tasks as well as their order, we made sure that the minimum number of required user inputs (e.g., head movement to the left) was the same for all subjects. In study mode, the app logged all user inputs together with a timestamp into a file. Wrong inputs could be determined via a comparison with the test plan. We had to manually log incorrectly recognized voice commands and unrecognized double blinks.

Following the testing of the app, we conducted an interview with each subject based on a questionnaire. In addition to data on demographics, we collected the subjects' subjective opinions on the input methods. For this purpose, they rated on Likert scales from 1 to 5 (1 = good, 5 = bad), among other things, how they liked the respective input method as well as additionally for all 3 action levels the usability, usefulness and fun factor.

6 Results

The results are based on the app log files, the erroneous entries we logged, and the interviews. 15 subjects (age: M = 30.33, SD = 14.00, 4 female, 11 male) participated in the user study. It took the subjects an average of 12.22 min (SD = 2.03 min, min = 9.00 min, max = 15.16 min) to complete all tasks with the app. Among the input methods, there were partly significant differences regarding the input speed. Table 1 shows the average input speed for each input method in minutes together with the standard deviation. The subjects were fastest with the hands-free input method timed scanning and blinking (M = 1.56 min), followed by head movements and the input method head movements and blinking with which the subjects took on average the third longest (M = 2.14 min) to complete the tasks. Voice control and especially QR code scan (M = 3.30 min) performed noticeably worse.

When looking at the percentage of tasks with at least one incorrect entry that occurred, the QR code scan (M = 61.94%) and voice control (M = 34.91%) input methods also performed the worst. We scored an incorrect input, for example, if the participants scanned the wrong QR code or the voice command was not correctly understood by the voice recognition. The input method head movements and blinking has the lowest error rate (M = 14.13%). The input methods timed scanning with blinking has with M = 23.48% a slightly worse error rate and head movements is in the middle. All error rates and their standard deviation is also shown in Table 1.

Table 1. Average time in minutes per input method to complete the tasks and the average percentage of tasks with at least one incorrect entry that occurred.

Input method	Time (min)	Error rate (%)
Head movements	2.01, SD = 0.25	29.03, SD = 12.44
Head movements and blinking	2.14, SD = 0.41	14.13, SD = 13.65
Timed scanning and blinking	1.56, SD = 0.22	23.48, SD = 35.42
Voice control	2.38, SD = 0.30	34,91, SD = 18.52
QR code scan	3.30, SD = 1.06	61.94, SD = 24.93

In the survey results, the 5 hands-free input methods perform partially differently. On a Likert scale of 1 to 5 (1 = good, 5 = bad), subjects rated the input method timed scanning and blinking (M = 4.07, SD = 1.03) the worst, followed by QR code scan (M = 3.60, SD = 0.74). The voice control (M = 2.07, SD = 0.70) and head movements (M = 2.13, SD = 1.13) input methods scored the best on average. The input method head movements and blinking (M = 2.60, SD = 0.83) were rated slightly worse by the test persons.

We also asked the subjects for a more detailed assessment of the 5 hands-free input methods regarding their operability (Table 2), usefulness (Table 3), and fun factor (Table 4) depending on the action levels A2, A4, and A8. The results show that the input methods timed scanning and blinking and QR code scan are rated notably lower than voice control and head movements. The head movements and blinking input method also performs somewhat worse in the detailed evaluation than the two previously mentioned input methods voice control and head movements.

Table 2. Evaluation of the 5 input methods in terms of their operability differentiated by the 3 action levels A2, A4 and A8 based on a Likert scale of 1 to 5 (1 = good, 5 = bad).

Input method	Action level 2	Action level 4	Action level 8
Head movements	1.60, SD = 0.91	2.07, SD = 1.16	2.80, SD = 1.15
Head movements and blinking	2.07, SD = 0.88	2.47, SD = 0.92	3.27, SD = 1.28
Timed scanning and blinking	2.53, SD = 1.36	3.07, SD = 1.22	3.87, SD = 1.36
Voice control	1.47, SD = 0.92	2.27, SD = 1.53	2.80, SD = 1.42
QR code scan	3.20, SD = 0.86	3.53, SD = 0.92	3.67, SD = 1.11

Table 3. Evaluation of the 5 input methods in terms of their usefulness differentiated by the 3 action levels A2, A4 and A8 based on a Likert scale of 1 to 5 (1 = good, 5 = bad).

Input method	Action level 2	Action level 4	Action level 8
Head movements	2.20, SD = 1.21	2.27, SD = 1.03	2.53, SD = 1.30
Head movements and blinking	2.27, SD = 0.88	2.33, SD = 0.82	2.80, SD = 1.01
Timed scanning and blinking	2.87, SD = 1.25	3.07, SD = 0.96	4.00, SD = 0.93
Voice control	1.80, SD = 0.86	2.07, SD = 1.03	2.40, SD = 1.12
QR code scan	3.47, SD = 0.83	3.67, SD = 0.72	3.60, SD = 0.91

Table 4. Evaluation of the 5 input methods in terms of their fun factor differentiated by the 3 action levels A2, A4 and A8 based on a Likert scale of 1 to 5 (1 = good, 5 = bad).

Input method	Action level 2	Action level 4	Action level 8
Head movements	2.00, SD = 1.20	2.43, SD = 1.22	2.67, SD = 1.18
Head movements and blinking	2.33, SD = 0.90	2.47, SD = 0.99	2.80, SD = 1.21
Timed scanning and blinking	3.00, SD = 1.31	3.40, SD = 1.18	4.00, SD = 1.07
Voice control	1.87, SD = 0.74	2.27, SD = 0.80	2.73, SD = 1.03
QR code scan	3.33, SD = 0.90	3.47, SD = 0.83	3.53, SD = 0.92

7 Discussion

When considering the results of the study and their generalization, several limitations must be considered:

- Participants had no discernible limitations in the use of their hands.
- The Google Glass is only one possible form of AR glasses, which is why the results cannot be transferred one-to-one to all AR glasses.
- The smart TV scenario we used in the user test is only one of many possible scenarios with AR glasses.
- The 15 participants, except for 3 of them, had no previous experience with Google Glass. Therefore, it cannot be ruled out that the results of the study, following a longer familiarization period, might be different.

Despite these limitations, we can draw the following conclusions from the results of the study. Technically, it is possible to develop apps for Google Glass that can be used well without involving the hands. This allows the Google Glass to be used as an input and output device to control a hand exoskeleton. In addition, it was possible to implement several hands-free input methods. The head movements, head movement and blinking, and timed scanning and blinking input methods achieved better average speeds in the measurement than voice control and QR code scan. The latter also scored two worse in terms of incorrect entries. In terms of reliability, timed scanning and blinking seem to be the most attractive. However, with regard to the error rate, the input methods head movements and head movements and blinking also still achieved acceptable values.

That not only the measurement results should be considered in further development is shown by the results of the subsequent survey, in which the input method timed scanning and blinking belong together with QR coder scan to the two worst input methods and voice control, despite its high error rate and slower average speed in the evaluation, achieves a high popularity in the subsequent survey. Therefore, in our opinion, voice control should not be excluded per se as a hands-free input method in the Google Glass, but work should be done on improving it. The results of the survey also show that the number of available control commands or the action levels only had a minor influence on the subjective reception of the 5 hands-free input methods. However, it could be observed that for all 3 factors operability, usefulness and fun the evaluation tended to worsen with the increase of input options or stagnated in individual cases. This could indicate that apps, which are used by means of hands-free input methods on the Google Glass, should only have 2 or a maximum of 4 options to choose from on a card or on the user interface.

8 Future Work

The next steps were to investigate whether there might be better understandable voice commands or whether an external service or a third-party voice recognition library would be better suited as an alternative to the Google Glass voice recognition. Subsequently, the user study should be repeated with improved voice control and then include test subjects with hand limitations in this phase of development. With regard to the subjective perception of the users, the 5 hands-free input methods developed should also be evaluated in other smart home and ambient assisted living scenarios – e.g., a hand exoskeleton – in order to rule out any influences of the smart TV on the evaluation of the input methods.

References

1. vom Stein, M., Günther, W.A., Knott, V., Bengler, K.: Augmented Reality im Flurförderzeug. Logistik für Unternehmen, 04-2015 (2015)
2. Enterprisewear blog - why the logistics industry is going hands-free, https://www.brainxchange.com/blog/why-the-logistics-industry-is-going-hands-free, last accessed 2022/04/08
3. Markovic, M., Dosen, S., Cipriani, C., Popovic, D., Farina, D.: Stereovision and augmented reality for closed-loop control of grasping in hand prostheses. J. Neural Eng. **11**, 046001 (2014)
4. Soekadar, S.R., et al.: Hybrid EEG/EOG-based brain/neural hand exoskeleton restores fully independent daily living activities after quadriplegia. Sci. Robot. **1** (2016)

Ontenna: Design and Social Implementation of Auditory Information Transmission Devices Using Tactile and Visual Senses

Tatsuya Honda[1,2](✉), Tetsuaki Baba[1], and Makoto Okamoto[3]

[1] Graduate School of Systems Design, Tokyo Metropolitan University, 1-1 Minami-Osawa, Hachioji-shi 192-0397, Tokyo, Japan
honda-tatsuya@ed.tmu.ac.jp, baba@tmu.ac.jp
[2] Fujitsu Limited, Shiodome City Center, 1-5-2, Higashi-Shimbashi, Minato-ku 105-7123, Tokyo, Japan
[3] Future University Hakodate, 116-2 Kamedanakano-cho, Hakodate 041-8655, Hokkaido, Japan
maq@fun.ac.jp

Abstract. Ontenna is a device that can be worn on the hair, earlobe, collar, or sleeve, and it transmits sound characteristics to the human body using vibrations and light. It can serve as an auxiliary acoustic sensory device for the Deaf and Hard of Hearing (DHH), whereas for others, it can serve as a novel acoustic perception device. A condenser microphone mounted on the main body of Ontenna acquires sound pressure data and drives the vibration motor and light-emitting diode in real-time according to the input signals. This allows the user to perceive various sonic features such as the rhythm, pattern, and strength of sound. Furthermore, by simultaneously controlling several Ontenna devices using a controller, rhythms can be transmitted to each user. In this paper, we present the design of Ontenna for DHH and its fabrication process, which was improved through digital fabrication methods. Additionally, we present case studies regarding the usage of Ontenna in a hearing-impaired school and case studies on the application of Ontenna in the entertainment field for hearing-impaired people and others. Furthermore, we discuss the effects of programming education using Ontenna.

Keywords: Deaf and hard of hearing · Sound · Tactile · Inclusive design · Programming education

1 Introduction

Members of the Deaf and Hard of Hearing (DHH) community find it difficult to perceive rhythms, patterns, sound loudness, and other sound characteristics. Therefore, it is difficult for DHH persons to regulate the loudness of their voice in speech practice and to match the rhythm of others during dance practice. Furthermore, in movie theaters, the DHH can only enjoy content based on visual information such as text. In sports venues, they may find it difficult to understand the atmosphere in terms of the cheering and excitement. Their sense of presence and unity may therefore be greatly inhibited

K. Miesenberger et al. (Eds.): ICCHP-AATE 2022, LNCS 13342, pp. 130–138, 2022.
https://doi.org/10.1007/978-3-031-08645-8_16

when simply mimicking the enjoyment of non-DHH persons. The authors learned sign language through connections with the DHH while at university. Moreover, they worked as sign language interpretation volunteers and established sign language circles while managing an NPO along with the DHH community. In 2014, based on the use of technology to convey sound to the DHH, the authors began research on the "Ontenna" user interface, which enables sound to be felt by the body [1] (Fig. 1).

Fig. 1. Ontenna is a user interface that enables the user to hear sound through his/her body via tactile feedback. Ontenna is worn on the hair of the person in the center of this figure and on the collar of the person on the right-hand side of this figure.

2 Related Work

In numerous studies, sound characteristics have been converted into visual and tactile information that is then presented to the DHH [2–8]. However, visual feedback increases the visual burden when visually transmitting sound information to the DHH, whose daily lives rely on visual information. Tactile feedback may inhibit movements of hands, arms, or feet, thereby placing a burden on the user when communicating in sign language or when performing physical actions. The ideas and opinions of the DHH were extracted through inclusive design techniques and repeated quick-prototyping using 3D printers, laser cutters, Arduino, and other digital fabrication technologies to design the optimal user interface for the DHH.

3 Study of the System Design

By obtaining real impressions from the use of prototypes, the DHH indicated aspects to be changed or improved. Table 1 summarizes the characteristics of each prototype, prototype users, interview period and frequency, opinions resulting from prototype implementation via managers and users, and considerations for improving upon this prototype.

Table 1. Changes in the Ontenna prototypes. We summarize the prototype evolution over four years from 2014 to 2017 in chronological order. Each prototype is presented with the year of development, image, number, description, characteristics, prototype testers, interview period and frequency, prototype implementation manager, user opinion, and aspects to consider for improving upon the prototype.

Year	2014	2014	2014	2015	2016	2017	2017	2017
Image								
Number	Prototype 1	Prototype 2	Prototype 3	Prototype 4	Prototype 5	Prototype 6	Prototype 7-1	Prototype 7-2
Description	Prototype that displays sound information using the sense of sight	Prototype that displays sound information using the sense of touch	Prototype for sensing sound through the hair	Prototype for sensing sound through the hair (standalone type)	Prototype for sensing sound through the hair (smaller type)	Prototype for sensing sound through the hair (Bluetooth type)	Prototype for sensing sound through the hair (Zigbee type)	Controller (Zigbee type)
Characteristics	· Realtime variation of light intensity according to sound pressure · More LEDs light up as the sound pressure increases	· Realtime variation of vibration intensity according to sound pressure · More arm vibration motors are driven as the sound pressure increases	· Realtime variation of light and vibration intensity according to sound pressure · Clip type that can be attached to hair · Exterior is produced by cutting an acrylic sheet with a laser cutter	· Realtime variation of light and vibration intensity according to sound pressure · External design using 3D printer · Design with greater awareness of accessories · Operates as a stand-alone unit	· Realtime variation of light and vibration intensity according to sound pressure · Exterior produced by cutting · Smaller than 2015 model	· Realtime variation of light and vibration intensity according to sound pressure · Equipped with Bluetooth for connection with smartphones · Interchangeable between simple and Bluetooth modes	· Realtime variation of light and vibration intensity according to sound pressure · 2-step slide switch · Connects to controller via Zigbee connection(2.4GHz) · Interchangeable between simple and Zigbee modes	· Simultaneous control of multiple Ontenna · Can be connected to audio equipment and microphones · External design using a 3D printer
Prototype testers	Approximately three people with severe hereditary hearing disabilities who are affiliated with an NPO. Age range: 30-59.	Approximately three people with severe hereditary hearing disabilities who are affiliated with an NPO. Age range: 30-59.	Approximately five people with severe hereditary hearing disabilities who are affiliated with an NPO. Age range: 20-69.	Approximately 10 people with severe hereditary hearing disabilities who are affiliated with an NPO. Age range: 20-69.	Approximately 20 people who are either students at schools for the deaf, persons with severe hereditary who are hearing disabilities affiliated with a DHH organization, or deaf persons. Age range: 10-39.	Approximately 10 people who are either students at schools for the deaf, persons with severe hereditary hearing disabilities who are affiliated with a DHH organization, or deaf persons. Age range: 10-39.	National test marketing was conducted. Approximately 100 people who are either students at schools for the deaf, persons with severe hereditary hearing disabilities who are affiliated with a DHH organization, or deaf persons. Age range: 10-59.	National test marketing was conducted. Approximately 100 people who are mainly either students at schools for the deaf, persons with severe hereditary hearing disabilities who are affiliated with a DHH organization, or deaf persons. Age range: 10-59.
Interview period and frequency	5 times over 1 month	5 times over 1 month	30 times over 6 months	60 times over 1 year	60 times over 1 year	30 times over 6 months	100 times over 2 years	100 times over 2 years
Prototype implementation manager	Independent production	Independent production	Independent production	Produced in cooperation with approximately four people, including a circuit board specialist university affiliate for substrate mounting, a design specialist university affiliate, and students for the exterior design.	Produced in cooperation with approximately 10 people, including group companies for substrate mounting and an in-house designer for the exterior design.	Produced in cooperation with approximately 10 people, including a prototype development support venture company for substrate mounting and an in-house designer for the exterior design.	Produced in cooperation with approximately 10 people, including a prototype development support venture company for substrate mounting and an in-house designer for the exterior design.	Produced in cooperation with approximately10 people, including a prototype development support venture company for substrate mounting and an in-house designer for the exterior design.
User opinions	"I could see flashing lights" "It's tiring to look at it for a long time" "I don't think I would want to use it regularly"	"It becomes sweaty and it tickles because the vibration motor is placed directly on the skin." "If it is placed on the arm, it would get difficult to do housework or to communicate in sign language."	"It's not a design for daily use because there are wires sticking out, etc." "It has sharp corners so I'm afraid of putting it on my head."	"The exterior was made on a 3D printer, so it really feels like a prototype." "The clip-part is weak."	"I want to experience the sound of films and music by connecting it to a smartphone."	"I want to be able to simultaneously control multiple Ontenna."	"I want a function to be able to turn ON/OFF the lights." "I want it to react to small sounds in quiet areas." "I want the current mode to be noticeable with just a glance." "I want to be able to attach it to something other than my hair."	"It's big." "It's difficult to understand how to use it." "I want to be able to charge it easily."
Aspects to improve for the next prototype	Determine a sound feedback method using the sense of touch as well as the sense of sight.	Investigate a structural design change to enable installation that facilitates the perception of vibrations without being attached to the skin.	Investigate standalone operation and an exterior design with curves.	Investigate the miniaturization of the overall product, and improvements to the design of the exterior and mount ability.	Investigate Bluetooth operation and smartphone connectivity.	Investigate the control of multiple Ontenna systems using Zigbee connection (2.4GHz)	Investigate additional functions for ON/OFF lights and sound zooming, as well as remodelling the slide switch and clip.	Investigate exterior design improvements, miniaturization, and charging using a magnet

The fabricated devices were loaned for a period of approximately one month to schools for the deaf in three locations across Japan that cooperated in the experiment to test these systems in real situations (Fig. 2). Concerns were raised pertaining to the difficulty of operation, inconvenience of charging, and weakness of the clip component. Furthermore, the students provided their opinions, stating the following: "I don't want to attach it to my hair because I have a cochlear implant," "It would be easier if it was attached to the earlobe," and "I would like to attach it to my collar." This feedback indicates differences in the preferred attachment method depending on the user. Accordingly, the system design was improved by changing the clip type to make it easier to attach to clothes, arms, and earlobes, among other locations.

Fig. 2. Demonstration at a deaf school.

4 Final Product

Ontenna is attached to the hair, earlobe, collar, or sleeve, and it has a user interface for physically sensing sound characteristics via vibrations and light. Sound characteristics transmitted after sensing sound pressures between 60 and 90 dB are converted to 256-stage vibrations and light intensities. The cadence patterns of the sound sources are converted in real-time such that sound rhythms, patterns, and volume can be perceived (see the left-hand side of Fig. 3).

Fig. 3. Left: Ontenna; Right: Controller

The controller can be used to control multiple Ontenna devices at the same time via the communication function. Because it uses a 920-MHz-band radio wave, there is little interference, and any number of Ontennas can be controlled within a 50 m radius (see the right-hand side of Fig. 3). In addition, it is possible to transmit sound information via AUX or MIC connections. The specifications of this system are presented in Table 2.

In June 2019, Ontenna was released as a product. Furthermore, Ontenna was freely distributed to 88 of 102 schools for the DHH in Japan (as of February 2022).

Table 2. Specifications

	Ontenna	Controller
Sound input	Internal electric condenser microphone (omnidirectional)	3.5-mm audio jack (TRS) for both line and mic inputs
Vibration motor	Maximum rated rotational speed (representative value) of approximately 12000 ± 3000 rpm	–
LED	Full-color LED; red LED charging light	Full-color LED; red LED charging light
Communication method	Specified low-power wireless transmissions (920 MHz band) STD-T108 ※ For use only in Japan	Specified low-power wireless transmissions (920 MHz band) STD-T108 ※ For use only in Japan
Radio law certification	–	Factory Design Certification 006-000687 Factory Design Certification 007-AB0237
PC connection	USB full-speed	USB full-speed
Power	Built-in lithium polymer rechargeable battery	Built-in lithium polymer rechargeable battery
Battery	200 mAh	200 mAh
Continuous usage time	Approximately 3 h	Approximately 3 h
Charging time	Full charge: approximately 8 h; 90% charge: approximately 4 h	Full charge: approximately 8 h; 90% charge: approximately 4 h
Operating temperature	0 °C to 35 °C	0 °C to 35 °C
Storage temperature	−15 °C to 50 °C	−15 °C to 50 °C
Measurements	W65 × D24 × H15 (mm)	Φ 60 × H22 (mm)
Weight	18 g	33 g

5 Usage Examples at Schools for the Deaf

Teachers at a school for the deaf asked students to trigger the LEDs after showing how Ontenna lit up when the teacher spoke. Accordingly, the students spoke more proactively than before such that Ontenna would light up, and they were able to control the volume of their voices. Moreover, they were able to understand that the strength of the light and vibrations changed according to the volume of the voice, and they modulated their voices to gradually become louder or quieter (Fig. 4). In addition, in a music class, Ontenna enabled students to adjust the strength of their breath while playing recorders. In a dance class, the controller enabled multiple students to synchronize their movements. The teachers provided the following feedback: "Rhythm could be transmitted to students from far away rather than by tapping them on the back," " During drum performances, it was easier to match the rhythms by showing the rhythm to multiple students simultaneously," and "It was easier to teach because individual students were accurately shown the rhythm".

Fig. 4. Left: voice training using Ontenna; center: recorder practice with Ontenna; right: dance practice with Ontenna

6 Usage Examples in Entertainment

Ontenna is also used in the field of entertainment. For example, when Ontenna was used in a soccer game, members of the DHH community commented, "I understood the rhythm of the chanting nearby," and "The silent tension that filled the stadium during a penalty kick was conveyed". When watching Kyogen, a traditional Japanese performance art, DHH patrons said, "I felt the vocal intonations" and "I could even sense the onstage footsteps". At a tap dance event, DHH patrons commented, "I was able to experience the rhythm of the tap dance in my body," and "It was fun because the vibrations and lights matched the dancing". Furthermore, the participants with normal hearing ability stated the following: "I had a strong sense of the ambience because of the vibrations" and "It was a lot of fun to experience the sense of oneness with the lights". After attending a ping-pong game, the DHH participants commented, "It was fun to experience the rhythm of the rally sounds" and "I could sense the different sound rhythms such as when it hit the net and during serves." Furthermore, those with normal hearing who also attended said the following: "It felt more real because of the sense of touch as well as the visuals and audio" and "I got a stronger sense of rhythms with smaller sounds." The system configurations for each event are illustrated in Fig. 5.

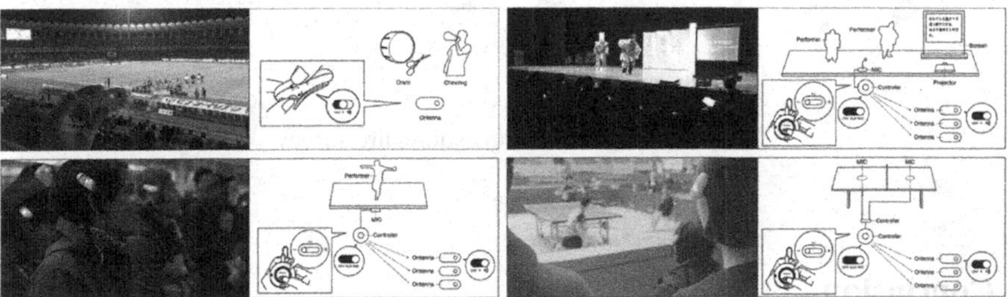

Fig. 5. Top left: watching a soccer game using Ontenna; top right: watching Kyogen using Ontenna; bottom left: watching tap dancing using Ontenna; bottom right: watching ping pong using Ontenna

7 Development and Release of the Ontenna Programming Education Environment

In December 2020, we released a programming environment using Ontenna, which has since been installed in over 80% of schools for the deaf in Japan. Using Scratch (https://scratch.mit.edu/), a visual programming tool, it is possible to change the color of the LEDs and the strength of the motors in Ontenna devices. We created an environment in which children with hearing impairments can overcome the obstacles they face at school by programming Ontenna themselves (Fig. 6). A questionnaire survey was conducted for seven classes in four schools where these systems were introduced. The responses were obtained using a 10-point scale, with 10 being the best and 1 being the worst. The results indicated the usefulness of the system (Fig. 7). In addition, the costs associated with internet-of-things (IoT) programming education, which is difficult to introduce due to financial constraints, were reduced by using Ontenna and PCs that were already present in the schools. In addition, by distributing instructional plans, lesson slides, and worksheets free-of-charge, we were able to reduce the learning burden of teachers.

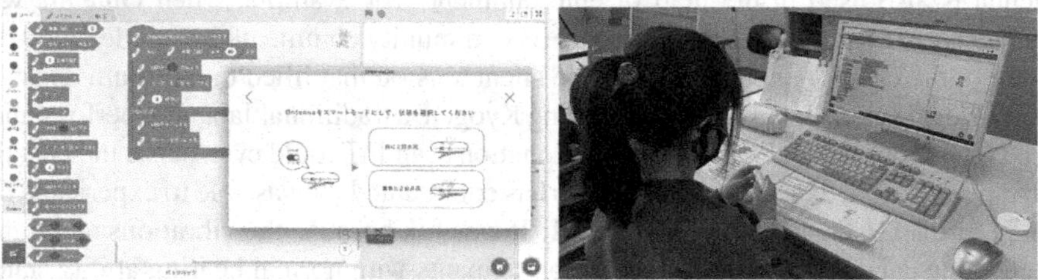

Fig. 6. Left: Ontenna programming environment; right: a deaf student programming their own ideas into Ontenna

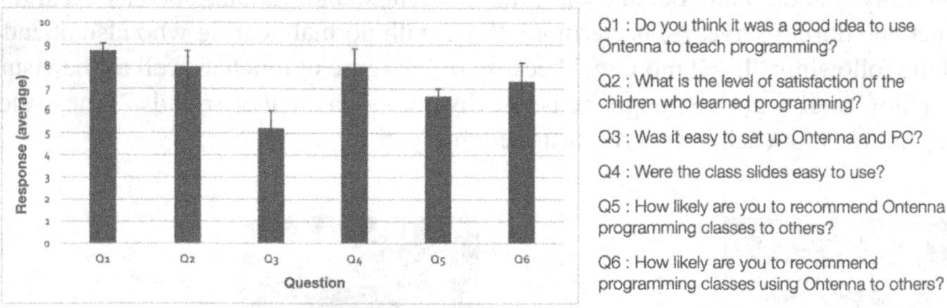

Fig. 7. Results of the questionnaire survey

8 Conclusion

In this report, we described the development of the Ontenna user interface for physically experiencing sound, which was researched and developed in cooperation with the DHH community. Case studies involving the use of Ontenna at schools for the deaf and in the field of entertainment were also presented. Ontenna was finalized as a product in June 2019, and it has been used for music and physical education lessons at schools for the deaf across Japan. In particular, changes were observed in speech and rhythm education applications upon the implementation of this system, where students who were not previously aware of sounds began to become interested in music and those who had difficulties understanding rhythms were able to accurately mimic rhythms. In the field of entertainment, including movies, traditional arts, and sports, Ontenna has been used to create novel spectator experiences for the DHH community. Furthermore, apart from DHH persons, Ontenna has been found to have potential use in creating added value for those with normal hearing in terms of their sense of realism and integration into an event. In addition, we developed a function that allows Ontenna to be programmed and made the educational environment available to schools for the deaf to promote programming education.

Acknowledgement. This work was supported by JST, CREST Grant Number JPMJCR1781, Japan.

References

1. Ontenna: A user interface that enables sound to be experienced through your body. https://ontenna.jp/en/
2. Gorman, B.M.: VisAural: a wearable sound-localisation device for people with impaired hearing. In: Proceedings of the 16th International ACM SIGACCESS Conference on Computers & Accessibility, pp. 337–338 (2014)
3. Hong, R., et al.: Video accessibility enhancement for hearing-impaired users. ACM Trans. Multimedia Comput. Commun. Appl. **7S**(1), 1–19 (2011)
4. Matthews, T., Fong, J., Mankoff, J.: Visualizing non-speech sounds for the deaf. In: Proceedings of the 7th International ACM SIGACCESS Conference on Computers and Accessibility, pp. 52–59. ACM (2005)
5. Azar, J., Abou Saleh, H., Al-Alaoui, M.: Sound visualization for the hearing impaired. Int. J. Emerg. Technol. Learn. (iJET) **2**(1), 1–7 (2007)
6. Sakajiri, M., Miyoshi, S., Nakamura, K., Fukushima, S., Ifukube, T.: Development of voice pitch control system using two dimensional tactile display for the deafblind or the hearing impaired persons. NTUT Educ. Disabil. **9**, 9–12 (2011)
7. Trivedi, U., Alqasemi, R., Dubey, R.: Wearable musical haptic sleeves for people with hearing impairment. In: Proceedings of the 12th ACM International Conference on PErvasive Technologies Related to Assistive Environments, pp. 146–151 (2019)
8. Shibasaki, M., Kamiyama, Y., Minamizawa, K.: Designing a haptic feedback system for hearing-impaired to experience tap dance. In: Proceedings of the 29th Annual Symposium on User Interface Software and Technology, pp. 97–99 (2016)

Usability Study of Tactile and Voice Interaction Modes by People with Disabilities for Home Automation Controls

Nadine Vigouroux[1(✉)], Frédéric Vella[1], Gaëlle Lepage[2,3], and Eric Campo[4]

[1] IRIT, CNRS 5505, Université Paul Sabatier, 118 Route de Narbonne, 31062 Toulouse, France
nadine.vigouroux@irit.fr
[2] GIHP, 10 Rue Jean Gilles, 31100 Toulouse, France
[3] UT2J, 5 Allée Antonio Machado, 31058 Toulouse, France
[4] LAAS-CNRS, Université de Toulouse, CNRS, UT2J, Toulouse, France

Abstract. This paper presents a comparative usability study on tactile and vocal interaction modes for home automation control of equipment at home for different profiles of disabled people. The study is related to the HIP HOPE project concerning the construction of 19 inclusive housing in the Toulouse metropolitan area in France. The experimentation took place in a living lab with 7 different disabled people who realize realistic use cases. The USE and UEQ questionnaires were selected as usability tools. The first results show that both interfaces are easy to learn but that usefulness and ease of use dimensions need to be improved. This study shows that there is real need for multimodality between touch and voice interaction to control the smart home. This study also shows that there is need to adapt the interface and the environment to the person's disability.

Keywords: Usability · Voice interaction · Tactile interaction · Smart house

1 Introduction

In France, the ELAN law of November 23, 2018[1] introduces the concept of inclusive housing and defines it as housing mode "intended for people with disabilities and the elderly who have the choice, as their main residence, of a grouped mode of living, among themselves or with other people (…) and accompanied by a social and shared life project". Due to the evolutions and changes in behavior that this new type of housing may entail, it seems interesting to study how the technological needs of people with disabilities could them to improve their living conditions in autonomy while taking into account their physical and material environment. Indeed, digital technologies have shown their potential to compensate for certain difficulties encountered in the daily life of people with disabilities in their homes. According to Khomiakoff [1], "assistive technologies can play a particularly important role in the choice to remain at home, or allow, in addition to adequate social support, greater autonomy and a better quality of

[1] Excerpt from Article L.281-1 of the CASF.

K. Miesenberger et al. (Eds.): ICCHP-AAATE 2022, LNCS 13342, pp. 139–147, 2022.
https://doi.org/10.1007/978-3-031-08645-8_17

life". However, the adequacy of the technological solutions developed to the real need of people with disabilities remains a challenge.

Vacher *et al.* [2] described an audio-based interaction technology that lets the user have full control over her home environment and at detecting distress situations for the elderly and visually impaired people. Varriale *et al.* [3] identified the role and function of home automation, for people with disabilities through a deep review, in particular they aim to highlight if and how home automation solutions can support people with disabilities improve their social inclusion. Cheng *et al.* [4] investigated the effects of button and spacing size on touchscreen performance by people with varying motor abilities. Mtshali and Khubisa [5] designed a smart home appliance control system for people with physical disabilities based on a voice digital assistant. Noda [6] reported that persons with disability could utilize the voice applications such as Google Home to control appliances in a smart house.

However, too few interfaces and smart home devices are not designed with people with disabilities and people with limited range of motion, sight, hearing or speech difficulties. In the framework of to the HIP HOPE project concerning a building on the Montaudran site in Toulouse (France) in which 19 inclusive housing units will be built, we conduct a pre-study on the tactile and vocal interaction modes for the home automation control of equipment by disabled people for an inclusive housing. In [7] the authors describe the respective rate of use of voice and touch commands and interaction errors due to their impairment.

Firstly, the paper briefly describes the experiment conducted in the Smart Home of Blagnac[2] in France. Then, we present and discuss the results of the USE and UEQ questionnaires.

2 Experiment

2.1 Material

We carried out the experimentation in the living lab MIB. It is a 70 m^2 apartment allowing to carry out design groups and experiments with end users (disabled and elderly people). It is composed of different rooms: living room, kitchen, corridor, bedroom, bathroom and toilet. It is equipped with various connected objects such as a removable sink and washbasin, lights, shutters, television, a fall sensor and an electric bed. It also has an infrastructure [8] to support communication between connected objects and control device, and microphones, cameras and motion sensors for sensors. Voice and/or touch interaction is used to activate the connected objects. The Amazon Fire Cube TV personal assistant realizes the voice interaction. The touch interface was designed under OpenHab's HABPanel and installed on a Samsung Tab A7 touch tablet. For example, the participants can formulate the command "open the living room shutter", "turn on the bedroom light" or call "help". In the same way, the tactile command, thanks to "presses/clicks" on a tablet allows to realize the same commands.

[2] MIB, http://mi.iut-blagnac.fr.

2.2 Population

7 persons with disabilities (1 mental disability, 4 motor disabilities including 2 with speech disorders, 1 visual and 1 hearing impairments) participated in this study (see Table 1). We recruited participants of all ages and with different impairments. This set of participants represents the population that will live in the HIP HOPE home automation flats. Table 1 also lists the home automation and assistive technologies desired by these individuals, collected from interviews.

Table 1. Table of participants.

Participant	Age/gender	Impairment	Activities	Technology needs for smart home
101	63/M	Hearing impairment	Pharmacist, now retired	Adapted intercom with high quality visuals to see the person and read their lips ; connected objects with visual feedback; flashing lights; app on phone to detect someone's presence or an abnormal noise.
102	72/M	Visual impairment	Computer science now retired	Easy to implement; efficient and responsive technology, limit the number of steps, preference for voice control with voice feedback on actions performed; home automation control (shutters, light, alarm) but with reliability and ease of use.
104	39/F	Cerebral palsy	Employee in an association and volunteer	Interfaces for home automation control (shutters, front door); voice control difficult in case of fatigue, so have the touch mode; connected intercom without the need to pick up the phone.
202	18/M	Trisomy syndrome	Student	Smartphone application to help organise activities, to encourage initiatives (coaching application).
204	19/M	Cerebral palsy	Student	Smartphone control system for gates, garages and front doors to be autonomous; smartphone remote control for TV, robotic arm.

(continued)

Table 1. (*continued*)

Participant	Age/gender	Impairment	Activities	Technology needs for smart home
300	38/F	Myopathy	Volunteer	Home automation to control the environment (with voice command); robotic arm (help for cutting, grabbing objects, grooming), adapted intercom (easy to open and to communicate).
302	70/F	Polio	Secretary, retired and volunteer	Opening of the gate from your home; automated bay window; automation control of equipment for individual and mobile homes; fall detector or easy emergency call.

2.3 Courses of the Experiment

First, we introduced the participants to the use of the two interaction modes (presentation by the experimenter and learning by the participant). Then they were asked to perform two scenarios (one controlled and one free). These scenarios included tasks (opening shutters, turning on lights, etc. see [7] for a detailed description). Subjects were free to use the tactile or voice command in any order they wished. At the end of the experiment, participants were asked to fill out questionnaires (Fig. 1).

Fig. 1. Courses of the experiment.

2.4 Questionnaires

We use two questionnaires: USE (Usefulness, Satisfaction, and Ease of use, [9]) and UEQ (User Experience Questionnaire, [10]) and a complementary questionnaire on interaction modalities (modality preference and multimodality).

The USE questionnaire consists of 30 items, divided into 4 dimensions (usefulness, ease of use, ease of learning, and finally satisfaction with its use). Each item is presented in the form of several statements to be noted from 1 to 7. 1 corresponds to "Very disagree" and 7 to "Very agree". The participants filled out the questionnaires just after the scenarios had been run, followed by a debriefing with the experimenters.

The UEQ questionnaire includes 26 items divided into 6 dimensions evaluating the *attractiveness* (general impression), *perspicuity* (easy to get familiar), *efficiency* (fast, efficient, organized), *dependability* (understandable, instinctive), *reliability* (control, predictable), *stimulation* (interest and motivation) and *novelty* (creative, innovative) of the system.

3 Results

Both interfaces were evaluated in a general way, without distinction between touch and voice.

3.1 Experimental Context

Table 2 illustrates the interaction environment (modality, device, tablet placement, mobility support for the participant). Participant 102 used only voice interaction (visual impairment) while participant 204 used only tactile interaction (speech impairment). The other 5 participants used all interaction modalities.

Table 2. Interaction environment.

Participant	101	102	104	202	204	300	302
Modalities	Touch and voice	Voice	Touch and voice	Touch and voice	Touch	Touch and voice	Touch and voice
Interaction devices			Help to open the voice channel		Joystick connected to the tablet		
Position of the tablet	In the hand	No use of the tablet	On the knees	In the hand	On the kitchen table (not mobile)	On the knees	Holds the tablet in one hand and touches with the other hand
Movement of the person	Without assistance	Without assistance	In an electric wheelchair	Without assistance	In an electric wheelchair	In an electric wheelchair	In an electric wheelchair
Touch interaction							

3.2 USE Questionnaire

The participant filled the questionnaire after the scenarios were played. For the analysis of these data, the 7 items were transposed to scores ranging from −3 (totally disagree) to 3 (totally agree) in order to have more contrasting results.

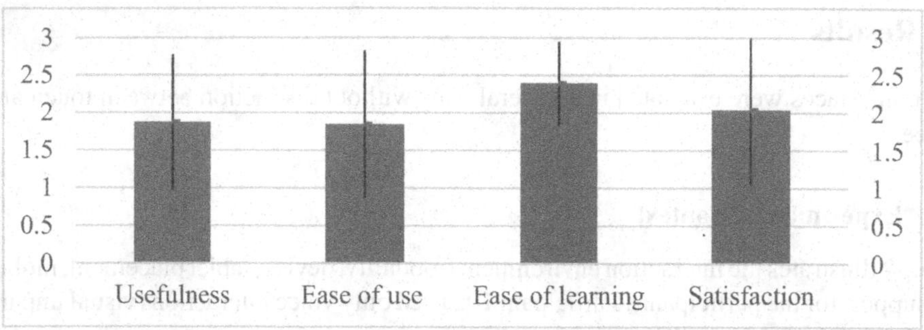

Fig. 2. Mean and standard deviation of the USE questionnaire score for the 7 participants.

Figure 2 shows the mean and standard deviation of the four dimensions of the USE questionnaire for 7 participants. The USE rating for *Ease of learning* (2, 4) and *Satisfaction* dimension (2) are good, even very good for *Ease of learning*. We can see that Usefulness and Ease of Use rating are similar (1.8). For 3 of the 4 dimensions, we find a significant standard deviation (±−0.9), except for the *Ease of learning* (±0.5).

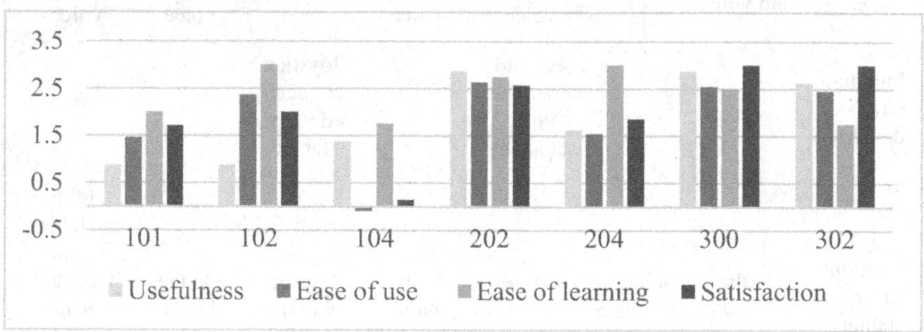

Fig. 3. USE values for each participant

Figure 3 shows that participants 101, 104 and 204 have some difficulty using the interaction modalities (*Ease of Use*) or even very serious difficulty using them (participant 104). These difficulties in using the interaction modalities resulted in a decrease in *satisfaction.* 4 participants found learning the interaction modalities very easy (>2.5) and 3 easy (>1.5). The Usefulness dimension was low for two participants (<1) and two quite low (>1 and <1.5).

3.3 UEQ Questionnaire

The UEQ is scored as the USE questionnaire. The UEQ value between −0.8 and 0.8 represent a more or less neutral evaluation of the corresponding dimension, values >0.8 represent a positive evaluation and values <−0.8 represent a negative evaluation. UEQ scores (*attractiveness, perspicuity, and stimulation*) are highly positive (>2) for four participants while the criteria *novelty* is lower (>1.5 and <1.8) for five participants as shown in Fig. 4. For participant 104, all dimensions of the UEQ questionnaire are <1.25. Negative values for the dimensions stimulation and novelty are also noted for participant 202.

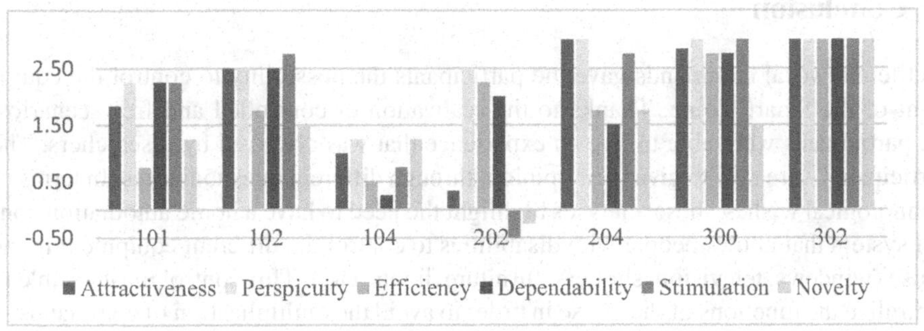

Fig. 4. Mean and standard deviation of the UEQ questionnaire score.

4 Discussion

Participants enjoyed participating in the experiment. They discovered the possibilities of voice and touch interaction with the connected objects of the smart home. The least positive scores were related to "ease of use" and "usefulness" of the USE questionnaire. Not all interface accessibility conditions were met for participants 101 (no magnetic loop and no visual feedback), 102 (no screen reader running on the tablet), 104 (severe speech difficulties and therefore recognition problem for the voice assistant). This study clearly shows that these interfaces alone are not sufficient and that the experimental environment must also incorporate assistive technologies for the hearing and vision impaired. The variability in *usefulness* dimension may be due to the limited exposure of participants to the use of the interactions. The need to repeat the experiment several times or to deploy these technologies in living spaces is necessary.

Regarding the results obtained during the use case script, some limitations were highlighted, such as the slow response time of the controlled equipment, the poor performance of the voice recognition (poor response formulation, difficulties in opening the recognition channel… [7]) and the reliability of the system with the Internet network. There is also a strong need for visual or audio feedback according to the participant's profile on the action performed on the touch. The results of the logs [7] show successions of touch pointing for which it will be necessary to identify if they are due to motor inabilities or to a response time of the home automation objects.

The question "*which interface do you prefer to use according to your abilities*" shows that all 7 participants would like to alternate between a tactile and oral modality. 5 would prefer voice interaction and 2 (101 and 104) would prefer touch interaction. Participant 104 suggested physical interaction buttons. The possibility to have a choice of interaction based on one's abilities, environmental choice: verbatim "*I find it very useful in certain contexts*", but also one's state (fatigue) is essential. The possibility to offer a multimodal interaction is also a request, because multimodality is considered in some cases as more efficient and faster. The low score of "novelty" dimension can be explained by the basic home automation controls for well-being.

5 Conclusion

Tactile and vocal commands gave the participants the possibility to control the equipment of the Smart Home. Thanks to the realization of controlled and free scenarios, the participants were able to live an experience that was observed by researchers. The participants were able to give their opinion, through different questionnaires. In terms of technological wishes, these analyses highlight the need to have a home automation control system that allows people with disabilities to control the different equipment in the house (windows, television, shutters, furniture, lights, etc.). This control must be able to centralize the functions of the house in order to avoid the multiplication of commands, it must also be customizable, mobile, understandable, easy to use and with several modes of interaction (touch or/and voice). However, these preliminary results must be put into perspective. Indeed, the people who carried out the tests were all technology-friendly and experienced.

Acknowledgment. The study is partially funded by the Occitanie Region (France). The authors thank the participants and the GIHP association.

References

1. Khomiakoff, R.: Handicap et technologies d'assistance: la place de la dimension subjective. Le Journal des psychologues **242**, 62–65 (2006). https://doi.org/10.3917/jdp.242.0062
2. Vacher, M., et al.: Experimental evaluation of speech recognition technologies for voice-based home automation control in a smart home. In: 4th workshop on Speech and Language Processing for Assistive Technologies, pp. 99–105 (2013). https://hal.archives-ouvertes.fr/hal-00953244
3. Varriale, L., Briganti, P., Mele, S.: Disability and home automation: insights and challenges within organizational settings. In: Lazazzara, A., Ricciardi, F., Za, S. (eds.) Exploring Digital Ecosystems. LNISO, vol. 33, pp. 47–66. Springer, Cham (2020). https://doi.org/10.1007/978-3-030-23665-6_5
4. Chen, K.B., Savage, A.B., Chourasia, A.O., Wiegmann, D.A., Sesto, M.E.: Touch screen performance by individuals with and without motor control disabilities. Appl. Ergon. **44**(2), 297–302 (2013). https://doi.org/10.1016/j.apergo.2012.08.004
5. Mtshali, P., Khubisa, F.M.: A smart home appliance control system for physically disabled people. In: 2019 Conference on Information Communications Technology and Society (ICTAS), pp. 1–5 (2019). https://doi.org/10.1109/ICTAS.2019.8703637

6. Noda, K.: Google Home: smart speaker as environmental control unit. Disabil. Rehabil. Assist. Technol. **13**(7), 674–675 (2018). https://doi.org/10.1080/17483107.2017.1369589
7. Vigouroux, N., Lepage, G., Campo, E., Vella, F.: Study of tactile and vocal interaction modes by disabled person for home automation controls in inclusive housing. In: 24th International Conference on Human-Computer Interaction. 26 June–1 July 2022 (2022). https://2022.hci.international/
8. van den Bossche, A., et al.: Specifying an MQTT tree for a connected smart home. In: Mokhtari, M., Abdulrazak, B., Aloulou, H. (eds.) ICOST 2018. LNCS, vol. 10898, pp. 236–246. Springer, Cham (2018). https://doi.org/10.1007/978-3-319-94523-1_21
9. Lund, A.M.: Measuring usability with the USE questionnaire. STC Usability SIG Newsl. **8**(2), 3–6 (2001). http://www.stcsig.org/usability/newsletter/0110_measuring_with_use.htm
10. Schrepp, M., Hinderks, A., Thomaschewski, J.: Construction of a benchmark for the User Experience Questionnaire (UEQ). Int. J. Interact. Multimedia Artif. Intell. **4**(Regular Issue), 40–44 (2017). https://doi.org/10.9781/ijimai.2017.445

Universal Access Panel: A Novel Approach for Accessible Smart Homes and IoT

Christoph Veigl(✉), Benjamin Klaus, Benjamin Aigner, and Manuel Wagner

UAS Technikum Wien, Höchstädtplatz 6, 1200 Vienna, Austria
veigl@technikum-wien.at

Abstract. Although various standards and guidelines for accessible design exist, many modern digital devices lack even basic accessibility features. In particular, touchscreens without haptic feedback and a highly complex menu navigation impose serious hurdles for many people – especially for people with disabilities and elderly persons. In this work, we present the *Universal Access Panel (UAP)* for enabling barrier-free access to home appliances and IoT devices. The system offers a novel, radically simple, multimodal user interface consisting of just a few interaction elements for accessing dedicated functions of the connected home. Using established APIs and communication protocols such as HomeConnect or OpenHab, various domestic appliances, consumer products and smart home devices can be controlled from a single, multimodal interaction console. The system has been designed in cooperation with visually impaired accessibility experts and a user study was conducted with people from the target group. The results show a high overall usability of the prototype.

Keywords: Home appliances · Disability · Accessibility · Multimodal user interface · Smart home · Internet-of-Things (IoT)

1 Introduction

Digital systems and connected devices have become an integral part of our living environment: Electronic 'companions' make our lives easier and safer and increase comfort in the modern home. Meanwhile, all manufacturers of home- and building technology are relying on 'smart' functions for their products. Many of these systems use touchscreens, LC displays or smartphone applications for interaction.

The United Nations Convention for the Rights of People with Disability (UNCRP) [1] is a comprehensive human rights treaty which entered into force on May 3rd, 2008 and has been ratified by 164 countries. In addition to establishing other fundamental rights, the UNCRP "requires countries to identify and eliminate obstacles and barriers and ensure that persons with disabilities can access their environment, transportation, public facilities and services, and information and communications technologies" (Article 9). Looking at every-day-products such as a kitchen stove, washing machine, dishwasher or other household appliances, we can see that accessible user interfaces for such products can be considered a human right covered by the UNCRP.

K. Miesenberger et al. (Eds.): ICCHP-AAATE 2022, LNCS 13342, pp. 148–158, 2022.
https://doi.org/10.1007/978-3-031-08645-8_18

1.1 Standards and Related Work

Most relevant standards and guidelines for accessible design of domestic appliances include the EN 301 549 (accessibility requirements for ICT products and services) by the European Telecommunications Standards Institute (ETSI) [2], the IEC 63008 (accessibility of household- and similar electrical devices) by the International Electrotechnical Commission [3] and several standards/technical reports of the International Organisation for Standardization, foremost the ISO TR 22411 [4] and the ISO 9241-20 [5].

The problem does not seem to be a lack of standardization or missing expertise in design-for-all principles, but rather a low level of acceptance of these principles in the industry. Although persons with disability could be an attractive customer group – and there is also evidence that accessible user interfaces are preferred by people without disabilities (see also: [9, 10]) – many modern household devices lack even basic accessibility features. In particular, missing haptic feedback and a high complexity of menu navigation impose serious hurdles for many people, especially for people with disabilities and elderly persons [6, 7]. According to the Home designed for all association[1], a vast majority of cooktops (hobs) available on today's market are completely unusable for blind people.

In a comprehensive study involving 52 people with different disabilities and ages, Lee et al. [8] identify a plethora of accessibility issues in modern home appliances and everyday-products, mainly involving problems in discovering functions, perceiving feedback and status messages, and reaching, grasping and controlling functions.

Serafin et al. [9] performed an evaluation of different feedback types for in-vehicle touchscreen systems and found a clear preference for haptic or auditory feedback in addition to the visual feedback. 60–80% of the test subjects would prefer a solution with haptic feedback (the test group consisted of persons without disabilities).

These results could be confirmed by Pitts et al. [10], who conclude in their research that haptic feedback significantly reduces visual workload as well as task completion times when working with touchscreens. They show that haptic feedback compensates information loss which occurs when visual feedback is degraded, and that multimodal (visual and haptic) feedback improves the overall user experience and confidence in the touchscreen interface.

Jiang et al. [11] point out a present trend in home appliance design towards excessive functions and complex operation (e.g. a typical modern microwave oven offers 80–160 functions) and that elderly people are not strongly present in current user experience design studies. They introduce four principles for user experience design, focused on elderly people with decreased learning abilities: Easy-to-Use, Easy-to-Operate, humanization (adequate sensory-, interaction- and emotional experience) and fault tolerance.

Although interesting concepts for multimodal interaction elements have been documented (e.g. the SmartKnob[2] design by Scott Bezek), to our best knowledge a flexible and accessible user interface for 'connected' household appliances does not exist.

---

[1] Home designed for all association: https://www.dbsv.org/home-designed-for-all.html.

[2] SmartKnob haptic input device: https://github.com/scottbez1/smartknob.

In this work, we present the *Universal Access Panel* (*UAP*) for enabling barrier-free access to home appliances and IoT devices. This system offers a novel, radically simple, multimodal interaction concept, consisting of just a few interaction elements for accessing dedicated functions of the connected home. Using established application programming interfaces (APIs) and communication protocols such as HomeConnect[3] or openHab,[4] various household appliances, consumer electronics products or smart home devices can be integrated and controlled from a single, multimodal interaction console.

2 Method

The system was planned and implemented in a participatory design process, involving two blind accessibility experts who work at the Austrian Federation of the Blind and Partially Sighted[5] (BSVÖ) and two experts from the Home designed for all association (one of them visually impaired). The functional prototype was created over a period of 18 months and evaluated with 5 persons from the target group. The development process consisted of three phases:

1. **Initial concept definition:** in the first meeting, ideas for the novel interaction concept were discussed and general requirements for the system were defined. For example, functional requirements guarantee haptic, visual and acoustic presentation of important information. Furthermore, various mechanical switches and motorized slider potentiometers were selected for purchase.
2. **Implementation with iterative feedback:** in several feedback rounds, the user experts contributed important design decisions to thc evolving prototype. The selection of mechanical switches was presented so that suitable components could be identified; form and function of the interaction elements and challenges/requirements for software features were discussed. Figure 1 shows design decisions in the process of the participatory development of the *UAP*.
3. **User study:** In February 2022, a functional prototype was presented to 5 blind or visually impaired participants and a qualitative user study was conducted. All users had to accomplish predefined tasks using the *UAP*; subsequently, user interviews were performed and the system was evaluated based on the System Usability Scale (SUS).

[3] HomeConnect standard: https://www.home-connect.com/.

[4] openHab: A vendor- and technology agnostic open source home automation software: https://www.openhab.org.

[5] Austrian Federation of the Blind and Partially Sighted: https://www.blindenverband.at/.

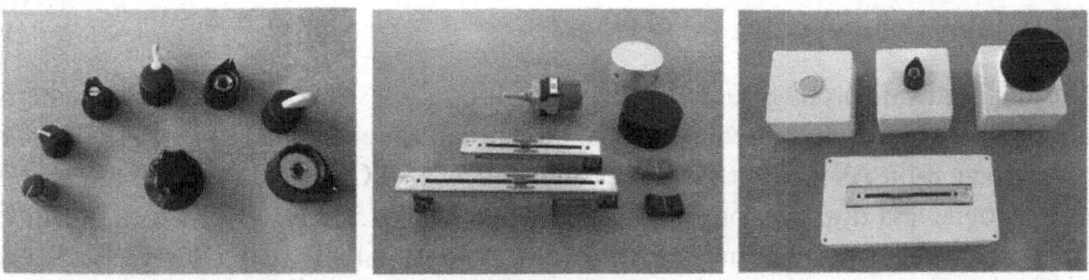

Fig. 1. Knob selection for step switch (left), motorized potentiometers (middle), modular interaction components (right)

3 Hardware Architecture

Figure 2 depicts an overview of the system architecture. For the main processing module, the M5Stack ESP32 Basic Core IoT development kit[6] was chosen. This module contains an Espressif ESP32 System-on-Chip (SoC) with dual-core Xtensa 32-bit LX6 microprocessor (up to 240 MHz system clock), built-in 16MB FLASH memory, WiFi- and Bluetooth capabilities. The M5Stack module offers a 2.0-inch color IPS display, an SD-card slot and an audio amplifier/speaker, which are important features for the multimodal characteristics of the access panel. The ESP32 SoC is fully supported with an open source toolchain (Espressif IDF[7]) and drivers/software libraries for all peripherals, as well as a full integration with a real-time operating system (FreeRTOS[8]).

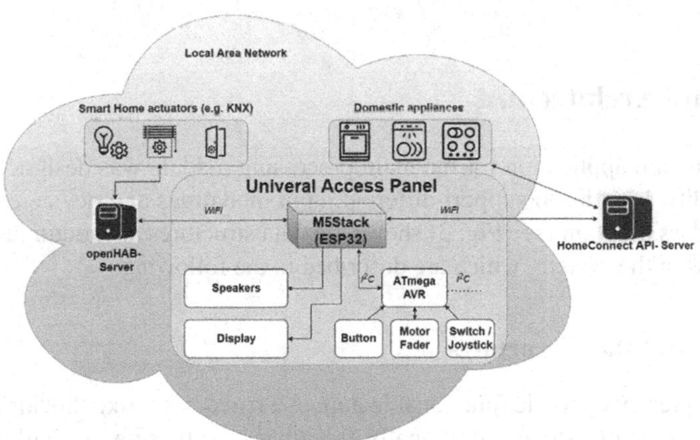

Fig. 2. System overview, Universal Access Panel component interconnection (green box). (Color figure online)

[6] M5Stack modular Open Source IoT Development platform: https://m5stack.com/.
[7] Espressif IDF ESP32 toolchain: https://docs.espressif.com/projects/esp-idf/.
[8] FreeRTOS Real Time Operating System: https://www.freertos.org/.

3.1 Modular Components

A modular hardware architecture was chosen, which allows the connection of interaction elements to the main module via I2C bus. One or multiple sensor/actuator elements are attached to an 8-bit AVR microcontroller which acts as I2C slave device. The AVR provides analogue and digital input/output and generates a 150 kHz PWM for controlling the motorized fader potentiometer. A custom PCB was made using the Open Source KiCad[9] design suite, in order to ease connection and reusability for multiple I/O modules. This architecture provides the flexibility to build *UAP*-variants for particular use cases with minor effort (e.g. a panel with 4 faders for controlling 4 different zones of a cooktop appliance). However, at a particular stage it was decided to focus on a specific panel configuration which is applicable for many different use cases (see Fig. 5). This configuration was utilized in the user study and consists of a) the main module (M5-Stack/ESP32 SoC), b) one interaction element for selection of device/function, c) one motorized fader potentiometer for parameter feedback and manipulation and d) one additional button for committing parameter selections or controlling selected functions. The 3d-printed enclosures were created using the Open Source FreeCad[10] 3d parametric modelling tool.

The main module establishes a wireless (WiFi-) connection to the LAN and accesses local services via an openHab instance which relays communication to other devices, e.g. a KNX/IP[11] gateway. Furthermore, functions of supported home appliances can be accessed via the HomeConnect-API[12] for connected home appliances which offers a cloud-based access to 15 appliance types of 9 major manufacturers of domestic appliances.

4 Software Architecture

The C++ software application for the main processing module was designed for maximum flexibility, in order to support different input modalities and device control standards. The class diagram (see Fig. 3) shows the data structures abstracting real devices and functions in the system, which are described in the following.

4.1 Classes and Data Structures

A *function* represents a single functional feature of a real device, like ‘hot air’ of an oven or ‘cooktop field 1’ of a stove. Additionally, functions can also refer to single standalone actions like switching a light, or closing shutters. *FunctionComposed* aggregates several single functions. Different kinds of functions are derived from a base function, depending on which API should be called (e.g. openHAB, HomeConnect, a generic REST API or any other kind of API).

[9] KiCad EDA - Schematic and PCB Design software: https://www.kicad.org/.

[10] FreeCAD 3D parametric modeler: https://www.freecadweb.org/.

[11] KNX fieldbus system for building automation: https://www.knx.org/.

[12] Home Connect API documentation: https://api-docs.home-connect.com/general.

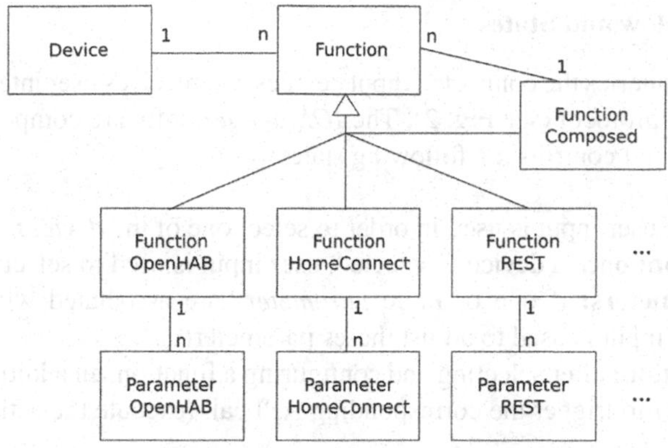

Fig. 3. Data structures/class diagram, representation of devices and functions in the *UAP*

A flexible number of *parameters* can be associated to a function. Parameters can be changed using a specific interaction component, e.g. the parameter 'temperature' of the function 'hot air' of an oven could be set using a slider. If a function offers more than one parameter (e.g. temperature and duration), different interaction components could be utilized in order to adjust these parameters individually, or default values for parameters could be used.

A *device* is the abstraction of either a single real device (like an oven or dishwasher with all its functions) or a collection of different functions of distinct real appliances which are thematically or spatially related (like the user's favorite functions, or functions located in the living room). Figure 4 shows the program flow of the software application running on the ESP32 SoC, illustrating the user interaction with the *UAP*.

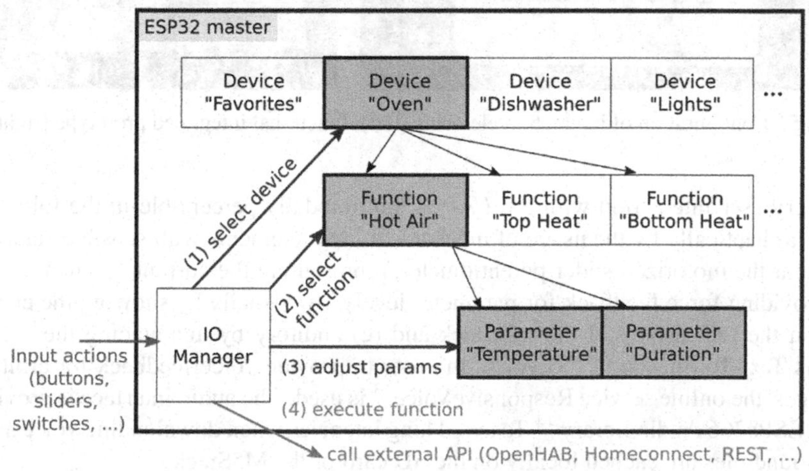

Fig. 4. Visualization of the program flow of the main software running on the ESP32 SoC

4.2 Program Flow and States

The ESP32 SoC queries the connected input devices and receives user interaction parameters via the I2C protocol (see Fig. 2). The *IOManager* software component processes this information and controls the following states:

- **Select device:** user input is used in order to select one of the *devices.*
- **Select function:** once a device is selected, user input is used to select a *function.*
- **Adjust parameters:** if one or more *parameters* are associated with the selected function, user input is used to adjust theses parameter(s).
- **Execute function:** after selecting and configuring a function, an additional user input is used in order to trigger the corresponding API call (execute the action).

5 Results

Figure 5 shows the final configuration of interaction elements and the functional integrated prototype of the *UAP* which was tested with persons of the target group.

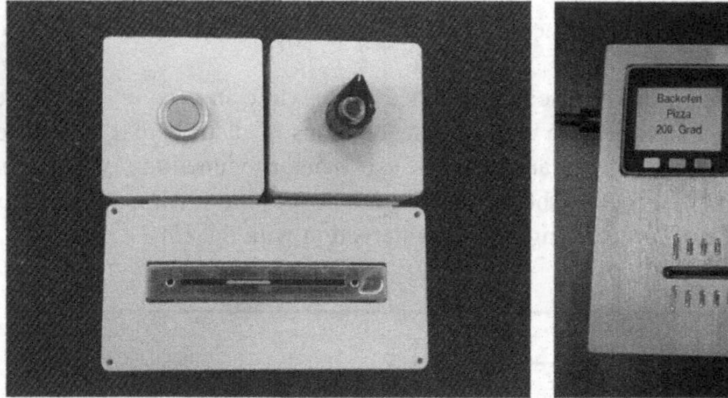

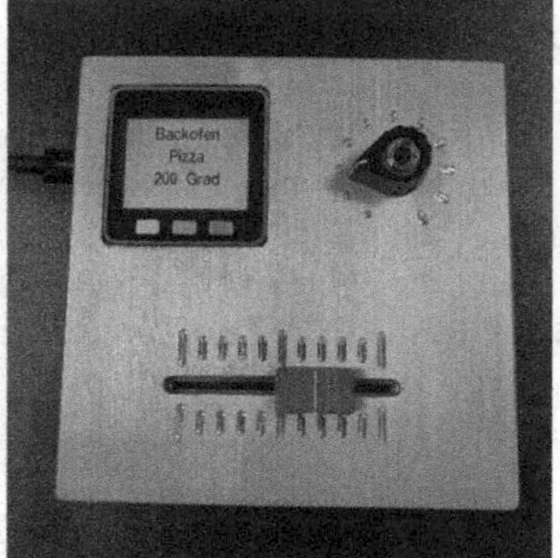

Fig. 5. Configuration of interaction elements (left), functional integrated prototype (right)

Every user interaction with the *UAP* is multimodally perceptible in the following ways: (a) haptically by the usage of mechanical input elements with sensible state – in particular the motorized slider potentiometer, representing the current parameter value and providing force feedback for parameter levels, (b) visually by showing the current state on the LC display of the M5Stack and (c) auditory by announcing the current state as Text-To-Speech (TTS) voice. In order to provide voice feedback for arbitrary messages, the online service ResponsiveVoice[13] is used. The audio interface is provided by the ESP8266 Audio library.[14] To avoid long latencies when downloading voice audio files, sound files are cached locally on the SD card of the M5Stack.

[13] ResponsiveVoice online TTS service: https://responsivevoice.org/.

[14] Audio Library for ESP8266 and ESP32 by Earle F. Philhower: https://github.com/earlephilhower/ESP8266Audio.

5.1 User Study

A user study was performed with 5 persons of the target group at the 'LivingLab' of UAS Technikum Wien in Vienna, Austria. Two of the participants were females and three were males in the age of 52 ± 20.16 years, four of them were blind and one visually impaired. The *UAP* was preconfigured for controlling different appliances in the 'LivingLab', including lights, shutters, oven and dishwasher. After signing the informed consent document, the participants were introduced to the functionality of the prototype. After getting acquainted with the setting, the users had to accomplish 8 tasks using the *UAP*, including turning on specific lights, starting and stopping the oven, and closing the shutters. The user study started with easy tasks, such as turning the lights on/off, followed by more complex tasks like changing parameters of running devices or stopping functions which are currently running. While the participants performed the tasks, occurring problems were observed. In a subsequent interview, all users were invited to share their thoughts and ideas for improvements. The tasks and observed problems are listed in Table 1.

A technical issue occurred during execution of task 4: the HomeConnect API was blocking remote access to a connected device because this device was accessed locally beforehand. During task 4, the study participants also experienced some difficulties when trying to start the washing machine with the required settings (Wool 60° – 1000 rpm). The reason for these difficulties was that in the current *UAP* implementation, only one parameter can be changed for a given device function (thus it is required to switch the device function if either temperature or rpm shall be changed). Furthermore, mentionable problems were observed during the final task, where the participants were asked to stop the running programs of the oven and the washing machine. In order to fulfil this task, it is required to navigate to the 'active functions' menu and press start button again, which caused some confusion for the participants.

Table 1. List of user study tasks including a description of occurring problems

Task	Description	Problems
1	Turn on the lights in the kitchen	None
2	Adjust the ceiling light to 70%	None
3	Lower the shutters and raise them again	None
4	Start the oven program *'Top and Bottom Heat'* with 80 °C	*API error: 'locked by local control'*- once
5	Start the dishwasher program *'Eco 50 °C'*	None
6	Start the washing machine program *'Wool 60 °C'* with a spin speed of 1000rpm	Confusing Parameter selection: only Temperature *or* RPM is adjustable
7	Change the oven program to *'Keep Warm'* with 60 °C	None
8	Stop the running program of the oven and the washing machine	Confusing: *'start'* button is also used for *'stop'*

Subsequently, all users completed 10 questions of the System Usability Scale (SUS) [12]. In total, the prototype scored 84.5/100 points in the SUS, indicating good overall usability. The most negative ratings were given for question 10 *"I needed to learn a lot of things before I could get going with this system"* (7/20 points agreeing) and question 6 *"I thought there was too much inconsistency in this system."* (5/20 points agreeing). The high inconsistency rating possibly resulted from an unexpected error that happened in multiple test sessions, causing some parameter values to change without user interaction. The highest positive score (20/20 points) was given for question 1 *"I think that I would like to use this device frequently"*, which shows an overall positive user experience of the participants. In general, it was observed that younger participants had fewer problems understanding the interaction concept than older ones, but even an 81-year-old person with visual disabilities could perform basic device control using the *UAP*, which would otherwise have been impossible due to the nature and complexity of the native touch-screen interfaces.

6 Discussion

A novel *Universal Access Panel* for improving the accessibility of connected devices and home appliances was developed in a participatory design process and evaluated by blind and visually impaired persons. The system provides multimodal feedback and enables access to household appliances and smart home functions which would otherwise be completely inaccessible to different user groups. While the overall feedback of the user evaluation was very good, some weaknesses of the current prototype became obvious: additional user input elements for repeating the last speech output, stopping a program or configuring more than one parameter would be useful. However, adding more interaction elements also makes the device more complex – therefore a proper "trade-off" between functionality and complexity must be found and further evaluated with users. Currently, the configuration of the panel is 'hardcoded' and it's not possible to change it dynamically. It is planned to provide an accessible web-based configuration manager which connects to the *UAP* and allows adjusting the system to the actual environment of the user.

We want to emphasize that one important purpose of the *UAP* is to present innovative concepts to the industry, to encourage manufactures to comply with existing accessibility guidelines and to pave the way for a better accessibility of household appliances in general. The goal remains – and it is even more relevant in today's digitally connected world: *Products and appliances shall be useable for everyone!*

Acknowledgement. This work was financially supported by the City of Vienna (Municipal Department for Economic Affairs, Labour and Statistics – MA23) in course of the project 'Wissensdrehscheibe für Barrierefreie Technologien' (MA23 project 26-02).

References

1. UN General Assembly, Convention on the Rights of Persons with Disabilities: resolution/adopted by the General Assembly, A/RES/61/106, 24 January 2007. https://www.refworld.org/docid/45f973632.html. Accessed 2 Apr 2022
2. European Telecommunications Standards Institute: ETSI EN 301 549 - V2.1.2 - Accessibility requirements for ICT products and services (2018)
3. IEC 63008: Household and Similar Electrical Appliances—Accessibility of Control Elements, Doors, Lids, Drawers and Handles. International Electrotechnical Commission, Geneva (2016)
4. ISO TR 22411: Ergonomics Data and Guidelines for the Application of ISO/IEC Guide 71 to Products and Services to Address the Needs of Older Persons and Persons with Disabilities. International Organization for Standardization, Geneva (2008)
5. ISO 9241-20: Ergonomics of Human-System Interaction—Part 20: Accessibility Guidelines for Information/Communication Technology (ICT) Equipment and Services. International Organization for Standardization, Geneva (2008)
6. Lee, J., Lau, S., Meijer, E., Hu, P.: Living longer: "with or without disability? A global and longitudinal perspective." J. Gerontol. Ser. A **75**(1), 162–167 (2020). https://doi.org/10.1093/gerona/glz007
7. Leporini, B., Buzzi, M.: Home automation for an independent living: investigating the needs of visually impaired people. In: Proceedings of the 15th International Web for All Conference (W4A 2018), pp. 1–9, April 2018. https://doi.org/10.1145/3192714.3192823
8. Lee, J.H., Kim, Y.M., Rhiu, I., Yun, M.H.: A persona-based approach for identifying accessibility issues in elderly and disabled users' interaction with home appliances. Appl. Sci. **11**(1), 368 (2021). https://doi.org/10.3390/app11010368
9. Serafin, C., Heers, R., Tschirhar, M., Ullrich, C., Ramstein, C.: User experience in the U.S. and Germany of in-vehicle screens with integrated haptic and auditory. SAE Trans. J. Passeng. Cars Mech. Syst. J. **116**(6), 357–364 (2007)
10. Pitts, M.J., Burnett, G., Skrypchuk, L., Wellings, T., Attridge, A., Williams, M.A.: Visual–haptic feedback interaction in automotive touchscreens. Displays **33**(1), 7–16 (2012). https://doi.org/10.1016/j.displa.2011.09.0
11. Jiang, B., Tian, L., Zhou, D.: User experience design research of new types of home appliances based on the analysis of the learning curve of the elderly. In: Zhou, J., Salvendy, G. (eds.) ITAP 2017. LNCS, vol. 10297, pp. 233–243. Springer, Cham (2017). https://doi.org/10.1007/978-3-319-58530-7_17
12. Bangor, A., Kortum, P., Miller, J.A.: The system usability scale (SUS): an empirical evaluation. Int. J. Hum.-Comput. Interact. **24**(6), 574–594 (2008)

BY

Technologies for Inclusion and Participation at Work and in Everyday Activities

Technologies for Inclusion and Participation at Work and in Everyday Activities
Introduction to the Special Thematic Session

Susanne Dirks(✉), Christian Bühler, and Bastian Pelka

TU Dortmund University, 44227 Dortmund, Germany
{susanne.dirks,christian.buehler,bastian.pelka}@tu-dortmund.de

Abstract. This session reflects R&D on technologies.

Keywords: User centered design · Participative research · People with disabilities · Accessibility · Assistive technology

1 Introduction

According to the UN Convention on the Rights of Persons with Disabilities (CRPD), people with disabilities should enjoy full participation in all areas of life. However, the extent of poverty and social exclusion in the 21st century in Europe and worldwide is still higher than one would assume. This affects people with disabilities in particular. According to current figures, more than 28% of people with disabilities in Europe are at direct risk of poverty and social exclusion. The risk for women with disabilities is even higher by two percentage points (29.5% to 27.5%) [1, 2]. In line with Sen's capability approach [3, 4] and the ICF [5], poverty and limited opportunities for participation depend on various factors. These include not only personal characteristics such as age and gender, but also the available resources and the environmental conditions in which people live.

Technologies and ICT have the potential to help marginalised groups overcome barriers to accessing information, communicating, and interacting with others. Assistive and adaptive technologies have already been used in the past, especially for people with motor or sensory limitations [6], to promote independence and participation. With further development of ICT (including mobile devices), more diverse support functions are increasingly available. For example, features such as text and speech recognition, the ability to change contrast and colour schemes, touch and gesture input, and screen magnification are increasingly available in everyday technologies [7]. However, for ICTs and digital technologies to enable the inclusion of persons with disabilities, not only technologies need to be developed, but also awareness and capacity building among different stakeholders to provide accessible services and environments [8].

The ability to participate in employment and to perform everyday tasks independently are essential prerequisites for overcoming poverty and social exclusion and for the mental health of people with disabilities [9–11].

K. Miesenberger et al. (Eds.): ICCHP-AAATE 2022, LNCS 13342, pp. 161–167, 2022.
https://doi.org/10.1007/978-3-031-08645-8_19

In the following sections, the potential uses of technology to support people with disabilities and their impact on participation and satisfaction in work environments and everyday activities are presented. This is followed by a brief presentation of the various workshop contributions, their integration into the scientific context and their applicability for people with disabilities.

2 Work and Employment

The possibility of work and employment is a determining factor for inclusion, but also for poverty and social exclusion. For example, significantly fewer people with disabilities are employed in the EU than people without disabilities (50.8% compared to 74.8%). This does not include people living in institutions. This means that in reality an even higher proportion of people with disabilities are not in employment. Furthermore, the figures do not give any information about the number of part-time workers, the quality of employment and whether this employment is in the open labour market or not [12]. Also, the type of disability has a significant impact on the employment rate. Statistics collected in Spain show that people with psychosocial disabilities are most affected by unemployment. People with learning disabilities also experience a higher rate of unemployment, with an estimated employment rate of 19.5% [13].

Not only disabilities per se, but also social barriers can lead to difficulties in finding a job – for example due to employers' prejudices, the accessibility of jobs or the inability to work full-time. Therefore, it is more difficult for disabled people to find and keep a job than for non-disabled people [14]. Employment and work are also important social activities. They offer the opportunity to socialise, interact, communicate, learn, and become independent from welfare and heteronomy.

Using appropriate assistive technology can make all the difference between being poor and being able to work and earn a living [15]. A number of studies have demonstrated a range of positive effects from the use of assistive technologies in the workplace, such as increased productivity, better self-esteem, higher attendance, and more hours of paid work [16]. Studies with vocational rehabilitation (VR) counsellors also show that assistive technologies can be increasingly effective in improving the employability and career progression of people with disabilities [17].

In many cases, assistive technologies are provided by employers or owned by the individual. Loan equipment or cost coverage by health insurance companies or insurances are rather the exception.

Based on existing studies on the role of assistive technologies in the employment of people with disabilities, the following findings emerge [15]: (1) people with disabilities are less likely to be employed than their non-disabled peers, (2) for people with disabilities who work, assistive technologies are an important feature of their jobs, (3) ICT is perceived as an important assistive technology in the workplace, (4) most technologies in the workplace used by people with disabilities are relatively simple and inexpensive, and (5) the success of assistive technology in the workplace depends on employees and employers having positive attitudes towards technology and embrace flexibility and problem-solving skills.

The pandemic led to a worldwide decline in productivity and a global recession. Unemployment, however, declined at a higher rate among workers with disabilities. The pandemic is also likely to have a negative impact on the job security of people with disabilities as they face more severe social and psychological consequences of COVID-19 [18]. The sudden shift to home-based work was also problematic for employees. Employees who worked from home during the shutdown reported missing the physical interaction with their colleagues and expressed concern about the blurring of boundaries between work and home life and the lack of necessary equipment and space to do their work at home [19]. Working exclusively or partly from home is a reasonable adjustment that can increase the accessibility of jobs for disabled workers and promote their retention in the labour force. Yet few studies to date have examined disabled workers' experiences of working from home. Pre-pandemic studies have shown that working from home helps disabled employees maintain their work routines as they have more control over their work schedule and tasks can be accommodated with fluctuating energy levels, pain, or medical appointments [20, 21]. Further research is needed on the specific impact of the pandemic on the effectiveness and well-being of people with disabilities at work.

3 Everyday Activities

Activities of daily living are tasks that are performed habitually or repeatedly at regular intervals and are often prerequisites for other activities. Examples of activities of daily living are dressing, eating, personal hygiene, toileting, or functional mobility. Activities of daily living are differentiated from productive activities such as paid work, volunteering, and education, and from leisure, recreational and social activities. Everyday activities are important because they help to maintain personal health, social life, and relationships with others [22].

The ability to care for oneself and carry out everyday activities independently plays a major role in the life satisfaction and well-being of people with disabilities. Everyday activities of people with disabilities often differ from those of non-disabled people in several ways. The existing disabilities may limit the extent to which they can participate in activities, increase the time required for activities of daily living or cause dependence on others [23, 24]. In addition, people with disabilities often perceive their social interactions and social network as limited [25].

Modern assistive technologies and ICT are increasingly available to support people with disabilities in various everyday activities. People with disabilities have access to a wide range of assistive technologies to support them in everyday activities, such as customizable wheelchairs and scooters, lifting systems, exoskeletons, or myoelectric prostheses [26, 27]. Alternative control systems, such as voice input and output systems or eye controls, can be used to operate ICT devices or smart home technologies [28–30]. Research on the effectiveness of assistive technologies for daily living has demonstrated the supportive role such devices have in maintaining, increasing, or delaying the decline of daily functions for people with disabilities and older adults. In addition, they can support the function and safety of family members, personal caregivers and others who work with people with disabilities in activities of daily living [30, 32].

4 Contributions

The contributions to this session integrate into this context and demonstrate the importance of progress in this domain. From the numerous submissions received, five got accepted for this session. The selected contributions present current research and development results that have great potential for improving the participation opportunities and well-being of people with disabilities in the context of work and everyday life.

- In the first article, technical solutions that can be used to support dressing are examined for their usability for people with dementia [33]. Dressing independently is a complex basic activity of daily living that is particularly challenging for people with dementia. Publications on different intelligent dressing systems, e.g., AID-ME or DRESS, are analyzed and evaluated regarding their suitability for persons with dementia. As a result, the authors show that many solutions are still too complex to be applied in practice. Furthermore, the systems only focus on certain aspects of dressing, e.g., recognizing dressing errors (AID-ME) or generating dressing suggestions. Some suggestions provide interesting ideas, but studies on their feasibility are still preliminary. The article reviews some of the approaches and discusses them critically.

  The second paper presents the results of a survey to determine the subjective perceptions of trainees and trainers regarding the digital transformation process in different vocational training institutions [34]. A total of three members of the institution's management, eight trainers and fifty-four trainees were interviewed. Among the trainees interviewed, many had a refugee or migration background, lacked language skills, and had learning difficulties. The study was conducted within the framework of the DIKOLF project, that aims to promote the digital and vocational participation of trainees with special needs. The results of the questionnaire survey show that all interviewed groups expect added value from the implementation of digital media in their institution. At the same time, the results confirm the continuing need for infrastructure in vocational education and training and vocational rehabilitation.
- The third article presents the most important results of the R&D project LernBAR (Learning based on Augmented Reality) [35]. The project focuses on renewing the vocational training in home economic services with the use of Augmented Reality (AR) and digital media. In the LernBAR project, a digital learning aid was developed for people with cognitive disabilities in vocational training in the field of home economics was designed, developed, and evaluated. An online learning platform with embedded AR learning stations was developed and evaluated with the target group. The developed app and the media were generally well accepted and evaluated as useful for training and exam preparation. The use of the app through the AR glasses (Hololens) was considered to be somewhat more difficult and tiring than through the tablet.
- The fourth study reports on a survey on the quality of work of Italian public administration employees, comparing a group of them working in traditional offices (control group) with another group working in home offices [36]. The aim of the project was to use a remote test to investigate the impact of "smart working" on the quality of work and satisfaction of the employees involved in the study. The results of the questionnaires showed that on average workers were satisfied with their work experience

and no significant differences were found between the two groups. However, both the efficiency and effectiveness results of the study showed that the participants who took the test at home were able to manage their time better and achieved better results than the participants who took the test in the office.

- The fifth paper presents the results of a study that aimed to investigate the success factors and challenges for people with disabilities in the home office [37]. For this purpose, employees from different work areas of a German university were interviewed. The aim of this mixed-methods study was to find out which technological and social factors influence the job satisfaction and quality of work of PWDs and to compare them with the work at the usual workplace. Thereby, already known influencing factors were investigated and new insights and ideas for improvements were generated. The results of the study show that the university's employees with disabilities rate working in a home office mostly positively. Above all, the increased flexibility and independence are seen as major advantages. In addition, barriers that occur in normal office environments, e.g., loud background noise or unwanted distractions, are reduced. However, even if the basic technical equipment is available, there is a lack of ergonomic equipment in the home office. Communication and support, especially from superiors, deans, and other departments, is perceived as insufficient and leads to frustration and stress in the work process. Good cooperation within the team as well as optimal technical equipment have a great influence on job satisfaction. All interviewees stated that a high degree of formal and interpersonal cooperation increases well-being, job satisfaction and motivation.

The studies presented in this session show various interesting approaches to support people with disabilities through the use of technology in work and training processes and in everyday activities. In order to protect people with disabilities from social exclusion and disadvantage and to help them to more self-determination and participation, complex devices such as AR glasses and self-learning systems as well as barrier-free digital environments and conventional assistive technologies are suitable. Last but not least, adequate organizational conditions and attitudes of caregivers, colleagues and supervisors are a fundamental prerequisite for improving the participation opportunities, social inclusion, and wellbeing of people with disabilities. The studies also showcase that the pandemic introduced wider availability of home office and ICT means for labor unleash positive aspects for PWD. The next years will show if this could lead to a better participation of PWD in the labor market.

Acknowledgment. The special topic session and this introduction are based on the joint work of scientists in the research cluster 'Technology for Inclusion and Participation' at TU Dortmund University [38].

References

1. European Disability Forum. Poverty and Social Exclusion of Persons with Disabilities. Chapter 2: Persons with disabilities and the risk of poverty and social exclusion. https://www.edf-feph.org/employment-policy/

2. European Commission. Proposal for a joint employment report from the commission and the council. https://ec.europa.eu/info/sites/default/files/2020-european-semester-joint-employment-report_en.pdf
3. Sen, A.: Inequality Reexamined. Clarendon Press, Oxford, England (1992)
4. Mitra, S.: The capability approach and disability. J. Disabil. Policy Stud. **16**, 236–247 (2006)
5. International Classification of Functioning, Disability and Health (ICF). https://www.who.int/standards/classifications/international-classification-of-functioning-disability-and-health
6. Borg, J., Östergren, P.-O., Larsson, S., Rahman, A.A., Bari, N., Khan, A.N.: Assistive technology use is associated with reduced capability poverty: a cross-sectional study in Bangladesh. Disabil. Rehabil. Assist. Technol. **7**(2), 112–121 (2012)
7. Thompson, S.: Mobile technology and inclusion of persons with disabilities. K4D Emerging Issues Report. Institute of Development Studies, Brighton, UK (2018)
8. Samant Raja, D.: Bridging the disability divide through digital technologies. Background Paper for the 2016 World Development Report: Digital Dividends. World Bank, Washington DC
9. Vornholt, K., et al.: Disability and employment – overview and highlights. Eur. J. Work Organ. Psychol. **27**(1), 40–55 (2018)
10. Schur, L.: The difference a job makes: The effects of employment among people with disabilities. J. Econ. Issues **36**, 339–347 (2002)
11. Baumgärtner, M.K., Böhm, S.A., Dwertmann, D.J.-G.: Job performance of employees with disabilities: interpersonal and intrapersonal resources matter. Equal. Divers. Incl. **33**(4), 347–360 (2014)
12. Informe 4 del Observatorio sobre Discapacidad y Mercado de Trabajo de la Fundación ONCE (2019). http://odismet.es/es/informes/
13. European Disability Forum. Poverty and Social Exclusion of Persons with Disabilities. Chapter 6: Employment of persons with disabilities. https://www.edf-feph.org/employment-policy/
14. Van der Zwan, R., De Beer, P.: The disability employment gap in European countries: what is the role of labour market policy? J. Eur. Soc. Policy **31**(4), 473–486 (2021)
15. Stumbo, N.J., Martin, J.K., Hedrick, B.N.: Assistive technology: impact on education, employment, and independence of individuals with physical disabilities. J. Vocat. Rehabil. **30**(2), 99–110 (2009)
16. Yeager, P., Kaye, H.S., Reed, M., Doe, T.M.: Assistive technology and employment: experiences of Californians with disabilities. Work **27**(4), 333–344 (2006)
17. Noll, A., Owens, L., Smith, R.O., Schwanke, T.: Survey of state vocational rehabilitation counselor roles and competencies in assistive technology. Work **27**(4), 413–419 (2006)
18. Scope. Disabled People Fear Being 'Pushed Out' of Post-Lockdown World as Shielding Pauses, online March 2022. https://www.scope.org.uk/media/press-releases/disabled-people-pushed-out-lockdown/
19. Chung, H., Seo, H., Forbes, S., Birkett, H.: Working from Home During the COVID-19 Lockdown: Changing Preferences and the Future of Work. University of Birmingham and University of Kent (2020). Online March 2022: http://wafproject.org/covidwfh
20. McNaughton, D., Rackensperger, T., Dorn, D., Wilson, N.: Home is at work and work is at home: telework and individuals who use augmentative and alternative communication. Work **2014**(48), 117–126 (2014)
21. Linden, M., Milchus, K.: Teleworkers with disabilities: characteristics and accommodation use. Work **2014**(47), 473–483 (2014)
22. Mallinson, T.R.: Activities of daily living. Encyclopedia Britannica, 24 November 2016. https://www.britannica.com/topic/activities-of-daily-living

23. Gaskin, C.J., Andersen, M.B., Morris, T.: Physical activity in the life of a woman with severe cerebral palsy: showing competence and being socially connected. Int. J. Disabil. Dev. Educ. **56**(3), 285–299 (2009)
24. Lutz, B.J., Bowers, B.J.: Disability in everyday life. Qual. Health Res. **15**(8), 1037–1054 (2005)
25. Isaksson, G., Skär, L., Lexell, J.: Women's perception of changes in social network after a spinal cord injury. Disabil. Rehabil. **27**(17), 1013–1021 (2005)
26. Schabron, B., Desai, J., Yihun, Y.: Wheelchair-mounted upper limb robotic exoskeleton with adaptive controller for activities of daily living. Sensors **21**, 5738 (2021)
27. Fritz, H., Patzer, D., Galen, S.S.: Robotic exoskeletons for reengaging in everyday activities: promises, pitfalls, and opportunities. Disabil. Rehabil. **41**(5), 560–563 (2019)
28. Poirier, S., Routhier, F., Campeau-Lecours, A.: Voice control interface prototype for assistive robots for people living with upper limb disabilities. In: 2019 IEEE 16th International Conference on Rehabilitation Robotics (ICORR), pp. 46–52 (2019)
29. Jamwal, R., Jarman, H.K., Roseingrave, E., Douglas, J., Winkler, D.: Smart home and communication technology for people with disability: a scoping review. Disabil. Rehabil. Assist. Technol. (2020)
30. Bissoli, A., Lavino-Junior, D., Sime, M., Encarnação, L., Bastos-Filho, T.A.: Human–machine interface based on eye tracking for controlling and monitoring a smart home using the internet of things. Sensors **19**, 859 (2019)
31. Hammel, J.: Aids for activities of daily living. Encyclopedia Britannica. https://www.britannica.com/topic/aids-for-activities-of-daily-living
32. Dirks, S., Bühler, C.: Assistive technologies for people with cognitive impairments – which factors influence technology acceptance? In: Antona, M., Stephanidis, C. (eds.) Universal Access in Human-Computer Interaction. Methods, Technologies, and Users: 12th International Conference, UAHCI 2018, Held as Part of HCI International 2018, Las Vegas, NV, USA, July 15–20, 2018, Proceedings, Part I, pp. 503–516. Springer, Cham (2018). https://doi.org/10.1007/978-3-319-92049-8_36
33. Ghezzi, S., Masciadri, A., Salice, F., Comai, S.: A Review on Technological Solutions Supporting People with Dementia in the Activity of Dressing. In: Lecture Notes …
34. Sube, L., Bühler, C.: Implications for digital transformation processes in vocational training of people with special needs. In: Petz, A., Hoogerwerf, E.-J., Mavrou, K. (eds.) Assistive Technology, Accessibility and (e)Inclusion, ICCHP-AAATE 2022 Open Access Compendium, accepted for publication, online. Johannes Kepler University Linz, Austria (2022). https://www.icchp-aaate.org
35. Wuttke, L., Söffgen, Y., Bühler, C.: Testing an augmented reality learning app for people with learning difficulties in vocational training in home economics – central results of the project LernBAR (Learning based on Augmented Reality). In: Lecture Notes …
36. Federici, S., et al.: Remote working: a way to foster greater inclusion and accessibility. In: Lecture Notes …
37. Dirks, S., Kurth, F.: Working from home in the COVID-19 pandemic - which technological and social factors influence the working conditions and job satisfaction of people with disabilities? In: Lecture Notes …
38. Research Cluster 'Technology for Inclusion and Participation', TU Dortmund University. http://tip.tu-dortmund.de/cms/de/Forschung/index.html

A Review on Technological Solutions Supporting People with Dementia in the Activity of Dressing

Sofia Ghezzi, Andrea Masciadri, Fabio Salice, and Sara Comai(✉)

Department of Electronics Information and Bioengineering, Politecnico di Milano, Milan, Italy
{sofia.ghezzi,andrea.masciadri,fabio.salice,sara.comai}@polimi.it

Abstract. In a world where the number of older people with dementia is steadily increasing, it is fundamental to develop and exploit technologies that support "ageing in place" and delay institutionalization, to lower the strain on the health care system. People with dementia need support from caregivers in performing many self-maintaining activities of daily living like, for example, dressing. This paper reviews the most relevant technological solutions proposed in the literature to support the activity of dressing in people with dementia.

Keywords: Assistive technology · Ageing · Activities of Daily Living (ADL) · Dressing

1 Introduction

The increasing ageing of the world population is shifting the focus on the pathologies that affect the elderly, among which there is dementia, one of the most diffused causes of disability and dependency [4].

Dementia is a group of chronic symptoms that affect the brain and progressively brings degeneration of cognition and capability to perform normal activities, such as eating or getting dressed, leading to disability and death [3,4].

There are different forms of dementia, depending on the specific pathology causing it, from Alzheimer's disease (AD, 60% of cases) to Lewy Bodies (DLB, the second most common - due to the abnormal aggregation of a synaptic protein), Frontotemporal Dementia (FTD - that may be either genetic or sporadic and causes atrophy of the frontal and temporal lobes), Vascular Dementia (VaD - primarily caused by a vascular damage or dysfunction, such as large vessel, small-vessel or cardioembolic disease), Mixed Dementia (a mix of AD and VaD, more common in 85+ people). AD is typically associated with memory loss and difficulty in learning, FTD usually causes language disturbance, DLB presents fluctuating cognitive disturbance and VaD is characterised by progressive problems in attention, planning and execution of tasks [1]. A common and very impacting aspect of dementia is functional disability in everyday activities that take place at home and in the community. They include: a) (Basic) Activities

K. Miesenberger et al. (Eds.): ICCHP-AAATE 2022, LNCS 13342, pp. 168–175, 2022.
https://doi.org/10.1007/978-3-031-08645-8_20

of Daily Living, i.e., self-maintaining skills such as bathing, toileting, dressing, eating, ambulating; b) Instrumental Activities of Daily Living, i.e., higher order skills such as managing finances, using the telephone, taking medicines, planning a meal, working, active problem solving. The functional disability develops progressively together with the syndrome, therefore people usually need support in Activities of Daily Living (ADL) following a specific order: firstly bathing, then dressing, grooming, toileting, walking and, finally, eating [15].

In this paper, we first introduce the problem of monitoring ADLs of Dementia patients in general (Sect. 2). Then, we focus on the technological solutions proposed for the activity of dressing (Sect. 3). Finally, we discuss the proposed solutions and draw our conclusions (Sect. 5).

2 ADL Monitoring of Dementia Patients

Many methods and scales for assessing functionality in dementia patients have been created. For example, the generic Katz Index of ADL is used by health care professionals to assess self-care functions: bathing, dressing, toileting, change of position (e.g., from sitting to standing), continence and eating [9]. The Lawton IADL considers higher degree functions such as using the telephone, shopping, preparing food, housekeeping, laundering, travelling with transportation, responsibility for their own treatments and managing finances [7].

In recent years, many technological solutions have been researched to provide automatic ADL recognition (i.e., which activity is being performed), like e.g., [22] and [19]. Wu et al. [22] recognize 16 household activities performed by a person wearing a RFID reader on a bracelet, by tagging with RFID tags 33 objects. To minimise labelling and human intervention, objects are automatically recognised from video data. A Dynamic Bayesian Network (DBN) model combines the aforementioned RFID readings and video to acquire object models and to infer the most likely activity; in the end, they recognise more than 80% of activities. In Stikic et al. [19], the authors integrated two different types of sensors, RFID tags on household objects and wearable accelerometer on the wrist, for inferring IADLs, such as cleaning windows, dusting, ironing etc. To cope with the gaps when there are no RFID readings or ambiguity with close readings of objects shared by different activites, accelerometer data are used, improving the recognition performance.

Despite the high number of works supporting performing ADL, not many of them target older people with dementia. Mynatt et al. [12] examine how to help older people with memory impairment to keep focus on a specific task after being interrupted. Cameras record when the person is cooking; in real-time, an operator selects the most important actions. These photograms of the actions are displayed on the screen in time order, to help the person keep track of what has been already performed.

A pervasive healthcare system based on computer vision to support the ADL washing hands was proposed by Mihalidis et al. [11]. This activity is seen as a series of tasks, such as opening the water tap, wetting hands, taking soap, rubbing soap, rinsing, closing the water and drying hands. A sensing agent recognizes body and hands position and infers what step is being carried out; color is used as a marker for objects), a planning agent understands if current step is correct or not and a prompting agent to provide guidance in case of mistake.

A field of research that has been attracting more and more interest in the last years is the use of vocal assistants. Reis et al. [16] investigate the potential to help reduce social isolation in the elderly using personal assistants such as Amazon Alexa, Google Assistant, Microsoft Cortana and Apple Siri. Tan et al. [20] developed the Eldercare Toolbox (a series of Alexa Skills) to support people with dementia. Thirteen skills provide support in the performance of activities by explaining them step by step (dressing, brushing teeth, using the stoves in the kitchen, using the mobile phone), providing Alzheimer and depression screening tools based on standardised public assessment tests, giving reminders about their diet, medications and the activities they should do everyday before going to bed and a game to elicit brain stimulation.

3 Dressing Activity

Able-bodied and able-minded people usually do not notice how complex it is to get dressed. More than 80% of caregivers (professionals or relatives) help people with dementia with ADLs; in particular, 61% help with dressing, 52% with feeding, 37% with bathing, 34% with toileting and 26% with continence care [2].

The works available in literature describing technologies that support the activity of dressing for the elderly or, more specifically, for people with dementia can be classified into three groups. Some works aim at providing recommendations before getting dressed, others analyse the activity while it is being performed, and others afterwards, as the person leaves the house.

Dressing Evaluation During the Activity. The work proposed by Kalimeri et al. [8] is one of the first approaches to recognise failures during dressing and, in particular, what garments are worn and in which order. Two different probabilistic approaches have been implemented to analyse the sparse, noisy RFID readings obtained by the RFID readers in the environment and tags on clothes. The first one uses a Layered Hidden Markov Model (LHMM) and follows dressing order to identify possible priority mistakes. The other probabilistic model is a Bayesian network. Antennas are in the cabin and clothes are tagged with two tags on the shoulders and one on the back. The possible states for the network nodes are: "put on"/ "not put on" and "right"/ "left side detected". These are also the types of mistakes. LHHM shows higher accuracy results and needs less effort for tagging objects, but is more precise in detecting if a garment is actually worn and not just held.

The system AID-ME developed by Matic et al. [10] integrates RFID readers and computer vision to recognise mistakes while the person is dressing. Firstly, they identify the most common types of mistakes among people with dementia:

Clothes in incorrect order, such as a t-shirt over a jacket; Clothes worn only partially, for example, not closing a zip; Clothes worn inside out; Too many clothes are worn and not appropriate for outside weather. They use three RFID antennas placed behind three booth walls; upper garments are tagged on the shoulders and on the back. Exploiting computer vision techniques, K-means clustering for colors and spatial analysis have been performed to identify if clothes were worn only partially. When combined together, the technologies proved to be able to predict to some extent three of the aforementioned mistakes.

Dressing failures were detected using computer vision from a single camera in Ruiz et al. [17]; the video was analysed using a newly developed temporal-relational visual grammar. The following types of mistakes are considered: 1) Temporal: the order in which garments are worn was wrong; 2) Relational: the relation between garment and body is wrong, e.g., jacket backwards; 3) Spatial: the garment is only partially worn. Temporal failures were correctly identified, whereas spatial and relational ones were more difficult. Nonetheless, the precision of the system was 91% in an 11-subjects trial.

Another proposed solution belonges to the smart wearables field: Chu et al. [6] developed the Autonomous Clothing Perception that combines RGB-D sensor and a series of smart sensors in clothes to detect if a person is dressing correctly. Using embedded sensors instead of computer vision has the advantage not to be limited by the colors of the garment. The case of a collared t-shirt with three buttons was implemented: capacitive sensors in the form of a fiber were sewn on the back and in the sleeves of a t-shirt, an IR-led was put in the front of the clothing item and contact switches in the buttons. An IR Camera (Kinect) was placed in front of the person to detect the IR led. Depending on the closed buttons and visible LEDs, the possible states for garments could either be: 1) Worn correctly; 2) Partially; 3) Backwards; 4) Inside out. Proof-of-concept testing showed that all four states could be correctly identified.

Dressing Evaluation During Activity and Feedback. A capability study for a personalised support for dressing in people with dementia, called DRESS, was developed by Burleson et al. [5]. It is based on an image recognition system that tracks the fiducial markers (similar to barcodes) on the clothes to determine their position, type, and orientation while the person is dressing. In case of mistakes, a recorded audio prompt with the caregiver's voice notes the nature of the mistake and gives indications for recovery actions; whereas, in case of correct steps, the audio is positive and encouraging. In case the person freezes while dressing, an alert is sent to the caregiver. The strength of the system is the capability to provide monitoring, identification of correct and wrong steps, feedback and also rectification of the mistake during activity performance. As mentioned, the system is equipped with many other sensors: motion sensor to understand if person is close to wardrobe, RFID reader in drawer to detect if clothes are moved, skin conductor sensor to sense physiological changes (in particular stress), ps3 eye camera, door sensor for detecting wardrobe door opening/closing. The prompts are provided through an iPod: video showed red/-green lights, audio played recorder's voice or a song to lower stress level. Results are encouraging: there were 10 misclassifications out of 22 shirt tests and 5 out of 22 for pants.

Dressing Evaluation After the Activity. Orr et al. [14] proposed a multi-agent approach to assist with dressing: the system offers a recommendation to the person leaving the house about how they should be wearing according to outside temperature. However, only one garment is considered, i.e. the coat. The Decision agent receives information from the Door (opening and closing events), from Coat (if it was worn or not by the person) and from the Temperature agent (outside temperature) and from these three pieces of information would tell the person if they should be wearing a coat because it is cold or take it off because it is hot. The system has only been simulated.

Dressing Recommendation Before the Activity. Finally, some proposals focus on recommending the correct garments. Among the technologies that have been investigated for monitoring and supporting dressing, social robots have been considered as well. In [21], an autonomous clothing recommendation system is used by the social robot Leia to recommend people a specific outfit, based on activity and personal experiences. More specifically, the considered variables are: outside weather, user's preferences, plans for the day, if such plans are outside or inside, and if they require athletic apparel. Proposed outfits can be accepted or partially/totally rejected, and the recommendation algorithm (based on multinomial logistic regression) would learn from the given feedback.

In Schaad et al. [18], the authors developed an intelligent wardrobe that generates clothing suggestions based on sensor data from the apartment, like inside temperature (using a Netatmo station), weather forecast, and today's events (from Google Calendar). Recommendations are shown on a tablet display on the wardrobe, together with all relevant information about the day. To facilitate the search, garments are marked on the tablet and in the closet with the same colour. One downside of the system is that it needs the user to turn it on and interact with the GUI.

4 Ethical Considerations

An important aspect of using technology for surveillance of people with dementia (or analogously intellectual disabilities) are the ethical concerns of such practices. Niemeijer et al. [13] consider the case of an institution. Usually the carer or institution point of view is examined (they focus on efficacy of the measures, security and lowered impact on carer), but "resident/person concerns" may clash with it. In fact, the right to independence and self-control of the person is limited by the duty to provide care and security of the personnel. A person with dementia may have limitations in cognitive capabilites, that could provoke dangerous situations to them or others; however, they should be respected as adults, with a narrower set of skills available [13]. Moreover, technology should be a support, not a substitute to personal care and contact with other people. Interactions with carers are for many patients the main social activity of the day and its reduction could cause social isolation. Also, care institutions should use technology wisely and not to cut personnel as a way to cut costs, or as an excuse not to train it properly, or to give a false sense of security [13].

5 Discussion and Conclusions

Dressing is a complex basic activity of daily living (BADL) that is particularly challenging for people suffering from dementia. Most studies that propose solutions that support this activity focus only on a single aspect at a time: giving a recommendation before getting dressed, analysing as the activity was being performed, or analysing afterwards, when the person left the house. An exception is represented by Burleson et al. [5] who implemented a multi-purpose system that monitors the activity and also gave context-aware feedback and guidance to the person in order to rectify their mistakes. The manifold of sensors and technologies of such solution was both its strength, since it could identify position and actions of the user in every moment and communicate with them (through colors, audio, music etc.), but also its weakness because of the complexity of deployment in a real-world environment. Using only computer vision for the analysis seems to be the least invasive technology, although the elaboration algorithm shows limitations (for example, people have to be manually selected). Combining other sensors (RFID tags in clothes or using specific barcodes for recognition) enables better identification. Works that focus on giving recommendations require some interaction from the user with the system, for example using a tablet, and there is no further verification that the advice has been actually followed.

The current state of the art on supporting the dressing activity in people with dementia presents still many issues. Many solutions are quite complex to be adopted in practice and focus only on particular aspects of the dressing activity. Some proposals provide interesting ideas, but studies on their feasibility are still preliminary.

Besides, when considering the possible applications of assistive technology for older adults, it is necessary to take into consideration that although some aspects or problems may be easily compensated by intelligent agents that can retrieve information that is not currently available to the user (for example, because they may not remember what they wore the previous days, or in which order clothes should be worn), other aspects still require human intervention. For example, if a person has physical limitations in reaching or lifting objects, standing and freely moving the limbs in order to wear garments, they will need the support of a caregiver. Moreover, configuration, deployment and maintenance of devices often require the presence of another person. One last important topic that should be considered is how the automation of everyday tasks is perceived by the users: older adults that live alone and/or have emotional or psychological disturbances, such as depression, might feel alienated and lonely if the amount of human interaction decreases because it is replaced with automatic devices.

However, given the problem of ageing population and considering that more than 80% of dementia patients need help from caregivers to perform everyday ADLs where dressing has a prominent place, we believe that further proposals and investigations in this field are needed to better understand the issues and targets that can be actually addressed with ICT solutions.

References

1. Dementia: a nice-scie guideline on supporting people with dementia and their carers in health and social care. british psychological society. https://www.ncbi.nlm.nih.gov/books/NBK55480/
2. e-Connected Family Caregiver: Bringing Caregiving into the 21st Century. https://www.caregiving.org/wp-content/uploads/2020/05/FINAL_eConnected_Family_Caregiver_Study_Jan-2011.pdf (2011), (accessed January 11 2021)
3. ICD Dementia. https://www.icd10data.com/ICD10CM/Codes/F01-F99/F01-F09/F03-/F03 (2021), (accessed October 14 2021)
4. Who Dementia. https://www.who.int/news-room/fact-sheets/detail/dementia (2021), (accessed October 14 2021)
5. Burleson, W., Lozano, C., Ravishankar, V., Lee, J., Mahoney, D., et al.: An assistive technology system that provides personalized dressing support for people living with dementia: capability study. JMIR Med. Inform. **6**(2), e5587 (2018)
6. Chu, M., Sun, Y.C., Ashraf, A., Alves, S.F., Nejat, G., Naguib, H.E.: Making dressing easier: Smart clothes to help with putting clothes on correctly. In: 2019 IEEE International Conference on Systems, Man and Cybernetics, SMC, pp. 3981–3986. IEEE (2019)
7. Graf, C.: The lawton instrumental activities of daily living (iadl) scale. Gerontologist **9**(3), 179–186 (2009)
8. Kalimeri, K., Matic, A., Cappelletti, A.: Rfid: recognizing failures in dressing activity. In: 2010 4th International Conference on Pervasive Computing Technologies for Healthcare, pp. 1–4. IEEE (2010)
9. Katz, S.: Assessing self-maintenance: activities of daily living, mobility, and instrumental activities of daily living. J. Am. Geriatr. Soc. **31**(12), 721–727 (1983)
10. Matic, A., Mehta, P., Rehg, J.M., Osmani, V., Mayora, O.: Aid-me: automatic identification of dressing failures through monitoring of patients and activity evaluation. In: 2010 4th International Conference on Pervasive Computing Technologies for Healthcare, pp. 1–8. IEEE (2010)
11. Mihailidis, A., Carmichael, B., Boger, J.: The use of computer vision in an intelligent environment to support aging-in-place, safety, and independence in the home. IEEE Trans. Inf Technol. Biomed. **8**(3), 238–247 (2004)
12. Mynatt, E.D., Melenhorst, A.S., Fisk, A.D., Rogers, W.A.: Aware technologies for aging in place: understanding user needs and attitudes. IEEE Pervasive Comput. **3**(2), 36–41 (2004)
13. Niemeijer, A.R., Frederiks, B.J., Riphagen, I.I., Legemaate, J., Eefsting, J.A., Hertogh, C.M.: Ethical and practical concerns of surveillance technologies in residential care for people with dementia or intellectual disabilities: an overview of the literature. Int. Psychogeriatr. **22**(7), 1129–1142 (2010)
14. Orr, C., Nugent, C., Wang, H., Zheng, H.: A Multi-agent approach to assist with dressing in a smart environment. In: Giokas, K., Bokor, L., Hopfgartner, F. (eds.) eHealth 360°. LNICST, vol. 181, pp. 220–223. Springer, Cham (2017). https://doi.org/10.1007/978-3-319-49655-9_29

15. Prizer, L.P., Zimmerman, S.: Progressive support for activities of daily living for persons living with dementia. The Gerontologist **58**(suppl_1), S74–S87 (2018)
16. Reis, A., et al.: Using intelligent personal assistants to assist the elderlies an evaluation of amazon alexa, google assistant, microsoft cortana, and apple siri. In: 2018 2nd International Conference on Technology and Innovation in Sports, Health and Wellbeing, TISHW, pp. 1–5. IEEE (2018)
17. Ruiz, E., Osmani, V., Sucar, L.E., Mayora, O.: Detecting dressing failures using temporal-relational visual grammars. J. Ambient. Intell. Humaniz. Comput. **10**(7), 2757–2770 (2019)
18. Schaad, P., Basler, S., Medini, M., Wissler, I., Bürkle, T., Lehmann, M.: «The intelligent wardrobe». Nursing Inf. 225, 213–217 (2016)
19. Stikic, M., Huynh, T., Van Laerhoven, K., Schiele, B.: Adl recognition based on the combination of rfid and accelerometer sensing. In: 2008 Second International Conference on Pervasive Computing Technologies for Healthcare, pp. 258–263. IEEE (2008)
20. Tan, K., Sekhar, K., Wong, J., Holgado, J., Ameer, M., Vesonder, G.: Alexa eldercare toolbox: A smarthome solution for the elderly. In: 2020 11th IEEE Annual Ubiquitous Computing, Electronics & Mobile Communication Conference, UEMCON, pp. 0806–0812. IEEE (2020)
21. Woiceshyn, L., Wang, Y., Nejat, G., Benhabib, B.: Personalized clothing recommendation by a social robot. In: 2017 IEEE International Symposium on Robotics and Intelligent Sensors, IRIS, pp. 179–185. IEEE (2017)
22. Wu, J., Osuntogun, A., Choudhury, T., Philipose, M., Rehg, J.M.: A scalable approach to activity recognition based on object use. In: 2007 IEEE 11th International Conference on Computer Vision, pp. 1–8. IEEE (2007)

Testing an Augmented Reality Learning App for People with Learning Difficulties in Vocational Training in Home Economics – Central Results of the Project LernBAR (Learning Based on Augmented Reality)

Laura Wuttke(✉), Christian Bühler, Anna Katharina Klug, and Yvonne Söffgen

Department of Rehabilitation Sciences, Research Unit of Rehabilitation Technology, TU Dortmund University, Emil-Figge-Str. 50, 44227 Dortmund, Germany
laura.wuttke@tu-dortmund.de

Abstract. This paper presents the main work and results of the completed R&D-project LernBAR (Learning based on Augmented Reality). The project ran from June 2018 to January 2022 and aimed to develop a digital learning assistance environment for people with cognitive disabilities in vocational training in the field of home economics. Therefor an online learning platform with embedded AR-learning stations was developed and evaluated with the target group. In the paper the qualitative and quantitative results of the formative evaluation of the project are presented and discussed, as well as the main results of an external evaluation.

Keywords: Augmented Reality · Vocational training · Digital media · Learning difficulties · Education · Home economics

1 Introduction

Vocational and educational training is a key factor for participating in working life. Especially for people with disabilities, who are not participating in the regular labour market to the same extend as people without disabilities do, a vocational training that brings out their individual educational potential is extremely important. The use of digital media in vocational training has the potential to enable people with disabilities to participate and qualify more independently, since it allows learning independent of time, place and without the need to have an instructor nearby. Also digital media can link learning and working, to promote work process-oriented learning. The possibility to prepare learning content in different ways (e.g., video, text, audio, etc.) has a great value for accessibility [1, 2].

K. Miesenberger et al. (Eds.): ICCHP-AATE 2022, LNCS 13342, pp. 176–182, 2022.
https://doi.org/10.1007/978-3-031-08645-8_21

A new educational technology innovation is the use of augmented reality (AR). AR is a media-supported extension of the real environment and presents additional information in the user's field of vision [3]. AR enables quick access to information, at the time needed, at the place needed, which makes it particularly attractive for use in a professional context. AR elements can be images, graphics and videos.

The project focuses on renewing the vocational training in home economic services with the use of AR and digital media. Although home economic services are gaining importance due to demographic change and the increasing employment of women, the number of new training contracts in this field has fallen by more than half over the course of the last decade [4]. At the same time home economics is an important sector in the training of people with disabilities [5]. In conclusion, there is a need for modernisation and digitalisation of the field, since digitalisation opens up opportunities for participation in education and, at the same time, basic qualifications can be acquired through the use of digital media. Therefor three institutions that offer vocational training in this field were partners in the project: Josefsheim Bigge gGmbH, Hannoversche Werkstätten gGmbH, Lebenshilfe Erfurt gGmbH.

The project takes up these challenges and supports the trainees through the development of a work process-oriented, inclusive e-learning offer both in the context of their daily work (AR application) and in preparation for their exams (Moodle e-learning platform). The AR-learning content is presented in a specially developed application via mixed reality data glasses from Microsoft (Hololens) [6] as well as mobile devices, such as tablets or smartphones, with an Android operating system. For the in-depth learning content the platform Moodle is used in the project to provide e-learning classes. Overall a total of 30 AR learning scenarios (10 per project partner) were developed. Learning contents are offered in various formats including picture galleries, videos and texts, as well as an AR template. The AR template is an image that can be displayed through the Hololens or through the tablet's camera as an extension of the real environment. The template image enables a direct comparison of the independently implemented task with a desired result.

The offer is targeted at participants from workshops for people with disabilities as well as trainers, so project goals were formulated and evaluated for both of these target groups. The project aimed to develop a practical, low-threshold offer for people with learning difficulties and therefor explore AR as a learning method in this context. Also strengthening digital competences of trainers was an important goal in the project. Therefor a media competence training was offered, as well as a low-threshold learning management system, so that trainers do not need programming skills to create AR learning contents themselves. This concept promotes the sustainability of the project.

In the following the methods and selected results of the project evaluation are presented and discussed, so it can be determined to what extend the project aims were achieved. The focus will be on the AR application since one main goal of the project was to evaluate the use of AR learning content in this context.

2 Methods

An essential part of the project was the formative evaluation using qualitative and quantitative methods. The evaluation was used to indicate the usability and acceptance of the digital learning offerings developed in the project.

The developed learning scenarios were successively tested at the partners' sites either by research personnel from TU Dortmund University or in the later course of the project by the partners themselves. The focus of the evaluation was on the aspects of usability and acceptance of the teaching and learning materials developed in LernBAR. The participants were recruited by the trainers of the project partners and the learning scenarios were tested by two to three participants each. The participants were informed in advance in detail about the procedure of the evaluation. Care was taken to ensure that everything was understood and that the trainees were aware of the voluntary nature of their participation. Data protection is ensured by anonymizing the answers. Due to the participatory approach of the project, the users were involved in the project from the beginning.

Behavioral observation is an established method of usability testing, as it has been shown to be an effective means of identifying usability problems [7]. Therefor an open, passive participant observation was conducted. The learners were given a task-based walkthrough to guide them through the trial. In order to draw conclusions about the comprehensibility of the learning content, control questions were asked during the walkthroughs. Observations were noted using observation sheets, that were developed based on the project's research interests.

Due to the effects of Covid-19 pandemic visits to the partners' sites became impossible during the course of the project, so observation data could only be generated for five learning scenarios.

In addition, a survey was conducted to accompany the trial. A questionnaire consisting of three parts was used for the survey, which concentrated on socio-demographic data, curiosity and fear of new technologies and usability and acceptance of the learning offer. In the questionnaire self-generated items were used as well as established scales like the "Technology Usage Inventory" (TUI) according to Kothgassner, Felnhofer et al. (2013) [8] - an established scale for measuring technology acceptance - and the "System Usability Scale" (SUS) according to John Brooke (1995) for measuring usability [9]. In line with the objective of the tests, only the pre-version of the TUI, consisting of the subscales "Curiosity" and "Technology Anxiety", was used. The original items of the TUI and the SUS were adapted for the project purposes. Abstract wording was replaced to enhance learner understanding. For example the original item 5 of the SUS uses the wording "I found the various functions in this system were well integrated", whereas the LernBAR-Version reads: "I found the app worked well".

3 Results

Quantifiable observation data could be generated for five learning modules, where a total of 17 learners were observed by staff of TU Dortmund University. The learners were between 17 and 56 years old. 29.4% (N = 5) of the learners were observed interacting with the LernBAR app on the Hololens and 70.6% (N = 12) were observed testing the app on a tablet. The results are presented along the observation categories "navigation", "design" and "content".

100% (N = 5) of Hololens users were able to find the app on the desktop and the majority were also able to scan (80%, N = 4). Among tablet users, 81.8% (N = 9) found the app on the desktop. 83.3% (N = 10) recorded that the scanning process was fully applicable and 16.7% (N = 2) recorded that it was rather applicable.

Learner interactions were also observed for confidence in navigating the media and navigating within the media view. For navigating the media – both on Tablet and Hololens – only the top two categories (fully applicable and rather applicable) were recorded, with 83,3% (N = 10) of the tablet users being able to navigate without any problems. For navigating within the media view observers noted fully applicable for 80% of the Hololens users (N = 4) and 72% of the tablet users. Only for one tablet user the category rather not applicable was chosen.

Three items were used in the observation to assess the design of the LernBAR app. For 100% (N = 5) of the learners, it was recorded as "completely true" that they recognized the app by its icon; for learners who used the tablet, this was true for 75% (N = 9) of the learners. For three learners (25%) this was recorded as "rather true". A key design aspect to observe was whether learners recognized that the media icons were selectable. This was fully applicable for 100% (N = 5) of the Hololens users and 75% (N = 9) of the tablet users.

In addition to quantitative observation, free observation notes were also made and summarized along the observation items. Qualitative observation results also provide very valuable information regarding the navigation, design and content of the LernBAR app.

The qualitative observation results include more than N = 12 in the evaluation, as the teachers made use of the possibility to make free observations or to note them down after handing over the trials. Some of the qualitative results are shown in the following.

Observers noted, that the option to operate the Hololens via voice control, was often not recognized by the learners. However using the voice control was in some cases desired, since the gesture control could lead to accidents like closing the entire app. All in all a preference for voice control was noted.

Also the scanning of the QR codes was more difficult on the tablet than on the Hololens since protective cover or incorrect handling complicated the process. Also the navigation between media and the function of the arrow buttons was sometimes not recognized. As for the learning content the observers noted some difficulties in understanding for example unfamiliar terms or contents that were presented in an abstract way. Also some comments were made about the design of the learning content, for example that subtitles should be shown longer. On the other hand speed of speech in the videos was praised.

Furthermore there are the results of the accompanying survey, of which an excerpt will be presented in the following. The results refer to 26/30 of the learning scenarios created. Two of the learning scenarios were used for pre-testing the learning materials, whereas another two scenarios could not be tested during the project period. A total of 68 learners took part in the trials. 77.9% (N = 53) of the participants were female, 22.1% (N = 5) male. The youngest participant was 16 years old, the oldest participant was 58 years old. A majority of the learners reported difficulties with thinking, learning or understanding, followed by difficulties with the mind, feelings and moods.

As the AR app was tested with both the Hololens and the tablet during the trials, the following results are reported separately according to the respective device. 21.2% (N = 12) of the learners used the LernBAR app with the Hololens, 78.9% (N = 45) of the learners tested the LernBAR app with the tablet. The app was assessed in terms of its user interface and its operation using a total of eight different items. Table 1 shows the learners' responses to selected items.

Table 1. Test results for the LernBAR app.

Item	Do not agree		Neither		Agree	
	Hololens	Tablet	Hololens	Tablet	Hololens	Tablet
Scanning was easy	1 9,1%	0 0,0%	5 45,5%	5 12,2%	5 45,5%	36 87,8%
You can see immediately what you can do in the app	0 0,0%	1 2,2%	7 58,3%	12 26,7%	5 41,7%	32 71,1%
I recognised what the symbols on the buttons mean	0 0,0%	0 0,0%	2 16,7%	12 26,7%	10 83,3%	33 73,3%
I could tap the buttons well	4 33,3%	2 4,4%	7 58,3%	6 13,3%	1 8,3%	37 82,2%
I realised how long the videos/galleries/texts are	2 16,7%	1 2,2%	3 25,0%	18 40,0%	7 58,3%	26 57,8%
I am tired after using the app	7 63,6%	34 75,6%	0 0,0%	8 17,8%	4 36,4%	3 6,7%
I knew how to close the app	1 9,1%	3 6,7%	4 36,4%	8 17,8%	6 54,5%	34 75,6%
Using the app was fun	0 0,0%	0 0,0%	0 0,0%	12 26,7%	10 100%	33 73,3%

The data analysis shows that both the user interface and the operation of the LernBAR app are assessed positively by the majority of the learners.

Learners were also surveyed about the learning contents and helpfulness of the app. The overall opinion to the statements "App is helpful for my work" and "App is helpful for my exam" are equally positive. Almost 70% of the tablet users agreed with both statements. Among the Hololens users, about 60% of the learners agreed with these statements (see Fig. 1).

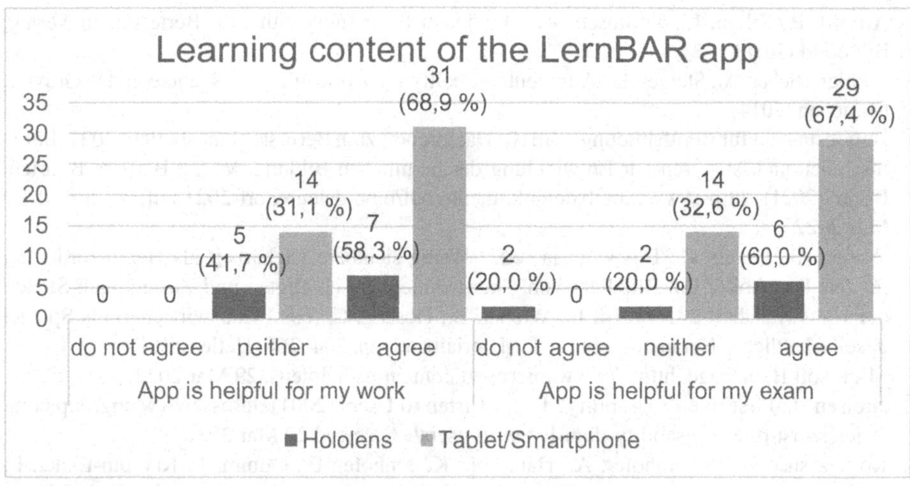

Fig. 1. Helpfulness of learning content.

4 Conclusions

In summary, the LernBAR offer was accepted by the learners and they perceived it as useful. This is of particular relevance with regard to further use of the developed teaching and learning materials. Some navigation problems that were identified could be addressed and strategies were developed to remedy them. Basically, it can be assumed that neither the design nor the operation lead to long-term usability problems. Rather, it must be taken into account that the trial was also the learners' first contact with the LernBAR app. There was no prior instruction in the structure of the learning offer. For this reason alone, it can be assumed that isolated difficulties will occur. In the future, this could be remedied by providing learners with instruction in the structure. Furthermore, the reported usability problems of the learners do not seem to diminish the acceptance of the offer. This can be proven by the statements and the survey data. In this respect, it can be assumed that the learners perceive a high level of benefit. The use of the learning offer goes hand in hand with added value for the learners.

Despite the positive findings, there are also limitations that have to be addressed. For example it is difficult to make a statement about the long-term use of the system or the learning contents. A sustainable use can only be ensured by the project partners of the practical institutions. Although media trainings and e-learning offers were developed to improve media competence of the trainers it cannot be ensured that this was sufficient enough to enable and motivate the trainers to use the technology and also create new learning content themselves to expand LernBAR.

References

1. Schmid, U., Goertz, L., Behrens, J.: Monitor Digitale Bildung. Berufliche Ausbildung im digitalen Zeitalter. Bertelsmann Stiftung (2016)

2. Arnold, P., Kilian, L., Thillosen, A.: Handbuch E-Learning, 5th edn. Bertelsmann Verlag, Bielefeld (2018)
3. Mehler-Bicher, A., Steiger, L.: Augmented Reality – Theorie und Praxis, 2nd edn. De Gruyter, München (2014)
4. Bundesinstitut für Berufsbildung [BiBB]: Datenreport zum Berufsbildungsbericht 2021. Informationen und Analysen zur Entwicklung der beruflichen Bildung. Verlag Barbara Budrich, Bonn (2021). https://www.bibb.de/dokumente/pdf/bibb-datenreport-2021.pdf. Accessed 29 Mar 2022
5. Wiener, B., Gotter, C.: Das kann ja Jede? Wenig sichtbare Facharbeit als Herausforderung für das Berufsbild. Ein Blitzlicht von Unternehmen, Beschäftigten und Zuständigen Stellen der Hauswirtschaft 2013/2014. In: Wiener, B., Hosang, C. (eds.) Hauswirtschaft als Spiegel gesellschaftlicher Herausforderungen. Materialband, pp. 204–268. Halle (2014)
6. Microsoft Homepage. https://www.microsoft.com/en-us/hololens. 29 Mar 2022
7. Nielsen, J.: First rule of Usability? Don't Listen to Users (2001). https://www.nngroup.com/articles/first-rule-of-usability-dont-listen-to-users/. Accessed 29 Mar 2022
8. Kothgassner, O.D., Felnhofer, A., Hauk, N., Kastenhofer, E., Gomm, J., Kryspin-Exner, I.: Technology Usage Inventory (TUI): Manual (2013). https://www.ffg.at/sites/default/files/allgemeine_downloads/thematische%20programme/programmdokumente/tui_manual.pdf. Accessed 29 Mar 2022
9. Brooke, J.: SUS: a quick and dirty usability scale. Usability Eval. Ind. **189** (1995). https://www.researchgate.net/publication/228593520_SUS_A_quick_and_dirty_usability_scale. Accessed 29 Mar 2022

Working from Home in the COVID-19 Pandemic - Which Technological and Social Factors Influence the Working Conditions and Job Satisfaction of People with Disabilities?

Susanne Dirks([✉]) and Frederike Kurth

TU Dortmund University, Emil-Figge-St. 50, 44227 Dortmund, Germany
susanne.dirks@tu-dortmund.de

Abstract. Objective: The project aims to determine the technological and social factors, which promote or hinder work success and job satisfaction of people with disabilities in home office situations.

Methods: A mixed-methods approach (online survey and expert interviews) with 13 participants with disabilities from different fields of university work was chosen.

Results: People with disabilities face significantly greater challenges in home office work than people without disabilities; lack of ergonomic equipment, non-accessible technologies, and difficulties in communicating and interacting with colleagues and superiors result in negative impacts on work processes and job satisfaction.

Conclusion: The outcomes of the presented research are a first approach to survey and evaluate the conditions and effects of home office work for people with disabilities. Further studies are needed to explore different areas of work and different types of disabilities in greater depth.

Keywords: Covid-19 pandemic · Home office · People with disabilities · Accessibility · Job satisfaction

1 Introduction

Professional work is an important part of social life. Job satisfaction and job achievements are important for companies as well as for the individual. The work environment and work conditions play a major role in this [1, 2]. Since the turn of the millennium, the number of employees making use of flexible working arrangements has steadily increased. Important preconditions for this were the increasing digitization of all working areas and the advances in information and communication technology (ICT). This has helped to make work organization more flexible in terms of time and place [3]. It has also facilitated interconnectivity by enabling workers to interact digitally with colleagues, managers, and other organizations [4].

In March 2020, due to the Covid-19 pandemic and the contact restrictions that came with it, many workplaces shifted to working in home office. Thus, many work

K. Miesenberger et al. (Eds.): ICCHP-AAATE 2022, LNCS 13342, pp. 183–191, 2022.
https://doi.org/10.1007/978-3-031-08645-8_22

processes conducted from home. The resulting changes in many work areas bring both challenges and new opportunities. There are already many studies on the benefits and disadvantages of telework and work-at-home on productivity and job satisfaction in general. The following aspects are often cited as advantages: greater autonomy, better work-life balance, higher productivity and reduced commuting times. However, the longer working hours, the overlapping of work and home life, and increased intensity of work are perceived as stressful [5, 6]. When an employee is predominantly or exclusively teleworking, there is often insufficient support from the company and the opportunity for career advancement is reduced [7].

Much less research has been done so far on how working from home affects the productivity and job satisfaction of people with disabilities (PWD). For PWD participation in work processes is often hampered by various types of technical and organizational barriers. The shift from the familiar accessible work environment to the private home office resulting from COVID-19 related restrictions has brought some extra challenges for this group of people [8].

The presented study examines the success factors and challenges for PWD in home offices, taking employees at a German university as an example. The research aimed to find out which technological and social factors influence the job satisfaction and the quality of work of PWD, to further investigate already known influencing factors from general research and to generate new insights and ideas for the improvement of working conditions in home environments for PDW.

2 Methods

To answer the research question, a mixed-method study was conducted. The sample of the survey consisted of employees of TU Dortmund University from different fields of work. The university as a governmental employer with many diverse workplaces provides an interesting and comprehensive research setting. In addition to research and teaching, university work involves activities from different service and administrative sectors, which require a higher level of education and offer good conditions for working at home. Due to the obligatory closure during the COVID-19 pandemic, TU Dortmund University provided various help offers, guidelines and software licenses, thus the prerequisites for home office work were guaranteed.

As the main interest of the study was to capture the general situation for employees with a disability, participants with different types of disabilities were included. The participants were contacted via the Disabled Persons' Association of TU Dortmund University and joined the study based on their personal motivation. A total of 13 people with physical disabilities, hearing impairments, visual impairments and mental disabilities participated in the study.

The participants worked in different fields of university work: research, accounting, administration, and secretary offices. 11 of the participants were working from home since spring 2020. Eight of the participants worked permanently in their home offices, the remaining three occasionally switched to their regular working environment. One person had been working from home for two years and six participants had already worked part-time at home before the pandemic. Table 1 shows an overview of the main demographic data of the participants. Participant 6 did not provide his/her personal data but completed the survey in all other aspects. Therefore, the data was also included in the evaluation.

Table 1. Demographic data of the participants.

ID	Gender	Age	Type of disability	Profession	h/week
1	M	28–55	Physical, visual	Computer Scientist	>35
2	M	28–55	Physical	Research Assistant	13–35
3	M	28–55	Visual	Research Assistant	>35
4	W	>55	Physical, Hearing	Accountant	>35
5	W	28–55	Physical	Administrative Employee	13–35
7	W	>55	Physical	Clerk	>35
8	W	>55	Physical, visual	Research Assistant	13–35
9	W	28–55	Physical	Clerk	>35
10	W	28–55	Mental	Secretary	13–35
11	W	28–55	Physical, hearing	Computer Scientist	>35
12	W	>55	Hearing	Research Assistant	>35
13	W	28–55	Physical	Research Assistant	>35

In the first phase of the project a survey was conducted to get an overview of the general situation of PWD in home working conditions. The questionnaire contained 41 questions organized in eight subgroups: (1) workplace setup, (2) ergonomics and accessibility, (3) changes in working style, (4) collaboration and communication, (5) effects due to Covid-19, (6) overall evaluation of home office, (7) demographic data, and (8) other. The questionnaire contained both open and closed questions.

The survey results were evaluated using a descriptive analysis approach [9]. For this purpose, the absolute and relative frequencies were calculated, and the respective results were summarized question by question. For the question on improvement priorities, the median was also determined to establish which issues most urgently need change or improvement.

After the initial analysis of the results of the questionnaire, it became apparent that some aspects of the survey needed to be examined in greater detail to get more precise results. For this, the Expert Interview method was chosen. In general, it is assumed that expert knowledge can be detached to some extent from the individual perspective. However, it needs to clear that expert knowledge is not generalizable in the same way as objective assessments [10]. The thematic focus of the interviews was on team collaboration and team communication, as this was the highest priority identified in the survey. The interviews further addressed the impact of working conditions on job satisfaction and the development of potential solutions. The interviews were conducted via zoom, recorded, and subsequently transcribed [11]. In addition, the transcripts receive a short case summary to be able to distinguish the interviews [12].

3 Results

In the following sections, the most important results of the survey and the interviews are summarized and explained.

3.1 Workplace Setup

Regarding the basic technical and technological equipment, the respondents were largely satisfied. The majority could either use existing equipment (computers, laptops, webcam, keyboard, and mouse) or equipment provided by the employer. One person received financial support for the purchase of new equipment from the Disabled Persons' Association of TU Dortmund University. In this case, the process was experienced as very time-consuming and complicated. However, most participants (9 out of 13) stated that further equipment is needed for optimal working conditions, e.g., larger screens, better headsets, height-adjustable desks, and further assistive technologies.

3.2 Ergonomics and Accessibility

The questions on accessibility were divided into spatial and technical accessibility. The necessary legroom under the table and corresponding movement areas were available in the home office for almost all participants. However, changing working positions was severely restricted because only a few people have height-adjustable desks in their home offices.

Almost all software programs used in daily work were accessible with the use of assistive technologies. Some people considered Skype, WebEx, Cisco Jabber, Confluence, Moodle, and the VPN client to be difficult or inaccessible. Respondents with sensory disabilities reported greater challenges in using communication software in specific situations. For example, the use of the chat function in a video conference was reported to be problematic for people with visual disabilities. The use of low-quality microphones or microphones integrated into webcams was experienced as challenging by participants with hearing disabilities. Some resources used for social exchange are inaccessible for visually impaired users. All these aspects lead to a higher level of strain or lack of participation opportunities for PWD in digital work environments. Table 2 shows the assessment of digital accessibility of the most used digital working environments. The numbers in the cells indicate the number of ratings for the respective level.

Table 2. Assessment of the accessibility of the most used working environments

	Accessible	Accessible with AT	Rather difficult	Not used
Skype	4	1	2	6
Zoom	9	1	1	2
WebEx	9	1	1	2
Cisco Jabber	4	0	1	8
Moodle	8	2	1	2
VPN-Client	10	0	2	1
Outlook Mail	12	1	0	0

3.3 Changes in Working Style

All respondents agreed that working from home brings greater flexibility and improves autonomy in performing work tasks. The flexibility created includes both flexibility of working days, working time and break times. In general, there were no problems with the timely completion of tasks even though 5 out of 13 people stated that actual processing times for individual tasks increased. Negative aspects included a disturbed work-life balance, reduced concentration, and a decrease in motivation. Four out of 13 respondents reported a decrease in motivation, work-life balance, and self-control. Five respondents noticed a decrease in their ability to focus over a longer period.

3.4 Communication and Collaboration

Communication and collaboration in the team under home office conditions was experienced as most changed and restricted. Communication with co-workers usually took place several times a week by telephone, email or video chat, personal contacts occurred only in exceptional cases. Communication with superiors took place via the same channels, but usually less frequently. The satisfaction with the cooperation in the team and the support provided by co-workers was assessed positively, the support provided by superiors was considered too low. Table 3 shows an overview of the 13 participants' satisfaction with the teamwork. The numbers in the cells indicate the number of ratings for the respective level.

Table 3. Participant's satisfaction with team cooperation

	Very much	Predominantly	Barely	Not at all
Receiving news	1	9	2	1
Team communication	0	10	2	1
Support from co-workers	3	7	3	0
Support from superiors	3	4	4	2

3.5 Effects Due to COVID-19

As expected, the pandemic-related alterations also had an impact on the working conditions and job satisfaction of PWDs. Contact restrictions were rated as the biggest additional constraint to working in a home office. All participants felt affected by this. One person remarked that she needs contact with people to keep from unlearning it and to have a distraction from herself from time to time. Other aggravating conditions were the close-down of leisure facilities (10/13), working with several people in home office (4/13), the lack of exercise in everyday life (2/13), the loss of accustomed routines (2/13) and domestic care for small children (1/13).

3.6 Overall Evaluation of Home Office

Based on the survey results, it can be concluded that PWD working at TU Dortmund University assess working in home office mainly positively. Eight of the 13 respondents were mostly satisfied with working from home and would welcome the opportunity to work from home even after the pandemic. Three of the participants who were hardly or not at all satisfied with working from home would not want to work from home for a longer period. In one case, the transition to working from home was so unsatisfactory that the employment contract was terminated prematurely.

Above all, the increased flexibility and autonomy are rated as a major advantage. Additionally, barriers that occur in normal office environments, e.g., loud background noise or unwanted distractions, can be reduced in the home environment. However, even if the basic technical equipment is provided, there is a lack of ergonomic equipment in the home office. Communication and support, especially from superiors, deans, and other departments, is rated as inadequate and leads to frustration and strains in the workflow. Poor communication and support lead to a lack of problem-solving ability and more difficult work processes.

The highest priority for improvements of working conditions relates to communication and interaction with colleagues and superiors. In addition to work-related and planned formal communication, informal communication in the digital space should also be improved to share experiences, to strengthen motivation, and to prevent the feeling of isolation. Improvements in software and programs, technical equipment, ergonomics and accessibility and the provision of furniture follow in descending order of priority. Table 4 shows the evaluation of the importance of the different improvement options.

3.7 Interview Results

The aim of the interviews in the second phase of the project focused on the difficulties encountered in cooperation and communication with co-workers and supervisors. A subgroup of five people from the survey respondents was interviewed. All interviewees had expressed interest in a follow-up conversation at the end of the survey. The conditions and regularity of working at home varied greatly among the interview participants. Some have been working exclusively from home since March 2020. Three of the interviewees were able to work in the office again soon after vaccinations. They worked in agreement

Table 4. Evaluation of the importance of the improvement options

	Rating (5 high – 1 low)
Communication and cooperation	5
Software and Programs	4
Technical equipment	4–3
Ergonomics and Accessibility	3
Furniture	1

with their colleagues and came to the office as needed, for example to check the mail. This was particularly important for the participant with mental health problems.

Digital collaboration and communication from home took place via Zoom and email for all participants. WhatsApp was also used and, depending on the team, additional programs such as Skype, Teams and Jabber were used for communication. All participants felt that working from home reduced interpersonal contact with their team members. For three participants, this was counteracted with the help of additional, informal online meetings. Satisfactory communication with superiors, as already seen in the questionnaires, was rather rare. It was more difficult to reach them for formal consultations and the informal exchange that usually took place in the corridors and at the coffee machines was missing.

Working from office resulted for all participants in a significant decrease in interpersonal contacts, which has even decreased over time. The limited personal exchange due to the absence of canteen and coffee conversations also led to limited job satisfaction. Online communication brought additional challenges, especially for people with hearing and visual disabilities, due to limited accessibility of the software and insufficient use of headsets, microphones, and cameras.

Strong communication and cooperation within the team as well as good technical equipment have a great influence on job satisfaction. All interviewees stated that a high degree of formal and interpersonal communication and cooperation increases well-being, job satisfaction and motivation. This includes not only communication per se, but also the attention and respect from co-workers and supervisors to the challenges that PWD face when working from home.

4 Conclusions

The data collection of the presented study provided important insights to the factors influencing productivity and job satisfaction of PWD when working from home. The following factors were identified as highly influencing: 1) ergonomic furniture, 2) appropriate audio and video transmission in video conferences, 3) use of appropriate and well-adjusted technology among all communication partners, 4) accessibility of digital resources, 5) appropriate selection of software programs, 6) regular exchange within the team and with superiors, 7) opportunities for professional and interpersonal communication, 8) mutual understanding and respect, and 9) balance between independence and commitment in the team. As other research not specifically related to PWD has also shown, home office working conditions in the context of the COVID-19 pandemic bring significant social challenges in addition to technical difficulties [13, 14]. For PWD, it seems to be particularly important that communication and cooperation with colleagues and superiors is continuous, supportive, and appreciative.

The presented research outcomes are a first approach to evaluate working conditions in home office for PWD on a rather small scale. Due to the increasing transfer of work processes to the home office and the very individual conditions and needs of PWD, studies of this kind need to be conducted with more participants. Although there are many fundamental factors that influence home office work regardless of an existing disability, it is important to explore different areas of work and different types of disabilities in a more detailed way. For an in-depth understanding of the long-term effects of home office work, it is further necessary to examine the development of work performance and job satisfaction in home office conditions over a longer period.

References

1. Brenke, K.: Home Office: Möglichkeiten werden bei weitem nicht ausgeschöpft. DIW Wochenbericht **5**(2016), 95–105 (2016)
2. Grunau, P., Ruf, K., Steffes, S., Dr. Wolter, S.: Homeoffice bietet Vorteile, hat aber auch Tücken. IAB Kurzbericht (November 2019)
3. European Commission, Employment, and social developments in Europe: Annual review. Publications Office of the European Union, Luxembourg (2018)
4. Eurofound, Telework and ICT-based mobile work: Flexible working in the digital age, new forms of employment series, Publications Office of the European Union, Luxembourg (2020)
5. Buomprisco, G., Ricci, S., Perri, R., De Sio, S.: Health and telework: new challenges after COVID-19 pandemic. Eur. J. Environ. Pub. Health **5**(2), em0073 (2021)
6. Mann, S., Holdswoth, L.: The psychological impact of teleworking: stress, emotions, and health. N. Technol. Work. Employ. **18**(3), 196–202 (2003)
7. Bloom, N., Liang, J., Roberts, J., Ying, Z.J.: Does working from home work? Evidence from a Chinese experiment. Q. J. Econ. **130**(1), 165–218 (2015)
8. Tang, J.: Understanding the telework experience of people with disabilities. Proc. ACM Hum. Comput. Interact. **5**(CSCW1), 1–27 (2021)
9. Döring, N., Bortz, J.: Forschungsmethoden und Evaluation in den Sozial und Humanwissenschaften (5. erweiterte Aufl.). Springer, Berlin (2016). https://doi.org/10.1007/978-3-642-41089-5
10. Helfferich, C.: Leitfaden- und Experteninterviews. In: Baur, N., Blasius, J. (eds.) Handbuch Methoden der empirischen Sozialforschung, pp. 559–574. Springer, Wiesbaden (2014). https://doi.org/10.1007/978-3-531-18939-0_39
11. Misoch, S.: Qualitative Interviews (2. erweiterte und aktualisierte Aufl.). Walter de Gruyter GmbH, Berlin (2019)
12. Kuckartz, U.: Qualitative Inhaltsanalyse. Methoden, Praxis, Computerunterstützung. 4. Auflage. Beltz Juventa, Weinheim; Basel (2018)

13. Franken, E., Bentley, T., Shafaei, A., Farr-Wharton, B., Onnis, L., Omari, M.: Forced flexibility and remote working: opportunities and challenges in the new normal. J. Manag. Organ. **27**(6), 1131–1149 (2021)
14. The impact of teleworking and digital work on workers and society. https://www.aceb.cat/images/The_impact_of_teleworking.pdf

Remote Working: A Way to Foster Greater Inclusion and Accessibility?

Stefano Federici[1], Giovanni Bifolchi[1(✉)], Maria Laura Mele[1], Marco Bracalenti[1], Maria Laura De Filippis[1], Simone Borsci[2], Giancarlo Gaudino[3], Massimo Amendola[3], Antonello Cocco[3], and Emilio Simonetti[4]

[1] Department of Philosophy, Social and Human Sciences, Education University of Perugia, Perugia, Italy
stefano.federici@unipg.it, gio.bifo@gmail.com
[2] Department of Learning, Data Analysis, and Technology – Cognition, Data and Education – CODE group, Faculty of BMS, University of Twente, Enschede, The Netherlands
[3] DGTCSI-ISCTI – Directorate General for Management and Information and Communications Technology, Superior Institute of Communication and Information Technologies, Ministry of Economic Development, Rome, Italy
{giancarlo.gaudino,massimo.amendola,antonello.cocco}@mise.gov.it
[4] Department of Public Service, Prime Minister's Office, Rome, Italy
e.simonetti@funzionepubblica.it

Abstract. The COVID-19 pandemic has brought several changes in everyday life, one of them being the application of Remote Working (RW). RW is the new way of working, thanks to this new modality all workers, with certain work requirements, were able to carry out their work from home without having to go to the office. Given the strict rules relating to lockdown, if this method had not been applied many people would not have been able to work and today many companies would probably be closed. But which advantages and disadvantages can RW have compared to classical work? Can it bring more inclusiveness and accessibility for every one or only for workers with specific requirements (for example, for workers that need to take care of family members with disabilities)? This paper attempts to answer these questions. The University of Perugia in collaboration with the Ministry of Economic Development has created the "Job-satisfying" project. In this project 24 participants were divided into two groups (home-space group and office-space group) and each of these had to complete some tasks and complete questionnaires. Generally, no significant difference emerged but some interesting results were encountered: those who took the experimentation from home, that have children, obtained higher scores relating to the sense of working autonomy, support from superiors and satisfaction of relationships at work. This data seems to argue that working from home can improve inclusiveness.

Keywords: Remote working · Smart working · Working from home · Inclusiveness · Accessibility

A. Mazzarini and I. Fagioli—Share authorship.
E. Gruppioni, S. Crea and N. Vitiello—Share the senior authorship.

K. Miesenberger et al. (Eds.): ICCHP-AAATE 2022, LNCS 13342, pp. 192–199, 2022.
https://doi.org/10.1007/978-3-031-08645-8_23

1 Introduction

Remote working (RW) has emerged as a solution to the limitations imposed by the COVID-19 outbreak. Recent estimates for the USA show that remote workers have quadrupled to 50% of the US workforce [1, 2]. Before the pandemic, Italy was the European country with the lowest share of teleworkers, with only 1% of remote workers [1]. During the March/June 2020 lockdown (Phase 1), the Minister of Public Administration in Italy declared that 90% of public sector employees were engaged in RW. The present study reports a survey on the work quality of employees at the Italian Public Administration (PA) by comparing a group of them working in traditional office-space (control group) with another group working in home-space (i.e., RW). The DGTCSI-ISCTI (Ministry of Economic Development, Directorate General for Communications Technology and Information Security – Higher Institute of Communications and Information Technologies), as part of the introduction of new RW methods in the PA, in collaboration with the University of Perugia and the Presidency of the Council of Ministers, initiated a research project called "Job-satisfying". The aim of the project was to investigate, through a remote usability test, the impact of "smart working" (or "lavoro agile", a term used in Italian law to refer to working from home or RW [3]) on the quality of work and satisfaction of the PA employees involved in the study.

Our drive for this survey emerged from wondering if RW, beyond just being a solution to the pandemic, could offer a beneficial solution (well-being) for workers with physical disabilities (e.g., walking disability) or working far away from home. Can RW present as an inclusive opportunity (inclusion) for those who have to manage the dual role of parent and worker or for those with non-binary gender identity and expression who experience barriers to sharing common workspaces (e.g., use of bathrooms). In other words, could RW give greater accessibility and inclusiveness to work?

Preliminary to this study, a literature review was conducted to identify which dimensions of work experience are able to mostly represent quality, efficiency and satisfaction in workplaces [4]. According to this systematic review, 10 dimensions emerged as the most relevant to measuring the experience of inclusiveness and accessibility in the RW condition: engagement with work (ENG), flexibility (FLEX), health and well-being (HEAL), layout and technology (LAY), organizational and job-related aspects (ORG), performance (PERF), personal needs and style (PERS), satisfaction (SAT), subjective gain (SUBJ) and work–life balance (WLB).

The purpose of the present study was to evaluate the work inclusiveness and accessibility of the Italian PA in the RW condition through the 10 dimensions mentioned above.

2 Method

The study is exploratory research involving voluntary PA employees, divided into two groups, who were assigned a work task to be carried out in work from home (home-space group) or from their own office (office-space group). In particular, the participants were asked to create a simple usability test of the website of the Ministry of Economic Development (https://www.mise.gov.it/). To carry out the task, the "eGLU-box PA 1.0" platform was used, a tool recently made available to all web editors of the PA for evaluating the usability of online services [5].

The proposed experimental design is correlational and semi-interventional, taking into consideration the working conditions (2x) of home-space versus office-space as independent variables (manipulated) and user experience (1x) in working technologies as the dependent variable (observed/experimental).

2.1 Participants

A total of 24 PA workers (12 males, 12 females) with an average age of 52 years (min. = 25; max. = 66; SD = 8.85; SE = 1.89) participated in the study. Out of 24 participants, 66% successfully completed the usability test ($n = 16$) but the remaining 33% did not complete the survey ($n = 8$). Among the participants who completed the usability test, nine (56.3%) belonged to the office-space group and seven (43.7%) to the home-space group.

2.2 Questionnaire and Measurements

A sociodemographic questionnaire gathered information about the participant's workplace (home-space/office-space), part-time/full-time job, travel time to the workplace and transportation to reach the workplace. In addition, personal details were asked: age, gender (as assigned at birth), gender identity, number of family members with and without disability, number and age of children, children in didactic learning and self-perception of housing quality (on a seven-point Likert-type scale, with a higher score meaning greater housing quality).

Four standardized scales were e also used to assess different dimensions associated with the worker's experience with the job conditions (home-space and office-space), as follows:

1. *Advantages and Disadvantages Scale* (ADV [6]). This is a 29-item self-report questionnaire to investigate WLB as the main dimension and ORG, LAY, HEAL, SUBJ and PERS as secondary dimensions. Answers are provided on a five-point Likert-type scale where 1 = "strongly disagree" and 5 = "strongly agree"; a higher score means greater advantages/disadvantages.
2. *Management Standards Indicator Tool* (MSIT [7]). This is a 38-item self-report questionnaire to assess FLEX as the main dimension and ORG and HEAL as secondary dimensions. Eight subscales can be obtained from this questionnaire: demands, control, peer support, managerial support, relationships, role clarity, support of change and work environment. The answers are provided on a five-point Likert-type scale where 1 = "never" and 5 = "always"; higher total scores mean greater management of and sociality at work.
3. *Individual Work Performance Survey* (IWPS [8]). This is a 27-item self-report questionnaire to assess PERF as the main dimension and ENG and HEAL as secondary dimensions. Three subscales can be obtained from this questionnaire: (i) task performance scale; (ii) contextual performance scale; and (iii) counterproductive work behavior scale. The answers are provided on a five-point Likert-type scale where

1 = "never" and 5 = "always"; a higher score means better work performance for scales (i) and (ii) but worse performance for the scale (iii).

4. *Work Related Basic Needs Satisfaction* (WRBNS [9]). This is an 18-item self-report questionnaire to assess the SAT dimension in three subscales: autonomy, competence and relatedness. The answers are provided on a five-point Likert-type scale where 1 = "strongly disagree" and 5 = "strongly agree"; a higher score means greater satisfaction of social and individual needs at work.

2.3 Procedure

An invitation was sent by the Department of Public Service to the management of the various Italian PAs to identify employees who were interested in voluntary participation in the research. Employees who replied to the invitation received an email explaining the survey procedure and a link to access an Internet platform where informed consent, a privacy statement, a sociodemographic questionnaire and measurements were administered. The time spent on the survey platform was recorded for each participant. After completing the questionnaire and measurements, the participants were briefed about the tasks to be carried out in the eGLU-box PA and the link to access it. The time spent on the eGLU-box PA platform to create a usability study was also recorded.

Participants logged into the eGLU-box PA platform with the credentials they were given by us. Their first task was to create a usability test related to the site of the Ministry of Economic Development (MISE). The participants then had to create tasks to be carried out on the MISE website. In Fig. 1 you can see the first task that all the participants had to create. Participants had to create a total of 4 tasks. After adding all the tasks, the participants validated the test, made it accessible, and invited a "test user".

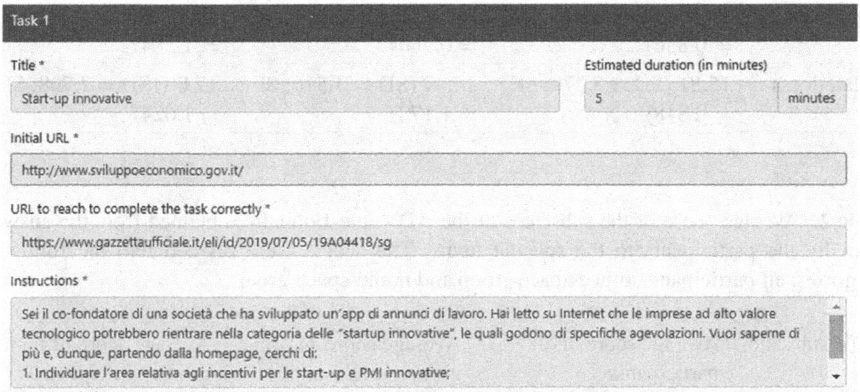

Task 1
Title *
Start-up innovative
Estimated duration (in minutes)
5 minutes
Initial URL *
http://www.sviluppoeconomico.gov.it/
URL to reach to complete the task correctly *
https://www.gazzettaufficiale.it/eli/id/2019/07/05/19A04418/sg
Instructions *
Sei il co-fondatore di una società che ha sviluppato un'app di annunci di lavoro. Hai letto su Internet che le imprese ad alto valore tecnologico potrebbero rientrare nella categoria delle "startup innovative", le quali godono di specifiche agevolazioni. Vuoi saperne di più e, dunque, partendo dalla homepage, cerchi di:
1. Individuare l'area relativa agli incentivi per le start-up e PMI innovative;

Fig. 1. Section to create tasks in eGLU-box PA.

3 Results

The average time taken to complete the survey was 12.64 h (SD = 42.01; SE = 10.51). More specifically, the office-space group took an average of 3.11 h (SD = 7.71; SE = 2.57) and the home-space group took an average of 24.90 h (SD = 63.45; SE = 23.98), showing a significant difference ($t[14] = -1.03$; $p = .03$); there was also a significant difference ($t[11] = -3.07$; $p = .02$) with regard to the time taken to complete the tasks in eGLU-box (26.00 min; SD = 15.09; SE = 4.18). However, there were no significant differences between the groups with regard to responses to the questionnaires or to the perception of housing quality (M = 5.94; SD = 1.65; SE = .41). The usability test conducted in eGLU-box PA was successfully completed by 85.7% of the home-space group and by 44.4% of the office-space group. In Table 1 it is possible to view the average scores of the participants regarding the WRBNS questionnaire. In Table 2 it is possible to view the average scores of the participants regarding the ADV questionnaire. In Table 3 it is possible to view the average scores of the participants regarding the MSIT questionnaire. In Table 4 it is possible to view the average scores of the participants regarding the IWPS questionnaire.

Table 1. Average score of the subscales of the WRBNS questionnaire, obtained from the answers given by the participants to the specific items. The scores were divided into the following categories: all participants, office-space group and home-space group.

WRBNS subscale	Average score of all participants	Average score of office group participants	Average score of home group participants
Autonomy	13.13 (SD = 3.845; SE = 0.961)	12.78 (SD = 3.1144; SE = 1.038	13.57 (SD = 4,860; SE = 1.837)
Competence	19.50 (SD = 3,425; SE = 0.856)	19.68 (SD = 2.958; SE = 0.986)	19.29 (SD = 4.192; SE = 1.584)
Relatedness	15.81 (SD = 3.270; SE = 0.818)	14.89 (SD = 3.516; SE = 1.172)	17.00 (SD = 2.708; SE = 1.024)

Table 2. Average score of the subscales of the ADV questionnaire, obtained from the answers given by the participants to the specific items. The scores were divided into the following categories: all participants, office-space group and home-space group.

ADV subscale	Average score of all participants	Average score of office group participants	Average score of home group participants
Advantages	48.56 (SD = 8.989; SE = 2.247)	49.33 (SD = 7,697; SE = 2,566)	47.57 (SD = 10,998; SE = 4,157)
Disadvantages	32.69 (SD = 10.562; SE = 2.641)	33.44 (SD = 11.260; SE = 3.753)	31.71 (SD = 10.388; SE = 3.926)

Table 3. Average score of the subscales of the MSIT questionnaire, obtained from the answers given by the participants to the specific items. The scores were divided into the following categories: all participants, office-space group and home-space group.

MSIT subscale	Average score of all participants	Average score of office group participants	Average score of home group participants
Demands	29.63 (SD = 5.691; SE = 1.423)	30.22 (SD = 7.345; SE = 2.448)	28.86 (SD = 2.795; SE = 1.056)
Control	20.81 (SD = 4,215; SE = 1,054)	22.78 (SD = 4.116; SE = 1.372)	18.29 (SD = 2.928; SE = 1.107)
Peer support	15.31 (SD = 3.554; SE = 0.888)	14.89 (SD = 3.855; SE = 1.285)	15.86 (SD = 3.338; SE = 1.262)
Managerial support	13.00 (SD = 4.546; SE = 1.137)	13.11 (SD = 4.595; SE = 1.532)	12.86 (SD = 4.845; SE = 1.831)
Relationships	16.19 (SD = 3.710; SE = 0.927)	15.67 (SD = 3.941; SE = 1.280)	16.86 (SD = 3.716; SE = 1.405)
Role clarity	22.13 (SD = 2.217; SE = 0.554)	21.56 (SD = 2.455; SE = 0.818)	22.86 (SD = 1.773; SE = 0.670)
Support of change	10.06 (SD = 1.982; SE = 0.496)	10.44 (SD = 2.068; SE = 0.689)	9.57 (SD = 1.902; SE = 0.719)
Work environment	10.94 (SD = 2.816; SE = 0.704)	11.33 (SD = 2.739; SE = 0.913)	10.43 (SD – 3.047; SE = 1.152)

Table 4. Average score of the subscales of the IWPS questionnaire, obtained from the answers given by the participants to the specific items. The scores were divided into the following categories: all participants, office-space group and home-space group.

IWPS subscale	Average score of all participants	Average score of office group participants	Average score of home group participants
Task performance scale	28.63 (SD = 3.948; SE = 0.987)	28.00 (SD = 4.062; SE = 1.354)	29.43 (SD = 3.952; SE = 1.494)
Contextual performance Scale	46.38 (SD = 8.421; SE = 2.105)	46.78 (SD = 8.258; SE = 2.753)	45.86 (SD = 9.263; SE = 3.501)
Counterproductive work behavior scale	17.00 (SD = 3.266; SE = 0.816)	16.67 (SD = 3.640; SE = 1.213)	17.43 (SD = 2.936; SE = 1.110)

4 Discussion

The results show no differences between the home-space and office-space groups in terms of questionnaire responses or usability test completion times. The results of the questionnaires showed that the workers were, on average, satisfied with their work experience and no significant differences were found between the two groups.

The only exception in performance between the two groups is the time elapsed from the moment the participants opened the instructions of the experimental tasks to the moment they decided to start the usability test (i.e., creating a usability study with the eGLU-box PA platform). However, the much higher times for starting the usability test in the home-space group did not affect the total time spent on completing the test in eGLU-box PA. In other words, the greater autonomy shown by the home-space group in the decision to start the task does not seem to affect its completion times (efficiency). Furthermore, a greater number in the home-space group (85.7%) correctly completed the usability test (effectiveness) compared to the office-space group (44.4%). Both the efficiency and effectiveness results show that the participants who took the usability test at home managed to better organize their time, with better results, than those who took the test from their office.

5 Conclusion

This paper is part of a project called "Job-satisfying" carried out by the Italian PA during 2021. The study is a preliminary feasibility study into the effects of working from home on Italian PA employees' well-being. The experiment consisted of four questionnaires to evaluate the most relevant dimensions of inclusiveness and accessibility in the RW condition [4]. The questionnaires were administered to two groups of participants conducting the usability test in two conditions, namely, home-space and office-space. All the participants performed the experimental tasks through a usability assessment web-based platform called eGLU-box PA, a tool developed by the PA to evaluate the usability of its digital platforms and services [10]. The results showed no differences in the overall experience between the two experimental conditions. However, differences in usability test completion rates were identified: more participants from the home-space group were able to complete the usability test (85.7%) in the eGLU-box PA compared to participants in the office-space group (44.4%). This result may indicate that working from home allows workers to achieve better performance results. Furthermore, the results showed that those in the RW condition were able to manage their time better than those who performed the experiment from the office, probably because of a higher level of autonomy in deciding when to start the usability test. We can say that RW or "smart working" allows for better accessibility, as the participants of this group have been able to manage their time better with very positive results, from their device in an easy way, all while staying at home.

In general, no significant differences were found between the two groups, but by analyzing the answers to the demographic questionnaire some interesting points emerged: those who have children and took the usability test at home obtained higher scores relating to the sense of working autonomy, support from superiors and satisfaction of relationships at work. This seems to argue that working from home can improve inclusiveness.

In future works, it is intended to extend the project to a larger number of PAs and investigate in greater depth the roles of the personal data variables of children and cohabitants in the family unit, the sharing of living and working spaces, the means of transport and the times used to go to work on the job performance and satisfaction of needs as perceived by the worker. Furthermore, it would be interesting to conduct a survey in which the worker performs his "everyday work".

References

1. Bonacini, L., Gallo, G., Scicchitano, S.: Working from home and income inequality: risks of a 'new normal' with COVID-19. J. Popul. Econ. **34**(1), 303–360 (2020). https://doi.org/10.1007/s00148-020-00800-7
2. Brynjolfsson, E., Horton, J.J., Ozimek, A., Rock, D., Sharma, G., TuYe, H.-Y.: Covid-19 and Remote Work: An Early Look at U.S. Data. NBER Working Paper 27344 (2020)
3. Gastaldi, L., Corso, M., Raguseo, E., Neirotti, P., Paolucci, E., Martini, A.: Smart Working: Rethinking Work Practices to Leverage Employees' Innovation Potential, pp. 337–347 (2014)
4. Federici, S., et al.: Measuring the experience of remote home workers: a scoping review. PsyArXiv, pp. 1–48 (19 November 2021). https://doi.org/10.31234/osf.io/8szwx
5. Borsci, S., Federici, S., Malizia, A., De Filippis, M.L.: Shaking the usability tree: why usability is not a dead end, and a constructive way forward. Behav. Inform. Technol. **38**, 519–532 (2019). https://doi.org/10.1080/0144929x.2018.1541255
6. Ipsen, C., van Veldhoven, M., Kirchner, K., Hansen, J.P.: Six key advantages and disadvantages of working from home in Europe during COVID-19. Int. J. Environ. Res. Public. Health **18**, 1826 (2021). https://doi.org/10.3390/ijerph18041826
7. Balducci, C., et al.: The validity of the short UK health and safety executive stress indicator tool for the assessment of the psychosocial work environment in Italy. Eur. J. Psychol. Assess. **33**, 149–157 (2017). https://doi.org/10.1027/1015-5759/a000280
8. Koopmans, L., Bernaards, C., Hildebrandt, V., van Buuren, S., van der Beek, A.J., de Vet, H.C.W.: Development of an individual work performance questionnaire. Int. J. Product. Perform. Manag. **62**, 6–28 (2013). https://doi.org/10.1108/17410401311285273
9. Colledani, D., Capozza, D., Falvo, R., Di Bernardo, G.A.: The work-related basic need satisfaction scale: an Italian validation. Front. Psychol. **9**, 1859 (2018). https://doi.org/10.3389/fpsyg.2018.01859
10. Federici, S., et al.: Heuristic evaluation of eGLU-Box: a semi-automatic usability evaluation tool for public administrations. In: Kurosu, M. (ed.) HCII 2019. LNCS, vol. 11566, pp. 75–86. Springer, Cham (2019). https://doi.org/10.1007/978-3-030-22646-6_6

Robotic and Virtual Reality Technologies for Children with Disabilities and Older Adults

Robotic and Virtual Reality Technologies for Children with Disabilities and Older Adults

Sanjit Samaddar[1](✉), Lorenzo Desideri[2], Pedro Encarnação[3], David Gollasch[4], Helen Petrie[1], and Gerhard Weber[4]

[1] Department of Computer Science, University of York, York YO10 5GH, UK
{sanjit.samaddar,helen.petrie}@york.ac.uk

[2] AIAS Bologna Onlus, Piazza della Pace 4/a, 40134 Bologna, Italy
ldesideri@ausilioteca.org

[3] Universidade Católica Portuguesa, Católica Lisbon School of Business and Economics, Palma de Cima, 1649-023 Lisbon, Portugal
pme@ucp.pt

[4] Technische Universität Dresden, Nöthnitzer Straße 46, 01062 Dresden, Germany
{david.gollasch,gerhard.weber}@tu-dresden.de

Abstract. Robotic and virtual reality technologies have been used with children with disabilities and older adults for different purposes. In this article, after summarising the characteristics of these technologies and listing various applications, we discuss the different challenges of developing them for children with disabilities and older adults, even if the intervention goals are similar. This sets the context for the articles addressing some of the identified challenges that were submitted to a special thematic session on robotic and virtual reality technologies for children with disabilities and older adults held at the ICCHP-AAATE 2022 conference.

Keywords: Human-robot interaction · Assistive robots · Virtual reality · Children with disabilities · Inclusive education · Older adults

1 Introduction

In the last few decades, there has been a significant interest in the use of robotic and virtual reality technologies with children with disabilities and older adults.

Robots are programmable mechanisms that move within a physical environment exhibiting a degree of autonomy. Its physical presence enables them to act upon the environment and to interact with people directly. Being programmable, capable of sensing the environment and of exhibiting different degrees of autonomy, robots can be used for different goals and adapt their behaviour in response to the environment and/or to the person they are interacting with. Robotic systems may also be a valuable tool in objectively assessing educational or therapeutic goals by registering all variables of interest during interventions. These features have motivated the development of robotic tools to assist children with disabilities and older adults [1–3]. Applications include the use of

K. Miesenberger et al. (Eds.): ICCHP-AAATE 2022, LNCS 13342, pp. 203–210, 2022.
https://doi.org/10.1007/978-3-031-08645-8_24

robots in a) inclusive education [4], allowing children to actively participate in the curricular activities (robotic assistive technologies to support manipulation), providing a direct application medium for the theoretical concepts under study (educational robotics), or interacting with children to support their learning (social robots acting as teachers or peers); b) cognitive therapy/training [5–7] (social robots that foster cognitive skills and language development); c) physical therapy/activity [8, 9] (robots designed to engage children and older adults in physical therapy/activity); d) stress and pain management [10–12] (social robots acting as companions of children or older adults with a chronic illness or undergoing medical and/or mental care); and e) promoting play for the sake of play [13, 14] (robots being the play object or providing a means to access to play).

Virtual reality (VR) environments are those in which a person "is totally immersed in, and able to interact with, a completely synthetic world" [15]. These lie in one extreme of the "virtuality continuum" [15], with real environments on the other extreme. In the middle are those environments mixing real (physical) and virtual (simulated) objects. Examples, from the real environments to the virtual reality environments extremes, are a) augmented reality, when virtual objects are overlaid on a view of the real environment; b) mixed reality, when real and virtual objects coexist and the user can interact with both; and c) augmented virtuality, when real objects are represented in a virtual environment. The term extended reality has been used to encompass all different combinations of real and virtual environments [16]. Extended reality systems allow for the involvement of persons in realistic virtual situations, substituting real-world experiences. That may be desirable, for example, when real-world experiences can put someone at risk (e.g., piloting a plane or performing a surgery), or are very difficult to replicate (e.g., walking on the Moon's surface). Virtual environments have also the potential of being more engaging to people, since they can be designed according to the user preferences. The main driver for extended reality systems has been the gaming industry, but many applications have been developed for children with disabilities and older adults [16–19]. Areas of intervention greatly overlap with the ones in which robots are being used, namely a) education [20], building augmented reality scenarios that enhance the learning experience or making available simulation scenarios for training skills; b) cognitive therapy/training [21] (virtual reality activities to train attention, memory, spatial orientation, social or communication skills); c) physical therapy/activity [22] (engaging serious games to increase adherence to physical exercises); d) stress and pain management [23, 24] (VR applications to divert attention from painful procedures or to help dealing with anxiety); e) promoting play for the sake of play [25].

Even though robotic and virtual reality technologies have been used with the two extremes of the age continuum, sometimes with similar goals, challenges in developing them for children and for older adults are different and reviewed in the following sections.

The references included in this introduction contain general literature reviews on the topics addressed in Sects. 2 and 3. For a list of references specific to each robotic application, please refer to: https://sites.google.com/view/robots4children/useful-references. Section 4 briefly summarises the articles submitted to the special thematic session on robotic and virtual reality technologies for children with disabilities and older adults held at the ICCHP-AAATE 2022 conference.[1]

2 Challenges in Developing Robotic and VR Technologies for Children with Disabilities

Advancements in robotics are determining important changes in the lives of children with disabilities. Most notably, with the advent of intelligent technologies capable of engaging people in social interactions, children can not only interact through technologies but also with technologies. In this view, over the last decade, research on robotics and other emerging technologies for children with disabilities has taken an important place in the development of more effective healthcare and educational intervention.

With reference to applying robots in healthcare settings, for instance, one of the most promising and researched application domains of socially assistive robots (SARs) is as support in treatment interventions for children with neurodevelopmental disorders. Most research in this application domain has been carried out with children with autism spectrum disorder (ASD) to foster the development of their social and communication skills. Physical rehabilitation is another area of intervention in which robotic technologies such as exoskeletons have been successfully applied (e.g., to reduce motor disability associated to cerebral palsy). In this rehabilitation context, interactive technologies such as those involving sensors linked to computer, immersive, or virtual reality systems can be employed in combination with exoskeletons to facilitate the child's engagement in a pleasant and motivating manner and, to a large extent, independent of staff direct and consistent guidance.

Despite the encouraging results from the application of robot-based activities in healthcare settings for treatment and rehabilitation, it should be recognized that research in these areas is still in its infancy. More evidence is needed, for instance, on the effectiveness of robot-based intervention protocols, as well as on demonstrating outcomes transferability from one context to another. In addition, the use of socially assistive robots in therapeutic/educational interventions for ASD has been recently criticized on the ground of ethical considerations. For example, it has been highlighted the risk of reducing human contact for children with ASD when using a SAR in therapy as well as educational sessions. Another critic is that there is no evidence that all children with ASD are attracted by artificial agents. To overcome such challenges, user-centred co-design methods should be followed, in which therapists, parents, children and other key stakeholders should play a central role in developing scenarios where robots may be useful tools in achieving child-centred goals.

With reference to applying robots in education, social robots have been shown to promote more learning gains and to evoke more expression of emotion through the creation of personalized learning ecosystems when compared to screen-based technologies

[1] Published in this chapter or in the corresponding chapters of Petz, A., Hoogerwerf, E.-J., Mavrou, K. (Ed.): Assistive Technology, Accessibility and (e)Inclusion, ICCHP-AAATE 2022 Open Access Compendium, accepted for publication; online: https://www.icchp-aaate.org, Johannes Kepler University Linz, Austria.

such as tablets. In these educational contexts, social robots may take on a variety of different roles, including that of tutors or peers.

Translating evidence into real educational practice, however, is challenging due to the lack of accessible indications and best practice examples on how teachers can use robots in their day-to-day activities. Therefore, it can be argued that currently the decision by teachers to use robots in their classrooms is often driven by availability and affordability of ready-to-use robot-based educational activities rather than by pedagogically sound considerations. Consequently, teachers' interest in adopting potentially useful robotic applications may be hindered by the difficulties they face in understanding the pedagogical value of robots as well as in integrating such innovative solutions within their settings. Furthermore, despite research having demonstrated promising applications of robots in school settings, teachers' attitudes towards robots are still mixed, as robots are not yet considered usable outside highly controlled settings or isolated structured interactions. Thus, there is a clear need to shift the focus of research from the development of educational robotic platforms to the learners, by examining the pedagogies and specific ways learners with diverse skills and capabilities undergo meaningful learning processes with robots.

3 Challenges in Developing Robotic and VR Technologies for Older Adults

Robots for older people are a promising and emerging technology which opens a set of new use cases and scenarios. Concerns on robot acceptance by older people have been relieved in recent years. One of such scenarios is Ambient Assisted Living (AAL) applications. AAL focuses on providing technical assistive solutions to older adults within their homes by means of smart technologies that are seamlessly embedded within the house or objects. Although the overall goal of AAL products and services is to enable older adults to age in place, most AAL solutions focus on medical aspects such as fall detection or recognizing and monitoring habits and activities of daily living (ADLs). Robots have been used in AAL settings when an embodied user agent might be a promising device, such as when interacting with a user for cognitive stimulation goals.

Next to activation and cognitive stimulation, further use cases come up in the field of a) agent-based cognitive behavioural therapy (CBT), when anxiety, social stress, depression and – worth to highlight – loneliness are increasing issues among the older fraction of our society; or b) supporting of people with early-stage dementia during ADLs. The COVID-19 pandemic revealed more use cases for socially assistive robots.

One of the challenges of using robots with older people is how to design human-robot interfaces (HRI). Humanoid robots, or at least the application of the human metaphor within the embodiment of robots, make voice interaction an obvious choice as primary interaction modality for service robots for older adults. Furthermore, natural-language-based interaction has made tremendous advances in the past decade, being voice assistants within smartphones and smart-speakers, such as Siri on iPhone and Alexa on Amazon's Echo devices, conspicuous examples. In terms of technology acceptance, recent studies show high motivation among older adults to use voice-controlled robots within their daily lives. To address usability and overall user experience, there is a considerable amount of work on designing strategies and guidelines for voice user interfaces (VUIs) within SARs for older adults and in elderly care. Beyond voice interaction, as robots potentially feature a wide set of sensors and actuators, further interaction techniques and multi-modal interaction gain interest, including sentiment, facial expressions or gestures recognition, or providing an enriched interaction environment by means of virtual, augmented or mixed reality. Use of VR technologies to help older people is a relatively new field with studies showing that VR can be used to help with clinical conditions, provide motivation for physical rehabilitation or to improve autonomy in day-to-day activities. Challenges highlighted are the need for more representative samples, longitudinal studies and further work with older adults to better understand how VR can be adapted to suit their needs.

For interactive systems, the well-established user-centred design process underlines the strong dependency of a satisfying design on the actual use cases. This is especially true for service robots that shall be used by older users. Challenges include not only developing functional robots, but also how the robot can actually help older people to age in place, taking into account possible age-related physical or cognitive limitations. Research supports a strong focus on and need for user-centred design and co-design workflows with older adults as target user group to move towards a technological – i.e. robotic – solution for our aging society with its stressed care sector.

4 Contributions to the ICCHP-AAATE 2022 Session

The contributions to this session held at the ICCHP-AAATE 2022 conference showcase the vast potential of robots and VR technologies to help children with disabilities and older adults. Combining contributions to the conference proceedings and open access compendium, the 11 articles included in this session provide a very interesting insight and possible solutions to the challenges listed in the previous sections.

On providing a robot supported education for children with ASD, Schulz et al. discuss a robot supported toolkit that aims to improve language, social and communication skills. The authors discuss ethical considerations required when working in the field and highlight the importance of involving all stakeholders to identify the challenges and contribute to a solution. Desideri argues the value of an immersive robotic telepresence system to help teachers deliver content by controlling a humanoid robot in group-based activities. Results from interviews with all the stakeholders suggest that, contrary to expectations from available literature, the predictable behaviour of a robot can be a limitation when working with children with ASD. The work presented shows how an immersive system can be flexible and allow teachers to adapt to the dynamic classes' scenarios. Finally, Chambers evaluates the effectiveness of a coding robot in classroom. Students with ASD used robots to solve coding tasks and then taught other students how to use the robots. The robots allowed for development of soft skills with both tasks, and allowed students to engage with their peers.

Zou et al. report on their work with teachers, speech therapists and psychomotor therapists to evaluate a Wizard-of-Oz interface to help children with dysgraphia. The authors present a multi-platform web interface communicating with a humanoid robot to provide different exercises and games. The final system was evaluated by 15 caregivers with positive results and suggestions for further improvements. Working with children with motor disabilities, Rojo et al. highlight the advantages of a custom exoskeleton to help with goal-directed rehabilitation tasks. The work shows the potential of having both robot-assisted and VR-based game solutions that engage children in rehabilitation tasks, and demonstrates the success of preliminary tests with end users.

To support disabled people, Bonarini provides examples of different robots that involve both players and their caregivers. The research highlights the benefits of both autonomous and remote-controlled robots, and how play can be facilitated and enjoyed by users. Van der Heide et al. describe interviews with dynamic arm support and robotic arm users to understand challenges faced by the users. Results show a need for more information and training, and the authors offer a protocol for this information provision. Thevin investigates how a VR sensitisation tool can help instructors working with blind and visually impaired people. Four professionals with different backgrounds helped co-designing the virtual environment and simulations. The article provides the perspective of instructors and answers questions around whether VR fulfils professional requirements and what the blockers might be.

The last three contributions discuss and present the acceptance of different robots for older and disabled people. Wasić et al. provide insight into the opinions and intention to use a mobile service robot from the perspective of caregivers and relatives of people with dementia. Results show more scepticism and lower acceptance among caregivers compared to relatives and authors discuss how perceived ease of use can be affected by those who are not the primary end user of the robot. An often-debated issue with robots is their appearance and how it impacts acceptance. Sehrt et al. investigate three different designs of a robot that fetches objects around a person's home. Evaluation involving both younger and older people show the difference of opinion between the two groups and re-iterated the importance of involving users in the robot design process. Finally, Prescott et al. explore design principles for social robots and present guidelines for ethical social robots with a view on "honest anthropomorphism".

While all these articles address different robotic and VR applications for different target groups, all show the critical value of user-centred co-design involving all stakeholders and illustrate methods to accomplish it. They also provide additional research evidence on the effective use of robotic and VR technologies for children with disabilities and older adults, contributing to improve the acceptance of these technologies.

Further research is still needed to assess the long-term effects of robotic and VR technologies, namely the transferability of acquired skills to other contexts. It is necessary to define standardised outcome measures such that robotic and VR interventions can be compared with other approaches. A wide consensus on the ethical use of these technologies is still to be achieved. More longitudinal studies in real-world application scenarios, involving larger samples in scientifically sound research methods, need to be conducted to prove beyond any doubt the value of robotic and VR technologies for children with disabilities and older adults. Once that is achieved, the cost of these technologies will go down, and intervention protocols and materials will be developed, allowing for its wide acceptance and use.

Acknowledgments. The work of Pedro Encarnação was partially funded by FCT – Fundação para a Ciência e a Tecnologia under the project UIBD/00470/2020.

References

1. Miguel Cruz, A., Rios Rincon, A.M., Rodriguez Dueñas, W.R., Quiroga Torres, D.A., Bohórquez-Heredia, A.F.: What does the literature say about using robots on children with disabilities? Disabil. Rehabil. Assist. Technol. **12**, 429–440 (2017)
2. Bedaf, S., Huijnen, C., van den Heuvel, R., de Witte, L.: Robots supporting care for elderly people. In: Robotic Assistive Technologies, pp. 309–332. CRC Press (2017)
3. Shishehgar, M., Kerr, D., Blake, J.: A systematic review of research into how robotic technology can help older people. Smart Health **7**, 1–18 (2018)
4. Pivetti, M., Di Battista, S., Agatolio, F., Simaku, B., Moro, M., Menegatti, E.: Educational Robotics for children with neurodevelopmental disorders: a systematic review. Heliyon. **6**, e05160 (2020)
5. van den Heuvel, R., et al.: The potential of robotics for the development and wellbeing of children with disabilities as we see it. Technol. Disab. **34**, 25–33 (2022)
6. Park, J., Baek, Y.E., Lim, B.L., Ko, H.: Robot-mediated interventions to enhance communication and social abilities of children and youth with disabilities: a review of the literature. Int. J. Spec. Educ. **36**, 99–112 (2021)
7. Yuan, F., Klavon, E., Liu, Z., Lopez, R.P., Zhao, X.: A systematic review of robotic rehabilitation for cognitive training. Front. Robot. AI **8**, 105 (2021)
8. Gonzalez, A., Garcia, L., Kilby, J., McNair, P.: Robotic devices for paediatric rehabilitation: a review of design features. Biomed. Eng. Onl. **20**, 1–33 (2021)
9. Fasola, J., Mataric, M.J.: Using socially assistive human-robot interaction to motivate physical exercise for older adults. Proc. IEEE **100**, 2512–2526 (2012)
10. Moerman, C.J., van der Heide, L., Heerink, M.: Social robots to support children's well-being under medical treatment: a systematic state-of-the-art review. J. Child Health Care **23**, 596–612 (2019)
11. Dawe, J., Sutherland, C., Barco, A., Broadbent, E.: Can social robots help children in healthcare contexts? A scoping review. BMJ Paediatrics. **3**, e000371 (2019)
12. Pu, L., Moyle, W., Jones, C., Todorovic, M.: The effectiveness of social robots for older adults: a systematic review and meta-analysis of randomized controlled studies. Gerontologist **59**, e37–e51 (2019)
13. den Heuvel, R.J.F., Lexis, M.A.S., Gelderblom, G.J., Jansens, R.M.L., de Witte, L.P.: Robots and ICT to support play in children with severe physical disabilities: a systematic review. Disabil. Rehabil. Assist. Technol. **11**, 103–116 (2016)
14. Espin-Tello, S.M., Gardeazabal, X., Abascal, J.: The use of robots for augmentative manipulation during play activities among children with motor impairment: a scoping review. Disab. Rehabilit. 1–15 (2022)
15. Milgram, P., Kishino, F.: A taxonomy of mixed reality visual displays. IEICE Trans. Inf. Syst. **77**, 1321–1329 (1994)
16. Margrett, J., Ouverson, K.M., Gilbert, S.B., Phillips, L.A., Charness, N.: Older adults' use of extended reality: a systematic review. Front. Virt. Real. **2**, 1–13 (2022)
17. da Cunha, R.D., Neiva, F.W., da Silva, R.L. de S.: Virtual reality as a support tool for the treatment of people with intellectual and multiple disabilities: a systematic literature review. Rev. Inf. Teór. Aplic. **25**, 67–81 (2018)

18. Cavus, N., Al-Dosakee, K., Abdi, A., Sadiq, S.: The utilization of augmented reality technology for sustainable skill development for people with special needs: a systematic literature review. Sustainability. **13**, 10532 (2021)
19. Fu, Y., Hu, Y., Sundstedt, V.: A systematic literature review of virtual, augmented, and mixed reality game applications in healthcare. ACM Trans. Comput. Healthc. **3**, 1–27 (2022)
20. Fernández-Batanero, J.M., Montenegro-Rueda, M., Fernández-Cerero, J.: Use of augmented reality for students with educational needs: a systematic review (2016–2021). Societies **12**, 36 (2022)
21. Bailey, B., Bryant, L., Hemsley, B.: Virtual reality and augmented reality for children, adolescents, and adults with communication disability and neurodevelopmental disorders: a systematic review. Rev. J. Autism Developm. Disord. (2021). https://doi.org/10.1007/s40489-020-00230-x
22. Wojciechowski, A., Wiśniewska, A., Pyszora, A., Liberacka-Dwojak, M., Juszczyk, K.: Virtual reality immersive environments for motor and cognitive training of elderly people - a scoping review. Hum. Tech. **17**, 145–163 (2021)
23. Arane, K., Behboudi, A., Goldman, R.D.: Virtual reality for pain and anxiety management in children. Can. Fam. Phys. **63**, 932–934 (2017)
24. Rawlins, C.R., Veigulis, Z., Hebert, C., Curtin, C., Osborne, T.: Effect of immersive virtual reality on pain and anxiety at a veterans affairs health care facility. Front. Virtual Real. **136** (2021)
25. Thach, K.S., Lederman, R., Waycott, J.: How older adults respond to the use of virtual reality for enrichment: a systematic review. In: 32nd Australian Conference on Human-Computer Interaction, pp. 303–313 (2020)

Creating a Robot-Supported Education Solution for Children with Autism Spectrum Disorder

Trenton Schulz(✉) and Kristin Skeide Fuglerud

Norwegian Computing Center/Norsk Regnesentral, Postbox 414, Blindern, 0314 Oslo, Norway
{trenton,kristins}@nr.no

Abstract. We introduce the ROSA project that aims to provide robot supported education in the areas of communication, language, and emotion for children with autism spectrum disorder. The background for the project is reviewed and the basic idea and components of the ROSA toolbox is presented. The initial project activities of the project so far have focused on ethical issues with having a robot assist in teaching children with autism, possible mechanisms for motivation, and performing an initial introduction of the robot to some classes. These activities have provided a good grounding for the future project work.

Keywords: Socially assitive robotics · Robots · Autism spectrum disorder · Children · Ethical reflection · Self-determination theory

1 Introduction

Autism Spectrum Disorder (ASD) is a disorder that is characterized by poor nonverbal conversation skills, uneven language development, repetitive or rigid language, and narrow interests in specific areas. Children with ASD can have difficulty understanding body language and the meaning and rhythm of words and sentences. This can lead to challenges developing social interaction and communication skills, which often form a basis for a child's ability to be independent and work and interact with people. Language skills are vital for education, expressing needs, and participating in society and work life [21].

Programs for improving the communication skills of children with ASD are recommended to: (*a*) begin at preschool and continue through school; (*b*) be tailored to the child's age and interests; (*c*) address communication and behavior; and (*d*) offer regular reinforcement of positive actions [8,20]. Special educators and teacher aids are often required to run these programs, but due to resource constraints, it can be difficult to recruit sufficient staff for these roles in all the schools that need them. Information and communication technology (ICT) resources may increase the quality of the children's support and reach additional children with ASD. We are currently working on a tool to support language development of children with ASD using social robots. Social robots interact

K. Miesenberger et al. (Eds.): ICCHP-AATE 2022, LNCS 13342, pp. 211–218, 2022.
https://doi.org/10.1007/978-3-031-08645-8_25

with people in a natural, interpersonal way, and socially assistive robotics (SAR) assist people by using a robot for social interaction (speech, gestures, and body language) [19].

Robots can be a good match to help children with ASD as robots can elicit motivation, provide physical presence, and a more tailored experience than other ICT solutions [2]. Robots can provide teachers with new tools [12] and deliver predictable behaviors and repetitive feedback. In addition, a robot can help build social behavior skills, teach, or demonstrate socially desirable behaviors to children with ASD who have trouble expressing themselves. Another benefit is that robots do not get angry, tired, or stressed, and they can be tailored to the needs of a specific child and used repetitively [10]. A child-sized or smaller robot is less intimidating than adults, and many children with ASD therefore feel safer interacting with social robots [19]. Children with ASD who had trained with robots paid closer attention during interactions with adults long after the robot training ended [19], and children with ASD were more likely to complete a treatment session when the session included a robot [26]. Other studies reported improved social skills, increased involvement, more positive behavior, and better social interaction [7,10,17,24].

A review of robots in ASD interventions defined four categories of intervention goals: social, communication, maladaptive behavior, and academic skills [2]. Most current studies, however, target only one of these goals, and they normally target only one kind of social robot. Research is needed on how social robots in general can meet the challenge of targeting all or a combination of the goals, in particular combining supporting social skills with language learning. Robots have been shown to be effective in teaching knowledge and skill-based topics, but research is needed on how effectively they teach language [3,13]. To our knowledge, there are no studies of robot-supported development of primary language skills for children with ASD nor any attempt to make the lessons work on multiple kinds of robots. To develop robots in this field, technological and multidisciplinary research is needed in human-robot interaction (HRI), human-computer interaction (HCI), robot-assisted learning, privacy, and ethics.

Our overall objective is to *use social robots to improve language, social, and communication skills for children with ASD*. We are researching how to best apply a robot for this activity by involving teachers, parents, and children in the design process, and to develop a toolbox that the teachers can use to personalize lessons for children with ASD. To meet this objective, we need to understand what possible scenarios work well for teaching children in this diverse group using a robot.

This paper is meant to introduce our research and provide some preliminary results on some of our activities we have already done with the children, parents and teachers. We introduce the toolbox, our activities, and discuss our preliminary findings and where we are going next.

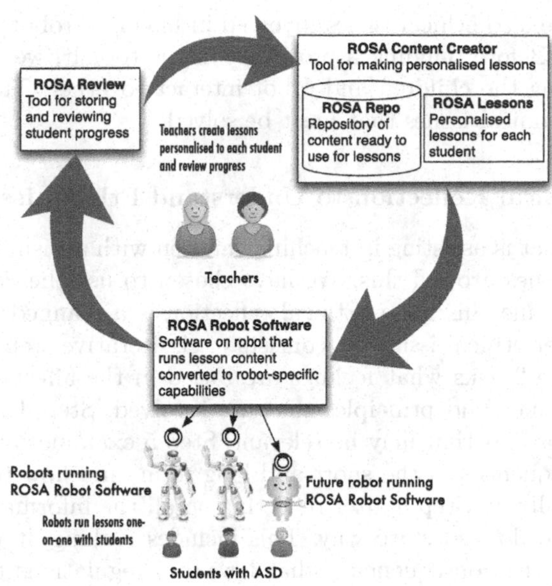

Fig. 1. The ROSA Toolbox consists of three parts: a content creator, software that runs on the robot for interpreting the lessons, and a review panel for teachers.

2 The ROSA Toolbox

We are working on building the RObot Supported Education for children with ASD (ROSA) toolbox to help meet our objective. The toolbox consists of three parts (Fig. 1): (a): ROSA Content Creator, a tool for teachers to easily create tailored one-on-one lessons for children with ASD; (b) ROSA Robot Software runs lesson content from the Content Creator customized to the robots' capabilities; and (c) ROSA Review, a tool for teachers to follow lesson progress and used as input for the next lesson. The goal of the toolbox is to make teachers more effective by providing tailor-made education plans for children with ASD and make it easy to follow the children's progress. For children with ASD, the toolbox's lessons will be tailored to their unique needs, increase the children's motivation for learning and result in children developing better language, social, and communication skills. The robot will present content customized to the robot's capabilities. The ROSA toolbox should provide tailored, motivating educational and communication support by exploring and exploiting the unique affordances of a social robot as an expressive medium and educational tool for children with ASD.

3 Understanding the Potential Users of the System

To ensure the success of the ROSA toolkit, we determined it was important to understand the different ways a robot can help with motivating children with autism. There are also ethical issues involved in having a robot assist in teaching the children. Before building a prototype of the toolkit, we gathered initial opinions on having the children and robot interact together. This activity also exposed some technical issues that must be solved.

3.1 Using Ethical Reflection to Understand Ethical Issues

Having a robot that is assisting in teaching children with autism forces to examine the ethical issues around this. We have chosen to use the *ethical reflection* model [1] to examine this issue. Ethical reflection is a planned and structured process to uncover ethical issues. It consists of six iterative steps. Step 1 states the problem. Step 2 asks what feelings are raised in the affected parties. Step 3 looks at the values and principles that are involved. Step 4 looks at potential laws or regulations that may be relevant. Step 5 examines alternatives that exist, their consequences in the short and long term, and how to prioritize the alternatives. Finally, in Step 6 after reflecting on all the information, one needs to decide what to do and state why. This includes looking at who is affected by the decisions, the consequences, what laws and regulations to consult, and making a plan to implement and possibly evaluate the measure.

As part of this ethical reflection, project partners and the scientific reference group were given a questionnaire that walked each person through the steps. An initial examination of the answers found general agreement on the goal that the robot should help improve teaching for children while taking into account each child's individual needs and the tension between keeping the lessons and robot reliable while doing iterative development on the lessons and robot. The partners discussed the challenge of getting proper informed consent and real user participation in the project from the children, teachers, and parents. Master students are further examining the answers from the questionnaires while the project is working on ways to increase participation with all the groups. We started the latter by presenting the project to the teachers and staff at our partner school and at parents' meetings. We have also held workshops with the teachers to find possible teaching scenarios that can be used to build the ROSA toolbox around.

3.2 Motivation and Motivation Mechanisms

Since the robot will serve as way of keeping children interested in the learning lessons, it is necessary to understand motivation and mechanisms that can help maintain or increase it. This has led us to examine different theories around motivation and how they relate to autism. There were three theories that are most often mentioned: (a) Theory of Mind (ToM) [27] (b)Social Motivation Theory (SMT) [6], and (c) Self-Determination Theory (SDT) [22]. The first two of these theories are in opposition to each other. ToM is the ability to attribute mental states to others to explain and predict behavior. Some argue that children with ASD have slower development of Theory of Mind. SMT is a combination from different disciplines and splits activities into different levels of social behavior, biological mechanisms, and evolution. For proponents of SMT, ASD is not an inability to develop ToM, but a lack of social motivation on all these levels. SMT, however, cannot explain all elements of ASD, something that critics have pointed out [11,18].

We have also investigated the general ideas of intrinsic motivation and extrinsic motivation and how these may be applied to learning goals and children with ASD [16]. Through our examination, we have found that SDT appears to be a good fit for how we should approach motivation in the project. SDT has its basis in the universal psychological needs of autonomy, competence, and relatedness [22]. SDT includes looking at intrinsic and extrinsic motivation through the concept of autonomous motivation and controlled motivation. Autonomous motivation is about having autonomy over your motivation and consists of intrinsic motivation and well-internalized extrinsic motivation. Controlled motivation is a collection of extrinsic motivation and some types of intrinsic motivation like ego. Some of this extrinsic motivation can be controlled through external factors, but also personal choice (self-determination). Applying this theory should mean that we take into consideration things that threaten the children's autonomy as this may ruin their motivation.

One way that we can build motivation it to try and tie rewards to things like circumscribed interests [14]. In addition, we have examined how other research projects have incorporated robots with mechanisms like games [15,23], music [25], unstructured play [4], and touch [5] into sessions between a robot and children with ASD and how well that can build motivation in the children. Our workshops with teachers have also provided some additional insights into how to incorporate these mechanisms into lessons.

3.3 Introducing the Robot to the Children

To get an idea about how the children would interact with the robot, we had the robot make a short trip to the school and introduce itself to the children. The robot, a Nao 5, was running a version of a language program that we have used in a different context [9]. Due to sickness and the pandemic, we were only able to visit a couple of classes, but the children in the classes seemed interested in the robot.

Even though we only could visit a couple of classrooms, it still provided us with a glimpse of some of the technical issues we needed to solve. The language program was not designed for the group of children and exhibited issues in speech recognition. This issue was compounded with problems in network connectivity, even when using the mobile network instead of local wireless, there were parts of the school where the connection to cloud services would drop or be slow. We also noticed some robustness issues with the communication between the robot and the software run on the phone. This provided insight into what needs to be considered to build a reliable system for the teachers and the children. Even though a program worked well in several other schools and group of children, it is not guaranteed to work in all situations.

4 Discussion and Future Activities

The activities so far in the project have shown the importance of including children, teachers, and parents in understanding the context and developing a solution. After several activities, there were challenges with getting all the participants on the same page, but this was solved through explanations. Using the collected information, we are beginning the work on creating prototypes and get feedback from the school about how well this can work in their classrooms. Otherwise, there are still issues around infection prevention during a pandemic. This is especially true for potential co-morbidities for some of the children at school.

On the technical side, there are still many issues that remain to be resolved. One of the biggest issue that we need to address is how to make the system easy to use for busy teachers and robust to problems with network connectivity. Also, while the software works on different generations of the Nao, we also have a goal that the software should work on different kinds of robots as well, and we are still looking to find the other robot.

Although there are many challenges that remain to be solved, we feel that anchoring our work in ethics, choosing a self-determination theory for modelling motivation, and including the school and parents in the design process should make it possible to overcome these challenges.

Acknowledgments. This work is partly supported by the Research Council of Norway as part of the RObot Supported Education for children with ASD (ROSA) project, under grant agreement 321821. We would also like to thank the other project members, and a special thank you to the teachers and students at *Frydenhaug skole* for their participation in the project.

References

1. Aadland, E., Eide, T.: Den lille etikkveilederen, Norway, KS, Oslo (2019)
2. Begum, M., Serna, R.W., Yanco, H.A.: Are robots ready to deliver autism interventions? a comprehensive review. Int. J. Soc. Robot. **8**(2), 157–181 (2016). https://doi.org/10.1007/s12369-016-0346-y
3. Belpaeme, T., et al.: Guidelines for designing social robots as second language tutors. Int. J. Soc. Robot. **10**, 325–341 (2018)
4. Brivio, A., Rogacheva, K., Lucchelli, M., Bonarini, A.: A soft, mobile, autonomous robot to develop skills through Play in autistic children. Paladyn. J. Behav. Robot. **12**(1), 187–198 (2021)
5. Burns, R.B., Seifi, H., Lee, H., Kuchenbecker, K.J.: Getting in touch with children with autism: specialist guidelines for a touch-perceiving robot. Paladyn. J. Behav. Robot. **12**(1), 115–135 (2021)
6. Chevallier, C., Kohls, G., Troiani, V., Brodkin, E.S., Schultz, R.T.: The social motivation theory of autism. Trends Cogn. Sci. **16**(4), 231–239 (2012)
7. Dautenhahn, K., Werry, I.: Towards interactive robots in autism therapy: background. Motiv. Challenges Pragmatics Cogn. **12**(1), 1–35 (2004)

8. Deafness and Other Communication Disorders (NIDCD), N.I. on: Autism Spectrum Disorder: Communication Problems in Children, NIDCD. (2015). https://www.nidcd.nih.gov/health/autism-spectrum-disorder-communication-problemschildren, (visited on December 11 2020)
9. Halbach, T., Schulz, T., Leister, W., Solheim, I.: Robot-enhanced language learning for children in Norwegian day-care centers. MTI **5**(12), 74 (2021)
10. Huijnen, C.A.G.J., Lexis, M.A.S., Jansens, R., de Witte, L.P.: How to implement robots in interventions for children with autism? a co-creation study involving people with autism, parents and professionals. J. Autism Dev. Disord. **47**(10), 3079–3096 (2017). https://doi.org/10.1007/s10803-017-3235-9
11. Jaswal, V.K., Akhtar, N.: Being versus appearing socially uninterested: challenging assumptions about social motivation in autism. Behav. Brain Sci. **42**, 1–73 (2019)
12. Jones, A., Castellano, G.: Adaptive robotic tutors that support self-regulated learning: a longer-term investigation with primary school children. Int. J. Soc. Robot. **10**(3), 357–370 (2018)
13. Kanero, J., Geçkin, V., Oranç, C., Mamus, E., Küntay, A.C., Göksun, T.: Social robots for early language learning: current evidence and future directions. Child Dev. Perspect. **12**(3), 146–151 (2018)
14. Kohls, G., Antezana, L., Mosner, M.G., Schultz, R.T., Yerys, B.E.: Altered reward system reactivity for personalized circumscribed interests in autism. Mol. Autism **9**(1), 9 (2018)
15. Lakatos, G., Wood, L.J., Syrdal, D.S., Robins, B., Zaraki, A., Dautenhahn, K.: Robot-mediated intervention can assist children with autism to develop visual perspective taking skills. Paladyn. J. Behav. Robot. **12**(1), 87–101 (2021)
16. Leafwing Center: Autism and Motivation in Children, LeafWing Center (2021). https://leafwingcenter.org/autism-and-motivation/, (visited on 08 June 2021)
17. Lee, C.-H.J., Kim, K., Breazeal, C., Picard, R.: Shybot: friend-stranger interaction for children living with Autism. In: CHI 2008 Extended Abstracts on Human Factors in Computing Systems, CHI EA 2008, pp. 3375–3380. Association for Computing Machinery (2008)
18. Livingston, L.A., Shah, P., Happé, F.: Compensation in autism is not consistent with social motivation theory. Behav. Brain Sci. **42**, e99 (2019)
19. Matarić, M.J., Scassellati, B.: Socially assistive robotics. In: Siciliano, B., Khatib, O. (eds.) Springer Handbook of Robotics, pp. 1973–1994. Springer, Cham (2016). https://doi.org/10.1007/978-3-319-32552-1_73
20. Olaff, H.S., Eikeseth, S.: Variabler som kan pvirke effekter av tidlig og intensiv opplaring basert pa anvendt atferdsanalyse (EIBI/TIOBA) (2015)
21. Parmenter, T.: Promoting Training and Employment Opportunities for People with Intellectual Disabilities: International Experience (2011)
22. Ryan, R.M., Deci, E.L.: Self-determination theory and the facilitation of intrinsic motivation, social development, and well-being. Am. Psychol. **55**(1), 68–78 (2000)
23. Sandygulova, A., et al.: Interaction design and methodology of robot-assisted therapy for children with severe ASD and ADHD. Paladyn. J. Behav. Robot. **10**(1), 330–345 (2019)
24. Simm, W., Ferrario, M.A., Gradinar, A., Whittle, J.: Prototyping 'clasp': implications for designing digital technology for and with adults with Autism. In: Proceedings of the 2014 Conference on Designing Interactive Systems, DIS 2014, pp. 345–354. Association for Computing Machinery, New York (2014)
25. Taheri, A., Shariati, A., Heidari, R., Shahab, M., Alemi, M., Meghdari, A.: Impacts of using a social robot to teach music to children with low-functioning autism. Paladyn. J. Behav. Robot. **12**(1), 256–275 (2021)

26. Van den Berk-Smeekens, I., et al.: Adherence and acceptability of a robot-assisted pivotal response treatment protocol for children with autism spectrum disorder. Sci. Rep. **10**(1), 8110 (2020)
27. Verbeke, E., Peeters, W., Kerkhof, I., Bijttebier, P., Steyaert, J., Wagemans, J.: Lack of motivation to share intention - primary deficit in autism? Behav. Brain Sci. **28**(5), 718–719 (2005)

A Wizard of Oz Interface with Qtrobot for Facilitating the Handwriting Learning in Children with Dysgraphia and Its Usability Evaluation

Jianling Zou[1(✉)], Soizic Gauthier[2,3], Salvatore M. Anzalone[1], David Cohen[2,3], and Dominique Archambault[1]

[1] CHArt Laboratory, Paris 8 University, Paris, France
jianlingzou93@gmail.com

[2] Department of Child and Adolescent Psychiatry, Pitié Salpêtrière University Hospital, Paris, France
soizic.gauthier@aphp.fr

[3] CNRS UMR 7222, Institut des Systèmes Intelligents et Robotiques, Sorbonne University, Paris, France

Abstract. This paper presents the design of a Wizard of Oz interface with a library of robot behaviors developed for caregivers on handwriting learning in children with dysgraphia. We assess the final version of the interface with 15 care participants during a single simulated session. All care participants fulfilled the System Usability Scale and Attrakdiff 2 scale. In sum, the results confirm the system's usability, but there is still room for improvement.

Keywords: Wizard of OZ interface · Social robot · Dysgraphia · Humain-robot interaction

1 Introduction

Handwriting is an essential skill to describe thoughts or objects, and express emotions. This ability seems natural for most people. However, some children demonstrate that their writing abilities are inconsistent with their ages. We call this disturbance in handwriting dysgraphia [5]. Children with dysgraphia are often viewed by teachers or parents as neglectful or lazy rather than being perceived as children suffering from a learning disability they cannot control. This situation directly impacts the children's self-esteem, self-confidence, and social relationships [4,6]. When handwriting difficulties are detected, children are usually addressed by occupational therapists with the approach focus on attention deficit that impacts handwriting automatization or on handwriting itself [6]. The pen-and-paper exercises which are very close to the tasks carried out in school will be proposed for remediation to automatize the writing process [3]. Some

Supported by National Research Agency (ANR) of France.

K. Miesenberger et al. (Eds.): ICCHP-AAATE 2022, LNCS 13342, pp. 219–225, 2022.
https://doi.org/10.1007/978-3-031-08645-8_26

children with dysgraphia express frustration, even refusal , regarding treatment sessions. The review of Cifuentes et al. highlight social robots are efficiently used to assist with therapies for children with NDD. And in the case of autism spectrum disorders, social robots can support clinical effectiveness of therapeutic session [13]. With the aim to facilitate the learning process of handwriting in children with dysgraphia and to break this vicious circle, we present the design of a tool based on a social robot. It's a Wizard of Oz interface which supports the caregivers in selecting the robot's behavior to apply the learning-by-teaching method to ask the child to teach the robot learning handwriting.

2 Methodology

Fig. 1. QTRobot's apperance. [Public domain] via symbioïde.

Fig. 2. Learning-by-teaching setup

Luxai's QTRobot[1] (Fig. 1) was chosen as the preferred social robot platform due to its expressive abilities in terms of social cues and, above all, broader facial expressions and good stability, with an appropriate size for interaction with children, of 64 cm . This social robot has been designed to increase therapy efficiency by encouraging active and engaged interaction [9]. Meanwhile, a serious game platform dedicated to practicing handwriting called Dynamilis[2] was used as a complementary tool to the robot. Among the various games provided by Dynamilis, the game that was used to train multi-features is co-writer. It was the best-suited game for our learning-by-teaching scenario. In this game, the child becomes the robot's teacher and teaches it how to write. In our previous work [7], Gargot et al. used the co-writer game between a Nao robot and a 10-year-old boy with a complex neurodevelopmental disorder combining developmental coordination disorder and severe dysgraphia. The structure of the study consisted of 20 consecutive weekly sessions (i.e., 500 min).

[1] Luxai's offical website : https://luxai.com/.

[2] The serious game "Dynamilis": https://dynamilis.com/en/.

As shown in Fig. 2, the robot is near the table and faces the child. The child has an iPad to play the serious game, and the caregiver has a tablet to control the robot. Meanwhile, the robot has a fake tablet to show the child that he is learning writing. This article focuses on evaluating the usability of the Wizard-of-Oz interface that caregivers will use during rehabilitation sessions. Another successive article will present the study of rehabilitation sessions and its result.

Following a literature review and an observatory study, we created the first set of behaviors based on the robot's role in our learning-by-teaching scenario of all of the significant robot-child interactions in the work indicated above [4]. Robot's complex behaviors involve gestures, speeches, and emotions. Gestures are predefined fluid movements created by physically moving the robot's joint while recording the dynamic of their different positions and angles, exploiting the gesture API built-in with the QTRobot. In addition, we have developed a standardized file format for these behaviors, keeping the name and the speed of the gesture, a sequence of facial expressions, and similar speeches. The program randomly selected one of these similar speeches when the behaviors were played to reduce repeatability and increase the robot's vitality.

There was a certain complexity in developing multi-platform interfaces because of different operating systems (such as Android, iOS, Windows) for various electronic devices that might be used in the future. In the end, we decided to build a web interface to adapt to multiple platforms. HTML 5, JavaScript, and CSS have been used for the web's front-end. Then, we used the Flask framework in Python as a server to ensure communication between the web and the robot. After every button click, the robot played the corresponding behavior through Robot Operating System (ROS). Furthermore, the user interface design followed Jakob Nielsen's ten usability heuristics [12]. After an iterative design with six children and six caregivers who participated in nine rehabilitation sessions (this study will be presented in another article), we invited fifteen caregivers (five teachers, five psychomotor therapists, five speech therapists) to evaluate the usability of the final version of our system. Table 1 describes each participant.

The evaluations were conducted in the form of single simulated sessions, each session was about an hour. After a tutorial about how to use the interface, every caregiver can test the interface in thier own way during half an hour. Then they were given some tasks and had to control the robot as if they were with a child. In the end, we asked the caregiver to complete two well-validated scales of user's experience evaluation: the French version of SUS (System Usability Scale) [8] and the Attrakdiff 2 scales [11]. In more detail, SUS is a Likert scale comprising ten items with a total score that varies between 0 and 100. AttrakDiff questionnaire is also a Likert scale containing twenty-eight items divided into four subscales, each comprising seven questions. The AttrakDiff subscales are as follows [10]:

- **Pragmatic quality (PQ)**: describes the usability of the product and indicates how well it enables users to achieve their goals (in the sense of realizing a task);
- **Hedonic-stimulation quality (HQ-S)**: indicates the extent to which the product can support the need for stimulation;

Table 1. Description of caregivers participants who carried on a final evaluation of system

Id.	Age*	Sex	Occupation	Years of experience*
ProFinal1	24	F	Psychomotor therapist	1
ProFinal2	27	F	Speech therapist	4
ProFinal3	22	M	Psychomotor therapist	1
ProFinal4	45	F	Psychomotor therapist	0 (2 years of internship)
ProFinal5	22	F	Psychomotor therapist	0 (2 years of internship)
ProFinal6	51	F	Speech therapist	26
ProFinal7	29	F	Speech therapist	3
ProFinal8	58	F	Teacher	36
ProFinal9	31	F	Speech therapist	4
ProFinal10	54	F	Speech therapist	21
ProFinal11	48	F	Teacher	25
ProFinal12	23	F	Psychomotor therapist	0 (2 years of internship)
ProFinal13	54	F	Teacher	25
ProFinal14	60	M	Teacher	37
ProFinal15	62	F	Teacher	32

**Age and years of experience at the research beginning*

- **Hedonic-identity quality (HQ-I)**: indicates to what extent the product allows the user to identify with it;
- **Overall attractiveness (ATT)**: describes the overall value of the product based on the perception of pragmatic and hedonic qualities.

We used the SUS to evaluate the WoZ interface and the AttrakDiff 2 to assess the robot's behaviors.

3 Result

At the final version of our system, we created 120 different behaviors classified into 33 menus according to their usage. In the interface presentation, we designed two web pages, one is the login page, and the other is the control page. The login page can collect the names of the participants, which can be included in some pre-programmed behaviors, where the robot calls their names for personalization. The control page includes the 33 menus into two tabs: scenario and game tab, reaction tab. As shown in the Fig. 3, we also used dividers to sub-categorize menus to make it easier for users to find the buttons they need quickly. When the user double-clicked the menu icon, all allocated buttons expanded in an ellipse, starting from the menu's position. Every button was in the same color as the icon of the menu it belonged to. Once the button was clicked on, the robot played the corresponding predefined behavior.

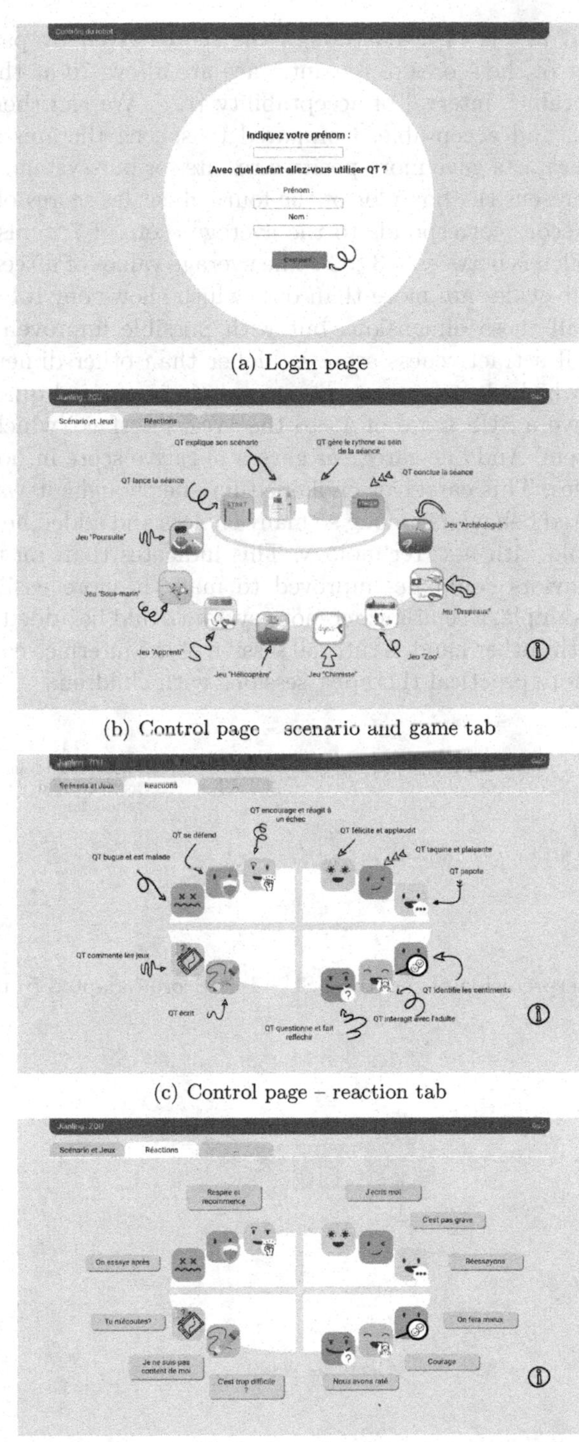

(a) Login page

(b) Control page – scenario and game tab

(c) Control page – reaction tab

(d) Buttons of a menu

Fig. 3. The final version of the Wizard of Oz interface

As illustrated in Fig. 4, even though the scores given by participants are spread out, most of the scores of our interface are above 70 at the SUS, which is in the "Acceptable" interval of acceptability [1,2]. We can therefore say our interface is good and acceptable. Compared to speech therapists or teachers, psychomotor therapists gave more positive results for our system. Furthermore, in Fig. 5, we represent the box-plot of the four sub-scales scores of Attrakdiff 2. Every sub-scale score corresponds to the average score of 7 items belonging to this sub-scale which is between −3 to 3. The average values of fifteen participants for these four sub-scales are more than one, which shows our robot's behaviors are positive in all these dimensions but with possible improvements.And the average of overall attractiveness score is higher than other dimension and has less dispersion, which shows in general our system is of good quality. However, one caregiver gave a SUS score of 45 to the WoZ interface, which corresponds to a "poor" system. And one caregiver gave a negative score in both AttrakDiff hedonic sub-scales. This caregiver explained he/she thought it was not easy to find the best-suited behaviors among so many choices and added he/she generally is not comfortable with new technology. This indicates that, on the one hand, the robot's behaviors could be improved to make it more easily usable and enjoyable. For example, a semi-autonomous system could be added to give choice suggestions. On the other hand, a tutorial session of the interface can be proposed to caregivers before practical therapist sessions with children.

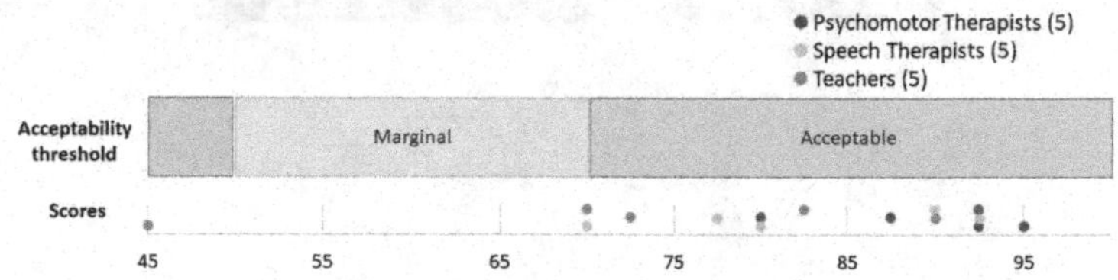

Fig. 4. Interpretation of the Total SUS Test Score (adapted from [1,2])

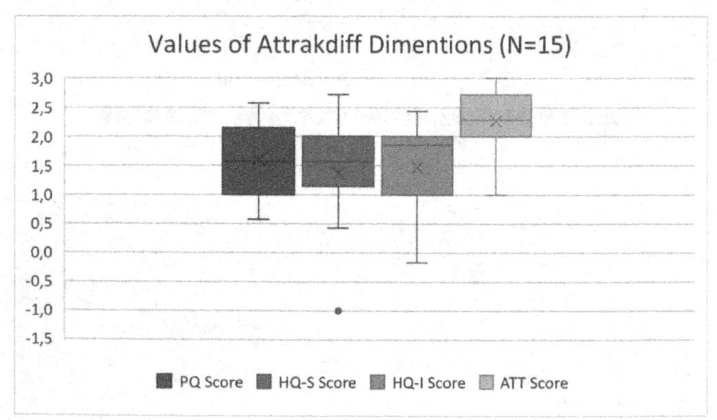

Fig. 5. Values of Attrakdiff dimensions (N=15)

4 Discussion and Conclusion

This work focused on developing a usable WoZ interface for caregivers adapted to multi-platforms to facilitate handwriting learning in children with dysgraphia. The WOZ interface presented was developed and updated based on our iteration development experience with six children and six caregivers, which will be presented in our successive article. We found our system to be positive based on the usability testing results we got for the final version. However, since all the participants did not test the system with real children in an actual situation, the score of the usability evaluation might be superior. Even though we mentioned before the evaluation that each scale should be used to assess the corresponding dimension (WoZ interface or robot's behavior), many participants indicated having difficulty evaluating them separately, which can be a bias of user test results. In the future, we will conduct practical experiments with more caregivers and children based on the original iteration development experience set up. This will provide the database for our next step in automating the robot and getting more user testing results.

References

1. Bangor, A., Kortum, P., Miller, J.: Determining what individual sus scores mean: adding an adjective rating scale. J. Usability Stud. **4**(3), 114–123 (2009)
2. Bangor, A., Kortum, P.T., Miller, J.T.: An empirical evaluation of the system usability scale. Intl. J. Hum. Comput. Int. **24**(6), 574–594 (2008)
3. Berninger, V.W., et al.: Treatment of handwriting problems in beginning writers: transfer from handwriting to composition. J. Educ. Psychol. **89**(4), 652 (1997)
4. Chung, P., Patel, D.R.: Dysgraphia. Int. J. Child Adolesc. Health **8**(1), 27 (2015)
5. Chung, P.J., Patel, D.R., Nizami, I.: Disorder of written expression and dysgraphia: definition, diagnosis, and management. Transl. Pediatr. **9**(Suppl 1), S46 (2020)
6. Feder, K.P., Majnemer, A.: Handwriting development, competency, and intervention. Develop. Med. Child Neurol. **49**(4), 312–317 (2007)
7. Gargot, T., et al.: It is not the robot who learns, it is me. treating severe dysgraphia using child-robot interaction. Front. Psychiatry **12**, 5 (2021)
8. Gronier, G., Baudet, A.: Psychometric evaluation of the F-SUS: creation and validation of the french version of the system usability scale. Int. J. Hum. Comput. Int. **37**(16), 1571–1582 (2021)
9. Grossard, C., Palestra, G., Xavier, J., Chetouani, M., Grynszpan, O., Cohen, D.: Ict and autism care: state of the art. Curr. Opin. Psychiatry **31**(6), 474–483 (2018)
10. Hassenzahl, M., Burmester, M., Koller, F.: Attrakdiff: Ein fragebogen zur messung wahrgenommener hedonischer und pragmatischer qualität. In: Mensch and Computer 2003, pp. 187–196. Springer (2003). https://doi.org/10.1007/978-3-322-80058-9_19
11. Lallemand, C., Koenig, V., Gronier, G., Martin, R.: Création et validation d'une version française du questionnaire attrakdiff pour l'évaluation de l'expérience utilisateur des systèmes interactifs. Eur. Rev. Appl. Psychol. **65**(5), 239–252 (2015)
12. Nielsen, J.: Ten usability heuristics (2005)
13. Valentine, A.Z., Brown, B.J., Groom, M.J., Young, E., Hollis, C., Hall, C.L.: A systematic review evaluating the implementation of technologies to assess, monitor and treat neurodevelopmental disorders: a map of the current evidence. Clin. Psychol. Rev. **80**, 101870 (2020)

POWERUP: A 3D-Printed Exoskeleton and Serious Games for the Rehabilitation of Children with Motor Disabilities

Ana Rojo[1,2](✉), Susana Del Riego[1], Cristina Sánchez[1], Eloy J. Urendes[1], Rodrigo García-Carmona[1], Sergio Lerma-Lara[3], and Rafael Raya[1,2]

[1] Departamento de Tecnologías de la Información, Escuela Politécnica Superior, Universidad San Pablo-CEU, CEU Universities, Madrid, Spain
ana.rojoagusti@usp.ceu.es

[2] Werium Assistive Solutions, Madrid, Spain

[3] Motion in Brains Research Group, Centro Superior de Estudios Universitarios La Salle, Universidad Autónoma de Madrid, Madrid, Spain

Abstract. Objective: This study presents the design and evaluation of goal-directed arm tasks using a customised exoskeleton for children with motor disabilities (MD). A further aim was to investigate the suitability of using video games or virtual reality as motivational technologies for gamified functional exercises. Methods: An upper limb exoskeleton and two gamified solutions adapted for functional exercises have been developed. Preliminary tests have been carried out with children with motor impairments and similar disorders to assess the level of satisfaction with the use of this proposed configuration. Results: The satisfaction results regarding the usability of the exoskeleton with these immersive gamified systems have been very positive, highlighting the ease of use, adaptability, comfort, lightness and safety of the exoskeleton. Preliminary validation results of the concept idea have also been excellent, as the exoskeleton system combined with the goal-directed tasks based video game has provided the user with the perception of control from the first session. The design, based on 3D printed materials, will allow the exoskeleton to be used more widely in day care centres due to its low cost and high usability. Conclusion: Training with gamified systems that motivate the patient to perform exercises together with exoskeletons that aid movement are positively accepted by children with motor disabilities. In addition, the use of an exoskeleton seems to improve the goals achieved by the children in the games.

Keywords: Exoskeleton · Motor disabilities · Rehabilitation · Serious games · Upper limb

1 Introduction

In this investigation, motor disabilities (MD) are defined as all motor or tonicity abnormalities of any origin. According to the WHO International Classification

K. Miesenberger et al. (Eds.): ICCHP-AAATE 2022, LNCS 13342, pp. 226–236, 2022.
https://doi.org/10.1007/978-3-031-08645-8_27

of Diseases, Ninth Revision (ICD-9) [1], motor disability diagnoses may include the presence of hemiplegia, quadriplegia, paraplegia, ataxy, athetosis and other motor disorders. Conventional treatments for children with MD comprise a combination of physiotherapy, orthotics and occupational therapy. Although there are still discrepancies about the most effective intervention therapies for this ailment, due to the complex nature of this type of injury [2], most physical intervention methodologies agree on the need to perform strength and repetition tasks [2–4]. Such tasks enable the patient to work on various parts of the body in a structured and separate manner.

However, in terms of motivation, traditional therapies present two main drawbacks: the monotony of the exercise and the lack of interesting stimuli for the patient to increase their motivation [5]. To mitigate this problem, several gamified solutions have been developed, but have required the design and creation of new hardware approaches that involve the installation of expensive equipment in the clinic or in the patient's home [6]. Nevertheless, a plausible solution to increase patient motivation and, consequently, positively influence their rehabilitation therapy without the need to create expensive hardware systems specifically tailored for children with motor disabilities is to use inexpensive commercial devices and generate gamified applications specific to this demand.

Concerning therapy feasibility, it should be considered that children with different motor disabilities often requires robotic assistance to perform certain movements. Lately, robotic rehabilitation has shown very positive results in preliminary studies [7–9]. Because of this, these gamified applications should tolerate the use of any external movement assistance equipment required by the child. Most existing videogame-based therapies focus on two fundamental properties: to induce as much immersion as possible and to accurately track the patient's movements. The former improves the user engagement in a task that is eminently physical, while the latter is necessary for assessing if the movements have been properly performed.

The reason why the Kinect device is one of the most widely used systems for motion capture in the field of physiological therapy is because it accurately captures the user movements [10,11]. However, it should be noted that this commercial system may lose tracking accuracy when exoskeletons or wearable robotic motion assistance systems are included. To deal with this limitation, wearable motion tracking systems for videogames (exergames) or virtual reality (VR) devices can be employed since their capability for accurate motion capture of the user head and hands movements precludes an immersive simulation and are compatible with the use of wearable robotics. The usage of VR headsets may be difficult or impossible for some children with MD, depending on the level of cognitive impairment and their cervical strength. For these reasons, children's preferences and physical condition must be properly assessed to choose, based on the characteristics of each patient, the appropriate technology for gamification applications. Several studies highlighted that rehabilitation solutions based on immersive environments are more effective than traditional [12] due to three essential qualities:

- Improve the patient's engagement: Exergames increase the user's energy expenditure and involve both cognitive and physiologically rewarding tasks [13]. These highly motivating activities likely promote game adherence.
- Provide physical fidelity to a real movement: The patient performs motions similar to those he would do in an analogous situation during their daily life.
- Provide cognitive fidelity to a real situation: The patient must perform the activities in an environment designed to be similar to the real world.

Different research studies have confirmed that exercises aimed at improving activities of daily living (ADL) have greater acceptance, increase motivation, and improve adherence to treatment [14,15]. Therefore, the exercises developed must have an intentional goal that makes the user perform one or more of the functional movements present in ADL. Taking all of this into account, it is expected these gamified immersive solutions specifically designed for upper limb rehabilitation exercises combinable with a custom exoskeleton will promote patient's immersion [16] and motivation. All in all, the objectives of this work are, first, to develop a solution that meets all the criteria listed before. And second, to perform a preliminary test to evaluate the satisfaction and usability of the approach.

2 Methods

The solution developed for this work, named "POWERUP" addresses the need to develop gamified scenarios playable with assistance or resistance robotics. Then, two technological solutions, designed for the cognitive level of children from 6 to 12 years, were created: a video game for reaching objectives and a virtual reality experience for interaction with objects, both adapted to be used with exoskeletons.

2.1 POWERUP Exoskeleton

The POWERUP exoskeleton for children aged 8–12 years old with different mortor disabilities implying upper limb limitations has been designed based on clinical and functional criteria defined by the clinicians of La Salle University (Madrid, Spain). This articulated system, built with 3D printing pieces with PLA filament (a thermoplastic monomer derived from renewable and organic sources), can be adapted to the arm length of the child. With 5 degrees of freedom (DoF), it allows the patient to perform functional tasks by providing stability and to assist or resist flexion and extension of shoulder and elbow joints keeping the wrist and the hand in neutral position. The system is composed of three segments (shoulder, arm, and elbow), which modular design allows for quick and intuitive assembly (see Fig. 1B). All the segments can be easily adjusted to the user's anthropometry by the physiotherapist. The flexion-extension movement of the shoulder and elbow joint is enabled by means of elastic bands, while the internal-external rotation of these joints is unrestricted. Elbow pronation is performed by means of a concentric circumferential mechanism on which the wrist is supported (see Fig. 1B).

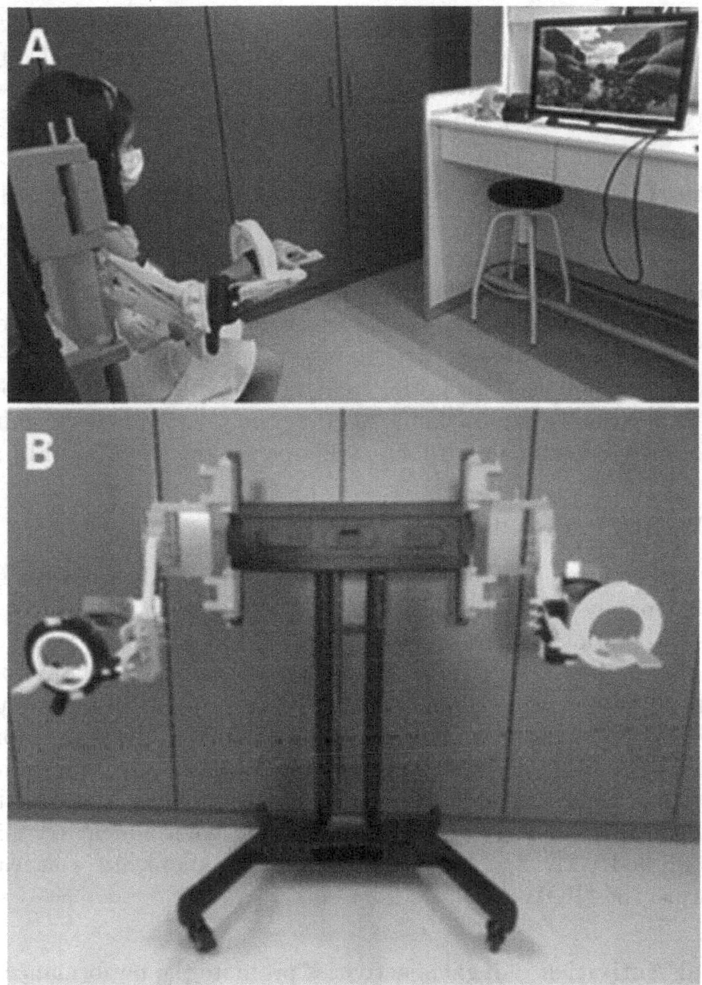

Fig. 1. A) Child using the upper limb exoskeleton and the video game. B) Exoskeleton structure for both upper extremities.

2.2 POWERUP Video Game

The POWERUP video game was generated using the Unity3D game engine v.2019.3. This video game is made up of a configuration interface of the game parameters, which is manipulated by the clinician, and the game interface for the patient. The interaction mode is based on user's arm kinematics to control a third-person avatar using the ENLAZA^{TM} sensor (Werium Assistive Solutions, Spain) [18]. This device contains an IMU module that integrates a 3-axis accelerometer, a 3-axis gyroscope and a 3-axis compass and transmits the angular data to the video game via Bluetooth.

Goal-Directed Tasks. All video game activities were developed following the direct manipulation paradigm i.e., the game consists of a virtual object that is manipulated via physical input device [19]. Using this paradigm solves the difficulties of interaction with peripherals that children with MD may face.

Videogame User Experience. In each one of the 5 scenarios of the video game, the child acts as the pilot of a vehicle (airplane, rocket, drone) or avatar (fairy, bird) which moves at a constant speed through a virtual scenario. When playing the game, targets positioned at a certain distance and height from the avatar appear. The positioning of these targets is defined by the range of motion (ROM) of the joint in question (wrist, elbow, shoulder), as determined by the clinician at the beginning. This initial configuration of difficulty, number of targets, targets positioning and maxima ROM of the joint, allows the definition of boundaries that set up a comfortable work area for the child (see Fig. 1A).

2.3 POWERUP VR Platform

The POWERUP Game Center was developed using the Unity3D game engine v.2019.2.13f, mainly using the collection of scripts and predefined elements of the Oculus Integration framework, which allows to build virtual reality solutions for the Oculus devices. This toolkit enabled the implementation of virtual space locomotion, 3D object interaction, 3D body physics within the virtual space and hand-tracking interaction. This whole VR platform is designed for the VR device Oculus Quest 2. While the practitioner or supervisor of the game session interacts with a computer application where the minimum game settings can be defined, the patient interacts with the virtual environment containing the different gamified activities. Both applications communicate with each other and constitute the "POWERUP Game Center" system.

Functional Activities. All game activities promote the performance of reaching movements that preclude the execution of functional tasks faithful to ADL. From the rehabilitation point of view, that is a clear advantage of using VR instead of exergames with exoskeletons, such as Armeo (Hocoma, Switzerland) [7], InMotion Arm Robot (Bionik Laboratory Corporation, USA), or the Diego and Amadeo (Tyromotion, Austria) [17].

VR Platform User Experience. At the beginning of the virtual experience and during each waiting time between the selection of the activities and its configuration, the user finds himself in a virtual environment that simulates a large ship, in which he is accompanied by non-playable characters. In this space, the user can gradually customize his cubicle by purchasing objects or toys in the virtual store. To be able to buy all these items, the user must pass levels in each game to be rewarded with coins.

Currently, the "POWERUP Game Center" platform offers 2 games: Cloud Room and Pirate Room, each with 3 gamified activities, which can be played with or without using an upper limb orthotics, as hand recognition is enabled. Therefore, the interaction mechanics of these games and activities are based on the achievement of objectives by grasping objects with virtual hands or colliding with them. In general, the objects are generated in front of the user and, if not reached, disappear after 10 s.

2.4 Procedure

The purpose of this preliminary test is to assess the participants' level of satisfaction with the games, in terms of usability with the gamified solutions, as well as to make a first approximation to the characteristics of the motor control of the participants.

Participants. Participants were recruited by the physiotherapists of the La Salle University (Madrid, Spain) according to the following inclusion criteria: (i) children aged 6 to 12 years, (ii) with appropriate or sufficient cognitive level to maintain attention and follow the video game dynamic, (iii) diagnosed with neuromuscular or neurological pathologies producing upper limb motor impairments. Ten children volunteered to participate in the preliminary test using the video game, but only seven children completed the 8 testing sessions. The participants had the following neurological pathologies: (2) spinal muscular atrophy, (3) right hemiparesis, (1) spastic tetraparesis and (1) cerebral palsy. Among the last 7 participants, three children volunteered to participate in the preliminary test using VR technology.

Video Game Experimental Trials. For this test, the participant was seated comfortably at 1.5 m from the screen on which the games were being played. Each participant performed several rounds of the video game, testing all scenarios configured with comfortable elbow ROM values for the user. All participants underwent 8 sessions working on shoulder and elbow flexion-extension and shoulder abduction-adduction movements. For each child, the exoskeleton was used on the most affected side and adjusted according to the needs of counter-gravity motion assistance by using rubber bands.

Virtual Reality Experimental Trials. For this test the user was seated in the center of a room, and, before starting, he/she had the interpupillary distance of the Oculus Quest 2 lenses adjusted to his/her needs and fitted the VR device to his/her head. Each participant tests all the activities (3) of each virtual room, which were configured according to a low level of difficulty and number of targets. Two of three participants completed all the rounds (5) of each activity until they obtained gratification (coins), while the third one abandoned the test shortly after starting.

2.5 Data Analysis

The analysis is focused on whether the approach, i.e., the combination of the POWERUP exoskeleton with the video game, results in a usable environment and provides the user with a sense of control of the system. To measure the degree of control and usability of the prototype, the success rate of each session and the ratio between the ideal measure and the successful one is recalculated from all the kinematic data measured by the inertial sensor. In this way, the end-point trajectory was acquired during each session. Later, based on the standardized indices computed by Armeo^{TM} Spring (Hocoma, AG, Swiss) [20], we have computed the global end-point path ratio (EPPR) defined as the ratio between the length of the end-point trajectory during the reaching movement and the ideal distance between the starting point and the target, for both vertical and horizontal movements.

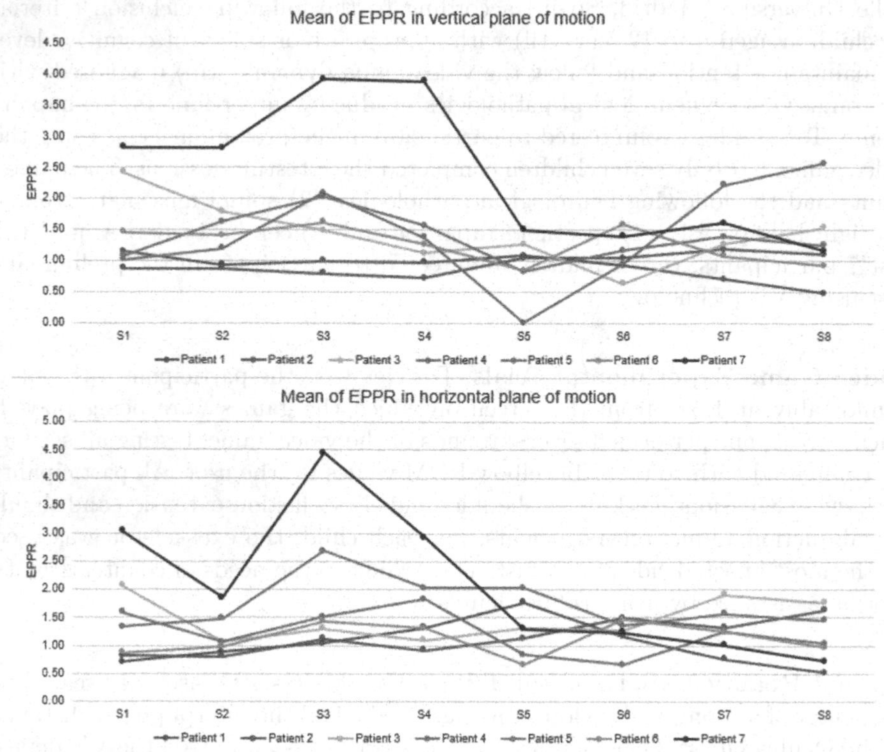

Fig. 2. Representation of the mean outcomes of EPPR for each session, participant and plane of movement.

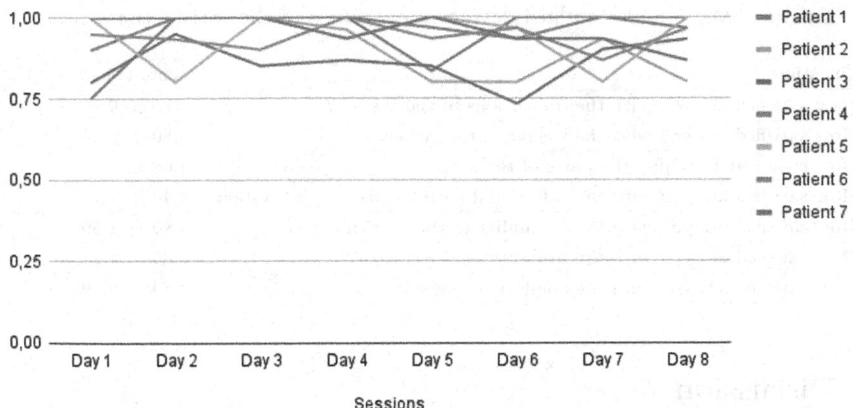

Fig. 3. Highest goal-achievement score per session and participant.

3 Results

The data analysis previously described and carried out with the aim of contrasting to what extent the combination of the exoskeleton with the video game interface can enhance the directed movement of the goal-reaching activities proposed.

Figure 2 shows the mean values of the EPPR of each plane of movement organized for users and sessions. The EPPR metric gives an appreciation of the directionality of the movement. Values close to 1 mean that the user has performed a movement whose trajectory is very similar to the ideal or minimum trajectory. Non-optimal trajectories are reflected by values below 1 when not enough movement was performed or, contrarily, by values above 1 when excessive movement was performed.

Consistent with the calculated EPPR results, the highest score of goal-achievements per session of each participant is shown in Fig. 3. Where the goal-achievement ratio of the video game is above 75% as a general pattern. Lastly, the average results of the satisfaction surveys on the use of the system are shown in the Table 1. This satisfaction questionnaire is based on a 5-point Likert scale, whereby each item of the questionnaire is scored from 1 to 5.

Table 1. Mean and standard deviation outcomes of the satisfaction survey

Question	Score (Mean $\pm$ SD)
How satisfied are you with the dimensions of the system?	4.20 $\pm$ 0.90
How satisfied are you with the weight of the system?	3.80 $\pm$ 0.96
How easy is it to adjust the parts of the system?	4.00 $\pm$ 1.11
How satisfied are you with the safety and harmlessness of the system?	4.40 $\pm$ 1.11
How satisfied are you with the durability of the system?	3.80 $\pm$ 1.50
How satisfied are you with the usability of the system?	4.60 $\pm$ 1.21
How satisfied are you with the comfort of the system?	3.80 $\pm$ 0.69

4 Discussion

The aim of this preliminary study was to validate the proof of concept by replicating the Armeo paradigm in a low-cost system customisable for each patient with a gamified environment that allows working in a specific work area. Thus, in general, the participants' satisfaction surveys on the exoskeleton highlighted the high satisfaction with the ease of use, adaptability and safety of the exoskeleton. Regarding the design of the exoskeleton, participants also rated the system's dimensions, weight and comfort very positively. In fact, these last aspects have been the main design requirements that clinicians expressed from the beginning and that researchers took into account during the process of creating and editing the prototype, as they are key points in the success of its use.

In addition, the results of the satisfaction questionnaire showed that the video game solution combined with the use of the exoskeleton is ideal for this purpose. Furthermore, it can be concluded that the key to motivate the subject has been the application of gamification strategies commonly used in commercial video games: 1) structure the game in progressive levels of complexity that force players to continuously surpass themselves in order to advance; 2) reward achievements; 3) use interesting narratives and high quality graphics to attract users. The aim of this work was not to develop a simple game for rehabilitation, but a virtual reality video game adapted to the interaction needs of children with MD.

With regard to the results of the preliminary test of the prototype with the video game, it should be noted that from the first to the last session, all patients showed a success rate of more than 75% in achieving the objectives of the video game. This value indicates that from the first moment, the use of this system provides the user with the perception of control and the necessary movement assistance to be able to exercise functional movements according to their maximum movement ranges of each joint. Although it is not possible to speak of a learning curve as a result of the outcomes, Fig. 3 shows a generalised success rate for all users, which confirms the viability of using the system. In addition, with the exception of participants 4 and 7, it can be seen that the rest of the participants achieve an average EPPR between 0.5 and 1.5 in both planes of movement throughout the sessions. Therefore, although the exoskeleton assists elbow flexion-extension, it has an effect on the participants' overall control of movement in both planes of motion.

Regarding the test experience with the virtual reality application, an important aspect to take into account is the patient's interest in video games. It was observed that of the three children who participated in the VR pretest, two of them quickly became involved in the game and even managed to perform movements that they had not been able to do so easily in the previous therapy sessions. In contrast, the other child, who did not have the same interest in video games, found the technology too overwhelming and cumbersome, and soon after the test began, he decided to stop playing. However, the game-based solution was accepted in all cases and none of the children dropped out of the test. We attribute this to the fact that a virtual reality experience might be more impactful than a video game, and not all children tolerate overstimulating environments. However, it was also observed that adherence to the video game was lower, as their motivational game strategy was not based on rewards for progressive improvement but on the score. Based on all these findings, the authors' recommendation is to use the VR solution with those children who show interest in the world of play, as a high level of motivation is clearly achieved. Finally, it is concluded that it is important to generate more immersive robot-assisted play solutions and to further investigate their potential positive effect on the functional rehabilitation of children with MD.

Acknowledgement. This research was funded by Ministerio de Ciencia, Innovación y Universidades, under the grant "Convocatoria Retos Investigación" with project reference RTI2018-097122-A-100.

References

1. World Health Organization. International classification of diseases [9th] ninth revision, basic tabulation list with alphabetic index. World Health Organization (1978). https://apps.who.int/iris/handle/10665/39473
2. Kwon, J.S., Park, M.J., Yoon, I.J., Park, S.H.: Effects of virtual reality on upperextremity function and activities of daily living performance in acute stroke: a double-blind randomized clinical trial. NeuroRehabilitation **31**(4), 379–385 (2011)
3. Howard, M.C.: A meta-analysis and systematic literature review of virtual reality rehabilitation programs. Comput. Hum. Behav. **2017**(01), 013 (2017)
4. Cheung, K.L., Tunik, E., Adamovich, S.V., Boyd, L.A.: Neuroplasticity and virtual reality. In: Weiss, P.L.T., Keshner, E.A., Levin, M.F. (eds.) Virtual Reality for Physical and Motor Rehabilitation. VRTHCA, pp. 5–24. Springer, New York (2014). https://doi.org/10.1007/978-1-4939-0968-1_2
5. Syed, U.E., Kamal, A.: Video game-based and conventional therapies in patients of neurological deficits: an experimental study. Disabil. Rehabil. Assist. Technol. **16**, 332–339 (2019)
6. Cano de la Cuerda, R., Munoz-Hellin, E., Alguacil-Diego, I., Molina-Rueda, F.: Telerrehabilitación y Neurología. Revista de Neurología. **51**(1), 49–56 (2010)

7. El-Shamy, S.M.: Efficacy of Armeo®robotic therapy versus conventional therapy on upper limb function in children with hemiplegic cerebral palsy. Am. J. Phys. Med. Rehabil. **97**(3), 164–169 (2018). https://doi.org/10.1097/PHM.0000000000000852
8. Lara S, L., et al.: Can robotic-based top-down rehabilitation therapies improve motor control in children with cerebral palsy? A perspective on the CPWalker project. Biomed. Res. Clin. Pract. **1**(1), 22–26 (2016). https://doi.org/10.15761/BRCP.1000106
9. Fasoli, S.E., Ladenheim, B., Mast, J., Krebs, H.I.: New horizons for robot-assisted therapy in pediatrics. Am. J. Phys. Med. Rehabil. **91**(11 Suppl 3), S280–S289 (2012). https://doi.org/10.1097/PHM.0b013e31826bcff4
10. Dimbwadyo-Terrer, I., et al.: Upper limb rehabilitation after spinal cord injury: a treatment based on a data glove and an immersive virtual reality environment. Disabil. Rehabil. Assistive Technol. **11**(6), 462–467 (2016)
11. Bayón, M., Martínez, J.: Rehabilitación del ictus mediante realidad virtual. Rehabilitación. **44**(3), 256–260 (2010)
12. Viñas-Diaz, S., Sobrido-Prieto, M.: Realidad virtual con fines terapéuticos en pacientes con ictus: revisión sistemática. Neurologia **34**(4), 255–277 (2019)
13. Maillot, P., Perrot, A., Hartley, A.: Effects of interactive physical-activity videogame training on physical and cognitive function in older adults. Psychol. Aging **27**(3), 589–600 (2012). https://doi.org/10.1037/a0026268
14. García García, E., Sánchez-Herrera Baeza, P., Cuesta Gómez, A.: Efectividad de la realidad virtual en la rehabilitación del miembro superior en la lesión de la médula espinal. Revisión sistemática. Revista de Neurología **69**(04), 135–144 (2019)
15. Sveistrup, H.: Motor rehabilitation using virtual reality. J. Neuroeng. Rehabil. **1**, 10 (2011)
16. Roberts, H., et al.: Constraint induced movement therapy camp for children with hemiplegic cerebral palsy augmented by use of an exoskeleton to play games in virtual reality. Phys. Occup. Ther. Pediatr. **41**(2), 150–165 (2021). https://doi.org/10.1080/01942638.2020.1812790
17. Esquenazi, A., et al.: A comparison of the ARMEO to tabletop assisted therapy exercises as supplemental interventions in acute stroke rehabilitation: a randomized single blinded study. PM&R **13**,(2020). https://doi.org/10.1002/pmrj.12397
18. Raya, R., et al.: An inexpensive and easy to use cervical range of motion measurement solution using inertial sensors. Sensors **18**(8), 2582 (2018). https://doi.org/10.3390/s18082582
19. Schneiderman, B.: Direct manipulation: a step beyond programming languages. IEEE Comput. **16**(8), 57–69 (1983)
20. Merlo, A., et al.: Upper limb evaluation with robotic exoskeleton. Normative values for indices of accuracy, speed and smoothness. NeuroRehabilitation **33**(4), 523–530 (2013)

Visual Impairment Sensitization: Co-Designing a Virtual Reality Tool with Sensitization Instructors

Lauren Thevin[1,2](✉) and Tonja Machulla[1,3]

[1] LMU Munich, Munich, Germany
tonja.machulla@ifi.lmu.de

[2] Université Catholique de l'Ouest, Angers, France
lauren.thevin@uco.fr

[3] Technical University Dortmund, Dortmund, Germany

Abstract. Sensitization procedures often make use of the simulation of visual impairments (VI). The use of Virtual Reality (VR) is particularly promising due to easy modification of the visual scenery and the high level of immersion. Existing implementations often focus on the demonstration of difficulties that arise from VI and do not embed the simulation into a structured sensitization procedure—they provide no information about adaptive behaviors, adaptations to the environment, or assistive technologies that can mitigate the problems experienced in the simulation. This can foster stereotypes of persons with VI as not being able to perform activities of daily living rather than sensitize with regard to their actual experiences. In this work, we co-designed a VR tool for professional sensitization sessions with a group of four sensitization instructors. The tool provides a large number of scripted interactions with the environment and allows the selective activation of different VI, barriers, and facilitators. Its design prioritizes the communication of solutions over the mere demonstration of what persons with VI cannot see.

Keywords: Virtual reality · Sensitization · Visual impairments

1 Introduction

Unstructured contact with people with impairments can result in stereotypes and negative attitudes [5]. For instance, sighted people often show misconceptions about the perceptual and behavioral consequences of visual impairments (VI). This is likely due to the fact that persons without VI rely heavily on visual information during daily activities (from grabbing a mug of coffee to negotiating obstacles and changes in level [12], to social interactions [19]). In fact, the subjectively perceived reliance on vision is so high that people without a VI may even feel uncomfortable using non-visual technology even if it imposes no extra costs [7,9]. As a result, they may be under the impression that having a VI is deleterious to performing daily activities autonomously. Sensitization is a

K. Miesenberger et al. (Eds.): ICCHP-AAATE 2022, LNCS 13342, pp. 237–246, 2022.
https://doi.org/10.1007/978-3-031-08645-8_28

structured procedure that aims to avoid such pitfalls. The goal is to convey a realistic impression of the abilities and challenges of persons with impairments in everyday life.

Critically, a sensitization procedure should convey the fact that a perceptual limitation or a VI does not necessarily lead to behavioral limitations [11,18], as described in the Disability Creation Process Conceptual Scheme [8]. Persons with VI often adapted their behavior to comply to the requirements of their residual vision, e.g., they bring a book close to their face to retain a standard reading speed. In addition, cognitive strategies can replace perceptual ones [10]. Virtual Reality (VR) approaches allow to generate arbitrary, high-fidelity stimuli and environments that can then be explored under simulated VI [6]. Unfortunately, digital simulation tools are often presented by themselves, i.e., without a systematic integration of interactions with the environment, responsible for the disabling situation [11,18]. Additionally, the emphasis is typically on the problems the VI introduces for persons without such impairements. An example would be the overlay of a virtual scotoma over real-world images without further instructions regarding compensation strategies that are typically used by persons with scotomas. Often, it is unclear whether these simulation tools increase awareness about an impairment, as intended, or whether they may even convey the wrong message (e.g., "low or no vision is the problem").

Critically, a sensitization procedure should convey the fact that a perceptual limitation or a VI does not necessarily lead to behavioral limitations [11,18], as described in the Disability Creation Process Conceptual Scheme [8]. Persons with VI often adapted their behavior to comply to the requirements of their residual vision, e.g., they bring a book close to their face to retain a standard reading speed. In addition, cognitive strategies can replace perceptual ones [10]. In this work, we collaborated over the course of six months with four sensitization instructors to study the field's needs and the relevance of VR for sensitization. In particular, VR and immersive visual interfaces provide flexible and controlled VI simulation and environment. In the proposed solution, and in contrast to previous work and in accordance with current models of how disability emerges, each disabling situation within the simulation is presented with compensatory solutions, either through behavioral strategies, environmental modifications, or assistive technologies. Further, we elicit misconceptions of the general public from the knowledge of the four instructors.

In sum, the main contributions of our work are: (1) a realistic and scripted scenario to study sensitization to VI in VR and in a real world setting, and (2) to our knowledge, the first study on sensitization including instructors as participants.

2 Related Work

2.1 Sensitization by Instructors: Tools and Theoretical Framework

Optical simulation goggles are widely used by instructors during sensitization. These glasses are modified to simulate VI, e.g., with a restricted acuity or field of view. Simulation goggles support sensitization to identify issues in daily life activities. In general, the instructors craft their own goggles, although commercial glasses exist (e.g. [2]). Aballéa and Tsuchiya [3] positively evaluated the feasibility of experiencing VI with glasses through three conditions of blurred vision. The instructors we interviewed (see our *Method*) use the Disability Creation Process Conceptual Scheme (DCPCS) [8]. The DCPCS posits that the disabling situation is modified by an interaction of personal factors (an impairment) with environmental factors (facilitators and barriers) and life habits (social participation or disabling situations). In particular for healthcare trainees, understanding VI in interaction with the environment is imperative to diagnose and propose solutions. Simulating impairments and disabilities without solutions may focus on problems only, convey the wrong messages and reinforce stereotypes and counterproductive beliefs, such as [16]: (i) The impairments and the disabilities are the problem or the source of the problem. In the worst case: the person with impairments is the source of the problem. (ii) The people with disabilities are not "capable"/"able". In the worst case: the impression that it is horrible to have an impairment, as it leads to not being able or autonomous. (iii) Feeling happy not having disabilities. (iv) There is nothing that can be done in case of disabilities and impairments. These wrong conclusions may have a huge impact, particularly for sensitization of relatives and caregivers. It may reinforce existing behaviors towards people with impairments, such as considering them as not autonomous (e.g., helping without asking, talking to the accompanying person), rather than adapting building and environmental conditions. By including non-personal factors in sensitization tools, it is possible to convey the following messages: (I) The interaction of impairment and environment is the source of the problem. (II) The impairment does not make somebody incapable, and strategies exist to overcome difficulties. (III) Not having pity for people with disabilities, but rather gaining awareness. (IV) We can propose solutions and modifications to make situations accessible and inclusive.

2.2 Visual Impairment Sensitization

Based on computer graphics, digital VI simulation tools were proposed in research as an alternative to the traditional simulation goggles. Computer serious games are an opportunity to sensitize, for instance with *Vie Ma Vue* [1]. The application proposes to play eight missions in school that may lead to difficulties for people with VI. The quiz at the end of every quest proposes adaptations and strategies. Multiple VR and virtual environment simulators were proposed. In [4], a virtual apartment, which can be explored with VI simulation to understand and recognize the problems described by a patient. However, this tool was not evaluated with participants. In 2011, Lewis et al. [14] proposed a realistic VR simulation in a restaurant environment, to raise awareness regarding the symptoms of eye diseases and demonstrate the difficulties and challenging tasks faced by people with VI. Four opticians validated the benefits of the Virtual Environment (VE) for VI simulation. An expert used the system for 15 min to verify the features. From our understanding of the experimental protocol, twenty-one participants explored the simulator in a one-by-one setting with two tasks (navigation, reading). They had pre-and post-exploration questionnaires about VI and of the problems faced by people with VI. The participants subjectively increased their understanding of problems faced by people with VI, and more participants were able to describe eye diseases. These studies demonstrate the interest for awareness about problems related to VI. However, they were not used by instructors running sensitization sessions. There are various works that use VI simulation in desktop and VR applications for sensitization [6,13,15,18]. The previous works validated the VI simulation in VR and VI simulation for sensitization. However, their conclusions answer only partially whether the objectives of instructors running a sensitization session are reached.

3 Method

Research Question: Our goal is to understand the factors that support and hinder sensitization in VR: Can VR fulfill the requirements of professional sensitization? The interactive design process, with stakeholders, enables to elicit the requirements of a professional sensitization system. These requirements are linked to VR systems, through prototyping and pretests. We gather these factors in an exploratory fashion.

Participants: Four instructors (all female) participated in the iterative design. They represent four occupations, i.e. O&M instructor, Orthoptist, Autonomy in daily life instructor, Consultant in adaptation and assistive technology. All work in a school for young people with VI. One of their responsibilities is to run sensitizations and train external groups regarding VI.

4 Results: Co-design of Environment and Visual Impairment Simulation in VR

4.1 Usual Settings for Sensitization

In the usual settings, the instructors use modified glasses to simulate VI. These are crafted from conventional glasses by frosting (blurred vision), by adding opaque tape on the glasses except a pinhole for tunnel vision, and by adding opaque circular patches and blurring the remaining vision for scotoma. The sensitization starts with a welcoming and a 15 min theoretical presentation by the orthoptist to the group to be sensitized (generally between 6 and 12 people). After the presentation, the group is split into 3 parts and each sub-group participates in 3 workshops of 30 min each. The workshops are i) navigation by the OM instructors, ii) assistive technology and tools by the Consultant, and iii) home and daily life activities by the Autonomy instructor. After the 1 h 30 of workshops, the participants have a 15 min debriefing with the instructors to comment on the scenario, the VIs, the disabling situations, and the solutions.

The participants can take up one of two roles: "experiencing a situation with VI" while wearing the glasses and performing interactions with the environment, or "observing the participants in situ".

4.2 Design Steps

The iterative process to arrive at the final prototype consisted of the study stages (a to c) and the design stages (1 to 5), depicted in Fig. 1. In the following, we provide detailed results for each of these stages.

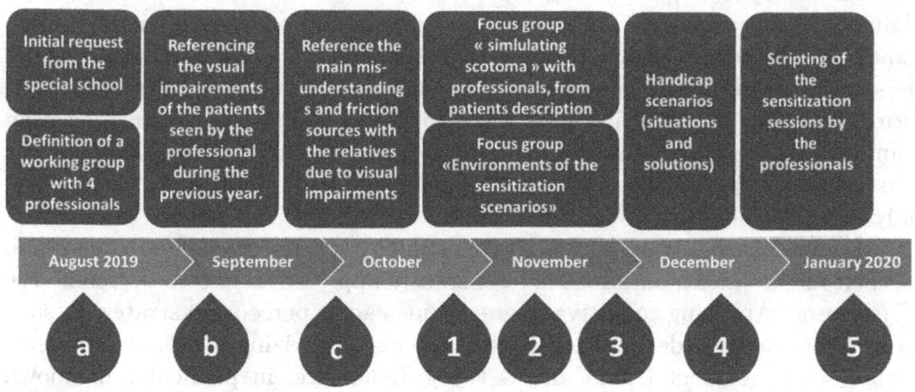

Fig. 1. Iterative design process, with the working group (stages a to c) and the co-designed prototypes (stages 1 to 5) before the final version.

a) In August 2019, we created the working group (WG) of four instructors (see participants subsection). We asked the WG about the objectives of a sensitization. There are three main types of participants in a sensitization session: wide audience, health-care professionals, and relatives. For all, the objectives are awareness about the main category of VI (**Objective O1**), and the associated problems for people with VI, if possible with a general awareness that solutions exist (**O2**). For health-care professionals and relatives, the sensitization aims to provide basic knowledge about the concrete solutions and typical compensatory strategies (**O3**). Finally, relatives may be interested in gaining knowledge about a particular type of VI (**O4**). Demonstrations that VR and visual impairment simulation support O1 and partially O2 is sufficiently covered in related work.

b) To define the VI to simulate (O1 and O4), we studied official sources (the WHO and national categories of VI). The Orthoptist send us the VI from the consultations the past year. These sources suggest to simulate the field of view, the acuity, and blind spots (scotoma), in particular central scotoma.

c) To bring awareness about the problem faced by people with VI, we asked the working group to identify common misconceptions about VI they encounter in their field work. We found three.

Misconception#1: Why does a person with VI perceive some things and not others (e.g., sees bread crumbs but not the bag on the floor, a bird but not a sign)? Reasons are the type of impairment (tunnel vision for the first example), and multi-sensory perception (bird singing). **Conclusion to avoid #1:** The person is acting in bad faith. **Requirement for sensitization #1:** Provide situations where we can observe variability of functional vision in daily life scenarios.

Misconception #2: Why does a person with VI not search for things (e.g., claiming "I do not have a fork") using strategies appropriate to their VI (e.g., fixating to the side of their blind spot). Reason: The VI is not perceptible to the person with VI themselves because "What is not seen does not exist". **Conclusion to avoid #2**: Waiting for people with VI to know their own limitation compared to the perceptual capacities of people without VI. **Requirement for sensitization #2**: Create a VI simulation where the VI itself is not perceptible, only its consequences.

Misconception #3: Why is the person with VI not paying more attention to their environment, and does not constantly apply strategies to overcome the VI? Reason: Applying cognitive strategies instead of perceptual strategies, such as imposing strict order on the environment or memorizing locations of objects requires a large mental load and is tiring. Therefore, in particular in known environments, the person may not double check if an object is correctly identified or if there are obstacles on the floor. **Conclusion to avoid #3**: Ask the person to compensate constantly for the VI, rather than adapt the environment (house, school) or the habits of the other co-users of the environments. **Requirement for sensitization #3**: Create interactive situations in adapted and non-adapted environments and habits, demonstrate the efficiency of cognitive strategies and environmental strategies, as well as the effort required for cognitive strategies.

Along these requirements, we developed six consecutive prototypes, each tested by the instructors of the WG.

1) The first **prototype 1** (Unity desktop app) simulated blurred vision, tunnel vision (with restricted camera field of view), and a scotoma in 3D environments of a classroom and of a living room (Requirement 1). We simulated auto-completion on the scotoma by progressively losing details when looking at an object (such as writing details) or progressively making small objects disappear in the center of the vision (Requirement 2). To answer the limitation of having only a 2D rendering, we created a Cardboard smartphone VR application, with 3DoF (degrees of freedom, as the user can only influence the angle of the view by turning the head).
2) As the field of view was not editable, we adapted the tunnel vision to be done with a smooth vignetting in the **prototype 2**.
3) To enable the trainees to move (moving closer is an adaptive strategies used for scotoma and blurred vision, and tunnel vision a major implication in

movement), we created the third **prototype 3** as a 6DoF VR VI simulation smartphone app. We integrated ARCore anchors to position the Cardboard camera at the position of the smartphone in the room in addition to VR stereoscopic rendering.

4) In order to add object manipulation, we moved to an HTC Vive Pro Eye application, to use eye-tracking, and with the possibility to enable and disable the visual impairments (O1, impact 2) in **prototype 4**.
5) In the **prototype 5**, we integrated complete scenarios of a sensitization session. Currently, we are finalizing the final application.

Final Prototype, Hardware and Software. We developed our application using Unity, SteamVR plugin, HTC Vive Pro with an integrated eye tracker, and its controllers. To simulate central scotoma without masking environment (i.e., no black spot visualization), we simulated an auto-completion (or auto-fill) phenomenon by modifying the appearance of the objects themselves. We can extend this technique virtually to any blind spot shapes, by changing the blind spot texture. Acuity is modified with a post processing blur effect on the camera. Tunnel vision is complicated to recreate in virtual reality without creating strong cybersickness by modifying the field of view of the virtual camera. We created two levels of tunnel vision. A first version (25°), not too obvious, uses two mechanisms (the reduced field of view in VR headset of 110° and a blur edge vignette). The second version is a pinhole recreated with a mask (3°). **Environment, Activities, Adaptation and Strategies**. We developed three virtual environments: i) an indoor environment with a living room and a kitchen; ii) a street environment with a pedestrian crossing, a bus stop, and the entrance of a school, and iii) a classroom environment. Since handicaps result from interaction with the environment, the users perform daily life tasks in these virtual environments, interacting with objects through the Vive controllers to learn adaptive strategies (moving, holding an object closer, manipulating a virtual magnifier). The scripted VR scenario includes 24 different interactive tasks to be performed by the trainees. The tasks were chosen from three areas, in which persons with VI commonly receive training: autonomy of daily life tasks, mobility and orientation tasks, and environmental adaptations & assistive technology-related tasks.

5 Discussion

Does Our VR Application Fulfill the Requirements for Structured Sensitization? The VR tool meets Requirement 1. It simulates specific challenges for each type of visual impairment in daily-life situations. Regarding Requirement 2, VR experiences were designed such that the VI itself is mostly imperceptible (see also [17]). For example, scotoma were not simulated as a black spot but rather as an area that is filled-in by the surrounding visual information. Lastly, the tool meets requirement 3, by providing a large number of scripted activities, allowing for the exploration of these activities with and without compensatory strategies as well as providing the possibility to display adaptations of the VR environment that act as facilitators and barriers.

Table 1. Steps of the scripted scenarios. Acronyms for VI(visual impairments) in the table: CS = central scotoma, BV = blurred vision, TV = tunnel vision, PH = pinhead vision. Acronyms for VE (virtual environments) in the table: LR = living room, K = kitchen, St =street, CR = classroom. Actions to perform in the sensitization scenarios (column 1), the associated VI simulated (col. 2), the proposed solution (col. 3).

Actions	VI / VE	Solutions
Find the remote controller	CS / LR	Organization, keep elements always at the same place
Turn on the TV and put the channel 15	CS / LR	Color (red button on-off), bigger button, standard tactile marker on the "5"
Watch the TV	CS / LR	Get closer and neofixation to have visual element outside of the scotoma
Read the journal	CS / LR	Get closer and neofixation, magnifier and e-magnifier
Go to the kitchen	CS / LR	Keep the floor free of obstacle (in the scenario kid toys), contrasted elements, all open or all closed doors
Find a can of bean	CS, BV / K	Get closer and neofixation, organize, use stickers with big police, use Penfriend stickers, close the closets door
Warm a deep pan	CS, BV / K	Contrasted fire places, logical location of the control buttons, physical buttons, contrasted and tactile indicators of the fire controlled by the button
Serve a liquid in a mug	CS, BV / K	Contrasted mug (depending on the liquid), sense of weight, index in the recipient for cold liquid, temperature on the exterior of the recipient (cold or warm), pitch of the sound, counting the time to fill a specific recipient, electronical sensors
Find a jogurt in a fridge	CS, BV / K	Organizing, contrasted tap on the edges of the frigde racks to understand the fridge organization even with the bloom from the fridge light, contrasted products
Open the door to go to outside with a key	CS, BV / K	Neofixation, organization
Find the number of the house and to go to the number 2	CS, BV / St	Logical research of visual cues, monocular glasses and e-magnifyer
Find the pedestrian crossing and reach it	TV, BV / St	Visual scanning to find the target and avoid obstacle, white cane
Find cues to decide how to cross and initiate the crossing	TV, BV / St	Search for traffic light, activate it through a button or a universal remote controller, listen the sound of the audio traffic light
Find the bus station and how to go to the city hall	TV, BV / St	Find the current stop and direction on the top of the bus station, search in the bus line map the stop, get closer to see the small letters
Find the entrance of the school (VR) or of the auditorium (glasses)	TV, BV / St	Find the signs with the names, and search the entrance doors with logical visual scanning
Count the number of steps	TV, BV / St	Use the line on the side of the stairs, standards (contrast and tactile warning bands)
Enter in the classroom and find and reach the black chair	PH / CR	Keep the floor free of obstacles, visual scanning
Find which of the 3 maps of the room is correct (VR) or draw the map of the room	PH / CR	Do not change the spatial organization, visual scanning
Read the content on the numerical board and find the newly added teachers written note	PH / CR	Good positioning regarding to the board, second screen for the student, control on light, police, size, color and contrast
Read exercise instructions	BV / CR	Chose the color of the paper depending on contrast (white) and photophobia (ivory), adapt the size and the police
Measure with a ruler the triangle sides	BV / CR	Chose an adapted ruler (high contrast and big police), and a highly contrasted figure
Calculate the sum of the triangle sides	BV / CR	Use a speaking and big police calculator
Read a corrected copy of a student with visual impairments	BV / CR	Write with a black and contrasted pen, avoid cursive writing, learn dactylography to write, read, proofread and review the written information
Find the Word icon on a computer desktop	BV / CR	Organize, use bigger icons and text, zoom tool

Limitations and Perspectives. In this work, we do not present quantitative results (including descriptive or inferential statistics). Our future work will be to verify the usability in a professional sensitization context in user study. In addition, we mainly address the potential of VR regarding the target group of health-care professionals, while close relatives and a more general audience would be relevant groups too.

Other Approaches to Sensitization. While VR demonstrated its potential for application in a sensitization context, we did not studied VR as a tool to replace current sensitization means as a full alternative but rather as an additional tool. Other approaches to sensitization exist, including being in contact with people with impairments. We believe that such direct contact with people is essential and should not be replaced with simulations. Our argument is that a first-person experience oriented solution can bring a phenomenological insight, and change beliefs from "I would never be able to do that with an impairment", to succeeding through compensation, adaption, and assistive technology use.

Acknowledgments. We thank IRSA - Alfred Peyrelongue Center and all their staff. We thank UNADEV for their support and funding.

References

1. Vie Ma Vue. https://www.reseau-canope.fr/vis-ma-vue/. Accessed 2020
2. Zimmerman Kit. www.lowvisionsimulationkit.com/. Accessed 2020
3. Aballéa, S., Tsuchiya, A.: Seeing for yourself: feasibility study towards valuing vi using simulation spectacles. Health Econ. **16**(5), 537–543 (2007)
4. Ai, Z., et al.: Simulation of eye diseases in a virtual environment (2000)
5. Barney, K.W.: The effect of two disability-awareness training models on stigmatizing attitudes among future healthcare professionals. The University of Utah (2011)
6. Boumenir, Y., Kadri, A., Suire, N., Mury, C., Klinger, E.: Impact of simulated low vision on perception and action. IJCHHD **7**(4), 441 (2014)
7. Delić, V., Vujnović Sedlar, N.: Stereo presentation and binaural localization in a memory game for the visually impaired. In: Esposito, A., Campbell, N., Vogel, C., Hussain, A., Nijholt, A. (eds.) Development of Multimodal Interfaces: Active Listening and Synchrony. LNCS, vol. 5967, pp. 354–363. Springer, Heidelberg (2010). https://doi.org/10.1007/978-3-642-12397-9_31
8. Fougeyrollas, P., Boucher, N., Edwards, G., Grenier, Y., Noreau, L.: The disability creation process model: a comprehensive explanation of disabling situations as a guide to developing policy and service programs. Scand. J. Disabil. Res. **21**(1), 25–37 (2019)
9. Gaudy, T., Natkin, S., Leprado, C., Dilger, T., Archambault, D.: Tampokme: a multi-users audio game accessible to visually and motor impaired people. In: CGAMES 20007, France. IEEE (2007). https://hal.archives-ouvertes.fr/hal-01125391
10. Giudice, N.A.: Navigating without vision: principles of blind spatial cognition. In: Handbook of behavioral and cognitive geography. Edward Elgar Publishing (2018)
11. Hogervorst, M., Van Damme, W.: Visualizing VI. Gerontechnology **5**(4), 208 (2006)

12. Houwen, S., Visscher, C., Lemmink, K., Hartman, E.: Motor skill performance of school-age children with VI. Dev. Med. Child Neurol. **50**(2), 139 (2008)
13. Klinger, E., Boumenir, Y., Kadri, A., Mury, C., Suire, N., Aubin, P.: Perceptual abilities in case of low vision, using a VR environment. In: ICVR, p. 63. IEEE (2013)
14. Lewis, J., Brown, D., Cranton, W., Mason, R.: Simulating VI using the unreal engine 3 game engine. In: SeGAH, pp. 1–8. IEEE (2011)
15. Maxhall, M., Backman, A., Holmlund, K., Hedman, L., Sondell, B., Bucht, G.: Participants responses to a stroke training simulator, vol. 4 (2002)
16. Silverman, A.M.: The perils of playing blind: problems with blindness simulation and a better way to teach about blindness. Braille Monit. **60**(6), 341–350 (2017)
17. Thévin, L., Machulla, T.: Three common misconceptions about VI. In: Demon 3DUI Contest IEEE VR (2020)
18. Velázquez, R., Sánchez, C.N., Pissaloux, E.E.: vi simulator based on the hadamard product. Electr. Notes Theor. Comput. Sci. **329**, 169–179 (2016)
19. West, S.K., Rubin, G.S., Broman, A.T., Munoz, B., Bandeen-Roche, K., Turano, K.: How does VI affect performance on tasks of everyday life?: the see project. Arch. Ophthalmol. **120**(6), 774–780 (2002)

Assessing Professional Caregivers' Intention to Use and Relatives' Support of Use for a Mobile Service Robot in Group Therapy for Institutionalized People with Dementia – A Standardized Assessment Using an Adapted Version of UTAUT

Catharina Wasić[1(✉)], Frank Bahrmann[2], Stefan Vogt[2], Hans-Joachim Böhme[2], and Elmar Graessel[1]

[1] Department of Psychiatry and Psychotherapy, Center for Health Services Research in Medicine, University Hospital Erlangen, Friedrich-Alexander-Universität Erlangen-Nürnberg (FAU), Schwabachanlage 6, 91054 Erlangen, Germany
catharina.wasic@uk-erlangen.de

[2] Faculty of Informatics/Mathematics, Department of Artificial Intelligence/Cognitive Robotics, University of Applied Science Dresden (HTW Dresden), Friedrich-List-Platz 1, 01069 Dresden, Germany

Abstract. Introduction: Care settings for people with dementia involve not only the individuals who are being cared for but also professional caregivers and relatives. Therefore, the use of a social robot also depends on professional caregivers' and relatives' acceptance of the robot.

Methods: We surveyed 29 relatives and 18 professional caregivers of institutionalized people with dementia in a nursing home in Germany. To assess acceptance, we used an adapted version of the Unified Theory of Acceptance and Use of Technology and the Almere model.

Results: Intention to use the robot by professional caregivers correlates positively with attitude, facilitating conditions and perceived usefulness as well as negatively with anxiety. Support of use by relatives correlates positively with attitude, perceived usefulness, facilitating conditions and social influence. Intention to use and support of use significantly differ between professional caregivers and relatives.

Conclusion: For professional caregivers and relatives that are not the primary users of the robot and only indirectly affected by the employment of a robot, perceived usefulness and attitude have a significant influence on the acceptance. Professional caregivers are more skeptical about social robots and have lower acceptance values compared to relatives.

Keywords: Robotics · Caregivers · Acceptance · Dementia · Residential facilities

K. Miesenberger et al. (Eds.): ICCHP-AAATE 2022, LNCS 13342, pp. 247–256, 2022.
https://doi.org/10.1007/978-3-031-08645-8_29

1 Introduction

The average global life expectancy increased over the last two decades by six years and demographic projections predict a continuation of this trend with a rising number of people with dementia [1–3]. Technical advances in medical treatments and processes are one reason for this trend [3]. Acceptance is a crucial prerequisite to aid implementation and optimize use of technical equipment [4]. Since the 1990s, researchers study the acceptance of different information systems in the health care sector, like electronic health records, telemedicine applications and handheld computers [4, 5]. In recent years, studies started to test robotic solutions for health care [6, 7]. Besides surgical robots and rehabilitation robots, social robots in particular are recognized for their potential uses in care settings, while not replacing professional caregivers [8], and research regarding this topic is expanding [6]. Assessing acceptance of a social robot is not only helpful to foster use, but also an ethical concern when vulnerable groups like people with dementia are involved.

1.1 Measuring Acceptance

In its general meaning acceptance implies receiving, agreeing to, or approving of something or someone [9]. Technology acceptance can either be defined as end-user satisfaction [10] or as the intention to use a technology [11].

The concept of intention to use was first conceptualized in the Technology Acceptance Model (TAM) by Davis [12] and is modelled after the behavioral theories of Fishbein and Ajzen [13]. TAM and its variations TAM2, TAM3 and the Unified Theory of Acceptance and Use of Technology (UTAUT) as well as adapted versions of these models have been widely used to study technology acceptance in the health care sector [5]. Heerink et al. [14] adapted the UTAUT model by Venkatesh et al. [15] to assess intention to use a social robot by elder adults and people with mild cognitive impairment, the Almere model.

1.2 Acceptance of Robots in Care Settings

Representative studies in Europe found that health professionals had a negative attitude towards robots and rated them as a risk in care settings [16, 17]. Acceptance of robots varied by the field of use: while support in physical tasks, monitoring and documentation was accepted by health professionals, support of emotional or social situations was not [18]. Reviews on TAM and its subsequent developments found that perceived usefulness, perceived ease of use, attitude and social influence can predict intention to use technology in health care [4, 5] and intention to use predicts the actual adoption of the robot in long-term use [19]. Intention to use a robot by older people with and without cognitive impairment can be predicted by perceived ease of use, perceived enjoyment, attitude, anxiety, trust, social influence, and perceived usefulness [14, 20–22]. The long-term use of a robot also increased perceived ease of use, attitude and perceived usefulness in people with dementia [23]. For informal caregivers social influence, facilitating conditions and effort expectancy could predict the intention to use technology with people with dementia [24] and interactions with the robot can increase a positive attitude towards it [25].

1.3 Research Aim and Hypothesis

"Care4All – Initial" was a pilot project designed to assess the feasibility and acceptance of a social robot in a psychosocial group therapy for people with dementia. While the body of research encompasses professional caregivers, informal caregivers and people with cognitive impairments alike, all participants of the studies were always the intended users of the technology. In the present study, most of the professional caregivers and all of the relatives questioned were not going to use the robot, though the robot employment could affect them as it was going to be within their workplace or concerning the residents they were related to. The present study therefore considers a broader view on acceptance by people being indirectly affected by the employment of a robot.

The main research aim was to identify, which aspects correlate with the acceptance of the professional caregivers and the relatives, even if they are not the users of the social robot. We adapted the Almere model and operationalized acceptance for professional caregiver using the construct intention to use. Since the relatives of the residents will not use the robot, we chose to adapt the construct into support of use. For the professional caregivers the robot was a workplace technology, whereas the relatives were further removed from the robot and or might view it from the perspective of the residents. Additionally, the literature suggests that professional caregivers may have a more negative attitude towards robots than relatives [16, 17]. Therefore, we formed the following hypothesis:

H_1 Professional caregivers and relatives differ significantly in intention to use and support of use, respectively.

Reviews of technology acceptance studies in the health care sector found evidence for the constructs perceived usefulness, perceived ease of use and attitude to influence intention to use [4, 5]. Our second hypothesis is therefore:

$H_{2.1}$ Intention to use in professional caregivers is highly correlated with perceived usefulness, perceived ease of use and attitude.

$H_{2.2}$ Support of use in relatives is highly correlated with perceived usefulness and attitude.

2 Methods

2.1 Design

As one part of the project "Care4All – Initial", we surveyed relatives and professional caregivers in a cross-sectional study regarding their acceptance of the robot. The robot was to be employed in a group therapy for institutionalized people with dementia [26]. We distributed questionnaires to professional caregivers and relatives who were affiliated with a nursing home in Dresden, Germany, before the employment of the robot started. For the research team, we pseudonymized or anonymized the survey.

Detailed information about the robot and its functions used in the group therapy [27] as well as results from RCTs on the effectiveness of the group therapy [28–30] can be found elsewhere.

2.2 Sample

To inform the relatives and professional caregivers about the study and the robot's employment, the nursing home management administered a leaflet. The leaflet detailed the robot's abilities and its role in therapy and showed pictures of it. The leaflet was send out a few weeks before questionnaires. The questionnaires included information and a consent form that referenced the leaflet.

We send out 80 questionnaires to the relative of the institutionalized people with dementia who had been noted as the primary contact in the care record and 80 questionnaires to professional caregivers. Participants were given two months to reply. Professional caregivers were send a reminder letter. Return rate was 36% for relatives (n = 29) and 22.5% for professional caregivers (n = 18).

All procedures were in accordance with the ethical standards of the institutional research committee, national legislation, and the 1964 Helsinki Declaration and its later amendments or comparable ethical standards. The study was approved by the Ethics Committee at the Friedrich-Alexander-Universität Erlangen-Nürnberg (No. 252_18 B). Informed consent was obtained from all participants involved as well as consent for publication in summarized form.

2.3 Instruments/Tools

We created a questionnaire based of UTAUT [15] and the Almere model [14]. Three different researchers and one language interpreter translated the items into German and back into English to ensure validity. Items were adapted so they referred to the use of a robot and the respective parties. Some of the constructs of the Almere model did not fit into the context of the study and were left out, since the questionnaire was administered before the robot's employment: perceived adaptability, perceived sociability, perceived enjoyment, social presence, trust and actual use. We expended the constructs perceived usefulness and perceived ease of use by incorporating items from performance expectancy, effort expectancy and self-efficacy from the UTAUT model. Each item is a statement to which the respondents had to rate their agreement on a five-point Likert scale (ranging from "not at all" to "entirely agree"). Age, gender and computer experience – and for professional caregivers, voluntariness of using the robot – were collected as well.

2.4 Analysis

The analysis was performed following the approach suggested by Heerink et al. [20]. First, we calculated total scores and Cronbach's alpha for each construct. Second, we performed descriptive statistics and correlations between constructs for professional caregivers and relatives separately. Finally, we calculated unpaired t-tests for the constructs between professional caregivers and relatives. We used IBM SPSS Statistics 24 [31] and Microsoft Excel 2016 [32] for the statistical analysis.

3 Results

The relatives were 40 to 89 years of age (M = 62.80, SD = 12.93) and usually female (65.4%). Professional caregivers were significantly younger than the relatives (28–60 years, M = 39.27, SD = 11.09, p < .001) and 68.8% were female.

For the relatives, all constructs had a good Cronbach's alpha value (.70 or higher) [20]. The professional caregivers had three constructs with lower Cronbach's alpha values: anxiety (.46), facilitating conditions (.45), and social influence (.58).

Figure 1 shows that except for anxiety, the professional caregivers gave lower ratings to all the constructs than the relatives did. We found significant differences between professional caregivers and relatives for the constructs attitude, perceived usefulness, and intention to use/support of use.

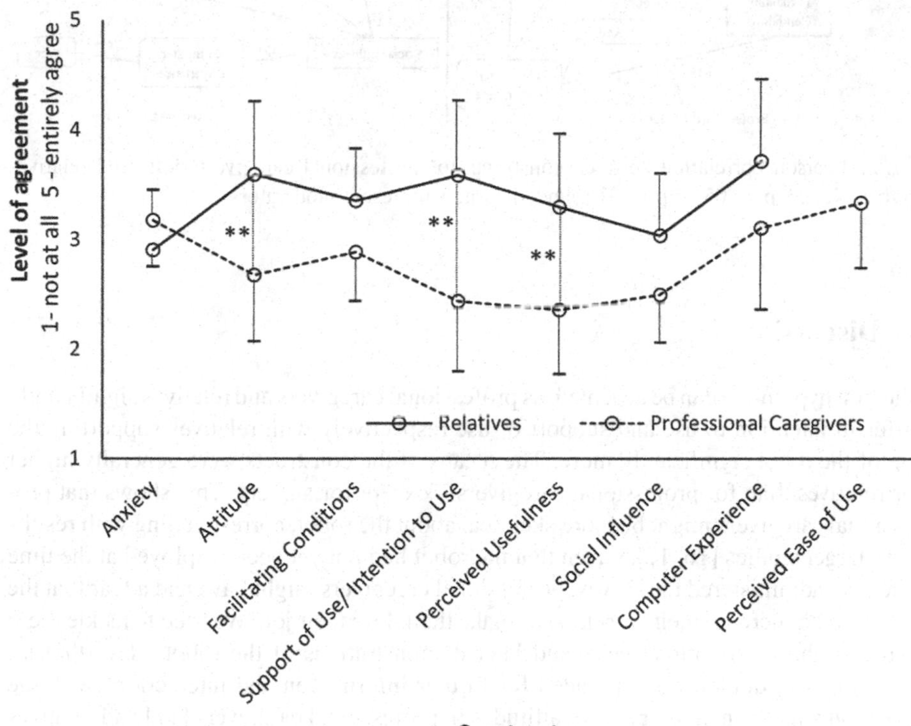

Fig. 1. Mean level of agreement with constructs by relatives and professional caregivers. Note. ** p < .01. Perceived ease of use was only measured for professional caregivers. Half standard deviation is noted for relatives and professional caregivers.

For professional caregivers the constructs attitude (ρ = .83, p < .001), facilitating conditions (ρ = .56, p = .017), and perceived usefulness (ρ = .97, p < .001) and anxiety (ρ = -.59, p = .011) correlated significantly with intention to use. For relatives the constructs attitude (ρ = .94, p < .001), facilitating conditions (ρ = .70, p < .001), perceived usefulness (ρ = .93, p < .001) and social influence (ρ = .84, p < .001) correlated significantly with support of use. Figure 2 details the correlations between the constructs and the moderators (age, gender, computer experience and voluntariness). For professional caregivers, social influence, gender and voluntariness did not correlate with other constructs. For relatives, gender did not correlate with other constructs.

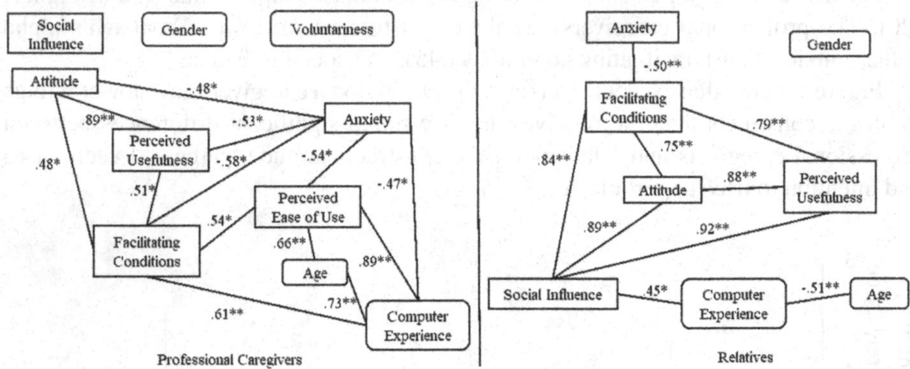

Fig. 2. Pearson correlation between constructs for professional caregivers (left) and relatives (right). Note. * p < .05 ** p < .01 rounded corners represent moderators.

4 Discussion

The first hypothesis can be accepted, as professional caregivers and relatives significantly differ in intention to use and support of use respectively with relatives supporting the use of the robot significantly more. The means of the constructs were generally higher for relatives than for professional caregivers – except for anxiety. This shows that professional caregivers might be more skeptical about the robot, corresponding with results from larger studies [16, 17]. Given that the robot had not yet been employed at the time when we administered the survey, professional caregivers might have had a fear that the robot would increase their workload or make them lose their job. We tried to tackle these issues in the information leaflet and later demonstrations of the robot. Nevertheless, these findings demonstrate the need for further information and interactions with the robot, which can increase positive attitudes in professional caregivers [17] and relatives [25].

We found significant differences between professional caregivers and relatives in age, attitude, perceived usefulness and intention to/support of use. The difference in age was to be expected as relatives can be spouses around the same age as the institutionalized people with dementia and professional caregivers are of working age. The significantly better attitude of relatives could be linked to the context of use. While the professional caregivers viewed the robot as a workplace technology, a potential burden, the relatives might have perceived the robot as a leisure time technology. This ties in with the significant difference in perceived usefulness. The relatives saw the robot as an additional source of entertainment and the professional caregivers as potentially increasing workload. The significant difference in intention to use/support of use may therefore be a direct result of the differences in attitude and perceived usefulness.

Hypothesis H2.1 can only be partially accepted. Perceived usefulness and attitude correlated significantly with intention to use for professional caregivers, perceived ease of use did not. Hypothesis H2.2 can be accepted as perceived usefulness and attitude significantly correlated with support of use. Other authors support our finding on perceived usefulness and attitude correlating to intention to use/support of use [4, 5, 14, 15, 20–22]. We also found significant correlations between the support of the robot use and social influence as well as between intention to use/support of use and facilitating conditions that are confirmed in other studies [14, 20–22, 24]. Facilitating conditions also correlated highly with other constructs for professional caregivers and relatives. This illustrates that the conditions of the robot employment affect different constructs and the overall acceptance of the robot.

The finding for perceived ease of use not correlating with intention to use is in contrast to recent research [4, 5, 22, 23]. The usefulness of a new technology might be especially important, if it is the first of its kind used within the environment. The nursing home did not use a robot beforehand. Therefore, the robot needed to proof that it was useful to be accepted. Perceived ease of use on the other hand becomes more important, if similar technologies are already in place or the usefulness is apparent. Like in the management of patient files, a file system is useful, analog as well as digital. A new electronic health record system needs to prove its advantage over the analog system by being easy to use as other studies indicate [33].

Contrary to the literature, social influence did not correlate with intention to use for the professional caregivers [4, 5] nor with any other construct. This finding might have different causes. Surveys in general tend to have a participation bias. This is notably true for studies where the participants were the intended users of the robot, since those who rejected the robot right away would refuse to participate. The professional caregivers in this study were only indirectly affected by the robot employment and would most likely not interact or work with the robot. The participation bias might therefore affect this study differently. Further, the employment of a robot in a group therapy for people with dementia in a nursing home is a new and innovative intervention, which could spark interest or rejection in the participants regardless of the opinion of others.

4.1 Strengths and Limitations

The sample size of both professional caregivers and relatives were rather low. This prevented us from using other statistical methods, like regressions, to produce further insight. This study was cross-sectional and therefore not able to examine a change in acceptance after the employment of the robot and collected in one nursing home. The findings should therefore be interpreted with caution. To our knowledge, existing studies encompassed professional caregivers, relatives and people with cognitive impairment, but they were all intended as primary users of the robot. Our work focused on assessing acceptance surveying the relatives of institutionalized people with dementia and professional caregivers who will not be directly involved with the robot employment. Assessing the acceptance of indirect users could provide guidance on aspects for general acceptance of robots in health care as well as involving them in further development. Therefore, we were able to provide a broad perspective and context of acceptance.

Future research could focus on studying intention to use/support of use in other settings, like adult day care, individual therapy or geriatric hospitals. A mixed-method approach with qualitative methods could contribute to more in-depth understanding of intention to use/support of use.

5 Conclusion

When assessing a mobile service robot employed in a group therapy for institutionalized people with dementia by professional caregivers and relatives that are not the primary users of the robot, perceived usefulness and attitude have a significant influence on the acceptance. Perceived ease of use may not be as important for new tasks or when the surveyed are not going to use the technology. Professional caregivers are more skeptical about social robots and have lower acceptance values compared to relatives.

Acknowledgments. This work is part of the project "Care4All – Initial", which was funded by the European Union via the European Regional Development Fund (ERDF), Grand number: 100294374. We thank the participants and the residential facility "Cultus gGmbH" in Dresden (Germany) for their cooperation.

References

1. United Nations, Department of Economic and Social Affairs, Population Division. World Population Prospects: The 2019 Revision (2019)
2. World Health Organization. WHO methods and data sources for life tables 1990–2019. Global Health Estimates Technical Paper WHO/DDI/DNA/GHE/2020.1 (2020)
3. United Nations, Department of Economic and Social Affairs, Population Division. World Population Ageing 2019 (ST/ESA/SER.A/444) (2020)
4. Holden, R.J., Karsh, B.-T.: The technology acceptance model: its past and its future in health care. J. Biomed. Inform. **43**, 159–172 (2010)
5. Rahimi, B., Nadri, H., Lotfnezhad Afshar, H., Timpka, T.: A systematic review of the technology acceptance model in health informatics. Appl. Clin. Inform. **9**, 604–634 (2018)
6. Wasić, C., Pendergrass, A., Böhme, H.J., Bahrmann, F., Graessel, E.: Feasibility, acceptance, and impact of socially assistive robots in non-drug interventions with people with dementia: a scoping review. Gerontechnology **20**, 1–25 (2020)
7. Alonso, S.G., Hamrioui, S., de la Torre Díez, I., Motta Cruz, E., López-Coronado, M., Franco, M.: Social robots for people with aging and dementia: a systematic review of literature. Telemed. J. E Health **25**, 533–540 (2019)
8. European Parliament. European Parliament Resolution of 16 February 2017 with Recommendations to the Commission on Civil Law Rules on Robotics (2015/2103(INL)). European Parliament, Strasbourg (2017)
9. Acceptance. Oxford English Dictionary, vol. 2020. Oxford English Dictionary (2010)
10. Brown, S.A., Massey, A.P., Montoya-Weiss, M.M., Burkman, J.R.: Do I really have to? User acceptance of mandated technology. Eur. J. Inf. Syst. **11**, 283–295 (2002)

11. Davis, F.D., Venkatesh, V.: A critical assessment of potential measurement biases in the technology acceptance model: three experiments. Int. J. Hum. Comput. Stud. **45**, 19–45 (1996)
12. Davis, F.D.: A Technology Acceptance Model For Empirically Testing New End-User Information Systems: Theory and Results. Massachusetts Institute of Technology (1985)
13. Fishbein, M., Ajzen, I.: Belief, Attitude, Intention and Behaviour: An Introduction to Theory and Research. Addison-Wesley, Reading (1975)
14. Heerink, M., Kröse, B., Evers, V., Wielinga, B.: Assessing acceptance of assistive social agent technology by older adults: the Almere model. Int. J. Soc. Robot. **2**, 361–375 (2010)
15. Venkatesh, V., Morris, M.G., Davis, G.B., Davis, F.D.: User acceptance of information technology: Toward a unified view. MIS Q. **27**, 425–478 (2003)
16. Rebitschek, F.G., Wagner, G.G.: Akzeptanz von assistiven Robotern im Pflege- und Gesundheitsbereich. Z. Gerontol. Geriatr. **53**(7), 637–643 (2020)
17. Turja, T., Van Aerschot, L., Särkikoski, T., Oksanen, A.: Finnish healthcare professionals' attitudes towards robots: reflections on a population sample. Nurs. Open **5**, 300–309 (2018)
18. Zöllick, J.C., Kuhlmey, A., Suhr, R., Eggert, S., Nordheim, J., Blüher, S.: Akzeptanz von Technikeinsatz in der Pflege. In: Jacobs, K., Kuhlmey, A., Greß, S., Klauber, J., Schwinger, A. (eds.) Pflege-Report 2019, pp. 211–218. Springer, Heidelberg (2020). https://doi.org/10.1007/978-3-662-58935-9_17
19. Vichitkraivin, P., Naenna, T.: Factors of healthcare robot adoption by medical staff in Thai government hospitals. Heal. Technol. **11**(1), 139–151 (2020)
20. Heerink, M., Krose, B., Evers, V., Wielinga, B.: Measuring acceptance of an assistive social robot: a suggested toolkit. In: RO-MAN 2009-The 18th IEEE International Symposium on Robot and Human Interactive Communication, pp. 528–533. IEEE (2009)
21. Wu, Y.H., Wrobel, J., Cornuet, M., Kerhervé, H., Damnée, S., Rigaud, A.S.: Acceptance of an assistive robot in older adults: a mixed-method study of human-robot interaction over a 1-month period in the Living Lab setting. Clin. Interv. Aging **9**, 801–811 (2014)
22. Piasek, J., Wieczorowska-Tobis, K.: acceptance and long-term use of a social robot by elderly users in a domestic environment. In: 2018 11th International Conference on Human System Interaction (HSI), pp. 478–482. IEEE (2018)
23. Ke, C., Lou, V.W.-Q., Tan, K.C.-K., Wai, M.Y., Chan, L.L.: Changes in technology acceptance among older people with dementia: the role of social robot engagement. Int. J. Med. Inform. **141**, 104241 (2020)
24. Dai, B., Larnyo, E., Tetteh, E.A., Aboagye, A.K., Musah, A.-A.I.: Factors affecting caregivers' acceptance of the use of wearable devices by patients with dementia: an extension of the unified theory of acceptance and use of technology model. Am. J. Alzheimers Dis. Other Demen. **35**, 1533317519883493 (2020)
25. Gross, H.-M., et al.: Further progress towards a home robot companion for people with mild cognitive impairment. In: 2012 IEEE International Conference on Systems, Man, and Cybernetics (SMC), pp. 637–644. IEEE (2012)
26. Böhme, H.-J., et al.: CARE4ALL-Initial. A new Human-Technology Interaction Concept for Care of People with Dementia. Zukunft der Pflege. Tagungsband der 1. Clusterkonferenz 2018 - Innovative Technologien für die Pflege, Oldenburg, pp. 152–157 (2018)
27. Bahrmann, F., Vogt, S., Wasic, C., Graessel, E., Boehme, H.-J.: Towards an all-day assignment of a mobile service robot for elderly care homes. Am. J. Nurs. Sci. **9**, 329–337 (2020)
28. Straubmeier, M., Behrndt, E.-M., Seidl, H., Özbe, D., Luttenberger, K., Gräßel, E.: Non-pharmacological treatment in people with cognitive impairment—results from the randomized controlled German Day Care Study. Dtsch. Arztebl. Int. **114**, 815–821 (2017)
29. Luttenberger, K., Hofner, B., Graessel, E.: Are the effects of a non-drug multimodal activation therapy of dementia sustainable? follow-up study 10 months after completion of a randomised controlled trial. BMC Neurol. **12**, 151 (2012)

30. Graessel, E., et al.: Non-pharmacological, multicomponent group therapy in patients with degenerative dementia: a 12-month randomised, controlled trial. BMC Med. **9**, 129 (2011)
31. IBM: SPSS Statistics. IBM Corporation, Armonk, NY (2016)
32. Microsoft Corporation: Microsoft Excel (2018)
33. Hsieh, H.-L., Kuo, Y.-M., Wang, S.-R., Chuang, B.-K., Tsai, C.-H.: A study of personal health record user's behavioral model based on the PMT and UTAUT integrative perspective. Int. J. Environ. Res. Publ. Health **14**, 8 (2017)

Development, Evaluation and Assessment of Assistive Technologies

Development, Evaluation and Assessment of Assistive Technologies

Introduction to the Special Thematic Session

Susanne Dirks[1(✉)], Christian Bühler[1], Peter Heumader[2], and Klaus Miesenberger[2]

[1] TU Dortmund University, 44227 Dortmund, Germany
{susanne.dirks,christian.buehler}@tu-dortmund.de

[2] Institute Integriert Studieren, Johannes Kepler University, Altenbergerstraße 69, Linz, Austria
{peter.heumader,klaus.miesenberger}@jku.at

Abstract. Individually adapted and usable assistive technologies are one of the essential prerequisites for empowering people with disabilities. Although a growing number of devices and assistive technologies are available, the proportion of technology abandonment is still very high. This is due to various aspects, which in part lie in the assistive technology itself, in the characteristics of the users or in the psycho-social environment. The diverse contributions in this session show interesting approaches on how to further improve the development, evaluation, and assessment of assistive technologies. The presented results entail important advances in providing people with disabilities with the technology they need in a more suitable and sustainable way.

Keywords: Assistive technologies · Participatory development · People with disabilities (PWD) · AT Abandonment · Outcome research

1 Introduction

According to the International Organization for Standardization ISO-9999:2016 [1], assistive technologies are devices, equipment, instruments, or software technologies that improve the participation opportunities and quality of life of people with disabilities [2]. Assistive technologies can be used in all areas of life. They facilitate self-care, help to lower healthcare costs and support people with disabilities to achieve greater autonomy. Examples of assistive technologies include sensory aids for sensory disabilities, prosthetics, wheelchairs, and exoskeletons for mobility impairments [3], telerehabilitation systems for barriers to accessing care, talkers and voice assistants for communication and social interaction, and social robots for mental well-being [4]. The wide range of assistive devices and the diversity of user groups make the development and provision of assistive devices challenging. Furthermore, the actual use of a particular assistive technology solution depends largely on the wishes and individual characteristics of the user and his or her living environment [5].

K. Miesenberger et al. (Eds.): ICCHP-AAATE 2022, LNCS 13342, pp. 259–266, 2022.
https://doi.org/10.1007/978-3-031-08645-8_30

Although people with disabilities as well as their relatives and caregivers generally consider the use of assistive technologies to be positive, many technologies are abandoned or not used sustainably [6–8]. The reasons for abandonment are manifold [9–11]. They can lie in the users themselves, in the assistive technology or be caused by the environment. A frequently mentioned problem is that the selected technology is too complex and not adapted to the real needs of the user [12]. Other studies indicate that assistive technologies are no longer used because the disabilities present have changed [13]. Other reasons for abandonment are environmental conditions or the acceptance of the assistive technology or the underlying limitation [14]. The demonstrably considerable extent of abandonment can be countered by appropriate approaches and methods at the levels of development, evaluation, and assessment of assistive technologies.

2 Development of Assistive Technologies

User-centered design and participatory approaches recognized as important success factor for R&D to reach a high level of usability and good user experience (UX). Through intensive cooperation with the future users of the devices and aids, the functions, complexity, usability, and design can be better adapted to the needs of the users [15, 16]. Despite the positive effects, user centered design and participatory approaches are often only an add-on to the development process, restricted to initial user requirements studies and a final product evaluation. Because of a lack of suitable concepts and methods of cooperation with different user groups, they come with some challenges and are often regarded as an additional burden in development projects. The challenges that arise in the participatory development of assistive technologies and ICT and corresponding solutions have been described in some newer studies [17].

This STS intends to provide an open and creative platform for further evaluating and reflecting the state of the art in participatory software development and discussing new and innovative ideas and concepts.

3 Evaluation and Assessment of Assistive Technologies

The terms ‘assessment’ and ‘evaluation’ are not always clearly distinguished in professional publications. However, since the goals of the two procedures are different, they need to be distinguished here. While an evaluation rates a person or a technology with regard to defined criteria, the goal of an assessment is to improve the quality of a product or a process [18].

While assistive technologies are undoubtedly empowering for people with disabilities, specific recommendations must be tailored to the individual’s needs. An evaluation process can help determine which technologies are most appropriate and effective for the individual to meet the needs of specific tasks in specific contexts. Evaluations should ideally be conducted in a way that identifies and assesses all the abilities, needs and routines in which the assistive technology will be used.

The more than 25-year-old observation by Stevens et al. that assistive technologies are evaluated insufficiently is still relevant today [19]. As in the field of development, there is still a lack of suitable methods for carrying out participatory evaluation processes that are aligned with the needs of the users and their caregivers [20]. The QUEST is one of the few methodological approaches that enables a structured evaluation of the satisfaction of the user with his/her assistive technology [21–23]. Even though the QUEST enables a standardized approach to evaluate the user satisfaction, other aspects relevant for a sustainable use of assistive technology are only partially captured.

The process of successfully bringing assistive technologies and people with disabilities together is a complex process that requires the collaboration of many different experts. With the Assistive Technology Assessment Model, a process description is available that explicates the relevant steps within the framework of a user-centered approach [24]. Assistive Technology Assessment does not only refer to the user and the assistive technology with its specific characteristics but also includes the psycho-social context of the technology application and its impact on the social inclusion and well-being of the user. Federici and Scherer therefore use the term 'assistive technology solution' instead of 'assistive technology' [24].

The contributions to this STS show innovative ways of evaluating and assessing assistive technologies.

4 Contributions

The relevance of the topic is also reflected in the diversity of the papers and presentations submitted to this workshop. In a competitive process, a total of thirteen contributions were selected, ranging from AI-based mediation of knowledge about assistive technologies [25], the selection of the appropriate technology [26], participatory development [30, 35] to the evaluation of assistive technologies in daily use [33].

The first contribution by Andrich [25] describes a model which has been developed to represent knowledge about assistive products, to feed an artificial-intelligence-based online system offering guidance to identify and select the assistive products that best suit individual needs (ASPREX). The paper describes the approach and results of building an ad hoc knowledge base on assistive technologies. An online system was used to collect the knowledge of individual experts from around the world who enter knowledge rules based on their personal expertise about the assistive technologies they know best.

The second paper by Heumader et al. [26] presents Buddy, a novel AI-powered approach to match the needs of users with cognitive disabilities with available AT solutions for working online. Based on user data collected through a questionnaire and simple games, and data provided by AT solution providers and AT users, Buddy recommends tools that support specific cognitive tasks of users. In addition to supporting people with cognitive disabilities, the approach also provides a rich source of research and development at all levels of the system.

The third paper presents two studies conducted by Aswad et al. [27] to create a sustainable, accessible, inclusive co-design toolkit for people with intellectual disabilities. The studies were based on the 'Co-Design programme' project, in which developers work together with people with cognitive disabilities as co-designers. The preliminary results reflect a positive view or experience of the co-design process by the designers and programmers involved. Especially the issues of accessibility, collaboration and communication were rated as relevant for co-design processes. Communication was seen as a key component by all participants, especially when it comes to facilitating or hindering the co-design process. Specific support measures seem to be most effective when aimed at facilitating effective communication between designers and co-designers.

The contribution of McDonnell [28] presents the results of the evaluation of a visual financial management system. The system was developed through a user-centered design process and was tested with 40 participants with different subjective numeracy skills. The visual system was developed using a visual representation of money instead of a traditional symbol-based application. The results of the study showed that the interactive visual system was the preferred design for the lower numeracy group compared to the symbolic system. It also improved the participants' financial awareness and consideration.

The fifth paper by Salatino et al. [29] reports how the provision of assistive technology assessment services succeeded for older adults with disabilities who were unable to access the service providers premises under COVID-19 conditions in Italy. The provision of mobility aids by the service provider during tele-assessments enabled the continuity of the service provision. The aids prescribed during the tele-assessments were found to be appropriate, with only a small percentage requiring revision. A questionnaire measured a high level of satisfaction with the service provided, with some respondents complaining about the length of the process, particularly in the initial period. The service professionals analyzed the process and refined the procedure for planning, collecting clinical information and organized evaluations.

The aim of the sixth study by Kortekaas and Zorn [30] was to gain insights into the concrete communication acts for participation practices in inclusive participatory virtual technology development processes and to reconstruct the interaction and participation practices with young people and professionals in an inpatient youth welfare facility. For this the first minutes of a participatory design workshop were analyzed with conversation analysis in order to find how promises for participation potential are or are not communicated. The results show how in a first minute of a "participatory" workshop the (possibly unconscious) communicational acts can contradict basic objectives of participatory design and of inclusion of people with special needs.

The following research papers were presented during the STS lectures. They are available in the ICCHP-AAATE 2022 Open Access Compendium.

The work of Corcuff et al. [31] aims to support the Municipality of Quebec, Canada, in improving the overall accessibility of best practices in knowledge mobilization. Preliminary results from the scoping review show the importance of involving all stakeholders throughout the research. Information sessions and reports need to be produced to promote knowledge, create an expert landscape to improve skills, and use interactive and diversified knowledge mobilization strategies (video, photovoice, journal) to facilitate implementation. These initial results, combined with the obstacles surveyed, will make it possible to jointly develop a knowledge mobilization intervention that is better adapted to the reality of community organizations.

The aim of the work of Rodríguez-Dueñas et al. [32] was the development of a teaching-learning strategy using a web-based simulation tool in an AT course that promotes the development of interprofessional skills through the process of developing a sensory toy for children with disabilities [32]. For this purpose, students of health sciences and engineering were brought together in an interprofessional development project. The results underline that interdisciplinary approaches are essential for designing ATs because they provide synergies that improve the quality of the products in terms of usability, appreciation of needs, and context-based suitability. Teaching AT interdisciplinary courses constitutes an opportunity to create significant learning opportunities to make students more aware of real needs.

The paper by Gantenbein et al. [33] presents a development project in which a wheelchair-mounted arm (MiAMove) support was developed with a user-centered design approach in close collaboration with a user with Spinal Muscular Atrophy. To assess long-term usability and impact on quality of life, several evaluation sessions were conducted over a two-year period of daily use. In the evaluation, the device proved to be robust and required minimal maintenance. User satisfaction with the device was found to be high. However, the observed decline in satisfaction after several months of use highlights the importance of assessing user satisfaction not only at the time of handover, but also after users have had sufficient time to fully explore the functions of the system and integrate it into their daily lives. The device has been shown to have a positive impact on users' independence, well-being, and quality of life.

The study of Fernandez-Rivera et al. [34] was based on an innovative co-design programme in collaboration with St John of God Community Services. In this program, third year computer science students work with service users with intellectual disabilities to develop digital applications. Co-design focus group sessions were held with the service users who were the participants in the co-design collaboration with SJOG services and TU Dublin. The data collected during these design sessions will be integrated into an accessible design toolkit that will be developed through a series of iterative workshops. The end result will be a sustainable resource that can be re-used in the co-design programme at TU Dublin, but also in the wider inclusive design community.

The penultimate article by Schmidt [35] presents research related to the use of Escape Games in technology teaching. An Escape Game is presented as an introduction to a participatory technology development process for everyday life solutions. The Escape Game focuses on the area of Smart Home and is aimed at young people in institutional welfare settings. Escape games are often closely linked to technology, as many commercial solutions are technology-based. This makes them an ideal way to provide non-technical people with a basic understanding of technology (in this case smart home technology). They introduce technology interactively and create an environment that allows experimentation. The paper gives insight into the development and evaluation of the Escape Game with the target group.

The contribution by Wilson et al. [36] presents results from the first phase of the Smart Dementia Care project. This project aims to develop an understanding of how best to develop digital tools that people with dementia and their caregivers will find useful and usable for care planning and goal setting. The paper describes how co-design is used to support people in the early stages of dementia to complete their daily tasks and engage in meaningful activities to extend their time of independent living. The co-design approach aims to go beyond participation and focus more on co-production, equal collaboration, and shared decision-making. An important element of co-design in this context is the development of a comprehensive understanding of living with dementia through initial exploratory interviews and discussions with both people with dementia and caregivers.

The many and diverse contributions to this STS show interesting approaches on how to further improve the development, evaluation, and assessment of assistive technologies. As already described at the beginning, assistive technologies that are individually suitable and easy to use are an essential prerequisite for enabling people with disabilities to participate in all areas of life. The ICCHP brings together researchers from a wide range of technical, social and life science disciplines. Only through collaboration and exchange can scientific and technological progress and ubiquitous digitization be shaped in a way that everyone benefits from its potential for social participation as well as personal development and wellbeing.

References

1. International Organization for Standardization. Assistive products for persons with disability: classification and terminology. https://www.iso.org/standard/60547.html
2. Tao, G., Charm, G., Kabacińska, K., Miller, W.C., Robillard, J.M.: Evaluation tools for assistive technologies: a scoping review. Arch. Phys. Med. Rehabil. **101**(6), 1025–1040 (2020)
3. Puyuelo-Quintana, G., Cano-de-la-Cuerda, R., Plaza-Flores, A., et al.: A new lower limb portable exoskeleton for gait assistance in neurological patients: a proof of concept study. J. Neuroeng. Rehabil. **17**, 1–16 (2020)
4. Broekens, J., Heerink, M., Rosendal, H.: Assistive social robots in elderly care: a review. Gerontechnology **8**(2), 94–103 (2009)
5. De Witte, L., Steel, E., Gupta, S., Delgado Ramos, V., Roentgen, U.: Assistive technology provision: towards an international framework for assuring availability and accessibility of affordable high-quality assistive technology. Disabil. Rehabil. Assist. Technol. **13**(5), 467–472 (2018)
6. Phillips, B., Zhao, H.: Predictors of assistive technology abandonment. Assist. Technol. **5**, 36–45 (1993)
7. Riemer-Reiss, M.L., Wacker, R.R.: Factors associated with assistive technology discontinuance among individuals with disabilities. J. Rehabil. **66**, 3 (2000)
8. Federici, S., Meloni, F., Borsci, S.: The abandonment of assistive technology in Italy: a survey of users of the national health service. Eur. J. Phys. Rehabil. Med. **52**, 516–526 (2016)
9. Martin, B., Mccormack, L.: Issues surrounding assistive technology use and abandonment in an emerging technological culture. In: Bühler, C., Knops, H. (eds.) 5th European Conference for the Advancement of Assistive Technology (AAATE 1999), p. 852. IOS Press, Düsseldorf (1999)
10. Scherer, M.J.: Living in the State of Stuck: How Technology Impacts the Lives of People with Disabilities, 2nd edn. Brookline Books, Cambridge (1996)
11. Petrie, H., Carmien, S., Lewis, A.: Assistive technology abandonment: research realities and potentials. In: Miesenberger, K., Kouroupetroglou, G. (eds.) ICCHP 2018. LNCS, vol. 10897, pp. 532–540. Springer, Cham (2018). https://doi.org/10.1007/978-3-319-94274-2_77
12. Lauer, A., Longenecker, R.K., Smith, R.O.: ATOMS project technical report—factors in assistive technology device abandonment: replacing 'abandonment' with 'discontinuance'. http://www.r2d2.uwm.edu/atoms/archive/technicalreports/tr-discontinuance.html
13. Jiménez-Arberas, E., Ordóñez-Fernández, F.F.: Discontinuation or abandonment of mobility assistive technology among people with neurological conditions. Rev. Neurol. **72**(12), 426–432 (2021)

14. Grott, R.: On technology abandonment or discontinuance. In: Assistive Technology Service Delivery, pp. 211–216. Academic Press, New York (2019)
15. Ko, A.J., Whitmire, E.: User Interface Software and Technology. https://faculty.washington.edu/ajko/books/uist/index.html
16. Miesenberger, K.: Best practice in design for all. In: Stephanidis (ed.): The Universal Access Handbook. CRC Press, Boca Raton (2009)
17. Antona, M., Stephanidis, C. (eds.): HCII 2019. LNCS, vol. 11572. Springer, Cham (2019). https://doi.org/10.1007/978-3-030-23560-4
18. Assessment vs. Evaluierung. Wo Liegt der Unterschied? https://www.onlineassessmenttool.com/de/wissenscenter/wissenscenter-assessments/assessment-vs-evaluierung/item10642
19. Stevens, R.D., Edwards, A.D.: An approach to the evaluation of assistive technology. In: Proceedings of the Second Annual ACM Conference on Assistive Technologies, pp. 64–71 (1996)
20. Mortenson, W.B., Demers, L., Fuhrer, M.J., et al.: Development and preliminary evaluation of the caregiver assistive technology outcome measure. J. Rehabil. Med. **47**(5), 412–418 (2015)
21. Demers, L., Weiss-Lambrou, R., Demers, L., et al.: Development of the Quebec user evaluation of satisfaction with assistive technology (QUEST). Assist. Technol. **8**(1), 3 (1996)
22. Wessels, R.D., De Witte, L.P.: Reliability and validity of the Dutch version of QUEST 2.0 with users of various types of assistive devices. Disabil. Rehabil. **25**, 267–272 (2003)
23. Colucci, M., Tofani, R., Trioschi, D., et al.: Reliability and validity of the Italian version of Quebec User Evaluation of Satisfaction with Assistive Technology 2.0 (QUEST-IT 2.0) with users of mobility assistive device. Disabil. Rehabilit. Assist. Technol. **16**(3), 251–254 (2021)
24. Federici, S., Scherer, M. (eds.): Assistive Technology Assessment Handbook. CRC Press, New York (2012)
25. Andrich, R.: A model to represent knowledge about assistive products. In: Miesenberger, K., Kouroupetroglu, G., et al. (eds). Computers Helping People with Special Needs. ICCHP 2022. Lecture Notes in Computer Science. Springer (2022)
26. Heumader, P., Murillo Morales, T., Miesenberger, K.: Buddy – a personal companion to match people with cognitive disabilities and AT. In: Miesenberger, K., Kouroupetroglu, G., et al. (eds.). Computers Helping People with Special Needs. ICCHP 2022. Lecture Notes in Computer Science. Springer (2022)
27. Aswad, E., Murphy, E., Fernandez-Rivera, C., Boland, S.: Towards an inclusive ci-design toolkit for the creation of accessible digital tools. In: Miesenberger, K., Kouroupetroglu, G., et al. (eds.). Computers Helping People with Special Needs. ICCHP 2022. Lecture Notes in Computer Science. Springer (2022)
28. McDonnell, M.: Evaluation a visual mobile banking app for users with low subjective numeracy. In: Miesenberger, K., Kouroupetroglu, G., et al. (eds). Computers Helping People with Special Needs. ICCHP 2022. Lecture Notes in Computer Science. Springer (2022)
29. Salatino, C., Gower, V., Malisano, L. et al.: How to ensure continuity of AT assessment services for frail people in times of pandemics: an Italian experience. In: Miesenberger, K., Kouroupetroglu, G., et al. (eds). Computers Helping People with Special Needs. ICCHP 2022. Lecture Notes in Computer Science. Springer (2022)
30. Kortekass, C., Zorn, I.: Paradox communication strategies as challenges for moderation in participatory design with youth with special needs in a residential youth facility - a conversation analysis. In: Miesenberger, K., Kouroupetroglu, G., et al. (eds). Computers Helping People with Special Needs. ICCHP 2022. Lecture Notes in Computer Science, Springer (2022)
31. Corcuff, M., Lamontagne, E.-M., Routier, F.: Knowledge mobilization strategies within a municipality to improve accessibility of the built environment: a research protocol. In: Petz, A., Hoogerwerf, E.-J., Mavrou, K. (eds.): Assistive Technology, Accessibility and (e)Inclusion, ICCHP-AAATE 2022 Open Access Compendium, accepted for publication. Johannes Kepler University Linz, Austria. https://www.icchp-aaate.org

32. Rodríguez-Dueñas, W.R., Aguia Rojas, K., Reyes, A.M.: How to promote the design of a sensory toy for children with disabilities through interdisciplinary teamwork: a classroom experience. In: Petz, A., Hoogerwerf, E.-J., Mavrou, K. (eds.): Assistive Technology, Accessibility and (e)Inclusion, ICCHP-AAATE 2022 Open Access Compendium, accepted for publication, Johannes Kepler University Linz, Austria. https://www.icchp-aaate.org
33. Gantenbein, J., Weber, M., Gassert, R., Lambercy, R.: Development of an assistive dynamic arm support for a user with spinal muscular atrophy – a retrospective analysis after two years of daily use. In: Petz, A., Hoogerwerf, E.-J., Mavrou, K. (eds.): Assistive Technology, Accessibility and (e)Inclusion, ICCHP-AAATE 2022 Open Access Compendium, accepted for publication, Johannes Kepler University Linz, Austria. https://www.icchp-aaate.org
34. Fernandez-Rivera, C., Boland, S., Aswad, E., Gilligan, J., Murphy, E.: AccessDesign: an inclusive co-design toolkit for the creation of accessible digital tools. In: Petz, A., Hoogerwerf, E.-J., Mavrou, K. (eds.): Assistive Technology, Accessibility and (e)Inclusion, ICCHP-AAATE 2022 Open Access Compendium, accepted for publication, Johannes Kepler University Linz, Austria. https://www.icchp-aaate.org
35. Schmidt, M.: Escape Games- an approach to start participative technology development. In: Petz, A., Hoogerwerf, E.-J., Mavrou, K. (eds.): Assistive Technology, Accessibility and (e)Inclusion, ICCHP-AAATE 2022 Open Access Compendium, accepted for publication, Johannes Kepler University Linz, Austria. https://www.icchp-aaate.org
36. Wilson, M., Doyle, J., Marron, A., et al.: Co-design to support engagement in activities of daily living and meaningful activities for people living with dementia. In: Petz, A., Hoogerwerf, E.-J., Mavrou, K. (eds.): Assistive Technology, Accessibility and (e)Inclusion, ICCHP-AAATE 2022 Open Access Compendium, accepted for publication, Johannes Kepler University Linz, Austria. https://www.icchp-aaate.org

A Model to Represent Knowledge about Assistive Products

Renzo Andrich(✉)

The Global Assistive Technology Information Network (EASTIN), Milan, Italy
renzo@andrich.cloud

Abstract. This paper describes a model which has been developed to represent knowledge about assistive products, to feed an artificial-intelligence-based online system offering guidance to identify and select the assistive products that best suit individual needs. In this model, each assistive product is described by a set of "knowledge rules" clustered round 15 chapters: 1) product identification data and overall description; 2) possible configuration variants; 3) optional components; 4) product goals; 5) indicated impairments and 6) contraindicated impairments; 7) indicated and 8) contraindicated environments; 9) other indicated and 10) contraindicated factors; points to consider in 11) selection, 12) fitting, 13) use and 14) maintenance/follow-up; and 15) sources/references. Each "knowledge rule" consists of a sentence – written in English language according to given guidelines – each containing a token of knowledge provided by an expert, based on scientific evidence or field experience; in this way, the knowledge base grows token by token thanks to the collective effort of a worldwide community of experts, each entering their own tokens on a voluntary basis. Today, the knowledge base includes about 2400 knowledge rules, mainly related to products belonging to the WHO APL (Assistive Product Priority List). It feeds an online guidance system called "Assistive Product Explorer" (ASPREX) which is currently under development by the World Health Organization within the GATE initiative (Global Collaboration on Assistive Technology). The model has shown able to represent knowledge about any categories of assistive products, and suitable for being fed by an open community of experts worldwide through the ASPREX system.

Keywords: AT information systems · Artificial intelligence · Guidance to AT choice

1 Background

Several countries have well-established national information systems on assistive products, which provide detailed and impartial information on the products available on the market. A well-known international information system also exists – the Global Assistive Technology Information Network (EASTIN) [1] which aggregates the basic contents of the major databases (currently from Germany [2], Italy [3], Denmark [4], Belgium [5], France [6], the UK [7], Australia [8], Israel [9] and the US [10]) to make it available through a single web interface all over the world in many languages. These information

K. Miesenberger et al. (Eds.): ICCHP-AAATE 2022, LNCS 13342, pp. 267–274, 2022.
https://doi.org/10.1007/978-3-031-08645-8_31

systems are a precious resource for people who need to know if any assistive solutions exist that suit their individual need, as well as for AT specialists who have clear ideas on the solutions to be recommended but need to know what brand/models the market is offering in that moment and where [11].

However, product information alone may be not enough; deciding what products are most appropriate to suit an individual need may be a challenging task, requiring guidance and often specialized professionals. In developed countries, these are available in AT assessment centers or specialized rehabilitation facilities; unfortunately, there are countries where these professionals are hardly reachable or do not even exist [12].

To help users self-assess their assistive technology needs and increase their ability to identify and select appropriate products, online guidance systems started appearing. The pioneer and the most well-known is the UK "AskSara" system [13], which mainly concerns daily living equipment and is quite popular in the UK as well in other English-speaking countries. Recently, other systems were launched in other countries making use of artificial intelligence techniques, such as the Israeli "ATvisor" [14] and the Canadian "Evika" [15]. Each of them has a different approach in relation to the range of products considered, the way to build their knowledge base, the actors involved in the contents, the search methods and the way search results are presented; all lead to recommendations on product brand/models contained in their databases.

Recently, within the GATE initiative (Global Collaboration on AT) [16], the World Health Organization also felt the need to develop a machine reasoning system which can help identify the most appropriate products based on a person's goals, circumstances, type of difficulties, level of ability, and life environment. It is expected that - especially in low resources countries – such a system can greatly favor informed and responsible choices of assistive products, by increasing task-shifting of AT provision to the non-specialist workforce at community level; and by increasing awareness about the complexity of the AT assessment and selection process, the risks associated to wrong choices and the competences needed case by case. The development of this artificial-intelligence-based system – now called the Assistive Product Explorer (ASPREX) – started at mid-2020 and is currently ongoing; an experimental version is now available for trial purposes providing guidance on assistive products belonging to the WHO APL (Assistive Technology Priority List) [17]. Within WHO, the term "product" is meant to indicate product categories (such as e.g., "manual wheelchair", "reading glasses", "communication software") with no reference to any brand/models.

2 Method

2.1 The ASPREX Concept

The ASPREX concept (Fig. 1) includes a public section providing information and guidance to find out the products which best meet the individual needs and circumstances; it also includes a knowledge-building system designed in such a way that it can be fed online by assistive technology experts all over the world, whether professionals or users, to continuously expand the knowledge base that drives the reasoning engine which provides guidance to the user.

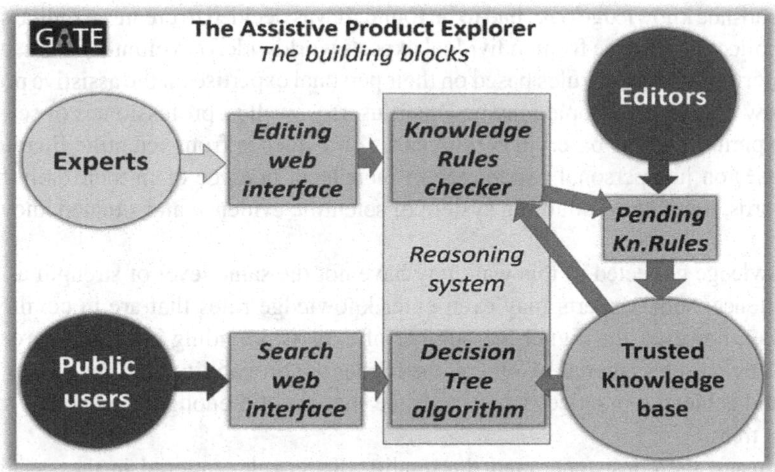

Fig. 1. The building blocks of the ASPREX system

2.2 The Challenge

Any reasoning system, whatever the technology, needs a reliable knowledge base and proper algorithms to extract the knowledge required in response to user requests [18]. Today's best-known artificial intelligence techniques draw knowledge from big data (large information sets reachable through the Web), make use of NLP (natural language processing) and have often some self-learning capability (ability to adapt themselves based on the interaction with the users); they work well when big data are available (millions of documents) and are used daily by massive amounts of users. Other systems, which don't need big data, are based on detailed models of their knowledge domains, often described through ontologies [19].

Excitement about the potential of artificial intelligence (AI) should not make us overlook the fact that either the knowledge or the algorithms are created by humans. AI does not do things that humans cannot do, it just does them faster. AI does not "invent" knowledge, it can only make inferences from available knowledge. Any recommendation generated by a reasoning system will be as reliable as is the knowledge feeding it. Therefore, when designing a reasoning system, the starting point is "what knowledge is available?", "where do we find it?", "who is providing it?".

An additional key question is "how reliable the system must be?" or "how critical would a wrong recommendation be for the user?". There are systems which harm nobody in case of imperfect recommendations (think e.g., a mistake made by an automatic translation system) while others may lead the user to misleading or harmful choices. Our system falls within the latter case, as wrong AT recommendations may be dangerous for the user.

2.3 The Need to Create an Ad-Hoc Knowledge Base

As no big data nor established knowledge models are available in the assistive technology domain, and reliability is of paramount importance, an efficient and sustainable way to build an ad-hoc knowledge base had to be found. It was decided to create an online system able to collect knowledge from individual experts worldwide, on voluntary basis, each of them entering knowledge rules based on their personal expertise on the assistive products they know best. These people may be expert users as well as professionals or scientists. Their expertise may be based in certain cases on evidence from scientific literature, in other cases on just personal experience in their local practice or in their daily life. In other words, it is a crowdsourcing system of scientific evidence and situated knowledge [20].

Knowledge collected in this way may have not the same level of strength as scientific evidence; some experts may even enter knowledge rules that are in conflict with each other; however, the higher the number of experts providing input and agreeing or disagreeing on rules entered by others, the higher the probability is to get "closer to the truth" and achieve a practice-based evidence that is solid enough to generate reliable decision trees.

To ensure the consistence and the quality of the rules entered in the system, the knowledge base is organized according to a precise structure and includes a rule-checking procedure combining NLP (natural language processing) and human supervision.

3 Results

The structure of the system's knowledge base is based on product records, each including the product identification and an unlimited number of knowledge rules.

Product identification data (chapter 1) include:

- The product name
- The product classification, according to both ISO 9999:2016 and the WHO APL
- Picture (a self-explanatory image with no reference to any specific brand/model)
- The product description (a concise text on what the product is and how it looks like).

Knowledge rules include:

- Rules describing product variations
  - Variants (chapter 2)
  - Accessories (chapter 3)
- Rules driving the "decision tree" of the recommending system
  - Goals (chapter 4)
  - Indicated impairments (chapter 5)
  - Contraindicated impairments (chapter 6)
  - Indicated environments (chapter 7)
  - Contraindicated environments (chapter 8)
  - Other indicated factors (chapter 9)
  - Other contraindicated factors (chapter 10)

- Rules providing guidance in the selection of the product item
  - Points to consider in the product selection (chapter 11)
  - Points to consider in the product fitting (chapter 12)
  - Points to consider in the product use (chapter 13)
  - Points to consider in the product follow-up (chapter 14)
  - Sources/references (chapter 15)

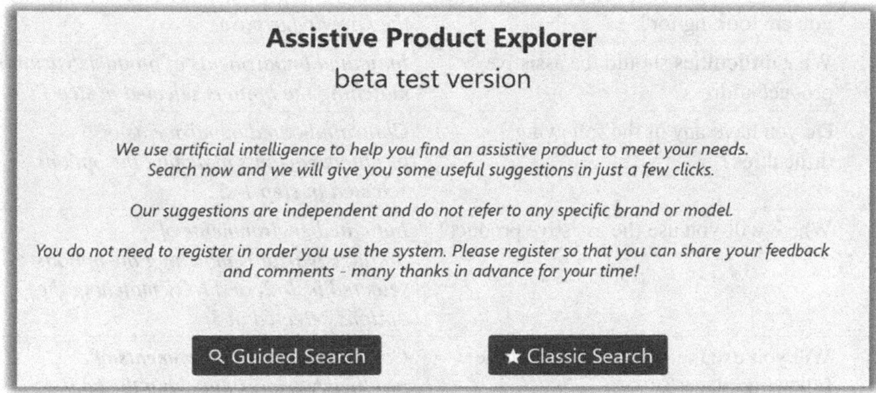

Fig. 2. The public side of the system (beta test for trial purposes)

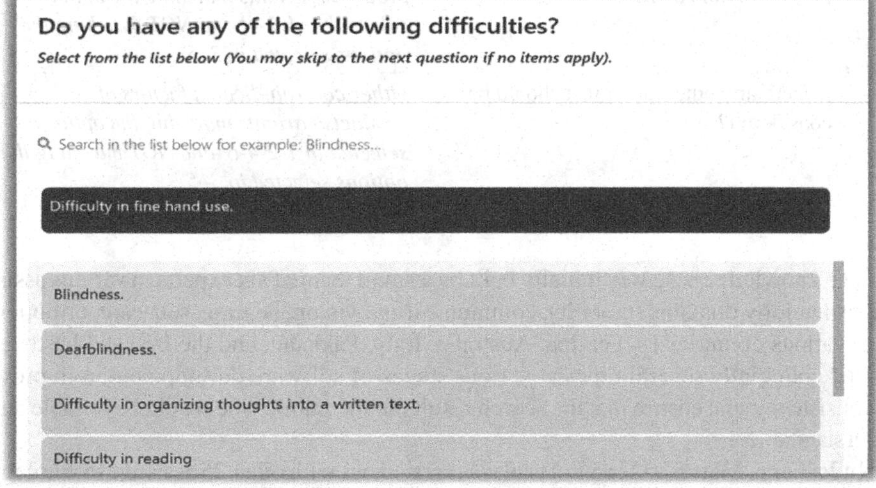

Fig. 3. Example of selection options (step 3)

This structure guides and facilitates the experts to write their knowledge rules in the password-protected side of the system; on the public side, it feeds the reasoning system which helps the users find products which may suit their needs. When choosing "Guided Search" in the public side of the system (Fig. 2), the reasoning system prompts the user with closed-ended questions and shows a list of choices depending on previous answers (Fig. 3). The maximum number of questions is seven, as shown in Table 1.

Table 1. The seven steps of a guided search ("decision tree")

Step	Question	Selection options
1	What are the goals of the assistive product you are looking for?	*Goals of all products/variants included in the knowledge base*
2	What difficulties should the assistive product address?	*Indicated impairments of products/variants matching the options selected in step 1*
3	Do you have any of the following difficulties?	*Contraindicated impairments of products/variants matching the options selected in step 1–2*
4	Where will you use the assistive product?	*Indicated environments of products/variants matching the options selected in 1–2, and NOT matching the options selected in 3*
5	Will you use the product in any of the following places?	*Contraindicated environments of products/variants matching the options selected in 1-2-4, and NOT matching the options selected in 3*
6	Is there any other factor the assistive product should address?	*Other indicated factors of products/variants matching the options selected in 1-2-4, and NOT matching the options selected in 3–5*
7	Is there any other factor that should be considered?	*Other contraindicated factors of products/variants matching the options selected in 1-2-4-6, and NOT matching the options selected in 3–5*

The knowledge base was initially built by a small team of six experts in various assistive technology domains (mobility, communication, vision, hearing, self-care, orthotics) from various countries (Argentina, Australia, Italy, Pakistan, and the US) and has been revised collegially several times at various stages of software development to improve its consistency and ensure that the search results in the public side would be reliable and understandable.

In January–March 2022 a pilot trial was carried out with other 25 assistive technology experts (users and professionals) from all over the world who volunteered to contribute by adding new knowledge rules (or countering rules entered by others and discussing until achieving consensus).

To date, the knowledge base contains about 2400 rules related to 73 products, 63 or which included in the WHO Assistive Product Priority List [17].

4 Conclusions

The model has shown able to represent knowledge about any categories of assistive products, and suitable to be fed by an open community of experts worldwide through the ASPREX system; the recommending system has shown understandable, straightforward, and fast from the user side, although some software improvements may be needed for better user-friendliness (Fig. 4).

To date, the main limitation lies in the small number of products included in the knowledge base, which currently covers well only the WHO APL products, while it should extend to the whole assistive product world. However, this is just the beginning, as the system is ready to welcome contributions by any expert from wherever in the world to continuously increase its contents.

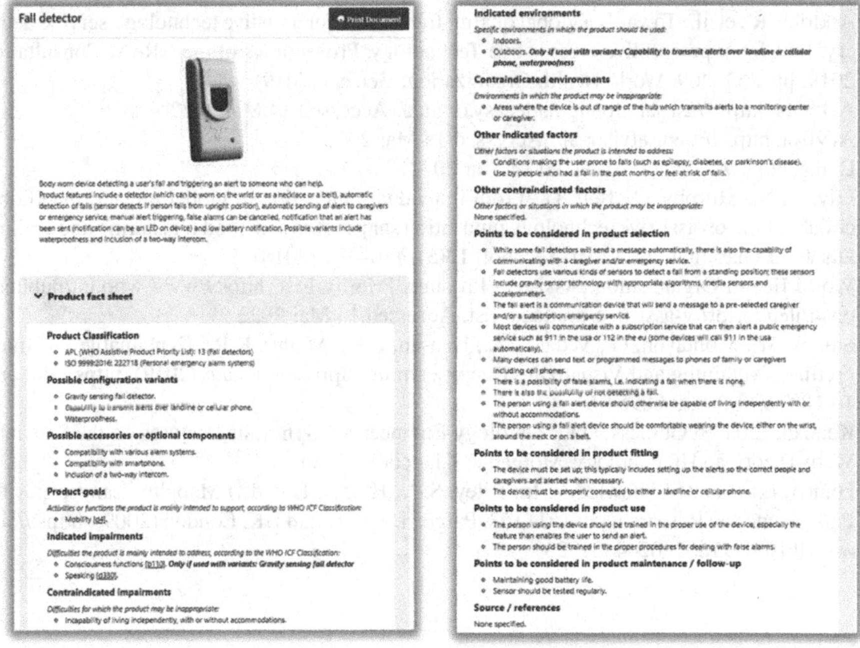

Fig. 4. Sample fact sheet of a product, showing its knowledge rules

Acknowledgements. This study was supported by the World Health Organization within the GATE initiative (Global Collaboration on Assistive Technology). Thanks to the WHO/GATE team (Geneva, Switzerland) for their collaboration in developing the ASPREX concept; to the GDI team (Global Disability Innovation Hub, London, UK) for reviewing the work at various stages; and to ICED team (International Centre for Evidence in Disability at LSHTM, London, UK) for participating in the discussions. Special thanks to the experts who helped the author build up the initial knowledge base of the system: Natasha Layton (Australia), Stefan Von Prondzinski (Italy), Gerald Weisman (USA), Silvana Contepomi (Argentina) and Hasan Minto (Pakistan).

References

1. EASTIN. http://www.eastin.eu/. Accessed 14 Mar 2022
2. REHADAT. https://www.rehadat-hilfsmittel.de/en/. Accessed 14 Mar 2022
3. Portale SIVA. http://www.portale.siva.it/en-GB/home/default. Accessed 14 Mar 2022
4. AssistData. https://hmi-basen.dk/en/indexdk.asp. Accessed 14 Mar 2022
5. VLIBANK. https://www.vaph.be/hulpmiddelen/databank. Accessed 14 Mar 2022
6. HANDICAT. https://handicat.com/. Accessed 14 Mar 2022
7. DLF ProAssist. https://dlfproassist.livingmadeeasy.org.uk//. Accessed 14 Mar 2022
8. Assistive Technology Australia. https://www.at-aust.org/. Accessed 14 Mar 2022
9. AZARIM. https://azarim.org.il/en/. Accessed 14 Mar 2022
10. GPII Unified Listing. https://ul.gpii.net/. Accessed 14 Mar 2022
11. Andrich, R., Mathiassen, N.E., Hoogerwerf, E.J., Gelderblom, G.J.: Service delivery systems for assistive technology in Europe: a AAATE/EASTIN position paper. Technol. Disabil. **25**(3), 127–146 (2013)
12. Andrich, R., et al.: Towards a global quality framework for assistive technology service delivery. In: Global perspective on assistive Technology, Proceedings of the GReAt Consultation 2019, pp. 263–269. World Health Organization, Geneva (2019)
13. AskSara. https://asksara.livingmadeeasy.org.uk/. Accessed 14 Mar 2022
14. AtVisor. https://www.atvisor.ai/. Accessed 14 Mar 2022
15. Evika. https://evika.io/. Accessed 14 Mar 2022
16. Layton, N., Murphy, C., Bell, D.: From individual innovation to global impact: the Global collaboration on assistive technology innovation snapshot as a method for sharing and scaling. Disabil. Rehabilitation. Assist. Technol. **13**(5), 486–491 (2018)
17. World Health Organization: Assistive Products Priority List. https://www.who.int/publications/i/item/priority-assistive-products-list. Accessed 14 Mar 2022
18. Samek, W., Montavon, G., Vedaldi, A., Hansen, L.K., Muller, K.R.: Explainable AI: Interpreting, Explaining and Visualizing Deep Learning. Springer, Cham (2019). https://doi.org/10.1007/978-3-030-28954-6
19. Kendall, E.F., McGuiness, D.L.: Ontology Engineering. Synthesis Lectures on the Semantic Web: Theory and Technology. Morgan & Claypool (2019)
20. Hunter, L.: Situated knowledge. In: Riley, S.R., Hunter, L. (eds.) Mapping Landscapes for Performance as Research, pp. 151–153. Palgrave Macmillan UK, London (2009). https://doi.org/10.1057/9780230244481_23

Buddy - A Personal Companion to Match People with Cognitive Disabilities and AT

Peter Heumader, Tomas Murillo-Morales(✉), and Klaus Miesenberger

Institut Integriert Studieren, Altenbergerstr. 69, 4040 Linz, Austria
{Peter.Heumader,Tomas.Murillo_Morales,Klaus.Miesenberger}@jku.at

Abstract. This paper presents a novel web-based repository and recommender system to match the requirements of users with cognitive disabilities with available AT solutions when working on the web. Based on personal data from users (questionnaire, simple games) stored in a profile and tool data provided by AT solution providers and AT vendors, Buddy recommends tools supporting particular cognitive needs of target users. Buddy intends to bridge the gap between the growing amount of AT solutions and the actual low level of uptake by involving all stakeholder groups in the value chain on the Buddy platform.

Keywords: Web accessibility · Cognitive accessibility · Assistive technologies · Recommender system

1 Introduction

Buddy is a R&D effort addressing the need to overcome the gap between the growing number of Assistive Technology (AT) available for people with cognitive disabilities when working on the web and the actual low level of uptake and use in practice [10].

Based on an analysis of the manifold reasons for low uptake (e.g. findability for independent access to tools and features, lacking customization and personalization, missing profile building and matching process, low incentive and missing training of the support/care environment, low/no interest in innovation at funding/commissioning/administrating level e.g. [2,11]), this paper presents a new and innovative web based approach to support the matching process of people with cognitive disabilities and AT. R&D lead to the development of *Buddy* providing:

1. A web **repository** to search, find, explore and exchange Assistive Technology (AT) more independently
2. An AI-based **recommender system** matching the user profile with parameters and functionalities of ATs. The recommender uses data provided by
   - users through answering questions and/or by playing a series of games to define the need of support for the different dimensions of cognitive skills

K. Miesenberger et al. (Eds.): ICCHP-AATE 2022, LNCS 13342, pp. 275–283, 2022.
https://doi.org/10.1007/978-3-031-08645-8_32

  - AT solution providers adding and categorizing their tools for the matching process
  - An explicit user-item rating mechanism feeding data into the recommender as well as providing an exchange/discussion platform on AT use.
3. A **quality assurance** back-end workflow to ensure that AT entries stored in the system are up-to-date and of relevance for target users.

Buddy is intended as a personal companion assisting users with cognitive disabilities and their support environment in finding the right AT solution for a successful web experience. It provides a new level of contact to users and a unique, rich and growing source for requirements elicitation for AT designers, developers, providers, commissioner and funders to better match ATs and functionalities towards needs of users and to support personalization.

2 End User Survey

Preparatory desktop research and online user interviews were conducted before designing *Buddy* in order to determine how persons with cognitive disabilities find, retrieve, and use AT, and to assess needs and problems in these processes. All in all, 88 individual responses to the online survey were gathered and analysed. 65 responses corresponded to Swedish participants, 20 answers came from Austria, 2 from the United Kingdom, and the remaining response came from Lithuania[1].

Participants where first queried regarding whether they were responding the questionnaire for themselves or for a third person (e.g. a caregiver responding on behalf of a disabled individual). As shown in Fig. 1, approximately half of the respondents reported answering for themselves, whereas the second half required some form of assistance in filling in the questionnaire. Therefore, the gathered responses are likely to cover a wide range of the cognitive spectrum.

Table 1. Usage of AT by questionnaire participants (answer counts).

Responding for:	Myself	A friend or relative	A person I support	Other	N/A	Total
Uses AT	15	5	4	2	2	28
Does not use AT	27	25	6	2	0	60
Total	42	30	10	4	2	88

Participants were additionally inquired about their current usage of AT. The collected answers are summarized in Table 1. These results suggest that not

[1] The full end user survey report is part of Buddy's "Report on User and Technical Requirements", publicly available at https://www.buddyproject.eu/main-results.

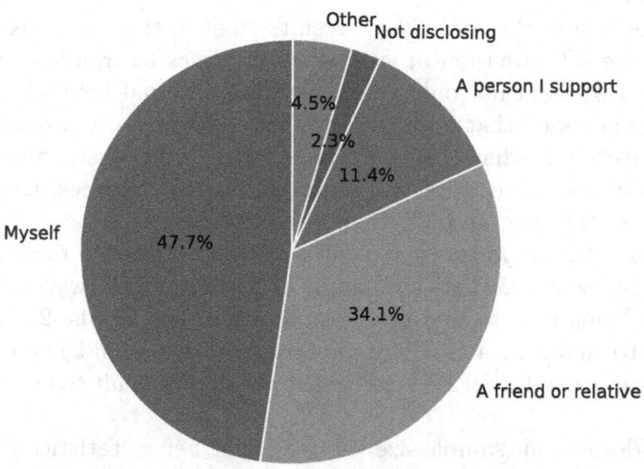

Fig. 1. Responses given by participants to the query "I am responding for...", as percentage of total gathered answers (88).

employing AT results in limited autonomy for the person (only 45% answered for themselves).

Regarding the type of AT employed, reading support tools were used by the majority of users (64%), followed by AT to support writing (43%). AT usage by support category is followed by understanding (36%), memory (32%), focus (29%), managing time (29%), calculation (25%), managing tasks (21%), and managing choices (29%). In addition, most respondents (71%) reported using more than one AT type. These results suggest that users commonly employ a combination of AT; consequently, potential users of AT are likely to find a centralized repository of AT helpful for finding the right solution for their individual needs.

Next, questions were posed on aspects related to finding, obtaining, and using AT. Participants were asked about the source of the AT they use. 54% of them reported that they downloaded a tool from the internet for free. 35% reported buying tools themselves, and only 30% obtained AT from a government agency, and/or from their school, employer, or similar. When asked whether it was easy to find AT that meets their needs, only one third of participants reported being able to find it without external help (more precisely, 15% reported having no problem at all to find AT whereas 18% stated that the process of finding AT could be improved despite managing it by themselves); on the other hand, 30% declared not being able to find a better tool, and 29% stated that they could find suitable AT only with help. Again, these results align with the assumption that a majority of users would benefit from a centralized intelligent repository that helps them in finding suitable AT by themselves.

In addition, 25% of users reported needing help in using AT even if they found a good solution for their needs. Help may be necessary in setting up tool preferences, installing the tool, learning how to use it, getting updates, and during regular use of the tool. These results suggest that there exists a significant gap in the AT provision process when it comes to training, support, and maintenance. Users did not only report needing external help when employing AT, but also expressed that current solutions ought to be improved - only 25% of surveyed users said that their current AT works flawlessly. Suggested areas of improvement include ease of use, more settings/preferences, need for better support such as training, and additional functionality.

Participants who reported not using AT were asked the reasons why they forgo it. 30% of them said that they simply do not need it. However, the majority reported not being able to find the right tool for their needs: 29% said not to know where to find AT, and 27% reported that they could not find AT that works for them. In addition, 5% said that it was too difficult to get the solutions they found.

In short, despite our sample size ($N = 88$) not being statistically significant, this preparatory research provides useful insights with regards to the barriers currently present in the AT provision process for persons with cognitive disabilities. The gathered answers suggest that there is an important need for a centralized repository with easily available and clear information about AT supporting cognitive user needs, including installation and usage instructions as well as clear classification and search functionality for tools according to the support categories they cover. Such a repository would also help mitigate the existing latency in regard to user needs, by letting users autonomously find AT for their specific support needs among the myriad of existing solutions. In turn, AT providers would also benefit from it by exposing their solutions to a large audience of potential users.

3 The Buddy Approach

The state-of-the-art analysis and a user-centered research, design and development approach based on the IPAR-UCD (Inclusive Participatory Action Research for User Centered Design) method [3] for including end-users as co-researchers, allowed us to specify, design and implement the concept and the components of Buddy. In addition, the different versions of the prototype and functionalities, developed in an cyclic agile approach, got evaluated by 18 end users with cognitive disabilities and from the neuro-diverse spectrum using the Think Aloud Protocol [9] and the Heuristic Evaluation [12] method, adapted to the requirements of the end users. Each component of Buddy is described next.

3.1 Accessible Web Repository of AT

Buddy intends to become a "one stop shop" for accessing ATs whose functionality hinges on a fully accessible Web application that serves as a central repository of individual AT tools and solutions enabling[2]:

[2] https://develop.buddyproject.eu/.

- Target users with a cognitive disability to search, (automatically) find, read about, download, and give feedback on AT solutions suitable for their individual support needs. This functionality is also useful for formal and informal care/support staff, teachers, trainers, employers, etc.; as well as administration and funding or commissioning bodies in search for AT.
- AT providers to add, describe, exchange, and get first hand feedback on their tools and solutions. Buddy invites AT solution providers but also other stakeholder to enter and categorize ATs into the public repository thereby exposing them to a suitable audience, see previous point.

The platform provides first hand access to end users, a communication and cooperation platform which is a rich source for AT providers to develop their tools further but also their market relations and cooperation. The cooperation with end user organizations, service provider organizations, administrative and political level will help to overcome reluctance and fears and should make Buddy the platform to be for the whole sector.

3.2 Profile Building via Traditional Forms and Gamification

To generate suitable AT recommendations for a specific user, the needs and preferences of that user must be known. In web accessibility, the key reference point for user needs are the standards of accessibility, namely, the standard EN 301 549 [5] and WCAG 2.1 [14]. However, none of these standards were conceived with the aim of proactively supporting cognitive user needs.

On the other hand, there exist guidelines issued by standardization agencies that do define cognitive accessibility. We have identified two such guidelines that had the most detailed definitions of cognitive user needs: namely [4] and [8]. To establish a relevant list of cognitive user needs to use as a basis for eliciting the user requirements, we mapped the definition of cognitive functions and needs in these guidelines against the cognitive abilities as defined in the international classification of functioning, disability and health [13] (the benchmark for defining human abilities and functions).

The list was also complemented by definitions of cognitive user requirements developed within research initiatives that explicitly look at requirements for the web, most notably the research conducted by the W3C COGA group [15]. The result was the following list of user needs for support that cover all required aspects:

- Reading
- Writing
- Understanding
- Calculation
- Focusing on a task or information, and keeping the focus
- Managing tasks (getting started and completing them)
- Memory
- Managing time (planning, allocating and controlling)

– Managing choices (evaluating options, deciding)

These preferences can be set by the user with a classic multi step web-form, where each step represents a user need mentioned above. However, previous projects and user involvement activities have shown that people with cognitive disabilities often struggle with long forms as they tend to be tedious and too complex. In addition, sometimes users do not know or are unable to express which types of support they need.

Therefore, a new innovative game-based approach [6] was implemented, in which users play mini games that aim to detect the users' needs for support. The games implemented address the cognitive dimensions/skills mentioned above. At the moment, 6 mini games have been developed covering 7 out of the 9 support categories. For further information on the gamification of user profile creation in Buddy, the reader is directed to [7].

With this gamification approach the capabilities of the user can be detected and added to his or her profile. The system allows and invites to do R&D for more and in particular more specific as well as attractive profiling games. Games have been developed and tested using the IPAR-UCD [3] approach to make sure that a high level of accessibility and usability is reached. The promising results invite to do more R&D to improve the approach.

3.3 AI Based Recommendations

Buddy uses both user profiles and AT entries stored in the repository as data sources for an intelligent recommender subsystem. Its main purpose is to find suitable ATs for specific users that may not be aware of their existence. In this manner, users are encouraged to try out new technologies that support their specific needs, thereby benefiting both users and AT vendors. The implemented hybrid recommender system hinges on two complementary methods:

- A knowledge-based recommendation approach that matches ATs to users directly by exploiting explicit knowledge about the support needs of users and support categories of ATs in the repository. A similarity score between ATs and the target user is computed, and the highest-scoring ATs may be recommended to the user.
- Data-driven recommendations that utilize user ratings of individual ATs to discover similar users and ATs regardless of their specific profiles. This system is inspired by well-established collaborative filtering methods commonly employed in e-commerce websites. Users are represented as a collection of score vectors, and similar ones to the target user are retrieved according to their similarity (Pearson's r correlation) in rating data-space. In this manner, suitable ATs for a target user may be found even if partial or incorrect knowledge about them is stored in the repository.

The final recommendations offered to a target user are based on a weighted mean of both scores in order to smooth the final score while benefiting from both techniques. Initially, more importance is given to the knowledge-based score. As more user ratings are inputted into the system, emphasis is placed on the data-driven scores. Specifically, the final likeness score $s(a_i, u_t)$ for target user u_t and a target AT entry a_i (yet unrated by u_t) is computed as follows:

$$s(a_i, u_t) = w \cdot d(a_i, u_t) + (1 - w) \cdot k(a_i, u_t) \tag{1}$$

where d is the data-driven score, k is the knowledge-based score, and $w \in [0, 1]$ is a dynamic weighting term that corresponds to the system's confidence on the accuracy of the data-driven score i.e. the more users have been considered in the computation of d, the higher the value of w, up to a value of 1.0 once 100 users have been taken into account.

This method is an instance of a distributed weighted hybrid recommender system [1]. Candidate AT entries a_i for user u_t are sorted according to their value of $s(a_i, u_t)$. The sorted elements are then offered as suggestions to the target user, in descending order.

3.4 Quality Assurance (QA) Back-End

Lastly, to guarantee the highest quality of the system, a web back-end is provided, which allows control of AT descriptions and categorization by expert users. A moderation process ensures that each AT entry available to end users in Buddy meets the necessary quality and relevance criteria.

Users with *AT moderator* privileges are informed each time a new AT entry has been added by an *AT vendor* user to the system. They may then proceed to review the entry (appropriateness of the solution, quality and ease of reading of its description, proper categorization, correct download links, etc.) following internal guidelines. Once the tool has been deemed appropriate for its inclusion to the repository, a new revision is published and made available to all end users, which may search for it manually ot get it automatically recommended if the solution matches their specific needs (c.f. Sect. 3.3).

Authors may edit their AT entries at any time, whereupon a new revision for the AT entry is created in the system. This new revision needs to go again through the QA workflow previously described. In this manner, Buddy allows AT vendors and providers to keep their solutions up to date in the repository while ensuring the quality of updated entries.

4 Conclusion

This paper presents a first prototype of an online platform that is able to recommend suitable AT to individual users with cognitive disabilities. The system intends to provide benefits to all stakeholder groups and to bridge the gap between potential and actual use of AT. It is intended and negotiated that the system is taken up by larger umbrella organizations to become sustainable and used at broad scale. It also provides a rich source for R&D at all levels of the system (e.g. user data for profiling, automatic/supported AT integration, AI based recommendation, platform features). Extension to other target groups is on the agenda for future R&D.

Acknowledgements. BUDDY has received funding from the European Commission's Work Programme for 2020 for Pilot Projects and Preparatory Actions in the field of Communications Networks, Content and Technology under grant agreement No LC-01610292/101018034 BUDDY.

References

1. Burke, R.: Hybrid recommender systems: survey and experiments. User Model. User Adap. Inter. **12**(4), 331–370 (2002)
2. Chadwick, D.D., Chapman, M., Caton, S.: Digital inclusion for people with an intellectual disability. In: The Oxford Handbook of Cyberpsychology (2019)
3. Cordula Edler, M.A.: IPAR-UCD – inclusive participation of users with cognitive disabilities in software development. In: Miesenberger, K., Manduchi, R., Covarrubias Rodriguez, M., Peňáz, P. (eds.) ICCHP 2020. LNCS, vol. 12376, pp. 43–50. Springer, Cham (2020). https://doi.org/10.1007/978-3-030-58796-3_6
4. European Telecommunications Standards Institute (ETSI): Human factors (HF); guidelines for the design of mobile ICT devices and their related applications for people with cognitive disabilities. ETSI EG 203 350 v1.1.1 (2016–11) (2016)
5. European Telecommunications Standards Institute (ETSI): Accessibility requirements for ICT products and services. Harmonised European Standard EN 301 549 v2.1.2 (2018–08) (2018)
6. Hautala, J., Heikkilä, R., Nieminen, L., Rantanen, V., Latvala, J.M., Richardson, U.: Identification of reading difficulties by a digital game-based assessment technology. J. Educ. Comput. Res. **58**(5), 1003–1028 (2020). https://doi.org/10.1177/0735633120905309
7. Heumader, P., Murillo-Morales, T., Miesenberger, K.: AI based recommendation and assessment of AT for people with cognitive disabilities. J. Technol. Pers. Disabil. **10** (2022)
8. International Organization for Standardization (ISO): Cognitive accessibility - Part 1: General guidelines. Standard ISO 21801-1:2020 (2020). https://www.iso.org/standard/71711.html
9. Lewis, C.: Using the "thinking-aloud" method in cognitive interface design. IBM TJ Watson Research Center Yorktown Heights (1982)
10. Miesenberger, K., Edler, C., Heumader, P., Petz, A.: Tools and applications for cognitive accessibility. In: Yesilada, Y., Harper, S. (eds.) Web Accessibility. HIS, pp. 523–546. Springer, London (2019). https://doi.org/10.1007/978-1-4471-7440-0_28
11. Miesenberger, K., Petz, A.: Easy to read on the web-state of the art and research directions. Procedia Comput. Sci. **27**, 318–326 (2014)
12. Nielsen, J.: How to conduct a heuristic evaluation. Nielsen Norman Group **1**(1), 8 (1995)
13. World Health Organization: International classification of functioning, disability and health: ICF (2001). https://apps.who.int/iris/handle/10665/42407
14. World Wide Web Consortium (W3C): Web Content Accessibility Guidelines (WCAG) 2.1 (2018). https://www.w3.org/TR/WCAG21/
15. World Wide Web Consortium (W3C): Making content usable for people with cognitive and learning disabilities (2020). https://www.w3.org/TR/coga-usable/

Towards an Inclusive Co-design Toolkit: Perceptions and Experiences of Co-design Stakeholders

Eamon Aswad[1,2], Emma Murphy[2(✉)], Claudia Fernandez-Rivera[2], and Sarah Boland[1,2]

[1] Saint John of God Liffey Services, Dublin, Ireland
{eamon.aswad,sarah.boland}@sjog.ie

[2] School of Computer Science, Technological University Dublin, Dublin 7, Dublin, Ireland
{emma.x.murphy,claudia.rivera}@tudublin.ie

Abstract. Participatory design holds great potential for the creation of inclusive technology but existing toolkits and resources to support co-design are not always accessible to designers and co-designers with disabilities. In this paper we present two studies to assist in facilitating the creation of a sustainable, accessible, inclusive co-design toolkit for individuals with intellectual disabilities i) exploration of the perceptions and experiences of lecturers (n = 5) and students (n = 5) involved in co-design activities via individual interviews and ii) a protocol and initial findings from focus groups with men and women with intellectual disabilities to inform on best co-design practices (n = 15). Positive reflections were reported on the co-design experience by all participants. Communication was highlighted as a theme that requires further attention and specific support during co-design processes with third level designers and co-designers with intellectual disabilities.

Keywords: Co-design · Inclusive design · People with intellectual disabilities

1 Introduction

The current project is based on an exploration of a "Co-Design Programme" which has been a collaboration project between two organizations in Dublin, Ireland: Technological University Dublin (TU Dublin) and St. John of God (SJOG) Liffey Services. Co-design refers to "collective creativity as it is applied across the whole span of a design process" [1], and it is an approach used in a variety of domains [2, 3] to provide beneficial outcomes for all parties involved. TU Dublin and SJOG have run an innovative co-design programme since 2016, where third year computer science students collaboratively design with SJOG service users to create accessible digital applications. These service users, further referred to in this paper as "co-designers", are men and women with intellectual disabilities, who have been involved in co-design activities with TU Dublin during their attendance at SJOG Liffey day centre services. The procedure of which has been published elsewhere [4]. This collaboration has generated a rich source of tacit knowledge on specific design tasks, methods and approaches that has potential

K. Miesenberger et al. (Eds.): ICCHP-AAATE 2022, LNCS 13342, pp. 284–292, 2022.
https://doi.org/10.1007/978-3-031-08645-8_33

benefits for both students and co-designers. The aim of this present study is to record and integrate the knowledge of stakeholders involved in a co-design programme to inform the generation of a sustainable co-design toolkit resource. The resulting toolkit is intended to strengthen engagement and better facilitate the co-design process and open other opportunities to engage in co-design for adults with intellectual disabilities. This project will also provide a practical solution to overcome some barriers to inclusive co-design for designers with disabilities.

2 Co-design: Benefits and Challenges

Understanding how a toolkit may assist the co-design process, requires an apprehension of codesign methodological advantages and disadvantages. Turner, Merle and Dichon [5] provide a review of co-design literature and suggest that assessment and value of co-design lies within four domains for the consumer or "co-designer": enjoyment, perceived control, pride of ownership and complexity. Leveraging these domains is suggested to enhance, not only the co-design process, but the resulting outcomes, such as toolkits. However, some common challenges in evaluating experience-based co-design are; power dynamics, methods for gathering experiences, design of improvements and ensuing implementation and impact [6]. Power dynamics are primarily cited in healthcare research, where status and identity come into play [7], this is less likely to occur when the process is centred around the co-designers, *for* the co-designers. Furthermore, specific processes can be implemented to increase this equity and engagement in co-designing with individuals with disabilities, such as a co-development opportunity, digital prototypes, non-finito features and inclusion of a proxy [8]. Focus groups have been used as a methodology for reporting and validating the experience of co-designers with disabilities [9]. The production of a tangible, practical co-designed toolkit that places the co-designers' opinions at the heart of the design, ensures subsequent follow up and impact. We aspire to address these complexities in experience-based co-design by assessing the collaborative process directly, engaging with stakeholders around their opinions of benefits, challenges and possible improvements. Thereby contributing to the literature on an archetype of "successful" co-designing, via the production of a comprehensive toolkit. This encompasses investigating an authentic collaborative approach that encourages equality and inclusivity.

Men and women with intellectual disabilities do not frequently take part in research [10]. Despite positive attitudes towards participation in research [11] and the necessity for greater representation. One barrier to recruiting individuals with intellectual disabilities is the complexity of the consent process. The requirement to protect vulnerable populations is evident, particularly in decision making, however, this may be at the cost of exclusion. Various modes of communication may be required so as inclusion and consent do not threaten exclusion of those unable to give an "autonomous or ideal consent" [12]. Therefore, we highlight the importance of an accessible protocol to engage individuals with intellectual disabilities to focus groups, and the proposed protocol focuses on co-designing accessible technologies.

This paper focuses on i) individual interviews with lecturers and students in TU Dublin who were involved in the co-design programme and ii) a protocol and initial findings from focus groups with the men and women who have been involved in the co-design collaboration with SJOG Services and TU Dublin. The data gathered will assist in developing an accessible co-design toolkit with SJOG services users with intellectual disabilities. We aspire to give a voice to a demographic of people, who historically, we're not invited to participate in software design and to leverage their lived experience, to support more universally designed technology.

3 Student and Lecturers Perceptions and Experiences of Co-design

Data was gathered qualitatively for this study via individual semi-structured interviews with lecturers and students in TU Dublin who were previously/currently involved in a Co-Design Project with SJOG co-designers. These co-design activities involved meeting together once per week over a semester-long module. While there was no formal co-design toolkit used, students and co-designers were introduced to design thinking tools such as Empathy maps [13] and "*I like, I wish, What if?*" [14] techniques to aid collaboration. These tools were modified to make them more visual, with icons and photos included to enhance accessibility for the co-designers.

3.1 Participants

The lecturers (n = 5) and students (n = 5) in the research were self-recruited after an invitation to participate was circulated via email by the principal investigator. All the lecturers had previously either been supervisors, module leaders or lecturers of the co-design programme based in TU Dublin. They had extensive experience with universal design and inclusive ICT. All the students were computer science undergraduate students, who had taken part in the co-design project during their third year in their undergraduate degree in TU Dublin (in 2020–2022). All the students had taken part in the online co-design programme due to COVID-19 but the lecturers had been involved in both online and previous in-person co-design activities. Three researchers individually interviewed each of the ten participants, with interviews ranging between 15–55 min.

3.2 Methods

A semi-structured interview script was created with open ended questions to elicit participants' perceptions and experiences of the co-design projects on the following themes: i) what worked well ii) what were the challenges iii) how the process could be improved. At the end of the individual interviews with the lecturers and students, they were invited to take part in an interactive focus group session with the SJOG co-designers. All participants agreed to be contacted to be involved in subsequent focus group sessions.

The interview data was analysed by the research team using the practical steps for thematic analysis as outlined by Clarke and Braun [15]. NVivo version 12 software was used to facilitate the coding and sorting process. Themes were highlighted via patterns emerging from the data set within each category. All themes were identified on a semantic level and were verified across both groups. Analysis was completed by two of the researchers, the third researcher facilitated any disagreements amongst the process of data analyses.

3.3 Results

The information provided by the lecturers and students assisted in the iteration process of the co-design focus groups. The primary aim was to evaluate the following themes: i) what worked well ii) what were the challenges and iii) how could the process be improved. Given the structure of the interviews, specific data directly related to the designer and co-designer's benefits (skills, novelty, perspective taking, empathy, inclusion) challenges (expectation management, conceptual difficulty, technical jargon), and impact (personal, professional, field) were identified. Further themes were also discovered, most notably, the themes of Communication, Accessibility and Collaboration.

Co-design Benefits. Both students and lecturers were forthcoming in describing the proposed benefits of their involvement in the co-design programme for both parties; the co-designers and the designers. Whilst a grade was the intention of the module for the students, this was not the only positive attained outcome as described in detail by Lecturer 3 "*Definitely it improved the potential of getting a job, 100% at a gruesome metric, that it was a real success in that way, improved their communication skills, their presentation skills, their interaction skills, and not least for their communications.*". The students reflected on the value of their learning within the module of; accessible design thinking, perspective taking, empathising, understanding the lived experience of others and interacting with a novel population "*it's the first time we're ever actually building something for someone and it was quite gratifying to see every Friday that the co-design team were happy to see us and to see that we were, implementing their ideas and we're actually listening to them, taking things on board.*" – Student 3. Furthermore, all participants reported a reciprocal relationship of fun, enjoyment, and friendship *"I'd like to think they really enjoyed it, because I really enjoyed it as well. You know, it really did seem like they enjoyed seeing us every Friday."* - Student 4.

Co-design Challenges. From the lecturers viewpoint, the challenges students faced the most revolved around being co-designers, leaving their technological comfort zone and "technical jargon" to engage in communication with a novel diverse population that requires a significant amount of "*soft skills*" and handling the honest criticism and redesigning that may be associated with it. All whilst balancing the group dynamics of the team project. "*So, for them was really to develop this empathy and the ability to understand what users were trying to say and analyse those data because they were, you know, students trained to make things. You know to create these circuits devices. So, for them I think was really a great opportunity to learn how to deal with people rather, than how to deal with technology.*" – Lecturer 2. The students also endorsed the demands of the group dynamics and limiting the use of technological jargon.

Communication was considered a central component by all participants, particularly within facilitating or hindering the co-design process, on both sides. "*Definitely with the communication. Sometimes at the start it was challenging. Definitely to encourage the co-designers to talk, but then to wait, say wait for three seconds after they finished speaking, to make sure, there's nothing else to say.*" – Lecturer 2. All students completed the co-design programme remotely. This was suggested to be less interactive for both students and co-designers and a preference was stated for face-to-face by all students. This was hypothesised to enhance the co-designing by process by providing more information for the students and being more tangible for the co-designers (prototyping, attention, senses).

Co-design Tools. In response to these challenges the students solicited their developed strategies to compensate, such as games *"I really think for this process the aspect of games really opened people up"*, online whiteboards, or prototyping tools *"for the bridge between us and the service users, we ended up using a website called Figma"*. However, in terms of co-design information sharing and communication, it was the tools developed at SJOG that were reported as most effective by the students.

All students remembered using some form of the tools *"we did use the "What IF" quite a lot because that was how we kept track of their needs and what they wanted to see. Because some of their requests just weren't feasible in the time that we had and that's something that we had to explain to them as well. But the "What IF" was very helpful because if we would send something on a Monday. They would update the "What if" during the week and then we'd have that information before coming into the meeting. So that was that was very helpful."* - Student 1. They also provided insight into how those tools were helpful. *"Yeah, absolutely because it just outlined in a very clear way, what they wanted to see from the app. Because verbal communication for them could have been tough at times. It outlined their thoughts and feelings and then we can react to that"*. – Student 2. *"So, they [the design thinking tools] effectively help shape their ideas and feedback. So like whatever they said like that was technically possible, like as far as our skills were like, we could do that and put it in for them."* – Student 3.

Accessibility and Collaboration. Accessibility and collaboration were two recurrent themes throughout the lecturer and student interviews. Accessibility was associated with a change in thinking about design for the students, how it impacts others, and the limitations others may possess. Students reinforced ideas of familiarity, functionality, universal and accessible design, ease of use and were determined to include these concepts in their own future designs, with some citing their final year project's revolving around accessibly designed projects. *"Nowadays it's not just good enough to make it work for you, you have to make it work for others as well"* – Student 5.

Accessibility of the interfaces being co-designed for the end user co-designers was a priority for all stakeholders and as highlighted above students appreciated that the design thinking tools were accessible to the SJOG co-designers. Interestingly, according to Lecturer 5, some computer science students struggled to understand some of the highly visual design thinking tools such as empathy maps as they require a different approach to processing and understanding information. *"In my experience some students find this type of visual information very easy...others would be more like a "computer science"...type of person"* – Lecturer 5. This is an important observation and highlights the need to acknowledge diverse capabilities and learning styles from both the perspective of students and co-designers in the creation and choice of accessible tools and supports.

The idea that the co-design project was a collaborative process was vehemently expressed by the students and lecturers, including items such as design collaboration, co-designer's needs, equality, listening and feedback, building rapport, information imparting, idea sharing and feelings. For the students, they suggested if they focused on understanding the needs and wants of the co-designers, their technical skills could fill the gap – *we really tried to focus on their input in our meetings, so we made it a very big part of our project to focus on what they wanted"* - Student 3. Although, it was understanding these needs and wants where the co-design tools were suggested to be necessary.

4 Iterative Focus Groups with Co-designers with Intellectual Disabilities

In total, five one-hour focus groups will be organised; one for every phase of design thinking (Empathise, Design, Ideate, Prototype, Test) as proposed in Hasso Plattner Institute of Design [16]. All the focus group sessions will have the same format, with some slight variations taking place between the sessions in terms of design process content. The first and last session place a higher emphasis on introductions and reflection, respectively.

4.1 Participants

Participants for the first two focus groups (n = 15) were recruited from St. John of God Liffey Services, and (n = 5) students and lecturers who previously participated in co-design activities. Participants self-recruited, through a gatekeeper, after reading the modified (highly visual), easy to read (included images, colour formatted) information leaflet and consent form that the gatekeeper will send to them.

4.2 Methods

During each focus group participants work together on a design challenge using some co-design tools to brainstorm ideas or to sketch a graphical user interface or give feedback on an existing design. The purpose of the focus group format is to recreate the context of the co-design process that the participants have already been involved in, this is to reduce the (possible negative) effect of introducing a new context to the participants. These series of focus group sessions mirror the codesign process. The intention of holding the focus group sessions within the same context of the codesign process, is twofold; to help minimise any discomfort to the participants as the context will be familiar and to allow participants to naturally provide and describe information about their experience while going through the same process.

The intended format of a single focus group session is welcome and introductions, ice breaker/warm up design task, content section, team discussions and reflections. At the end of the focus group session, participants will be asked some questions for feedback. Some sample questions are: "How did you find this co-design session?", "How did you find communicating with the students in this co-design session?", "What could have made this co-design session better for you?".

4.3 Initial Findings from Focus Groups with Men and Women

At the time of writing this paper, two focus group sessions of the design phases have taken place and we would like provide some observations to better assist others within in this space. Preliminary focus group findings from the co-designers themselves, reinforced some of the previous theme outlined in study 1, most notably; "It makes me feel important", "we want our own designs", "Teamwork", "helping", "fun", "new people", "friends". Similar to the student's experience – it is quite difficult for the co-designers to name or label what they don't like, perhaps not wanting to be wrong or to offend someone. Focus group co-designer participants preferred more visualisations or tools to assist in this form of comprehension. A commonly occurring issue in within research is biasing individuals or influencing their answers whether knowingly or not, this can be even more pronounced in more vulnerable populations. In order to make sure that support staff or facilitators do not bias the co-designers, great care and attention needs to be paid to language, prompts and turn-taking in the sessions.

5 Discussion

While the primary outcome of the co-design project was a co-designed app that was developed, it is evident that more benefits were attained and challenges/barriers are present – for both the co-designers and designers, albeit, in different forms. The fundamental similarities underpinning this programme as cited by the students and lecturers was the challenge of communication, for SJOG co-designers to advocate for themselves and most importantly, what they don't like (response bias), while the students were challenged to speak colloquially removing their technological jargon, enjoyment and engagement in a novel experience, with novel individuals and the resulting outcomes of learning, inclusion and a physical project to represent the collaborative work.

The themes revealed, are quite similar to the benefits proposed by Turner, Merle and Dichon [5] for the co-designers, particularly in terms of "enjoyment" and "sense of ownership". Of the barriers described by Colin Gibson et al., [17], we subscribe that "overly complex concepts" is an evident challenge to those with intellectual disabilities within co-design and that it is essential that tools are developed to reduce these challenges, for example by providing a template to break down difficult concepts. This particular barrier was also reported by the students and lecturers in terms of "abstracting".

6 Limitations

It is acknowledged that the students who agreed to provide information on their experience in the co-design project, may have been more likely to be the students who had a positive experience.

7 Conclusion

In qualitative interviews student and lecturer participants who engaged in the co-design process reported their experience of the benefits and challenges of this interactive process, within the computer science domain. Communication was highlighted as a central theme within this process, particularly in supporting and engaging individuals with intellectual disabilities in co-design via tools made for co-design. Actively involving individuals with disabilities in co-design research is essential but can be an elaborate process that may place an impetus on researchers. We have provided a detailed description of a co-design focus group protocol and research consent procedure, potentially providing valuable insight for other researchers, particularly around involving individuals with intellectual disabilities in informed research practices of co-design. These exploratory studies are an important part of facilitating the creation of a sustainable, accessible, inclusive co-design toolkit.

Acknowledgments. This research is supported by the Irish Research Council (www.research.ie). We would also like to thank all participants for their time, enthusiasm and valuable input.

References

1. Sanders, E.B.-N., Stappers, P.J.: Co-creation and the new landscapes of design. CoDesign **4**(1), 5–18 (2008). https://doi.org/10.1080/15710880701875068
2. Bolger, P., Brereton, P., Grant, O., Torney, D.: Better together: knowledge co-production for a sustainable society. In: Better Together: Knowledge Co-production for a Sustainable Society. White Paper, pp. 1–104. Royal Irish Academy (2021)
3. Boyd, H., McKernon, S., Mullin, B., Old, A.: Improving healthcare through the use of co-design. NZ. Med. J. **125**(1357), 76–87 (2012)
4. Boland, S., Mooney, E., Gilligan, J., Bourke, P., Bourke, D.: A Co-design Partnership to Develop Universally Designed ICT Applications for People with Intellectual Disability (2018)
5. Turner, F., Merle, A., Diochon, P.F.: How to assess and increase the value of a co-design experience: a synthesis of the extant literature. In: Mass Customization, Personalization, and Co-creation: Bridging Mass Customization and Open Innovation, December 2011
6. Dimopoulos-Bick, T., Dawda, P., Maher, L., Verma, R., Palmer, V.: Experience-based co-design: tackling common challenges. J. Health Des. **3**(1), 86–93 (2018). https://doi.org/10.21853/jhd.2018.46
7. Donetto, S., Pierri, P., Tsianakas, V., Robert, G.: Experience-based co-design and healthcare improvement: realizing participatory design in the public sector. Des. J. **18**(2), 227–248 (2015). https://doi.org/10.2752/175630615x14212498964312
8. Sitbon, L., Farhin, S.: Co-designing interactive applications with adults with intellectual disability. In: Proceedings of the 29th Australian Conference on Computer-Human Interaction (2017). https://doi.org/10.1145/3152771.3156163
9. Kidney, C.A., McDonald, K.E.: A toolkit for accessible and respectful engagement in research. Disabil. Soc. **29**(7), 1013–1030 (2014). https://doi.org/10.1080/09687599.2014.902357
10. Cook, T., Inglis, P.: Participatory research with men with learning disability: informed consent. Tizard Learn. Disabil. Rev. **17**(2), 92–101 (2012). https://doi.org/10.1108/13595471211218875
11. Conroy, N.E., McDonald, K.E., Olick, R.S.: A survey study of the attitudes and experiences of adults with intellectual disability regarding participation in research. J. Intellect. Disabil. Res. **65**(10), 941–948 (2021). https://doi.org/10.1111/jir.12877
12. Doody, O.: Ethical challenges in intellectual disability research. Mathews J. Nurs. Health Care **1**(1), 1–11 (2018)

13. d.school (n.d.) Empathy Map. http://dschool-old.stanford.edu/wp-content/themes/dschool/method-cards/empathy-map.pdf
14. d.school (n.d.) I Like, I wish, What if. http://dschool-old.stanford.edu/wp-content/themes/dschool/method-cards/i-like-i-wish-what-if.pdf
15. Clarke, V., Braun, V.: Thematic Analysis. Encyclopedia Critical Psychology, pp. 1947–1952. Springer, New York (2014). https://doi.org/10.1007/978-1-4614-5583-7_311
16. Hasso Plattner Institute of Design: An Introduction to Design Thinking: Process Guide (2010). https://web.stanford.edu/~mshanks/MichaelShanks/files/509554.pdf
17. Colin Gibson, R., Dunlop, M.D., Bouamrane, M.-M.: Lessons from expert focus groups on how to better support adults with mild intellectual disabilities to engage in co-design. In: The 22nd International ACM SIGACCESS Conference on Computers and Accessibility (2020). https://doi.org/10.1145/3373625.3417008

Evaluating a Visual Mobile Banking App for Users with Low Subjective Numeracy

Alexander Stewart and Marian McDonnell(✉)

Institute of Art, Design and Technology, Dun Laoghaire, Dublin, Ireland
marian.mcdonnell@iadt.ie

Abstract. Financial well-being is one of the many aspects of life affected by low numeracy. Digital banking interactions use numerically symbolic-based interactions. However, one of the critical learning difficulties often associated with low numeracy, a magnitude-processing deficit, is directly impaired by associating symbolic numbers with their equivalent magnitude. Using a user-centered design process, a visual financial management system was created. It was then tested with 40 participants of various reported subjective numeracy scores. The visual system was designed using a visual representation of money instead of a traditional application, which is purely symbolic-based. The study results indicated that the interactive visual system was the preferred design compared to the symbolic system for the lower subjective numeracy group. Furthermore, it also improved financial awareness and consideration across all ranges of numeracy.

Keywords: Assistive technology · Inclusion · Subjective low numeracy · Money management · Usability

1 Introduction

1.1 Low Numeracy

Numeracy can be defined in two ways, mathematical skills, which are taught, and skills applied in everyday life [1]. The Organisation for Economic Co-operation and Development reported that in 2016, 25% of adults in Ireland received a score lower than a level 1 in mathematical abilities, which ranks Ireland 18th for numeracy skills [2]. At this level of numeracy skills, performing anything other than basic arithmetic becomes difficult. Comparatively, at level 2, people possess the ability to process numbers in a relatable context where the mathematical content is explicit [3]. Research conducted by the Institute of Education London found that low numeracy has impacts on the economic, social and health areas of daily life [4]. OECD also reported a correlation between low numeracy and a lower level of trust in others, as well as a low engagement in community activities and political process' [5]. However, a lower ability in numeracy has been noted to affect an adult's motivation and effort to learn and improve their numeracy [6]. There are several factors, which cause low numeracy. A common factor is a special learning difficulty in math's (SLDM) or developmental dyscalculia. A characteristic of dyscalculia

K. Miesenberger et al. (Eds.): ICCHP-AAATE 2022, LNCS 13342, pp. 293–300, 2022.
https://doi.org/10.1007/978-3-031-08645-8_34

is a number sense deficit, which heavily affects a person's ability to learn arithmetic [7]. This is the sole deficit of the condition and, as such, can be found to affect people who otherwise have normal intelligence and cognitive functioning. Dyscalculia is estimated to have a prevalence of 5–7% [8], which is approximately the same as dyslexia, yet it has not been afforded the same degree of attention. This deficit is identified as an impairment of the ability to process symbolic representation of numbers and their magnitude equivalent [9]. This impairment also heavily affects the ability to carry out estimation tasks [10]. Studies have shown a direct correlation between mathematical achievements and a number sense deficit [11]. Because of this, a person's ability to confidently and successfully perform everyday numerical activities can be limited [12].

1.2 Measuring Low Numeracy

The challenge of adult low numeracy is identifying a number sense deficit or other factors that impact numeracy skills [13]. To help to identify low numeracy, experts often use scales such as the Lipkus numeracy scale to gauge the level of numeracy skills [14]. This scale is calculated based on an objective numeracy test. These objective measures have been a critical indicator quantifying numeracy skills, but there have been comparable success using subjective numeracy measures. The Subjective Numeracy Scale (SNS) test differs from a traditional objective test, as it involves a self-reported measure of perceived ability to perform mathematical tasks [15]. The SNS test is also faster to complete and evokes fewer adverse reactions, which encourages participation more than the objective numeracy test. A study conducted in 2007 aimed at validating the subjective numeracy scale compared to an objective scale showed that the SNS scale held up considerably well compared to the established objective numeracy measures [16]. It also provides some additional qualitative improvements to traditional objective tests. As a result of this, the comparability of the SNS to traditional methods of predicting numeracy abilities allows for an alternative way of qualifying the intended user group for this project [17].

1.3 Mobile Banking

Low numeracy skills can lead to several financial difficulties when conducting everyday banking tasks. To date, there are no mobile banking (MB) apps that genuinely address the abilities of users with low numeracy or subjective low numeracy. Financial mistakes, overspending, fraud and other financial vulnerability are all issues, which face users with a lower level of numeracy skills. A refined understanding of low numeracy users and how they interact with MB services is key to providing assistive features within MB apps. Studies have shown the benefits assistive technology can have when assisting users with cognitive impairments to make better decisions [18]. To facilitate this in a MB context, the design must utilise evolving features such as visual displays, error prevention, and intuitive interaction design principles. Tailoring these design aspects to reflect users' cognitive processing abilities with a lower level of numeracy could provide a wide range of benefits. Designing these features with a better understanding of users with low numeracy could create alternative systems that do not require a moderate to high numeracy ability.

2 Research Objectives

Many leading mobile banking apps attribute their success to a user-centred design approach (UCD), focusing on users, tasks, and use environments [19]. Although most users have experienced the benefits of improved mobile banking services, users are not provided with an alternative interactive system for performing numerical tasks. Mobile banking app features fail to provide an inclusive method of performing a numerical task for users with low numeracy. Offering choice for conducting tasks is a crucial principle behind inclusive design [20]. The goal of this research will focus on developing and evaluating an alternative to traditional numerical design systems used in a mobile banking app. Evaluation will be carried out using the Usability Satisfaction and Ease of use (USE) questionnaire. The USE scale is a measure created to assess the subjective usability of an application across four subscales; Usefulness, Ease of Use, Ease of Learning and Satisfaction. The statements are rated on a 7-point Likert scale, where 1 is 'Strongly Disagree' and 7 is 'Strongly Agree'. The overall Cronbach's alpha for the USE scale was found to be 0.98 [21].

To achieve this, the research question posed is:

1. Do individuals, with low SNS scores, report higher usability with the visually design application compared to a traditionally designed application?

Three hypotheses will be required to test research question 1:

H1: There will be a difference for the participants on their USE scores depending on the condition (visually designed application compared to a traditionally designed application) to which they are assigned.

H2: There will be a difference for the participants on their USE score depending on their subjective numeracy group (low-medium, medium-high).

H3: There will be a significant interaction between the assigned test condition and numeracy.

3 Method

3.1 Research Design

The research activities conducted during this project were structured around a User Centred Design (UCD) approach. The research framework is structured around three phases, first to explore the user's needs and define their problems. The second phase is to synthesise and refine potential design solutions, which address the user needs specified in the first phase. The goal of the final phase is to validate the design solution with the intended users. The first iterations of the design system were by primary and secondary data gathered in the project's first phase. The primary research methodologies conducted during the first phases of the project were a series of semi-structured Subject Matter Expert (SME) interviews and a user survey on mobile banking users. The secondary research activities were made up of an initial literature review, followed by competitor analysis and task analysis of other mobile banking apps. Figure 1 represents the timelines of research activities conducted throughout the project. Table 1 contains a description of each of the primary research activities.

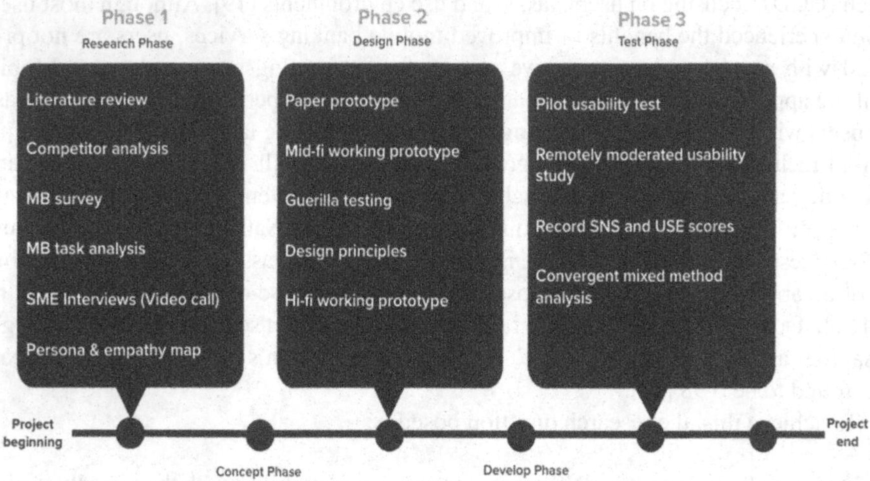

Fig. 1. Research activity timeline

After the initial research conducted in phase 1, the data and insights gathered were used as design input into phase 2. Within this phase, the aim was to refine the MB design requirements for users with subjective low numeracy. Using these refined design requirements, a non-symbolic based number system was developed using Balsamiq, a lo-fi mockup design software. The goal of the lo-fi prototyping design system was to test the feasibility of the design variations. Once the scope of the lo-fi design had been narrowed through various iterations, the selected design was developed into a working prototype for a mobile device.

Table 1. Primary research activity detail

	User Survey	SME Interview	Guerilla testing	Usability study
Participants	60+ (as many as possible)	2 (SNA, Education specialist)	20 x 2	40 (Mix of age,sex and numeracy abilities)
Measures	Likert scale, single answer & free text	Qualitative questions	Task time, success rate, and Qualitative feedback	SNS and USE
Analysis	Cross tabulation and chi-square analysis	Thematic analysis	Issue prioritization analysis	Convergent parallel mixed method analysis

Fig. 2. Traditional and visual prototype

The first round of user testing was conducted with 20 applied psychology students using the remote user testing software Maze. For each prototype feature, the desired task flow was defined within the lo-fi prototype, and participants were asked to complete the following tasks:

1. Can you find your transactions from yesterday?
2. Can you find how much you spent in December, in restaurants?
3. Can you create a budget of €250 for Groceries and House, occurring monthly?
4. Can you find how much you can spend from your budget each day?
5. Can you send €120.50 to your contact, Ben Simon?

The quantitative and qualitative feedback obtained during this user testing provided an insight into the number systems performance. The primary theme identified related to the symbolic representation of the numbers. Recommendations from the group mainly focused on re-designing the number blocks to be more representative of money as opposed to ambiguous blocks representing numbers. The quantitative data gathered using Maze also backed up these key themes discussed post-testing. Heatmaps and miss click rates were also a primary indicator of areas within the lo-fi prototype, which performed well or not. Considering both the qualitative and quantitative data gathered during the first round of users testing, the second iteration of the prototype focused on improving the interactive visual number system and moving the prototype version to a hi-fi design. The first design problem focused on making the visual number system more reflective of real money. For this, a number of solutions were produced to test their feasibility. These solutions were then presented to a low numeracy accessibility expert who previously consulted on the project. Aspects of two of the design solutions were their preference. Post consultation, the two best features of the solutions were combined.

This included a note type design with an inner circle, coins that were circular in form, as well as colours reflective of real money.

The final usability study was designed to be completed by participants unmoderated. Each participant was assigned a test condition, the visual prototype or the traditional prototype (see Fig. 2), and was categorised into a Low-Medium, Medium-High group based on their SNS score. Both the test condition and the numeracy groups were the independent variables of the study. The dependent variable of the study was the USE scores. The USE questionnaire conducted collected both quantitative data and qualitative data. As the usability study was a between-group study, two prototypes needed to be developed: the visual prototype and the traditional prototype. The prototypes were the same except for the inclusion or exclusion of the visual number display. The visual prototype contains the visual interactive system, which had been iteratively developed based on user testing and feedback. This solution has a visual representation of numbers as well as supporting symbolic representation, requiring users to tap numbers to add or subtract them when managing finances. The traditional system contains only the symbolic representation of numbers. The interactions are the same in all banking apps, requiring users to type in number amounts to add or subtract.

4 Results and Discussion

Participants were gathered using convenience snowball sampling and aged between 18 and 65+ years old (M = 34.67, SD = 9.4), 59% of the participants were female, and 41% were male. 70% of the participants had higher education. As the study design was a between-groups study, a 2 × 2 factorial between groups two-way ANOVA was conducted using IBM's SPSS. This analysis aimed to examine any relationship between subjective numeracy and the recorded subjective usability of each prototype. To ensure the data assumptions were not violated during the study, both a Shapiro-Wilk test of normality and a Levine's test of homogeneity was conducted prior to analysis. The results of the Shapiro-Wilk test revealed an acceptable distribution of data, while a test statistic of $p = 0.311$ for Levine's test of homogeneity was recorded. This met the assumption of the homogeneity of variance. No outliers were reported in the SPSS output. The first hypothesis associated with the research question stated there would be a difference in the participants on their USE scores depending on their assigned condition. The statistical test used to prove this hypothesis recorded a result of $F(1,36) = 0.388$, $p = 0.537$, with an effect size of n2 = 0.011. These results support accepting the null hypothesis and rejecting the alternative. The second hypothesis stated that there would be a difference in the participants USE scores depending on their assigned subjective numeracy group (low-medium, medium-high). This was proven to be statistically significant $F(1,36) = 4.784$, $p = 0.035$, with a reported power of 0.567. Thus, the hypothesis was accepted. The third hypothesis stated that the interaction between the assigned test condition and the participants reported SNS would be significant. The statistical analysis reported $F(1,36) = 8.097$, $p = 0.007$, with a large effect size of n2 = 0.184. This result proved the level of significance required to accept the hypothesis.

4.1 Subjective Numeracy and the Visual Prototype

Although the results of this study suggested a slight difference reported in the USE scores across both of the prototypes, there was a significant difference in USE scores when compared with the assigned numeracy group. The Low-Medium numeracy group reported a significantly higher subjective usability score when using the visual prototype. In contrast, the Medium-High group reported a significantly lower usability score when using the visual prototype. Using the traditional prototype, the Low-Medium numeracy group reported a slightly lower usability score than the Medium-High group. The prototype does allow users with a lower numeracy ability to carry out financial tasks in an alternative method. This feature has not been previously offered in current banking apps. The result of the study also supported the impact this has on the overall usability of the prototype, as a significantly higher usability score was recorded in the lower numeracy group for the visual prototype. Even with the potential discrepancies, which may have occurred during the subjective numeracy reporting compared to a participant's objective numeracy, the study results still maintain that lower numeracy groups report a significantly higher usability score using the visual prototype. The unreliability factor in the subject numeracy reporting could have affected the overall reported usability scores reported for each of the prototypes, but not to the point in which the results of the study should be deemed invalid.

4.2 Strengths and Limitations

The main strength of the study was the use of a user centred design approach. A limitation of the study was the relatively small sample size (N = 40). Given the smaller sample size, fewer participants within the Low-Medium (N = 13) participated in the study. Generally, the mix of ages was quite good. However, the 65+ group was not well represented within this study. The educational level was also disproportionately spread, as no participant indicated they had a level of education lower than secondary level, and 70% of participants indicated they have a level three or equivalent level of education.

As there is a high rate of comorbidity between dyscalculia and dyslexia, a future research study involving participants diagnosed with dyslexia would provide an ever-greater insight into the overall usability of the prototype.

References

1. Skills for Life 2011, PIAAC 2014, National Numeracy YouGov Survey 2014: Low levels of numeracy are a long-term problem for the UK. National Numeracy YouGov Survey 2014(2014)
2. OECD: Skills Matter: Further Results from the Survey of Adult Skills. OECD Publishing, Paris (2016)
3. OECD: Literacy, Numeracy and Problem Solving in Technology-Rich Environments: Framework for the OECD Survey of Adult Skills. OECD Publishing (2012). https://doi.org/10.1787/9789264128859-en
4. Lister, J.: The impact of poor numeracy skills on adults, research review. Prepared for NIACE by the National Research and Development Centre for Adult Literacy and Numeracy (NRDC) at the Institute of Education (IOE), University of London, June 2013

5. Grotlüschen, A., Mallows, D., Reder, S., Sabtini, J.: Adults with low proficiency in literacy or numeracy. OECD Education Working Papers, No. 131. OECD Publishing, Paris (2016)
6. Ofsted: Tackling the challenge of low numeracy skills in young people and adults (100225). The Office for Students in Eductation, Children's services and Skills, Manchester (2011)
7. Butterworth, B., Laurillard, D.: Low numeracy and dyscalculia: identification and intervention. ZDM **42**, 527–539 (2010)
8. Shalev, R.S.: Prevalence of developmental dyscalculia. In: Berch, D.B., Mazzocco, M.M. (eds.) Why is Math So Hard for Some Children? The Nature and Origins of Mathematical Learning Difficulties and Disabilities, pp. 49–60. Paul H. Brooks Publishing, Baltimore (2007)
9. Szucs, D., Devine, A., Soltesz, F., Nobes, A., Gabriela, F.: Developmental dyscalculia is related to visuo-spatial memory and inhibition impairment. Cortex **49**(10), 2674–2688 (2013)
10. Morsanyi, K., Bers, B.M., O'Connor, P.A., McCormack, T.: Developmental dyscalculia is characterized by order processing deficits: evidence from numerical and non-numerical ordering tasks. Dev. Neuropsychol. **43**(7), 595–621 (2018)
11. Halberda, J., Mazzocco, M.M., Feigenson, L.: Individual differences in non-verbal number acuity correlate with maths achievement. Nature **455**, 665–668 (2008)
12. Schelifer, P., Landerl, K.: Subitizing and counting in typical and atypical development. Dev. Sci. **14**, 280–291 (2011)
13. Siemann, J., Petermann, F.: Innate or acquired? – disentangling number sense and early number competencies. Front. Psychol. **9**, 571 (2018)
14. Lipkus, I., Samsa, G., Rijmer, B.K.: General performance on a numeracy scale among highly educated samples. Med. Decis. Making **21**(1), 37–44 (2001)
15. Fagerlin, A., Zikmund-Fisher, B.J., Ubel, P.A., Jankovic, A., Derry, H.A., Smith, D.M.: Measuring numeracy without a math test: development of the Subjective Numeracy Scale. Med. Decis.Making **27**, 672–680 (2007)
16. Zikmund-Fisher, B.J., Smith, D.M., Ubel, P.A., Fagerlin, A.: Validation of the subjective numeracy scale: effects of low numeracy on comprehension of risk communications and utility elicitations. Med. Decis. Making **27**(5), 663–671 (2007)
17. Mera, C., Ruiz-Cagigas, G., Navarro-Guzmán, J. I., Aragón-Mendizábal, E., Delgado, C., Aguilar-Villagrán, M.: PP designed for early math training. Magnitudes Comparison. In: Proceedings of the 5th International Conference on Technological Ecosystems for Enhancing Multiculturality, Article 65, 1–8. Association for Computing Machinery, New York (2017)
18. Davies, D.K., Stock, S.E., Wehmeyer, M.L.: A palmtop computer-based intelligent aid to increase independent decision making. Res. Pract. Persons with Severe Disabil. **28**(4), 182–193 (2003)
19. Usability.gov: User-Centered Design Basics (n.d.). Retrieved from Usability.gov: https://www.usability.gov/what-and-why/user-centered-design.html. Accessed 3 Dec 2021
20. Swan, H., Pouncey, I., Pickering, H., Watson, L. (n.d.) https://inclusivedesignprinciples.org/
21. Gao, M., Kortum, P., Oswald, F.: Psychometric evaluation of the USE (usefulness, satisfaction, and ease of use) questionnaire for reliability and validity. In: Proceedings of the Human Factors and Ergonomics Society Annual Meeting, vol. 62, no. 1, pp. 1414–1418 (2018)

How to Ensure Continuity of AT Assessment Services for Frail People in Times of Pandemics: An Italian Experience

Claudia Salatino[1(✉)], Valerio Gower[1], Lia Malisano[2], Chiara Folini[1], Maurizio Saruggia[1], Rosa Maria Converti[1], Francesco Zava[1], and Marina Ramella[1]

[1] IRCCS Fondazione Don Carlo Gnocchi ONLUS, Milan, Italy
csalatino@dongnocchi.it
[2] Università degli studi di Milano, Milan, Italy

Abstract. After an initial lock-down phase in 2020, the measures subsequently adopted in Italy to limit the spread of the SARS-CoV-2 virus made it impossible for people residing in nursing homes to have contacts with the outside world. Here we want to report how the DAT (Home automation, Assistive Technology and Occupational Therapy) service of Fondazione Don Carlo Gnocchi in Milan, Italy, was able to give continuity to the provision of assistive technology assessment services for older adults with disability who were not able to reach the DAT premises due to social restrictions. In the period 2020–2021, remote AT assessments were organized using a Tele-rehabilitation platform so that the physiatrist in charge of prescribing the assistive devices, supported by a therapist specialized in AT, could connect remotely from the DAT service to nursing homes in the Milan area. There, a rehabilitation professional would participate to the visit. 94 older adults with disability in 2020 and 2021 were able to take advantage of mobility assistive technology assessments provided remotely by DAT service AT professionals. The assistive devices prescribed were found to be appropriate, only a small percentage needed to be revised or were refused. High levels of satisfaction with the service provided were measured through KWAZO questionnaire among users of the service. 80% of the interviewees declared that it might be useful to keep the possibility of carrying out remote AT assessments in the future, even when the state of emergency for the COVID-19 pandemic will be finished.

Keywords: Tele-rehabilitation · AT assessment · AT services

1 Background

The fragile population, such as the older adults with disability, was severely impacted by the COVID-19 pandemic. After an initial lock-down phase in 2020, the measures subsequently adopted in Italy to limit the spread of the virus made it impossible for people living in nursing homes to have contact with the outside world. The aim of this paper is to describe how the DAT (Domotica, Ausili, Terapia Occupazionale - Home

The original version of this chapter was revised: Acknowledgment section with funding was added. The correction to this chapter is available at https://doi.org/10.1007/978-3-031-08645-8_64

K. Miesenberger et al. (Eds.): ICCHP-AAATE 2022, LNCS 13342, pp. 301–309, 2022.
https://doi.org/10.1007/978-3-031-08645-8_35

Automation, Assistive Technology and Occupational Therapy) service of Fondazione Don Carlo Gnocchi (FDG) in Milan, Italy, developed a new remote Assistive Technology (AT) assessment procedure to give continuity to the service dedicated to older adults with disability.

2 Methods

FDG has different facilities distributed throughout Italy, in 12 of these an AT service (SIVA: Servizi di Informazione e Valutazione Ausili-AT Information and Assessment services) is available with a showroom and professionals with a wide experience in AT for the independence of people with disabilities [1]. In the FDG research center (IRCCS Santa Maria Nascente) in Milan the SIVA service is part of DAT. The DAT offers a comprehensive rehabilitation pathway that includes occupational therapy training, individualized AT counselling and education towards independence [2]. The DAT professional team is prepared to help the patients find solutions to problems that they have experienced in daily life (mobility, communication, computer access, personal care, home adaptation…) and in any context (domestic life, school, workplace, social activities…).

In the initial phase of the COVID-19 lockdown in Italy, most of the outpatient services were suddenly interrupted. In such a context, FDG immediately decided to work at implementing Tele-Rehabilitation (TR) services in order to give patients the possibility to continue their rehabilitation pathways. In the very first phase, from March to May 2020, the implemented solution consisted in using some of the most common video-conferencing platforms (e.g. Microsoft Teams and Skype, Google Meet, etc.). Such solutions, although having the advantage that many patients and clinicians were already accustomed to their use, were however not suitable to be used in the long run due to two main limitations. The first one is related to the certification of the platform. The Medical Device Regulation (MDR) of the European Union (EU) requires any software solution that provides information used to take clinical decisions (either diagnostic or therapeutic) to be certified as medical device class IIa. Moreover, according to the rules set out in the General Data Protection Regulation (GDPR) of the EU, special attention has to be paid to the protection of health-related data. The use of cloud-based services for which there is no direct control on where the data centres are based is not recommended for the exchange of health-related data between patients and clinicians. The second limitation is related to the difficulties of integrating general-purpose video-conferencing platforms with the existing Hospital Information Systems (HIS) which is something that, in contrast with the goal of TR to optimize resources and costs, creates additional administration burdens.

FDG therefore started a scouting process to identify the most suitable telemedicine platform among the ones available on the market. A set of selection criteria was defined by involving clinicians working in different areas such as paediatric neuropsychiatry, adult neurological and orthopaedic rehab, home care services and AT. The involved clinicians, by exploiting their previous experiences in the use of general purpose video-conferencing platforms to provide TR services, were able to formulate a set of functional and usability requirements which encompassed both the healthcare professionals' and patients' points of view.

The most relevant requirements identified included:

- the presence of video-communication functionalities, to be able to provide synchronous TR services (i.e. with the telepresence of the clinician/therapist). The video-communication system had to be able to connect multiple people at the same time (e.g. one therapist with two patients or two therapists with one patient);
- the video-communication system had to be suitable for mobile devices (smartphone and tablet) as well, through the browser or a dedicated app;
- the possibility to exchange files (e.g. video, images, documents, etc.) between clinicians and patients in a secure way through the platform;
- the possibility to share the screen and send text messages during the therapeutic session;
- the possibility to provide asynchronous TR services, by allowing the clinician to set-up a personalized plan of activities for the patient to be performed autonomously at home. The asynchronous TR system should allow the clinician to link specific contents to the exercise (e.g. video, documents, etc.) and to register the patient feedback on the performed activities;
- the compliance with MDR and GDPR, including the adoption of best practices for data protection such as the encryption of personal and sensitive data;
- the possibility of integrating the platform with the existing HIS.

This last point includes the possibility of integrating the TR platform with: a) FDG authentication servers (i.e. the possibility for healthcare professionals to log-in with the company credentials), b) the Master Patient Index (MPI) of FDG (i.e. the database of patient personal data), and c) the existing software solutions for managing clinicians' agendas and producing clinical and administrative/financial reports. All the integration had to be made through HL7 protocols.

In Italy, the first attempt to provide a legislative framework for the delivery of telemedicine services was made by the Italian Ministry of Health in 2014, with the document entitled "national guidelines on telemedicine" which, however, did not provide a specific definition, nor concrete indications for the implementation of TR services. Although some experiences of TR had been promoted by Italian regional health authorities in experimental form before 2020, it was only in November 2021, that is several months after the pandemic outbreak, that an official document was issued by the Ministry of Health including national indications for the delivery of TR services. In this context, as of 2020, most of the telemedicine platforms available on the market as commercial medical device CE marked products were not specifically focused on TR. Several prototypes, developed within research and innovation projects, existed however, which represented the solid basis for the implementation of specific TR functionalities.

The platform that has eventually been selected is Maia, produced by the Italian company ab medica srl. Maia, formerly known as Telbios Connect and produced by the Italian SEM Telbios, is the result of several research and innovation projects of the company Telbios that involved FDG as clinical partner [3]. All of the functionalities listed in the requirements above have been gradually implemented in the platform, which has been progressively rolled-out in 12 different FDG facilities starting from June 2020.

The roll-out of the new technological system required an initial experimentation period in which organizational solutions were identified that were useful for achieving the maximum effectiveness of the rehabilitation intervention. The system in fact offered a great opportunity but strategies for use, organization and planning had to be identified that would allow to overcome the limits of not having the patient in presence.

In the 2020–2021 period remote AT assessments were organized so that the physiatrist responsible for assistive devices (ADs) prescription, supported by a therapist specialized in AT, could connect remotely from the DAT service to nursing homes in Milan area. In the first phase video-conferencing platforms were used, and subsequently the TR platform described above was adopted.

Before the tele-visit, documentation about the subjects was required which allowed AT experts to get an idea of the possible assistive solutions useful for each of them; this documentation included disability certification, request for AT assessment by the doctor in charge of the subjects, information about diagnosis, functional limitations, the results of the evaluation with clinical scales such as MMSE (Mini-Mental State Examination) and Barthel Index for functional evaluation. Subjects diagnoses were classified using ICD9.

The AT assessment consists of one or more tele-visits. During the first one the assessment team is composed by: the DAT physiatrist, DAT therapist and the nursing home therapist together with the patient. The nursing home rehabilitation professional supports the clinician's decision for the most adequate assistive solution and takes the measurements useful to set up the appropriate assistive device (AD). During the tele-visit the prescription was entered in the online system provided by the regional health system and the report of the examination was written (see Fig. 1).

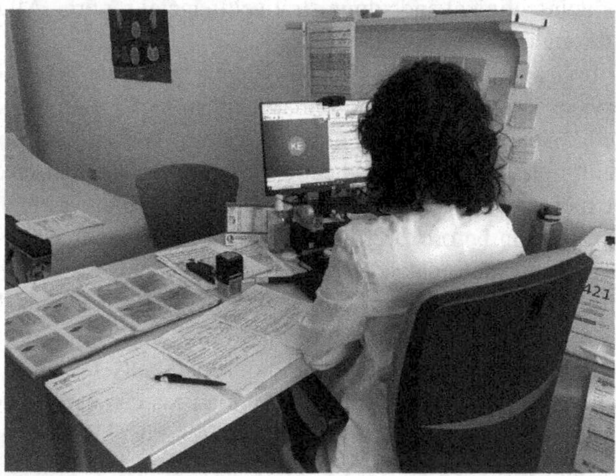

Fig. 1. The setting of the tele-visit: the physiatrist, connected remotely to the nursing home, is preforming online the prescription of the ADs identified

In complex cases a second tele-visit can be performed before prescription in presence of an orthopaedic technician (chosen by the patient).

The prescribed ADs can be provided by the local health authorities warehouse or by a private AT company. An orthopaedic technician delivers the ADs to the nursing home and makes adjustments and customizations on site, in order to improve the fitting. The rehabilitation professional of the nursing home verifies if the ADs delivered are appropriate, if not a prescription revision can be requested and the ADs provided can be rejected and replaced.

The tele-visit is organized so that a maximum of 6 nursing home residents in need for an assistive solution could be evaluated in a single session.

The revised prescriptions, the rejected ADs and a perceived satisfaction questionnaire were chosen as quality indicators of the provided service.

Among AT outcome assessment instruments [4, 5] KWAZO questionnaire [6] was chosen to evaluate the nursing homes therapists' satisfaction.

KWAZO is composed of seven questions about the quality of the AT service delivery process (Accessibility, Information, Coordination, Knowledge, Efficiency, Participation, Instruction). In the Italian [7] version the respondent is requested to rate his/her degree of satisfaction with each indicator on a 5-point Likert scale ('not at all satisfied', 'not satisfied', 'more or less satisfied', 'satisfied', and 'very satisfied') (see Table 1).

Table 1. KWAZO questionnaire questions and domains.

Item ID	Question	Domain
K1	Could you always reach the service delivery professionals easily?	Accessibility
K2	How clear was the information about the application and the possible solutions that the service delivery professionals gave you?	Information
K3	How well was the cooperation and the communication between the different service delivery professionals?	Coordination
K4	Did the service delivery professionals have sufficient know how?	Know-how
K5	Was your application handled quickly and efficiently?	Efficiency
K6	Were your own opinion and wishes considered in choosing an assistive device?	Participation
K7	Was the use of the assistive device well explained to you?	Instruction

We performed a qualitative descriptive analysis of data of tele-AT assessment performed in 2020 and 2021.

3 Results

During 2020–2021, 12 nursing homes had used the service and 94 residents (73 females and 21 males; mean age 86 years; SD 9.62; range: 47–100) were tele-visited. Among them, 30 had hypokinetic syndrome, 10 hemiplegia, 9 senile dementia, 7 Alzheimer's disease, 7 cerebral vascular disease, 7 vascular dementia, 5 brain degeneration, 6 Parkinson's disease, 4 cerebrovascular disease and others pathologies or functional limitations.

The following mobility ADs were prescribed: 59 tilting push wheelchairs, 33 light self-propelled wheelchairs and 2 electronic wheelchairs. The average cost for the regional health service was respectively of 2343 euros for wheelchairs push tilting, 1217 euros for self-propelled wheelchairs, 1244 euros for electronic wheelchairs (see Table 2).

Table 2. ADs prescribed to the 94 subjects involved in the study KWAZO questionnaire questions and domains.

Mobility AD	Number	Average cost
Tilting push wheelchairs	59	2343 €
Light self-propelled wheelchairs	33	1217 €
Electronic wheelchairs	2	1244 €

In 3 cases (3.2%) it was necessary to review the prescription, since, when the ADs were provided, they were no longer adequate to the resident's situation; in 2 cases (2.1%) the AD provided was inappropriate and it was rejected.

The KWAZO questionnaire was proposed to the rehabilitation professionals involved in the tele-AT-assessments to evaluate their perceived satisfaction with the service provided. 5 questionnaires were collected, the average score obtained was 4.2. Items which obtained highest scores (4.8) were in information, coordination and know-how domains (items K2, K3, K4). The participation domain (item K6) obtained 4.6, while instruction domain (item K7) obtained 4.4. The efficiency domain (item K5) obtained 3.2 while the lowest score (3.0) was accessibility (item K1) (see Table 3).

Table 3. KWAZO scores obtained from nursing homes (NH) therapists.

Item ID	NH1	NH2	NH3	NH4	NH5	Mean score obtained
K1	2	2	4	3	4	3.0
K2	5	5	4	5	5	4.8
K3	5	5	5	4	5	4.8
K4	5	5	5	4	5	4.8
K5	3	3	2	3	5	3.2
K6	5	5	5	4	4	4.6
K7	5	5	5	4	3	4.4

4 interviewees (80%) declared that it might be useful to maintain the remote AT assessments in the future, even when the state of emergency for the COVID-19 pandemic will be finished, 1 did not express any opinion.

4 Discussion

The subjects to whom the tele-AT-assessments were provided were fragile people with comorbidities; while social distancing measures were active they were forbidden to go out of their residences and, even later on, it was safer and more prudent to limit traveling.

The AT tele-assessments, provided by DAT, made it possible to maintain service continuity, to respond to the unmet needs of older people.

The AT assessment consisted of one or more tele-visits. The assessment team was composed by: the DAT physiatrist, DAT therapist and the nursing home therapist in presence of the patient. The nursing home rehabilitation professional supported the clinician's decision for the most adequate assistive solution and took the measurements useful to set up the appropriate assistive device (AD).

The ADs prescribed during the tele-AT-assessments were found to be appropriate, only a small percentage (3.2%) needed to be reviewed and the prescription was then modified. In 2.1% of cases the device delivered could not be fitted or personalized adequately, was rejected and so substituted.

High levels of satisfaction with the service provided were detected through KWAZO questionnaire in information, coordination, know-how, participation and instruction domains. The main complains were about the waiting time to access the AT tele-assessment, especially in the first period and the length of the process.

The entire AT provision process includes assessment, prescription, delivery, verification and involves many actors (AT services, regional health system, AT companies). The DAT service analysed and improved the phases of the process in which it is involved (assessment and prescription): the aim was to reduce waiting times and to optimize the procedures for information/documents collection and assessment planning. DAT service could not reduce the length of the process due to the case complexity (which needed a higher number of tele-visits) and to the delivery waiting time.

5 Limitations of the Study

Due to time limitation a small number of KWAZO responses could be obtained. In the future greater consideration should be given to the users' satisfaction with the service, collecting more interviews; the same limitation reduced the possibility to analyse more deeply the outcomes of ATs provided, for example the AT's effects on the life of the residents or the achievements of the goals of the different stakeholders.

6 Conclusions

The pandemic has forced IT companies to develop remote work tools and healthcare facilities to engage in their use. These remote work tools allow an optimization of available resources and facilitate alternative and accessible ways to deliver rehabilitation services.

During COVID pandemics the availability of a TR platform allowed DAT to ensure AT service continuity, to organize tele-assessments and so to prescribe ADs for nursing homes residents.

The roll-out of the new technological system required an initial experimentation period in which technological and organizational solutions were identified that were useful for achieving the maximum effectiveness of the TR interventions with AT.

Usually AT assessments require the presence of the patient. In this particular situation it was possible to use the TR platform and complete the entire AT process remotely because of the presence, besides the patient, of the nursing home rehabilitation professionals who supported the DAT team in the prescription.

Prescribed ADs were found to be appropriate, interviewed users of the service were satisfied.

The authors and users of the service consider it useful to maintain and, if possible, further expand the possibility of carrying out remote AT assessments using the TR platform available, reducing traveling of frail people.

Acknowledgement. This work was supported and funded by the Italian Ministry of Health - Ricerca Corrente.

References

1. Andrich, R., Caracciolo, A., Johnson, I.: Individual assessment for assistive technology solutions: reflections on a thirty-year experience. Technol. Disabil. **25**(3), 147–158 (2013). https://doi.org/10.3233/TAD-130379
2. Andrich, R., Gower, V., Converti, R.M.: The DAT service, an integrated approach to improve in-dependence at home. In: Challenges for Assistive Technology, pp. 579–588. IOS Press (2007)
3. Realdon, O., et al.: The technology-enhanced ability continuum-of-care home program for people with cognitive disorders: concept design and scenario of use. In: Cipresso, P., Serino, S., Ostrovsky, Y., Baker, J.T. (eds.) MindCare 2018. LNICSSITE, vol. 253, pp. 64–73. Springer, Cham (2018). https://doi.org/10.1007/978-3-030-01093-5_9
4. Salatino, C., Pigini, L., Andrich, R.: How to measure the impact of assistive technology solutions on the person's quality of life? In: GOODTECHS 2018: Proceedings of the 4th EAI International Conference on Smart Objects and Technologies for Social Good, pp. 238–242 (2018). https://doi.org/10.1145/3284869.3284910
5. Desideri, L., et al.: Using a standard procedure to assess assistive technology service delivery outcomes: a proposal from the Italian Network of Independent Assistive Technology Centres. In: Global Perspectives on Assistive Technology, pp. 269–283. WHO (2019). https://apps.who.int/iris/bitstream/handle/10665/330371/9789241516853-eng.pdf#page=278. Accessed 29 Mar 2022
6. Desideri, L., Brandan, V., Bitelli, C., De Witte, L.: The employment of KWAZO with parents of children with disabilities in an Italian region: preliminary data on scale adaptation and validation. In: Assistive Technology Research Series (2013)
7. Desideri, L., Bizzarri, M., Bitelli, C., Roentgen, U., Gelderblom, G.J., De Witte, L.P.: Implementing a routine outcome assessment procedure to evaluate the quality of assistive technology service delivery for children with physical or multiple disabilities: perceived effectiveness, social cost, and user satisfaction. Assist. Technol. **28**(1), 30–40 (2016). https://doi.org/10.1080/10400435.2015.1072592

Communication Styles as Challenges for Participatory Design Process Facilitators Working with Young People with Additional Needs in a Residential Care Setting

A Conversation Analysis

Caroline Kortekaas and Isabel Zorn(✉)

TH Köln University of Applied Sciences, Gustav-Heinemann-Ufer 54, 50968 Köln, Germany
isabel.zorn@th-koeln.de

Abstract. Communication styles may play an important part in promoting or discouraging genuine engagement in participatory design, all the more so where design projects involve young people with additional needs receiving social work support. While technology designers may seek to set up a participatory process, the – possibly unconscious – communicative acts and language employed by a facilitator may play a crucial role in supporting or undermining participatory strategies, even where the participatory methods employed are appropriate to the planned process. This study presents findings of a conversation analysis undertaken on the opening minutes of a virtual participatory design workshop, showing how the sequence analyzed sets up a basis for participation that appears contradictory within itself.

Keywords: Conversation analysis · Participatory design · Communication styles · Virtual collaboration · Residential care for young people · Ethics

1 Introduction

Supporting skills for managing day-to-day life tasks is a core aspect of the remit of residential care settings for young people with and without disabilities alike. The design of appropriate technologies may benefit this endeavor [1]. In this context, we assume that participatory design methods could constitute a suitable approach to identifying young people's needs and their potential for input into the design of such tools [2], engaging clients, professionals, and developers in a co-design process. The communicative acts and language employed, possibly unconsciously, by a facilitator of such a process may act together with appropriate participatory methods to support participatory strategies in this context, or they may, contrastingly, undermine these methods and strategies.

The objectives of participatory design, its methods, and potential obstacles to its aims are well described in the literature, and a growing body of research explores participatory design processes conducted with people with disabilities or additional health or educational needs. The present study builds on this work by considering the potential

K. Miesenberger et al. (Eds.): ICCHP-AAATE 2022, LNCS 13342, pp. 310–319, 2022.
https://doi.org/10.1007/978-3-031-08645-8_36

effect of details of communication styles in promoting or blocking genuine participation. We proceed from the assumption that this possible impact of communication styles may be all the stronger where participatory design projects work with young people with additional needs in social care settings, to which subtle barriers to equal participation and uncertainties around the voluntary nature of client involvement in activities are inherent.

2 Participatory Design with Young People with Disabilities or Additional Educational Needs

Participatory technology design aims to involve future users of technologies in the design process as equal partners, to the end of understanding and including their views and accurately meeting their needs. In this context, genuine participation manifests as sharing in decision-making processes, from which ensues an ability to influence these processes' outcome [7]. Sharing control, sharing expertise and inspiring change are among the outcomes cited as the principal objectives of user participation in the development of digital technologies [3]. Models of participatory processes in research and development projects distinguish among various degrees of participation and describe challenges to genuine participation which may, for instance, involve "participants" effectively being used simply as providers of information or a failure to include them in a project's decision-making stages [5, 6]. Participating future users of products or services may have less control over the process than researchers or developers, who act as organizers and facilitators, and interpret the needs and views expressed [3]. Current research in this area evidences a lack of systematic reflection on and exploration or classification of methodological and research practice around the ambitions or assertions underlying and accompanying the establishment of participatory processes in technology development [4]. It is crucial in this context to consider interventions by researchers in these processes as key factors in user participation and needs analysis [3]; a particular area requiring increased analysis is the very beginning of a project [4]. In this light, and considering, from a critical perspective, whether the objectives of "participation" can hold up in practice, Vine et al. note the power of researchers when they "engage in acts [that] configure[e] participation." [3] It is some of these acts that our paper will analyze.

Participatory design research with people with learning disabilities is a growing field [refer to the good overview in 8]. Describing methods for, and obstacles to, participatory design with this group of people [12], authors in this area advocate for the extension and adaptation of existing participatory methods to the end of facilitating engagement among people with intellectual disabilities as valuable members of participatory design teams. The use of asset-based approaches to encourage participants' creative expression appears to be a helpful participatory strategy [13]. The likewise growing body of research on participatory design with children and young people who have additional needs has thus far tended to neglect residential care settings and the associated specific conditions and challenges [9]. Kinnula and Iivari [10] propose a framework for participatory design with children that takes their rights, potential, and needs for support into account, arguing that children's participation should be meaningful, effective, contextual, political, and educational. The authors outline the framework's purposes as giving children access to real responsibility and influence and enabling them to have a part in defining the goals of the activity [10]. Druin shows that current participatory processes may fall short of this aim, finding that children in participatory design processes fall into one of four roles, user, tester, informant, or design partner [11], which differ, inter alia, in the degrees of power and opportunities to take control associated with them.

The study described here will contribute to exploring participation by children with additional educational and support needs in care settings, proceeding from an interactionist point of view. Motivation is a central issue here. Constraints on time, resources, or motivation may be among the factors blamed for lacking participation; the reasons behind these constraints, specifically in relation to motivation, require closer analysis. Involving non-specialists in design processes requires time and resources for on-boarding, explanation and education; inadequate provision for these in project planning may itself stem from time constraints. In some instances, participants may sense that a "participatory" project in fact lacks truly participatory structures, thus experiencing a drop in motivation. In the project analyzed for this study, the researchers were not fully satisfied with the extent of the young people's participation. It is tempting to attribute a lack of motivation among young clients of social work projects to presumed individual characteristics of these clients, labeling them, for instance, "difficult to motivate". The aim of the study was to progress beyond this potentially reductive perspective and identify possible issues with the project's design and the researchers' actions that may serve as blocks to motivation and whose resolution may reverse these challenges.

The study set out here analyzes the opening interaction sequence of a participatory workshop to the end of uncovering communication behavior – which may be unconscious – that could act to subtly undermine the participatory process the project intends. It aims to gain knowledge of the specific acts of communication that take place in virtual participatory technology development processes with inclusive objectives, and reconstructs to this end the practices of interaction and participation that are observable in a specific project involving residents and professionals in a care setting for young people with additional needs. Our guiding research question revolved around identifying the communication styles used by the facilitator in this project and ascertaining the extent to which the interaction observed sets out the objectives of the participatory process and the young people's opportunities for participation.

3 Methodology

This study centers on a participatory design research project for the development of technologies to support young people with additional needs in carrying out everyday tasks. The project took place in a residential care setting for young people located in Germany. During the Covid-19 pandemic, when restrictions on entry to the setting were in force, the participatory design workshops took place as videoconferences, giving rise to additional challenges occasioned by the home's poor technological infrastructure, the lack of direct contact between participants and facilitator, limited opportunities for small talk to relax the atmosphere, and a highly focused workshop setting. A further challenge consisted in motivating the young people to engage in the process, as it was not possible to determine definitively whether their involvement was truly of a voluntary nature or whether social workers within their care setting had placed them under a degree of pressure or expectation to take part.

3.1 Methods

This qualitative study used a combination of ethnomethodological conversation analysis (with sequential analysis), multimodal conversation analysis, and video interaction analysis [14–16]. The aim of sequential analysis is the reconstruction of "how participants in conversations collectively organize their interaction as a step-by-step, reciprocally interrelating process of meaning-making and [of the] production of interactional structures" [17, transl.]. It aims to identify the role of discourse in this interaction, with the ultimate objective of understanding how and why people act through communication; in this context, it seeks to understand "why that now" [19: 299], that is, to what a communicative act responds and what, in turn, it prepares. The communication styles identified in such analysis are of relevance because they have worked at least once, regardless of whether they occur in a large or smaller number of similar conversational situations.

3.2 Sample

The data stem from one participatory design workshop conducted in virtual format in a residential care setting for young people with additional needs located in Germany. The workshop was the sixth in a series that took place within an inclusive participatory technology development project with a group of male residents of a care and support setting for young people with additional needs in the kitchen of their group home. Restrictions on entering the setting during the Covid-19 pandemic meant the workshop took place via videoconferencing. The workshop involved six residents (T) and a research project team member (MA 04), a young male computer scientist who had no background or experience in working with people with additional needs. The six young participants were male teenagers aged 14–16, some of whom had mild learning disabilities, some of whom had suffered trauma due to their experience of being a refugee, and all except one of whom had very limited proficiency in the German language.

The teenagers sat around the table in their residential kitchen with one iPad at the head of the table displaying the researcher, who spoke to them via Zoom (Fig. 1). The sample of the conversation we analyze is the opening phase of the sixth workshop, whose objective was to develop ideas for technical solutions to some of the challenges of everyday life for this group of people on the basis of the technological knowledge the participants had acquired in the previous workshop. All workshops were virtual videoconference workshops.

3.3 Procedures

A recording was made of the Zoom session, giving total data material of 90 min' duration. From this recording, we selected the relevant opening sequence and made a transcription using GAT-2 [18] and a descriptive presentation of it. There ensued an open-ended cyclical process of analysis using sequential analysis [19] and ensuring that any interpretation made was demonstrable on the basis of the data [15, 20]. The analysis further made reference to existing studies and to robust concepts for the structuring of interactions [17].

The analysis of the transcript sought to identify interpretations of why particular utterances occur at the specific moment of their production and to understand their place in the sequence of turns, that is, which turn each utterance responds to and which subsequent turn it prepares [15]. The following modalities may be of interest during the analysis: changes of speaker, adjacency pairs, turns initiated by a particular speaker or by others, repairs to misconceptions of turns by the same speaker or by others, co-constructions, terminations of topics or interactions, preferences and disparities, and overlaps. Our analysis further seeks to examine features of recipient design to the end of analyzing practices around participation, specifically uncovering forms of inclusion and exclusion [20]. Sequences in which symmetry or asymmetry of interaction becomes apparent are of particular interest due to their high relevance to the intended interactive construction of a partnership of equals that underlies the participatory design process.

4 Findings of the Conversation Analysis

Figure 1 shows the setting as seen from the point of view of the facilitator, MA 04, through a camera and laptop positioned at the head of the kitchen table. Six teenagers sit around the table as the facilitator opens the workshop.

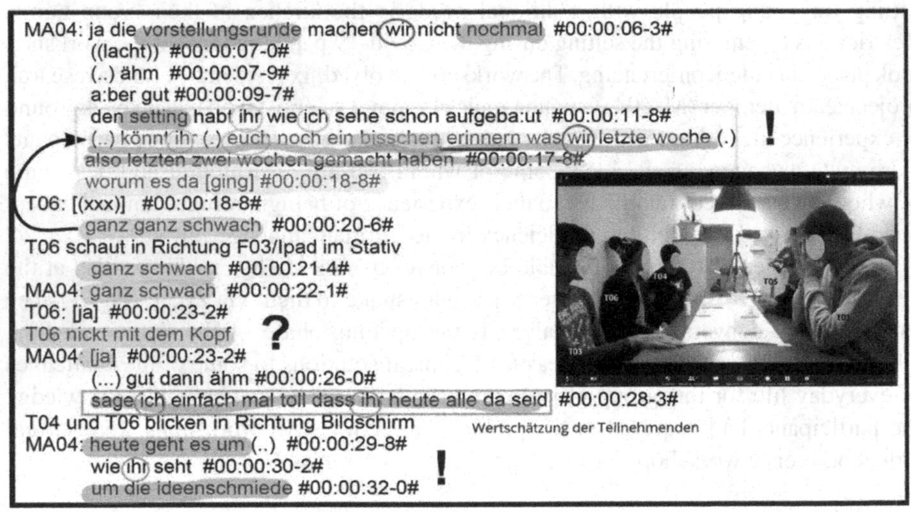

Fig. 1. Conversation analyses of the participatory design workshop transcript

Translated conversation:

MA4: well, the introductions we won't do again.
((laughs))
(..) um
Bu:t ok
I see you've set up the setting alrea:dy
(..) can you (.) remember a little bit of what we (.)
did last week, well, last two weeks
what it was [about]
T6: [(xxx)]
[a] very very little bit
T6 looks toward the iPad
just a very little bit
MA4: just a very little bit
T6: yeah. T06 nods his head.
MA4: yeah.
Ok. Then um
I just want to say it's great that you're all here today.
T4 and T06 look toward the screen
MA4: Today's about
as you can see
about the ideas workshop

We identified five distinct communication styles used by the facilitator during the opening minute of the workshop:

Style 1: Assumption of sole decision-making authority and laying down of the procedures for the workshop. The lack of protest from the young people at this juncture permits an interpretation of agreement between facilitator and participants that it is in the facilitator's power to decide on the course of events and the choice of methods.
Style 2: Othering. The facilitator defines the participants as a group separate from himself by addressing them as "you" and referring to himself as "I" and to his point of view ("I see you've set up the setting already"). This differentiation between two groups in the interaction represents an "othering" of the participants, especially because the facilitator attributes differing competencies, prerequisites and expectations to the participants and to himself when he asks the others about their memory of the previous session assuming that they will only remember a "little bit". He constructs an asymmetry between the one with the knowledge (himself) and those "others" whose task is to remember and report back, like students in a school setting. There is a similar asymmetry in his construction of himself as the decision-maker and the others as those who need to follow his decisions.
Style 3: Inclusion. This style contrasts with Style 2 and entails the facilitator using "we," as in "we won't [redo the introductions]"and "what we did last week". This style has the potential to bring the group together as a unit of equal participants, but it does not predominate in this sequence.

Style 4: Teacher-like question. This style has strong similarities to classroom settings, with the facilitator taking the role of "teacher" whose right it is to ascertain the state of the knowledge held by his "pupils." This style lays bare an asymmetry of knowledge between the participants and the facilitator. The question may seek to produce a consensus and/or a shared understanding of the project's intent and current stage; however, the facilitator fails to address the participants' inability to remember much of the last session's work, instead leaving the matter aside and continuing with the plan for the current workshop. This means that the aim of creating shared understanding remains unachieved, which may be interpretable as a serious mistake on the facilitator's part due to the crucial importance of shared understanding to a participatory process on equal terms. There are no indications in this part of the sequence as to the participants' motivation for involvement in the project.
Style 5: Valuing voluntary participation. The facilitator places a positive emphasis on the participants' voluntary attendance, to which the participants respond with nonverbal signals, turning their heads toward the screen where he appears. This style shows appreciation for the participants, acknowledging and valuing their willingness to engage in the project.

5 Analysis and Conclusions

Analysis of this opening interaction uncovered the facilitator's strict adherence to the planned workshop schedule; he chooses not to pursue the participants' lack of memory of the previous session, nor explore their potential interests, and instead to press on with the activities scheduled for that day. He does not, at this stage, give any indication of opportunities for participants to co-structure the workshop, whose contours appear fixed and predetermined, undermining the intent of participatory design to create an open, flexible process that encourages all stakeholders to share in decisions about what to do. This preimposition of a structure may act as an obstacle to participatory engagement among the group.

We note a paradox in the facilitator's juxtaposition of communication styles 2, which we have termed "othering," and 3, which we call "inclusion." There is a risk here that the facilitator may find himself reproducing existing (institutionally conditioned) asymmetry rather than establishing an equal partnership, particularly if the "othering" manifests alongside asymmetrical power relations - which appears to be the case in view of the facilitator's assertive setting of the agenda at the outset of the sequence. The appreciation of the participants' voluntary engagement in Style 5 may be open to question; the institutionalized setting of a residential care home for young people may – and seemingly did, in earlier workshops in the series - feature a more general pattern of interaction in which resident social workers frequently talk clients into taking part in activities and check their attendance.

We may interpret the communication styles identified in this sequence as problematic in the sense that they do not seem to signal genuine opportunities for participation. A full understanding of the young participants' role in this design process would require further analysis. We might speculate that, in line with the four roles identified by Druin [11], young people might rather be directed into acting as testers of a method than embark on a process of becoming genuine decision-making partners in the design process.

The findings of this analysis demonstrate how, in the opening minute of a "participatory" workshop, a facilitator's (possibly unconscious) communicative acts may undermine fundamental objectives of participatory design and of inclusive work with people with additional needs. It could be (and indeed was) the case that in the further course of the workshop the facilitator provided for a greater degree of participation, asking the group for suggestions on how to proceed or which topics to choose. However, the initial interaction studied here opened the session and therefore set its tone. Conversation analysis, however, does not aim at explaining why a group behaves in a certain way. It aims simply at explaining what happens in a specific sequence.

What does this analysis have to communicate to us about planning participatory design projects? If we aim for equal participation, we should avoid interactions and planned procedures outlines that may undermine this objective, such as interactions interpretable as othering, as teacher-like, or as assuming sole decision-making authority. Further research might usefully analyze whether, and the extent to which, such interaction styles commonly occur in failed participatory design projects.

We may assume that inexperienced facilitators from academic fields will find convening meetings with young people in residential care settings a challenge. There appears to be a need for provisions to help facilitators handle uncertainty or nervousness that may give rise to contradictory communication styles that undermine fundamental objectives of participatory design. Ethical issues are also of relevance here; young people who were perhaps initially promised higher levels of active participation may feel mocked or misled, which could be deleterious to the trust in their self-efficacy that is often a key objective of social work supporting vulnerable clients in institutional settings. The use of a co-facilitator who is experienced in this area of work and can employ appropriate communication strategies may be a necessary investment to the end of enabling genuine inclusion of young people with additional needs in meaningful, effective, contextual, and educational co-design [12] in which they can access power and control over structural elements of the process [10].

Acknowledgement. The INTIA project, of which the work underlying this paper was part, was funded by the German Federal Ministry of Education and Research and the European Social Fund (funding code 13FH534SX7) from 2019 to 2023 as part of the funding program "Lebensqualität durch Soziale Innovation (FH-Sozial)".

We extend our thanks to Katherine Ebisch-Burton for her assistance with language editing and in improving the article's structure, precision and focus.

References

1. Schiffhauer, B.: Assistive Technologien in der Sozialen Arbeit. In: Kutscher, N., Ley, T., Seelmeyer, U., Siller, F., Tillmann, A., Zorn, I. (eds.) Handbuch Soziale Arbeit und Digitalisierung, pp. 265–275. Beltz Juventa, Weinheim [u.a.] (2020)
2. Ferati, M., Babar, A., Carine, K., Hamidi, A., Mörtberg, C.: Participatory design approach to internet of things: co-designing a smart shower for and with people with disabilities. In: Antona, M., Stephanidis, C. (eds.) UAHCI 2018. LNCS, vol. 10908, pp. 246–261. Springer, Cham (2018). https://doi.org/10.1007/978-3-319-92052-8_19

3. Vines, J., Clarke, R., Wright, P., McCarthy, J., Olivier, P.: Configuring participation. In: Mackay, W.E., Brewster, S., Bødker, S. (eds.) Proceedings of the SIGCHI Conference on Human Factors in Computing Systems. CHI Conference on Human Factors in Computing Systems, CHI 2013, Paris France, 27 April 2013–02 May 2013, pp. 429–438. ACM, New York (2013). https://doi.org/10.1145/2470654.2470716
4. Bischof, A., Kurze, A., Totzauer, S., Storz, M., Freiermuth, M., Berger, A.: Living Labs zur Initiierung von Partizipation in der HCI (2018)
5. Wright, M.T., Unger, H. von, Block, M.: Partizipation der Zielgruppe in der Gesundheitsförderung und Prävention, 1st edn. In: Wright, M.T. (ed.) Partizipative Qualitätsentwicklung in der Gesundheitsförderung und Prävention, pp. 35–52. Verlag Hans Huber, s.l. (2010)
6. Straßburger, G., Rieger, J.: Bedeutung und Formen der Partizipation - Das Modell der Partizipationspyramide, 2nd edn. In: Straßburger, G., Rieger, J. (eds.) Partizipation kompakt - Für Studium, Lehre und Praxis sozialer Berufe, pp. 12–39. Beltz Juventa, Weinheim (2019)
7. Straßburger, G., Rieger, J.: Partizipation kompakt – Komplexe Zusammenhänge auf den Punkt gebracht. In: Straßburger, G., Rieger, J. (eds.) Partizipation kompakt - Für Studium, Lehre und Praxis sozialer Berufe, 2nd edn., pp. 230–240. Beltz Juventa, Weinheim (2019)
8. Edler, C.: e-Inclusion – Inklusive-Partizipative Forschung und Entwicklung, User-Centred Design und Empowerment. Orientierungen für einen Ansatz der Forschung und Entwicklung (F&E) gemeinsam mit Menschen mit kognitiven Behinderungen. Dissertation, Pädagogische Hochschule Ludwigsburg (2020)
9. Schmier, A., Zorn, I.: Literaturreview zu partizipativer Technologieentwicklung in der Behinderten- und Erziehungshilfe im Kontext Sozialer Arbeit. Soziale Passagen eingereicht
10. Kinnula, M., Iivari, N.: Manifesto for children's genuine participation in digital technology design and making. Int. J. Child Comput. Interact. **28**, 100244 (2021). https://doi.org/10.1016/j.ijcci.2020.100244
11. Druin, A.: The role of children in the design of new technology. Behav. Inf. Technol. **21**, 1–25 (2002). https://doi.org/10.1080/01449290110108659
12. Spencer González, H., Vega Córdova, V., Exss Cid, K., Jarpa Azagra, M., Álvarez-Aguado, I.: Including intellectual disability in participatory design processes: methodological adaptations and supports. In: Del Gaudio, C., et al. (eds.) Proceedings of the 16th Participatory Design Conference 2020 - Participation(s) Otherwise - Volume 1. Participatory Design Conference 2020, PDC 2020 - Participation Otherwise, Manizales Colombia, 15 June 2020–20 June 2020, pp. 55–63. ACM, New York (15 June 2020). https://doi.org/10.1145/3385010.3385023
13. Raman, S., French, T.: Enabling genuine participation in co-design with young people with learning disabilities. CoDesign (2021).https://doi.org/10.1080/15710882.2021.1877728
14. Ayaß, R.: Konversationsanalytische Medienforschung. M&K (2004).https://doi.org/10.5771/1615-634x-2004-1-5
15. Tuma, R.: Video-Interaktionsanalyse. In: Moritz, C., Corsten, M. (eds.) Handbuch Qualitative Videoanalyse, pp. 423–444. Springer, Wiesbaden (2018). https://doi.org/10.1007/978-3-658-15894-1_22
16. Deppermann, A.: Sprache in der multimodalen Interaktion. In: Deppermann, A., Reineke, S. (eds.) Sprache im kommunikativen, interaktiven und kulturellen Kontext, pp. 51–86. De Gruyter, Berlin, Boston (2018)
17. Deppermann, A.: Konversationsanalyse: Elementare Interaktionsstrukturen am Beispiel der Bundespressekonferenz. In: Staffeldt, S., Hagemann, J. (eds.) Pragmatiktheorien. Analysen im Vergleich, pp. 19–47. Stauffenburg, Tübingen (2014)
18. Selting, M., Auer, P., Barth-Weingarten, D., Bergmann, J.: Gesprächsanalytisches Transkriptionssystem 2 (GAT 2). Gesprächsforschung - Online Zeitschrift zur verbalen Interaktion, pp. 353–402 (2009)

19. Schegloff, E.A., Sacks, H.: Opening up Closings. Semiotica (1973). https://doi.org/10.1515/semi.1973.8.4.289
20. Hitzler, S.: Recipient Design in institutioneller Mehrparteieninteraktion. Gesprächsforschung - Online-Zeitschrift zur verbalen Interaktion, pp, 110–132 (2013)

ICT to Support Inclusive Education - Universal Learning Design (ULD)

ICT to Support Inclusive Education - Universal Learning Design (ULD)
Introduction to the Special Thematic Session

Marion Hersh[1](✉) and Barbara Leporini[2]

[1] Biomedical Engineering, University of Glasgow, Glasgow G12 8LT, Scotland
marion.hersh@glasgow.ac.uk
[2] ISTI-CNR, Via G. Moruzzi, 1, Pisa, Italy
barbara.leporini@isti.cnr.it

Abstract. This short paper presents six papers discussing different features of and approaches to inclusive education, including audio access to admissions tests, accessibility and usability, the use of assistive technology to support inclusion and teacher education. They are introduced by a brief discussion of inclusive education and the role of accessibility and usability and assistive technology in supporting it.

Keywords: Inclusive education · Accessibility · Usability · Assistive technology · Teacher education · Audio access

1 Introduction

It has been suggested that full educational inclusion requires physical, academic and social inclusion [1]. The Convention of the Rights of Persons with Disabilities [2] recognises iinclusivee education as a human right. The principles of the Education for All movement [3] have been incorporated into the policies and legislation of many countries. Education is vital both for personal development and employment opportunities. People with a postsecondary education qualification are significantly more likely to get a job e.g. [4] and the correlation may be even stronger for disabled people [5]. Disabled students have comparable entry qualifications [6], but are underrepresented in further and higher education [7] and obtain poorer degree results. This considerably reduces their employment opportunities [8, 9] particularly when combined with attitudinal and other barriers [10, 11].

The value of inclusive education in mainstream schools is being increasingly recognised including through legislation e.g. for 97% of all learners to be included in mainstream schools in Denmark [12]. However moves to educating disabled students in mainstream schools are taking place at different rates in different countries.

ICT (information and communication technologies) can be used to support inclusion by providing different ways of representing information, expressing knowledge and engaging in learning, including assessment. This involves both general learning technologies and assistive technologies designed specifically for disabled people. This has

K. Miesenberger et al. (Eds.): ICCHP-AAATE 2022, LNCS 13342, pp. 323–327, 2022.
https://doi.org/10.1007/978-3-031-08645-8_37

the further advantages of teaching ICT skills, which are becoming increasingly important and drawing on the increasing popularity and motivating effects of using ICT, particularly amongst young people. However, ICT is not a universal solution and its successful use requires appropriate inclusive pedagogical strategies and teacher education. It also needs to be fully accessible and usable by all students. Accessibility is the system feature which ensures it can be used in particular by disabled people, including those who rely on assistive technology [13]. Usability is based on the principles of effectiveness, efficiency and satisfaction to make the process of interaction and use of both content and functions simpler, more intuitive and satisfying. There is discussion in the literature of the value of combining accessibility and usability so that disabled people are not only able to use particular systems find it easy to do so [14]. This is illustrated by the discussion in the next section of a learning platform which is accessible to screen reader users, but not very useable.

These two principles are important for all digital resources and systems, and really crucial in the field of education. In this case, it is important that the learner can focus on learning and that the system or resource does not introduce unnecessary barriers that may distract the student or even prevent learning [15]. For these reasons, when designing and developing solutions, including those based on ICT, it is crucial to always take account of the principles of accessibility and usability in the design.

2 Session Papers

Inclusive education should cover both online education/eInclusion and in person education. The papers in this session focus on eInclusion and the use of ICT to support it. This is very important, but should be considered complementary to rather than instead of in person/classroom inclusion. The six conference session papers published in this chapter are wide ranging and include audio access to admission exams, accessibility of open education resources, usability of an accessible learning platform, two papers on assistive technology and teacher education on inclusion.

All stage of education should be accessible, including admissions. In their paper 'Simulating the answering process of dyslexic students for audio versions of the common test of university admissions', Masashi Hatekayami and Akio Fujiyoshi from Ibaraki University in Japan propose a method for evaluating audio admissions tests. The audio tests are aimed particularly at dyslexic students and the initial university admissions test (Common Test) which is taken by over half a million students in Japan each year. The evaluation is carried out by non-disabled students due to few dyslexic students yet having sufficient qualifications to apply for university. In the audio test, the scanner on top of a Speakun reading device scans an invisible 2-dimensional code and the corresponding text is read. It can be listened to via a headphone or built-in speaker at half to twice reading speed. To prevent non-disabled students reading the text it was replaced by hard to read glyphs based on the original characters. Tests with four university students found that they could complete the test in the time allowed (one and a half times that for the regular test) and three of them did better than average. However, they found the audio test more tiring and difficult and to require more time than the standard test. Technology to support audio tests is very useful and the approach to evaluation is interesting. However, it does not consider possible differences in audio processing between dyslexic and non-disabled students and that dyslexic students may use both audio and written information.

All aspects of education systems should be accessible and usable to all students. This includes institution websites, learning management systems and resource materials. Two papers in the session consider accessibility (and usability).

In 'Gauging awareness of accessibility in open educational resources' Oriane Pierrès and Alireza Darvisha from Zurich University of Applied Sciences, Switzerland, used interviews to investigate the accessibility of open educational resources. These are educational materials that can be used by everyone free of charge and with few restrictions. 17 semi-structured interviews were carried out with university personnel in 15 countries who create, teach about or support the creation of open educational resources (OERs). 12 participants considered accessibility in terms of meeting the needs of disabled learners, whereas others had a broader definition based on meeting the needs of all users including those of 'low socioeconomic status'. 14 participants tried to make OERs accessible and nine of them tested their content for accessibility issues. The difficulties of creating accessible OERs included the time involved with accessibility involving additional work to make adjustments or learn how to make OERs accessible. Participants realised they needed more knowledge of accessibility and considered this generally lacking amongst OER developers. Knowledge about making maths formulae and tables accessible was particularly limited.

Leaning content and technologies need to be easy to use as well as accessible. In 'Usability of an accessible learning platform – lessons learnt', Leeve Wilkens and Christian Bühler from TU Dortmund, Germany evaluate the usability of the Degree 4.0 learning platform with nine disabled and non-disabled students. Accessibility features of this platform include the ability to operate all functions including the video player and editor via a keyboard and to switch audio descriptions and subtitles on and off. One usability test with a visually impaired student was carried out in person with the others carried out on zoom with screen sharing to allow observation by researchers who were present for one of the six usability tests and not for the five others. Participants were asked to 'think aloud'. The usability task involved editing a video sequence. All participants completed the task, but the time required varied by a factor of five. All participants found the platform accessible. Screen reader users were able to access everything with a keyboard, but experienced problems due to inaccurate or incorrect labelling. There were also problems due to lack of knowledge of how codes worked. Three participants had usability scores below 70, which is considered a problem. A visually impaired participant had the lowest score of 17.5. This indicates the importance of considering usability as well as accessibility. There is a risk that users will abandon systems with poor usability e.g. which take to long to use even if they are theoretically fully accessible.

Two papers consider the use of assistive technology to support inclusion. 'Requirements for assistive technology by disabled students in higher education' by Inguna Griskevica, Dace Stiegle and Dina Bithere from the University of Liepaja, Latvia presents the results of a study to support the development of an evaluation tool for the requirements of disabled students in higher education. This involved analysing policy documents and research on inclusive education. This led to the choice of inclusive education, universal design and universal design for research approaches to tool development. Data was collected on a random basis from students in any level of education in Cyprus, Greece, Larvia and Slovenia. 65% of participants were found to require assistive technology to some extent. This is a very high percentage and its implications require further investigation. The main types of assistive technologies required were found to be mentor (42%), psychologist (31%) and assistant (16%). However, this refers to types of support generally provided by people rather than technology.

'Video screen commentary system supporting online learning of visually impaired students' by Dong-Yeon Park and Soon-Bum Lin of Sookmyung Women University, Korea presents a system for automatically adding audio commentary to a video screen to improve the understanding of visually impaired students. This involves identifying the start of new slides, adding commentary files for each slide and merging the commentary video with the original video. The commentary file includes all text from the slide in an appropriate reading order, captions for graphics, either provided on the slide (or created using Microsoft's Azure Cognitive Services Computer Vision), and structural information for tables. The commentary files are inserted when the screen changes in the original video and the commentary and videos merged to form a single video. Eight blind and blindfolded non-disabled students evaluated the system. The use of video commentary was found to improve understanding to a statistically significant extent.

Teachers need appropriate education and training to apply inclusive approaches. 'How to overcome eInclusion – Inclusive education going digital: the education of "digital scouts"' by Claudia Mertens of the University of Bielefeld, Germany presents a two-phase approach to educating students in teacher education ('digital scouts') on inclusion. The first theoretical phase involved the presentation of inclusive digital teaching materials and concepts. In the second practical phase 14 digital scouts worked in pairs with students with learning disabilities or cognitive impairments in inclusive settings in seven mainstream schools. The aim was to support the disabled students using digital media to learn to teach them about media. The materials used were developed using universal design for learning principles. Group interviews with these students were used to investigate their experiences and found that they had both learnt to use media and learnt about them and enjoyed the involvement of the digital scouts. E-portfolios of self-reflection were used to investigate the digital scouts' experiences and found that they had increased their competence in digital teaching and sensitivity to universal design for learning.

This conference session also includes seven scientific contributions which are part of in the Open Access Compendium (OAC) and one in the Inclusion Forum. The OAC paper are:

- 'Accessibility Standards and Laws: Implementation for Successful Digital Education within the Eurozone',
- 'Digi-ID: co-creating accessible digital skills education to enhance health, well being and social inclusion for people with accessibility needs',
- 'Information Technologies in Teaching to Play the Piano for Children with Disabilities',
- 'Polygraf Online – video-conferencing system for accessible remote and hybrid teaching',
- 'Training to implement inclusive distance higher education', and
- 'Universal Design of Inquiry-Based Mathematics Education in Universities'.

Many of these papers discuss the use of technology and accessibility features which should be part of good practice when designing and developing technologies to support inclusive education. A substantial proportion of the papers deal with the more topical issue of the accessibility of distance education and communication systems. There is a need for research to start now to prepare for the possible future use of these systems in remote or blended learning to contribute to ensuring full access for all.

References

1. Qvortrup, A., Qvortrup, L.: Inclusion: dimensions of inclusion in education. Int. J. Incl. Educ. **22**(7), 803–817 (2018)
2. UN. Convention of the Rights of Persons with Disabilities (2006). https://duckduckgo.com/?q=Convention+of+the+Rights+of+Persons+with+Disabilities+%28UN%2C+2006&ia=web
3. UNESCO. Dakar Framework for Action, Education for all Meeting our Collective Commitments 2000 (2000). http://unesdoc.unesco.org/images/0012/001211/121147e.pdf. Accessed 11 Sept 2017
4. Hutcheon, E.J., Wolbring, G.: Voices of "disabled" post secondary students: examining higher education "disability" policy using an ableism lens. J. Divers. High. Educ. **5**(1), 39 (2012)
5. Burgstahler, S.: The role of technology in preparing youth with disabilities for postsecondary education and employment. J. Spec. Educ. Technol. **18**(4), 7–19 (2003)
6. Fuller, M., Bradley, A., Healey, M.: Incorporating disabled students within an inclusive higher education environment. Disab. Soc. **19**(5), 455–468 (2004)
7. Konur, O.: Teaching disabled students in higher education. Teach. High. Educ. **11**(3), 351–363 (2006)
8. Barnes, H., Thornton, P., Maynard Campbell, S.: Disabled People and Employment: A Review of Research and Development Work. York Publishing Services, York (1998)
9. Szeto, A.Y.J.: Assistive technology and rehabilitation engineering. In: Assistive Technologies: Concepts, Methodologies, Tools, and Applications, pp 277–331. Information Science Reference, Hershey (2014)
10. Daone, L., Scott, R.: Ready, willing, and disabled: survey of UK employers. London, Scope (2003). https://www.scope.org.uk/Scope/media/Images/Publication%20Directory/Ready-willing-and-disabled.pdf?ext=.pdf. Accessed 11 Sept 2017
11. Roberts, S., Heaver, C., Hill, K., et al.: Disability in the Workplace: Employers' and Service Providers' Responses to the Disability Discrimination Act in 2003 and Preparation for 2004 Changes. Department of Work and Pensions Research Summary, London (2004)
12. Andersen, H.V., Sorensen, E.K.: Technology as a vehicle for inclusion of learners with attention deficits in mainstream schools. Eur. J. Open Dist. E-learn. **19**(2), 720–730 (2015)
13. Petrie, H., Kheir, O.: The relationship between accessibility and usability of websites. In: Proceedings of the SIGCHI conference on Human factors in computing systems, pp. 397–406 (2007)
14. Leporini, B., Paternò, F.: Applying web usability criteria for vision-impaired users: does it really improve task performance? Intl. J. Hum. Comput. Interact. **24**(1), 17–47 (2008)
15. Vlachogianni, P., Tselios, N.: Perceived usability evaluation of educational technology using the System Usability Scale (SUS): a systematic review. J. Res. Technol. Educ. 1–18 (2021). Accessed 21 Nov 2016

Simulating the Answering Process of Dyslexic Students for Audio Versions of the Common Test for University Admissions

Masashi Hatakeyama and Akio Fujiyoshi(✉)

Graduate School of Science and Engineering, Ibaraki University, Hitachi, Japan
{22nm742n,akio.fujiyoshi.cs}@vc.ibaraki.ac.jp

Abstract. For the introduction of audio versions of the Common Test for University Admissions in Japan, this study proposes a method to evaluate the feasibility of audio versions of tests with non-disabled students by simulating the answering process of dyslexic students. Since the number of dyslexic students with enough learning achievement levels is still small in Japan, the evaluation of the feasibility has to be done by recruiting non-disabled students as experimental participants. In order to put non-disabled students in the print-disabled situation, we replace all characters of test booklets with hard-to-read ones using vertex-reduced glyphs. As a result of a pilot evaluation of the audio version with hard-to-read test booklets, they seem to be usable for the evaluation of the feasibility of audio versions of the Common Test for University Admissions.

Keywords: Test accommodations · Audio versions of tests · Extended testing time · The dyslexic · University admissions

1 Introduction

The Common Test for University Admissions (formerly known as the National Center Test) is the joint first stage achievement test for admissions into all national and local public universities as well as many private universities in Japan. Every year, about 530,000 students take it. As for students with disabilities, special accommodations regarding testing media such as large-print-format test and braille-format test have been administered [1]. However, these testing media are not enough for dyslexic students. They are only allowed to ask proctors to read aloud some part of documents in problems. In most advanced countries, audio versions of tests such as MP3 audio, DAISY (Digital Accessible Information System) or computer screen readers are available [2–4]. Audio versions of the Common Test for University Admissions are urgently required.

The authors have been studying auditory testing media for the National Center Test. It is not easy to take the National Center Test with ordinary auditory testing media because the documents are very long and the document structure very complicated. First, the DAISY version of the test was studied [5]. Afterwards, utilizing invisible 2-dimensional codes and digital audio players with a

K. Miesenberger et al. (Eds.): ICCHP-AAATE 2022, LNCS 13342, pp. 328–334, 2022.
https://doi.org/10.1007/978-3-031-08645-8_38

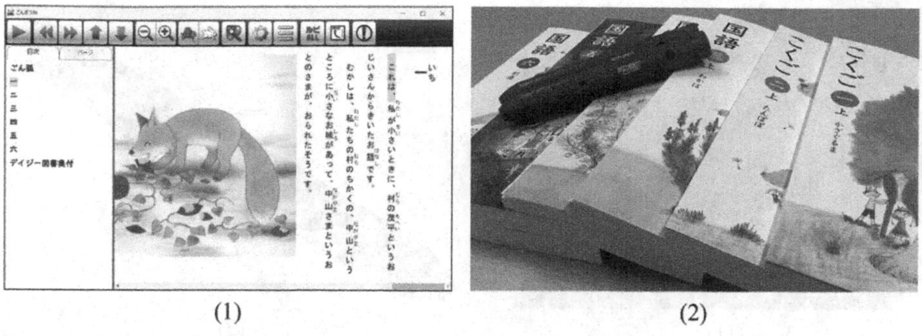

(1) (2)

Fig. 1. (1) Multimedia DAISY textbooks and (2) Multimodal textbooks

2-dimensional code scanner, two types of new auditory testing media, audio tests with document structure diagrams [6] and multimodal tests [7] were developed. The result of the evaluation showed that, if we give adequate extended time, the two types of new auditory testing media offer fair accommodation to dyslexic students to take the National Center Test.

Unfortunately, audio versions of the National Center Test were not administered because there were no requests from dyslexic students for the administration of audio versions of the test. Around 2010, the number of dyslexic high school students who had access to audio study materials was quite limited in Japan. In 2008, "Barrier-free textbook law" was administered, and Japanese Ministry of Education, Culture, Sports, Science and Technology started to give supports for the production and supply of audio study materials. Since 2008, multimedia DAISY textbooks (Fig. 1 (1), used by 14,211 students in 2020) have been provided by Japanese Society for Rehabilitation of Persons with Disabilities. Since 2012, multimodal textbooks utilizing invisible 2-dimensional codes and digital audio players with a 2-dimensional code scanner (Fig. 1 (2), used by 1,468 students in 2020) [8] have been provided by the author's laboratory in Ibaraki University. The first generation of dyslexic students who have started going to school with audio study materials are getting ready to take the Common Test for University Admissions. Now is the time to re-emphasize the necessity and feasibility of audio versions of the test.

However, the limitations of extended time is a big issue for the Common Test for University Admissions. The results of the evaluation of auditory testing media in [6,7] suggested that more than double time is necessary for the fairness of the test. Since 10 tests (60–80 min testing time with 15 min instructions) are tightly scheduled in 2 days, the extended time cannot exceed a half (50%) of regular testing time. Though it may not be the best solution, we decided to study the feasibility of audio versions of the Common Test with a half or less extended time.

This study proposes a method to evaluate the feasibility of audio versions of tests with non-disabled students by simulating the answering process of dyslexic students. Since the number of dyslexic students with enough learning achieve-

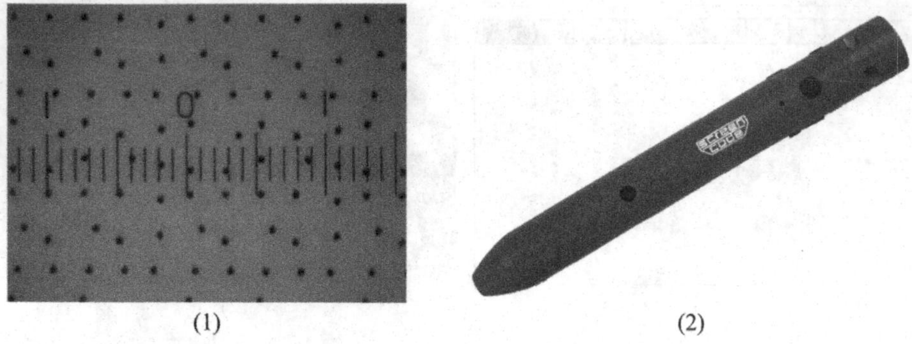

(1) (2)

Fig. 2. (1) Screen code and (2) Speakun

ment levels is still small in Japan, the evaluation of the feasibility has to be done by recruiting non-disabled students as experimental participants. In order to put non-disabled students in the print-disabled situation, we replace all characters of test booklets with hard-to-read ones using vertex-reduced glyphs. As a result of a pilot evaluation of the audio version with hard-to-read test booklets, they seem to be usable for the evaluation of the feasibility of audio versions of the Common Test for University Admissions.

2 Trial Production of Audio Versions of the Common Test for University Admissions

Utilizing invisible 2-dimensional codes and digital audio players with a 2-dimensional code scanner, audio versions of the Common Test for University Admissions are produced by way of trial. The Common Test consists of a total of 30 separate tests in 6 subjects. We choose 1 test in Japanese language, 1 test in English language, 2 tests in mathematics, 2 tests in science, and 3 tests in social studies for the trail production.

2.1 Specification of the Trial Production of Audio Versions

This audio versions are modeled after the multimodal tests proposed in [7]. We employ 'Screen Code', an invisible 2-dimensional code system developed by Apollo Japan Co., Ltd. Dots of Screen Code are arranged at intervals of about 0.25 mm, and the size of a code is about 2 mm square (Fig. 2 (1)). Since the intervals are large enough for the size of dots themselves, dots are almost invisible. As a reading device for the audio version, we employ 'Speakun' developed by Apollo Japan Co., Ltd (Fig. 2 (2)). Speakun has a 2-dimensional code scanner at its top.

The use of the multimodal tests is quite easy, and so almost no training is necessary. When a 2-dimensional code is scanned with it, the corresponding reading voice is reproduced. We can listen to the sound through a headphone or

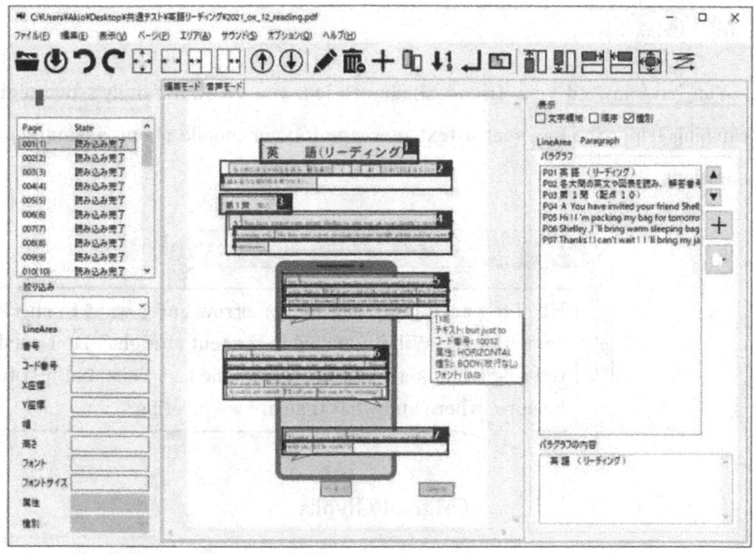

Fig. 3. Multimodal publication producer

built-in speaker. The sound volume and talk speed can be adjusted by touching special 2-dimensional codes. The talk speed can be selected from 2.0× (fastest), 1.5×, 1.0× (default), 0.75×, and 0.5× (slowest). The sound data is stored in an SD memory card.

The arrangement of Screen Code on the test booklets was done with 'Multimodal Publication Producer' (Fig. 3) [9]. It has been developed in the author's laboratory for the efficient production of multimodal textbooks.

For reading voice, we decided to use speech synthesis technology because reading voice of tests should be neutral. Japanese documents are read by 'Voice Sommelier' developed by Hitachi Solutions Create, Ltd., and English documents are read by 'Microsoft Zira Desktop' and 'Microsoft David Desktop'.

2.2 Vertex-Reduced Glyphs

In order to put non-disabled students in the print-disabled situation, hard-to-read characters using 'vertex-reduced glyphs' were developed. Glyphs of a character in a TrueType outline font consist of a sequence of line segments and curves. A vertex-reduced glyph is obtained from the original glyph by erasing pre-defined amount of its components uniformly. For the English language test booklet, all Latin alphabet characters are replaced, and for the test booklets of the other subjects, all Japanese and Chinese characters are replaced. Figure 4 shows original glyphs and vertex-reduced glyphs in English language test booklet.

Vertex-reduced glyphs are designed so that they resemble original Latin alphabet characters though they need to be un-readable.

第1問 (配点 10)

A You have invited your friend Shelley to join you on your family's overnight camping trip. She has sent a text message to your mobile phone asking some questions.

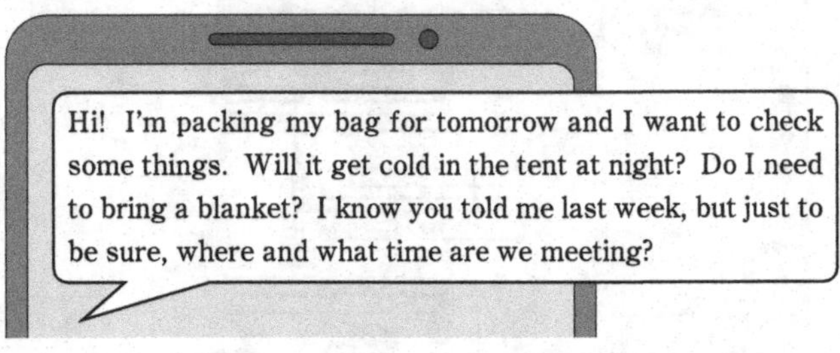

Original Glyphs

第1問 (配点 10)

Vertex-Reduced Glyphs

Fig. 4. Part of test booklet with original glyphs and vertex-reduced glyphs

3 Pilot Evaluation

3.1 Experiment Setting

As for experimental participants, 4 university students who have taken the National Center Test were employed. 2 participants took the audio version in English language, and the other 2 participants took the audio version in Japanese language. Tests in languages are selected because the amounts of their documents are larger than the other subjects. Since the time limit of the regular tests is

80 min, we set the time limit of the audio versions 120 min (a half-time extended). Participants were given time to practice the usage of digital audio players with a 2-dimensional code scanner before the experiment.

3.2 Result

All participants could finish taking the audio version within the time limit. The result of the experiment is shown in Table 1. The 'average scores' mean the average scores of the regular tests taken by about 500,000 students. Three participants could get more than the average score of the regular tests. All participants used 2.0× talk speed for the most part.

Table 1. Result of the audio version for the participants

Participant	Score	Subject	Full score	Average score
A	140	Japanese language	200	117.51
B	123			
C	44	English language	100	58.80
D	59			

After the experiment, participants were asked to answer questionnaires. The result of the questionnaires is shown in Table 2. The responses were chosen from five possible choices.

Table 2. Result of the questionnaires

Question	A	B	C	D
More tired than regular test?	Agree	Strongly	Strongly	Strongly
More difficult than regular test?	Strongly	Strongly	Strongly	Agree
More time needed than regular test?	Strongly	Strongly	Strongly	Strongly
Prefer audio versions?	Disagree	Disagree	Never	Never
Speed of reading voice?	Excellent	Good	Good	Good
Quality of reading voice?	Fair	Good	Fair	Excellent

4 Conclusion

A method to evaluate the feasibility of audio versions with non-disabled students by simulating the answering process of dyslexic students was proposed, and an experiment was conducted with non-disabled students. Since three participants could get more than the average score of the regular tests, we think that the feasibility of audio versions of the Common Test for University Admissions was affirmed. The score of the remaining participant was nearly average. As all participants answered the audio version is more difficult than regular test, the usability of the audio version should be improved. In order to confirm the feasibility of audio versions of the Common Test, we plan to conduct experiments with a large number of participants giving audio versions in all 6 subjects.

Acknowledgements. This work was supported by JSPS KAKENHI Grant Number JP22H01030.

References

1. Fujiyoshi, M., Fujiyoshi, A.: Estimating testing time extension ratios for students with disabilities from item cumulative curves. In: New Developments in Psychometrics: Proceedings of the International Meeting of the Psychometric Society IMPS 2003, pp. 265–272 (2001)
2. Allman, C.: Making tests accessible for students with visual impairments -A guide for test publishers, test developers, and state assessment personnel-. American Printing House for the Blind (2004)
3. Mandinach, E.B., Bridgeman, B., Cahalan-Laitusis, C., Trapani C.: The Impact of Extended Time on SAT Test Performance, College Board Research Report No. 2005–8, ETS RR-05-20, pp. 1–35 (2005)
4. College Board, Services for Students with Disabilities, Accommodations on College Board Exams. https://accommodations.collegeboard.org/
5. Fujiyoshi, M., Fujiyoshi, A.: A new audio testing system for the newly blind and the learning disabled to take the National Center Test for University Admissions. In: Miesenberger, K., Klaus, J., Zagler, W.L., Karshmer, A.I. (eds.) ICCHP 2006. LNCS, vol. 4061, pp. 801–808. Springer, Heidelberg (2006). https://doi.org/10.1007/11788713_117
6. Fujiyoshi, M., Fujiyoshi, A., Aomatsu, T.: New testing method for the dyslexic and the newly blind with a digital audio player and document structure diagrams. In: Miesenberger, K., Klaus, J., Zagler, W., Karshmer, A. (eds.) ICCHP 2010. LNCS, vol. 6179, pp. 116–123. Springer, Heidelberg (2010). https://doi.org/10.1007/978-3-642-14097-6_20
7. Fujiyoshi, M., Fujiyoshi, A., Ohsawa, A., Aomatsu, T., Sawazaki, H.: Development of new auditory testing media with invisible 2-dimensional codes for test-takers with print disabilities. In: Miesenberger, K., Karshmer, A., Penaz, P., Zagler, W. (eds.) ICCHP 2012. LNCS, vol. 7382, pp. 116–123. Springer, Heidelberg (2012). https://doi.org/10.1007/978-3-642-31522-0_17
8. Fujiyoshi, A., Fujiyoshi, M., Ohsawa, A., Ota, Y.: Development of multimodal textbooks with invisible 2-dimensional codes for students with print disabilities. In: Miesenberger, K., Fels, D., Archambault, D., Peňáz, P., Zagler, W. (eds.) ICCHP 2014. LNCS, vol. 8548, pp. 331–337. Springer, Cham (2014). https://doi.org/10.1007/978-3-319-08599-9_50
9. Takaira, T., Tani, Y., Fujiyoshi, A.: Development of a unified production system for various types of accessible textbooks. In: Miesenberger, K., Bühler, C., Penaz, P. (eds.) ICCHP 2016. LNCS, vol. 9758, pp. 381–388. Springer, Cham (2016). https://doi.org/10.1007/978-3-319-41264-1_52

Gauging Awareness of Accessibility in Open Educational Resources

Oriane Pierrès(✉) and Alireza Darvishy

Zurich University for Applied Sciences, Steinberggasse 13, 8400 Winterthur, Switzerland
{oriane.pierres,alireza.darvishy}@zhaw.ch

Abstract. Open Educational Resources (OERs) have been widely promoted in the higher education community in recent years. However, the accessibility of OERs for people with disabilities has received relatively little attention. This paper presents the results of interviews carried out with people at higher education institutions worldwide who are involved in the creation and implementation of OERs. The goal is to gauge the awareness of accessibility issues in OERs. This paper raises the following research questions: How much do OER creators know about accessibility? What measures are needed to ensure accessibility in OERs? Results suggest that OER creators are aware about some issues around accessibility, but they still need further training on how to solve them. OER creators lack time, skills, and awareness to create accessible OERs. Support from specialists and colleagues and hands-on trainings can help cope with these challenges.

Keywords: Open educational resources · Accessibility awareness · Higher-education

1 Introduction

The term "Open Educational Resources" (OERs) was first adopted by the UNESCO in 2002 [1]. OERs are defined as educational materials (i.e., for teaching, learning, and research) that can be used, adapted, and redistributed by anyone, free of charge and with no or few limitations [2]. These materials are often in digital format, though not always.

Digital technologies offer tremendous potential for inclusion of people with disabilities. Online materials are usually more accessible than materials given in the classroom [3]. At the same time, these same technologies can also result in further exclusion of this group if their specific needs are not considered. For instance, digital content becomes inaccessible if there are no captions in a video or if they are not compatible with screen reading software [3]. For that reason, content creators need to know how to produce accessible content.

The importance of and potential for accessibility in OERs has been noted since their beginnings. The 2007 Cape Town Open Education Declaration and the 2012 Paris OER Declaration both noted the unique opportunities offered by OERs for providing "alternative and accessible formats of materials for learners with special educational needs" [4]. More recently, in 2019, UNESCO presented a series of recommendations on

The original version of this chapter was revised: this chapter was previously published non-open access. The correction to this chapter is available at
https://doi.org/10.1007/978-3-031-08645-8_64

K. Miesenberger et al. (Eds.): ICCHP-AAATE 2022, LNCS 13342, pp. 335–342, 2022.
https://doi.org/10.1007/978-3-031-08645-8_39

OERs; these recommendations touch on the importance of accessibility for individuals with disabilities multiple times [4]. A recent systematic literature review found that although this political recognition has led to an increase in research on the accessibility of OERs since 2014, research remains limited to a few countries [5]. Thus, this paper seeks to highlight the importance of the topic as well as the need for further trainings.

Despite the adaptable nature of OERs, their content is not automatically accessible for people with disabilities [6]. A recent survey found that OER librarians have a basic understanding of accessibility [7], while a different study found that researchers do not know how to create accessible PDFs [8]. It is therefore not clear whether OER creators are aware of accessibility issues.

2 Methods: Semi-structured Interviews

Semi-structured interviews were conducted because this method provides detailed information while leaving space to identify factors that were not found in the literature. The interview script was developed based on the literature. Before starting the interviews, the script interview was tested with an OER specialist to guarantee that the script was understandable and logically structured. Interviews were led online via Microsoft Teams or Zoom.

People working at or with universities who create, teach about, or support the creation of OERs were selected for semi-structured interviews. To reach out to OER creators, various "country champions" from the OER World Map [9] were contacted. Country champions were selected because they are more likely to have extensive knowledge and experience with the creation of OERs. Lecturers registered on the OER World Map and who were active in the last year were also contacted. Additionally, a call for participants was also posted in three different networks of OER creators. Interviewees were informed that questions will be about OER accessibility. However, the term accessibility was not explicitly defined to minimize self-selection bias, i.e., to avoid that only people who know about accessibility issues for people with disabilities accept the invitation.

In total, 17 persons were interviewed. Ten of these were country champions according to the OER World Map, the remaining 7 were OER experts reached through OER university network. Interviews lasted between 15 and 60 min. Participants came from all over the world: Australia (1), Austria (1), Brazil (1), Canada (2), Chile (1), Columbia (1), France (1), Greece (1), India (1), Italy (1), South Africa (1), South Korea (1), Sweden (1), Switzerland (2), and United States of America (1). Most participants worked in a university (see Table 1) and created OERs themselves or provided support and training to create OERs.

Before starting the interviews, participants were given an overview of the aim of the research. Participants consented to record the interviews. All interviews were transcribed with automatic transcription and then corrected by a human. The transcripts were coded in two cycles: the first aimed at summarizing the information, and the second sought to find patterns in the codes [10].

Table 1. Repartition of the participants' workplace.

Workplace	Number of participants
University	13
Non-governmental organisation	2
Library	1
International organization	1

3 Results

3.1 Awareness with Accessibility and Definition

Level of Awareness. Overall, interview participants had at least heard about accessibility (Fig. 1). Most of the participants (10) have a medium level knowledge of accessibility of digital content. They could name some issues that people with disabilities face with digital content, but they recognized that they still have more to learn. Only four participants had a high-level knowledge of accessibility, i.e., they assessed themselves as very familiar, could name several issues, and routinely consider accessibility in their design. Three participants had a rather low level of awareness, i.e., they had heard of accessibility but did not know much about existing solutions.

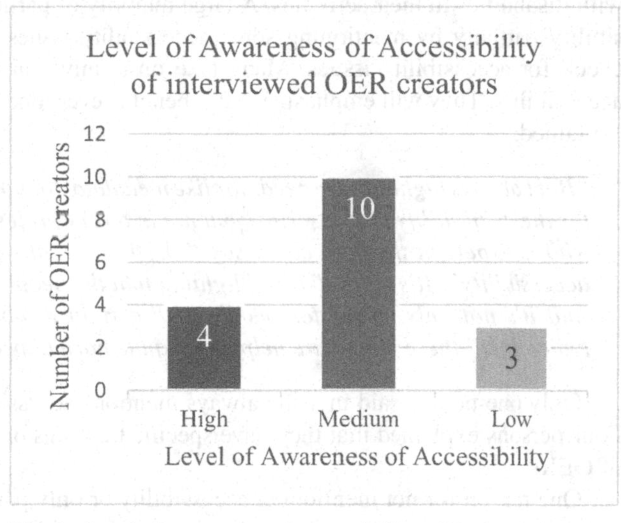

Fig. 1. Level of awareness of accessibility of the interviewed OER creators (N = 17)

Definition of Accessible OERs. Participants usually reckoned that the term accessibility has several meanings. Twelve participants mentioned that accessible OERs means accounting for the needs of learners with disabilities.

Still, many participants defined accessibility as focusing on users' needs and their background. In that case, the term of accessible OERs was defined broadly, it went beyond the focus on the needs of persons with disabilities. Participant 1 gave a good example of this broader definition of accessibility:

"It's putting the end user first, thinking about who is going to use this. [...] And then knowing your audience. At [our university], [...] we have a cohort that includes a lot of people who are low socioeconomic status. A man who works 20 or more hours a week on top of studying. They often have families. So, knowing the people, and then putting yourself in their shoes and saying "OK well, what would make this difficult for me to access?""

Apart from these definitions, seven participants defined accessibility as ensuring that materials are free on the internet and that it is legally allowed to use and reuse OERs thanks to open licenses.

3.2 Promotion of Accessible OERs

The fifteen interview participants who organize trainings or hold presentations to advocate for the creation of OERs were asked whether they promote accessibility for people with disabilities in their activities. A large majority of participants only promote accessibility partially by mentioning some accessibility issues or advising to use a list to check for accessibility issues. Many take on a universal approach without calling it accessibility. They will emphasize that it benefits everyone. For instance, participant 15 explained:

"But I always highlight the needs for like metadata, for no music in the background, for the availability of transcripts, but not in a very professional way that a person who is expert in the field could say "oh, this is really a helpful introduction to accessibility". It's more like highlighting that the people should be aware of this. And it's not only meant for people with certain disabilities or needs. It's like typically all these things are helpful for quite normal people as well."

Only one person said that she always mentions accessibility in her talks on OERs. Four persons explained that they have specific trainings or support on the accessibility of OERs.

One reason for not mentioning accessibility or only partially is that accessibility is considered an advanced topic. People learning about OERs first need to learn about the legal aspects of open licenses before they can learn about accessibility.

3.3 Creation of Accessible OERs

Creation Process of Accessible OERs. In general, at the institutional level, there is no clear guidelines or policies that require OERs to be accessible. Seven participants explained that they did not have any guidelines. In comparison, only four participants mentioned the use of an official guideline by their university about accessibility.

Fourteen participants said that they reduce barriers to access OERs for people with disabilities. However, not everyone is using accessibility standards nor testing their content. In fact, among these participants, only nine test their content for accessibility issues themselves (manual checks or with automatic tools), with the help of specialists, or with co-evaluation. Four participants are also mostly following universal design.

Type of Accessible Content. Most common features that participants considered to create accessible OERs are alternative text for images and adding captions or transcript to video or audio (Fig. 2). Captions and transcripts are nevertheless often said to be time intensive. Participants also mentioned that they check (often manually) that colors and fonts are accessible.

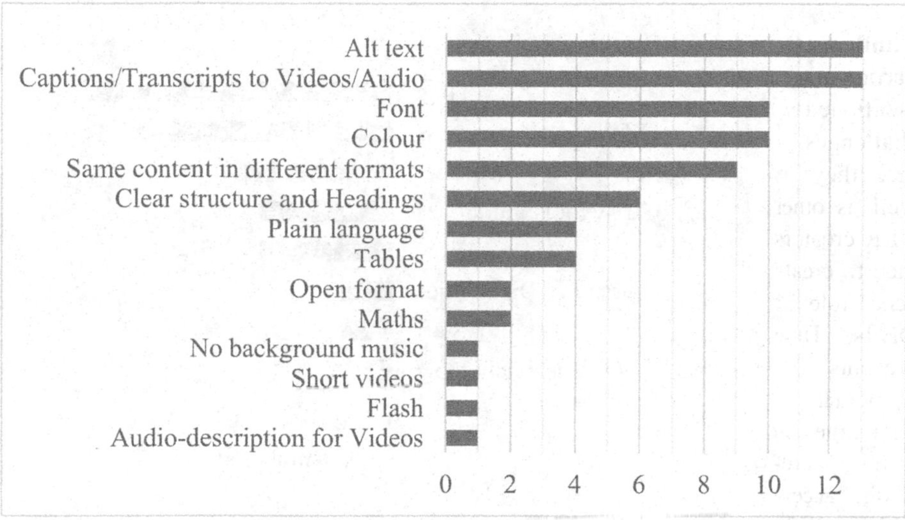

Fig. 2. Content elements that participants pay attention to in their creation of accessible OERs (N = 17)

Although it is possible that math formulas are not common content of the interviewed participants, it appears that participants knew less about how to make math accessible. They were also less aware with how to design accessible tables.

3.4 Motivation for the Creation of Accessible OERs

According to de Bie et al. [11], there are five factors that can encourage lecturers to teach in a more inclusive and accessible manners: legislation, ethical obligation, pedagogical motivation, being nice, and profits. These categories were used to analyse the interviews. To the exception of two participants who mentioned the law as a reason to create accessible OERs, there are two main reasons that motivate participants to create accessible OERs. The first one is ethical obligation. Ten participants explained that for open education to be really open, it has to be accessible to people with disabilities. Some participants said that people with disabilities cannot be locked out, education is a human right, and it is a matter of epistemic justice to guarantee that content is useful to as many people as possible. Participant 1's answer summarizes well this motivation:

> *"I think that the question should be you know why aren't we making them accessible? I think that if we are serious about making education as accessible as possible, about making it equitable, then that means thinking about everybody."*

The second motivation is pedagogical and is closely related to the first one as two participants explained that accessibility is about ensuring that students achieve learning outcomes.

3.5 Challenges and Opportunities for the Creation of Accessible OERs

Challenges. Participants mentioned challenges that they as well as other OER creators face to create accessible OERs. Time presents a particular challenge in terms of creating accessible OERs (Fig. 3). Accessibility can be perceived as an additional work because they need adjustments to the content or because creators need to learn how to make OERs accessible.

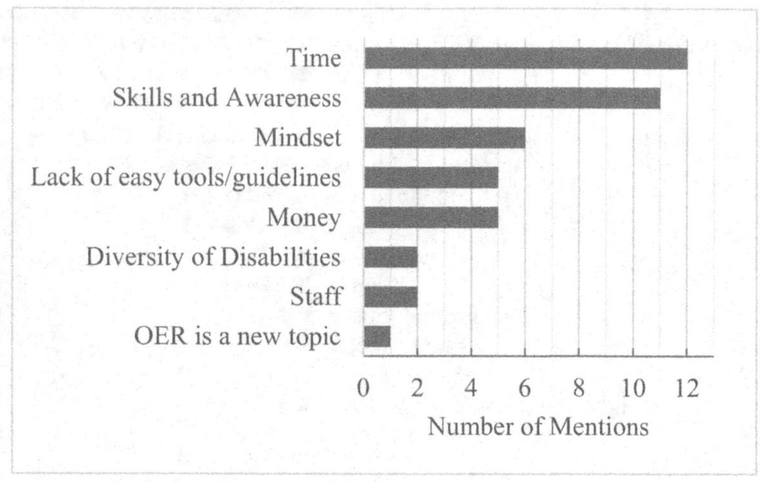

Fig. 3. Challenges to create accessible OERs according to interviewees (N = 17)

Skills and awareness are also lacking. Participants recognized that they need to learn more and also stressed that in general OER creators are unaware of the issues.

Accessibility is also something that is not yet integrated in the mindset of people and institutions. It is not necessarily demanded by universities or OER publishers. There is not necessarily support and recognition for the work done. Two participants explained that people talk late about accessibility and is more an afterthought in the creation process.

Among other challenges are the lack of money invested for accessibility, the lack of easy-to-use tools or guidelines, the lack of staff. Two participants explained that the nature of disabilities is in itself a challenge because disabilities are diverse, there are many needs to cover. Hence, it is difficult to create an OER that is truly accessible to everyone. Furthermore, one participant explained that when OER is a new topic, they must first be convinced to provide open content and mentioning accessibility complexifies the discourse.

Opportunities. Eight participants mentioned that it helps them when they get support from specialists (Fig. 4). Two also explained that OER can be co-created (with colleagues or learners). This way, different perspectives and needs can be considered in the creation process. Five participants stressed that trainings explaining why OERs must be accessible are helpful. In particular, they stress the importance to explain why OERs have to be accessible, how it impacts learners, and give examples.

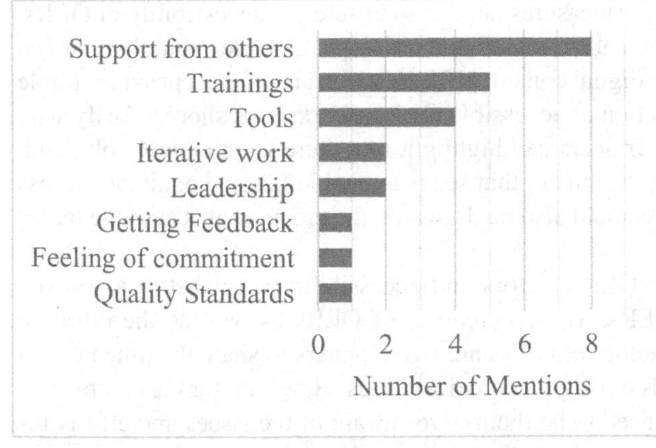

Fig. 4. Elements that help create accessible OERs (N = 17)

Automated tools and open software are also said to facilitate the creation of accessible OERs.Institutions or persons in leading positions can also support the creation of accessible OERs. In particular, leaders or publishers can also help by requiring accessible OERs (thus making it legitimate to invest time and money). One participant also mentioned that platforms can provide quality standards, or scores for accessibility to indicate the OER is accessible or not. Moreover, one participant explained that her feeling of commitment towards students helped overcome challenges to create accessible OERs.

Two participants also provided workarounds to the challenge of creating accessible OERs. They explained that OERs can be adapted overtime (by the same person or others). This iterative work thus reduces the difficulty to account for all the needs at once in a restricted time.

4 Discussion and Conclusion

First, this paper raised the question how much OER creators know about accessibility. Similar to the results of the survey with OER librarians [6], OER creators have a basic understanding of accessibility and only about half of the interviewed participants look proactively for accessibility issues. In this study, more than half of participants were country champions which meant that they were more likely to be aware of the issues. Yet, even among them, few really knew how to address accessibility issues. This highlights that accessibility awareness is still not widespread. Moreover, accessibility is often mentioned as an advanced topic for creators starting to learn about open education. This indicates that only advanced OER creators are likely to consider accessibility issues. Moreover, accessibility is usually not required to publish OERs or integrated into OER guidelines (when they exist). This could reinforce the fact that accessibility is often considered late in the design process and is seen as an afterthought.

Moreover, several interviewed OER creators recognize that accessibility can benefit everyone. On the one hand, this can give accommodations for people with disabilities without having them to ask for it. On the other hand, the accessibility of universal design varies depending on the type and degree of disability [3]. For instance, the use of captions in videos is not systematic because it is time intensive. For someone whose native language is not the one of the lecture, captions make learning easier. Comparatively, a student who is deaf simply cannot access the content of the video without captions. Therefore, while it is helpful to emphasize that many benefit from accessible content, special needs must be addressed because they are not affected the same way.

Second, this study looked for measures needed to ensure the accessibility of OERs. The lack of skills and awareness calls for hands-on trainings. Complex guidelines are an additional barrier to accessible digital content [12]. Hence, trainers must provide simple guidelines to facilitate the creation of accessible OERs. Workshops should clarify why accessibility in OERs matter. Trainers can highlight that there is an ethical obligation inherent to the open education movement that seeks to enable fair and equitable access to education. Special attention should also be drawn on the creation of accessible tables as well as math formulas.

Finally, the community of OER creators and accessibility specialists was proven useful to create accessible OERs. The co-creation of OERs as well as the effort to iteratively improve the accessibility of OERs are two manners to share the time needed to account for the various needs of people with disabilities. However, for the community to improve accessibility, they need to be themselves aware of the issues and efforts for accessibility be recognized as a standard of quality.

References

1. Johnstone, S.M.: Open educational resources serve the world. Educause Quart. **28**(3), 16 (2005)
2. UNESCO. Open Educational Resources. Accessed 03 Feb 2022
3. Fichten, C., Olenik-Shemesh, D., Asuncion, J., Jorgensen, M., Colwell, C.: Higher education, information and communication technologies and students with disabilities: an overview of the current situation. In: Seale, J. (ed.) Improving Accessible Digital Practices in Higher Education, pp. 21–44. Springer, Cham (2020). https://doi.org/10.1007/978-3-030-37125-8_2
4. UNESCO. Recommendation on Open Educational Resources (OER). Accessed 03 Feb 2022
5. Zhang, X., et al.: Accessibility within open educational resources and practices for disabled learners: a systematic literature review. Smart Learn. Environ. **7**(1), 1–19 (2020)
6. Clinton-Lisell, V., Legerski, E.M., Rhodes, B., Gilpin, S.: Open educational resources as tools to foster equity. In: Ozaki, C.C., Parson, L. (eds.) Teaching and Learning for Social Justice and Equity in Higher Education, pp. 317–337. Palgrave Macmillan, Cham (2021). https://doi.org/10.1007/978-3-030-69947-5_15
7. Schultz, T.A., Azadbakht, E.: Open but not for all: a survey of open educational resource librarians on accessibility. Coll. Res. Libr. **82**(5), 755 (2021)
8. Jembu Rajkumar, A., Lazar, J., Jordan, J.B., Darvishy, A., Hutter, H.-P.: PDF accessibility of research papers: what tools are needed for assessment and remediation? In: Hawaii International Conference on System Sciences (2020)
9. OER World Map. https://oerworldmap.org/resource/. Accessed 03 Feb 2022
10. Miles, M.B., Huberman, A.M., Saldana, J.: Qualitative Data Analysis. Sage (2013)
11. de Bie, A., Marquis, E., Suttie, M., Watkin-McClurg, O., Woolmer, C.: Orientations to teaching more accessibly in postsecondary education: mandated, right, pedagogically effective, nice, and/or profitable? Disab. Soc. 1–26 (2020). https://www.tandfonline.com/doi/full/10.1080/09687599.2020.1848803?scroll=top&needAccess=true
12. Kulkarni, M.: Digital accessibility: challenges and opportunities. IIMB Manag. Rev. **31**(1), 91–98 (2019)

Usability of an Accessible Learning Platform – Lessons Learned

Leevke Wilkens(✉) and Christian Bühler

Department of Rehabilitation Technology, TU Dortmund University, Dortmund, Germany
{leevke.wilkens,christian.buehler}@tu-dortmund.de

Abstract. As part of the project "Degree 4.0 - Digital Reflective Teacher Education 4.0: Video-based - Accessible – Personalized", a digital learning platform for teacher training is developed and researched. This learning platform is designed with accessibility in mind. However, technical accessibility should always be supplemented by usability, so that both are considered. Usability tests with students can help to understand if a learning platform is inducing or reducing the extraneous cognitive load of a task. This paper presents the results of usability tests conducted during the development process and derived lessons learned for further development.

Keywords: Accessibility · Usability · Learning platform

1 Introduction

Colleges and universities have changed in recent years. Due to the ratification of the UN Convention on the Rights of Persons with Disabilities (CRPD) in 2009, in which the participation of all people in the education system is enshrined in Article 24, universities, as part of the education system, are also responsible for enabling participation for a heterogeneous student body [1]. As part of the project "Degree 4.0 - Digital Reflective Teacher Education 4.0: Video-based - Accessible – Personalized", a digital learning platform for teacher training at TU Dortmund University is developed and investigated. The subjects involved (German, Computer Science, Mathematics, and Music) develop video-based digital teaching and learning formats for reflective teacher training. The subproject Rehabilitation Sciences focuses on the adaptivity and accessible design of the learning platform and the videos [2]. In this paper, results from usability tests of the Degree 4.0 platform and derived lessons learned for further development are presented.

2 Framework

The use of digital media offers great potential for the participation of students with disabilities in tertiary education. However, at the same time, new risks of exclusion arise if the accessibility of these technologies is not taken into account [3, 4].

Fernandez [5] highlights that, especially in tertiary education, "ableist dynamics and 'disabling' ideologies" still shape the spaces in which teaching and learning take

K. Miesenberger et al. (Eds.): ICCHP-AAATE 2022, LNCS 13342, pp. 343–350, 2022.
https://doi.org/10.1007/978-3-031-08645-8_40

place. Often, the technologies used are not designed with accessibility in mind [3], and improvements are always costly and time-consuming [6].

Nevertheless, in recent years the awareness for accessible learning platforms increased. By now, there are platforms designed explicitly with accessibility in mind (e.g. ATutor), or platforms were further developed, such as Ilias or Moodle [7]. Also, for accessible videos, it is now widely known that captions and audio descriptions are needed, but accessible video players pose new challenges here. For example, Wild [8] found out that only Able Player and OzPlayer do not contain any show-stoppers. But if the aim is to edit videos for a specific learning task, these players do not have the needed functionalities. To our knowledge, there is no accessible, browser-based video editing tool, which can be implemented in a specific learning platform.

While the Degree 4.0 platform is still under development, the platform is already in use in teacher education at TU Dortmund University. At the moment, the learning platform includes a course structure in which different tasks can be presented to students. The overall aim of these tasks is to initiate reflection using videos. The video-based reflection process is a central focus of the project. The editing functionalities annotation, coding, and cutting were implemented. It is also possible to switch subtitles and audio descriptions on and off as required. For this purpose, the audio description is uploaded to the learning platform as an additional MP3 and integrated into the video so that the video's audio track is changed depending on the selection. If necessary, an extended audio description is designed. In this case, the gap in the audio track is lengthened using a still image [9]. Because it is possible to turn the audio description on and off, the still images are also seen if someone is watching the video without audio description. Thus, all students work with the same video, which simplifies collaborative editing by a heterogeneous group. The platform and functionalities can be operated via the keyboard, which was tested manually. Additionally, an evaluation of the accessibility of the platform with WAVE by WebAim [10] showed nearly no errors, only some form labels were missing, or buttons were empty. These errors can be corrected quickly.

3 Method

Technical accessibility should always be supplemented by user tests so that not only technical accessibility but also usability is evaluated. Therefore, usability and accessibility should be considered as two criteria that contribute to the quality improvement of a product [11]. However, even if technical accessibility is granted, problems in usability still may prevent students from using the learning platform [12]. Thus the usability tests aimed to identify usability issues, which can be addressed in further development. Usability tests were carried out with students with and without study-relevant impairments who work on tasks on the learning platform and are recorded in the process using think-aloud. In addition, a short questionnaire using the System Usability Scale (SUS) [13] was implemented following the usability test.

3.1 Procedure

The usability testing procedure and task were developed in a joint effort by the sub-project Rehabilitation Sciences. Before the usability tests started, the participants had to log in to the learning platform. After this first log-in, they were assigned to the course created for the usability tests. The video used is an image film of TU Dortmund University, where a student with visual impairment shows why he decided to study at TU Dortmund University. Captions and audio descriptions, created by DoBuS, were provided for the video. After a first orientation on the learning platform, the participants were asked to set three codes and to write an annotation on the video. The task was functionality-oriented rather than content-oriented. Thus the code or the annotation did not have to be set at the correct point in the video. In the next phase of the task, the participants should cut the video corresponding to the set codes. The cut video sequences are automatically in chronological order. The participants then had the task of changing the order.

3.2 Participants

In total, nine students of TU Dortmund University participated. Some were recruited via a newsletter by Service Center for Students with Disabilities (DoBuS). Seven participants reported no disabilities, and two used screen readers due to their visual impairment. It was irrelevant in which course of study they were enrolled. Additionally, student assistants, who did not know the learning platform in advance and students enrolled in a master's degree Rehabilitation Sciences course, took part in the usability tests (Table 1).

Table 1. Participants

Participant	Device	AT	Setting
P1	Computer with Windows 10	Jaws	In Person
P2	Computer with Windows 10	–	Remote, unmoderated
P3	Laptop with MacOS	–	Remote, unmoderated
P4	Laptop with MacOS	–	Remote, unmoderated
P5	Laptop with Windows 10	–	Remote, unmoderated
P6	Laptop with Windows 10	–	Remote, unmoderated
P7	Laptop with Windows 10	NVDA, Windows Screenenlarger	Remote, moderated
P8	Laptop with Windows 10		Remote, moderated
P9	Laptop with Windows 10	–	Remote, moderated

Except for one usability test with a student with visual impairment, all usability tests were conducted remotely moderated and unmoderated. This one test was carried out in person at a working space of DoBuS. The testing was recorded, the moderator was present and helped out when the participant asked for support.

The remote, moderated usability tests were conducted during a recorded Zoom-Session. The participants shared their screens, so the moderators could follow what they were doing. The semi-structured interview was conducted afterwards. Additionally, five remote, unmoderated usability tests were conducted. Again, the participants recorded their screen and the audio during the testing and handed it in. In this case, no semi-structured interview was conducted.

3.3 Think-Aloud

The "thinking aloud" method is used to get an impression of which content or navigation links students notice [4]. A short semi-structured interview was conducted afterwards depending on the extent of the students' comments during the "Thinking aloud" phase. In this interview, concrete follow-up questions are asked, which on the one hand, clarify open questions of the researchers about the student's actions, and on the other hand, take up further aspects. For example, which elements and contents do the students find difficult or easy to work with (ibid.).

3.4 System Usability Scale

The SUS is a ten-item long 5-point Likert scale to assess the subjective assessment of the usability of a system [13]. By 2013, the SUS was cited in more than 1.200 publications in various contexts [14]. The items of the SUS "cover a variety of aspects of system usability, such as the need for support, training, and complexity" [13]. However, it is important to note that only the overall SUS score can be interpreted as "scores for individual items are not meaningful on their own" [13]. The SUS scores range from 0 to 100. The higher the score, the higher the subjective usability of the system (ibid.).

4 Results

A first usability indicator is the extent how far the participants could fulfill the given task. A second indicator for usability is the time needed.

All participants were able to fulfill the task, with differing extent of support. However, the duration of the usability tests varied from 00:31 to about 02:38 in two sessions. Derived from the length of the usability tests, we can assume that solving the task on the learning platform takes longer for students who use a screen reader (02:15 h; 02:38 h). This was already assumed before the learning platform was developed. In an interview upfront, one interviewee stated that, regardless of the accessibility of the website, operating a website with a screen reader takes more time [15].

4.1 SUS

The SUS scores of the participants ranged from 17,5 to 87,5 ($M = 62,2$; $SD = 23,93$). The lowest score was from one of the screen reader users. The interpretation of this SUS score needs to be done carefully because one screen reader user uses his screen reader only for office applications; otherwise, he uses his smartphone with the respective voice-over function. Thus the score might also be influenced by difficulties with the screen reader rather than the platform itself. Applying acceptability scores to interpret the SUS scores means that most participants ($n = 6$) rated the usability of the system as acceptable (in the 70 s), at the same time 3 participants rated the below 70, which indicates that the learning platform has usability issues, which cause for concern [16].

Considering that the learning platform is just the means to learn and initiate reflection, these scores should also be of concern for lecturers using the learning platform because it may be difficult to differentiate whether there are difficulties with the task itself and the respective learning objective with the learning platform.

4.2 Usability

Overall, all participants could solve the given task, differing in the time required. Nevertheless, the screen reader users had problems if a label was not correctly named. For example, participant 1 could not turn on the audio description because the respective button was called "audio track" (P1, l. 64). For other users, the audio description itself led to some problems: the used still images to lengthen the gaps in the audio track in the video were interpreted as internet problems (P1, l. 21; P3, l. 9; P8, l.38) or as problems in the video itself (P6, l. 23). Even though information about the used still images was integrated into the first task description.

Furthermore, there is a button "Active" Annotation respective Coding for both annotation and codes. "Active" Annotation respective Coding displays annotation or codes which are set at this particular moment. Thus, the number of active annotation or codes varies during the video. This functionality was often mistaken with the total number of codes or annotations the participant set. So participants thought the set coding was not saved because the active codes displayed zero active codes (P1, l. 106–107,147; P5, l. 47–48; P6).

To set a code on the video, the participants had to differentiate whether an already existing code is supposed to be assigned to the video or if it is the task to develop a new code with a new name and color and then assign it to the video. This differentiation is necessary because these are two different functionalities: For the first case, one has to use the functionality "Create a Code" for the second case, one has to use the functionality "Code-List", there new codes can be added. These new codes than can be chosen to "Create a Code". This differentiation and two steps caused confusion when the participants had the task to name a new code and then place it in the video (P1, l.190; P4, l. 38; P87, l. 155,158). When a new code is added to the Code-List, choosing a color with names and not just the RGB-Code is possible. However, while it was helpful that the screen reader read out the name, the name of the color "Monza" was unfamiliar and therefore hard to remember for the screen reader user (P7, l. 185–187).

Also difficult for screen reader users was sometimes the labeling of the buttons itself. Even though they were named according to the functionality, one screen reader user did not listen to the full name. Instead, the user listened to the first words and then moved on if the name did not seem promising (P7, l. 5; l. 15).

Furthermore, while some participants stated that the automatic saving of the rearranged order of the video cuts is quite helpful (P1, l. 354; P7, l. 92), others were looking for a saving button and worried that their new order was not saved (P9, l. 158).

Another important aspect is the familiarity with the learning platform. As one participant put it: "But if you know that, then it's actually super easy" (P7, l. 93).

5 Lessons Learned

Having accessibility in mind when developing or implementing a new learning platform in higher education is crucial. Only with accessible tools and material can everyone fully participate. Nevertheless, also for an accessible learning platform, usability is crucial because usability problems can prevent students from using the accessible learning platform [12] or increase the "extraneous cognitive load", which can impede the learning process [17]. Especially, when working on a complex task, for example, with videos, the students must concentrate on the given task rather than on the technical realization on the learning platform. Thus it is essential to keep the "extraneous cognitive load," which is caused, e.g., by the design of the learning environment, as low as possible [17, 18].

In the Degree 4.0 project, we achieve a high accessibility level of the learning platform. Still existing accessibility problems will be solved in the ongoing development process. The presented results are only derived from a small test sample. Thus the results must be interpreted with caution. Nevertheless, the usability tests revealed issues that need to be considered in the accessible design.

For example, it is not sufficient when the buttons and links are clearly labeled. The important information must come first, so screen reader users do not miss important information due to their tempo while operating the learning platform. Thus, the labeling process has to be done carefully. This also became obvious with the names of the colors. Even though it was stated that it was helpful, that the colors had names instead of the RGB code. If the names of the colors are unfamiliar, it was hard to remember.

Another surprising issue is the difficulties the participants had to differentiate between actually setting a code on the video and creating a new code followed by setting this code. In order to consider such problems upfront, it might be necessary that students participate in the development process. So not just lecturers, who are familiar with working with videos and coding process and software developers are part of the development process. On the other hand, this wording "Code", "coding" is derived from qualitative content analysis, a well-known analysis method from social sciences [19].

In summary, it can be said that usability is indeed an essential criterion so students in lectures can easily use a complex learning platform. However, the SUS scores and the large standard deviation illustrate that the usability is ranked quite differently by different users. This might be partly due to the small sample. Nevertheless, in an accessible and inclusive learning and teaching environment, everyone should be considered despite the number of people. Even though, the platform is supposed to be intuitive it is important that it takes time to get to know a new software. Therefore, it is reasonable to think about training material for students to familiarize themselves with the learning platform, who have problems operating the learning platform or who need more general information on how to edit videos. This could be additional material, which students can access upfront or a tutorial, so students have the opportunity to make themselves familiar with the soon to be used learning platform or the wording in video editing. When providing additional support, it is necessary to consider assistive technology so all students have the same level of support. This is especially important, because it cannot be assumed that all students who use assistive technology have the needed media competencies top use new software or learning platforms from the beginning. Thus, support services are crucial [20].

In further usability tests during the development of the Degree 4.0 platform, it is planned to involve more students who use different assistive technology.

Acknowledgments. The project on which this report is based was funded by the BMBF Bundesministerium für Bildung und Forschung [Federal Ministry of Education and Research] under the funding code 16DHB2130. The responsibility for the content of this publication lies with the authors.

References

1. Dannenbeck, C., Dorrance, C., Moldenhauer, A., Oehme, A., Platte, A.: Inklusionssensible Hochschule. Zur Einführung in diesen Band. In: Dannenbeck, C., et al. (eds.) Inklusionssensible Hochschule. Grundlagen, Ansätze und Konzepte für Hochschuldidaktik und Organisationsentwicklung, pp. 9–21. Verlag Julius Klinkhardt, Bad Heilbrunn (2016)
2. Degree 4.0: Startseite (2022). https://degree.tu-dortmund.de/
3. Burgstahler, S.: Opening doors or slamming them shut? Online learning practices and students with disabilities. Soc. Incl. **3**, 69–79 (2015). https://doi.org/10.17645/si.v3i6.420
4. Kumar, K.L., Owston, R.: Evaluating e-learning accessibility by automated and student-centered methods. Education Tech. Research Dev. **64**(2), 263–283 (2015). https://doi.org/10.1007/s11423-015-9413-6
5. Fernandez, S.: Making space in higher education: disability, digital technology, and the inclusive prospect of digital collaborative making. Int. J. Incl. Educ. **25**, 1375–1390 (2019). https://doi.org/10.1080/13603116.2019.1610806
6. Bühler, C., Burgstahler, S.E., Havel, A., Kaspi-Tsahor, D.: New practices: promoting the role of ICT in the shared space of transition. In: Seale, J. (ed.) Improving Accessible Digital Practices in Higher Education. Challenges and New Practices for Inclusion, 1st edn., pp. 117–141. Palgrave Pivot, London (2020)
7. e-teaching.org: Barrierefreiheit: Inklusives E-Learning (2022). https://www.e-teaching.org/didaktik/konzeption/barrierefreiheit
8. Wild, G.: The inaccessibility of video players. In: Miesenberger, K., Kouroupetroglou, G. (eds.) ICCHP 2018. LNCS, vol. 10896, pp. 47–51. Springer, Cham (2018). https://doi.org/10.1007/978-3-319-94277-3_9
9. Wilkens, L., Heitplatz, V.N., Bühler, C.: Designing accessible videos for people with disabilities. In: Antona, M., Stephanidis, C. (eds.) HCII 2021. LNCS, vol. 12769, pp. 328–344. Springer, Cham (2021). https://doi.org/10.1007/978-3-030-78095-1_24
10. WAVE: WAVE Help. What is WAVE and how do I use it? https://wave.webaim.org/help (o.J.)
11. Casare, A.R., da Silva, C.G., Martins, P.S., Moraes, R.L.O.: Usability heuristics and accessibility guidelines. In: Ossowski, S. (ed.) Proceedings of the 31st Annual ACM Symposium on Applied Computing, pp. 213–215. ACM, New York, NY (2016). https://doi.org/10.1145/2851613.2851913
12. Cooper, M., Colwell, C., Jelfs, A.: Embedding accessibility and usability: considerations for e-learning research and development projects. ALT-J Res. Learn. Technol. **15**(3), 231–245 (2007). https://doi.org/10.1080/09687760701673659
13. Brooke, J.: SUS: A 'Quick and Dirty' Usability Scale (1996). https://hell.meiert.org/core/pdf/sus.pdf
14. Brooke, J.: SUS: a retrospective. J. Usability Stud. **8**, 29–40 (2013)
15. Wilkens, L., Bühler, C., Bosse, I.: Accessible learning management systems in higher education. In: Antona, M., Stephanidis, C. (eds.) HCII 2020. LNCS, vol. 12189, pp. 315–328. Springer, Cham (2020). https://doi.org/10.1007/978-3-030-49108-6_23

16. Bangor, A., Kortum, P., Miller, J.: Determining what individual SUS scores mean: adding an adjective rating scale. J. Usability Stud. **4**, 114–123 (2009)
17. Sweller, J., van Merrienboer, J.J., Paas, F.G.C.: Cognitive architecture and instructional design. Educ. Psychol. Rev. **10**, 251–296 (1998)
18. Syring, M., Bohl, T., Kleinknecht, M., Kuntze, S., Rehm, M., Schneider, J.: Videos oder Texte in der Lehrerbildung? Effekte unterschiedlicher Medien auf die kognitive Belastung und die motivational-emotionalen Prozesse beim Lernen mit Fällen. Zeitschrift für Erziehungswissenschaft (2015). https://doi.org/10.1007/s11618-015-0631-9
19. Mayring, P., Gläser-Zikuda, M., Ziegelbauer, S.: Auswertung von Videoaufnahmen mit Hilfe der Qualitativen Inhaltsanalyse - ein Beispiel aus der Unterrichtsforschung. Medienpädagogik, pp. 1–17 (2005)
20. Drolshagen, B., Klein, R.: Medienkompetenz blinder und sehbeeinträchtigter Studierende - eine Frage der Gestaltung passgenauer Übergänge. In: Drolshagen, B., Schnurnberger, M. (eds.) Sehen in Kontexten. Perspektiven auf Wahmehmung, Sehbeeinträchtigung und Blindheit, pp. 144–161. Edition Bentheim, Würzburg (2019)

Assessment Requirements of Disabled Students in Higher Education

Ingūna Griškēviča[1], Dace Stieģele[1(✉)], Dina Bethere[1(✉)], Ines Kožuh[2(✉)], Matjaž Debevc[2(✉)], Ioannis Gialelis[3(✉)], Andreas Papalambrou[3(✉)], and Eva Papadopoulos[4(✉)]

[1] Liepaja University, Liepāja, Latvia
{inguna.griskevica,dace.stiegele,dina.bethere}@liepu.lv
[2] Maribor University, Maribor, Slovenia
{ines.kozuh,matjaz.debevc}@um.si
[3] Patras University, Patras, Greece
jgialel@upatras.gr, andreas@papalambrou.gr
[4] Social Innovation Center LTD., Nicosia, Cyprus
eva.papadopoulos@csicy.com

Abstract. According to research data, students with special needs face higher academic, psychological and social problems in higher education. Research shows that European countries have different understandings of what constitutes a disability and what is needed to include students with special needs in higher education. The Erasmus + partnership project "Smart Solutions for the Inclusion of Students with Disabilities in Higher Education" aims to develop integrated digital assistive technology services for higher education processes. Within the framework of the first stage of the project, the project partners have developed a tool for assessing the requirements of students with special needs for higher education. The article aims to reflect the process of developing an assessment tool and to describe the guidelines for developing the tool, which was determined by a theoretical analysis of selected data sources, inclusion and education policy documents using induction, deduction, and comparison methods. The evaluation tool developed was used to collect data for the identification of the needs of students for inclusive education. The comparative data from Latvia, Slovenia, Greece and Cyprus about the requirements of students in higher education are analyzed and presented.

Keywords: Assistive technologies · Higher education · Inclusive education · Special needs · Students · Technical aids

1 Introduction

Introduction Inclusive higher education is one of the priorities of modern social development. This is confirmed by several important international and local documents. The UN

The original version of this chapter was revised: Missing special characters and typing errors in some of the authors' names have been corrected. The correction to this chapter is available at https://doi.org/10.1007/978-3-031-08645-8_64

K. Miesenberger et al. (Eds.): ICCHP-AAATE 2022, LNCS 13342, pp. 351–359, 2022.
https://doi.org/10.1007/978-3-031-08645-8_41

General Assembly (UN General Assembly 2015) resolution "Transforming Our World: A 2030 Agenda for Sustainable Development" adopted in 2015 included among its 17 sustainable development goals the goal of "Providing inclusive and quality education and promoting lifelong learning for all". The goal is to ensure equal access to all levels of education and vocational training for vulnerable people, including people with disabilities, by 2030. The "UN Convention on the Rights of Persons with Disabilities" (hereinafter "the Convention") (2007) also requires its member states to ensure equal access for persons with disabilities to tertiary, vocational, adult, and lifelong learning, and to reasonable adjustments to implement this option. The main goal in education of the European Disability Strategy 2010–2020. (European Commission 2010) is to promote inclusive education for pupils and students with disabilities. The European Commission has identified inclusion and gender equality as one of the six dimensions of the development of the European Education Area (European Commission 2020). The renewed EU Agenda for Higher Education emphasizes the unique role of higher education in building a successful, inclusive society and notes that higher education institutions provide students with advanced knowledge, skills, and competencies, complementing society's human capital and promoting social mobility and inclusion (European Commission 2017). Researchers in Europe and around the world have focused on exploring the conditions for inclusive higher education (Riddell 2016; McNicholl et al. 2019; Kottmann et al. 2019; Jung 2003). Research shows that the use of digital assistive technologies in higher education can ensure the academic involvement and social participation of students with special needs, as well as promote inclusion (McNicholl et al. 2019; Samant Raja 2016).

Erasmus + KA2 Strategic Partnership project no. 2020–1-LV01-KA203-077455 "Smart Solutions for Inclusion of Students with Disabilities in Higher Education" (hereinafter the Project) aims to develop integrated digital assistive technology system services for higher education processes. The results obtained and the products developed during the project can make a significant theoretical and practical contribution to the implementation of inclusive higher education and can contribute to further research in this field. As part of the first phase of the project, a tool for assessing the requirements of students with disabilities for higher education was developed at the Institute of Educational Sciences of the University of Liepaja in cooperation with the project partners from Social Innovation Center LTD (Cyprus), University of Patras (Greece) and University of Maribor (Slovenia).

The current study aimed to establish guidelines for the development of an evaluation tool and collected data about the requirements of the disabled students in higher education. The guidelines for the development of the evaluation tool were determined by performing a theoretical analysis of selected data sources – global and European inclusion and education policy documents and studies on the conditions for providing inclusive education (Riddell 2016; McNicholl et al. 2019; Namkung and Peng 2018; Jung 2003; Goegan et al. 2018 etc.) using a type of literature review study with induction, deduction, and comparison approach.

2 Inclusive Higher Education as a Prerequisite for Equally Accessible Lifelong Learning

There is a lack of detailed statistics on how many students with hearing loss are currently included in HE. Worldwide, more than 1 billion people live with some form of disability [4], and in the student population over 10% have at least one special educational need [5]. The European figures show that the percentage of students with disabilities included in HE is even 25% or above in some national cases. A similar trend has been observed in the USA [6]. Regarding hearing loss, statistics show that, in Slovenia, 1% of deaf people had HE in 2011 [7].

The needs and requirements of students with hearing loss are very heterogeneous. Those related to communication seem to be the most important. No two students with hearing loss are the same. They either need technical adaptations at HE institutions for Assistive Technology (AT) to be used efficiently, or they rely more on visual communication approaches due to sign language use [8]. Another type of needs and requirements are related to the availability of personnel at the HE institutions who may assist students when they need certain adaptations.

3 Needs of Assistive Technologies for Inclusive Higher Education

Firstly, support as human resources may include sign language interpreting, as those students who use sign language as a preferred means of communication are reported to have more significant difficulties during the speech-based education process [9]. For instance, in some European countries, students have a right to a sign language interpreter according to the Act on the Use of the National Sign Language [10]. Nevertheless, several issues appear in this regard. Namely, there is a lack of sign language interpreters according to the needs, not all of them have tertiary education to be able to interpret the content from various disciplines professionally, and the available number of sign language interpreter hours financed by the State does not cover the actual needs [11]. These issues are even more evident when the education process is held online, or when a combined approach is performed of online and face-to-face education processes.

Secondly, while teachers are advised to tailor their teaching styles to individual needs, they are frequently unaware of how to perform such adaptations appropriately [12]. They may follow specific guidelines in one-to-one communication and communication in a group.

Thirdly, in the HE process, technical aids may have a vital role for students with hearing loss. During the COVID-19 pandemic such technology has turned out to be an efficient support when the education process has been altered [1, 13]. However, it is significant that students with hearing loss and practitioners in HE are informed about available technologies that may assist them. Thus, we present a response to these needs and requirements which was examined in the international project [3].

4 Development of a Tool for Assessing the Requirements of Students with Disabilities in Higher Education

The Erasmus + KA2 Strategic Partnership project "Smart Solutions for Inclusion of Students with Disabilities in Higher Education" [3] has been implemented to respond to the needs and requirements of students with hearing loss in HE. The project aims to develop integrated digital AT system services for students with various types of disabilities (hearing, vision, physical, developmental, learning and mental) and promote their access to HE.

In the third phase of the project, the partners analyse contemporary ATs and other contemporary tools for disabled students, as well as design and develop the information toolkit about these technologies, which is foreseen to be published as open-source software. In what follows, we provide the results where we examined ATs, mobile and other technologies, assisting students with hearing loss in HE.

5 Method

5.1 Sample

The data collected for this study were dispersed in the four countries involved in this research piece; Latvia, Cyprus, Slovenia and Greece. Participants were recruited randomly with the prerequisite that they were studying in any of the following Educational Institutions; Primary, Secondary General, Secondary Vocational, Incomplete Tertiary and Tertiary Education. Participants participated online using the Smart Solutions Platform that University of Patras created. Prior to completing the questionnaire, participants were required to select their country and thus the equivalent country language; Latvian, Greek, Slovenian, Greek.

5.2 Instrument

Participants were presented with a set of questions, initially with demographic related questions requiring them to select their Country, Age, Gender, Level of Education, followed by Question 5; "I need/would need support in the study process". Participants who responded with "a little" to "very much" support were presented with the full list of questions; total of 25, whereas the ones who responded "Not at all" were only presented with an overall of 11 questions. Apart from the demographic related questions, some of the questions were quantitative using Likert scale ("1 - Not at All" to 5 – "Very Much") and finally a few qualitative open ended questions were included. Likert skale and scoring of questions: all questions excluding the demographics and qualitative questions were scored ranging from 1 –"Not at All", 2 – "A Little", 3 – "Some", 4 – "A Lot" and 5 – "Very Much". List of questions that required scoring is listed in Table 1.

Table 1. Requirements of disabled students in higher education survey questions.

Questions	Response	Score
I need/would need support in the study process	A little	2
I need/would need support in the study process for VISUAL PERCEPTION	Some	3
I need/would need support in the study process for AUDITORY PERCEPTION	A little	2
I need/would need support in the study process for READING COMPREHENSION	A lot	4
I need/would need support in the study process for COMPREHENSION OF WRITTEN TEXT	A lot	4
I need/would need support in the study process for WRITTEN EXPRESSION	Very much	5
I need/would need support in the study process for VERBAL COMMUNICATION	Very much	5
I need/would need support in the study process for EMOTIONAL RESILIENCE	Very much	5
I need/would need support in the study process for PERSISTENCE	A lot	4
I need/would need support in the study process for MENTAL STABILITY	Very much	5
I need/would need support in the study process for PHYSICAL STABILITY	Some	3
I need/would need support in the study process for MOBILITY	Very much	5
I need/would need support in the study process for ROOM CUSTOMIZATION	Very much	5
I have information about assistive technologies	Very much	5
I would like to use an assistive technologies I use assistive technologies	Very much	5
I need/would need additional assistive technologies in the study process	Some	3
In the study process I need/would need to acquire additional skills for the use of assistive technologies	Some	3
I need/would need the other additional support in the study process	A lot	4

5.3 Data Analysis

Data analysis was conducted to answer the following questions: (1) What constitutes impairment and what are the requirements for the inclusion of students with disability in higher education? (2) Where there is lack of professional support and assistance and adequate staffing for the inclusion of students with disability in higher education? (3) Whether there are limited opportunities for assistive technologies in education for persons with disabilities in higher education? (4) What are the needs for adequate training of teaching staff to meet the needs of disabled students in higher education? (5) What lack of understanding of the need for integrating assistive technologies in education for persons with disabilities in higher education?

6 Results

In Chart 1 the dispersion of respondents who do not require assistive technologies (not at all) is demonstrated versus those who need them to some degree. At least 20% of respondents were in no need for assistive technologies (AT) with Slovenia scoring 50% of their sample not in need for AT. Overall, 65% of the respondents were in need for AT to some degree.

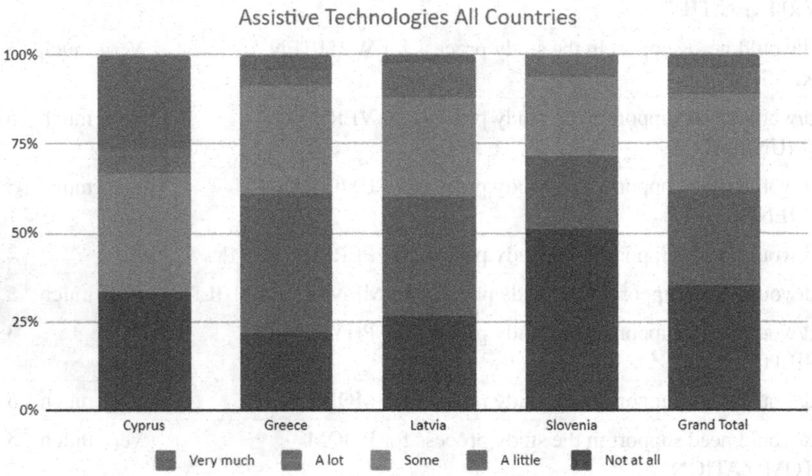

Chart 1. Requirements of assistive technologies by countries.

For the purposes of establishing of what constitutes disability for those respondents that responded with at least 'a little' when asked if they '..need/would need support in the study process. A Pearson's r correlation was conducted to identify the relationship between each of the types of the Assistive Technologies. Overall for the students that took part in this research, higher level of need/potential need for assistive technologies was positively correlated to the need for every type of Assistive Technologies that was included in this research as demonstrated in Table 2. With regards to having access to information, the results on Table 3, show that the relationship between students who scored higher on 'needing assistive technologies and having information about AT' was generally low across all parameters. Additionally, 'I would like to use an assistive technologies' was also not strongly correlated with the need for AT, r = .29, and 'I use assistive technologies' is in a similar position r = .28. Generally the two strongest relationships were those of "I need/would need the other additional support in the study process.", and "I need/would need additional assistive technologies in the study process", r = 36 and .38 respectively. Those respondents (20) who did not Use AT, when asked which ones additional AT are needed in the study process, 65% did not know or could not suggest any AT that are needed. The rest of the 35%, focused on computer tools or technology gadgets like 'speech to text software', colour coding notes, audiobooks, better reading programs and speech recorders. As shown in Table 4, the results that derived from the qualitative analysis regarding the types of AT respondents 'need/would need additional assistive technologies in the study process' there are three main categories to be considered, the major one being the mentor with 42%, followed by a Psychologist 31% and an assistant 16%.

Table 2. Relationship between the needs and required types of assistive technologies

Types of needs	Requirements of assistive technologies
Visual perception	$.722^{**}$
Auditory perception	$.750^{**}$
Reading comprehension	$.743^{**}$
Comprehension of written text	$.749^{**}$
Written expression	$.756^{**}$
Verbal communication	$.730^{**}$
Emotional resilience	$.754^{**}$
Mental stability	$.738^{**}$
Physical stability	$.706^{**}$
Mobility	$.713^{**}$
Room customization	$.694^{**}$

$N = 225, p < 0.05^*, p < 0.01^{**}$

Table 3. Relationship between requirements for assistive technologies and access to information

Requirements for assistive technologies	Access to information
Have information about AT	$.184^{**}$
Would like to use AT	$.293^{**}$
Already use AT	$.276^{**}$
Need for additional AT	$.360^{**}$
Need for additional skills in use of AT	$.208^{**}$
Need additional human support	$.383^{**}$

$N = 225, p < 0.05^*, p < 0.01^{**}$

Table 4. Additional needs of human support to assistive technologies

Requirements for assistive technologies	Assistant	Mentor	Psychologist	Other
100%	16%	42%	11%	31%

7 Conclusions

From the finding of this research we can conclude that for the sample of students that have participated, there is a strong correlation between students who '*need support In the study process*' and all the kinds of impairments that would need Assistive Technologies (AT) for that were included in this research. Counteracting that, there is a low positive correlation between students needing support and having information about AT. Additional to that, the students who did not Use AT, when asked which ones additional AT are needed in the study process, 65% did not know or could not suggest any AT that are needed, but also many of those who had been using AT could not make suggestions for more AT tools. This is a clear indication that more information must be made available to students. Finally, the type of support that students with needs for AT needed were the one of a Mentor, by 42%.

References

1. Aljedaani, W., Aljedaani, M., AlOmar, E.A., Mkaouer, M.W., Ludi, S., Khalaf, Y.B.: I cannot see you—the perspectives of deaf students to online learning during COVID-19 pandemic: Saudi Arabia case study. Educ. Sci. **11**(11), 712 (2021)
2. World Federation of the Deaf Homepage. http://wfdeaf.org/news/resources/access-to-higher-education-for-deaf-students-during-the-covid-19-pandemic/. Accessed 3 Feb 2022
3. Smart Solutions for the Inclusion of Students with Disabilities in Higher Education Homepage. https://sssd-he.liepu.lv/. Accessed 3 Feb 2022
4. World Health Organization Homepage. https://www.who.int/news-room/fact-sheets/detail/disability-and-health. Accessed 3 Feb 2022
5. Petretto, D.R., et al.: The use of distance learning and e-learning in students with learning disabilities: a review on the effects and some hint of analysis on the use during COVID-19 outbreak. Clin. Pract. Epidemiol. Mental Health CP & EMH **92**(17), 92–102 (2021)
6. McNicholl, A., Casey, H., Desmond, D., Gallagher, P.: The impact of assistive technology use for students with disabilities in higher education: a systematic review. Disabil. Rehabil. Assist. Technol. **16**(2), 130–143 (2021)
7. Slovenian press agency Homepage. https://english.sta.si/2905068/equal-opportunities-ombudsman-says-deaf-disadvantaged-in-education. Accessed 3 Feb 2022
8. Smith, D.H., Andrews, J.F.: Deaf and hard of hearing faculty in higher education: enhancing access, equity, policy, and practice. Disabil. Soc. **30**(10), 1521–1536 (2015)
9. Richardson, J.T.E., MacLeod-Gallinger, J., McKee, B.G., Long, G.L.: Approaches to studying in deaf and hearing students in higher education. J. Deaf Stud. Deaf Educ. **5**, 156–173 (2000)
10. World Federation of the Deaf Homepage. https://wfdeaf.org/news/the-legal-recognition-of-national-sign-languages/. Accessed 3 Feb 2022

11. Vrtačič, V.: Vloga tolmača za slovenski znakovni jezik v procesu visokošolskega izobraževanja gluhih (The role of the sign language interpreter for Slovene sign language in the process of higher education of the deaf). Fakulteta za uporabne družbene študije v Novi Gorici, Nova Gorica (2014)
12. Kermit, P.S., Holiman, S.: Inclusion in Norwegian higher education: deaf students' experiences with lecturers. Soc. Inclusion **6**(4), 158–167 (2018)
13. Lazzari, M., Baroni, F.: Remote teaching for deaf pupils during the Covid-19 emergency. In: Proceedings of the 14th International Conference on e-Learning 2020, Lisbon, Portugal, 15–17 December 2020, pp. 170–174 (2020)
14. Debevc, M.: Dostopnost digitalnih produktov za vse (Accessibility of digital products for all), 1st edn. Univerza v Mariboru Univerzitetna založba, Maribor (2021)
15. International Telecommunication Union. https://www.itu.int/dms_pub/itu-t/opb/tut/T-TUT-FSTP-2020-ACC.WEBVRI-PDF-E.pdf. Accessed 3 Feb 2022
16. Debevc, M., Milošević, D., Kožuh, I.: A comparison of comprehension processes in sign language interpreter videos with or without captions. PLoS ONE **10**(5), e0127577 (2015)
17. National Deaf Center. https://www.nationaldeafcenter.org/news/auto-captions-and-deaf-students-why-automatic-speech-recognition-technology-not-answer-yet. Accessed 3 Feb 2022
18. Sparkes, M.: What is a metaverse. New Sci. **251**(3348), 18 (2021)
19. Duan, H., Li, J., Fan, S., Lin, Z., Wu, X., Cai, W.: Metaverse for social good: a university campus prototype. In: Proceedings of the 29th ACM International Conference on Multimedia, pp. 153–161. ACM, China (2021)

Video Screen Commentary System Supporting Online Learning of Visually Impaired Students

Dong-Yeon Park and Soon-Bum Lim(✉)

Department of IT Engineering, Graduate School, Sookmyung Women's University, Seoul, Korea
yeon0729@sookmyung.ac.kr, sblim@sm.ac.kr

Abstract. Because visually impaired students cannot use visual materials in a non-face-to-face lecture system, their understanding of the class content decreases, leading to an infringement of their right to learn. In this paper, we therefore propose a service that automatically provides voice commentary on a video lecture screen to increase the class understanding of visually impaired students. First, to provide an appropriate description of each screen, the screen switching point and the slide number in the video are identified using a similarity analysis algorithm applied between the frame and image. Subsequently, commentary files are created around the text, image, and table in each slide, and commentary voice files are generated using text-to-speech technology. Finally, the original lecture and commentary videos are merged according to their order of appearance on the slide. We conducted a usability evaluation experiment by organizing an assessment using blind students and non-disabled students who had their vision blocked. As the results indicate, the understanding of the lecture content increased when the students heard the explanation on the screen when using the proposed service. Through this evaluation, we confirmed that the proposed service assists in the learning of visually impaired students.

Keywords: Video commentary · Visually impaired student · Non-face-to-face

1 Introduction

1.1 Research Background

To prevent the spread of Covid19, most educational institutions have introduced non-face-to-face lecture systems [1]. A non-face-to-face lecture system indicates a system built to use an existing lecture system anywhere through the web [2]. Among these, video lectures most frequently used for non-face-to-face lectures [3].

With the introduction of new lecture systems, visually impaired students have faced various problems. The most significant problem among them is a poor understanding of the content of the class [4]. Visually impaired students previously used a screen-reader program in a web environment [5]. However, a screen reader cannot read the video screen. Therefore, students do not know what content is on the screen. This has led to a decrease in the understanding of the class content of visually impaired students and difficulties in participating in class, thereby leading to a situation in which many visually

K. Miesenberger et al. (Eds.): ICCHP-AAATE 2022, LNCS 13342, pp. 360–368, 2022.
https://doi.org/10.1007/978-3-031-08645-8_42

impaired students have taken a leave of absence, infringing on their right to learn [4, 6]. Therefore, in this study, we propose an automatic voice commentary service using a lecture video screen to enhance the understanding of classes and guarantee the right of visually impaired students to learn.

1.2 State of Art

Governments and support centers for disabled students in educational institutions have proposed alternatives to solving the aforementioned problems. One alternative is to recruit and match helper students according to the number of classes taken by the visually impaired students. Matched helper students can write commentary files on the lecture materials during a designated class. However, this method is expensive owing to the need for helper students, and because a lengthy period allowing the commentary files to be written in person is required. Such an approach also makes it difficult to mobilize the manpower required to solve other problems [4, 6].

Studies have also been actively conducted on analyzing the current situations and problems and on pointing out the limitations of existing alternatives. Shin analyzed the experience of teachers in visually impaired schools [7]. As the results of the analysis indicate, schools for the visually impaired have responded by recording voice files in person for each specific subject or have used auxiliary engineering devices for visually impaired students. However, the study noted that it is difficult to manage such classes in comparison to those in previous years because it is difficult to ascertain the progress being made and deliver the class content. Lewis also pointed out that if classes are conducted through the current lecture platform, there is a limit to the transfer of knowledge in comparison with an existing approach [8]. Accordingly, the author emphasized the importance of narrowing the information gap. Various studies have also been conducted to solve these problems and support the digital information accessibility and learning activities of visually impaired students. Although graphs are typically used to effectively visualize and provide information in the fields of mathematics and statistics, it is difficult for visually impaired students to obtain information through such means. Na therefore studied the use of automatic description generation technology for mathematical graphs provided to visually impaired students [9]. In addition, Park analyzed the level of understanding and degree of satisfaction regarding learning by comparing and evaluating three reading methods to find the optimal approach to reading formulas for blind students [10]. Finally, to deal with web accessibility, Park developed an optional focusing interface-based mobile voice web browser that selectively enlarges the web content for low-vision learners [11].

2 Approach

The workflow of this system is as follows. First, the instructor uploads the lecture material (pdf) and lecture video (mp4) to the system. The system then captures the switching point of the uploaded videos through a screen analysis (Sect. 2.1). Next, the system matches the order of the slides appearing at the time of the screen transition through an image similarity analysis and a natural language similarity analysis (Sect. 2.2). Meanwhile, the system creates a commentary text file regarding the text, image, and table of each slide by using the lecture materials, and then converts them into mp3 files using the text-to-speech (TTS) engine (Sect. 2.3). After converting the TTS commentary voice files into video files, they are combined according to the screen switching time and number. Finally, they are merged into a single video file (Sect. 2.4). Through this approach, the visually impaired can use the lecture video provided with voice commentary of the information displayed on the screen (Fig. 1).

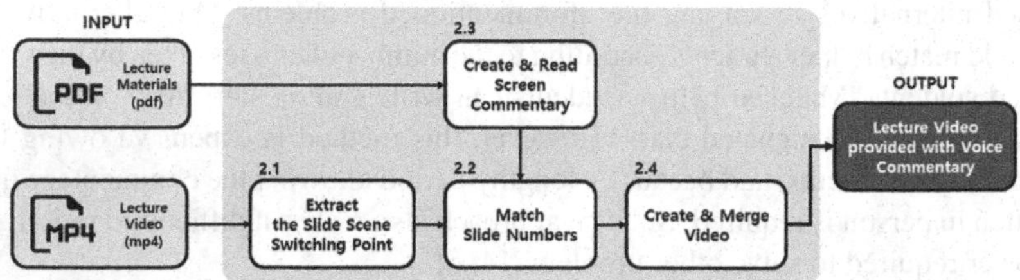

Fig. 1. Workflow of automatic commentary system using video lecture screen

2.1 Extracting the Slide Scene Switching Point

First, we must determine when the screen changes during a lecture video. To do so, we use the PySceneDetect library to extract and store the time and frame when a switch occurs. At this time, the sensitivity threshold is set to the lowest level such that all possible turning points can be extracted. However, we need to filter them again owing to the unnecessary overlapping of scenes. We therefore compared the similarity between the front and rear scenes using the scikit-learn image library. As a result, we confirmed that when the similarity decreases to below 95%, we can extract the time point at which different slides were switched. Through the above processes, we extracted the time and frame at which the screen was switched in units of slides within a lecture video.

2.2 Matching Slide Numbers of Video Frames and Lecture Materials

To provide explanations on the lecture screen to visually impaired students, we must know the screen appearing at each transition point. Therefore, we designed match algorithms that compare the similarities between the lecture material page and the screen frames of the slide.

(1) Image Hashing: The image hash function converts the input image into a string hash value of a fixed length. Using this function, we converted the frame image extracted from the video and the original image extracted from the lecture material into hash values. By comparing the Jaccard similarity between the two strings, we determined that the two images showed the same slide when the similarity value was the highest.

(2) Comparison of the Image Feature Points (ORB Algorithm): Among the various feature point extraction algorithms, we used the Oriented FAST and Rotated BRIEF

(ORB) algorithm because it demonstrated the fastest computational speed and can consider the rotation and direction. Using the ORB algorithm, we extract and matched the feature points of each frame and slide image. We judged whether they were on the same slide when the number of matching feature points was the largest.

(3) Text Similarity: First, all texts on the screen for each frame were extracted using the Tesseract library. We then extracted all texts for each original slide image using the pdfplumber library. Next, we compared the text similarity between them. We also determined whether these two images exhibited the same slide when the similarity value was the highest.

(4) Mixed Similarity (2 + 3): Finally, we used the ORB algorithm and text similarity comparison method. First, the text was extracted, and the similarity of the method described in the third step was compared. When the maximum similarity is lower than a specific threshold point, an ORB algorithm (image feature point extraction) is applied to find the most similar slide for each frame.

We tested the matching accuracy of the previously proposed algorithm using 10 lecture materials including text, images, and tables. As a result, the fourth method using text extraction and the ORB algorithm together showed the highest performance (Fig. 2).

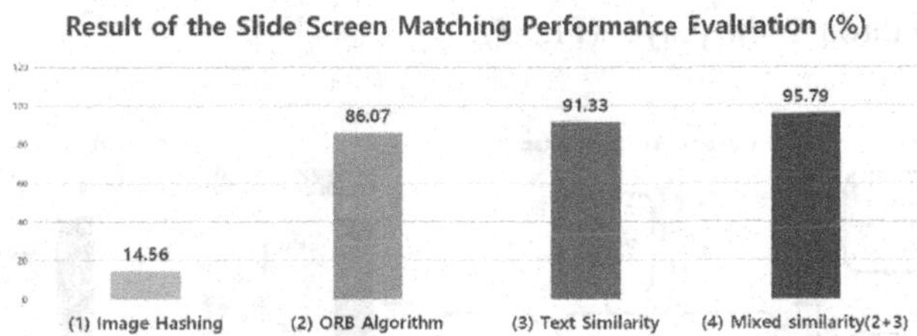

Fig. 2. Results of slide screen matching performance evaluation

2.3 Creation and Reading a Screen Commentary

If slide matching is completed, commentary files to be provided for each slide screen are required. Appropriate commentary files were created for each slide using the lecture material file.

- **Text:** Using the pdfplumber library, all texts in the slide are extracted according to the general reading order and added to the commentary file.
- **Image:** If a caption provides a description of the image, it is added to the commentary file. However, if captions are not provided, new captions are created using Microsoft's Azure Cognitive Services Computer Vision and added to the commentary file.
- **Table:** The rows and columns of the table, that is, the structural information, are identified, and each cell is accessed individually to add the contents in the form of "N row M column CONTENT."

When a commentary file is created for a slide, it should be read by a voice. To achieve this, we used the gtts library provided by Google to create an mp3 file of a voice reading the commentary file.

2.4 Video Creation and Merging

Finally, to generate a video to which the voice commentary is provided, the slide commentary video and the original video must be combined according to the order of appearance of the slide. Therefore, commentary video files are generated using a previously generated TTS voice and the moviepy library. At this time, a lecture material page suitable for the corresponding slide number is displayed on the screen. If commentary video files for all slides are generated, the videos are combined in order. Commentary video files are appropriately inserted at the time of a screen change in the slide units in the original lecture video. Finally, the videos are merged and exported as a single lecture video.

In this way, visually impaired students can receive information on the current slide number, content, and instructor's lecture video through a single video without having to use lecture materials and lecture videos separately. Using the slide switching time and a dedicated player, visually impaired students can freely move the video playback time in units of slides. In addition, if a repeated voice commentary is provided through a repeated slide screen movement of the instructor, the student can omit the voice commentary for the slide screen through the player (Fig. 3).

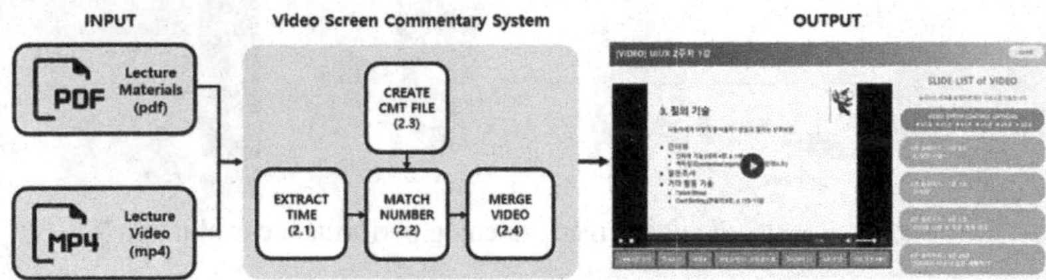

Fig. 3. Implementation result of the voice commentary system

3 User Study

3.1 Usability Evaluation Design

We conducted a usability evaluation to confirm whether the method proposed in this study actually helps with learning. We checked three aspects in the evaluation. First, did the student obtain a better overall understanding of the lecture when listening to the commentary (understanding)? Second, is the method of explaining the screen easy to use (satisfaction)? Third, are the student satisfied with the explanatory service and willing to use it (survey)? Four non-disabled students and four blind students who have taken non-face-to-face lectures participated as evaluators. To participate in the evaluation, non-disabled students covered their eyes with blindfolds.

Table 1. Evaluation tasks for service usability evaluation

Classification	Task	Explanation
Understanding, Satisfaction	Select lecture type	• Three types of lectures (Text/Image/Table)
	Take a lecture	• Capture 2 videos for each lecture type
	Quiz & Satisfaction	• Take quizzes about the contents of the lecture • Satisfaction with the content and explanation of each lecture (5-point Likert scale)
Survey	Response to survey	• Overall service satisfaction (5-point Likert scale) • Willingness to use the service (5-point Likert scale) • Parts requiring improvement

The evaluation task was organized as shown in Table 1 above. To avoid being affected by the major and prior knowledge of the students, the lecture field selected was one in which the major did not overlap with any students. In addition, to prevent biased results according to the lecture, the description of the lecture is random; however, the ratio of descriptions of the lecture by each evaluator should be the same. The evaluation was conducted within approximately 40 min to 1 h per student in a quiet environment where the evaluators could concentrate, and it took approximately one week to finish all evaluations.

3.2 Evaluation Result

The experiment results are as follows: When voice commentary on the video lecture screen was provided, the score was approximately 14.58 points higher than when it was not. The results of the F-test confirmed that the population variance of the two groups was the same. As a result of conducting a t-test on the equivalent variance assumption, it was confirmed that the difference in scores between the two groups was statistically significant ($p = 0.035 < 0.05$). Thus, we know that if a voice commentary is provided it will be effective in allowing the students to understand the contents of the lecture (Fig. 4).

We compared the satisfaction score according to the presence or absence of an explanation. As a result, the satisfaction level when a commentary was provided for the lecture was approximately 0.84 points higher than when it was not provided (3.38 > 2.54). We then confirmed that there was a difference in satisfaction depending on the existence of a commentary ($p = 0.010 < 0.05$). As a result of comparing the satisfaction scores according to lecture types, it was confirmed that the difference in such scores widened further when explanations were provided for objects such as pictures and tables (Figs. 5 and 6).

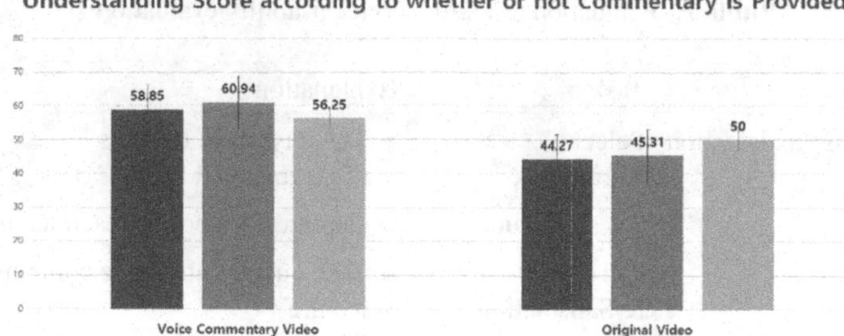

Fig. 4. Understanding score graph

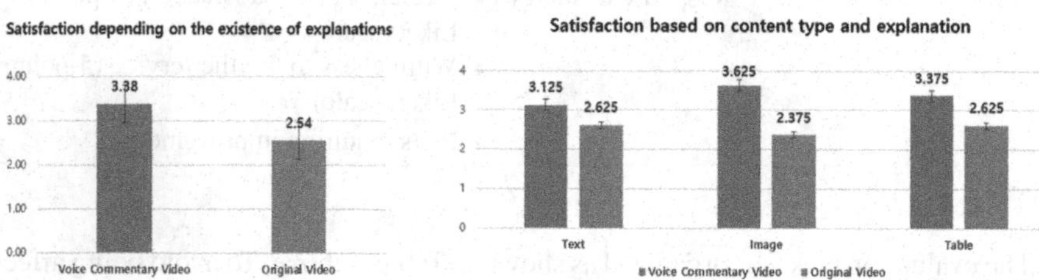

Fig. 5. Satisfaction score

Fig. 6. Satisfaction score by lecture type

We checked whether the overall service satisfaction was slightly higher than 3 points (i.e., 3.38), which indicates "normal." We also confirmed that the willingness-to-use score was 4 points, which indicates "good to use." However, the satisfaction score of the blind group was slightly lower than that of the non-disabled group. We estimate this phenomenon to be due to the fact that the actual users of this service were those of the blind group, and thus the system's usability was evaluated more calmly in terms of actual use.

Some complaints were commonly mentioned, including the following: "I can't feel a clear distinction between paragraphs in the explanation." "The speed of the voice commentary is too fast," and "The vocal spaces of the commentary voice are awkward." At this time, problems such as voice speed can be solved by using an appropriate dedicated player. However, to solve the other problems, we need to improve the algorithm used to generate the commentary text and voice files.

4 Conclusion

In this study, we proposed an automatic video lecture voice explanation service to ensure the right to learn and improve the class understanding of visually impaired students. As a result of analyzing a usability evaluation for the proposed service, we confirmed that it was easier to understand the contents of a lecture when voice commentary was provided.

However, the method proposed in this study has two limitations. First, it only provides explanations for static content. Factors that hinder an understanding of the lecture content include the absence of screen descriptions and an abuse of new handwriting or indicator pronouns on the screen. It is therefore possible to provide appropriate explanations of these dynamic elements. Second, the approach only works in slide-type lecture materials and videos, such as PowerPoint. Because most lectures use this format, we conducted the study based on the slide method. However, there are cases in which classes are written on a blackboard or practiced on a screen. Therefore, further research is needed to overcome these limitations and provide appropriate explanations, even in more diverse environments.

However, the method proposed in this study has two limitations. First, it only provides explanations for static content. Factors that hinder the understanding of the lecture contents include the absence of screen descriptions and an abuse of new handwriting or indicator pronouns on the screen. Therefore, it is possible to provide appropriate explanations of these dynamic elements. Second, the approach only works in slide-type lecture materials and videos, such as PowerPoint. Because most lectures use this format, we conducted the study based on a slide method. However, there are cases in which classes are written on a blackboard or practiced on a screen. Therefore, further research is needed to overcome these limitations and provide appropriate explanations, even in more diverse environments.

Acknowledgements. This research was supported by the Step 4 BK21 Plus program through the National Research Foundation (NRF) funded by the Ministry of Education of Korea.

References

1. Park, D.Y., Kang, S.J., Kim, Y.J., Lim, S.B.: Analysis on the guarantee of learning rights for the visually impaired student in the online learning system. In: Proceedings of the Korea Multimedia Spring Academic Presentation Conference, pp. 574–575 (2021)
2. Lee, S.H., Lee, B.H.: Current status of support for the disabled and policy tasks following the COVID-19 outbreak. Health Welfare **22**(3), 7–34 (2020)
3. Shin, Y.S., Cha, H.M.: A study on the teaching experience of visually impaired school teachers according to the Corona 19 situation. Korean J. Vis. Impairment **36**(4), 147–168 (2020)
4. Lewis, S.: Education for students with visual impairments in the time of Coronavirus: an approach to education through videoconferencing. J. Vis. Impair. Blind. **114**(3), 171–172 (2020)
5. Na, H.W., Kim, J.E., Dong, S.Y.: An automatic generation method of mathematical graph descriptions for visually impaired students. J. HCI Soc. Korea **16**(1), 5–13 (2021)
6. Yook, J.H., Lim, S.B., Park, S.J., Kim, M.J.: An analysis on comprehension of high school mathematics by voice-reading types for the Korean blind. J. Nonlinear Convex Anal. **22**(10), 2191–2202 (2021)
7. Park, J.H., Lee, H.N., Shin, J.E., Dong, S.Y., Lim, S.B.: Mobile voice web browser for the low vision. J. Korea Multimedia Soc. **23**(11), 1418–1427 (2020)
8. Lee, D.J., Kim, M.S.: University students' perceptions on the practices of online learning in the COVID-19 situation and future directions. Multimedia-Assist. Lang. Learn. **23**(3), 359–377 (2020)
9. Lee, Y.S., Shin, D.K.: An investigation of the implementation of online classes in the untact era caused by the COVID-19 pandemic. J. Curriculum Eval. **23**(4), 39–57 (2020)

10. Kim, J.W., Park, Y.S., Kim, K.Y., Yang, K.S.: An analysis of college professors' and students' perceptions and experiences of online classes under the COVID-19 situation. Educ. Res. **80**, 33–58 (2021)
11. Buzzi, M.C., Buzzi, M., Leporini, B.: Accessing e-learning systems via screen reader: an example. In: Jacko, J.A. (ed.) HCI 2009. LNCS, vol. 5613, pp. 21–30. Springer, Heidelberg (2009). https://doi.org/10.1007/978-3-642-02583-9_3

Inclusive Education Going Digital: The Education of "Digital Scouts"

Claudia Mertens(✉)

Bielefeld University, Universitätsstraße 25, 33615 Bielefeld, Germany
claudia.mertens@uni-bielefeld.de

Abstract. The paper presents the approach of the so-called Digital Scouts. Teacher students of a German University were educated in e-learning in inclusive school settings. Having dealt with the accessibility of digital materials (on the basis of scientific criteria catalogues) the students created e-learning materials for pupils with special educational needs (SEN) in a project phase (media projects) – giving respect to the Universal Design for Learning (www.cast.org).

After that the Digital Scouts spent four lessons at comprehensive schools and augmented school staff. The practical phase aimed at promoting digital literacy in early grades for students with learning and mental disabilities.

The paper shows the improvement of the digital skills of the students (via interview studies) and the improvement of the inclusive skills of the future teachers in e-learning contexts and media education (via portfolio analyses).

All in all, it can be summarized that the students with and without handicaps in inclusive settings profited from the project with regard to their digital skills. The Digital Scouts reported positive effects with regard to their sensitivity towards pupils with SEN in the context of e-learning and media education. In the portfolios the Digital Scouts reflected the chances and risks of using digital media when trying to empower pupils with and without SEN. They stressed the necessity of a good teacher-student-relation and they reported that because of the project they could cope more easily with uncertainty in inclusive settings. It became clear that schools need a better internet and that teachers need better technical training.

Keywords: Inclusion · Digital change · Digital media · Media education

1 Education of So-called "Digital Scouts"

Although schools in Germany dispose of more media equipment than before Covid 19, the individual support of pupils with special educational needs in inclusive settings is still to be improved. The concept of the so-called "Digital Scouts" (DSs) (= students in teacher education) by Mertens & Kamin faces this challenge. The project DILBi stands for: "**D**igital **I**nclusive professiona**L**isation of teachers **Bi**elefeld" and consists of two phases: In the seminar "Inclusion meets digitalization" students at Bielefeld University (Germany) were educated in inclusive media education (= step 1, funded by "Qualitätsfonds für die Lehre") before they worked as tutors in seven comprehensive schools in Northrhine Westfalia, NRW, (= step 2, funded by "Stifterverband für die

K. Miesenberger et al. (Eds.): ICCHP-AAATE 2022, LNCS 13342, pp. 369–376, 2022.
https://doi.org/10.1007/978-3-031-08645-8_43

deutsche Wissenschaft"; the project was chosen – amongst others - out of more than 500 applications). The aims of both projects were to raise future teachers' and teachers' awareness of digital, inclusive teaching concepts and to empower every pupil in the class – regardless of any form of disability. The results of DILBi[100] - including a self-study course – are presented on www.digi-klusion.de.

Description of the Theoretical Phase (= step 1): In the seminar "Inclusion meets digitalization" the criteria for the choice of inclusive materials were discussed. We focused on the WCAG 2.1 standards and cooperated with the project ITM (itm-europe.org; cf. Bierschwale et al. 2020) to work out a catalogue for checking whether documents are accessible or not. In the seminar existing digital materials were evaluated according to the potential for empowerment by the teacher students.

Apart from this, we discussed the TPACK model (Mishra and Koehler 2006), which was adapted by Marci-Boehncke (2018) to give respect to (cf. Delere et al. 2020). The students were invited to use material which was created according to the principles of the universal design for learning (https://www.cast.org/impact/universal-design-for-learning-udl) so that the material was accessible to everybody in the class and free of technical barriers. The UDL guidelines ask for multiple forms with regard to the "why of learning" (multiple means of engagement), "the what of learning" (multiple means of representation) and "the how of learning" (multiple means of action and expression) (cf. CAST 2021).

Yet, knowing the rules for automated document remediation tools and accessibility checkers alone is not sufficient: What is needed is a positive attitude towards inclusion. On the international level, we see several assessment efforts to describe the competencies needed (like e.g. https://iaap-dach.org/iaap-dach-2/zertifizierungen.html or https://www.accessibilityassociation.org/s/accessible-document-specialist#memberSec), but in Germany, the focus on inclusive media education is only just starting (cf. Bosse et al. 2019). Therefore, input with regard to inclusive education was given by external experts (https://inklusive-bildung.org/en/about-us).

Furthermore, a self-study course was offered as a preparation for the practical phase. Digital inclusive teaching materials and concepts for teacher education were then created by the teacher students, as e.g. HP5 Quizzes about the Olympic Games, explanatory videos about how to log in with ZOOM, etc.

Description of the Practical Phase (= step 2): Fourteen Digital Scouts were taught with regard to inclusive media education. The scouts were all preparing their master degree of teacher education. They worked in seven comprehensive schools (5th and 6th grades) in inclusive settings with some of the pupils with learning disability or mental disability. The reason for focusing on this area of SEN was that for pupils with learning disabilitites, such as e.g. ADHDS, it is especially challenging to use digital media: These pupils need a clear structure. Yet, the internet is not structured at all. We felt, that the one-to-one support in the DILBi project could be a help.

The teacher students did pair work for the didactic conception of their units and they discussed in small teams how to use the digital materials in inclusive settings. The aim of the practical phase was to support the pupils a) with regard to the use of media (= learning *with* media) and b) media education (= learning *about* media) in four lessons/units. The ideas were shared amongst the Digital Scouts teams and the supervising teachers. In this way, interaction was initiated between students, teachers and the university (cf. Fig. 1). Thus, two/three phases of teacher education worked together – which is a novum in Germany (cf. https://www.uni-due.de/comein/).

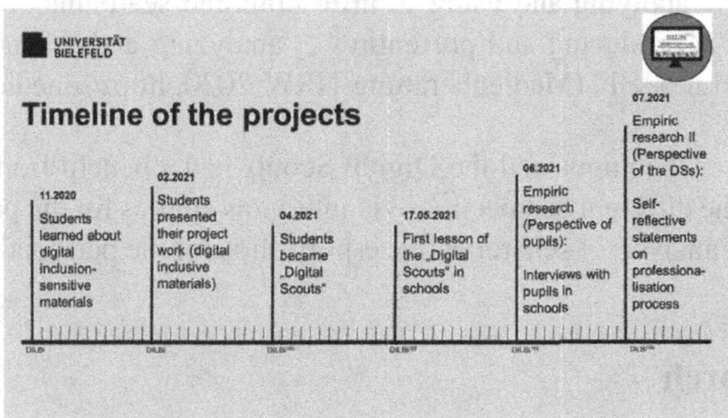

Fig. 1. Timeline of the projects

2 Theoretical Framework

The theoretical basis of our project was – in addition to a paper edited by the German Ministry - the DigCompEdu model (Redecker 2017): "As educators face rapidly changing demands, they require an increasingly broader and more sophisticated set of competences than before. In particular, the ubiquity of digital devices and the duty to help students become digitally competent requires educators to develop their own digital competence" (Redecker 2017).

According to this framework educators need competencies in six areas: "Area 1: Professional Engagement Using digital technologies for communication, collaboration and professional development. Area 2: Digital Resources Sourcing, creating and sharing digital resources. Area 3: Teaching and Learning Managing and orchestrating the use of digital technologies in teaching and learning. Area 4: Assessment Using digital technologies and strategies to enhance assessment. Area 5: Empowering Learners Using digital technologies to enhance inclusion, personalization and learners' active engagement. Area 6: Facilitating Learners' Digital Competence Enabling learners to creatively and responsibly use digital technologies for information, communication, content creation, wellbeing and problem-solving" (Redecker 2017, p. 16).

These competencies are reflected similarly in the above-mentioned paper of the German Ministry, Northrhine-Westfalia, in the so-called "Orientation framework for teachers in a digitalized world" (Eickelmann 2020). As this document is binding for teacher education in NRW we used it to derive our coding categories. For analyzing the development of the teacher students this document was used as a starting point for MAXQDA coding - with deductive categories from the above-mentioned document such as "teaching", "educating", "supporting learning and performing", "counselling" and "developing schools". Inductive categories were created from the material.

For the perspective of the pupils, two other papers published by the German Ministry (KMK 2016, 2021) were used as a basis. They are specified for NRW in the "Medienkompetenzrahmen NRW". This paper describes the media competencies pupils should have at the end of their school careers. Here, the areas of competence that pupils shall acquire are: "applying and using", "informing and searching", "communicating and cooperating", "producing and presenting", "analyzing and reflecting" and "solving problems and modell" (Medienberatung NRW 2020, https://medienkompetenzrahmen.nrw.)

To see whether the pupils and the Digital Scouts had a benefit from the project we did research on the different perspectives via interview studies for the perspective of the pupils and via an analysis of self-reflective e-portfolios for the perspective of the Digital Scouts.

3 The Research

3.1 Phase I: The Pupils' Perspective

Methodoloy. We did group interview studies on experience, feedback and motivational aspects of students with 18 pupils and transcribed the 10 interviews. The interviews were analyzed via a qualitative content analysis according to Mayring (2015) with MAXQDA. Deductive items were derived from the so-called "Medienkompetenzrahmen" (= official document on media competence education for pupils, Medienberatung). Inductive categories, which were derived from the interview material itself, were added.

Results. The quotations from the interviews are translated in the text. Yet the original wording is kept in the footnotes for scientific transparency.

The results showed that there was both a progress in learning to use media ("I've just learned how I can create the background. A photo, any photo. I can choose the background photo in TEAMS-, where I show myself"[1]) as well as a progress in the learning about media ("I also learnt that in the internet you should not write back immediately or meet people if you don't know them" (see footnote 1)).

Several pupils stressed the positive motivational impact of the Digital Scouts ("well, I would like to work more with you - So I would like to continue working with you because it's fun and yes-. B3: Me too"[2]) but they criticized again and again the insufficient infrastructure ("I don't get much of it because we have got a bad internet connection[3]").

The overall positive feedback goes along with background information from a brainwriting with the teachers (= mentors of the DSs). The teachers considered the presence of the Digital Scouts as very helpful: "Pupils realize that they can benefit from being media-literate. They see dangers that they might not have recognized before[4]".

[1] Ich habe gerade was-, das alles gelernt, wie ich kann den Hintergrund machen. Ein Foto, egal welches Foto. Da kann ich Hintergrund bei den Teams-, wo ich mich zeige [einstellen].

[2] Also ich würde mit Ihnen mehr– Also ich würde gerne mit Ihnen weiterarbeiten, weil es macht Spaß und ja-. B3: Ich auch.

[3] Mir bringt das nicht viel. Wir haben schlechtes Internet.

[4] Schüler erkennen, dass sie Vorteile daraus ziehen können, wenn sie sich gut mit unterschiedlichen digitalen Angeboten auskennen. Sie sehen Gefahren, die sie davor vielleicht nicht erkannt hätten.

The pupils could benefit as far as the technical use of media is concerned but also as far as the knowledge *about* media is concerned (Fake News, Hate Speech, data privacy, etc.).

3.2 Phase II: The Perspective of the Digital Scouts

Methodology. As mentioned above the e-portfolios of the digital scouts were used to get an insight into the Digital Scouts' view on the project. In the portfolios the Digital Scouts self-reflected their professionalization process with regard to Universal Design for Learning and with regard to being sensitive to the special concerns of pupils with additional support need.

Once again, a content analysis (Mayring 2015) was used to analyze the portfolios. Items were deduced from the official document for teachers in a digitalized world "Orientierungsrahmen für Lehrkräfte in der digitalisierten Welt" (Eickelmann 2020) and inductive categories were added from the portfolios. The portfolios were then analyzed in pair-work ("principle of four eyes") with the research staff being educated in a training phase to increase the interrater-reliability.

Major Outcomes. All Digital Scouts mentioned an increase in their competence in digital teaching. Most of the Digital Scouts reported being more sensitive when using digital media: "I have definitely learned to familiarize myself with new platforms and digital tools and to use them profitably for students[5]". Apart from this a higher sensitivity for the diverse needs of students/effect on attitude towards inclusion is reported: "It was also made clear to me once again how much effort is needed for good inclusive teaching. However, it also became clear that the effort was worth it and that the students cooperated very well and I had the feeling that all students were able to use their strengths. Due to the practical phase, I definitely improved handling and also perceiving inclusive learning groups[6]".

Moreover, the Digital Scouts mentioned a higher sensitivity for the Universal Design for Learning: "As all students in my learning group had different SEN I had to think about how to reach the kids via different channels. I tried to use the visual and the acoustic channel. I also paid attention to a motivation and simple way of speaking[7]". And they pointed out a risen awareness for the chances of digital media in inclusive settings: "I see some advantages of digital media for inclusive settings, as e.g. the individualization

[5] Ich habe definitiv gelernt mich selbst in neue Plattformen und digitale Hilfsmittel einzuarbeiten und diese gewinnbringend für Schüler*innen zu nutzen.

[6] Genauso wurde mir noch einmal deutlich gemacht, mit wieviel Aufwand ein guter inklusiver Unterricht zusammenhängt. Es wurde aber auch deutlich, dass sich der Aufwand lohnt und die SuS sehr gut mitgearbeitet haben und ich das Gefühl hatte, dass alle SuS ihre Stärken einbringen konnten. Durch die Praxisphase habe ich definitiv eine Verbesserung in meinem Umgang und auch der Wahrnehmung von inklusiven Lerngruppen gespürt.

[7] Dadurch, dass die Kinder in meiner Lerngruppe unterschiedliche Förderschwerpunkte hatten, musste ich mir überlegen, wie ich die Kinder auf den unterschiedlichsten Kanälen erreichen kann. Somit wurde darauf geachtet, dass sowohl der visuelle und die akustischen Kanäle angesprochen wurden. Ebenfalls wurde auf eine motivierende und einfache Sprache geachtet.

of learning[8]". This risen awareness seems to be due to the hands-on experience in the schools.

Interestingly enough the Digital Scouts did not only see the potential of digital media only but they also considered the risks of digital media in inclusive settings, which can be exemplified with the help of the following quotation: "For the perspective of inclusion I see the risk that because of the high amount of solo work the kids with SEN don't want to integrate in the learning group and isolate themselves. This is not the aim of inclusion but it could happen because of the high amount of solo work[9]".

Due to the experience of distance learning during the COVID 19 phase it became clear that the teacher-student relationship is very important: "Because of the video platform it was difficult for me to establish a relationship with the pupils[10]".

Last but not least there is a risen competence to deal with ambiguity: "Yet, I could profit a lot with regard to using digital media – especially the fact that you should always have a plan "B" in case of technical problems[11]" or "I learnt once more to deal with uncertainty[12]".

4 Conclusion

To summarize, we can say that all in all, the project was a success. All participants – students, teachers and Digital Scouts – had a benefit. The concept of Digital Scouts may be one step to overcome digital exclusion. The cooperation of the first and the second phase of teacher education is highly recommendable. Yet, the project should not be misunderstood in the sense of "the more practical periods the better". All practical experiences need to be reflected upon. Theoretical concepts are needed to put the practical experience into a bigger context. This can be reached via the method of portfolio writing for the future teachers. The use of portfolios starts from the assumption that self-reflective portfolios are an adequate means to make implicit knowledge explicit, to put "lessons learnt" into a bigger context, and to transfer the knowledge to future situations (Häcker 2017, p. 22; cf. Bräuer 2016; Brunner et al. 2017; Koch-Priewe and Störtländer 2016).

Yet, for the future, the scope of the project should be adapted. If the Digital Scouts spend a longer period at the schools it is possible to have active media projects with the pupils (like recording podcasts or trying blog-writing etc.). This was not possible here due to the lack of time.

8 Ich sehe einige Chancen in den digitalen Medien unter der Perspektive der Inklusion, wie z.B. dass individuell auf die Schüler*innen eingegangen werden kann.

9 Für die Perspektive der Inklusion sehe ich das Risiko, dass sich durch den großen Anteil der Einzelarbeit der digitalen Medien, die Kinder mit einem inklusiven Hintergrund, nicht weiter in die Lerngruppe integrieren wollen und immer mehr abschotten. Dies ist nicht der Sinn von Inklusion, könnte aber durch die vermehrte Einzelarbeit an Medien passieren.

10 Durch die Video-Plattformen ist es mir schwerer gefallen, die Beziehungskompetenz zu den Schüler*innen zu erweitern.

11 Allerdings konnte ich in Bezug auf den Einsatz von digitalen Medien einiges mitnehmen – insbesondere die Erkenntnis, dass man auch immer einen Plan B in der Tasche haben sollte, falls die Technik mal wieder nicht das macht, was man eigentlich möchte.

12 Ich haben noch einmal mehr gelernt mit Kontingenzen also Unsicherheiten umzugehen.

It became clear that there is a gap between university standards on the one hand and the practice in schools as far as the technical equipment and the access to internet are concerned on the other hand. Although concepts for digital media education do exist, it is hard to put the concepts into practice if the teachers encounter technical problems in school. Sometimes the teachers had the technical expertise but they could not download an app e.g. and install it because the IT department would have been needed to give the allowance first.

As a general conclusion, both from step one and step two of the study, we can say that schools need better internet/better technical support structures. Last but not least teachers need more technical training and especially didactic training in “inclusive media education”.

References

Bierschwale, C., Vogt, M., Andersen, K.N., Bagger, A., Macchia, V.: Qualitätskriterien von inklusiven Bildungsmedien im Fach Mathematik – Theoretische und empirische Rahmenbedingungen. k:ON – Kölner Online Journal für Lehrer*innenbildung **2020**(2), 1–25 (2020). https://doi.org/10.18716/ojs/kON/2020.2.01

Bosse, I., Kamin, A.-M., Schluchter, J.-R.: Medienbildung für alle: Inklusive Medienbildung – Zugehörigkeit und Teilhabe in gegenwärtigen Gesellschaften. In: Brüggemann, M., Eder, S., Tillmann, A. (eds.) Schriften zur Medienpädagogik. Medienbildung für alle – Digitalisierung. Teilhabe. Vielfalt, vol. 55, pp. 35–52. kopaed, München (2019)

Bräuer, G.: Das Portfolio als Reflexionsmedium für Lehrende und Studierende, 2nd edn. Verlag Barbara Budrich (2016)

Brunner, I., Häcker, T., Winter, F. (eds.): Das Handbuch Portfolioarbeit, 5th edn. Klett Kallmeyer, Seelze (2017)

CAST: Until learning has no limits®: https://www.cast.org/. Accessed 30 Sept 2021

Delere, M., Marci-Boencke, G., Schmidth, J.S., Werner, L.: Was sie wissen, was sie brauchen: Zum medientechnischen und mediendidaktischen Reflexionsbewusstsein von Grundschullehrkräften. k:ON - Kölner Online Journal für Lehrer*innenbildung **1**(1), 23–42 (2020)

Eickelmann, B.: Lehrkräfte in der digitalisierten Welt. Orientierungsrahmen für die Lehrerausbildung und Lehrerfortbildung in NRW. Medienberatung NRW (ed.) (2020). https://www.medienberatung.schulministerium.nrw.de/_Medienberatung-NRW/Publikationen/Lehrkraefte_Digitalisierte_Welt_2020.pdf. Accessed 30 Sept 2021

Häcker, T.: Grundlagen und Implikationen der Forderung nach Förderung von Reflexivität in der Lehrerinnen- und Lehrerbildung. In: Berndt, C., Häcker, T., Leonhard, T. (eds.) Reflexive Lehrerbildung revisited. Traditionen – Zugänge – Perspektiven, pp. 21–45. Klinkhardt, Bad Heilbrunn (2017)

KMK – Kultusministerkonferenz: Bildung in der digitalen Welt: Strategie der Kultusministerkonferenz. Berlin (2016)

KMK. Lehren und Lernen in der digitalen Welt. Ergänzung zur Strategie der Kultusministerkonferenz “Bildung in der digitalen Welt” (Beschluss der Kultusministerkonferenz vom 09.12.2021) (2021). https://www.kmk.org/fileadmin/veroeffentlichungen_beschluesse/2021/2021_12_09-Lehren-und-Lernen-Digi.pdf. Accessed 31 Mar 2022

Koch-Priewe, B., Störtländer, J.C.: Portfolio in Schule und LehrerInnenbildung. Zur Einschätzung neuerer Entwicklungen. In: Ziegelbauer, S. Gläser-Zikuda, M. (eds.) Das Portfolio als Innovation in Schule, Hochschule und LehrerInnenbildung. Perspektiven aus Sicht von Praxis, Forschung und Lehre, pp. 265–279. Verlag Julius Klinkhardt, Bad Heilbrunn (2016)

Marci-Boehncke, G.: Von der integrierten zur inklusiven Mediennutzung. In: Hug, T. (ed.) Medienpädagogik: Herausforderungen für Lernen und Bildung im Medienzeitalter, pp. 49–64. Innsbruck University Press, Innsbruck (2018)

Mayring, P.: Qualitative Inhaltsanalyse. Grundlagen und Techniken, 12th revised edition. Beltz, Weinheim/Basel (2015)

Medienberatung NRW: Medienkompetenzrahmen NRW (2020). https://medienkompetenzrahmen.nrw/fileadmin/pdf/LVR_ZMB_MKR_Broschuere.pdf. Accessed 30 Sept 2021

Mishra, P., Koehler, M.J.: Technological pedagogical content knowledge: a framework for teacher knowledge. Teach. Coll. Rec. **108**(6), 1017–1054 (2006). https://doi.org/10.1111/j.1467-9620.2006.00684.x

Redecker, C.: Europäischer Rahmen für die Digitale Kompetenz Lehrender: DigCompEdu. Seville (2017). https://ec.europa.eu/jrc/sites/default/files/digcompedu_german_final.pdf. Accessed 30 Sept 2021 (translated by Goethe Institut 2019, edited by: Punie, Yves)

Design for Assistive Technologies and Rehabilitation

A Multidisciplinary Approach for the Designing and Realization of Customized High Performance Prostheses by Continuous Fiber Additive Manufacturing

Milutin Kostovic[1], Gennaro Rollo[1], Andrea Sorrentino[1], Eleonora Ticli[1], Cristina De Capitani[1], Simone Pittaccio[2], Jacopo Romanò[2,3], Lorenzo Garavaglia[2], Fabio Lazzari[2], Enrico Bassani[2], Fabio Storm[4], Claudio Corbetta[4], Marco Tarabini[5], Paola Saccomandi[5], Giada Luppino[5], Davide Paloschi[5], Andrea Canegrati[5], Luca M. Martulli[5], Andrea Bernasconi[5], Mauro Rossini[6], Marino Lavorgna[1(✉)], and Emanuele Gruppioni[7]

[1] CNR-IPCB, Lecco, Italy
marino.lavorgna@cnr.it
[2] CNR-ICMATE, Lecco, Italy
[3] Politecnico di Milano - CMIC, Milan, Italy
[4] Scientific Institute IRCCS E. Medea, Bosisio Parini, Lecco, Italy
[5] Department of Mechanical Engineering, Politecnico di Milano, Milan, Italy
[6] Villa Beretta, Rehabilitation Center, Costa Masnaga, Lecco, Italy
[7] INAIL, Centro Protesi, Vigorso di Budrio, Bologna, Italy

Abstract. Additive Manufacturing (AM) techniques have attracted great interest in sectors with high benefit such as the Medtech. The AM of continuous fiber reinforced composite is a technology that, although still in its initial development, appears to be very promising. The AM process could be particularly interesting for the production of prosthetic devices for sports (ESAR devices such as foot or foil). In this work, is explored the potential of additive manufacturing in the field of prosthetics of the lower limb through an multidisciplinary approach, involving several competences from the clinical evaluation, integration of biomechanics, development of new composite and hybrid materials based on polymers, carbon fibres and metal inserts, and implementation of optical sensors with their integration in the composites for the continuous monitoring of prosthetic devices and their durability.

Keywords: Additive manufacturing · Prosthetic device · Optical sensors

M. Kostovic and G. Rollo—Contributed equally to the manuscript.

K. Miesenberger et al. (Eds.): ICCHP-AAATE 2022, LNCS 13342, pp. 379–386, 2022.
https://doi.org/10.1007/978-3-031-08645-8_44

1 Introduction

In recent years, Additive Manufacturing (AM) techniques have attracted great interest in the customization of medical devices. However, the current use of these technologies is limited to the prototyping of new products. The advantages offered by AM compared to traditional production processes, including the possibility of obtaining customized objects, the flexibility in the creation of complex shapes and the reduced initial costs for infrastructures, are considerable and represent the driving force for the future diffusion of these innovative technologies [1, 2].

In recent years, the possibility of producing fiber-reinforced composites with short and long fibers is arousing great interest. The development and diffusion of 3D printing of fiber-reinforced composites could limit some problems of conventional technologies (such as wet lay-up, resin transfer molding, vacuum bag, lamination and autoclave curing), among which it is worth underlining the excessive use of handwork, the lack of repeatability, the high cost and the limited geometries [3, 4].

Orthopaedic prostheses represent a typical sector in which AM technologies can lead to considerable progress. Their traditional production process is very complex, and consists of several steps (from the realization of the negative mold, to the positive mold, up to the trial prostheses necessary to arrive at the perfect customization of the final product). The final result depends on the skills and abilities of expert technicians [5]. The AM process could be particularly interesting for the production of prosthetic devices for sports (ESAR devices such as foot or foil) being characterized by reduced volumes, and functional properties (energy recovery capacity, rigidity, viscoelasticity) that must be designed in order to optimize performance according to the physical characteristics of the patient.

The aim of this work is to explore the potential of additive manufacturing in the field of prosthetics of the lower limb (foot and lamina for adaptive sport) through an holistic and multidisciplinary approach, involving several competences from the clinical evaluation of requisites and analysis of movement (comparing the behaviour of traditional and innovative prostheses), to integration of biomechanics, development of new composite and hybrid materials based on polymers, carbon fibers and metal inserts, definition of new hierarchical designing tools from material, to topography up to the prostheses, and implementation of optical sensors with their integration in the composites for the continuous monitoring of prosthetic devices and their durability (see Fig. 1).

This contribution, which is split into four parts according to the main pillars of the project, overviews the main hypothesis and the rationale with the preliminary results produced during the first year.

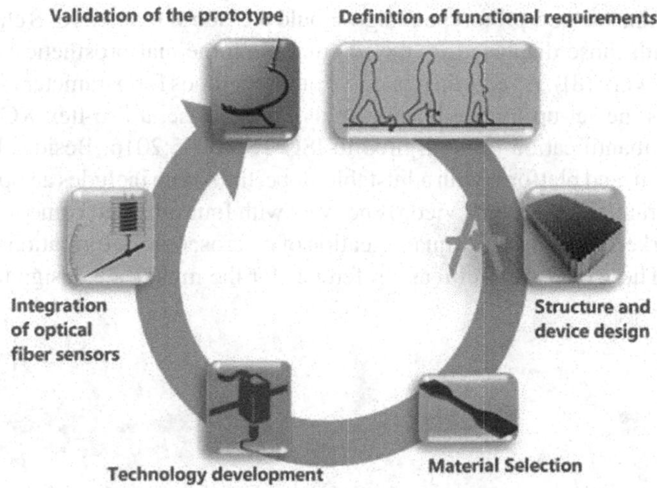

Fig. 1. Scheme of the project, which highlight the multidisciplinary of the methodological approach.

2 Definitions of Requisites and Biomechanic Analysis

The project investigates the feasibility by AM of sports foot prostheses with a general range of characteristics similar to commercial devices Pro-Flex XC (Össur) or Variflex (Össur). The target user is a young adult of 80 kg with unilateral trans-tibial amputation doing regular and intense physical exercise. Our prospective volunteer wears model Pro-Flex XC.

A list of basic requirements for further concept and prototype development has been chosen in accordance with evidence drawn from the technical (ISO 22675, ISO 10328, ISO 16955) and scientific literature [6, 7] and cross-checked with the independent opinions of 7 clinical experts from the extended working group. It includes functional parameters to be identified primarily via gait analysis (value and symmetry of step length, ground reaction force, speed, stance duration, knee flexion moment); technical parameters to be obtained from prototype loading trials (local stiffness and damping behaviour), biometric measurements (alignment of the loading axis and dorsiflexion angle) or estimated with mathematical models (roll-over shape: ROS); as well as material properties (elastic moduli, hysteresis), to be assessed through mechanical tests. The standard also include specifications for structural testing in view of medical device certification: these were considered but not conducted as a complete set during the design phase. We wish to verify that the obtained prototypes possess similar values for the parameters in this list, as the reference commercial prostheses. To illustrate the method, Fig. 2 shows preliminary 2D finite-element numerical simulations run on a starting-point design of the prosthesis, mimicking Variflex. Here, the model thickness was modified in order to study the ROS sensitivity to homogenous rigidity changes. Similarly, by introducing localised modulations in thickness, shell/core arrangement, and material properties, it is expected that the ROS can be adjusted and customised. We set as a requirement, that the new prototype design should provide simulated ROS characteristics consistent with those displayed by the reference commercial prosthetic feet (see also experimental work [8]). As a further example of the methods for parameter identification, Fig. 3 depicts the set-up for the loading trials. In this case, a Pro-flex XC (size 26) is subjected to quantification tests inspired to ISO/TS 16955:2016. Besides loading axis along the pylon, and platform with adjustable slope, the set-up includes an optoelectronic stereophotogrammetry system (Vicon) endowed with four infra-red cameras and passive reflective markers, which allows quantification of macroscopic deformations during load application. These data are useful as a reference for the multiscale design task.

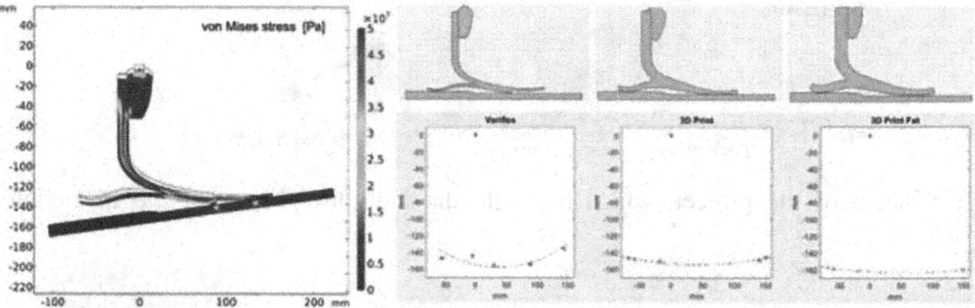

Fig. 2. Anisotropic 2D finite-element model for the prediction of roll-over shape (ROS). It highlights ROS curvature changes produced by variations in thickness (stiffness).

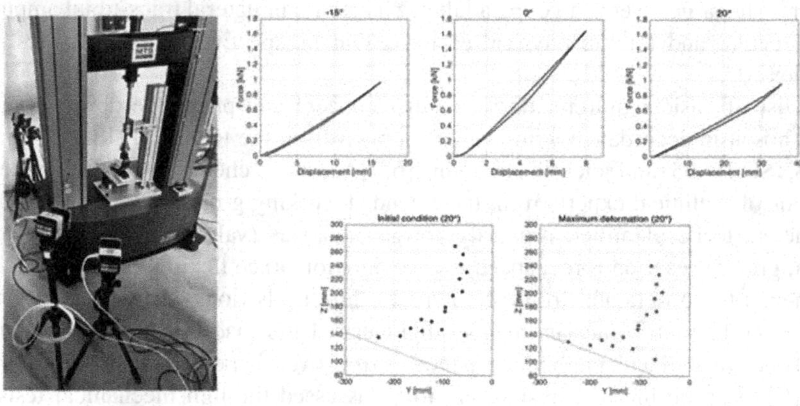

Fig. 3. Set-up for prosthesis testing. Top graphs display mechanical characteristics for different platform angles. The point clouds in the bottom graphs represent marker positions at the start and end of the loading phase.

3 Multiscale Designing: From Composite, to Structure up to the First Concept

The design of any structure or component requires, as input, the knowledge of its material properties and the capability of predicting them. Composite materials are heterogeneous and anisotropic materials, whose mechanical properties are dependent on several factors. The prediction of their mechanical properties is not trivial, and historically required the development of several mathematical theories. On the other hand, 3D printed structures often features distinct meso-structures, like the infill and the skins, each with its own features and properties. Each of these meso-structures requires dedicated material model to predict their contribution to the overall part mechanical performance. Predicting the material properties of 3D printed composite parts is a challenging task [4].

To tackle such task, numerical simulations adopting anisotropic material models and homogenised properties of core and skins. Classical Laminate Theory (CLT) was adopted to consider the anisotropic material properties, since 3D printed composites have a similar morphology to laminated ones [4].

Several modelling approaches, involving numerical simulations were thus performed to tackle this task. First, a commercially available prosthetic foot, namely an Össur Pro-Flex, was considered as reference. This prosthesis is made of carbon fibres laminate. The stiffnesses of this prosthesis at the three main phases of the walk (heel-strike, mid-stance and tow-off) were evaluated by Finite Element Analysis and set as constraints for the optimized 3D printed foot.

An FE beam model was then used for the optimization of the novel 3D printed prosthetic, after being validated against 3D shell models. This optimisation involved geometrical parameters like the thickness of the cross-section and portion of the skins and the geometrical details of the upper part of the prosthesis (shape, curvature, relative position to the constraint point).

Once a general design was obtained with the optimisation tool, a full 3D simulation was performed on the obtained geometry. This allowed the assessment of the stiffness and strength of the component to further validate the optimisation tool and improve and refine the design. The obtained prosthesis was thus 3D printed and tested. The experimental results could thus provide further validation to the adopted modelling approach and highlight potential necessary improvements.

4 Materials and Technologies for Additive Manufacturing

The AM of continuous fiber composites in thermoplastic material (possibly reinforced with other particles and short fibers), can represent a valid technological alternative for the realization of new prosthetic devices at low costs while maintaining the lightness, the properties dynamic – mechanical (energy recovery, stiffness, viscoelasticity) and durability (fatigue resistance) [9]. On the other side the selection of polymeric materials occurred with attention to the materials currently available for additive manufacturing (thermoplastics with short and continuous fibers) and laminated composites (thermoplastics). A commercial Nylon loaded with short carbon fibers was selected, and reinforced with continuous glass fibers or continuous carbon fibers. This material is particularly suitable for the realization, through 3D printing, of prosthetic components with adequate mechanical properties and durability [10]. The main feature of Nylon filled with Carbon is undoubtedly the excellent weight/stiffness ratio: the best-known properties of carbon, i.e. lightness and strength, blend with the mechanical and thermal properties of nylon (strength and durability) to create a material easily printable and extremely versatile. Carbon-filled nylon also has excellent sliding properties and is therefore less abrasive than nylon filled with short glass fiber. Carbon also confers superior thermal conductivity, which results in rapid dissipation of frictional heat, critical for sliding applications [11].

Using 3D printing technology together with fiber-reinforced polymer materials and continous carbon fibers, a first prototype of the prosthesis was printed. Mechanical characterizations for the comparison between the traditional prosthesis and the 3D printed prosthesis are currently in progress.

5 Development of Optical Fiber Sensors Integrated in Printed Composites/Structures

The proper functioning of a prosthetic device is of fundamental importance to ensure a long-lasting and effective sustain for the daily-life and athletic activities of the patient. The continuous monitoring of the prosthesis allows obtaining real-time diagnostic information, with the advantage of promptly detecting failures and their causes. The concept of durability can in fact be related to both prosthesis' mechanical resistance in terms of material strength and flexibility, but also, under a wider prospective, to the evolving clinical condition of the amputated limb that can cause discomfort during the prosthesis employment. In this scenario, AM offers the great opportunity of easily integrating sensors in printed structures, creating therefore "smart" devices that can be useful for researchers in the biomechanical field. Sensorized devices can help clinicians in identifying gait-related problematics and in taking corrective actions accordingly to each patient's needs [12]. Fiber Bragg Grating (FBG) sensors are a well-known and still spreading technology in the medical field [13]. As a fact, they are widely used for temperature [14], pressure, force and strain measurements [15] thanks to their biocompatibility, lightweight and miniaturized structure and for the possibility of multiplexing signals coming from different measurement points using a single glass fiber [16]. In particular, the use of FBGs for biomechanics and rehabilitation has gained interests in last decade [17]. Galvão et al. explored the possibility of exploiting FBGs for prostheses strain measurements considering a traditionally manufactured prosthesis through carbon fiber fabric lamination. At the best of our knowledge, still no attempt of using FBGs in 3D printed prosthetic devices has been concluded.

For the aim of this project, a series of bespoke experiments has been conducted in order to understand requisites for the FBGs to be employed as strain sensors in a 3D printed prosthetic limb. For what concerns the glass fiber, attention was posed to the choice of the coating material and to the coupling mode with the composite structure. Both polyamide and acrylate coating fibers have been tested in 3D printed samples having the same characteristic of the prototype. Fibers have been embedded in the samples during the AM process, and the ability of FBG of measuring the samples deformation has been evaluated using a tensile test machine. Samples have been tested under gradually incremented imposed strain in a quasi-static condition but also under dynamic load condition with imposed cyclic deformation in order to verify sensor response to dynamic excitation such as the one coming from sport activities with use of the prosthesis.

A study has also been conducted to understand the most effective positioning of FBGs with respect to the composite material, testing both embedded and on-surface solutions. The functional and mechanical evaluation of both solutions has been tested, and the on-surface application has been chosen in order to ensure an easy access to sensors in case of maintenance and substitution.

For what concerns the interrogator system, a lightweight portable device by Redondo Optics Inc has been selected [17]. The optical interrogator is able to detect up to 4 FBGs on 12 different channels. Moreover, the device has an integrated Wi-Fi module for real-time data transfer and therefore does not require any cable for data acquisition.

The possibility of integrating the acquired signals in an Artificial Intelligence Neural Network (ANN) is presently under investigation. The aim is creating a system able to extract relevant features from optical signals and to derive useful gait parameters, such as gait symmetry or body oscillation in the medio-lateral plane. As a preliminary simulation, pending the first sensorized prototype, signals have been acquired with notch accelerometers positioned on a subject hip and foot and walking on a treadmill. The final goal is that of trying to correlate features coming from different body parts, and to train the ANN to work with foot signals and to derive from them all missing parameters of interest. This analysis would help clinicians in the diagnostic of gait problematics and in the interpretation of complex strain signals not related to gait parameters in an immediately understandable way.

Acknowledgements. The authors are grateful to Centro Protesi INAIL for supporting this study through the PROFIL Project (FILamenti multimateriali per la realizzazione di PROtesi personalizzate ad alte prestazioni con focus su adaptive sport).

References

1. Roland, K., Jin, Y., Wensman, J., Shih, A.: Additive manufacturing of custom orthoses and prostheses-a review. Addit. Manuf. Part A **12**, 77–89 (2016)
2. Vahid, M., Bakhsheshi-Rad, H.R., Ramakrishna, S., Razzaghi, M., Berto, F.: A brief review on additive manufacturing of polymeric composites and nanocomposites. Micromachines **12**(6), 704–728 (2021)
3. Rochlitz, B., Pammer. D.: Design and analysis of 3D printable foot prosthesis. Period. Polytech. Mech. Eng. **61**(4), 282–287 (2017)
4. Melenka, G.W., Cheung, B.K.O., Schofield, J.S., Dawson, M.R., Carey, J.P.: Evaluation and prediction of the tensile properties of continuous fiber-reinforced 3D printed structures. Compos. Struct. **153**, 866–875 (2016)
5. BHAT. Sandesh Ganapati. Design and Development of a Passive Prosthetic Ankle. Arizona State University (2017)
6. Hansen, A., Starker, F.: Prosthetic foot principles and their influence on gait. In: Handbook of Human Motion, pp. 1343–1357. Springer, Cham (2018). https://doi.org/10.1007/978-3-319-14418-4_74

7. Sagawa, Y., Jr., Turcot, K., Armand, S., Thevenon, A., Vuillerme, N., Watelain, E.: Biomechanics and physiological parameters during gait in lower-limb amputees: a systematic review. Gait Posture **33**(4), 511–526 (2011)
8. Curtze, C., Hof, A.L., van Keeken, H.G., Halbertsma, J.P.K., Postema, K., Otten, B.: Comparative roll- over analysis of prosthetic feet. J. Biomech. **42**, 1746–1753 (2009)
9. Chacón, J.M., Caminero, M.A., Núñez, P.J., García-Plaza, E., García-Moreno, I., Reverte, J.M.: Additive manufacturing of continuous fibre reinforced thermoplastic composites using fused deposition modelling: effect of process parameters on mechanical properties. Compos. Sci. Technol. **181**, 107688 (2019)
10. Tavangarian, F., Proano, C.: The need to fabricate lower limb prosthetic devices by additive manufacturing. Biomed. J. Sci. Tech. Res.| BJSTR. MS.ID.002772
11. Matsuzaki, R., et al.: Three-dimensional printing of continuous-fiber composites by in-nozzle impregnation. Sci. Rep. **6**, 23058 (2016)
12. Chadwell, A., et al.: Technology for monitoring everyday prosthesis use: a systematic review. J. NeuroEng. Rehabil. **17**(1) (2020). BioMed Central. https://doi.org/10.1186/s12984-020-00711-4
13. Ochoa, M., Algorri, J.F., Roldán-Varona, P., Rodríguez-Cobo, L., López-Higuera, J.M.: Recent advances in biomedical photonic sensors: a focus on optical-fibre-based sensing. Sensors **21**, 6469 (2021). https://doi.org/10.3390/s21196469
14. Bianchi, L., Korganbayev, S., Orrico, A., De Landro, M., Saccomandi, P.: Quasi-distributed fiber optic sensor-based control system for interstitial laser ablation of tissue: theoretical and experimental investigations. Biomed. Opt. Exp. **12**(5), 2841–2858 (2021)
15. Paloschi, D., Bronnikov, K.A., Korganbayev, S., Wolf, A.A., Dostovalov, A., Saccomandi, P.: 3D shape sensing with multicore optical fibers: transformation matrices versus Frenet-Serret equations for real-time application. IEEE Sens. J. **21**(4), 4599–4609 (2020)
16. Correia, R., James, S., Lee, S.W., Morgan, S.P., Korposh, S.: Biomedical application of optical fibre sensors. J. Opt. **20**(7), 073003 (2018). https://doi.org/10.1088/2040-8986/AAC68D
17. Mendoza, E.A., Esterkin, Y., Andreas, T.: Low Power, Low Cost, Lightweight, Multichannel Optical Fiber Interrogation System for Structural Health Management of Rotor Blades (2019)

Mechanical Arm for Soft Exoskeleton Testing

Mario Covarrubias Rodriguez[3(✉)], Ignacio Amui[3], Youssef Beik[3], Gabriele Gambirasio[3], Marta Gandolla[1,2], Elena Bardi[2], and Emilia Ambrosini[1,2]

[1] NearLab, Department of Electronics, Information and Bioengineering, Politecnico di Milano, 20133 Milan, Italy
[2] Department of Mechanical Engineering, Politecnico di Milano, 20156 Milan, Italy
[3] Virtual Prototyping and Augmented Reality Lab, Department of Mechanical Engineering, Lecco Campus, Politecnico di Milano, Milan, Italy
mario.covarrubias@polimi.it

Abstract. Soft robotic exoskeletons offer multiple advantages in the field of motor rehabilitation and assistance with activities of daily living This paper reports the design process of a mechanical arm for upper-limb soft exoskeleton testing. The main requirement of the test bench was to simulate five degrees of freedom (DOF) of the human arm, and in particular i) shoulder flexion/extension, ii) shoulder adduction/abduction, iii) shoulder medial rotation/lateral rotation, iv) elbow flexion/extension and v) forearm supination/pronation. An additional requirement included the possibility to alternatively lock each DOF. The final concept was designed using Autodesk Inventor and it is composed of 32 parts, 18 of which were particularly designed for this application. Topological optimisation and Finite Element Method (FEM) analysis were performed to some custom components to obtain the final design. The final concept was manufactured by means of additive manufacturing of PLA (polylactic acid) and laser cutting of PMMA (poly methyl methacrylate) sheets. After testing and validation, the prototype was able to meet the desired requirements and it can be used for soft-exoskeleton testing.

Keywords: Motor rehabilitation · Exoskeleton · Industrial sector · Upper limb · User feedback

1 Introduction

Robotic exoskeletons have been increasingly studied in the field of biomedical engineering [1]. These devices can be used for the rehabilitation and assistance of people affected by motor impairment as a consequence of neurological or neuro muscular disorders. Soft exoskeletons, also referred to as exosuits, offer the possibility to assist the user when performing physical tasks and simultaneously guarantee enough flexibility and comfort by adjusting to the wearer's body, making them good candidates to assist the wearer with daily activities [2].

K. Miesenberger et al. (Eds.): ICCHP-AAATE 2022, LNCS 13342, pp. 387–394, 2022.
https://doi.org/10.1007/978-3-031-08645-8_45

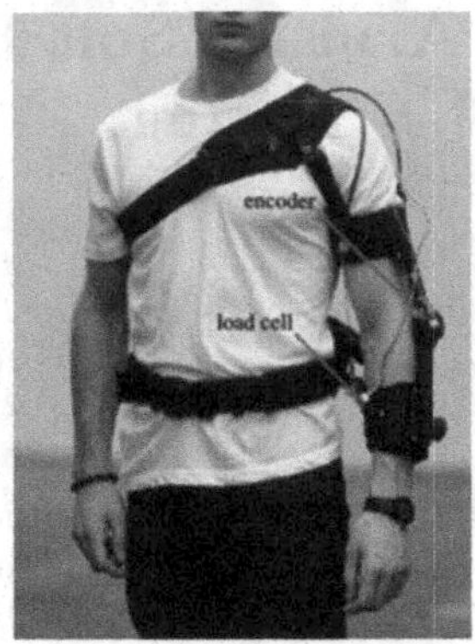

Fig. 1. Example of upper-limb assistance exoskeleton. [4]

Among the possible types of actuators that can be used with exosuits, electric motors which employ cable driven transmission seem to be the most promising in terms of ease of control. An example of a cable-driven exosuit for upper-limb assistance was developed by [3,4] and is shown in Fig. 1.

Although exosuits are a promising technology in the field of assistive devices, they are still in a preliminary development phase and few degrees of freedom (DOFs) are actuated simultaneously, mainly to preserve portability, which is a key feature. We believe that more effort should be put in optimizing the cable routing and understanding the effect of the actuation on non-targeted joints.

Indeed, the development of these assisting devices requires a deep understanding of bio-mechanics and anatomy. To create a high-performance exoskeleton, an extensive design process must be carefully followed. It is important to consider factors such as safety, comfort and most importantly optimization of the forces, which should accurately adjust to the biological moments created at the arm joints level. The testing procedure is an essential part of the design process and thus requires high-quality testing components that can replicate the final operation of the device. The aim of this project is to design a test-bench for the testing of a upper limb assistive soft exoskeleton.

The mechanism initially used for testing is shown in Fig. 2-a. and lacks features which are essential to perform accurate measurements and to test the device for different arm configurations. The test-bench is composed of a two degree-of-freedom metallic arm with a couple of anchor points to which a string is attached, as shown in Fig. 2-b. The string is connected to a motor which drives one of the two DOFs, e.g. shoulder flexion or elbow flexion.

Project Proposal and Requirements. The proposal for the improved test-bench was based on multiple requirements and criteria. The foremost criterion was the resemblance from a kinematic point of view of the mechanism to that of an actual human arm, in terms of both degrees of freedom and dimensional parameters. The dimension of the final device was based on the statistical data published by [5] on the human upper extremity dimensions. Considering the

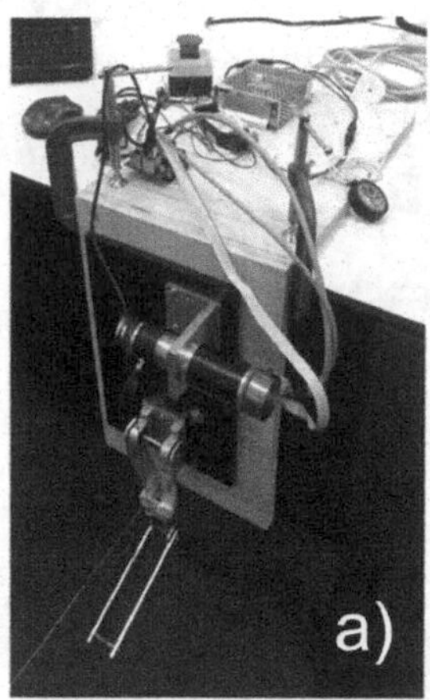

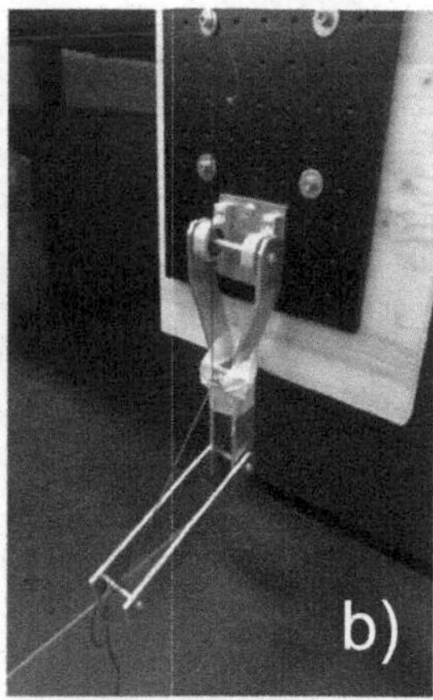

Fig. 2. First prototype of the mechanical arm.

male mean values of the lengths of the arm and the forearm, an approximated ratio of 1.25:1 was estimated between these two parts of the arm. Therefore, the final design dimensions were set to stay close to this ratio.

The human arm is composed of 7 DOFs nonetheless two of them are for positioning of the hand (i.e., end-effector) - wrist flexion/extension and the wrist abduction/adduction - which are out of scope when designing a device to assist upper limb movements. Therefore for this project, we have considered as requirement the 5 DOFs associated to the development of the upper-limb exoskeletons.

Therefore, the degrees of freedom required for this application are:

- Shoulder flexion/extension
- Shoulder adduction/abduction
- Shoulder medial rotation/lateral rotation
- Elbow flexion/extension
- Forearm supination/pronation

An additional requirement was the possibility for the user to lock certain degrees of freedom at a certain angle, to test the device at different configurations. This requirement applied only to the shoulder adduction/abduction, the shoulder medial rotation/lateral rotation and the forearm supination/pronation. With the aim of allowing the user to perform analyses for different cable-routing designs, the user should be able to move the anchor points to different locations of the arm. Being the string tension controlled by the DC motor, the different locations of the anchor point permit the study of the forces needed to move certain degrees of freedom when the string is attached to different parts of the arm. Therefore, this requirement was of utmost importance for the purpose of this research. The initial model has the DC motor and the mechanical arm placed on the same plane which is perpendicular to the working table. The requirement was to move the location of the motor to the upper part of the base, on the plane

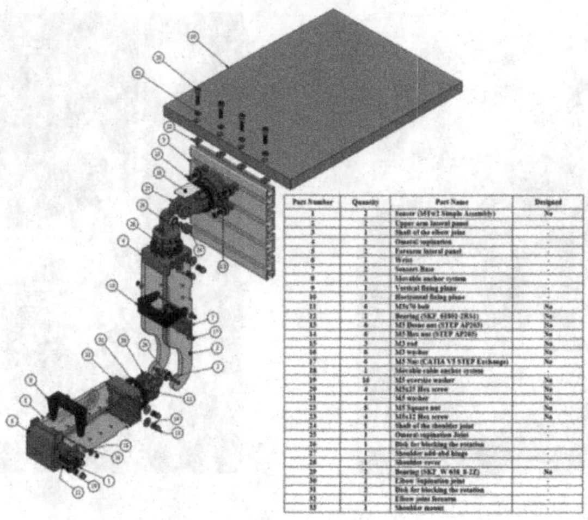

Part Number	Quantity	Part Name	Designed
1	2	Sensor (MTw2 Simple Assembly)	No
2	2	Upper arm lateral panel	-
3	1	Shaft of the elbow joint	-
4	1	Omeral supination	-
5	2	Forearm lateral panel	-
6	1	Wrist	-
7	2	Sensors Base	-
8	1	Movable anchor system	-
9	1	Vertical fixing plane	-
10	1	Horizontal fixing plane	-
11	4	M5x70 bolt	No
12	1	Bearing (SKF_61802-2RS1)	No
13	6	M5 Dome nut (STEP AP203)	No
14	6	M5 Hex nut (STEP AP203)	No
15	3	M3 rod	No
16	8	M3 washer	No
17	6	M5 Nut (CATIA V5 STEP Exchange)	No
18	1	Movable cable anchor system	-
19	10	M5 oversize washer	No
20	4	M5x25 Hex screw	No
21	4	M5 washer	No
22	3	M5 Square nut	No
23	4	M5x12 Hex screw	No
24	1	Shaft of the shoulder joint	-
25	1	Omeral supination Joint	-
26	1	Disk for blocking the rotation	-
27	1	Shoulder add-abd hinge	-
28	1	Shoulder cover	-
29	2	Bearing (SKF_W 618_8-2Z)	No
30	1	Elbow Supination joint	-
31	2	Disk for blocking the rotation	-
32	1	Elbow joint forearm	-
33	1	Shoulder mount	-

Fig. 3. Assembly and Bill of Materials

parallel to the working table. This was required as to resemble more accurately the final application of the soft exoskeleton which would have the motor placed distally with respect to the arm of the user (e.g., on the back). In this way is possible to correctly study what the behaviour of the string would be in the real application. Moreover, the attachment of the motor to the base should allow to change the position of the motor if required by the researcher.

For the purpose of measuring the orientation, acceleration and angular velocity of the arm, an inertial measurement unit (IMU) must be mounted on both the arm and the forearm.

The sensors to be used are the MTw series manufactured by Xsens Technologies B.V. which offer a wireless configuration. The locations of the sensors were specified by the user later in the design process, based on the digital model created. Lastly, to simulate the effect of the weight when a person grabs certain objects, the arm should allow the attachment of weights no heavier than 3 kg at the end of the forearm, where the wrist is located.

Digital Mock Up. The starting point of the project was focused on designing the mechanical arm using Autodesk Inventor software, which has high flexibility in terms of simulating the required degrees of freedom and FEM analysis, including static and dynamic behaviour of the model under certain conditions. As shown below, the final model of the mechanical arm is composed of 33 different parts highlighted by the balloons and named in the Fig. 3. The total mass of the physical model of the mechanical arm was 0.82 kg excluding the horizontal and vertical fixing plane.

There are 14 components which are excluded from design part as they were available in the Inventor library. However, the remaining 19 parts were designed to meet project requirements introduced in the previous section of this paper.

2 Topological Optimization

The digital model of the mechanical arm underwent various physical modifications throughout the design process. Most of these modifications had as objective the reduction of weight and consequently the optimization of material and production time (since components have been realized through additive manufacturing). The optimization process was performed in Autodesk Inventor by using the Shape Generator command. The topological optimization, summarized in Fig. 4, relies on the inputs given to the software related to boundary conditions, applied forces and pressures, areas to be preserved, symmetry planes and volume percentage reduction desired. After correctly setting the inputs, the software generated a model with recommended modifications to achieve the reduction in volume.

Fig. 4. Topological optimization

From the first draft until the final concept, some components particularly related to the joints had their shapes and thus weight reduced by a significant percent. In contrast, other components such as the lateral panels did not undergo a significant topological optimization as to maintain the structural stability and weight distributed along the structure. In addition, as the production will be done by additive manufacturing, the components will have a rectilinear infill pattern of 20%, already reducing the weight by a significant amount. The removal of material was done mainly in areas where the stresses were significantly low, and the accumulation of material was unnecessary. The failure condition was set to yield strength of the material. The material used for the creation of the parts was polylactic acid (PLA), however, as Autodesk Inventor does not contain this material in its default libraries, acrylonitrile butadiene styrene (ABS) was used for the simulations. Both materials have similar mechanical and physical properties, which is why it was considered as the most suitable solution.

3 Numerical Model Validation

Given the list of requirements, the mechanical arm should withstand a maximum load of approximately 3 kg, corresponding for example, to double the weight of a water bottle held by a human arm. Therefore, it was essential to perform a structural analysis to study the response of the mechanical arm when an external force is applied. Static stress analysis is a type of structural analysis that can be effectively carried out by means of a finite element model. This analysis is a common procedure in mechanical design to investigate stress, strain, and ensure that failure is avoided during the operation. Inventor software provides a practical tool for such analysis, which was used to conduct some stress inspection. In order to have more accurate results and reduce the computational time, only the components which were considered to be critically loaded were analysed. These components were the wrist and the elbows shaft shown in Fig. 5-a.

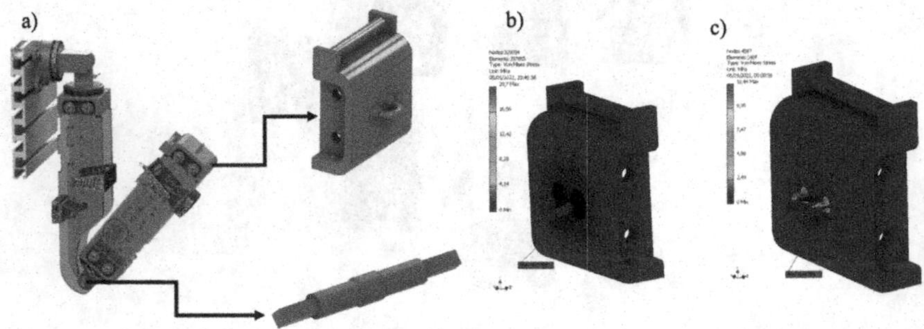

Fig. 5. FEM analysis.

Polylactide (PLA) was used as material for 3D printing the component mentioned for the stress analysis. For the stress analysis it was required by Inventor software to choose the material properties, including the mechanical thermal and strength of the PLA. However, this material was not defined in the inventor library. Therefore, a new material was created and added to the library of Inventor, considering [6] as reference the material properties are shown in Fig. 5-b and 5-c.

4 Results and Validation

The validation of the mechanical arm was based the following steps:

1. Testing of the required DOFs on the physical model, as well as evaluating the correct operation of the locking system. The system showed a correct operation, thus this point was confirmed.
2. Applying a static load on the wrist corresponding to 3 kg of mass in order to check if the FEM static analysis performed in Inventor was valid.

The first condition was studied by fixing the test bench on a table and connecting the wrist to the anchor bases at the forearm and the upper arm by means of the string. By pulling the string, it was possible to analyse the motion of the arm. The second condition was validated by attaching a load equivalent to 3 kg and observing the deflection behaviour of the most critical components. The physical model was able to withstand the load applied considering the initial boundary conditions.

5 Conclusions and Future Work

The 5 °C of freedom required for the test bench to represent the behavior of the real arm were implemented successfully. The implemented setup gives the possibility to lock each DOF at any position. Although, the locking system could be slightly improved by updating the interference between the locking disk and the Omeral Supination which guarantee that the locking disk will not have any displacement while the arm is moving. The FEM analysis demonstrates that the mechanical arm will not fail under static load considering with a load applied of 30N with having the possibility to increase the load but should consider that the safety factor is 3.38 when 3 kg load is added. However, further analysis could be implemented, such as dynamic analysis. A further improvement can be applied by studying a different coupling in the joints for Omeral and Forearm Supination: by changing the design of the joints it is possible to increase the resistance under static load. Right now the joints are kept together through shrink fit of its elements; exploiting the employment of Seiger disks (as happened in the Arm Adduction/Abduction joint) we can increase the maximum axial load that can be bothered by the joint, increasing the safety coefficient. 3D printing technology using PLA material demonstrated to be promising technology for additive manufacturing, in this project it exhibited a high precision and high strength to weight ratio. Therefore, it can be used in many fields. However, the employment of different additive manufacturing techniques (like selective laser sintering) can help in obtaining a denser material and a higher dimensional precision, providing great improvements both in the mechanical resistance and in the working principle (in particular for the locking system).

References

1. Gassert, R., Dietz, V.: Rehabilitation robots for the treatment of sensorimotor deficits: a neu-rophysiological perspective. Neuroeng. Rehabil **15**(1), 1–15 (2018). https://doi.org/10.1186/s12984-018-0383-x
2. Thalman, C., Artemiadis, P.: A review of soft wearable robots that provide active assistance: trends, common actuation methods, fabrication, and applications. Wearab. Technol. **1**, e3 (2020). https://doi.org/10.1017/wtc.2020.4
3. Wang, Z., Cai, Z., Cui, L., Pang, C.: Structure design and analysis of kinematics of an upper-limbed rehabilitation robot. MATEC Web Conf. **232**, 02033 (2018). https://doi.org/10.1051/matecconf/201823202033

4. Xiloyannis, M., Chiaradia, D., Frisoli, A., Masia, L.: Physiological and kinematic effects of a soft exosuit on arm movements. J.NeuroEng. Rehabilit. **16** (2019). https://doi.org/10.1186/s12984-019-0495-y
5. ñzaslan, A., Koß, S., ñzaslan, Tufücu, H.: Estimation of stature from upper extremity. Military Med. **171**(4), 288–291 (2006). https://doi.org/10.7205/MILMED.171.4.288
6. Farah, S., Anderson, D.G., Langer, R.: Physical and mechanical properties of pla, and their functions in widespread applications-a comprehensive review. Adv. Drug Deliv. Rev. **107**, 367–392 (2016)

Hybrid Manufacturing of Upper-Limb Prosthesis Sockets with Improved Material Properties

Simone Pittaccio[1(✉)], Marino Lavorgna[2], Jacopo Romanò[1,3], Andrea Sorrentino[2], Pierfrancesco Cerruti[2], Gennaro Rollo[2], Chiara Ascione[2], Maria Grazia Raucci[2], Alessandra Soriente[2], Viviana Casaleggi[4], Lorenzo Garavaglia[1], Fabio Lazzari[1,3], Rosa Zullo[2], Angelo Davalli[4], and Emanuele Gruppioni[4]

[1] CNR-ICMATE, Lecco, Italy
simone.pittaccio@cnr.it
[2] CNR-IPCB, Lecco, Italy
[3] Politecnico di Milano - CMIC, Milan, Italy
[4] Centro Protesi Inail, Centro Protesi, Vigorso di Budrio, Italy

Abstract. This paper describes the design and manufacturing process of an advanced socket for upper limb prostheses. This device uses synergies between smart materials such as phase change materials (PCM), reduced graphene oxide (rGO) and a 3D printed metastructure to improve ergonomics and thermal comfort. Virtual prototyping was combined with traditional fabrication techniques to obtain a biocompatible, user centered device, whose main advantage is an improved thermal behavior. Besides feasibility and biocompatibility tests, the paper describes the results of a preliminary trial involving a volunteer with upper limb amputation. It was observed that the use of an inner metastructure provides basic mechanical stability and improves resin flowability. The combination of PCM and rGO delay the increase in inner socket temperature during physical exercise on a treadmill, which induced a feeling of freshness and dryness and improved the comfort for the user. These findings, despite their preliminary nature, suggest that advanced modifications of the materials and technologies involved in the production of prosthetic sockets are able to generate appreciable benefits in terms of usability.

Keywords: 3D printing · Prosthesis comfort · Graphene

1 Introduction

Prostheses play a substantial role in supporting the social and work reintegration of people who have undergone an upper-limb amputation, however excessive weight or an unnatural feel of those devices may often limit their comfort and acceptability [1] therefore there is a basic interest in improving their characteristics and function. The socket is a critical interface between the user's (natural) stump and the prosthetic (artificial) device, so it ought to possess appropriate load transmission ability, stability and control,

K. Miesenberger et al. (Eds.): ICCHP-AAATE 2022, LNCS 13342, pp. 395–402, 2022.
https://doi.org/10.1007/978-3-031-08645-8_46

alongside efficient fitting characteristics [3]. Several patents tackled the improvement of comfort, and temperature control (cooling) [4].

The present paper is principally focussed on the re-design of the inner socket, an important element of the system directly involved in the interfacial transfer of external loads to the limb stump, and in regulating the heat exchanges between the skin surface and the environment.

To aid in the re-design of the inner socket, additive manufacturing techniques were integrated in the traditional fabrication process, in order to allow a more versatile design approach and favour multi-material integration. The function of these materials should not just be to provide structural stability and load bearing, but also to address the thermoregulation of the stump. Phase-change materials (PCMs), which consist of alkane waxes often embedded in polymeric shells, absorb large amount of heat from the environment as the solid-to-liquid phase transition takes place [5–7]. In the present context, PCMs can be incorporated into innovative prostheses and may contribute to optimise the heat transfer from the limb to the outside environment [8]. Recent studies also demonstrate that the use of graphene can improve electrical conductivity, thermal stability and mechanical properties in the production of multi-functional textiles [9–11]. Graphene is an excellent thermal conductor with a large specific surface area, especially when it is in form of reduced graphene oxide (rGO) [12].

The objective of this study is to propose a combined solution for reducing weight and improving the thermal behaviour of the socket, with expected improvements in overall users' comfort. The principal approach adopted for the study relies on the selection and application of innovative materials. In addition to the modification of the acrylic resin with PCMs and rGO, the creation of a 3D-printed metastructure to reinforce and lighten the socket structure is included. The present solution, with some modifications can be integrated with a smart-textile liner with EMG sensing capability [7].

2 Design Concept

Aiming to reconcile rather binding requirements on socket shape with the desire to improve lightness and comfort, the concept design includes:

- strict geometrical reference to a professionally-stylised stump replica;
- re-definition of the composite materials, using an additively-manufactured metastructure to reinforce the resin and facilitate its lamination;
- improvement of the thermal properties of the resin by addition of phase change materials (PCM);
- improvement of the thermal properties of the knit sleeves (reinforcing fabrics) by adsorption of reduced graphene oxide (rGO);

The co-lamination of the metastructure, modified reinforcing fabrics and modified resin is expected to provide a socket with adequate mechanical properties, longer heating times and lower weight.

3 Materials and Methods

3.1 Virtual Prototyping of the Socket and Topological Considerations

The surface of the stylised stump replica was digitalised using a structured-light 3D scanner (Artec EVA, Artec3D). A triangulated mesh was reconstructed (Artec Studio 13, Artec3D), simplified, and then imported into Rhinoceros 5 (McNeel) with Grasshopper, by which the socket design process was implemented. A semi-automated routine was developed, able to create a trabecular metastructure (named '*Hypermat*') for the socket. The topological features in the metastructure are imparted using a Voronoi tessellation, which originates from a distribution of points on the anatomical surface, and can be controlled at user-interface level in the Grasshopper routine. In particular, the operator can modify: the number and density of the cells, resulting in trabeculae of variable thickness in different regions of the socket; the principal orientation paths, along which the cells are distributed in the axial and circumferential directions of the forearm; the insertion of regions with a pre-established shape (such as apertures for the EMG sensors), which determine an organic adaptation of the tessellation pattern, so that they can be coherently included within the metastructure; other global parameters such as the overall thickness of the structure.

Preliminary FEM simulations under Comsol Multiphysics 5.5 (COMSOL Inc.) were run to optimise topological features (Fig. 1 - Left). In particular, utilising a constant thickness for the trabeculae may cause plastic strain concentration due to a lack of material in regions with large cells. This problem appears to be minimised if the thickness of the trabeculae is made proportional to the cell size. Early transition to plastic behaviour was also observed around triangular cells, which were therefore avoided in the following tests.

By modifying the cell orientation paths, it is possible to obtain different metastructures with varying degrees of anisotropy and provide distinctive structural/functional contexts for regions of the stump with specific characteristics (Fig. 1 – Right).

3.2 Additive Manufacturing

The *Hypermat* metastructure was produced in two half-shells using fused-filament deposition of ABSplus (Dimension Elite, Stratasys). The shells were built with a printing layer thickness of 0.15 mm and 100% filling. The building direction was perpendicular to the stump axis, close to the radio-ulnar direction. After printing, the support material was removed from the shells; the metastructure was then exposed for 45 min to a controlled atmosphere with high saturation of acetone vapours, to obtain a smooth finish.

3.3 Modification of the Lamination Resin and Reinforcing Fabrics

The thermal properties of a common resin (acrylic resin: Laminhartz, Acrylhartz and catalist, purchased by Otto Bock, Germany) were modified by using a selected mixture of phase change microcapsules (purchased from Microtek Lab) characterized by phase transition temperatures compatible with the management of heat released by human

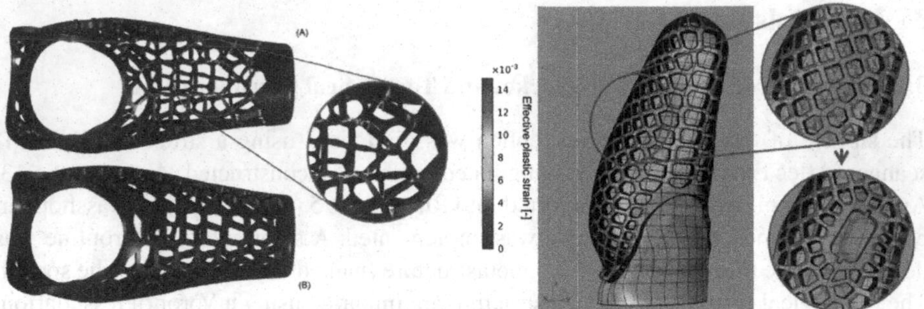

Fig. 1. *Left*. Results of preliminary FEM simulations. Plastic strain field for a velar-dorsal load of 25N on the distal end. The models were implemented as Voronoi-tassellated metastructures with trabeculae of constant thickness (A) and with thicknesses proportional to the cell size (B). Notice that in (A) strain concentration occurred particularly around cells with triangular morphology (detail), which were avoided in (B). *Right*. Example of *Hypermat* metastructure with anisotropic cell distribution. It is possible to observe principal orientation paths in the axial and circumferential directions, as well as the metastructure adapted for the insertion of fixed-shaped EMG sensors.

body. Acrylic resin was added with 40wt% of PCMs and mixed by hand up to get a homogeneous dispersion.

The Perlon® fabric (Perlon Elastic Stockinette white, 6 cm of diameter, purchased by Ottobock, Germany), which is based on nylon fibres and is commonly used for the lamination of acrylic-based composites for traditional upper limb prosthesis sockets, was modified by depositing on its yarns a continuous layer of rGO. In detail, the graphene-modified fabric was prepared by chemically reducing the Graphene Oxide powder (produced by Hummers' method according to the procedure previously adopted by some of the authors [13]) with L-ascorbic acid in presence of the tubular fabric. After this process, the Perlon fabric, which is initially white, becomes completely dark grey, due to the presence of the rGO layer homogeneously deposited on the nylon fibres.

3.4 Biocompatibility Studies: Indirect and Direct Tests

The biocompatibility of standard and new laminates was tested according to ISO 10993-5 and 10993-12. The elution test (cytotoxic indirect assay) was performed by adding 1.0 mL of sterile and complete DMEM solution (extraction vehicle) to 0.2 g of material at 37 °C according to ISO 10993-5/10993-12 guidelines. After 72 h of elution time, the conditioned media (eluants) were removed and 500 μL were pipetted into a 48-well plate previously seeded with murine fibroblasts L929 at 80% of confluence, and incubated for further 24 h (exposure time). Alamar blue assay (AbD Serotec, Milan, Italy) was used to evaluate the cell vitality according to the manufacturer's instructions. Absorbance was measured at wavelengths 540 and 600 nm by using a UV-Vis spectrophotometer (Victor X3, Perkin Elmer).

3.5 Co-lamination of the Socket

The co-lamination procedure was carried out by an orthopaedic technician expert in the conventional socket lamination technique. The modified process includes layering of one Perlon fabric modified with rGO, the two half-shells of the *Hypermat* metastructure, a second Nylon/Perlon fabric without rGO, followed by perfusion under vacuum with acrylic resin with 40% PCM and suitable solvents to control the viscosity (acetone). Once curing is complete, the socket shell is dismounted from the stump replica and is finished by hand.

3.6 Preliminary Performance Tests with a Volunteer

One individual (male, 65 years old) with a right trans-radial amputation volunteered for the current study. The volunteer was a long-time user of traditional and innovative upper-limb prosthetics. After signing informed consent for the procedures connected with the research, he made himself available for acquisition of the stump geometry by a trained orthopaedic technician, and participation in the tests to evaluate the performance of the new prosthesis socket.

Three thermocouples (TC1, TC2 and TC3) have been employed to measure temperature: TC1 on the medial aspect of the stump (wrist flexors); TC2 on the lateral aspect of the stump (wrist extensors); TC3 away from the body, to monitor the room temperature. The test protocol included three successive evaluation periods, each lasting ca. 30 min:

Rest 1: Wearing the prosthesis at rest;
Treadmill: Wearing prosthesis during fast walking on a treadmill;
Rest 2: Wearing the prosthesis at rest.

At the end of each period, the temperature of the contralateral limb was checked with the subject at rest. After the test, the volunteer was interviewed about his experience with the device.

The same protocol was repeated with the volunteer's own traditional device. In both cases, during the tests the inner socket was covered by the same outer socket (traditional material).

4 Results

4.1 Cytotoxicity: Indirect and Direct Tests

The quantitative results of the indirect contact assay after 24 h of exposure time (elution time: 72 h) on L929 cells are reported in Fig. 2 - *Left*. The innovative materials (reported in the figure as new) produce no negative effect on L929 cell vitality, with respect to the control (cells at contact with no-conditioned medium) Light microscopy results reported in Fig. 2 – *Right* support the same outcome in terms of cell viability for traditional and new materials, compared to control plate.

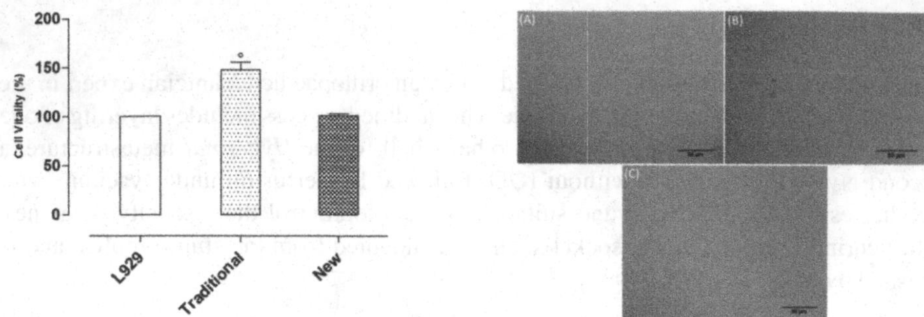

Fig. 2. *Left.* Cell vitality: Elution studies (indirect assay) performed using L929 cell line. Effect of eluants (72 h of elution time) from traditional and new laminates on cell vitality after 24 h of exposure time. Data are expressed as Cell vitality (%) normalized to plate control (L929). Results are mean ± standard error of the mean (SEM) of 3–4 experiments. $p < 0.001$ vs L929. *Right.* Optical microscopy images of L929 for traditional (B) and new based-materials (C) conditioned media compared to control L929 (A) after 72 h of elution time and 24 h of exposure time. Scale bar = 80 μm.

4.2 Prosthesis Socket Prototypes

A first prototype of the prosthesis socket (Fig. 3) has been manufactured. The geometry was obtained from the stylised gypsum cast of a right upper-limb with trans-radial amputation. The modified resin, albeit more viscous than the basic formulation, flowed well during the lamination procedure. The presence of the *Hypermat* appeared to facilitate uniform spreading of the resin, by breaking the fluid mass and holding parts of it in the cells while the rest of it got progressively pushed forward.

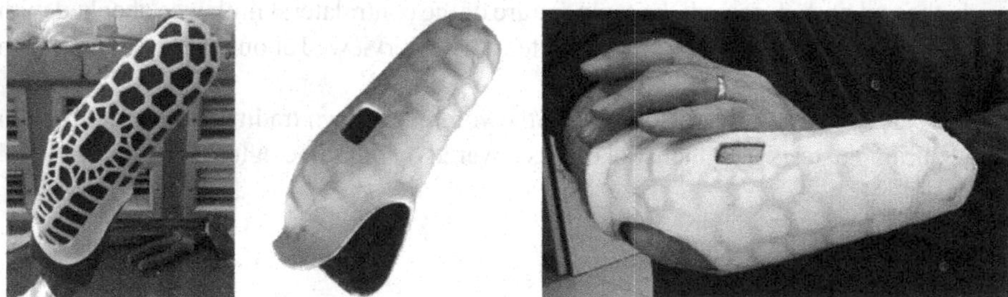

Fig. 3. *Left*: *Hypermat* metastructure just before the lamination process. The black knit sleeve of Nylon/Perlon modified with rGO is visible. *Middle*: *Hypermat* metastructure embedded in the resin modified with PCM after the lamination process. Right: Volunteer wearing the prototype of the prosthesis socket. The socket weighed 165 g.

The reduction in shear stress possibly also depended on the rather sparing use of knit sleeves (only 5 rather than the usual 6 or 8), whose reinforcing action was partially taken over by the solid metastructure. The final overall mass of the socket was 165 g.

4.3 Preliminary Performance Tests with a Volunteer

The test was conducted in order to follow the temperature evolution at the interface between the stump and prosthesis under different physical conditions (rest and fast walking on treadmill). The temperature was recoded with a multichannel thermometer, which simultaneously acquired temperature signals from 3 thermocouples (Fig. 4). It appears that during the Treadmill phase the temperature curves for the socket fabricated with the modified resin have a lower slope than those for the traditional socket. Moreover, it can be observed that the temperature crossed the 32 °C (discomfort) threshold earlier with the traditional socket. This happened although in the modified socket test the temperature of the contralateral limb rose 5 °C warmer (35 °C vs. 30 °C) after the Treadmill phase than in the traditional socket test (likely due to an incidentally higher movement intensity/exertion). Finally, the feelings verbally expressed by the patient upon doffing the prosthesis fabricated with the modified resin, which was of dryness and freshness. An immediate and direct measure of the limb temperature at this point indicated 30 °C.

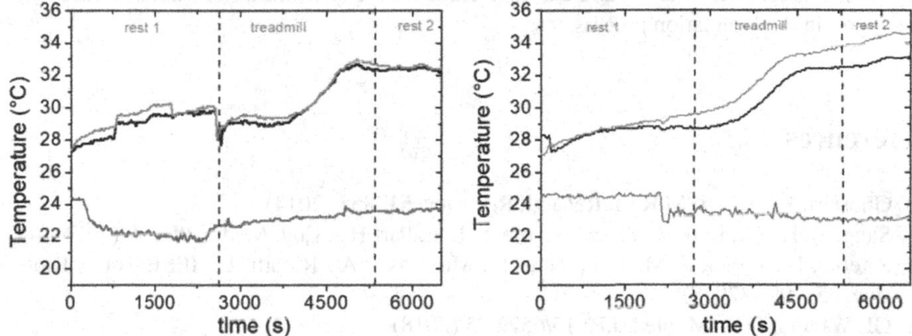

Fig. 4. Results of temperature monitoring referred to TC1 (black), TC2 (red) and TC3 (gray) of the socket produced with traditional (*left*) and modified (*right*) laminates. (Color figure online)

5 Discussion and Conclusions

The present prototype of socket with modified materials is proposed as a new concept in upper-limb prosthesis design. The study suggests that the introduction of new materials and fabrication technologies like additive, could improve aspects such as comfort and tolerability. The use of composite and hybrid structures, including modifications of the conventional resins and reinforcing fabric sleeves, besides the introduction of additively-manufactured metastructures with structural and process-easing capabilities, could improve thermal control in the socket. The combined use of PCMs and rGO in the socket material synergistically produces an enhancement of the heat storage effects. The mechanism can be explained by an improved heat conductivity of the resin in the intimate thickness of the shell (rGO near the skin), and a subsequent heat storage by the PCMs. Overall, the new socket delayed temperature increase during rest and gym exercise. The presence of the *Hypermat* metastructure improves the overall flowability during lamination, allowing the use of PCMs concentrations as high as at least 40wt%, which are essential to favour heat absorption.

The preliminary test with a volunteer, although insufficient to draw final conclusions, showed that this patient's subjective impression was of an improved dryness and freshness, which paired with the quantitative observation that, with the modified socket, the temperature increase during exercise was delayed with respect to the traditional socket. More subjects will be enrolled in future to confirm the current evidence.

Although the adoption of new and hybrid manufacturing techniques could pose questions in practical terms, it is expected that appropriate guidelines and well thought-out virtual design systems could smooth transition towards a more integrated approach to the production of advanced prostheses.

Acknowledgements. The authors are grateful to Centro Protesi Inail for supporting this study through the MAPS Project (Multimaterials for Adapted Prosthetic Sockets). They also thank Giuseppe Andreoni, Paolo Perego and Roberto Sironi (Politecnico di Milano) for useful scientific discussions; Enrico Bassani and Nicola Bennato (CNR-ICMATE) for technical support in the additive manufacturing process; and Giovanni Hamoui, Pietro Morara and Mario Vertucci (Inail) for support in the lamination process.

References

1. Ghoseiri, K., Safari, M.R.: J. Rehabil. Res. Dev. **51**, 855 (2014)
2. Sang, Y., Li, X., Luo, Y.: Proc. Inst. Mech. Eng. Part H J. Eng. Med. **230**, 239 (2016)
3. Paternò, L., Ibrahimi, M., Gruppioni, E., Menciassi, A., Ricotti, L.: IEEE Trans. Biomed. Eng. **65**, 1996 (2018)
4. GL Walters, D.S., Montez, J.P.: 15/652,695 (2018)
5. Sharma, A., Tyagi, V.V., Chen, C.R., Buddhi, D.: Renew. Sustain. Energy Rev. **13**, 318 (2009)
6. Fatih Demirbas, M.: Energy Sources Part B Econ. Plan. Policy **1**, 85 (2006)
7. Huang, X., Alva, G., Jia, Y., Fang, G.: Renew. Sustain. Energy Rev. **72**, 128 (2017)
8. Wernke, M.M., Schroeder, R.M., Kelley, C.T., Denune, J.A., Colvin, J.M.: J. Prosthetics Orthot. **27**, 134 (2015)
9. Ersoy, M.S., et al.: 5th International Istanbul Text Congress, vol. 82 (2015)
10. Cai, G., Xu, Z., Yang, M., Tang, B., Wang, X.: Appl. Surf. Sci. **393**, 441 (2017)
11. Gan, L., Shang, S., Yuen, C.W.M., Xiang Jiang, S.: Compos. Sci. Technol. **117**, 208 (2015)
12. Hidayah, N.M.S., et al.: AIP Conf. Proc. **1892** (2017)
13. Hummers, W.S., Offeman, R.E.: J. Am. Chem. Soc. **80**, 1339 (1958)

Sensor-Based Task Ergonomics Feedback for a Passive Low-Back Exoskeleton

Mattia Pesenti[1(✉)], Marta Gandolla[1,2], Carlo Folcio[3], Sha Ouyang[3], Luigi Rovelli[3], Alessandra Pedrocchi[1], Mario Covarrubias Rodriguez[3], and Loris Roveda[4]

[1] NearLab, Department of Electronics, Information and Bioengineering, Politecnico di Milano, 20133 Milan, Italy
{mattia.pesenti,alessandra.pedrocchi}@polimi.it

[2] Department of Mechanical Engineering, Politecnico di Milano, 20156 Milan, Italy
marta.gandolla@polimi.it

[3] Virtual Prototyping and Augmented Reality Lab, Department of Mechanical Engineering, Lecco Campus, Politecnico di Milano, Milan, Italy
mario.covarrubias@polimi.it

[4] Istituto Dalle Molle di studi sull'Intelligenza Artificiale (IDSIA), Scuola Universitaria Professionale della Svizzera Italiana (SUPSI), Università della Svizzera Italiana (USI), 6962 Lugano-Viganello, Switzerland
loris.roveda@supsi.ch

Abstract. Low-back exoskeletons are a wide-spreading technology tackling low-back pain, the leading work-related musculoskeletal disorder in many work sectors. Currently, spring-based (i.e., passive) exoskeletons are the mostly adopted in the industry, being cheaper and generally less complex and more intuitive to use. We introduce a system of interconnected wireless sensing units to provide online ergonomics feedback to the wearer. We integrate the system into our passive low-back exoskeleton and evaluate its usability with healthy volunteers and potential end users. In this way, we provide the exoskeleton with a tool aimed both at monitoring the interaction of the system with the user, providing them with an ergonomics feedback during task execution. The sensor system can also be integrated with a custom-developed Unity3D application which can be used to interface with Augmented- or Virtual-Reality applications with higher potential for improved user feedback, ergonomics training, and offline ergonomics evaluation of the workplace. We believe that providing ergonomics feedback to exoskeleton users in the industrial sector could help further reduce the drastic impact of low-back pain and prevent its onset.

Keywords: Low-back pain · Exoskeleton · Industrial sector · Ergonomics · User feedback · Usability

---

This research has received funding from the European Union's Horizon 2020 research and innovation programme, via an Open Call issued and executed under Project EUROBENCH (grant n. 779963) - XSPINE and REMOTe_XSPINE projects.

K. Miesenberger et al. (Eds.): ICCHP-AAATE 2022, LNCS 13342, pp. 403–410, 2022.
https://doi.org/10.1007/978-3-031-08645-8_47

1 Introduction

Exoskeletons are among the mostly widespread assistive technologies since the last two decades. Robotic exoskeletons are more and more used for rehabilitation and neuro-rehabilitation. Exoskeletons are also used to provide assistance to disabled or impaired people with daily-life activities. In this context, industrial exoskeletons are an emerging topic [2]. Their aim is to support workers with either tiring or non-ergonomic tasks, preventing or mitigating the impact of low-back pain [5,9]. Indeed, low-back pain and other work-related musculoskeletal disorders are among the most common causes of disability for workers in the field of automotive, logistics, aerospace, and other industrial sectors [20].

Passive exoskeletons are currently the most adopted in the industrial context. While research on active exoskeletons is ongoing, their higher potential is not yet fully exploitable, and comes with higher cost and complexity [15]. Passive exoskeletons are typically actuated by means of springs or elastic elements and thus provide assistance in a repeatable and intuitive way. With this in mind, we designed a system of interconnected Wireless Sensing Units. We opted for the integration of such sensors in a passive low-back exoskeleton. Of course, the same technology could be integrated in active exoskeletons as well. Being wearable, the system could be easily worn as a standalone system, either for ergonomics training or when exoskeleton assistance may be not necessary.

State of the Art. Work-related musculoskeletal disorders (WRMD) are a significant issue that spans many work sectors. Poor ergonomics is well know to cause musculoskeletal disorders. This phenomenon is recently being studied not only in the industrial sector, but also in constructions [18], agriculture [4], clinical laboratories [7], healthcare [8], dental practice [6], surgery [17], and many more. Here, we focus on the industrial sector, in which the dominant WRMD is low-back pain.

Several strategies have been recently proposed to mitigate and prevent low-back pain and ergonomics-related musculoskeletal disorders for workers. Worker feedback and workplace improvements have been suggested to improve task ergonomics with the aim of reducing the spread of low-back pain and other disorders [13]. Participatory ergonomic interventions is often a common and cost-effective strategy. Specifically, ergonomic training by an expert ergonomist was found to be the most common intervention [19]. On the other hand, novel sensor-based assessment and feedback tools are being developed. The ErgoTac [11] is a wearable device that embeds a reduced-complexity biomechanical model aimed at giving online tactile feedback to the wearer. It was recently evaluated in a simulated industrial setting to provide ergonomic postural adjustments [10]. Similarly, the Smart Workwear System [12] is a wearable sensor system that provides haptic feedbacks for ergonomics interventions. The *ErgoTac* requires external inertial sensors (IMU) and ground reaction force measurements. Sensor data is fed to the human biomechanical model that provides online estimates of joint overloading, then used to provide ergonomic feedback. On the other hand, the *Smart Workwear System* is focused on the upper limbs and exploits only postural data and ergonomic-derived thresholds to provide user feedback.

In the literature, there is no record of a sensor-based ergonomic feedback device embedded in an exoskeleton.

Aim of the Work. Our aim is to exploit the higher level of technological readiness of passive exoskeletons and improve their end-user acceptability embedding some *intelligence* in a simple yet effective mechanical design. Specifically, in this work we present a sensor-based system for a passive low-back exoskeleton aimed at providing online feedback on task ergonomics to the wearer. We exploit wireless inertial measurement units with sensor fusion and Unity3D for virtual/augmented-reality-ready kinematic reconstruction and task ergonomics.

2 The Low-Back Exoskeleton

Currently available low-back exoskeletons are designed in order to reduce the stress on the musculoskeletal system, and in particular on the lumbo-sacral (L5-S1) joint. A trade-off among several requirements is often to be solved, with particular attention to output power (i.e., provided assistance), freedom of motion and user ergonomics, and manufacturing cost. As a result, the most widely adopted low-back exoskeletons rely on passive actuation, as discussed above.

Here, we exploit our low-back exoskeleton – shown in Fig. 1-(a). Its design consists of three main elements: the backbone-tracking kinematics, the wearable suit, and the passive actuation system. The goal of the backbone-tracking kinematic structure is to follow the motion of the human spine, and in particular of the second thoracic vertebra (T2), allowing the wearer to move as naturally and unconstrained as possible. In order to achieve this, its elements are obtained from a user-centric optimization process. A subject-specific structure can be designed and manufactured to achieve optimal tracking of the backbone, adapting the exoskeleton to the wearer. The kinematic structure presented in [16] was equipped with a passive actuation system, shown in Fig. 1-(b).

3 Sensor-Based Ergonomics Feedback

The passive exoskeleton for the low-back described above (cf. Fig. 1) has been equipped with a set of wireless Inertial Measurement Units (IMU). Each sensing unit is made of a low-power micro-controller with built-in Wi-Fi connectivity (WeMos D1 Mini), a 9-axis IMU (InvenSense MPU-9250), a buzzer for user feedback, and a 3.7 V Lithium polymer (LiPo) battery. Each Wireless Sensing Unit (WSU) is rigidly attached to each of the four links of the exoskeleton, thus tracking the motion of the wearer. Specifically, we are interested in monitoring position and motion of the two legs, the hips, and the trunk.

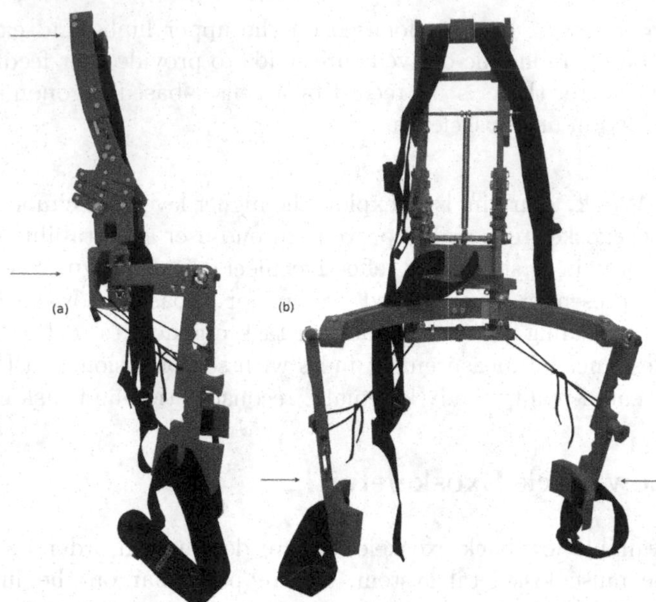

Fig. 1. Our low-back exoskeleton featuring the backbone-tracking kinematic structure (a) and passive actuation (b). WSU's are shown with blue arrows.

The WSU's can work in two modalities. In the *stand-alone mode*, each sensing unit is calibrated while the wearer is standing in upright position, and can track user motion with respect to the gravity vector. This means that while the wearer is standing still, the relative angle measured by each WSU is zero. In the *interconnected mode*, all four WSU's can be connected to a computer and provide data to a custom application developed in Unity3D. In this case, data from all sensors is used for the kinematic reconstruction of the pose of the human wearing the exoskeleton.

In the stand-alone mode, each WSU measures the orientation of its reference body segment. 9-axis IMU data (3-axis accelerometer, 3-axis gyroscope, and 3-axis magnetometer) is sampled at 50 Hz. The internal Digital Motion Processor is then exploited to compute quaternion data online by means of sensor fusion. The unit then compares the computed orientation with a reference value that sets the ergonomics threshold for each task. We set the *safe* range of motion for each monitored joint according to state-of-the-art ergonomics. For load lifting from the ground, for example, we set the threshold of trunk forward bending to 45°. Un-assisted forward trunk bending between 20° and 60° is beyond the acceptability threshold accoring to RULA [14] (RULA score +3), and bending past 60° further increases the risk score (RULA score +4). If the measured orientation overcomes the threshold, the buzzer is used to provide localized feedback to the user. The quaternions of each sensor are also converted to Euler angles for easier visualization of the orientation. Specifically, Euler angles can be streamed

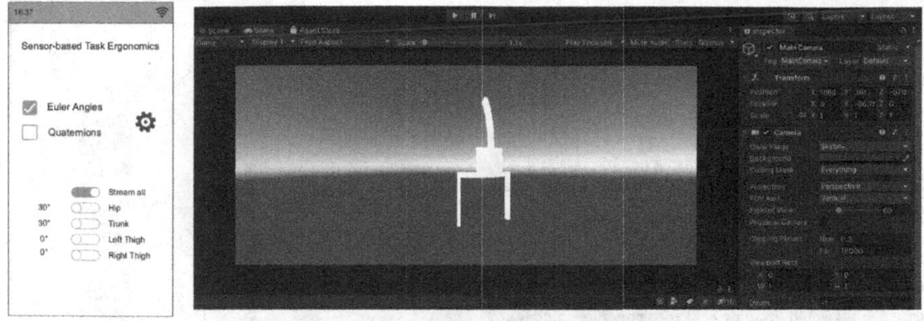

Fig. 2. Smartphone application (left) and Unity3D framework for kinematic reconstruction and task ergonomics (right).

over Wi-Fi either to a computer or to a custom-made smartphone application. This application can be used for online visual feedback, or to save and store data for later analysis. The smartphone application (app) is shown in Fig. 2-(a).

In the inter-connected mode, all the WSU's are connected to a computer and stream quaternion data to a custom-developed Unity3D application. The application – shown in Fig. 2-(b) – is used for kinematic reconstruction from sensor data. This allows to visualize online the motion of the wearer while they are using the exoskeleton. In this way, the task can be monitored considering the overall posture, thus providing a higher-level ergonomics feedback to the user. Unity3D allows to integrate data from the sensing units and could be exploited to deploy augmented/virtual-reality tools for operator training and task ergonomics feedback. Moreover, this data could also be exploited for operator monitoring in the developing context of smart factories.

4 Usability Evaluation

The overall system, that consists of the exoskeleton and the wireless sensing units, has been tested with healthy volunteers. In particular, we recruited 2 healthy subjects and 4 healthy workers of the logistic sector, for a total of 6 healthy male subjects (age: 37 ± 18.10 years; height: 1.79 ± 0.07 m, weight: 76.67 ± 9.43 kg).

To each subject, we submitted the System Usability Scale (SUS) [3] to evaluate the overall usability of the system. The SUS is a commonly used tool that measures the usability of a new technology. It is a ten-question survey that investigates usability, effectiveness, and perceived complexity. It was introduced as a *quick and dirty* survey to have an idea of end-user's acceptability. Each item of the SUS is evaluated with a 5-point Likert scale (i.e., ranging from *Strongly Disagree* to *Strongly Agree*). The global score – computed from the question scores q as shown in Eq. 1 – is obtained in a 0–100 scale. Then, we interpreted the results according to Bangor's guidelines [1]. Specifically, these set a threshold

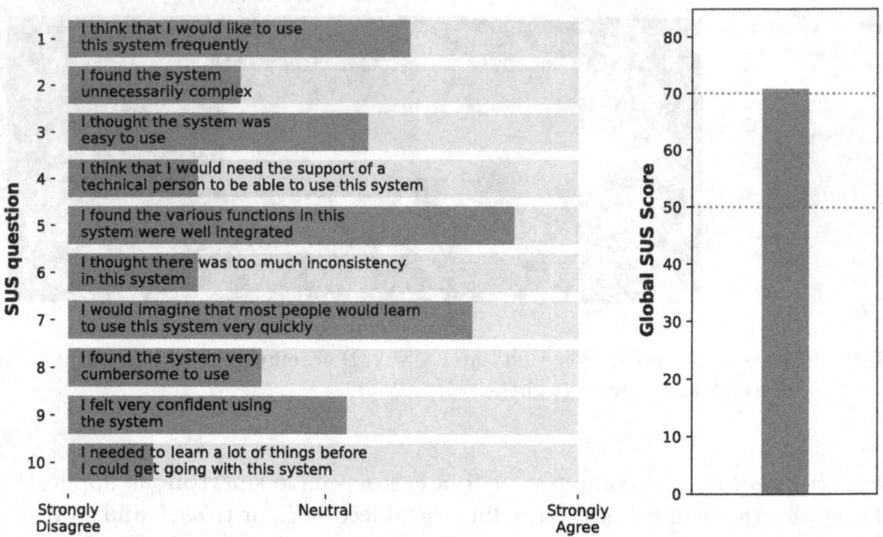

Fig. 3. SUS questionnaire: average score for each question (left panel) and average global SUS score (right panel).

for end-user acceptability at 70/100, also suggesting that scores below 50 should raise major concerns, while scores of 85 or higher indicate exceptional usability.

$$\mathrm{SUS} = 2.5 \cdot \left(\sum_{i=1,3,5,7,9} (q_i - 1) + \sum_{j=2,4,6,8,10} (5 - q_j) \right) \tag{1}$$

For our system, the average score of the SUS was found to be 70.83, as shown in Fig. 3. In the plot, we also show the average of each of the 10 questions of the survey.

5 Discussion

We have introduced a sensor-based, task-aware ergonomics feedback for a passive low-back exoskeleton. We described the wireless sensing units that were designed and attached to the exoskeleton in order to monitor the body segments of interest for industrial workers. Each sensor can provide online feedback to the wearer while they are executing tasks that require assistance at the level of the lumbosacral joint. The overall architecture described above also features a smartphone application and a custom-developed Unity3D application for kinematic reconstruction. With this framework, we can achieve both online user feedback for task ergonomics – aimed as an intra-task corrective action – and offline task analysis – to improve long-term ergonomics for the users of the exoskeleton.

We showed the results of a SUS questionnaire submitted to 6 healthy subjects who evaluated rather positively the system. Indeed, the average score of 70.83

is just above the recommended acceptability threshold according to Bangor's interpretation of the SUS. Being a scale to evaluate products to be commercialized, we are rather satisfied of the score obtained by our prototype. Evaluating a prototype with a usability scale allows to involve end users in the design process. User feedback will be exploited to improve the re-design of the device, aiming at higher overall usability for the final device.

5.1 Conclusion

With this work, we have shown and tested a proof-of-concept of a sensor-based system for online task ergonomics. Although few similar systems exist, our is the first to be featured on a (passive) exoskeleton for the industrial sector. A similar framework could be used to measure and investigate several other kinematic and non-kinematic features, including other non-invasive human-monitoring sensors. Augmented- or virtual-reality could be integrated aiming at achieving either online operator feedback or operator training, respectively. Depending on the context, several technological solutions could be exploited to provide online user feedback limiting the invasiveness of the device and maximizing its efficacy.

The development of the system will continue treasuring the user feedback obtained with the SUS questionnaire. User testing will also continue throughout the process, extending also the evaluation to female subjects. The major limitation of this study is indeed the study population, consisting of 6 male subjects.

In conclusion, we believe that featuring a passive exoskeleton with smart, wireless sensing units could increase the end-user acceptability of exoskeletons in the industrial field and further improve task ergonomics and thus the efficacy of the exoskeleton and the assistance it provides.

Acknowledgements. The authors would like to thank the volunteers that participated in the prototype evaluation.

MG and AP hold shares in AGADE s.r.l., Milan, Italy.

References

1. Bangor, A., Kortum, P.T., Miller, J.T.: An empirical evaluation of the system usability scale. Int. J. Hum. Comput. Interact. **24**(6), 574–594 (2008)
2. Bogue, R.: Exoskeletons-a review of industrial applications. Indust. Robot Int. J. (2018)
3. Brooke, J.: Sus: a "quick and dirty' usability." Usab. Eval. Indust. **189**(3) (1996)
4. Davis, K.G., Kotowski, S.E.: Understanding the ergonomic risk for musculoskeletal disorders in the united states agricultural sector. Am. J. Indust. Med. **50**(7), 501–511 (2007)
5. De Looze, M.P., Bosch, T., Krause, F., Stadler, K.S., O'sullivan, L.W.: Exoskeletons for industrial application and their potential effects on physical work load. Ergonomics **59**(5), 671–681 (2016)
6. De Sio, S., et al.: Ergonomic risk and preventive measures of musculoskeletal disorders in the dentistry environment: an umbrella review. PeerJ **6**, e4154 (2018)

7. Haile, E.L., Taye, B., Hussen, F.: Ergonomic workstations and work-related musculoskeletal disorders in the clinical laboratory. Lab. Med. 43(suppl_2), e11–e19 (2012)
8. Hamid, A., Ahmad, A.S., Dar, S., Sohail, S., Akram, F., Qureshi, M.I.: Ergonomics hazards and musculoskeletal disorders among workers of health care facilities. Curr. World Environ. **13**(2) (2018)
9. Kermavnar, T., de Vries, A.W., de Looze, M.P., O'Sullivan, L.W.: Effects of industrial back-support exoskeletons on body loading and user experience: an updated systematic review. Ergonomics **64**(6), 685–711 (2021)
10. Kim, W., Garate, V.R., Gandarias, J.M., Lorenzini, M., Ajoudani, A.: A directional vibrotactile feedback interface for ergonomic postural adjustment. IEEE Trans. Haptics (2021)
11. Kim, W., Lorenzini, M., Kapıcıoğlu, K., Ajoudani, A.: Ergotac: a tactile feedback interface for improving human ergonomics in workplaces. IEEE Robot. Autom. Lett. **3**(4), 4179–4186 (2018)
12. Lind, C.M., Diaz-Olivares, J.A., Lindecrantz, K., Eklund, J.: A wearable sensor system for physical ergonomics interventions using haptic feedback. Sensors **20**(21), 6010 (2020)
13. Loske, D., Klumpp, M., Keil, M., Neukirchen, T.: Logistics work, ergonomics and social sustainability: empirical musculoskeletal system strain assessment in retail intralogistics. Logistics **5**(4), 89 (2021)
14. McAtamney, L., Corlett, E.N.: Rula: a survey method for the investigation of work-related upper limb disorders. Appl. Ergon. **24**(2), 91–99 (1993)
15. Pesenti, M., Antonietti, A., Gandolla, M., Pedrocchi, A.: Towards a functional performance validation standard for industrial low-back exoskeletons: state of the art review. Sensors **21**(3), 808 (2021)
16. Roveda, L., Savani, L., Arlati, S., Dinon, T., Legnani, G., Tosatti, L.M.: Design methodology of an active back-support exoskeleton with adaptable backbone-based kinematics. Int. J. Indust. Ergon. **79**, 102991 (2020)
17. Schlussel, A.T., Maykel, J.A.: Ergonomics and musculoskeletal health of the surgeon. Clin. Colon Rectal Surg. **32**(06), 424–434 (2019)
18. Valero, E., Sivanathan, A., Bosché, F., Abdel-Wahab, M.: Musculoskeletal disorders in construction: a review and a novel system for activity tracking with body area network. Appl. Ergon. **54**, 120–130 (2016)
19. Van Eerd, D., et al.: Process and implementation of participatory ergonomic interventions: a systematic review. Ergonomics **53**(10), 1153–1166 (2010)
20. Vos, T., et al.: Global, regional, and national incidence, prevalence, and years lived with disability for 310 diseases and injuries, 1990–2015: a systematic analysis for the global burden of disease study 2015. The Lancet **388**(10053), 1545–1602 (2016)

Implementation and Evaluation of a Control System for a Hand Exoskeleton on Mobile Devices

Sebastian Koch([✉]), Tobias Ableitner, and Gottfried Zimmermann

Hochschule der Medien, Responsive Media Experience Research Group, Nobelstraße 10, 70569 Stuttgart, Germany

sebastian@koch.cf, tobias.ableitner@googlemail.com, gzimmermann@acm.org

Abstract. Anyone could suffer a stroke, which is one of the major causes of disability in the adult population. Survivors often experience problems due to paralysis and spasticity and thus require constant help, as even the simplest everyday tasks can pose an insurmountable challenge. To help those affected, the KONSENS research project led by the University Hospital in Tübingen developed a hand exoskeleton that can also be used by stroke patients.

The goal of this work is to implement a control for this exoskeleton on Google Glass, as well as Android smartphones and smartwatches. Then we evaluated the resulting prototype with students of Stuttgart Media University and acquaintances of the author. The focus of this work is on the comparison of user acceptance and suitability of ten different input and output methods such as voice control, eye tracking or touch input on three mobile devices. It was found the user acceptance and suitability of controlling the system using touch input was highest, while eye tracking and head movements was lowest.

Keywords: Accessibility · Augmented reality · Assistive technology · Input and output methods · Hand exoskeleton · User acceptance

1 Introduction

After brain or spinal cord injuries such as a stroke, hand impairments including a loss of muscle strength, apraxia or ataxia, spasticity or paralysis can occur [3]. A stroke affects an estimated 270,000 persons in Germany each year [6], around a quarter of which suffer from permanent physical limitations as a result [7]. This impairment results in a significant loss of autonomy and quality of life for the affected persons, both in their professional and private lives [2]. By using a hand exoskeleton, physicians can restore at least part of the hand functionality [4], such as the ability to independently eat or drink [5].

However, further challenges accompany the control of this hand exoskeleton regarding human-machine interaction for different people—such as the elderly.

K. Miesenberger et al. (Eds.): ICCHP-AAATE 2022, LNCS 13342, pp. 411–419, 2022.
https://doi.org/10.1007/978-3-031-08645-8_48

For example, a visually impaired user cannot benefit from the hand exoskeleton if they cannot control it—because they are unable to read its control unit. Additionally, [1] found that the control system needs to be as inconspicuous as possible to prevent further ostracization of affected persons in public.

In this work, we designed a user interface for a hand exoskeleton developed by the research project KONSENS under the direction of the University Hospital Tübingen, Germany. Then we implemented the resulting concept natively for Google Glass as well as Android devices smartphones and smartwatches. A variety of different input methods can be used to control the system—namely voice and touch input, as well as eye and head movements.

We evaluated the application with students at Stuttgart Media University and acquaintances of the authors. In particular, we compared the user acceptance and suitability of the different input methods on the respective output devices.

2 Methodology

The study participants were tasked with using ten different combinations of input and output modalities (hereinafter called input-output-combination) to select between two and four icons. Each arrangement of icons within the user interface (hereinafter called icon-position-combination) contains exactly one correct icon, which was marked with a smiley, while the others were marked as wrong using a cross icon. An exemplary icon-position-combination can be seen in Fig. 1.

Fig. 1. One of the five icon-position-combinations implemented for this study—namely IPC4. Here the bottom icon is marked as the correct one.

In the actual control system, the icons would instead show the possible actions of the exoskeleton, e.g. display two different grip types to be selected, depending on the object to be grabbed. This study aims to find the optimal number of icons and their positions, to aid in the further development of the system.

In total, five different icon-position-combinations were used for each input-output-combination, each measured twelve times with uniformly distributed icons. To prevent the participants from guessing subsequent icons, two additional icons were randomly inserted into each icon-position-combination. These additional icons were not considered for this study.

The input-output-combinations tested were distributed over a Latin square to reduce systematic errors. Additionally, the order of the icon-position-combinations containing the same number of icons was alternated between participants. Each participant was allowed to familiarize themselves with each input-output-combination during an unmeasured run.

The following input-output-combinations were part of the study. The naming convention used derives from previous work by [1]:

I2O2 Touch input on smartphone (tapping)
I2O1 Touch input on smartwatch (swiping)
I6O5 Touch input on Glass (swiping)
I7O2 Voice input on smartphone (German)
I7O1 Voice input on smartwatch (German)
I7O5 Voice input on Glass (German, via smartphone)
I8AO5 Head movements on Glass (pitch/yaw axes)
I8BO5 Head movements on Glass (pitch/roll axes)
I9AO5 Eye movements on Glass (glance with blinking)
I9CO5 Eye movements on Glass (item scanning with blinking)

Also, the following icon-position-combinations were part of the study:

IPC2a Two icons horizontally arranged
IPC2b Two icons vertically arranged
IPC3a Three icons in a triangle (hypotenuse at bottom)
IPC3b Three icons in a triangle (hypotenuse at top)
IPC4 Four icons in a square

Following the experiment, a survey was conducted. Each participant was instructed to order the input-output-combinations tested according to their subjective preference. In addition, data on the subjects' demography and pre-existing conditions was recorded pseudonymously.

The study took place over several weeks with students of media informatics, mobile media and audiovisual media at Stuttgart Media University who can be assumed to have an above-average affinity with technology and acquaintance of the author. Participants had approximately 45 min using the input-output-combinations and 10 min answering the survey. Participants from Stuttgart Media University were compensated for their time.

3 Results

A total of twenty persons (age: M = 31.1 SD = 13.31) participated in the study. Of these ten were male, ten female and none diverse.

3.1 Comparison of Icon-Position-Combination Variants

Overall, no significant difference could be found between the icon-position-combination variants with the same number of icons in each case. Table 1 shows an overview of the measured data for the tested icon-position-combinations.

Table 1. Comparison of input errors [‰], time needed for a correct input [s] and the bandwidth [bit/s] using the different icon-position-combinations

	Input errors		Time needed		Bandwidth	
	M	SD	M	SD	M	SD
IPC2a	54.95	257.7	1.60	0.90	1.61	0.80
IPC2b	61.54	312.5	1.65	0.93	1.55	0.74
IPC3a	73.37	290.5	1.60	0.81	2.40	1.09
IPC3b	52.06	237.9	1.61	0.85	2.36	1.13
IPC4	83.26	333.5	1.63	0.89	3.15	1.49

Figure 2 shows the errors [‰] with the different icon-position-combinations. No significant difference could be found between IPC2a and IPC2b (t = 0.54; p = 0.59); likewise, no significant difference could be found between IPC3a and IPC3b (t = 1.89; p = 0.06).

Figure 3 shows time needed for a correct input [s] with the different icon-position-combinations. No significant difference could be found between IPC2a and IPC2b (t = 1.38; p = 0.17); likewise, no significant difference could be found between IPC3a and IPC3b (t = 1.49; p = 0.14).

Figure 4 shows bandwidth [bit/s] which was achieved with the different icon-position-combinations. No significant difference could be found between IPC2a and IPC2b(t = 1.91; p = 0.06); likewise, no significant difference could be found between IPC3a and IPC3b (t = 0.78; p = 0.44).

3.2 Comparison of Input-Output-Combination Variants

Overall, no significant difference could be found between the input-output-combination variants with the same number of icons in each case. Table 2 shows an overview of the measured data for the tested input-output-combinations.

The highest bandwidth was achieved by using touch on the smartphone, followed by touch on the smartwatch and smart glass. The bandwidth when using head movements was the next highest. A significant difference was found between

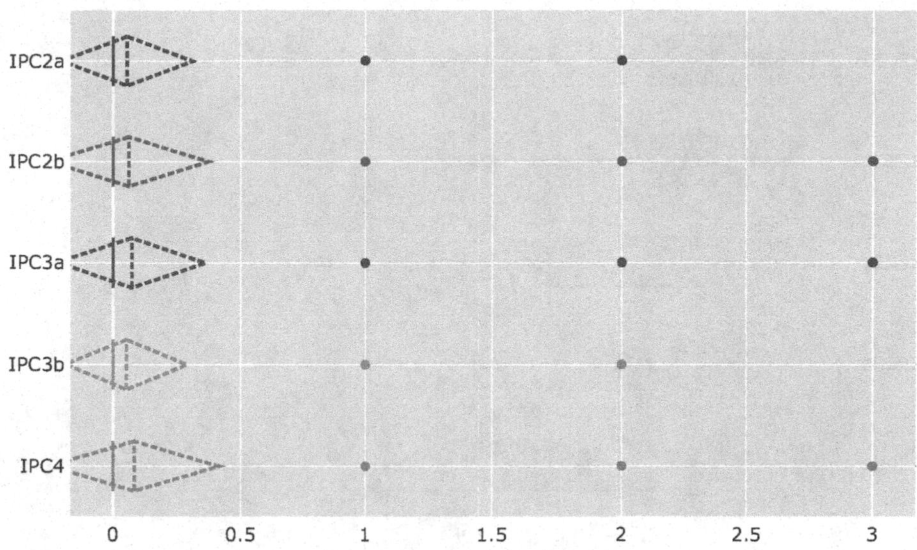

Fig. 2. Comparison of the number of incorrect inputs made using the different icon-position-combinations.

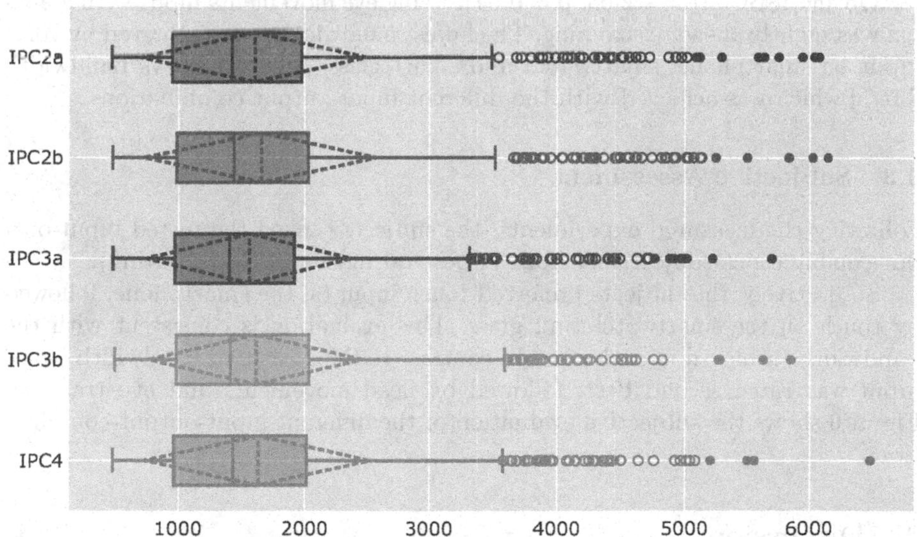

Fig. 3. Comparison of the time needed for a correct input using the different icon-position-combinations.

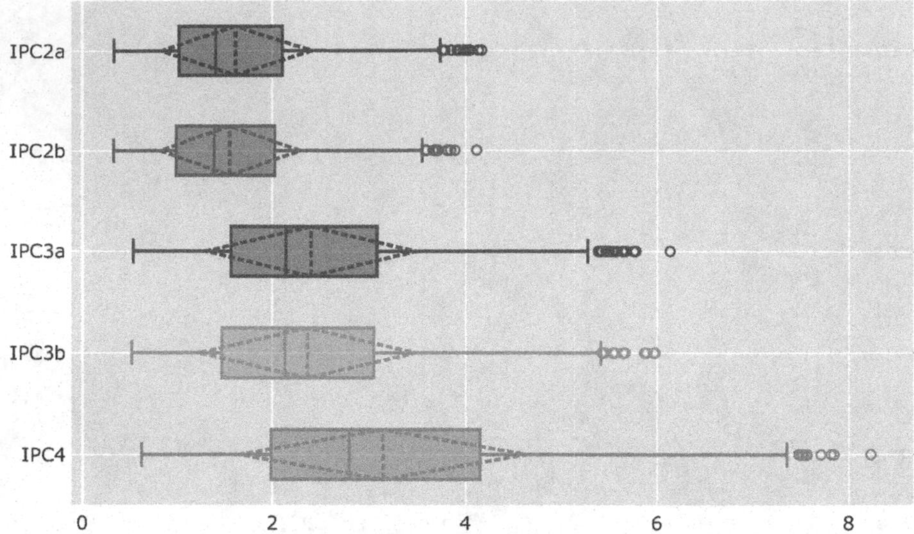

Fig. 4. Comparison of the bandwidth using the different icon-position-combinations.eps

I8AO5 and I8BO5 ($t = -2.03$; $p = 0.04$). Using eye movements input with glancing was slightly ahead of scanning. The lowest bandwidths were achieved by voice input on smartphone, smartwatch and smart glass. Figure 5 shows bandwidth [bit/s] which was achieved with the different input-output-combinations.

3.3 Subjective Assessment

Following the measured experiments, the subjects ranked the tested input-output-combinations subjectively from 1 (best rating) to 10 (worst rating).

Subjectively, the subjects preferred touch input on the smartphone, followed by touch on the smartwatch and glass. This evaluation is consistent with the bandwidths achieved in each case. In contrast to the measured bandwidth, voice input was rated second best, followed by head movements and eye tracking. Figure 6 shows the subjective evaluation of the different input-output-combinations.

4 Discussion

As this work could show in a preliminary study, the most suitable way to control a hand exoskeleton is touch input, whereby a smartphone and a smartwatch were somewhat preferred over a smart glass. This confirms the results by [1] according to which, the touch-based input-output-combinations were preferred by the participants. But this work could not confirm the hypothesis posed by [1] that spectacle wearers were more willing to use the Google Glass, as opposed

Table 2. Comparison of input errors [‰], time needed for a correct input [s] and the bandwidth [bit/s] using the different input-output-combinations

	Input errors		Time needed		Bandwidth	
	M	SD	M	SD	M	SD
I2O2	4,18	64,55	0,74	1,84	3,94	1,37
I6O5	26,32	170,83	1,29	0,73	2,54	1,04
I2O1	3,38	58,07	1,16	0,65	2,86	1,22
I7O5	36,33	187,29	2,04	0,72	1,54	0,80
I7O1	23,38	151,25	1,99	0,71	1,57	0,68
I702	32,91	188,53	1,91	0,59	1,60	0,70
I8AO5	98,59	367,26	1,58	0,92	2,19	1,00
I8BO5	46,18	234,10	1,41	0,74	2,30	0,95
I9AO5	216,17	528,10	1,93	1,10	1,89	1,04
I9CO5	152,06	419,24	2,00	0,98	1,85	1,26

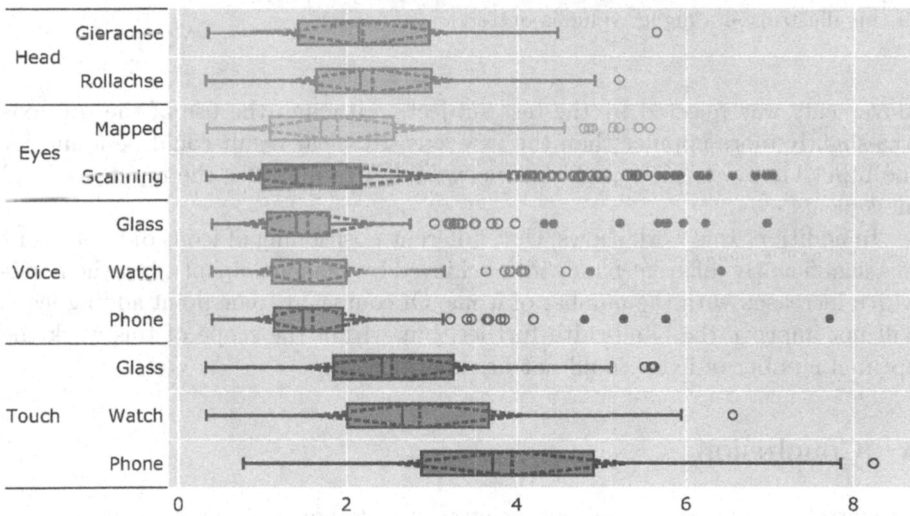

Fig. 5. Comparison of the bandwidth using the different input-output-combinations.

to non spectacle wearers. This could be due to the fact, that spectacle wearers could not wear their normal glasses and thus were less able to comfortably view the display.

Furthermore, it could be shown that voice input on a smartphone was more accepted than on a smartwatch and a smart glass – although technical limitations of current mobile devices may have influenced the results. Input via head

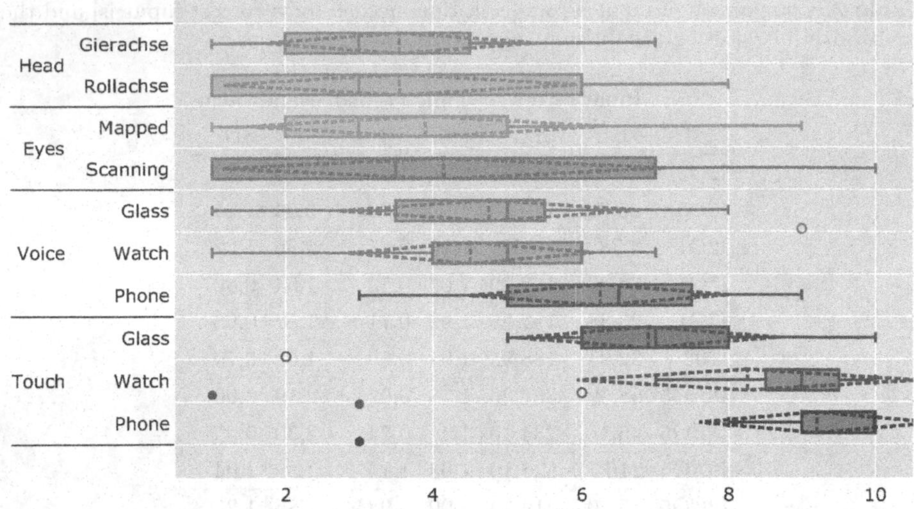

Fig. 6. Subjective evaluation in comparison of the tested input-output-combinations. In this illustration a higher value is better.

movements was rejected by the test subjects, although the use of the roll axis was slightly more popular than the yaw axis. No clear result could be found for the input via eye tracking, which was evaluated similarly as the input via head movements.

In addition, this work shows, that different positioning of icons did not result in a significantly different bandwidth achieved by the participants, but the bandwidth increased with the number of icons. Of course, at some point adding icons will not improve the bandwidth further, but within the scope of this work the optimal number of icons could not be determined.

5 Conclusion

A control system or a hand exoskeleton was designed and implemented as a native application for mobile devices. With the help of a hand exoskeleton, physicians can restore at least a part of the hand function of e.g. stroke patients [4]. The affected people can thereby regain a certain autonomy and quality of life [2].

This work evaluated different icon-position-combinations on different input-output-combinations. No significant difference could be shown between icon-position-combinations with the same number of icons, but it was shown that the achieved bandwidth increases with the number of icons (up to four icons were tested). It was shown, that the input using touch was both most effectively used and rated highest by the participants. This implies touch input is most suitable for controlling a hand exoskeleton among the input methods tested.

6 Future Work

In the next step, these experiments should be repeated with additional test persons in order to consolidate the preliminary findings. It is particularly important to investigate whether and for which groups of persons eye tracking control is feasible. The application should also be tested together with the hand exoskeleton in a realistic context by actually affected persons in order to be able to assess the developed control. For example, it could turn out that affected persons are less comfortable with touch input, because both hands would be blocked – one by the hand exoskeleton, the other by the input. It is at least conceivable that in this group, input via voice control will prove to be more effective than touch control.

References

1. Ableitner, T., Soekadar, S., Schilling, A., Strobbe, C., Zimmermann, G.: User acceptance of augmented reality glasses in comparison to other interaction methods for controlling a hand exoskeleton: a study among technology-oriented young persons. In: Mensch und Computer 2019 - Workshopband, No. MuC'19, pp. 178–184. Association for Computing Machinery, Hamburg (2019). https://doi.org/10.18420/muc2019-ws-616
2. Bakula, M., Kovačević, D., Sarilar, M., Palijan, T., Kovač, M.: Quality of life in people with physical disabilities. Collegium Antropol. **35**(Suppl. 2), 247–53 (2011)
3. Sanborn, M., Smith, L.J., Malhotra, N.R.: The Trauma Manual: Trauma and Acute Care Surgery, 4 edn. Lippincott Williams & Wilkins, A Wolters Kluwer Business, Philadelphia (2013). https://doi.org/10.1016/B978-0-12-374245-2.00015-2
4. Schabowsky, C.N., Godfrey, S.B., Holley, R.J., Lum, P.S.: Development and pilot testing of HEXORR: hand EXOskeleton rehabilitation robot. J. NeuroEng. Rehabilit. **7**(1), 36 (2010). https://doi.org/10.1186/1743-0003-7-36
5. Soekadar, S.R., et al.: Hybrid EEG/EOG-based brain/neural hand exoskeleton restores fully independent daily living activities after quadriplegia. Sci. Robot. **1**(1), 1–8 (2016). https://doi.org/10.1126/scirobotics.aag3296
6. Villringer, A., et al.: Schlaganfallhäufigkeit und Versorgung von Schlaganfallpatienten in Deutschland. Aktuelle Neurologie **37**(07), 333–340 (2010). https://doi.org/10.1055/s-0030-1248611
7. Ward, A., Payne, K.A., Caro, J.J., Heuschmann, P.U., Kolominsky-Rabas, P.L.: Care needs and economic consequences after acute ischemic stroke: the Erlangen Stroke project. Eur. J. Neurol. **12**(4), 264–267 (2005). https://doi.org/10.1111/j.1468-1331.2004.00949.x

Design and Administration of a Questionnaire for the User-Centered Design of a Novel Upper-Limb Assistive Device for Brachial Plexus Injury and Post-stroke Subjects

Michele Francesco Penna[1,2](✉), Emilio Trigili[1,2], Loredana Zollo[3], Christian Cipriani[1,2], Leonardo Cappello[1,2], Marco Controzzi[1,2], Stefania Dalise[4], Carmelo Chisari[4], Emanuele Gruppioni[5], Simona Crea[1,2], and Nicola Vitiello[1,2]

[1] The BioRobotics Institute, Scuola Superiore Sant'Anna, Pisa, Italy
michelefrancesco.penna@santannapisa.it

[2] Department of Excellence in Robotics & AI, Scuola Superiore Sant'Anna, Pisa, Italy

[3] Research Unit of Advanced Robotics and Human-Centered Technologies, Università Campus Bio-Medico di Roma, Rome, Italy

[4] Department of Neuroscience, University of Pisa, Pisa, Italy

[5] Centro Protesi INAIL di Vigorso di Budrio, Bologna, Italy

Abstract. This study presents the results of a focus group with post-stroke and brachial plexus injury subjects, aiming at defining the functional and technical requirements of a novel upper-limb (UL) assistive device. According to participants' responses, the device will integrate an UL exoskeleton, functional electrical stimulation, and a sensory feedback glove, to restore both motor and sensory functions.

Keywords: User-centered design · Wearable robotics · Functional electrical stimulation

1 Introduction

Human upper-limb (UL) biomechanics guarantees a sophisticated synergy of motor and sensory capabilities during the execution of activities of daily living (ADLs) [1, 2]. The occurrence of UL impairments, due to either traumatic or non-traumatic events, may affect the execution of common ADLs, reducing the subjects' quality of life. Several approaches have been proposed for supporting the recovery of UL motor and sensory functions. Portable orthoses can be used to increase subject's autonomy and independence in ADLs. Passive orthoses, such as arm slings, splints, or braces, are used when dealing with unrestricted wearability and portability constraints. Since passive orthoses do not integrate power sources and actuators, these devices provide a non-adaptive assistance, depending on the physical interaction with the user. On the other hand,

E. Gruppioni, S.Crea and N. Vitiello—Share the senior authorship.

K. Miesenberger et al. (Eds.): ICCHP-AAATE 2022, LNCS 13342, pp. 420–427, 2022.
https://doi.org/10.1007/978-3-031-08645-8_49

active orthoses, i.e., exoskeletons, are based on both a physical and a cognitive human-robot interaction, due to the presence of actuators and control algorithms. Therefore, the exoskeleton can be used to observe the user's residual movement capability, and amplify it according to adaptive control strategies [3, 4]. Exoskeletons can be also integrated with functional electrical stimulation (FES) in hybrid systems, for improving the user's muscular activity and output force, taking advantage of the lightness and ability to reduce muscle atrophy of the FES [5]. Finally, the recovery of sensory capabilities can be addressed using non-invasive sensory feedback systems, already widely applied in UL prosthetics to improve hand motor control [1, 6]. Indeed, the implementation of a supplementary *augmented feedback*, e.g., auditory, visual, or haptic, to sensory impaired subjects, could lead to an improvement in motor performances and to a stimulation of neural plasticity [7].

In the preliminary design phases, an assistive device that embeds such variety of features should be conceived with a user-centered approach, to identify a list of needs and priorities that favors its usability and acceptability. In this perspective, focus groups, i.e., interviews where questionnaires are administered to potential final users, are used to assess the acceptability of the device [8], and to define the functional and technical requirements according to the final users' needs [9, 10].

The aim of this study is to investigate the needs and opinions of people suffering from UL impairments, namely brachial plexus injury (BPI) and post-stroke (PS) subjects, for the definition of functional and technical requirements of a new UL assistive device for ADLs support. In particular, the interrogation addressed (i) a shoulder-elbow-hand exoskeleton, (ii) functional electrical stimulation (FES) and (iii) the use of a sensory feedback glove. Although some studies have investigated the opinions of BPI and PS subjects on these technologies [10, 11], and their effectiveness has been proven [12–16], a comprehensive synthesis is still missing. Therefore, we designed *ex-novo* two different questionnaires for PS and BPI subjects. The questionnaires were administered to five BPI and seven PS subjects, in dedicated focus group sessions with each subject. The work is structured as follows: in Sect. 2 the two questionnaires are presented and the statistical analysis on subjects' answers is described. Section 3 presents the results of the interviews. Finally, results are discussed in Sect. 4.

2 Materials and Methods

2.1 Questionnaires

Two questionnaires, i.e., one for BPI subjects and one for PS ones, were custom-designed in collaboration with INAIL Prosthesis Centre (Vigorso di Budrio, Italy), Sant'Anna School of Advanced Studies (Pisa, Italy), Campus Bio-Medico University of Rome (Rome, Italy) and University Hospital of Pisa (Pisa, Italy).

The questionnaires were administered in Italian, at a single time point (no follow-up). The BPI questionnaire was administered via teleconference, while the PS one via in-person interview by a physician at University Hospital of Pisa (Pisa, Italy). Any additional comments of the participants were noted by the administrators. The questionnaire addressed five main categories (Table 1). (i) *Participant's information*: the participants were asked to answer to open-ended questions about demographic and clinical information. (ii) *Current assistive device*: the participants were asked to answer to both open-ended questions and multiple-choice questions (Likert scale, 6 elements) about assistive devices that they currently use, if any, assessing their level of satisfaction in terms of features of the device and movements that the device assists. (iii) *New assistive device:* the participants were asked to rank order, in terms of priorities, the features that a new UL assistive device should possess, and the movements or daily-life activities for which they would prefer to receive assistance from the device. In the first case, the participants were asked to rank order the following device's features: *Appearance, Comfort, Weight, Reliability, Noisiness, Battery life, Water resistance, Portability, Easy maintenance.* In the latter case, the participants were asked to rank order the following activities: *Reaching, Grasping, Manipulating, Lifting an object, Carrying an object, Lifting the arm, Performing repetitive movements.* (iv) *FES*: the participants were asked open-ended questions about their previous experiences with FES, if any. Moreover, participants' opinions on the use of FES in a new assistive device for amplifying the muscular activity, were investigated using multiple-choice questions. (v) *Sensory feedback glove*: the acceptability of wearing a sensory feedback glove during ADLs was assessed using multiple-choice questions. Finally, the participants were asked to rank order (i) different types of sensory information and (ii) different types of stimulation they would require from a sensory feedback glove. In the first case, participants were asked to rank order the following sensory information: *Contact with external objects, Force level applied, Type of contact surface, Materials' elasticity, Temperature.* In the latter case, the participants were asked to rank the following types of stimulation: *Vibration, Continuous pression, Acoustic signal, Light signal.* The PS questionnaire was slightly modified with respect to the BPI one, to account for the differences in terms of residual capabilities between the two groups. First, during PS subjects' interviews, the physician noted the scores in the Ashworth and Medical Research Council (MRC) scales. Then, the description of the current assistive device was slightly shortened for PS subjects since most of the participants did not use assistive devices in their daily life.

Table 1. Description of items in the questionnaires for BPI and PS subjects.

Category	Description	Question type– BPI subjects	Question type– PS subjects
(i) Participant's information	Gender, age, year, and cause of the adverse event	Multiple-choice, free responses	Multiple-choice, free responses
	Ashworth and MRC scales score	/	Multiple-choice
(ii) Current assistive device	Type of assistive device, participation in the choice of the device, use of the device in everyday life	Free responses	Multiple-choice

(continued)

Table 1. (*continued*)

Category	Description	Question type– BPI subjects	Question type– PS subjects
	Satisfaction of the features and assistance provided by the current assistive device	Likert scale, 6 items	/
	Perceived autonomy during ADLs, while wearing the assistive device	Likert scale, 6 items	Likert scale, 6 items
(iii) New assistive device	Priority of characteristics for the choice of a new assistive device	Rank ordering	Rank ordering
	Priority of movements that the device should assist	Rank ordering	Rank ordering
	Acceptability of possible features of the assistive device (surface sensors, additional backpack for electronics)	Multiple-choice, free responses	Multiple-choice and free responses
(iv) FES	Description of the previous experience with FES	Multiple-choice, free responses	Multiple-choice, free responses
	Acceptability of the FES in a new assistive device	Multiple-choice	Multiple-choice
(v) Sensory feedback glove	Priority of sensory information to receive during ADL tasks	Rank ordering	Rank ordering
	Priority of type of stimulation for sensory feedback	Rank ordering	Rank ordering

2.2 Statistical Analysis

A statistical analysis was performed on participants' answers from rank ordering questions in category (iii), i.e., *New assistive device*. The lowest rank order value was assigned to missing responses, assuming that the subject did not consider these factors as fundamental for the design of the device [9].

The normality of the data was assessed using the Shapiro-Wilk test. Since data did not meet the normality assumption, the Kruskal-Wallis test by ranks was used to perform post-hoc paired comparisons between items. All statistical analyses were performed using a significance level $\alpha < 5\%$. For post-hoc paired comparisons, the Bonferroni correction was applied to adjust the level of significance according to the number of comparisons.

3 Results

A total of 5 BPI and 7 PS subjects completed the questionnaires, with a median (IQR) age of 37 (24.5) and 64 (7) years respectively; the adverse event causing the UL impairment occurred at a median (IQR) age of 28 (11) years for BPI subjects and 62 (8.5) years for PS ones. The PS subjects had a median Ashworth score of 2 for the elbow and 1 for the fingers, and a median MRC score of 0 for shoulder abductors and 1.5 for elbow flexors. Four BPI subjects and three PS currently use passive UL assistive devices. Between the BPI subjects, two of them use devices for arm weight compensation, while the others use braces for elbow-wrist assistance. The features of the current assistive device that most satisfy BPI subjects are the weight, the encumbrances, and the ease of cleaning. Considering the priorities identified for the choice new assistive device, the answers to rank ordering questions showed statistically significant differences ($p = 0.00003$ for priority of characteristics for the choice, $p = 0.00087$ for priority of ADL tasks that the device should assist). On the one hand, regarding the priorities of features of the new assistive device, *Comfort* and *Reliability* are the most important features identified (Fig. 1(a)). Post-hoc pairwise comparisons showed statistical differences between *Comfort* and *Reliability* and the three lowest ranked items on average, i.e., *Water resistance*, *Easy maintenance*, and *Appearance*. Notably, out of nine items, the *Appearance* feature was ranked 6th by PS subjects and 9th from BPI ones. On the other hand, regarding the priorities of ADL tasks where assistance is required the most, *Grasping*, *Manipulating*, and *Reaching an object* were the highest ranked task, on average (Fig. 1(b)). The *Grasping* task showed statistical differences with respect to the two lowest ranked tasks, i.e., *Lifting the arm* and performing *Repetitive movements*. The task with higher priority for PS subjects was *Reaching* (1st on average), while BPI subjects ranked *Grasping* and *Manipulation* tasks as the most important ones. Outlier answers can be observed for *Grasping*, *Manipulating,* and performing *Repetitive movements.* All the BPI subjects and one PS had previous experience with FES, in rehabilitation scenarios. All PS subjects and three BPI ones would like to benefit from FES to amplify the muscle activity during ADLs. All the subjects would use a glove for sensory feedback. Both PS and BPI subjects identified *Contact with the external objects* as the best sensory information to receive and the *Vibration* as the best feedback method.

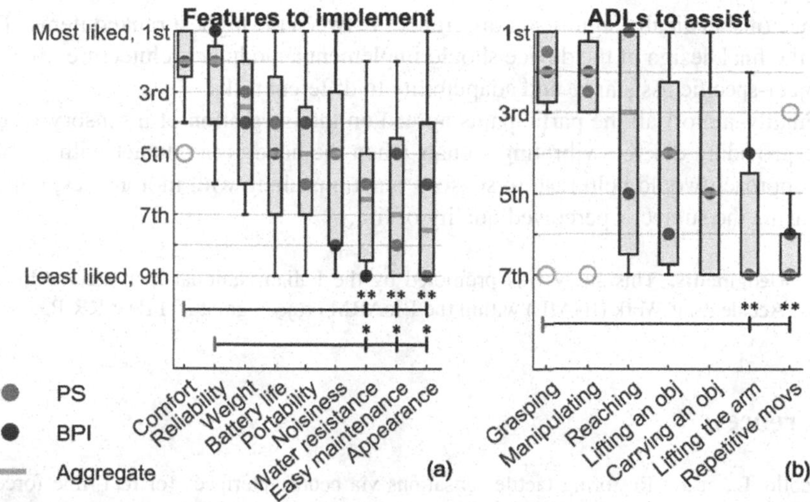

Fig. 1. (a) Priority of features that a new assistive device could implement; (b) priority of movements that the device should assist. Blue and red dots represent the median rank for BPI and PS subjects; yellow boxplot shows the aggregate data. Horizontal bars mark statistical differences in pairwise post-hoc comparison between the item marked green and the other items ($*p < 0.05$, $**p < 0.01$), after applying the Bonferroni correction. (Color figure online)

4 Discussions

The objective of the study was to assess the needs and opinion of a pool of BPI and PS subjects, to define the functional and technical requirements of a novel assistive device for ADLs support.

First, significant differences between the participants' responses were observed, particularly regarding the features that the novel assistive device should implement. This result, which is in line with the literature [10], is caused by the differences in the residual capabilities of the subjects and it is fundamental for the definition of functional and technical requirements of the new device. The functionality and reliability of the device is generally preferred to its appearance. However, while PS subjects rank the *Appearance* item as the least important characteristic (9th on average), BPI ones consider it more important (6th on average), probably due to the age difference between the subjects (PS subjects are 27 years older than BPI ones on average). The weight of the device is a fundamental design constraint, since the final device should maximize the assistance provided while minimizing the weights loaded on the subject's UL.

Second, as regards the ADL tasks to assist, most of the participants agree that the device should aid in reaching, grasping, and manipulation tasks. Thus, elbow flexion/extension movement and grasp primitives should be assisted by the device. Moreover, some subjects would benefit from assistance at the shoulder level, providing gravity compensation of the arm weight. Since most of the subjects would accept the use of FES, the final device can implement a hybrid robot-FES architecture, to maximize the benefits of both systems [17]. However, priorities of ADL tasks that the new device should assist are highly subject-dependent, as shown by numerous outlier responses and the absence of statistically significant differences between the highest ranked items. Therefore, the final design of the device should implement a modular architecture, to provide a subject-specific assistance and adaptability to different tasks.

Finally, almost all the participants agreed on the integration of a sensory feedback glove providing discrete vibrating signals when the hand is in contact with an object. This approach would help restore sensory functions along with motor ones, hopefully increasing the subject's perceived quality of life.

Acknowledgments. This study was promoted by the Italian National Institute for Insurance against Accidents at Work (INAIL) within the BioARM project, grant n° PR19-RR-P3.

References

1. Zollo, L., et al.: Restoring tactile sensations via neural interfaces for real-time force-and-slippage closed-loop control of bionic hands. Sci. Robot. (2019). https://doi.org/10.1126/scirobotics.aau9924
2. Chen, W., Xiong, C., Huang, X., Sun, R., Xiong, Y.: Kinematic analysis and dexterity evaluation of upper extremity in activities of daily living. Gait Posture **32**(4), 475–481 (2010). https://doi.org/10.1016/j.gaitpost.2010.07.005
3. Pons, J.L.: Rehabilitation exoskeletal robotics. IEEE Eng. Med. Biol. Mag. **29**(3), 57–63 (2010). https://doi.org/10.1109/MEMB.2010.936548
4. Trigili, E., et al.: Design and experimental characterization of a shoulder-elbow exoskeleton with compliant joints for post-stroke rehabilitation. IEEEASME Trans. Mechatron. **24**(4), 1485–1496 (2019). https://doi.org/10.1109/TMECH.2019.2907465
5. Stewart, A.M., Pretty, C.G., Adams, M., Chen, X.: Review of upper limb hybrid exoskeletons. IFAC-Pap. **50**(1), 15169–15178 (2017). https://doi.org/10.1016/j.ifacol.2017.08.2266
6. Clemente, F., D'Alonzo, M., Controzzi, M., Edin, B.B., Cipriani, C.: Non-Invasive, temporally discrete feedback of object contact and release improves grasp control of closed-loop myoelectric transradial prostheses. IEEE Trans. Neural Syst. Rehabil. Eng. **24**(12), 1314–1322 (2016). https://doi.org/10.1109/TNSRE.2015.2500586
7. Cappello, L., Baldi, R., Frederik, L., Cipriani, C.: "Chapter 6 - Noninvasive augmented sensory feedback in poststroke hand rehabilitation approaches. In: *Somatosensory Feedback for Neuroprosthetics*, B. Güçlü, Ed. Academic Press, 2021, pp. 207–244 (2021). https://doi.org/10.1016/B978-0-12-822828-9.00006-X
8. Shore, L., de Eyto, A., O'Sullivan, L.: Technology acceptance and perceptions of robotic assistive devices by older adults – implications for exoskeleton design. Disabil. Rehabil. Assist. Technol., 1–9 (2020). https://doi.org/10.1080/17483107.2020.1817988
9. Fanciullacci, C., et al.: Survey of transfemoral amputee experience and priorities for the user-centered design of powered robotic transfemoral prostheses. J. Neuro Eng. Rehabil. **18**(1), 168 (2021). https://doi.org/10.1186/s12984-021-00944-x
10. Boser, Q.A., Dawson, M.R., Schofield, J.S., Dziwenko, G.Y., Hebert, J.S.: Defining the design requirements for an assistive powered hand exoskeleton: a pilot explorative interview study and case series. Prosthet. Orthot. Int. **45**(2), 161–169 (2021). https://doi.org/10.1177/0309364620963943
11. Hill, D., Holloway, C.S., Ramirez, D.Z.M., Smitham, P., Pappas, Y.: What are user perspectives of exoskeleton technology? a literature review. Int. J. Technol. Assess. Health Care **33**(2), 160–167 (2017). https://doi.org/10.1017/S0266462317000460

12. Crea, S., et al.: "Feasibility and safety of shared EEG/EOG and vision-guided autonomous whole-arm exoskeleton control to perform activities of daily living. Sci. Rep., **8**(1), 1 (2018). https://doi.org/10.1038/s41598-018-29091-5
13. Ronsse, R., Vitiello, N., Lenzi, T., van den Kieboom, J., Carrozza, M.C., Ijspeert, A.J.: Human–robot synchrony: flexible assistance using adaptive oscillators. IEEE Trans. Biomed. Eng. **58**(4), 1001–1012 (2011). https://doi.org/10.1109/TBME.2010.2089629
14. Pilla, A. et al.: Robotic Rehabilitation and Multimodal Instrumented Assessment of Post-stroke Elbow Motor Functions—A Randomized Controlled Trial Protocol. In: *Front. Neurol.*, vol. 11, 2020, Accessed: Mar. 21 (2022). https://doi.org/10.3389/fneur.2020.587293
15. Howlett, O.A., Lannin, N.A., Ada, L., McKinstry, C.: Functional electrical stimulation improves activity after stroke: a systematic review with meta-analysis. Arch. Phys. Med. Rehabil. **96**(5), 934–943 (2015). https://doi.org/10.1016/j.apmr.2015.01.013
16. Bolognini, N., Russo, C., Edwards, D.J.: The sensory side of post-stroke motor rehabilitation. Restor. Neurol. Neurosci. **34**(4), 571–586 (2016). https://doi.org/10.3233/RNN-150606
17. Popović, D.B.: Chapter 20 - Hybrid FES-robot devices for training of activities of daily living. In: Rehabilitation Robotics, Colombo, R., Sanguineti, V., Eds. Academic Press, 2018, pp. 277–287 (2018). https://doi.org/10.1016/B978-0-12-811995-2.00020-5

Multimodal Wearable System for Motor Rehabilitation: Usability and Acceptability

Paolo Perego[1,2(✉)], Roberto Sironi[1,2], Martina Scagnoli[1], Maria Terraroli[1], Carlo Emilio Standoli[1], and Giuseppe Andreoni[1]

[1] Laboratory TeDH - Technology and Design for Healthcare, Department of Design, Politecnico di Milano, Milan, Italy
paolo.perego@polimi.it

[2] Sensibilab, Polo Territoriale di Lecco, Politecnico di Milano, Milan, Italy
http://www.tedh.polimi.it/,http://www.sensibilab.lecco.polimi.it/

Abstract. Wearables are one of the most promising technology for easing the transition towards a personalized medicine, bringing healthcare and rehabilitation from hospitals to homes. Wearables inherently carries with them all the problems of small, portable devices and technologists. These problems could be related to the design phase as the real needs of the user are often not taken into consideration. This paper aims to describe the design and application of a new method for usability and acceptability evaluation of wearable devices, which can be applied after the first low fidelity prototype or and the end of development phase in order to evaluate how easy the system is to use, when comfortable and invasive, but above all if it reflects.

Keywords: Wearable design · Rehabilitation · Usability protocol · Co-design · User-centered design

1 Introduction

Population aging and especially Covid-19 pandemic situation are leading most of society to reshape healthcare systems, transforming a system based on hospital care into a system in which care is more personal, personalized and delocalized within homes. These circumstances changed people habits, and also healthcare system has been forced to evolve, changing protocols and medical environments, bringing prevention, diagnosis and treatment no longer in clinics, but in everyone's houses.

In this transition, advanced technologies play a fundamental role transforming the cure in care and improving patients and caregivers life quality.

In this day and age, wearable devices could be the best solutions in term of costs/services ratio for monitoring people outside hospitals. Wearables are one of the most promising technology which can help in the transaction from

K. Miesenberger et al. (Eds.): ICCHP-AAATE 2022, LNCS 13342, pp. 428–436, 2022.
https://doi.org/10.1007/978-3-031-08645-8_50

today medicine (based on cure and treat people) towards a more personalized, predictive, preventive and participatory medicine [1].

Wearables are by definition instruments that are in close contact with the human body; for this reason human factor and usability are fundamental and need to be considered and tested during all the development phases. Current wearable solution for telemedia and tele-rehabilitation often came from consumer products, and for this reason are cumbersome and developed for use in other areas and with different users; these because the design phase does not take into consideration all the actors and the stakeholders who can operate and wear the system. Moreover, the use of small and wearable technologies requires dealing with different barriers related to the users' health status, which cab further undermine the effectiveness of the diagnosis/treatment due to the difficulty of use.

Starting from a wearable system developed involving directly the various stakeholders from the earliest stage of design [2], this paper aims to define a usability and performance validation approach applied for the testing of wearable sensing platform.

2 Materials and Methods

The MW (Multimodal Wearable) system is a wearable system designed for monitoring and evaluating motor rehabilitation activities in post-stroke patients. MW born form a project funded by "Centro Protesi" Inail, one of the research centers of the National Institute for Insurance against Accidents at Work in Italy. MW is a suit embedding sensors to monitor rehabilitation sessions or supporting the restart of working activities without affecting functions and/or mobility. The hardware components are small devices to be worn and placed into the dedicated receptacles mounted on the suit, and the smartphone app to start/stop/record sessions's data complete the system. The suit is composed in two parts, upper and lower body, which consists in a long sleeves shirt and trousers each of which has 7 hooks for connecting sensors. Based on the rehabilitation exercise, a full-body or an half-body configuration can be worn. The suit would result in an increase of comfort and efficacy of the therapy.

As described above in the introduction paragraph, the main core of the MW project is the migration form the classic clinics rehabilitation, to a more personal and comfortable home rehabilitation. This objective underline the importance of co-designing the entire system directly with users and stakeholders in order to be able to correctly respond to their needs and desires.

The MW system was developed based on User-Centred Design (UCD) full-stack ten tails (FSTT) approach defined by Perego et al. [3]. The FSTT approach is based son ISO9421 UCD that consists in for main stages: brief and user definition, co-design, features definition, developing and testing.

As described by the FSTT the testing stage is not related only to the last part of the design, but is consistent with all the development approach. As show in Fig. 1, the FSTT is not a linear sequential method, but consists of a continuous circular process of product/service improvement until the performances required by all the stakeholders are achieved.

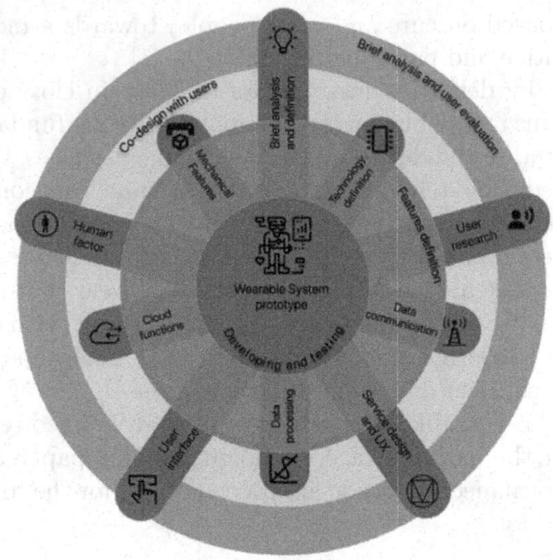

Fig. 1. Overview of the Full-stack ten tails (FSTT) approach.

The design iterations end only when the required performance off all the users and stakeholder are satisfied: both patients and doctors, nurses, physioterapists, relatives...

Having to meet the requirements of a plethora of different users and stakeholders, testing and iteration processes could become very time-consuming and expensive. For this reason, the drafting of an analysis and testing protocol is a mandatory part of the FSTT approach.

As for the FSTT approach, four main steps for the protocol definition are defined:

1. *Goals definition*
   The goals of the testing protocol is the outcome that designers desire from the test. It can consists in perceived comfort test regarding sensitized clothing, usability of the system, battery duration or system performances. Tasks definition needs to be strictly related to goals in order to optimize times and costs of carrying out the tests.
   In the use case of MW system, the expected goals/outcomes for the performance and usability protocols are:
   – Usability
   – Perceived comfort
   – Performance
   The goals of testing include establishing a baseline of user performance, establishing and validating user performance measures, and identifying potential design concerns to be addressed in order to improve the efficiency, comfort, and end-user satisfaction.

In order to have an index of performance, a baseline needs to be provided; for this reason, the performance test compares data of the MW system with respect to a gold standard technology. For this purpose, BTS mocap system and/or Xsens wearable mocap system, in standard protocol and movements of the upper limb according to Garofalo et al. 2009 [5], is used as comparison. The usability and perceived comfort tests focus on determining the design inconsistencies and usability problems during the use of the system (e.g. dress/undress problem, placement of the devices, functional performance, comfort problem).

2. *Tasks definition*
The main tasks of the system are defined during the initial definition stage in which a task analysis is executed. Task analysis is the process of learning about users by observing them in action to achieve a goal. Tasks analysis helps identify the tasks that applications must support. The tasks definition of the protocol drafting retraces the initial task analysis, to test all the main tasks that the user will perform within the system.
The task for usability test and performance test are different. Performance test is going to acquire the upper limb movements using both MW system and a gold standard. Comparison of the range of motion and angle patters in a timer normalized series is considered for validating and reliability assessment. The usability tasks were derived from test scenarios developed from use cases and/or with the assistance of a participant-matter expert. Preliminary sessions carried out during the development phase of the project have provided necessary input to the definition of this test plan and related protocol. Due to the range and extent of functionality provided in the application, and the short time for which each participant is available for the test, the tasks are the most common and relatively complex of available functions. The tasks are identical for all participants of a given user role in the study.
The usability testing protocol consists of 3 steps or phases:
Phase 1: observing the MW system and touching it; The facilitator and the project team members introduce MW system with its general description. The users can touch the system and devices but not wear and use it. Then, the user fills in the short questionnaire for this phase and describing product expectations.
Phase 2: wearing the system and preparing, before the rehabilitation session. The user is asked to wear the MW system. Ability to self-wearing the MW system and related time will be recorded. Non-critical errors will be eventually noted. The user has also to place the devices into the corresponding receptacles. In case of need of assistance, the facilitator will support the user in wearing the MW system and this operation is noted. Also in this second case wearing time will be recorded and non-critical errors will be eventually noted.

Phase 3: after having undressed the MW system and after the rehabilitation session.
The user activates the recording app on the smartphone. The user starts the simulated rehabilitation session for 10 min. At the end of this session, the user is asked to undress the MW system. Ability to self-undressing the MW system and related time will be recorded. Non-critical errors will be eventually noted. In case of need, the facilitator will assist the user in undressing the MW system and this operation is noted. Also in this second case wearing time will be recorded and non-critical errors will be eventually noted. After all these tasks, the user fills in the short final questionnaire for this phase and to verify the matching of the initial product expectations.

3. *Definition of the users:*
As for the ideation and product/service design phase, the definition of the users is a fundamental part for the protocol definition. The protocol needs to take into consideration different users, based both on expertise and other characteristics such as age, sex, schooling, disabilities...
All these characteristics, together with the cognitive age, digital literacy contribute to the acceptance of digital technologies [4]. Choosing the types of users for carrying out the tests is essential in order not to have final bias on the acquired data. For example, choosing users and experts in the field of mobile technologies can cause a wrong evaluation of the acceptability and usability of the system, as they are accustomed to the technology and are already aware of all those mental paths necessary for the use.
The usability testing includes 2 categories of users: direct users and caregivers, both considered primary users. Secondary users such as those participating in MW cleaning/maintenance and other secondary functions or in relation to the product lifecycle are not considered in this test plan due to the Covid-19 pandemic emergency which strongly affects the original protocol plans.
Having to test usability, perceived comfort and performances and having a fairly high number of stakeholders and type of users, the definition of the users for the tests can be different depending on the defined goals and tasks. In MW tests, the performance test is carried put on a sample of 5 healthy participants preferably ranging from the 5th female percentile in stature (about 155 cm) up to the 95th male percentile (about 185 cm). The user panel for the acceptability and usability test is designed as follows:
   - 5 health participants (also the same of the performance test);
   - 5 rehabilitation therapists/caregivers leading the therapeutic rehabilitative session and supporting some tasks (e.g. wearability, undressing the suit, first configuration...);
   - 5 patients or fragile people - the direct users - with acquired or congenital functional limitation running rehabilitation sessions.

Due Covid-19 emergency, the last 5 users only visual insect the MW system and fill in the assessment questionnaire without wearing and testing it for safety reason.
According to Faulkner [6], the above described sample is coherent to reach a confident value of 90%.
All users needs to be aged 18 or more and sign the informed consent. The panel need to possibly be gender balanced. The participants try to complete a set of representative task scenarios presented to them in as efficient and timely a manner as possible, and to provide feedback regarding the usability and acceptability of the user interface. The participants are directed to provide honest opinions regarding the usability of the application, and to participate in post-session subjective questionnaires and debriefing.
Moreover, the participants are going to receive an overview of the usability test procedure, equipment and methods before acceptance and participation to the test.

4. *Metrics definition*
   Metrics are fundamental to quantify the tasks outcomes. Depending on the number and type of tasks and goals, different evaluation metrics can be defined. These can be metrics derives dorm standardized methods (for example standardized usability test such as the SUS and the QUIS questionnaire), or associated with numerical values defined by the designer. In this second case the Likert scale is the most used and consists of a scale used to represent people's attitude to a topic.
   Usability metrics refers to user performance measured against specific performance goals necessary to satisfy usability requirements. Scenario completion success rates, adherence to dialog scripts, error rates, and subjective evaluations will be used. Time-to-completion of scenarios will also be collected.
   Three questionnaires will be administered to participants in three steps of user experience and usability of the product:
   - Showing the MW suit and system before wearing it;
   - After having worn the MW system;
   - At the end of the session, after having undressed the MW suit.

   The questionnaires are based on the Visual Analog Scale (VAS) or the Likert scale, each question with the proper resolution 5/7/9 points according to the validated semantic scale. A body part discomfort score complements the questionnaire. Some performance measures (e.g. time to complete the task) are recorded as well.
   Other two metrics are include in the protocol: successful self wearability/undressing (0/1 - N/Y, binary value); self wearability/undressing time (time in seconds with 2 decimals).
   Completion rate is recorded for any session; completion rate is the percentage of test participants who successfully complete the task without critical errors (Fig. 2).

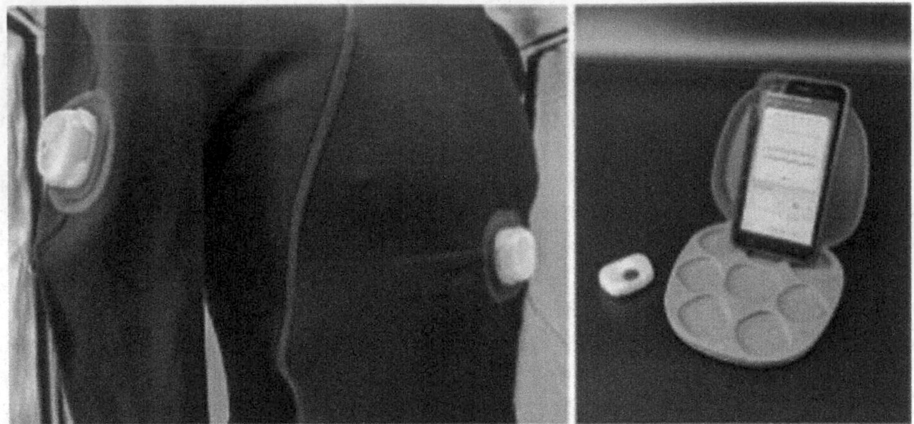

Fig. 2. The MW sensorized suit with the sensors, battery charger and mobile app.

3 Results and Discussion

15 participants (6 males and 9 females, aged between 25 and 60 years) participated to the usability tests. Out of total of 15 participants, 5 are healthy participants, 5 are therapists from the Centro di Riabilitazione Villa Beretta (CRVB) Valduce Hospital, 5 are participants with pathologies under treatment at CRVB. The factors that influence or not the digital acceptance by people are strongly linked with the same factors that determine the usability of a digital interface. Usually users with low digital acceptance, who tend not to be attracted to the products/services provided by digital and make very little or almost no use of them, are the same who, when interfacing with them, have greater difficulties in using them. This is because their low exposure to these interfaces does not put them in the position of being able to correctly recognize and use the design patterns that are usually implemented in digital interfaces. For this reason an heterogeneous sample of participants was selected; however all participants were in possession and regularly used a smartphone.

Wearability tests and surveys has been executed by healthy participants and therapists, and after that a standardized questionnaire (SUS - System Usability Scale) [7] has been administered to them; the SUS has been accompanied by other questions based on the Likert scale in order to measure the degree of acceptability of the system. For the pathological participants it has not be possible to carry out the wearability tests for precautionary reasons due to the Covid-19 pandemic emergency. The results (Fig. 3) emerged from the final overall evaluation show that there is an excellent adherence between the high initial expectations of the participants involved and the post-test evaluation of the system. This reasons that the system responds to the expected users' needs, in particular thanks to the first co-design phase that characterized the MW project. In general, the perceived quality of the system is high, a score that is substantially confirmed by the parameters analyzed in the usability assessment.

It should be emphasized that the quality of the information received by the system, the overall acceptance and appropriateness of the operations carried out by MW reach an optimal score (>6/7) while the other evaluation parameters are at very good values, close to the optimal. The slightly lower scores relate to wearability (4.1/5) and aesthetic acceptability (5.40/7) underlines the opportunity to improve the system, by working on the suit design and aesthetics and the methods of wearing and unwiring. The usability test also measured the wearing times of the system, which is around four minutes for dressing, and around a minute and half for undressing.

Finally, the mobile application developed to detect data has been tested by users; this App has an overall acceptability high score SUS 75.5/100 and in particular, by the category of users for which it was developed, the therapists, the score achieved has been 87.5/100.

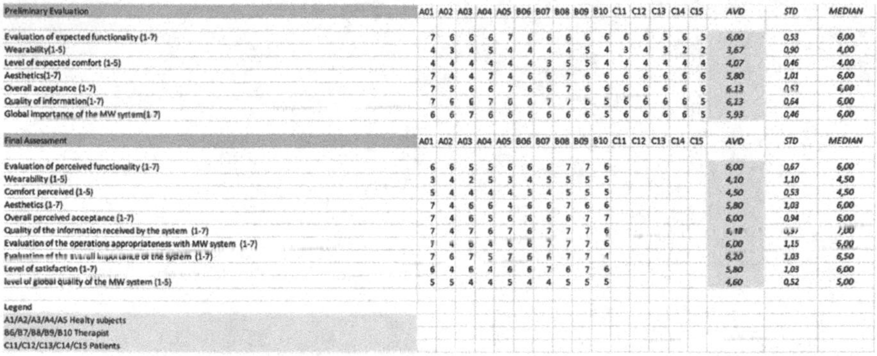

Preliminary Evaluation	A01	A02	A03	A04	A05	B06	B07	B08	B09	B10	C11	C12	C13	C14	C15	AVD	STD	MEDIAN
Evaluation of expected functionality (1-7)	7	6	6	6	7	6	6	6	6	6	6	6	5	6	5	6,00	0,53	6,00
Wearability(1-5)	4	3	4	5	4	4	4	4	5	4	3	4	3	2	2	3,67	0,90	4,00
Level of expected comfort (1-5)	4	4	4	4	4	4	3	5	5	4	4	4	4	4	4	4,07	0,46	4,00
Aesthetics(1-7)	7	4	4	7	4	6	6	7	6	6	6	6	6	6	6	5,80	1,01	6,00
Overall acceptance (1-7)	7	5	6	6	7	6	6	7	6	6	6	6	6	6	6	6.13	0,52	6,00
Quality of information(1-7)	7	6	6	7	6	6	7	7	6	5	6	6	6	6	5	6,13	0,64	6,00
Global importance of the MW sytem(1-7)	6	6	7	6	6	6	6	6	6	5	6	6	6	6	5	5,93	0,46	6,00
Final Assessment	**A01**	**A02**	**A03**	**A04**	**A05**	**B06**	**B07**	**B08**	**B09**	**B10**	**C11**	**C12**	**C13**	**C14**	**C15**	**AVD**	**STD**	**MEDIAN**
Evaluation of perceived functionality (1-7)	6	6	5	5	6	6	6	7	7	6						6,00	0,67	6,00
Wearability (1-5)	3	4	2	5	3	4	5	5	5	5						4,10	1,10	4,50
Comfort perceived (1-5)	5	4	4	4	4	5	4	5	5	5						4,50	0,53	4,50
Aesthetics (1-7)	7	4	6	6	4	6	6	7	6	6						5,80	1,03	6,00
Overall perceived acceptance (1-7)	7	4	6	5	6	6	6	6	7	7						6,00	0,94	6,00
Quality of the information received by the system (1-7)	7	4	7	6	7	6	7	7	7	6						6,18	0,97	7,00
Evaluation of the operations appropriateness with MW system (1-7)	7	4	6	4	6	6	7	7	7	6						6,00	1,15	6,00
Evaluation of the overall importance of the system (1-7)	7	6	7	5	7	6	6	7	7	4						6,20	1,03	6,50
Level of satisfaction (1-7)	6	4	6	4	6	6	7	6	7	6						5,80	1,03	6,00
level of global quality of the MW system (1-5)	5	5	4	4	5	4	4	5	5	5						4,60	0,52	5,00

Legend
A1/A2/A3/A4/A5 Healty subjects
B6/B7/B8/B9/B10 Therapist
C11/C12/C13/C14/C15 Patients

Fig. 3. The chart shows the results of the usability test.

Acknowledgments. This work has been supported by "Centro Protesi INAIL" - Vigorso di Budrio (BO), Italy, the main research center of the National Institute for Insurance against Accidents at Work. The authors would also like to thank all the focus group participant for their willingness and patience, and to eng. Angelo Davalli, eng Emanuele Gruppioni and eng. Rinaldo Sacchetti of INAIL Centro Protesi for supervising the research.

References

1. Flores, M., Glusman, G., Brogaard, K., Price, N.D., Hood, L.: P4 medicine: how systems medicine will transform the healthcare sector and society. Pers. Med. **10**(6), 565–576 (2013)
2. Perego, P., Scagnoli, M., Sironi, R.: Co-design the acceptability of Wearables in the Healthcare field. In: Proceeding of EAI HealthyIoT 2021–8th EAI International Conference on IoT Technologies for HealthCare, 24–26 November 2021 (2021)

3. Perego, P., Sironi, R., Scagnoli, M., Fusca, M., Gruppioni, E., Davalli, A.: Multimodal wearable system for motor rehabilitation - design perspective and development. In: Perego, P., TaheriNejad, N., Caon, M. (eds.) ICWH 2020. LNICST, vol. 376, pp. 99–106. Springer, Cham (2021). https://doi.org/10.1007/978-3-030-76066-3_8
4. Eastman, J.K., Iyer, R.: L'impatto dell'etá cognitiva sull'uso di Internet degli anziani: un'introduzione alle implicazioni di politica pubblica. Int. Stud. **29**(2), 125–136 (2005)
5. Garofalo, P., et al.: Inter-operator reliability and prediction bands of a novel protocol to measure the coordinated movements of shoulder-girdle and humerus in clinical settings. Med. Biol. Eng. Comput. **47**(5), 475–486 (2009)
6. Faulkner, L.: Beyond the five-user assumption: benefits of increased sample sizes in usability testing. Behav. Res. Methods Instrum. Comput. **35**(3), 379–383 (2003)
7. Kortum, P.T., Bangor, A.: Usability ratings for everyday products measured with the system usability scale. Int. J. Hum. Comput. Interact. **29**(2), 67–76 (2013)

Training with a Mobile FES-cycling System: A Case Study with a Spinal Cord Injured Pilot to Investigate Performances Optimization

Federica Ferrari[1(✉)], Nicole Sanna[2], Paolo Brambilla[2], Francesca Dell'Eva[1], Simona Ferrante[1], Marco Tarabini[2], Alessandra Pedrocchi[1], and Emilia Ambrosini[1]

[1] NearLab, Department of Electronics Information and Bioengineering, Politecnico di Milano, Milan, Italy
federica.ferrari@polimi.it

[2] Department of Mechanical Engineering, Politecnico di Milano, Milan, Italy

Abstract. Cycling by means of Functional Electrical Stimulation (FES) has proven to be a valid technique for the rehabilitation of patients with Spinal Cord Injuries (SCI). In particular, it can be seen not only as a therapeutical approach but also as an accessible form for people with disabilities to perform sport activity. In this case study, carried out in collaboration with INAIL Centro Protesi within the project FES-leg, a mobile FES-cycling system designed to provide real-time outcome measures about cycling performance is presented. A commercial passive recumbent trike has been adapted for use by cyclists with neurological conditions by adding two four-channel stimulators and a measuring system composed by an encoder, sensorized pedals and a heart rate sensor. Preliminary results with a single SCI pilot are shown, proving the feasibility of the system and the importance of constant training to increase motor performances. Furthermore, new sensor-based measures are proposed, and the possibility to exploit them to validate stimulation strategies and to optimize training performances is presented.

Keywords: Cycling · Spinal Cord Injury · Functional Electrical Stimulation · Sport therapy

1 Introduction

Most of the rehabilitation strategies after Spinal Cord Injuries (SCI) or strokes, exploit non-invasive techniques to maintain joint mobility of the affected limbs and to alleviate from secondary symptoms such as osteoporosis, spasticity and chronic pain. Important elements of these therapies are intensive and repetitive training, motivation, and potentially interactive devices [1].

Among these options, one is represented by Functional Electrical Stimulation (FES), a technique used for artificially eliciting muscle contractions, by applying

K. Miesenberger et al. (Eds.): ICCHP-AAATE 2022, LNCS 13342, pp. 437–444, 2022.
https://doi.org/10.1007/978-3-031-08645-8_51

trains of low-level electrical pulses to the intact peripheral motor nerves. As a neurorehabilitation approach that excites the muscles directly, FES has been widely used both as an assistive device to provide functional movement, but also as a therapeutic option, promoting recovery of motor functions and blood circulation, improving cardio-pulmonary fitness, increasing muscle trophism and range of motion, and decreasing bone demineralzation [2].

In the last decade, the combination of FES with cycling has renovated its interest, as a leading example of "Sport Therapy", since cycling can be maintained for reasonably long periods, maximizing activity dependent neuroplasticity [6].

The practice of FES-cycling 2–3 times per week for 10 weeks in individuals with SCI showed improvement in body composition, metabolic and neural factors in lower extremity, which is particularly important in individuals who experience the effects of chronic paralysis [3]. Moreover, FES-cycling provides an accessible form of exercise for people with limited possibility to participate in other forms of exercise, thus adding psychological benefits to the aforementioned therapeutical ones, favoring social inclusion and more engaging rehabilitation sessions. During FES-cycling, muscles groups of the lower limbs are stimulated sequentially, trying to emulate their physiological activation patterns. The stimulation strategy is defined by means of a look-up table specifying the range of the crank angle in which each muscle has to be stimulated to generate the cycling movement. In addition to the ranges, spatial and temporal characteristics of the stimulation wave-form can be manipulated as well, by adjusting different parameters (i.e., current amplitude, pulse width, and frequency). These parameters, together with the stimulation ranges, affect the resulting cycling performances.

Beside its benefits, some limitations are still related to this exercise because of its low metabolic efficacy (the ratio between external work output and metabolic energy input) and the early fatigue onset due to FES fibers recruitment, which affects the exercise performances, compared to volitional cycling [4]. In particular, the inefficacy of artificially muscle contraction and the critical muscle condition of the pilots are responsible of a very low power output produced during cycling. Some of the challenges of FES-cycling can be faced by the proposed system, which is able to provide outcome measures to precisely monitor the user's performance and the physiological state during the exercise. In this way, the stimulation parameters can be adjusted automatically to the needs of the user in order to delay the on-set of fatigue and to induce desired movements in an optimal way [5].

In this perspective, we present a mobile FES-cycling system designed to give real-time outcome measures and to allow the optimization of cycling performances, with the aim to maximize the efficacy of FES and minimize the early occurrence of muscle fatigue. Preliminary results on a single pilot with complete SCI showed significant performance improvement after a period of exercise and confirm the feasibility and the stability of the mobile FES-cycling system.

This work was performed in collaboration with INAIL Centro Protesi, within the project FESleg.

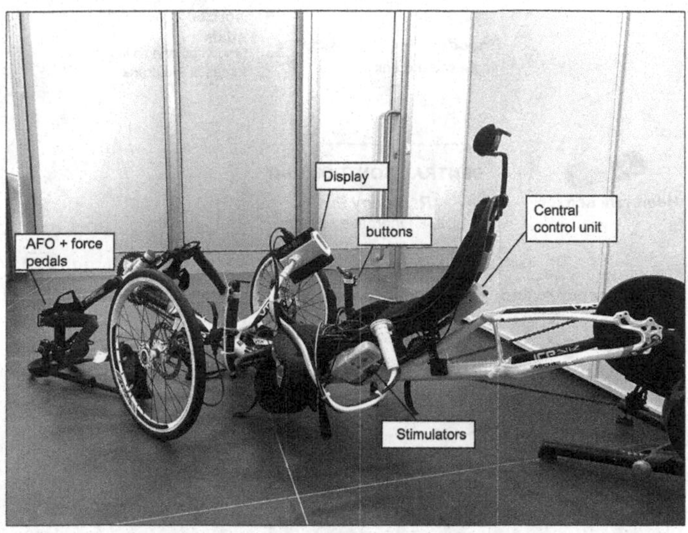

Fig. 1. Experimental set-up

2 The Mobile FES-cycling System

The complete system set-up is shown in Fig. 1. A commercial recumbent trike (ICE VTX^{TM}, 2017) has been adapted to be used by subjects with reduced mobility in conjunction with two four-channel current-controlled stimulators (RehaMove3^{TM}, Hasomed GmbH). Two ankle-foot orthoses (AFOs) have been developed to constraint the movement of the legs in the sagittal plane and lock the ankle angle at 90°. The control software of the system runs on a Raspberry Pi 4 model B with a Raspbian operating system - a Linux based Distribution. The control unit and all the electronic components are stored in a 3D printed box, which is located on the back of the seat and allows to make the trike comfortable to be used also in outdoor conditions. A power bank is used to power the system. A magnetic absolute encoder (AksIM^{TM}) has been placed at the crank to measure in real-time the crank angle with a sample frequency 200 Hz and a resolution of 16 bits (0.0055°). The current value of the crank angle is used to sequentially stimulate the different muscle groups of the lower limbs (i.e., quadriceps, gluteal muscles, hamstrings, and gastrocnemius) during each cycle. The muscle activation ranges are identified using a biomechanical model of FES-induced cycling implemented in MATLAB/Simulink® (The MathWorks, Inc. USA). The model of the FES-activated muscles was derived from the work of Riener et al. [7], and proved its ability to model fes-cycling in [8]. Within the stimulation environment the procedure described in [9] has been carried out to compute the stimulation angular range as the one in which each muscle gives a functional contribution to the cycling movement. Surface self-adhesive electrodes (Pals® from Axelgaard Manufacturing Co. Ltd.) are used to activate muscle delivering rectangular biphasic pulses, which are completely balanced in

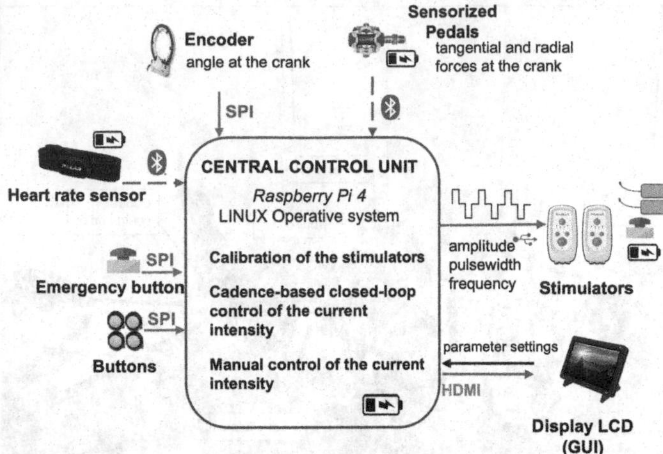

Fig. 2. System diagram

charge. The system also includes Bluetooth Low Energy (BLE) sensors to add the number of information that the device can provide. A heart rate sensor (H10 thoracic band by Polar) has been integrated to monitor the pilot's physical condition and send to the control unit the heart rate and the R-R interval with a sample frequency 1 Hz. Finally, two commercial MTB/quick release pedals (X-Power, SRM GmbH) are connected to the AFO to measure the radial and tangential forces exerted by each leg on the pedals (sample frequency 200 Hz). Based on these quantities, it is possible to compute the power output and evaluate the performances using specific indices such as smoothness and symmetry of movement. During the use of the trike, the subject could interact with the system through 4 buttons and a Graphical User Interface (Fig. 2) via an LCD Display, developed to enhance user's autonomy and system portability (Fig. 2). The system's modalities include the possibility to pedal at a fixed cadence thanks to the inclusion of a Proportional Integrative (PI) control which regulates the current intensity delivered to each muscle in such a way that a predetermined target cycling cadence is maintained. The target cadence can be set at the beginning of the training and modified during the session. The action of the PI is performed at the same way on all the muscle groups, while the initial and saturation values are characteristic for each muscle. The frequency of the stimulation and the pulse width can be set constant at a specific value at the beginning of the training. A second modality includes the possibility to regulate manually the intensity of the current delivered to each muscles independently. During the training the user can visualize useful data about stimulation (current intensity, pulse width and frequency), training session (elapsed time, measured force and actual cycling cadence) and system state (pedals and stimulators' residual battery charge). The trike is also equipped with an emergency button which immediately switches off the stimulation in case of emergency (Fig. 3).

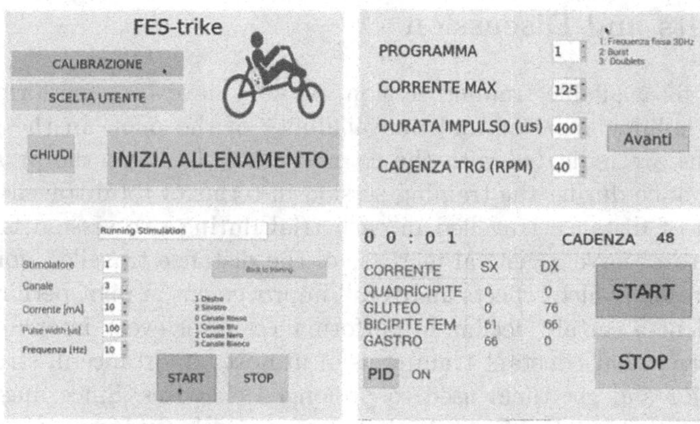

Fig. 3. Graphical User Interface

3 The Pilot

One single subject (38 years, 63 kg, 1.83 m) with complete SCI (T5, ASIA A, 2 years post-injury) participated in this case study. The participant gave his informed consent to the study. The Ethical Committee of Politecnico di Milano approved the study in September 2019.

4 Experimental Protocol and Outcome Measures

The trainings were conducted at Politecnico di Milano, Polo di Lecco, since July 2021. The experimental protocol consisted in 40 min sessions performed twice a week. During each session, four consecutive 10-minute trials were performed, with 6 min of rest between them. A smart trainer (KICKR from Wahoo Fitness^{TM}) substitutes the back wheel, and its resistance value was kept fixed for all the trials. The PI control was used in all the trials to maintain a fixed cadence. The target cadence was kept constant during each session and increased over time: starting from a target cadence of 30 RPM in session 1, we increased it to 35 RPM from session 16 on and to 40 RPM starting from session 33.

All the training specifications are listed in Table 1. The outcome measures used to assess performance improvements and the effect of muscular fatigue were the net time to reach saturation (i.e. the time elapsed from the beginning of the exercise until the maximum current value was reached), and the distance traveled within a session.

5 Results and Discussion

Out of the 62 available training session, only 44 have been performed due to closing for holiday vacation and unavailability of the pilot. In the graph, the interruptions are indicated with the colored areas. In Fig. 4 the progression of the performance during the training session in terms of total travelled distance as the sum of distance travelled in each trial during one session is shown. It is possible to observe a general increase of the distance travelled, for the same session duration, which reflects an overall improvement in pilot performances. It is also evident a certain decline in performances after every interruption. This result confirms that constant training is of utmost importance in strengthening weak muscles and get them used to prolonged exercises. Since muscles under stimulation fatigue early, it is likely that during a prolonged exercise, at a certain point they start to exert lower forces with the same amount of current delivered. Thus, one of the outcome measures that better represents the effect of muscle

Table 1. Training specifications

Initial currents	
Quadriceps	80 mA
Hamstrings	80 mA
Gastrocnemious	70 mA
Gluteus	70 mA
Other specifications	
Frequency	40 Hz
Pulsewidth	400 μs
Target cadence	30/35 rpm
Saturation current	120 mA

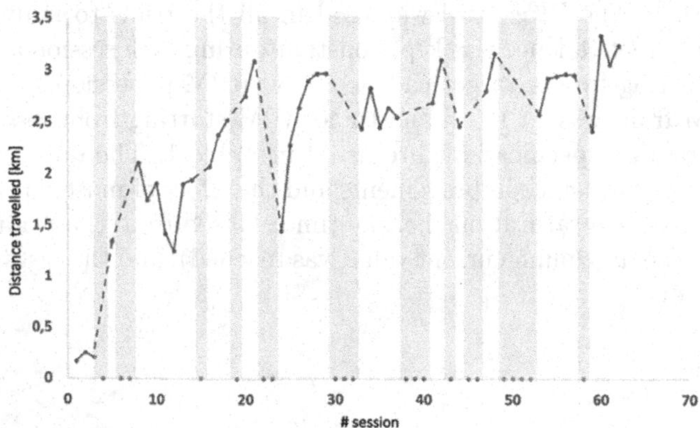

Fig. 4. Mean distance travelled over 4 trials for each available session

fatigue is the time elapsed between the beginning of the training and the point in which the saturation current is reached: the earlier the onset of muscle fatigue, the earlier the onset of saturation point. When saturation point is reached the system is limited in delivering an higher intensity of current to maintain the target cadence, thus the cadence starts decreasing due to the decrease of force applied by the muscles at the crank. Figure 5 reports the mean saturation time over the 4 trials for each session. Overall, the time to reach saturation showed a constant trend over the available sessions. This is due to the fact that the saturation time strongly depend on the target cadence: typically, the higher the pedaling cadence maintained, the lower the time to reach muscle fatigue onset. Therefore, since target cadence was increased to 35rpm from session 16 and to 40rpm from session 33, it is still not evident a constant increase of the saturation time over time, which is instead evident from the distance travelled (Fig. 4). Nevertheless, it showed a significant decrease after each interruption, meaning that the muscles needed a certain recovery after some days of pause to provide the same forces with the same amount of current and target cadence. Thus, the pilot showed an earlier onset of muscle fatigue after a pause.

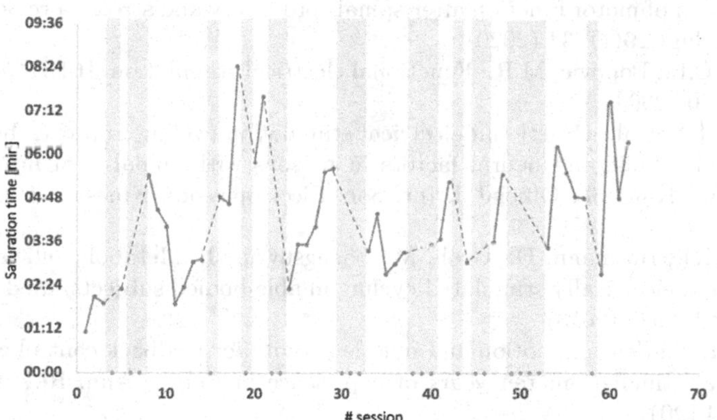

Fig. 5. Mean time to reach saturation over 4 trials for each available session

6 Conclusions and Future Developments

To conclude, in this paper a FES-cycling system to allow SCI subjects to perform rehabilitation and sport exercises is presented. The set-up can be used in an easy and safe manner, is portable and is adaptable to the anthropometric characteristics of the pilot. A sustained and constant use of the presented FES-cycling system has reported good results in terms of performances. In future, the analysis of the acquired data such as the force exerted at the pedals and the heart rate will allow to improve the measures of the performances and to better address the effect of muscular fatigue. In particular, relying on outcome measures, new experimental protocols will be proposed with the aim to investigate and optimize stimulation strategies, comparing different stimulation ranges and stimulation patterns. Moreover, based on sensor-based measures, it would be possible to implement control strategies to efficiently and automatically modulate the stimulation parameters during the training sessions in order to assure a symmetrical and physiological pedaling movement. To improve the engagement and the motivation of the pilot during the training session, a video-based platform will be included within the system to add the possibility to ride in a virtual reality environment. The final aim of this project will be the participation to the FES-bike discipline at Cybathlon 2024 [10].

Acknowledgements. This work was performed at WE-COBOT Lab - Politecnico di Milano Polo territoriale di Lecco, in collaboration with Centro Protesi INAIL within the project FESleg (PR19-RR-P5). We also thanks Axelgaard Manufacturing Ltd for donating us the stimulation electrodes.

References

1. Marquez-Chin, C., Popovic, M.R.: Functional electrical stimulation therapy for restoration of motor function after spinal cord injury and stroke: a review. Biomed. Eng. Online **19**(1), 34 (2020)
2. Lynch, C.L., Popovic, M.R.: Functional electrical stimulation. IEEE Control. Syst. **28**, 40–50 (2008)
3. Griffin, L., et al.: Functional electrical stimulation cycling improves body composition, metabolic and neural factors in persons with spinal cord injury. J. Electromyogr. Kinesiol.: Official J. Int. Soc. Electrophysiol. Kinesiol. **19**(4), 614–622 (2009)
4. Hunt, K.J., Hosmann, D., Grob, M., Saengsuwan, J.: Metabolic efficiency of volitional and electrically stimulated cycling in able-bodied subjects. Med. Eng. Phys. **35**(7), 919–925 (2013)
5. Schauer, T.: Sensing motion and muscle activity for feedback control of functional electrical stimulation: ten years of experience in Berlin. Ann. Rev. Control **44**, 355–374 (2017)
6. Newham, D.J., Donaldson, N.: Supplement FES cycling. Acta Neurochirurgica **97**(Pt 1), 395–402 (2007)
7. Riener, R., Fuhr, T.: Patient-driven control of FES-supported standing up: a simulation study. IEEE Trans. Rehabil. Eng. **6**(2), 113–124 (1998)
8. Wiesener, C., Schauer, T.: The Cybathlon RehaBike: inertial-sensor-driven functional electrical stimulation cycling by team Hasomed. IEEE Robot. Autom. Mag. **24**(4), 49–57 (2017)
9. Ambrosini, E., Ferrante, S., Schauer, T., Ferrigno, G., Molteni, F., Pedrocchi, A.: An automatic identification procedure to promote the use of FES-cycling training for hemiparetic patients. J. Healthcare Eng. **5**(3), 275–291 (2014)
10. Cybathlon Homepage. https://cybathlon.ethz.ch/en. Accessed 30 Mar 2022

Towards an Ontology-Based Decision Support System to Support Car-Reconfiguration for Novice Wheelchair Users

Daniele Spoladore[1,2](✉), Turgut Cilsal[1], Atieh Mahroo[1], Alberto Trombetta[2], and Marco Sacco[1]

[1] Institute of Intelligent Industrial Technologies and Systems for Advanced Manufacturing (STIIMA) National Research Council of Italy, Milan, Italy
{daniele.spoladore,turgut.cilsal,atieh.mahroo, marco.sacco}@stiima.cnr.it

[2] Department of Pure and Applied Sciences, Insubria University, Varese, Italy
alberto.trombetta@uninsubria.it

Abstract. The ability to drive a vehicle is fundamental to fostering people's independence, especially people characterized by physical disability. European regulations foresee that these drivers' cars need to undergo a process of adaptations that may involve modifying the vehicle's mechanics and adding specific driving aids depending on the particular driver's health condition. Since drivers can have access to different configurations for their vehicles, they may not be familiar with driving aids and how they modify the driving activity. To help drivers understand the possible car configurations and their aids, this work proposes an ontology-based decision support system (DSS) to identify the possible configurations and explicit the list of driving aids and mechanical modifications that the vehicle must equip. The DSS leverages ontology-based knowledge representation within the Rip@rto research project to determine and illustrate the possible car configurations. Also, taking advantage of a driving simulator and cognitive assessment of drivers, the DSS may support clinical personnel in defining restrictions and limitations to the use of vehicles for some drivers. This paper presents the ontology engineering process, delving into the domain analysis, conceptualization, and development phase of the DSS prototype, and sketches the future research directions.

Keywords: Ontology engineering · Ontology-based decision support system · Car configuration · Drivers with disability

1 Introduction

The ability to drive a vehicle is fundamental to fostering people's independence. Impairments deriving from traumatic accidents can cause this ability to deteriorate, especially when the impairments result in a permanent disability to the lower or upper limbs. In such a scenario, people affected by disability may be forced to rely on a wheelchair or prosthetics to perform several activities of daily life, including driving.

K. Miesenberger et al. (Eds.): ICCHP-AAATE 2022, LNCS 13342, pp. 445–452, 2022.
https://doi.org/10.1007/978-3-031-08645-8_52

However, these types of aids are not enough to ensure safe driving: in fact, cars are designed for people not characterized by physical disability (e.g., cars have pedals, sticks, knobs, etc. that are designed for "regular" people). Therefore, regular cars need to undergo a process of adaptations that may involve both modifying the vehicle's mechanics and adding specific driving aids – depending on the specific driver's health condition.

These vehicular modifications may also be a legal requirement that countries foresee to allow drivers with a disability to regain access to a driving license. In particular, in some European countries, the "special driving license" is granted by a medical committee. The medical professionals, taking into account the driver's health status and his/her impairments, can specify a set of driving aids, mechanical modifications and restrictions to the use of vehicles according to their expertise and local regulations. At the end of this clinical evaluation phase, the driver is granted a "special driving license", which replaces his/her original (and "regular") driving license. The special driving license lists the mandatory adaptations and modifications that the driver's car must have, and specifies the sets of physical aids (e.g., prosthetics, wheelchair, glasses, etc.) that the driver must use while driving. In particular cases, this type of license can also state some restrictions the driver must respect when driving (e.g., he/she is forbidden from driving for periods of time longer than a specific amount, he/she is restricted from driving in specific hours of the day or of the night, he/she is prohibited driving on highways, he/she must drive with another driver in the passenger seat, etc.).

While European countries are facing the effort to homogenize the various local regulations for special driving licenses, drivers characterized by disabilities are not familiar with the driving aids and possible modifications that their vehicles may undergo. To help these drivers to understand the possible car configurations and their aids, this work proposes an ontology-based decision support system (DSS) to identify the possible configurations – determined according to the driver's health condition – and to explicit the list of driving aids and mechanical modifications that the vehicle must have. The proposed DSS is one of the outputs of Rip@rto, a national research project financed by the Italian National Institute for Insurance against Accidents at Work (INAIL). Rip@rto foresees the development of a novel and immersive driving simulator to help drivers with disabilities get re-acquainted with their driving skills. During the driving simulation sessions, drivers are monitored via an EEG system to evaluate their cognitive performance in different and common driving situations (e.g., turning the vehicle, driving in metropolitan areas, driving in the highways, driving under different weather conditions, etc.). Along with the driving simulator, the possibility to provide a DSS based on expert and consolidated knowledge can act as a tool to support drivers with disability in understanding the possible modification of their vehicles. It can also help clinical personnel (not directly involved in granting the special driving license) to better understand the motivations behind some reconfiguration of the driver's car and the restrictions prescribed by specialized health professionals. The development of the ontology underlying the DSS must leverage both expert and consolidated clinical knowledge and take into account the Italian regulations for granting the special driving license.

2 European and Italian Regulations for Special Driver License

Even though many European local laws already foresee the special driving license for people with physical disabilities, the procedures and regulations are not homogeneous among various countries [1]. Nevertheless, in the last decade the European Union has started to rationalize the different local regulations, for instance with the Directive 2015/653 related to driving licenses, which Italy also adopted in 2016 and 2017 [2].

In Italy, the process for selecting what aids and modifications need to be adopted on a driver's vehicle must take into account both an evaluation of the driver's physical disability – under a physical and cognitive perspective – and the provisions described in national and European regulations. This evaluation is conducted by specialized health professionals. Also, the process takes into account the fact that it may be necessary to limit the driver's possibility to drive under certain circumstances.

While this process is transparent for clinical personnel, drivers who require their cars to be adapted are not familiar with the driving aids or the mechanical adaptations that could be mounted on their vehicles. Also, some disability conditions may require the driver's decisions on which adaptations he/she may want to use to drive, as various car configurations could be potentially set up for the driver's car according to national regulations.

3 Rip@rto Ontology

Considering the very rigid and regulated framework of the Italian (and European) laws describing the different modifications to vehicles and the health conditions for which the modifications are mandatory, the ontology appears to be a promising tool for knowledge representation. In fact, a computational ontology – i.e., a formal and shared conceptualization of a domain of knowledge [3] – enables a first-order logic-based representation of the regulations and their underlying concepts and relationships. Also, by leveraging on rules, the ontology can act as a backbone for an application DSS [4], which can be used to show drivers the adaptations that laws foresee for his/her car. Finally, the possibility to explain the inferences produced by ontology can support clinical personnel not directly involved in the process for granting the special driving license.

The ontology engineering process takes advantage of the findings of ontology development in the healthcare domains [5]: for Rip@rto, considering the relevance of structured sources of knowledge such as the regulations, the development of the ontology took advantage of a classical waterfall methodology [6] leveraging on the cooperation and expertise from clinical personnel from INAIL. The following subsections delve into the main phases of Rip@rto ontology engineering.

3.1 Domain Analysis and Knowledge Elicitation

The domain of candidate drivers applying for the special driving license involves several aspects that should be taken into account: the impairment conditions, the driving aids and their configuration.

According to the regulations mentioned in Sect. 2, the impairment conditions that are considered relevant for a candidate driver accessing the special driving license are two: a single impairment condition (i.e., an impairment occurring to a single limb) or a double impairment condition (i.e., an impairment occurring to two limbs). While the first category can involve only lower or upper limbs exclusively, the second category foresees the possibility of an impairment characterizing one upper limb and a lower limb. The Italian regulation foresees all the possible impairment conditions that can characterize a driver, which can range from a limitation of the functions of a single arm to more complex conditions (e.g., a myoelectric prosthetic to one of the arms and, at the same time, a complete functional limitation to a lower limb).

Therefore, a candidate driver can have only one impairment condition, which can be characterized by one of the 14 single impairments codes or one of the 130 double impairments codes. The impairment codes are named with integer ranging from 1 to 5, with the numbers from 1 to 3 dedicated to the representation of arm and hands-related impairments (with capital letters "A", "B", and "C" specifying different types of upper limb disability), and the numbers 4 and 5 reserved for lower limbs. By adding literal codes after each number, it is possible to specify whether the candidate driver wears a prosthetic (e.g., "1PM" indicates a person without an arm wearing a myoelectric prosthetic; "3PE" indicates a person without a hand or a comparable functional limitation wearing an aesthetic prosthetic). Double impairment conditions involving the same limbs (upper or lower) are represented with a juxtaposition of two codes (e.g., "2 + 3PM" indicates an arm characterized by agenesis or partial anatomical loss, and an arm characterized by the loss of a hand or comparable functional limitation supported by a myoelectric prosthetic): for this type of conditions, the side characterized by the most severe impairment needs to be specified. Double impairment conditions involving an upper limb and a lower limb present a juxtaposition of two integer numbers, which can also be completed with letters indicating whether the driver wears a prosthetics and specifying the side of the impairment (using "s" for left and "d" for right). For instance, "2PEs + 4d" indicates a driver with an aesthetic prosthetic on his/her left arm (due to agenesis or partial anatomical loss) and a non-functional right leg.

With regard to the cognitive function of the candidate drivers, clinical personnel conduct examinations with tests to verify the compatibility of each candidate with the driving tasks. Since Rip@rto foresees the possibility to acquire data from EEG, sensors and simulation sessions to provide a preliminary assessment of the level of risk perceived by the driver and of stress, these data can be used to inform clinical personnel in suggesting whether the candidate driver should be subjected to some limitations in the use of the car. Codes from "61" to "69" provide a list of limited uses (e.g., "61" suggests driving in day time journeys, "62" limits the radius of the journeys, "64" limits the speed to a specific amount).

The driving aids foreseen by the regulation are 57 and they involve different types of gearshift and transmission, clutch, accelerator, adaptations to car pedals and underbody, steering wheel, rear-view and lateral mirrors, and driver's seat. Each driving aid is coded with numbers from the European Directive 2015/653: for example, the code "40" describes modified steering wheels and contains subcodes for their descriptions (e.g., "40.05" indicates an adapted steering wheel; "40.14" stands for a steering wheel that can be controlled with one hand). Codes from "01" to "03" indicate those aids that a driver must wear to drive (e.g., "01.01" prescribes glasses, "01.02" prescribes contact lens, "03.01" prescribes an upper limb prosthetic/orthosis).

The driving aids are grouped into configurations, sets of aids and adaptations (each specified with their codes) that are thought to support drivers in particular impairment conditions: for each condition, at least one configuration must be available. For example, a candidate driver with an impairment condition specified as "2PEd + 4d" (aesthetic prosthetic to right arm and absence of functionality to the right leg) can take advantage of a configuration composed of "40.01" (Steering with maximum operation force of x N, with x being defined by clinical personnel), "40.11" (Assistive device at steering wheel), "35.02" (Control devices operable without releasing the steering device), and "03.01" (upper limb prosthetic/orthosis). Some configurations may be suitable for drivers with different impairment conditions, while some conditions may take advantage of different configurations.

3.2 Conceptualization

Taking the considerations described in the domain analysis above, the conceptual map deriving from the regulations and the discussion with INAIL personnel is reported in Fig. 1.

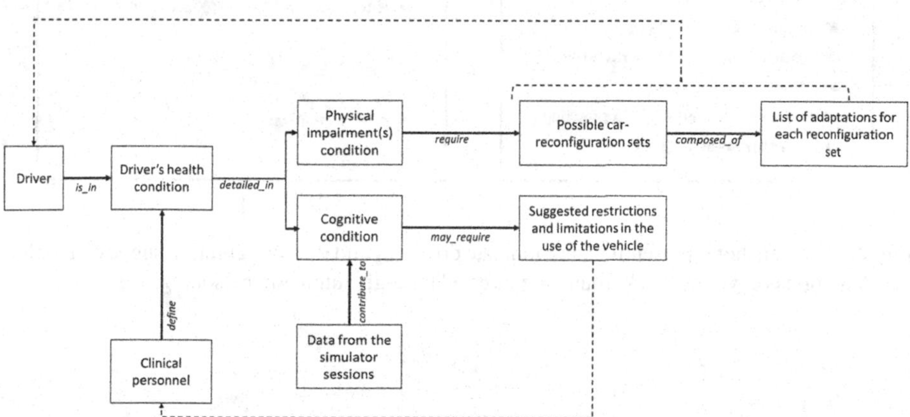

Fig. 1. An informal schema representing the different areas involved in the development of the DSS. Dotted lines indicate which DSS's outputs are delivered to drivers and clinical personnel.

3.3 Implementation and Development

The Rip@rto ontology is structured in a TBox (containing the classes and properties necessary to represent the knowledge), ABox (for modeling instances), and RBox (dedicated to rules, expressed with Semantic Web Rule Language (SWRL) [7]).

The model is developed with W3C-endorsed languages Resource Description Framework (RDF) [8] and Ontology Web Language (OWL) [9] (with Description Logic – DL profile), with the support of SPARQL [10] for query language, and makes use of well-established ontology design patterns in the fields of health (for example, the content patterns connecting an individual to his/her health condition [11]). The prototypical ontology of Rip@rto is composed of more than 2100 axioms, 310 individuals, 230 classes, and 180 rules to connect each impairment condition to its configurations. Using the Pellet DL reasoner engine [12], it is possible to explicit all the information entailed in the Rip@rto ontology.

To enable the possibility to indicate in which side the driving aids should be equipped, taking into account the candidate driver's most impaired side, some configurations specify the side on which it should be located. For example, for a candidate driver characterized by a "1B" single impairment condition on the right side, the configuration "04" (composed of the driving aids "40.01" and "10.02") is inferred to be located on the left side, so that the driver can use the aids (Fig. 2).

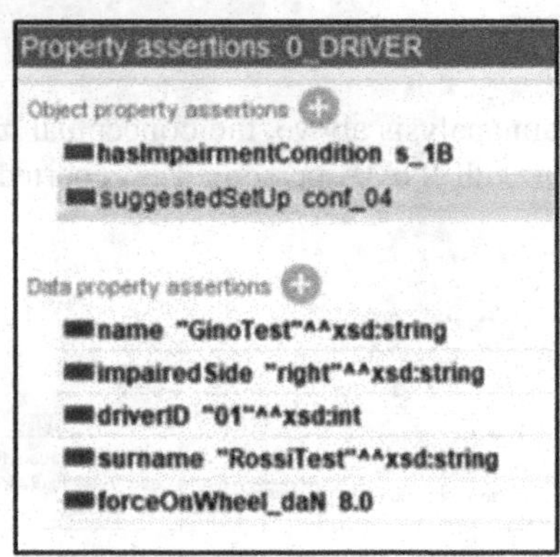

a

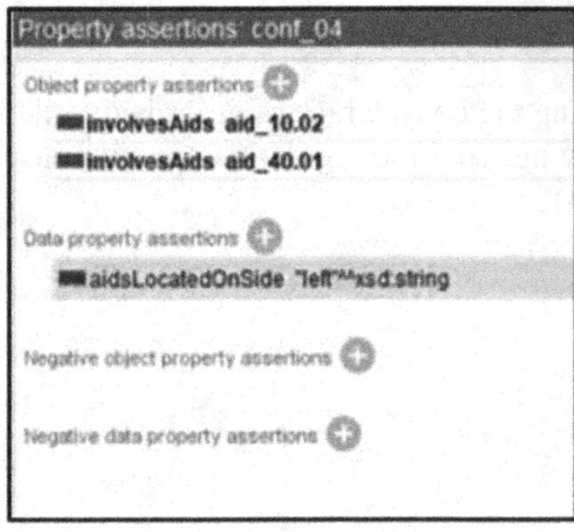

b

Fig. 2. A screenshot representing the candidate driver (a) and the configuration suggested for him (b). Assertions on yellow background are inferred through automatic reasoning.

A simple SPARQL query (Fig. 3) allows information retrieval about the candidate drivers modeled in the ontology and the configurations (and driving aids) proposed for each of them.

```
PREFIX owl: <http://www.w3.org/2002/07/owl#>
PREFIX rdf: <http://www.w3.org/1999/02/22-rdf-syntax-ns#>
PREFIX rdfs: <http://www.w3.org/2000/01/rdf-schema#>
PREFIX rip:<http://www.stiima.cnr.it/spoladore/Rip@rto#>

SELECT ?name ?sur ?cond ?configuration ?aids WHERE {
        ?user a rip:Canditate_driver ;
        rip:hasImpairmentCondition ?cond ;
        rip:name ?name ;
        rip:surname ?sur ;
        rip:suggestedSetUp ?configuration .
        ?configuration a rip:Car_configuration ;
        rip:involvesAids ?aids .
}
```

Fig. 3. A SPARQL query for retrieving any candidate driver, his/her impairment condition, and the car configurations (and driving aids) inferred for him/her.

4 Discussion and Future Works

The ontology-based DSS Rip@rto, in its prototypical state, can return the car configurations foreseen by the European and Italian regulations, specifying the driving aids and where they should be placed within the vehicle – using only the candidate driver's impairment conditions as an input. Although this DSS is still a prototype, the DL underlying the ontology proves to be expressive enough to represent the various cases (i.e., candidate drivers and their impairment conditions), with SWRL rules able to identify the different configurations a driver's car can accept.

Nonetheless, to support candidate drivers in getting familiar with the driving aids and their location inside the car and the mechanical adaptations their vehicle has to sustain, the Rip@rto DSS needs to be used in an application. Therefore, the development of a visual application – able to illustrate the drivers the shape, the functioning and the position of the driving aids in the car – is a fundamental step in this direction. With the application, drivers can get some more information about specific configurations, and – in case of multiple configurations available – they can select the one they believe to be most appropriate (with the support of clinical personnel).

Finally, Rip@rto needs to integrate data from the sensors investigating the level of risk perceived by the drivers and the amount of stress the driving activity in the simulator exerts on them. This information can be incorporated as input in the ontology to help clinical personnel define whether a user should be restricted in the use of vehicles. Therefore, the data from simulation and cognitive measurements would serve as an input for a second set of SWRL rules able to suggest one or more of the limited use codes presented in the European and Italian regulations.

5 Conclusion

This paper introduces the development of a Decision Support System dedicated to drivers characterized by impairments, who need to adapt their vehicles to be granted a special driving license. Drivers may not be familiar with the driving aids they need to adopt and use while driving, however these aids are necessary for them to be able to drive safely. After a discussion on the current European and Italian regulations on this matter, this work presents the ontology underlying the DSS, delving into its engineering process. The Domain analysis, conceptualization and development phases introduce the formalization of a candidate driver, his/her impairment condition, and the possible car configurations he/she can take advantage of. Also, the ontology-based DSS can illustrate for each car configuration the list of specific driving aids that must be equipped on the driver's vehicle. Taking advantage of the Rip@rto research project outputs, the DSS will integrate data gathered from driving simulation sessions and sensors to provide a representation of cognitive-related measurements (perceived risk, stress) and to support clinical personnel in defining the potential limitations in the use of a vehicle for a candidate driver.

References

1. European Commission: Commission Directive (EU) 2015/653 of 24 April 2015. https://eur-lex.europa.eu/legal-content/EN/TXT/?uri=CELEX%3A32015L0653
2. Italian Government: Decree 285/1992 (and successive modifications) "New highway Code, road safety and vehicle use in Italy", 1992. https://www.aci.it/i-servizi/normative/codice-della-strada.html
3. Gruber, T.R.: A translation approach to portable ontology specifications. Knowl. Acquis. **5**, 199–220 (1993)
4. Blomqvist, E.: The use of Semantic Web technologies for decision support–a survey. Semantic Web. **5**, 177–201 (2014)
5. Spoladore, D., Pessot, E.: Collaborative ontology engineering methodologies for the development of decision support systems: Case studies in the healthcare domain. Electronics **10**, 1060 (2021)
6. Uschold, M., Gruninger, M.: Ontologies: Principles, methods and applications. knowl. Eng. Rev. **11**, 93–136 (1996)
7. Horrocks, I., Patel-Schneider, P.F., Boley, H., Tabet, S., Grosof, B., Dean, M.: SWRL: A semantic web rule language combining OWL and RuleML. W3C Member Submission **21**, 1–31 (2004)
8. Pan, J.Z.: Resource Description Framework. In: Staab, S., Studer, R. (eds.) Handbook on ontologies. IHIS, pp. 71–90. Springer, Heidelberg (2009). https://doi.org/10.1007/978-3-540-92673-3_3
9. Antoniou, G., Van Harmelen, F.: Web ontology language: Owl. In: Handbook on ontologies. pp. 67–92. Springer (2004). https://doi.org/10.1007/978-3-540-24750-0_4
10. Sirin, E., Parsia, B.: SPARQL-DL: SPARQL Query for OWL-DL. In: OWLED. Citeseer (2007)
11. Spoladore, D., Mahroo, A., Trombetta, A., Sacco, M.: DOMUS: A domestic ontology managed ubiquitous system. J. Ambient Intell. Hum. Comput. **13**(6), 3037–3052 (2021)
12. Sirin, E., Parsia, B., Grau, B.C., Kalyanpur, A., Katz, Y.: Pellet: a practical OWL-DL reasoner. J. Web Seman. **5**, 51–53 (2007)

A Model-Based Framework for the Selection of Mechatronic Components of Wearable Robots: Preliminary Design of an Active Ankle-Foot Prosthesis

Alessandro Mazzarini[1,2(✉)], Ilaria Fagioli[1,2], Emilio Trigili[1,2], Tommaso Fiumalbi[1,2], Stefano Capitani[1,2], Emanuele Peperoni[1,2], Emanuele Gruppioni[3], Simona Crea[1,2], and Nicola Vitiello[1,2]

[1] The BioRobotics Institute, Scuola Superiore Sant'Anna, Pisa, Italy
alessandro.mazzarini@santannapisa.it
[2] Department of Excellence in Robotics & AI, Scuola Superiore Sant'Anna, Pisa, Italy
[3] Centro Protesi INAIL di Vigorso di Budrio, Bologna, Italy

Abstract. This paper presents a dynamic modelling approach to aid the selection process of actuation components during the design of wearable robots. As a case study, an application of the model to the preliminary design of a fully active ankle prosthesis is presented.

Keywords: Actuators · Wearable robotics · Active ankle prosthesis

1 Introduction

The advent of active wearable robots has implied a new set of requirements regarding devices' safety, power consumption, and weight. Actuators have become essential components that allow the robot to move and perceive interaction forces [1]. In this framework, choosing the appropriate components becomes critical to keep low weight and encumbrance while satisfying biomechanical requirements [2–4]. The development of actuators for robotic devices is still primarily guided by engineers' experience, instead of relying on a model that matches requirements and components' capabilities considering the dynamics of a task execution [5]. Moreover, hardware selection is often based on strict upper bounds on requirements that must be met, leading to mechatronic components oversizing [6, 7]. Additionally, the choice of actuators in robotics is made of antagonistic requirements. For example, high torques and high velocities are often required in daily-life activities like ground-level walking [8]: in this case, choosing a specific reduction gear is critical. Indeed, a high torque is achieved by using high-ratio transmission at the expense of lower output velocity and larger size, weight, and cost.

A. Mazzarini and I. Fagioli—Share authorship.
E. Gruppioni, S. Crea and N. Vitiello—Share the senior authorship.

K. Miesenberger et al. (Eds.): ICCHP-AAATE 2022, LNCS 13342, pp. 453–460, 2022.
https://doi.org/10.1007/978-3-031-08645-8_53

Springs placed in parallel to the actuator can reduce the torque and power requirements of the actuator [8, 9] whereas springs placed in series to the actuator help regulate joint torque and offer shock tolerance [10, 11]. Avoiding oversizing of mechanical components is particularly critical in the prosthetic field, where the encumbrance and weight of the device must not be greater than those of the missing limb [12].

Motivated by these considerations, we present a dynamic modelling approach to guide the choice of actuation components of a wearable robot, considering the biomechanical requirements in terms of joint torques and velocities in the main tasks the device should assist. The novelty of this approach resides in the possibility to simulate different working conditions by giving as input to the model data either found in literature or extracted by ad-hoc acquisitions. Such a dynamic model can provide quantitative estimates of current absorption, power generation, torque, and speed during the functional tasks the device is assisting aiding components' selection. This allows to optimize the most critical aspects in the design of a wearable robot, like weight, encumbrance, battery duration and electrical consumption. Hereby, we present a use case for the preliminary design of an active ankle prosthesis with series and unidirectional parallel elasticity, for which desired actuation components can be selected based on a prototypical Ground Level Walking (GLW) task to assist.

2 Theoretical Framework and Methodology

The modelling approach we present allows extracting key motor functioning features, such as the torque and velocity profiles during a work cycle, current consumption, and power expenditure, given the motor's characteristics and the desired task to assist. A working cycle is defined as a specific task's desired position, velocity, and force profiles. The basic model we used as a footprint of our dynamic simulations computes the total torque exerted by the motor as the sum of three main contributions:

$$\tau_M = J \cdot \ddot{\theta}_M + B \cdot \dot{\theta}_M + \frac{\tau_L}{rr} \tag{1}$$

where θ_M is the motor's position, τ_L is the load torque on the motor, rr is the reduction ratio of the gearbox, if present, and J and B are the equivalent inertia and the damping term of the actuation unit, respectively. We assumed the current I_M supplied to the motor to be proportional to the torque through the torque constant k_t:

$$I_M = \frac{\tau_M}{k_t} \tag{2}$$

The saturation current limits I^+_{max} and I^-_{max} can be computed by taking into consideration the supply voltage V and the counter-electromotive force (back-EMF), $k_e \cdot \dot{\theta}_M$:

$$I^+_{max} = \frac{V - k_e \cdot \dot{\theta}_M}{R}, \quad I^-_{max} = -\frac{V + k_e \cdot \dot{\theta}_M}{R} \tag{3}$$

where k_e is the back-EMF constant, R is the motor's thermal resistance, and $\dot{\theta}_M$ is the motor speed. Once the required motor velocity is known, the instantaneous voltage V_M, electrical power P_M and energy consumptions E are respectively computed as in [8] and [13]:

$$V_M = k_e \cdot \dot{\theta}_M + R \cdot I_M \tag{4}$$

$$P_M = V_M \cdot I_M \tag{5}$$

$$E = \int P_M dt \tag{6}$$

The model can also help in selecting batteries to power the motor by estimating the number of work cycles that could be performed with a battery charge. Indeed, given the nominal voltage V_b, the capacity C_b and the weight w of a battery cell, the energy density U can be computed as:

$$U = \frac{V_b \cdot C_b}{w} \tag{7}$$

By multiplying the battery energy density by the total battery weight w_{tot}, it is possible to find the total energy the battery can supply, E_{tot}. The total battery weight is given by multiplying the weight of a single battery cell w by the number of cells n, which depends on the motor voltage characteristics. Lastly, the device's autonomy in terms of work cycles S is computed as the ratio between E_{tot} and E, defined as the energy required by the motor in a single work cycle:

$$S = \frac{E_{tot}}{E} \tag{8}$$

3 Use Case

The dynamic model presented in this work has been used for the preliminary design of a fully active ankle prosthesis for transtibial amputees. The prosthesis has been conceived to embed a Series Elastic Actuator (SEA) [10] and a unidirectional parallel torsional spring (Fig. 1). The latter engages with the SEA when the ankle joint angle θ_{ref} goes beyond a specific angle θ_{eng}.

We decided to assess the prosthesis' performance during GLW, the primary goal for gait restoration [1]. We extracted the ankle angle profile θ_{ref} and torque profile τ_{ref} from a biomechanical dataset [14] as inputs to the model. The duration of the work cycle was set to one second, in accordance with gait parameters reported in the literature [15]. When the unidirectional, torsional parallel spring is engaged, it produces a torque τ_p that reduces the motor's burden during dorsiflexion [16]:

$$\tau_l = \tau_{ref} - \tau_p \tag{9}$$

$$\tau_p = \begin{cases} K_p \cdot (\theta_{ref} - \theta_{eng}) & if\ \theta_{ref} \geq \theta_{eng} \\ 0 & otherwise \end{cases} \tag{10}$$

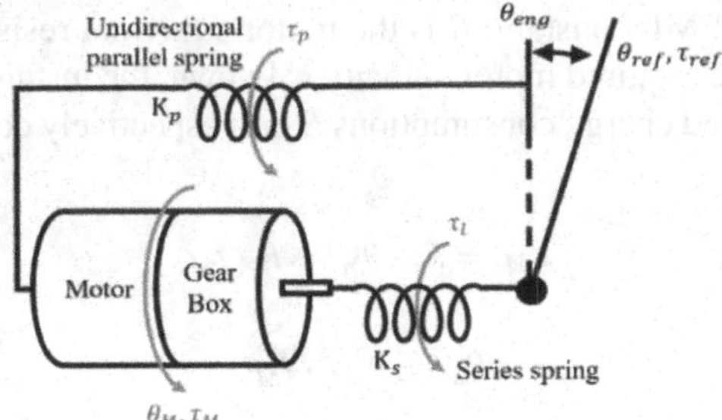

Fig. 1. Schematic representation of the mechanical structure of the active ankle prosthesis.

where τ_l is the torque at the SEA's output. To account for the presence of the torsional series spring of elastic constant K_s, the motor velocity is expressed as:

$$\dot{\theta}_M = rr \cdot \left(\frac{\tau_L}{K_s} + \dot{\theta}_{ref}\right) \tag{11}$$

In our simulation, a Harmonic Drive (HD) was employed as the reduction stage of the motor. Since the damping term B of Eq. (1) is not *apriori* known, the term $B \cdot \dot{\theta}_M$ can be approximated as a generalized losses term B_{loss}, which is the sum of a static contribution B_{st} and a dynamic contribution B_{dyn} [17]:

$$\begin{aligned} B_{loss} &= B_{st}(\dot{\theta}_M) + B_{dyn}(\dot{\theta}_M) \\ &= \text{sign}(\dot{\theta}_M) \cdot \tau_{st} \cdot e^{-|\dot{\theta}_M|} + \text{sign}(\dot{\theta}_M) \cdot \left(p_1 + p_2 \cdot |\dot{\theta}_M| + p_3 \cdot \dot{\theta}_M^2\right) \end{aligned} \tag{12}$$

where τ_{st} is the HD's starting torque, and p_1, p_2, p_3 are the coefficients of a second-order polynomial that determines the no-load running torque as a function of the motor speed. Table 1 and Table 2 report the inputs and the outputs of the model.

Table 1. Inputs required by the model.

Input		Measurement unit
Motor	Back-EMF constant k_e	$\frac{V \cdot s}{rad}$
	Torque constant k_t	$\frac{Nm}{A}$
	Thermal resistance R	Ω
	Supply voltage V	V
Harmonic drive	Reduction ratio rr	#
	Starting torque τ_{st}	Nm
Spring	Series stiffness K_s	$\frac{Nm}{rad}$
	Parallel stiffness K_p	$\frac{Nm}{rad}$
	Engagement angle θ_{eng}	deg

(continued)

Table 1. (*continued*)

Input		Measurement unit
Work cycle	Ankle angle profile θ_{ref}	deg
	Ankle torque profile τ_{ref}	Nm
CAD	Inertia J	$kg \cdot m^2$
Battery	Nominal capacity C_b	Ah
	Nominal voltage V_b	V
	Cell weight w	kg
	Number of cells n	#

Table 2. Outputs of the model.

Output	Measurement unit
Motor current I_m	A
Motor voltage V_m	V
Motor power P_m	W
Energy E	J
Motor speed $\dot{\theta}_m$	rpm
Motor torque τ_m	Nm
Number of work cycles S	#

Since the selection and sizing of one actuation component strongly affect the choice of other elements of the architecture (and vice-versa), the design process was inherently iterative. A pool of mechatronic components was selected by considering weight, height, and encumbrance requirements [6]. We also required the parallel spring to exert a peak torque of at least 40 Nm, approximately 1/3 of the biomechanical peak torque generated by a subject of 90 kg. Following these considerations, dynamic simulations were carried out by evaluating possible combinations of five components: the motor, the harmonic drive, the series spring, the parallel spring, and the engagement angle of the parallel spring. During the evaluation of different combinations, three main requirements were taken into consideration: (i) the current to be within the thermal limits for the whole task, defined as three times the rated current (namely the overload region); (ii) the required motor velocity not to exceed the no-load velocity of the motor and the maximum input velocity to the gearbox; (iii) the motor torque not to exceed the repeatable maximum torque of the gearbox. If more combinations satisfied these three requirements, the combination with the lowest energy consumption was selected to ensure increased battery life. Figure 2 shows the simulation output obtained using a 24 V frameless motor, a Harmonic Drive CSD-20-2A with a reduction ratio of 160:1, a series spring stiffness of 1200 Nm/rad, a parallel spring stiffness of 250 Nm/rad, and an engagement angle of 0°. Stiffness values were obtained by FEM simulations of custom-made torsional springs. The stiffness value of the series spring was chosen in order to provide shock tolerance without adding excessive delay in the system's dynamic response, according to similar studies [8, 18]. For the parallel spring, FEM simulations were carried out to grant that the custom-made design could bear a torque up to 70 Nm and deform up to the biomechanical dorsiflexion peak, which corresponds to 15°, without yielding. We obtained a maximum absolute motor current of 16 A, a maximum absolute motor speed of 6500 rpm, and a maximum absolute SEA torque of 54.5 Nm. All the values were within the physical limits of the chosen components (Fig. 2c, -d and -e). In fact, even if the current goes over the safety region delimited by the value of the rated current, this is acceptable since it only occurs for a small portion of the work cycle. Moreover, the estimated prosthesis autonomy using six Panasonic NCR18650PF cells is of 4200 strides, which is in line with the reported daily activity of transtibial amputees [19].

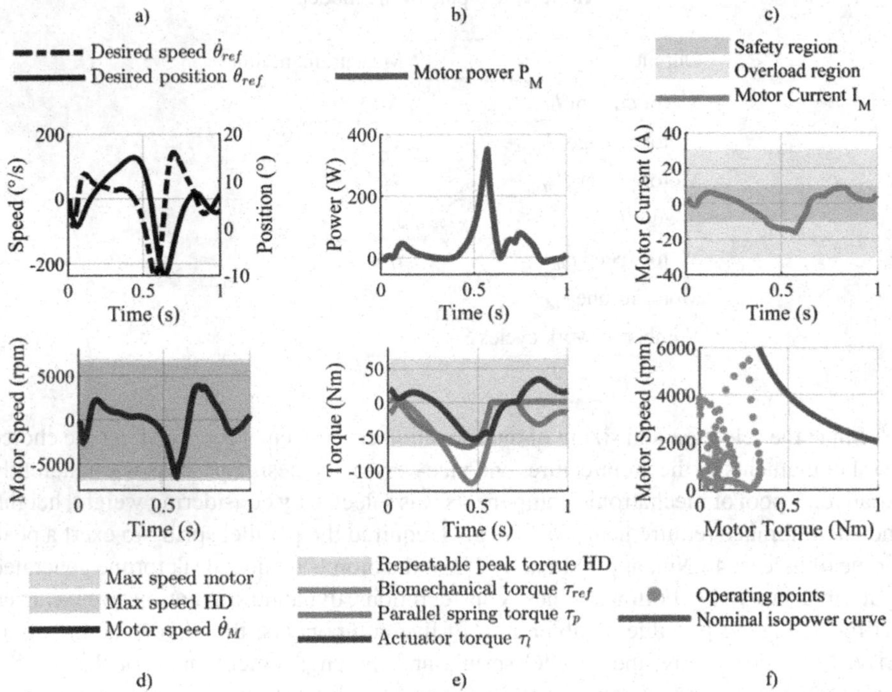

Fig. 2. Output of the dynamic simulation. a) Input biomechanical position and speed in a work cycle, b) output motor power, c) output current and safety limits of the motor, d) output motor speed and safety limits of the motor and HD, e) output actuator and parallel spring torques compared to the biomechanical torque and HD safety limits, f) output operating points and nominal isopower curve. All the estimates given by the model satisfy the requirements set.

4 Summary and Future Perspectives

We presented a dynamic model that estimates the torque, current, power consumption and speed requirements of an actuator during a prototypical task. We used this approach to iteratively refine components selection of a fully active ankle prosthesis. We believe that this methodology represents a viable framework for developing prostheses and orthoses that satisfy biomechanical requirements while balancing weight, power, and encumbrance requirements of the actuation units, as well as battery lifespan. We also believe that the strength of our model is that it allows to account for the dynamics of the biomechanical system within the design loop of a wearable device. Although we presented a case study for a series-elastic actuator, the proposed approach can be easily generalized to any actuation unit's architecture, given the knowledge of a few specific parameters of its components and the dynamics of the tasks to be assisted. In case the modeled architecture employs a transmission system different from the Harmonic Drive, such as planetary gearheads or Bowden cables, a proper modelling of its friction losses and non-linearities will be required. Future work will expand the model to include the system's bandwidth estimation and an analysis of the thermal limits. Moreover, the model estimates will be benchmarked against experimental results from the active ankle prosthesis under development.

Acknowledgements. This study was supported by the projects PPR-AI 1-2 MOTU and PR19-PAI-P2 MOTU++, both promoted by INAIL (Centro Protesi, Budrio, Italy).

References

1. Grimmer, M.: Powered Lower Limb Prostheses, p. 168 (2015)
2. Baldoni, A., Cempini, M., Cortese, M., Crea, S., Carrozza, M.C., Vitiello, N.: Design and validation of a miniaturized SEA transmission system. Mechatronics **49**, 149–156 (2018). https://doi.org/10.1016/j.mechatronics.2017.12.003
3. Giovacchini, F., et al.: A light-weight active orthosis for hip movement assistance. Rob. Auton. Syst. **73**, 123–134 (2015). https://doi.org/10.1016/j.robot.2014.08.015
4. Lanotte, F., et al.: Design and characterization of a multi-joint underactuated low-back exoskeleton for lifting tasks. In: Proceedings of the IEEE RAS EMBS International Conference on Biomedical Robotics and Biomechatronics, vol. 2020, pp. 1146–1151, November (2020). https://doi.org/10.1109/BioRob49111.2020.9224370
5. Malzahn, J., Roozing, W., Tsagarakis, N.: The compliant joint toolbox for MATLAB: an introduction with examples. IEEE Robot. Autom. Mag. **26**(3), 52–63 (2019). https://doi.org/10.1109/MRA.2019.2896360
6. Calanca, A., et al.: Actuation selection for assistive exoskeletons: matching capabilities to task requirements. IEEE Trans. Neural Syst. Rehabil. Eng. **28**(9), 2053–2062 (2020). https://doi.org/10.1109/TNSRE.2020.3010829
7. Au, S.K., Weber, J., Herr, H.: Biomechanical design of a powered ankle-foot prosthesis. In: 2007 IEEE 10th International Conference on Rehabilitation Robotics, ICORR 2007, pp. 298–303 (2007). https://doi.org/10.1109/ICORR.2007.4428441
8. Au, S., Berniker, M., Herr, H.: Powered ankle-foot prosthesis to assist level-ground and stair-descent gaits. Neural Netw. **21**(4), 654–666 (2008). https://doi.org/10.1016/j.neunet.2008.03.006

9. Ferris, A.E., Aldridge, J.M., Rábago, C.A., Wilken, J.M.: Evaluation of a powered ankle-foot prosthetic system during walking. Arch. Phys. Med. Rehabil. **93**(11), 1911–1918 (2012). https://doi.org/10.1016/j.apmr.2012.06.009
10. Pratt, G.A., Williamson, M.M.: Series elastic actuators.pdf. In: Intelligent Robots and Systems 95. Human Robot Interaction and Cooperative Robots, pp. 399–406 (1995)
11. Trigili, E., et al.: Design and experimental characterization of a shoulder-elbow exoskeleton with compliant joints for post-stroke rehabilitation. IEEE/ASME Trans. Mechatron. **24**(4), 1485–1496 (2020). https://doi.org/10.1109/TMECH.2019.2907465
12. Voloshina, A.S., Collins, S.H.: A Review of Design and Control Approaches in Lower-Limb Prosthetic Devices, pp. 1–21 (2019)
13. Verstraten, T., Furnemont, R., Mathijssen, G., Vanderborght, B., Lefeber, D.: Energy consumption of geared DC motors in dynamic applications: comparing modeling approaches. IEEE Robot. Autom. Lett. **1**(1), 524–530 (2016). https://doi.org/10.1109/LRA.2016.2517820
14. Bovi, G., Rabuffetti, M., Mazzoleni, P., Ferrarin, M.: A multiple-task gait analysis approach: Kinematic, kinetic and EMG reference data for healthy young and adult subjects. Gait Posture **33**(1), 6–13 (2011). https://doi.org/10.1016/j.gaitpost.2010.08.009
15. Isakov, E., Keren, O., Benjuya, N.: Trans-tibial amputee gait: time-distance parameters and EMG activity. Prosthet. Orthot. Int. **24**(3), 216–220 (2000). https://doi.org/10.1080/03093640008726550
16. Lawson, B.E., Mitchell, J., Truex, D., Shultz, A., Ledoux, E., Goldfarb, M.: A robotic leg prosthesis: design, control, and implementation. IEEE Robot. Autom. Mag. **21**(4), 70–81 (2014). https://doi.org/10.1109/MRA.2014.2360303
17. Papadopoulos, E.G., Chasparis, G.C.: Analysis and model-based control of servomechanisms with friction. J. Dyn. Syst. Meas. Control Trans. ASME **126**(4), 911–915 (2004). https://doi.org/10.1115/1.1849245
18. Liu, J., et al.: Optimization and comparison of typical elastic actuators in powered ankle-foot prosthesis. Int. J. Control Autom. Syst. **20**(1), 232–242 (2022)
19. Klute, G.K., Berge, J.S., Orendurff, M.S., Williams, R.M., Czerniecki, J.M.: Prosthetic intervention effects on activity of lower-extremity amputees. Arch. Phys. Med. Rehabil. **87**(5), 717–722 (2006). https://doi.org/10.1016/j.apmr.2006.02.007

Pointing Gestures for Human-Robot Interaction in Service Robotics: A Feasibility Study

Luca Pozzi[1](✉), Marta Gandolla[2], and Loris Roveda[3]

[1] Mechanical Department, WE-COBOT Lab (Polo Territoriale di Lecco), Politecnico di Milano, Lecco, Italy
luca.pozzi@polimi.it
[2] Mechanical Department, Politecnico di Milano, Milano, Italy
[3] Istituto Dalle Molle di Studi sull'Intelligenza Artificiale (IDSIA), Scuola Universitaria Professionale della Svizzera Italiana (SUPSI), Università della Svizzera italiana (USI), Lugano, Switzerland

Abstract. Research in service robotics strives at having a positive impact on people's quality of life by the introduction of robotic helpers for everyday activities. From this ambition arises the need of enabling natural communication between robots and ordinary people. For this reason, Human-Robot Interaction (HRI) is an extensively investigated topic, exceeding language-based exchange of information, to include all the relevant facets of communication. Each aspect of communication (*e.g.* hearing, sight, touch) comes with its own peculiar strengths and limits, thus they are often combined to improve robustness and naturalness. In this contribution, an HRI framework is presented, based on pointing gestures as the preferred interaction strategy. Pointing gestures are selected as they are an innate behavior to direct another attention, and thus could represent a natural way to require a service to a robot. To complement the visual information, the user could be prompted to give voice commands to resolve ambiguities and prevent the execution of unintended actions. The two layers (perceptive and semantic) architecture of the proposed HRI system is described. The perceptive layer is responsible for objects mapping, action detection, and assessment of the indicated direction. Moreover, it has to listen to uses' voice commands. To avoid privacy issues and not burden the computational resources of the robot, the interaction would be triggered by a wake-word detection system. The semantic layer receives the information processed by the perceptive layer and determines which actions are available for the selected object. The decision is based on object's characteristics, contextual information and user vocal feedbacks are exploited to resolve ambiguities. A pilot implementation of the semantic layer is detailed, and qualitative results are shown. The preliminary findings on the validity of the proposed system, as well as on the limitations of a purely vision-based approach, are discussed.

Keywords: Human-Robot Interaction · Pointing · Service robotics · Action detection

K. Miesenberger et al. (Eds.): ICCHP-AAATE 2022, LNCS 13342, pp. 461–468, 2022.
https://doi.org/10.1007/978-3-031-08645-8_54

1 Background

The term *robot* was introduced in 1920 by the Czech playwright Karel Čapek in his sci-fi drama "R.U.R" [15], adapting a Slavic word for *forced labor*. Although the term remains unchanged, robots trascended their original role of tireless factory workers and nowadays promise to assist humans in many different contexts. Enhanced hardware functionalities can be combined with artificial intelligence algorithms, so to let the robots work autonomously in unstructured environments. As a consequence, Service Robotics (SR) is gaining popularity and robots are being deployed in public places such as hotels, airports or hospitals, as they can increase productivity, guaranteeing service consistency [14]. With particular reference to the healthcare sector, burdened by the ageing of the world population and professional staff shortage, SR offers an appealing solution to relief the medical personnel and to improve the quality of the cares [10].

Though non-social service robots exist (*e.g.* for cleaning, monitoring...), the use of SR might have a great impact in supporting heterogeneous and personalized tasks execution in an unstructured environment. In this sense, Human-Robot Interaction (HRI) and SR become closely linked fields. In particular, for some applications, HRI arises as a mandatory requirement, as the robot must be able to understand the user's commands. The most relevant communication means are referable to the senses of hearing, sight, and touch, either alone or combined [8]. When thinking about communication, speech is usually the first concept that comes to mind, as it is a behavior we voluntarily practise every day. However, available text-to-speech and speech recognition models are characterized by a strong computational load *vs* naturality trade-off, limiting their application [3]. A simple yet effective solution is represented by touch screens, although the resulting interaction is impoverished [3]. Beside that, motion and touch sensors can be used to feel the user's proximity and possibly infer his/her behavior (*e.g.* hugging a toy robot) [3]. However, physical interaction introduces some issues related to sanitization when the robot is shared among several users, particularly relevant in healthcare settings. One further valuable communication mean is represented by gestures, either as a source of information about the user's attitude (*i.e.* body language) or as voluntary commands sent to the robot [6]. The latter (*i.e.* action detection) still represent an open research issue and it has been selected as the preferred human machine interaction strategy in the proposed framework.

2 Related Work and Paper Contribution

Pointing gestures are a popular choice for HRI, as they are a natural way to drive another's (*i.e.* the robot) attention. Nickel and Stiefelhagen [7] fused skin-color map and disparity images to achieve communication with a domestic robot. The findings of their work identified pointing as a viable way for object selection in an household scenario (90% of correct target identification), despite a limited geometrical accuracy (average error of 16.9). To achieve more accurate detection performance, available methods often introduce constraints, thus limiting the problem complexity at the cost of generality. Some of them require the user to wear a sensor, such as in Gromov and colleagues work [5], in which an inertial measurement unit placed on the wrist allows to control a drone's flight. This kind of methods is hardly scalable, as the number of users grows, and requires to know the operators in advance. Another possibility is to constrain the gesture execution to ease its recognition. Azari and colleagues [1] tested their method on a mobile robot, achieving a 0.5 m error at a 5.5 m distance. However, the pointing is assumed to be done putting the index finger between the eyes and the point of interest, thus reducing the user's freedom of movement. Likewise, the problem can be simplified assuming a fixed (and optimal) relative position between the camera and the user. This has been done in the work from Showers and Si [13], who fused visual and audio information to discriminate between objects in close vicinity. The idea of multimodal communication is appealing, as it could both improve the accuracy of the detection and help in achieving a more natural interaction. Voice could be used as a trigger for the gesture detection, as in Bolt's pioneering work [2]. In his study, a user moves a cursor on a screen by pointing at it and, with the voice command "there", can select the current position as the desired one.

In this work, we propose the HRI system to leverage on color and depth images to detect pointing gestures, allowing the user to request for a service. The system is complemented with audio capabilities to concur in resolving ambiguities and to alternatively send feedbacks to the robot or the user. The goal is not limited to achieve a robust identification of the object/area selected through pointing, but also to trigger the proper robot action, based on the object's characteristic and the surrounding context. Thus, the main contribution of the present paper are:

- the development of a HRI system
  - enabling a natural interaction with the robot (*i.e.* not imposing any constraint nor on the user behavior nor on his/her position),
  - relying exclusively on sensors that can be easily mounted on a service robot (namely an RGBD camera and a microphone), hence not requiring to place any sensor on the user;
- an application of said HRI system on a service robot.

3 Materials and Methods

3.1 Two-Layers HRI System

The conceived HRI system is composed of two levels, namely the *perceptive* and the *semantic* layer, as depicted in Fig. 1.

The perceptive layer has three main functions:

i mapping the objects available for interaction, combining autonomous navigation and object detection;

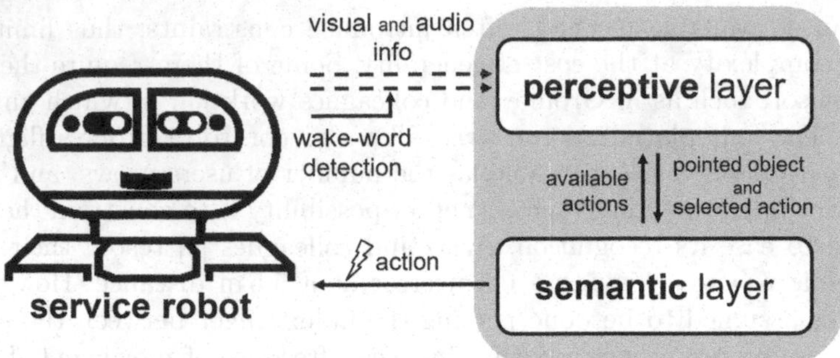

Fig. 1. Schema of the application functioning. The HRI system, with its two layers, is represented against a grey background. Arrows represent the messages exchanged between the building blocks. Dashed arrows represent conditional connections, as the stream of audio and video information is subordinate to the wake-word detection.

- ii detecting the indicated direction, after having applied user tracking and action detection methods;
- iii listening to the user's audio feedback, *e.g.* when the user is prompted to give a voice command to select the actions listed by the semantic layer.

The semantic layer is in charge of determining which actions, in the current context, are available for a given object. The actions may be linked to the object itself (*e.g.* a fetch-and-retrieval task), or depend on the presence of other items (*e.g.* the action *pour* when pointing to a bottle, is made available only if there is a cup in the surroundings), or require collaboration with the user (*e.g.* to unscrew the bottle cap with a one-armed robot).

To avoid having the described system running continuously, a wake-word detection system (similarly to what happens with Google Assistant or Amazon Echo) could be introduced. This would be beneficial both to relief the computational load on the robot's computer, as well as to avoid privacy issues. Indeed, triggering the a robot interaction by saying the wake-word, the user would give an implicit consensus to be tracked and listened.

3.2 Robotic Platform

The framework is implemented and tested on a mobile service robot (*TIAGo* robot, *PAL Robotics*) [11]. The mobile base, equipped with a *SICK* laser, and the *Orbecc Astra S* RGBD camera enable the environment mapping. The same camera is exploited to capture the user's motion. For voice interaction, the *Super-Beam Stereo Array Microphone* (*Andrea Electronics*) and a 5W speaker are used [11]. The robot and the location of the mentioned devices are depicted in Fig. 2

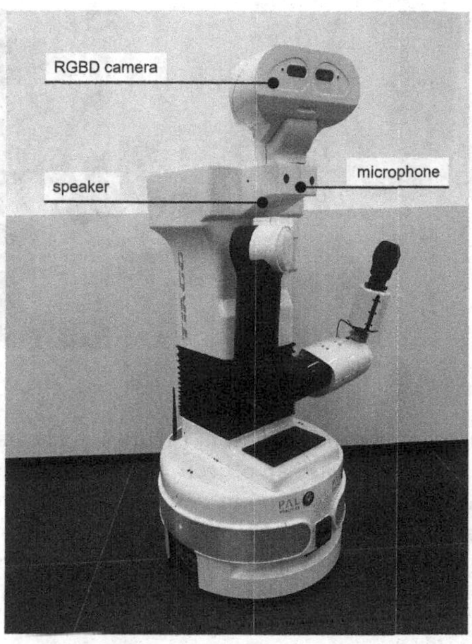

Fig. 2. TIAGo, the service robot used to test the proposed framework. The locations of the onboard sensors used for HRI are highlighted.

4 Pilot Implementation

A pilot implementation of the perceptive layer, exploiting a state-of-the-art 2D keypoints extraction model and simple heuristics for action detection, led to the qualitative result shown in Fig. 3.

The Lightweight OpenPose [9] pre-trained model is exploited for keypoint detection on the RGB images. The model has been selected as it is an implementation of the popular OpenPose method [4], optimize to run in real-time on a CPU. The joints positions are then brought to the 3D space relying on the information from a synchronous pixel-aligned depth image. The RGB and depth image are considered as synchronized if the time difference between their acquisition stamps fall within a $3 \cdot 10^{-2}s$ interval. The arms movement are analyzed to estimate their kinetic energy as described by Shan and collaborators in [12]. Accordingly to the cited method, the kinetic energy estimate of a set of points at time i is defined as the sum of the points' estimates, *i.e.*

$$E(P_i) = \sum_j E(P_i^j) \tag{1}$$

where $E(P_i^j)$ is the estimated kinetic energy of a single joint, computed as

$$E(P_i^j) = \frac{1}{2}(v_i^j)^2 = \frac{1}{2}\left(\frac{P_i^j - P_{i-1}^j}{\Delta T}\right)^2 \tag{2}$$

(a) (b)

Fig. 3. Application functioning demonstration. Figure (a) The user is in the robot view and has raised his arm to point toward an object. The robot has previously mapped the object on the table, and thanks to a keypoint detection network, assesses the indicated direction and thus the selected object. Figure (b) Scene reconstruction made by the robot: white circles represent objects; the red dot is the user's wrist and the red line the pointed direction; the orange circle accounts for the robot position. (Color figure online)

where ΔT is the time elapsed between the receipt of samples $i-1$ and i. The kinetic energy estimate for each arm is therefore obtained substituting Eq. 2 into Eq. 1, *i.e.*

$$E(P_i) = \sum_j \frac{1}{2} \left(\frac{P_i^j - P_{i-1}^j}{\Delta T} \right)^2 \tag{3}$$

where $j = shoulder,\ elbow,\ wrist$. A threshold value is experimentally tuned to discriminate between the motion and rest condition of each arm.

A pointing gesture is assumed to be composed of three phases: arm lifting, stationary stance (*i.e.* pointing) and arm return. The action starts with the two arms in rest condition. If one arm starts moving upward (*i.e.* E overcomes the threshold and the wrist is moved away from the ground plane), the arm lifting phase is entered. Then, if the arm stops, the line passing through the elbow and the wrist joint is assessed as the indicated direction. The subsequent movement is recognized as the arm return phase. During the lifting and the stationary phases, the contralateral arm must be kept still, otherwise the movement is classified as a non-relevant gesture. To reduce the sensitivity to the noise in the arm poses, the transition from the rest to the motion condition is triggered only if three consecutive above-threshold values of E are received (and vice versa when switching from motion to rest). This sketched action detection system is false positives-prone, as several arm movements share the same features. However, it must be noticed that, being the interaction intentionally triggered by the user, the impact of this issue is limited.

Overall, the perceptive layer can run on a *AMD Ryzen7* 8-cores CPU at a rate of $\approx 4Hz$.

5 Preliminary Findings

The initial work on the perceptive layer allowed the authors to better understand the limits and the potential of a fully vision-based approach. Though the described system is able to assess a good estimate of the indicated direction, the perception layer must be refined to improve the accuracy and, most importantly, the robustness. Indeed, the current implementation is sensitive to variations in light condition and user-robot relative position. As far as performance is concerned, the proposed implementation can work in real-time for the task at hand on a standard CPU. The speed rate, indeed, is sufficient to recognize pointing gestures, characterized by a considerable static phase. Nevertheless, the perceptive layer would benefit of a faster pose estimation algorithm as it would enable to use the same approach on more dynamic gestures. Moreover, it would be useful to associate a confidence score to the geometrical information, *e.g.* the variance of the detected direction in the last n samples (as in [13]). In addition, the implementation of a vocal feedback system would allow to make the robot aware of any mistake in perception. This would both prevent the execution of undesired actions and pave the way for a learning-based improvement of the performance.

6 Conclusions

The authors acknowledge the limitations of a preparatory study lacking of a robust experimental evaluation. Nevertheless, the proposed architecture for a HRI system is sound and the provided pilot implementation of the perceptive layer represents an intriguing starting point for the project development. The proposed HRI framework would only relying on the robot's onboard instrumentation (*i.e.* RGBD camera, microphone and speaker), enabling a natural connection with a mobile service robot. Indeed, the method introduces a minimal overhead to trigger the interaction (as easy as saying a couple of words) and does not impose any constraint nor on the user behavior nor on the ambient. Ultimately, the spontaneity of the interaction represents the greatest strength of the presented HRI framework, as it is a fundamental requirement to achieve users' acceptance.

References

1. Azari, B., Lim, A., Vaughan, R.: Commodifying pointing in HRI: simple and fast pointing gesture detection from RGB-D images. In: 2019 16th Conference on Computer and Robot Vision (CRV), pp. 174–180 (2019). https://doi.org/10.1109/CRV.2019.00031
2. Bolt, R.A.: "Put-That-There": voice and gesture at the graphics interface. In: Proceedings of the 7th Annual Conference on Computer Graphics and Interactive Techniques, pp. 262–270, SIGGRAPH 1980. Association for Computing Machinery, New York, NY, USA (1980). https://doi.org/10.1145/800250.807503

3. Bonarini, A.: Communication in human-robot interaction. Curr. Robot. Rep. **1**(4), 279–285 (2020). https://doi.org/10.1007/s43154-020-00026-1
4. Cao, Z., Simon, T., Wei, S.E., Sheikh, Y.: Realtime multi-person 2D pose estimation using part affinity fields. In: CVPR (2017)
5. Gromov, B., Abbate, G., Gambardella, L.M., Giusti, A.: Proximity human-robot interaction using pointing gestures and a wrist-mounted IMU. In: 2019 International Conference on Robotics and Automation (ICRA), pp. 8084–8091 (2019). https://doi.org/10.1109/ICRA.2019.8794399
6. Ji, Y., Yang, Y., Shen, F., Shen, H.T., Li, X.: A survey of human action analysis in HRI applications. IEEE Trans. Circuits Syst. Video Technol. **30**(7), 2114–2128 (2020). https://doi.org/10.1109/TCSVT.2019.2912988
7. Nickel, K., Stiefelhagen, R.: Visual recognition of pointing gestures for human-robot interaction. Image Vis. Comput. **25**(12), 1875–1884 (2007)
8. Onnasch, L., Roesler, E.: A taxonomy to structure and analyze human–robot interaction. Int. J. Soc. Robot. **13**(4), 833–849 (2020). https://doi.org/10.1007/s12369-020-00666-5
9. Osokin, D.: Real-time 2D multi-person pose estimation on CPU: lightweight OpenPose. arXiv preprint arXiv:1811.12004 (2018)
10. Ozturkcan, S., Merdin-Uygur, E.: Humanoid service robots: the future of healthcare? J. Inf. Technol. Teach. Cases 20438869211003905 (2021). Prepublished 23 June 2021
11. Pagès, J., Marchionni, L., Ferro, F.: TIAGo: the modular robot that adapts to different research needs (2016)
12. Shan, J., Akella, S.: 3D human action segmentation and recognition using pose kinetic energy. In: 2014 IEEE International Workshop on Advanced Robotics and its Social Impacts, pp. 69–75 (2014). https://doi.org/10.1109/ARSO.2014.7020983
13. Showers, A., Si, M.: Pointing estimation for human-robot interaction using hand pose, verbal cues, and confidence heuristics. In: Meiselwitz, G. (ed.) SCSM 2018. LNCS, vol. 10914, pp. 403–412. Springer, Cham (2018). https://doi.org/10.1007/978-3-319-91485-5_31
14. Wirtz, J., et al.: Brave new world: service robots in the frontline. J. Serv. Manage. **29**, 907–931 (2018). https://doi.org/10.1108/JOSM-04-2018-0119
15. Čapek, K., R.U.R.: Rossum's Universal Robots. Aventinum (1920)

Assessment of the Usability of an Innovative Assistive Swimsuit

Giuseppe Andreoni[1,2](✉), Luciano Bissolotti[3], Eleonora Castagna[4], Giulio Valagussa[4], Francesco Mondini[5], Alberto Paleari[6], and Simone Pittaccio[7]

[1] Laboratory TeDH - Technology and Design for Healthcare, Department of Design, and Sensibilab, Polo Territoriale di Lecco, Politecnico di Milano, Milan, Italy
giuseppe.andreoni@polimi.it
[2] IBFM – CN, Segrate, Milan, Italy
[3] Casa di Cura Domus Salutis, Brescia, Italy
[4] Istituto Villa Santa Maria, Como, Tavernerio, Italy
[5] AUS Niguarda Onlus, Milan, Italy
[6] Dipartimento di Scienza dei Materiali, Università degli Studi Milano-Bicocca, Milan, Italy
[7] CNR-ICMATE, National Research Council of Italy, Lecco, Italy

Abstract. Wearable systems, or even more simply wearables, are a wide variety of body worn objects and accessories that in the last decade have been introduced in our availability. The aim of this paper is to propose a structured methodology to conduct usability analysis with wearables and describe it through its application on a wearable system for water rehabilitation. AQTIVO is a new corset co-design with users (patients and caregivers) and to validate its usability we carried out a test with 30 subjects and 10 caregivers in 2 water rehabilitation sites. The AQTIVO usability was very satisfactory. Young users. Indeed, it allowed new rehabilitation exercises (flotation, prone transfer). In adults, AQTIVO system improved the buoyancy task provided more support in dynamic tasks. Support from the caregiver was also reduced by using the brace in all subjects. Also the aesthetics was positively evaluated.

Keywords: Wearable assistive systems · Usability analysis · UCD methodology · Rehabilitation swimsuit

1 Introduction

1.1 A Subsection Sample

Wearable systems, or even more simply wearables, are a wide variety of body worn objects and accessories that in the last decade have been introduced in our availability. Main applications are in sport, fitness, and healthcare, where system's usability is not just a simple quality but even a requirement. Despite this priority few studies have face this aspect, mainly adopting simple questionnaires to investigate it [1]. Usability is essential to match user's acceptance of the product-service system like a wearable, but also its proper use, the reliability of the data measured by it, up to the motivation and engagement

K. Miesenberger et al. (Eds.): ICCHP-AAATE 2022, LNCS 13342, pp. 469–476, 2022.
https://doi.org/10.1007/978-3-031-08645-8_55

of the overall approach or service that the system implements [2, 3]. The aim of this paper is to propose a structured methodology to conduct usability analysis with wearables and describe it through its application on a wearable for water rehabilitation.

AQTIVO is a swimsuit supporting fragile user during in-water rehabilitation session increasing support without affecting mobility (Fig. 1). This would result in an increase of comfort, duration, and efficacy of the therapy. AQTIVO was designed to meet the following requirements:

- modularity and adaptability both for anthropometry and for functional requirements
- need to have buoyancy supports and weights for different parts of the body (head, trunk, limbs) according to individual characteristics (type of disability, shape and body mass)
- Functionality in different activities (simple float, swimming).
- Ability to manage changes in attitude (prone, supine, floating in standing)
- Materials suitable for body contact due to their safety and softness characteristics
- Aesthetic pleasantness
- Attention to the ergonomic aspects of usability and wearability.

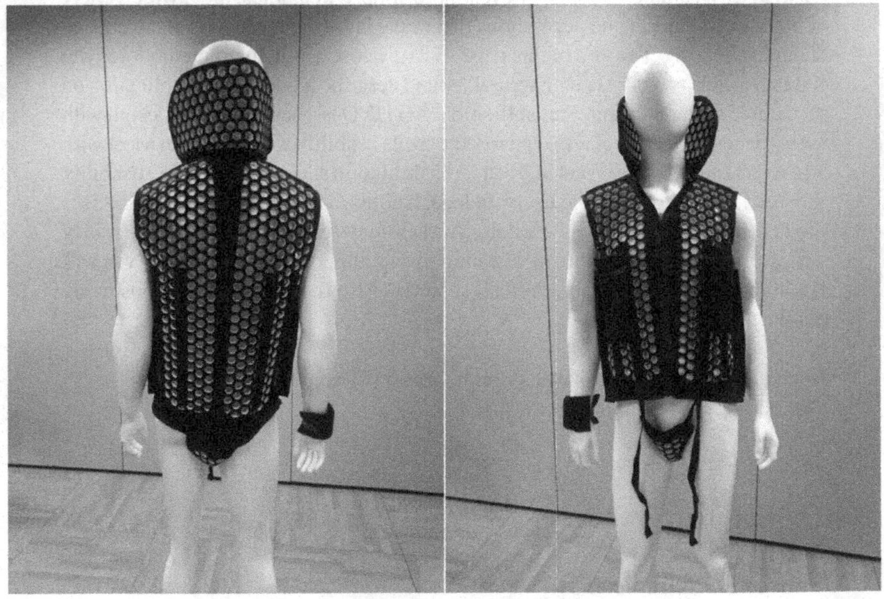

Fig. 1. The AQTIVO swimsuit for water rehabilitation.

The AQTIVO swimsuit was developed in the frame of the CREW project funded by Fondazione Cariplo (Milan, Italy) in a co-design approach of systems for rehabilitation and wellness for fragile people. During co-design activity a set of usability requirements were set up in relation to the target population and at the end of the production of the final system, a dedicated phase of assessment of usability, perceived comfort, and performance was programmed to validate product acceptance or the needed refinements.

2 Materials and Methods

2.1 Test Protocol

Step 1: Users definition. This system has 2 categories of users: direct users and caregivers, both considered primary users.

Secondary users such as those participating in cleaning/maintenance and other secondary functions or in relation to the product lifecycle were considered not relevant so excluded by the test plan.

30 subjects (15 adults and 15 teenagers < 18yrs) with motor impairments of different aetiology and 10 caregivers (water rehabilitation therapists) took part to the usability validation study.

Step 2: Task analysis to set up the usability test protocol and assessment criteria. A preliminary set of observation were carried out with 3 subject aged 16–42: they were given the system and a general instruction of the product scope, we observed their behaviour and listened to their think aloud comments. This activity led to identify the following requirements for the usability protocol:

- 3 macro-tasks were relevant: wearing the system, using the system, undressing the system; the support of the caregiver could be a relevant parameter to be assessed in all phases, as well as some temporal measurements can assess the overall usability (e.g. in wearing or undressing it). A detailed sub-sequencing of micro-tasks was also developed. The task descriptions have been reviewed by the project team to ensure that the content, format, and presentation are representative of real use and substantially evaluate the total application. The project team agreed and accepted it prior to developing the protocol for the usability test that will consider the most common and relatively complex functions. The tasks are identical for all participants of a given user role in the study.
- Some functional parameters are relevant to usability (speed, number of foot/arm-strokes).
- Aesthetics plays a relevant role in system's acceptance too, so it is impacting on usability and should be included in the evaluation.

The presence of a facilitator during the usability tests was chosen so to help in the long assessment that such a system was requiring. The facilitator directly followed the session staying on the side of the pool video-recording the session according to the users' consent. The usability testing protocol consisted of 3 steps or phases as here described:

- Phase 1: out of the water, before the rehabilitation session.
- Phase 2: in the water, carrying out the rehabilitation session distinguishing 2 moments:
    - Phase 2a: During the water rehabilitation session in the pool, without wearing the system.
    - Phase 2b: During the water rehabilitation session in the pool, wearing the system.
- Phase 3: out of water, after the rehabilitation session.

The facilitator was in charge of administering the questionnaires to the participants after each of the 3 phases (Fig. 2).

Fig. 2. Example of the starfish position wearing the AQTIVO system during buoyancy tasks.

Step 3: Prepare and optimize the tools for the usability analysis. For the investigation of user experience and usability of the product, the questionnaires were based on the Visual Analog Scale (VAS) or the Likert scale, each question with the proper resolution 5/7/9 points according to the validated semantic scale. A body part discomfort score complemented the questionnaire, when necessary, in particular when studying body regions and physical interface with the system. Also, the main performance measures (time to complete the task, number of armstroke/footstroke while swimming) were recorded as relevant to usability.

The usability and the performance was to be analysed in a with/without the system approach: thus the test needs to be repeated twice, wearing the system and without it. This is crucial for the protocol and for the statistical methods in data analysis.

Step 4: Experimental tests. 30 subjects and 10 caregivers were recruited for the usability study with the following inclusion criteria:

- Subjects: fragile people with acquired or congenital functional limitation running rehabilitation session in water (pool or sea), aged 8 or more, eligible to water rehabilitation/ psychomotor activity upon physiatrist visit according to clinical assessment and rehabilitative needs;
- Caregivers: professionals with specific license for water rehabilitation leading the therapeutic rehabilitative session and supporting some tasks (e.g. wearability, undressing the swimsuit, …). Some caregivers assisted more subjects in water-rehabilitation.

In case the participants were aged under 18 years, parents would have provided the informed consent to participate to the usability test, and, in case of need, the caregiver can support the user in providing answers to questionnaire items.

The usability testing protocol consisted in the observation of one rehabilitative session and the administration of the questionnaires to the users for each dyad. In each session, in one half the subject is asked to perform activities without the swimsuit, in the other half he/she is asked to perform water rehabilitation with the swimsuit. The order will be randomized to avoid polarization effects or fatigue influence on the results. After each task, the facilitator recorded the answers of the participant for the post-task questionnaire.

3 Results and Discussion

3.1 Children

USER	S01	S02	S03	S04	S05	S06	S07	S08	S09	S10	S11	S12	S13	S14	S15	AVD	STD	MEDIAN
Water Entry (0/1)	1	1	0	0	0	1	1	1	1	1	1	0	1	1	1	0,73	0,46	1,00
STATIC TASK	S01	S02	S03	S04	S05	S06	S07	S08	S09	S10	S11	S12	S13	S14	S15	AVD	STD	MEDIAN
Support by water (0-10)	0	7,5	0	4	7	5		7	3	1	0	6	3	0	0	3,11	2,98	3,00
Appropriatess of support (1-7)	2	6	1	6	5	6		2	3	2	0	5	2	1	2	3,07	2,09	2,00
Importance of water support (1-7)	2	2	1	2	5	4		3	3	2	2	6	2	1	1	2,57	1,50	2,00
Level of support by caregiver (0-7)	6	5	7	6	2	0		0	0	5	5	5	0	0	0	2,93	2,84	3,50
DYNAMIC TASK	S01	S02	S03	S04	S05	S06	S07	S08	S09	S10	S11	S12	S13	S14	S15	AVD	STD	MEDIAN
Freestyle- prone translation time*	22	18					21	12	20		12		11	8,1	8,1	14,75	5,62	12,20
Freestyle- prone translation acts*							19						9	11	6	11,25	5,56	10,00
Fatigue (VAS 0-10)	4,5	8	3,5				10	8	7	10	4	6	3	1	0	5,42	3,29	5,25
Importance of water support (1-7)	5	1	2				2	3	5	2	5	3	6	6	6	3,83	1,85	4,00
Level of support by caregiver (0-7)	0	0	7				0	0	0	5	0	5	0	0	0	1,42	2,61	0,00
Backstroke- supine translation time*	22	25	0				22	18	10				12	10	7	14,04	8,30	12,00
Freestyle- prone translation acts*							24	21					10	12	7	14,80	7,33	12,00
Fatigue (VAS 0-10)	8,5	8	3,5	5	1	2	10	7	4	10		2	7	8	3	5,64	3,08	6,00
Level of water support (VAS 0-10)	5	1	1	2	0	3	2	3	4	2		3	5	1	4	2,57	1,55	2,50
Level of support by caregiver (0-7)	0	0	7	6	2	5	0	0	0	5		3	0	0	0	2,00	2,66	0,00
Water Exit (0/1)	1	1	0	0	0	1	1	1	1	1	0	0	1	1	1	0,67	0,49	1,00
non riesce																		
*significant only with respect to same subject																		

Fig. 3. Usability assessment data in children without AQTIVO.

Expected and Perceived Comfort. The expected results were confirmed with limited differences (Fig. 3).

The perceived functionality improved by 0.4 points on average while the fairly negative judgment of a single subject slightly penalized (−0.2 points) the comfort and wearability that otherwise would be confirmed in their judgment, that was, however, positive (4.2 out of 5 and 6.4 out of 7).

All the values of the quality and acceptance parameters were largely positive up to excellence (i.e. score > 6) for functionality, aesthetics and global acceptance.

Functionality. For the (static) buoyancy task, the perceived level of support in the water paradoxically decreased slightly with the swimsuit, while the level of appropriateness of the perceived support and its relevance for buoyancy increased in the expected way. Coherently, the request for assistance from the caregiver decreased.

In dynamic tasks (swimming/transfer prone and supine) the perception of better support and less fatigue was confirmed, especially in backstroke swimming, but, on the contrary, there was no reduction in transfer times. Again, in coherence with expectation, there was a significant reduction in caregiver support (Fig. 4).

WATER ENTRY	S01	S02	S03	S04	S05	S06	S07	S08	S09	S10	S11	S12	S13	S14	S15	AVD	STD	MEDIAN
Water Entry (0/1)	1	1	0	0	0	1	1	1	1	0	1	0	1	1	1	0,67	0,49	1,00
Level of received assistance (VAS 0-10)	0	0	10	10	10	4	0	0	0	5	0	10	0	0	0	3,27	4,48	0,00
STATIC TASK	S01	S02	S03	S04	S05	S06	S07	S08	S09	S10	S11	S12	S13	S14	S15	AVD	STD	MEDIAN
Support by water (0-10)	1	5	8	6	7	6	10	7,5	8	4		9	6	10	9	6,89	2,48	7,25
Appropriatess of support (1-7)	6	4	7	6	6	6	3	3	6	5		7	6	7	6	5,57	1,34	6,00
Importance of water support (1-7)	6	5	6	5	6	5	6	3	5	5		6	6	5	6	5,36	0,84	5,50
Level of support by caregiver (0-7)	0	2	2	5	5	0	0	0	0	6		3	0	0	0	1,64	2,24	0,00
DYNAMIC TASK	S01	S02	S03	S04	S05	S06	S07	S08	S09	S10	S11	S12	S13	S14	S15	AVD	STD	MEDIAN
Freestyle- prone translation time*	26	13					23	8,9	20	2	17		11	9,8	6,1	13,61	7,64	11,77
Freestyle- prone translation acts*	0	0					22	0					9	13	8	7,43	8,28	8,00
Fatigue (VAS 0-10)	7	8				0	10	8	5	9	3		0	4	2	5,09	3,56	5,00
Importance of water support (1-7)	6	6				4	5	6,5	5	5	6		6	7	7	5,77	0,93	6,00
Level of support by caregiver (0-7)	0	0				6	0	0	0	4	0		0	0	0	0,91	2,07	0,00
discomfort to comfort (VAS 0-100)	80	85				80	100	85					20	80	100	78,75	25,18	82,50
Backstroke- supine translation time*	34	30					25	20					11	9	7	19,41	10,78	19,72
Freestyle- prone translation acts*	0	0					22	19					9	13	9	10,29	8,52	9,00
Fatigue (VAS 0-10)	8,5	5	0	5	1	0	10	8		9		1	0	7	4	4,50	3,77	5,00
Level of water support (VAS 0-10)	6	6	5	5	6	4	5	6		5		6	7	7	7	5,77	0,93	6,00
Level of support by caregiver (0-7)	0	0	2	5	2	0	0	0		4		2	0	0	0	1,15	1,72	0,00
discomfort to comfort (VAS 0-100)	80	90	70	70	90	80	100	80				80	100	80	100	85,00	10,87	80,00
WATER EXIT	S01	S02	S03	S04	S05	S06	S07	S08	S09	S10	S11	S12	S13	S14	S15	AVD	STD	MEDIAN
Water Exit (0/1)	1	1	0	0	0	1	1	1	1	1	1	0	1	1	1	0,73	0,46	1,00
Level of received assistance (VAS 0-10)	0	0	10	10	10	4	0	0	0	0	0	10	0	0	0	2,93	4,53	0,00

Fig. 4. Usability assessment data in children with AQTIVO.

Wearability and Comfort. The subjects are divided into 2 categories: who managed to self-wear the system or not. In any case, the wearing time is quite limited and on average equal to 1 min 15 s and with low inter-subject variability. The perceived comfort scored a quite positive evaluation (75 out of 100) with a slight but not significant improvement compared to the initial expectations generated only by observing the system.

3.2 Adults

Expected and Perceived Comfort. The expected results were confirmed with limited and not always improving differences. The perceived functionality was slightly lower than expected (−0.2 points) but above all it was the perceived comfort that records the most significant worsening of the judgment (almost 1 point). It is probably the factor that drags down the global acceptance of the AQTIVO System, not so relevant (−0.4 points), but which is affected by the negative judgment on the support and on the perceived global quality.

The aesthetic judgment was very good and strongly increased after the test and the wearability operations: the score improves by 0.4 points on average.

Functionality. For the (static) flotation task, by wearing the AQTIVO suit the subjects improved all the parameters, in an appreciable average value. The level of appropriateness of the perceived support and its relevance for buoyancy increased as expected. Coherently, the request for assistance from the caregiver consistently decreased.

In the dynamic tasks (swimming/prone and supine transfer) the perception of better support and less fatigue was confirmed, especially in freestyle swimming. Caregiver support also decreased as expected (Figs. 5 and 6).

USER	T01	T02	T03	T04	T05	T06	S01	S02	S03	S04	S05	S06	S07	S08	S09	S10	S11	S12	S13	S14	S15	S16	AVD	STD	MEDIAN
Water Entry (0/1)	1	1	1	1	1	1	1	0	1	1	1	1	1	1	1	1	1	1	0	1	1	1	0,88	0,34	1,00
STATIC TASK	T01	T02	T03	T04	T05	T06	S01	S02	S03	S04	S05	S06	S07	S08	S09	S10	S11	S12	S13	S14	S15	S16	AVD	STD	MEDIAN
Support by water (0-10)	1	1	1	2	1	1	1	4	3	2	5		4	4	6	8	6	6	1	4	4	1	3,93	2,09	4,00
Appropriatess of support (1-7)	5	4	5	4	4	4	4	4	4	4	4		4	4	6	6	5	6	4	6	4	5	4,67	0,90	4,00
Importance of water support (1-7)	6	4	4	4	4	4	4	4	4	3	4		4	4	5	5	5	5	4	5	4	5	4,33	0,62	4,00
Level of support by caregiver (0-7)	0	0	0	0	0	0	5	1	1	5	0		3	4	0	0	0	0	6	4	4	4	2,47	2,23	2,00
DYNAMIC TASK	T01	T02	T03	T04	T05	T06	S01	S02	S03	S04	S05	S06	S07	S08	S09	S10	S11	S12	S13	S14	S15	S16	AVD	STD	MEDIAN
Freestyle- prone translation time*																							#DIV/0!	#DIV/0!	#NUM!
Freestyle- prone translation acts*																							#DIV/0!	#DIV/0!	#NUM!
Fatigue (VAS 0-10)	0	0	0	0	0	0	3		3	4	1		4	5	1	6	5	4	10	5	4	4	4,21	2,19	4,00
Importance of water support (1-7)	4	4	4	4	4	4	3		3	4	4		4	4	5	5	5	5	3	5	5	4	4,21	0,80	4,00
Level of support by caregiver (0-7)	0	0	0	0	0	0	5		3	4	0		0	0	0	0	0	0	7	0	0	1	1,43	2,34	0,00
Backstroke- supine translation time*																							#DIV/0!	#DIV/0!	#NUM!
Freestyle- prone translation acts*																							#DIV/0!	#DIV/0!	#NUM!
Fatigue (VAS 0-10)	0	0	0	0	0	0	3		3	3	2		3	3	1	6	5	5	10	1	1	4	3,57	2,41	3,00
Level of water support (VAS 0-10)	4	4	4	4	4	4	3		3	3	4		4	4	5	5	4	4	2	4	3	4	3,71	0,83	4,00
Level of support by caregiver (0-7)	0	0	0	0	0	0	5		3	5	0		0	0	0	0	0		7	0	0	4	1,85	2,58	0,00
Water Exit (0/1)	1	1	1	1	1	1	1	0	1	1	1		1	1	1	1	1	1	0	1	1	1	0,87	0,35	1,00

Fig. 5. Usability assessment data in adults without AQTIVO.

WATER ENTRY	T01	T02	T03	T04	T05	T06	S01	S02	S03	S04	S05	S06	S07	S08	S09	S10	S11	S12	S13	S14	S15	S16	AVD	STD	MEDIAN
Water Entry (0/1)	1	1	1	1	1	1	1	0	1	1	1		1	1	1	1	1	1	0	1	1	1	0,87	0,35	1,00
Level of received assistance (VAS 0-10)	0	0	0	0	0	0	0	10	0	0	0		0	0	0	0	0	0	10	0	0	0	1,33	3,52	0,00
STATIC TASK	T01	T02	T03	T04	T05	T06	S01	S02	S03	S04	S05	S06	S07	S08	S09	S10	S11	S12	S13	S14	S15	S16	AVD	STD	MEDIAN
Support by water (0-10)	4	1	4	3	4	4	5	6	5	5	6		6	6	6	6	5	5	5	6	5	4	5,40	0,63	5,50
Appropriatess of support (1-7)	5	5	5	5	5	5	5	5	5	4	5		6	6	6	6	5	5	5	5	5	4	5,13	0,64	5,00
Importance of water support (1-7)	5	3	4	4	5	4	5	4	5	4	5		5	5	5	6	5	6	4	5	4	5	4,87	0,64	5,00
Level of support by caregiver (0-7)	0	0	0	0	0	0	4	5	1	2	0		2	2	0	0	0	0	6	1	0	5	1,87	2,13	1,00
DYNAMIC TASK	T01	T02	T03	T04	T05	T06	S01	S02	S03	S04	S05	S06	S07	S08	S09	S10	S11	S12	S13	S14	S15	S16	AVD	STD	MEDIAN
Freestyle- prone translation time*																							#DIV/0!	#DIV/0!	#NUM!
Freestyle- prone translation acts*																							#DIV/0!	#DIV/0!	#NUM!
Fatigue (VAS 0-10)	1	1	1	1	0	0	4		3	3	2		3	4	1	1	1	1	10	3	4	3	3,07	2,30	3,00
Importance of water support (1-7)	2	3	3	3	4	3	5		5	4	6		4	5	5	6	5	6	5	5	5	4	5,00	0,68	5,00
Level of support by caregiver (0-7)	0	0	0	0	0	0	3		0	2	0				0	0	0		7	0	0	2	1,27	2,20	0,00
discomfort to comfort (VAS 0-100)	0	10	0	0	0	30	0	0	0	0	0				35	5			0			0	5,00	12,25	0,00
Backstroke- supine translation time*																							#DIV/0!	#DIV/0!	#NUM!
Freestyle- prone translation acts*																							#DIV/0!	#DIV/0!	#NUM!
Fatigue (VAS 0-10)	1	1	1	1	0	0	4		3	3	2		3	3	1	1	2	2	10	3	2	4	3,07	2,20	3,00
Level of water support (VAS 0-10)	2	3	4	3	4	4	5		5	4	6		4	6	5	6	5	6	5	5	4	4	5,00	0,78	5,00
Level of support by caregiver (0-7)	0	0	0	0	0	0	3		0	2	0		1			0	0	0	7			1	1,40	2,22	0,00
discomfort to comfort (VAS 0-100)	0	0	0	0	0	30	0	0	0	0	0		60		35	5						0	12,50	22,68	0,00
WATER EXIT	T01	T02	T03	T04	T05	T06	S01	S02	S03	S04	S05	S06	S07	S08	S09	S10	S11	S12	S13	S14	S15	S16	AVD	STD	MEDIAN
Water Exit (0/1)	1	1	1	1	1	1	1	1	1	1	1		1	1	1	1	1	1	0	1	1	1	0,93	0,26	1,00
Level of received assistance (VAS 0-10)	0	0	0	0	0	0	1	9	0	0	0		0	4	0	0	0	0	10	0	0	0	1,60	3,38	0,00

Fig. 6. Usability assessment data in adults with AQTIVO.

Wearability and Comfort. Most of the subjects were able to wear AQTIVO autonomously and in a short time (about 40 s) with a median value of 30 s and the longest time equal to 1 min 30 s. Undressing was very quick and quite easy. The overall perceived comfort was very positive (75 out of 100).

Comments. Some comments from users and caregivers offered interesting suggestions for system improvement. Most of the comments focus on buoyancy requiring more support and modularity for its regulation. A dedicated extension for supporting the legs were requested by some caregivers for the children rehabilitation. The second set of comments focuses on the characteristics of the corset and points out the criticality of the buckles and the introduction of an intermediate size for a better adaptation to anthropometric characteristics. Local discomfort (in the neck and upper trunk region) due to friction between the body and a not well-fitting suit were registered in few cases, thus encouraging a better definition of sizes and their adaptability to body morphology.

4 Conclusions

The usability of wearable system is a key factor for their success. In this experience we faced the assessment of a passive swimsuit supporting water rehabilitation. Overall, the AQTIVO usability was very satisfactory, in particular for young users. Indeed, in some children, the swimsuit allowed activities previously not possible with some subjects (flotation, prone transfer). For adults, AQTIVO brace achieved a good and positive evaluation. The best results were in functionality: for the buoyancy task all the parameters improved by wearing the AQTIVO, and in the dynamic tasks the perception of better support and less fatigue was confirmed, especially in freestyle swimming. Also the support from the caregiver was reduced by using the brace. The aesthetics was good, while the perceived quality and comfort can be improved.

Acknowledgements. This project was supported by a grant from Fondazione CARIPLO under the call Cariplo CREW (Codesign for REhabilitation and Wellbeing), that is an action of the Cariplo Foundation aimed at researching and implementing innovative technological solutions for the qualification, rehabilitation and well-being of people with temporary, permanent or advancing age-related frailty or disabilities.

References

1. Keogh, A., Argent, R., Anderson, A., Caulfeld, B., Johnston, W.: Assessing the usability of wearable devices to measure gait and physical activity in chronic conditions: a systematic review. J. NeuroEng. Rehabil. **18**, 138 (2021)
2. Standoli, C.E., et al.: Practicing the Test of new system-services for elderly care: how to introduce and measure user experience and related outcomes. In: Andreoni, G., Mambretti, C. (eds.) Digital Health Technology for Better Aging. RD, pp. 229–243. Springer, Cham (2021). https://doi.org/10.1007/978-3-030-72663-8_14
3. Harte, R., et al.: A human-centered design methodology to enhance the usability, human factors, and user experience of connected health systems: a three-phase methodology. JMIR Hum. Factors **4**(1), e8 (2017)

Design of a Car Simulator to Assess Driving Capabilities in People with Disability

Giovanni Tauro[1](✉), Davide Felice Redaelli[1], Le An Dao[1], Alfonso Mastropietro[2], Marta Mondellini[1], Fabio Storm[3], Vera Colombo[1], Sara Arlati[1], Ileana Pirovano[2], Mattia Chiappini[3], Carla Dei[3], Luca Greci[1], Matteo Malosio[1], Giovanna Rizzo[2], Gianluigi Reni[3], and Marco Sacco[1]

[1] Istituto di Sistemi e Tecnologie Industriali Intelligenti per il Manifatturiero Avanzato, Consiglio Nazionale, Rome, Italy
giovanni.tauro@stiima.cnr.it

[2] Istituto di Tecnologie Biomediche, Consiglio Nazionale delle Ricerche, Segrate, MI, Italy

[3] IRCCS E. Medea – Associazione La Nostra Famiglia, Bosisio Parini, LC, Italy

Abstract. Disabilities related to motor and/or cognitive impairment may impact driving abilities. The project Rip@rto aims at supporting INAIL personnel during the evaluation of the residual capabilities of people with disability who apply for a driving license. The newly designed simulator presents new features compared to the current state of art. It will provide a realistic 3D environment and a mechatronic platform to improve the realism of the driving experience. The simulator will also allow collecting objective (mental workload) and subjective (stress, risk perception, user-experience) data to support the operator's decision.

Keywords: Driving with disabilities · Virtual environments · Assistive and assessment technology · Mental workload · User experience

1 Introduction

In Italy, people with disability can obtain a so-called "special driving license," enabling them to manage a vehicle equipped with specific assistive devices autonomously and safely [1]. Within this context, the National Institute for Insurance against Accidents at Work (INAIL) offers free consulting services to people who want to (re)obtain the driving license before being reviewed by Local Medical Committees, i.e., the juridical bodies entitled to release such special driving licenses. In particular, INAIL examines license candidates and suggests: (i) whether the person can drive safely and (ii) which assistive devices can support and secure him/her in the vehicle. To do this, operators take advantage of a residual capabilities evaluator (RCE) [2], i.e., a tool able to assess the residual functions of the upper and lower limbs, the reaction times, and some sensory-related variables.

Though effective, the current RCE allows testing only motor and (partially) sensory abilities via single stereotypical tasks that are serially proposed to the person. This makes the whole assessment limited in terms of realism and ecological experience. Indeed, the

K. Miesenberger et al. (Eds.): ICCHP-AAATE 2022, LNCS 13342, pp. 477–483, 2022.
https://doi.org/10.1007/978-3-031-08645-8_56

RCE does not allow simulating a longer driving experience and assessing all those cognitive and emotional (e.g., stress-related) variables that are generally challenged during driving.

2 Aims

The presented project, namely Rip@rto, aims at advancing the state-of-the-art by designing and developing a realistic car simulator enabling INAIL operators to assess motor, sensory, cognitive and emotional parameters within a realistic and safe driving experience.

The car simulator developed within Rip@rto will enable the measurements of objective variables during the execution of single tasks, thus allowing the continuity of the data collection done until now and in a structured and longer driving experience. Such experience will be customized by the INAIL operators depending on the user's medical records. For instance, in the case of a person with only motor impairment, the user will be proposed with scenarios requiring sudden braking or harsh steering. Instead, people with cognitive disabilities will be proposed with longer experiences – up to 45 min –to assess their sustained attention and concentration throughout time.

3 Simulator Components

The Rip@rto simulator will be composed of a mechatronic platform allowing for the reproduction of the frontal and lateral accelerations; a real vehicle will be anchored on such a platform. In fact, using a real vehicle represents the only solution to mount and assess the usefulness of all the commercially-available assistive devices, as it would happen in an on-road test.

The virtual environment will be displayed on a hemicylindrical projected screen with at least a 2-m diameter.

3.1 Hardware

As mentioned, one of the main requirements for the Rip@rto simulator is the use of an entire real car, thus not considering only seats, pedals, and steering wheel or the front cockpit, as in most of the simulators. The motion platform will have important dimensions to support and move the entire vehicle while ideally allowing the widest range of motion possible.

Most of the simulators typically have maximum pitch and roll angles of about 25° because, as reported by W. Riley Garrot [3], instead of real accelerations acting on the driver's body, the simulators work with the sensations of movement. Going beyond the limits of 0.4–0.5 radians (about 23–29°) of inclination, the person would perceive the rotation as is, instead of a lateral-frontal acceleration sensation. Moreover, Murgovski [4] states that a driver starts to feel rotation at a rate bigger than 0.2 rad/s. Thus, we made a preliminary analysis implementing one of the Motion Cuing Algorithms (MCA) [5], which enables moving the platform with its motion limits to reproduce the sensation of the cockpit movements with the highest fidelity possible.

In particular, we adopted the Classical Washout Filter (CWF), also known as Classical Motion Cueing Algorithm, to analyze the relationship between platform dimensions and the ability to recreate the movement sensation for the simulator driver, not only considering the pitch and roll angles but also the horizontal translations (sway and surge). We can consider that, even if a standard car can reach about 1g in extreme braking or turning conditions, the simulators can only reproduce a small part of the forces and mostly work on the transient sensation rather than the sustained accelerations. For more details about the algorithms and sensation error evaluation, we referred to [5, 6]. We analyzed both cases of turning at a constant speed and of an instantaneous braking condition, at first with no motion platform limits and then considering a common commercial solution. The final considerations about the sensation error, which is the difference between the perceived accelerations on the simulator and on the real car movement, can be summarized as follows:

- Roll angle is very important for steady lateral accelerations, as the example of a wide roundabout or a long highway turning, while could be limited for frontal breaking-speeding accelerations;
- Horizontal translations are necessary to emulate the transient and high-frequency movements;
- Inclining the motion platform can be good for steady accelerations but introduces additional accelerations depending on the center of rotation's position, which can be tricky for the overall perception.

3.2 Software

Rip@rto virtual environments will be developed with Unity. Blender and 3D Studio Max will be employed to model 3D environment features.

The single tasks will be reproduced to be as similar as possible to the original tasks currently present in the RCE. However, given the additional features of this simulator, whenever possible, we will try to contextualize these tasks. For instance, in the case of assessing the force modulation on the accelerator pedal, a vehicle with an unpredictable behavior will be placed in front of the users' virtual car. When peripherical vision is tested, a stimulus will appear at the edge of the semi-cylindrical screen while driving on an urban route.

We designed a modular software architecture relying on blocks to generate customizable, controllable, and realistic scenarios on demand. This choice will facilitate the INAIL operator to choose the best combination of elements (e.g., curves, roundabouts) and tasks (e.g., cross a regulated/unregulated cross, management of unpredictable events) to evaluate the person with a disability. The scenario generation logic will be supported by a consistent User Interface (UI) dedicated to the operator that will allow him/her to easily navigate through the customizable options accelerating the environment configuration process before the test. Once the operator makes his/her choices and selects the whole experience duration, the application will generate a random path combining blocks containing the selected features. In this way, if the person has to be re-assessed, e.g., with a different combination of assistive devices, he/she will not be enabled to rely on memory – rather than on attention – to complete the assessment successfully.

Each block incorporates different elements such as urban streets, suburb area streets, and highways and may present one or two travel directions, speed limits, and overtaking opportunities. Additional elements will be traffic lights, pedestrians crossing path, intersections, and turns. Unpredictable events, such as sudden crossing, angry drivers, distracting and occluding elements, will also be inserted [7]. The operator will also have the chance of setting the meteorological condition (e.g., adding fog or setting a night sky) and the traffic level, thus acting directly on the general driving difficulty. Each driving experience will last from 10 to 45 min.

4 Measures

One of the aims of Rip@rto is the quantitative assessment of both objective and subjective variables potentially affecting drivers' abilities and safety to assist operators' decisions.

4.1 Cognitive Workload

Driving a car is a complex activity requiring different simultaneous skills, considerable cognitive effort, and rapid decision making. All these aspects affect the driver's cognitive workload (CW), defined as "a hypothetical construct that describes the extent to which the cognitive resources required to perform a task have been actively engaged by the operator" [8]. An optimal level of CW is necessary to accomplish a task correctly, and excessively high or low CW levels can reduce the overall performance [9], leading to potentially threatening conditions for driving safety. Therefore, CW will be evaluated in Rip@rto as follows.

Objective EEG Quantification. Since CW changes are associated with the brain's power oscillation [10, 11], they will be quantitatively assessed by the electroencephalography (EEG) technique. The Workload Index (WLI), defined as the ratio between the θ (4–8 Hz) and α (8–13 Hz) spectral power bands recorded respectively at the frontal (Fz) and parietal (Pz) midline scalp electrodes, will be considered as the main metric.

Subjective Quantification. The perceived CW and how it changes depending on the task and its relationship with the EEG signal will be evaluated using the National Aeronautics and Space Administration Task Load Index (NASA-TLX) [12], and it will be administered after the overall driving experience and after every task requiring it. NASA-TLX has good psychometric properties [13, 14], and it will allow identifying which subjective factor among the six proposed (mental demand, physical demand, temporal demand, effort, performance, and frustration) will contribute more to increasing the user's cognitive load.

4.2 Risk Perception and Driving Stress

Environmental, psychological, and vehicle design factors contribute to how a person behaves while driving. Risk perception is qualified as a significant component in driving behavior, especially regarding road safety. The driving experience can lead to an improvement in the perception of danger, defined as the disposition to recognize in advance dangerous situations related to traffic [15, 16]. This ability, even before being conscious, manifests itself on a somatic level in an anticipatory way [17, 18] influencing the driver's decision-making in risk contexts, with important consequences on road safety [19]. In the context of driving simulators, experiments have shown that experienced drivers, when faced with a danger, develop greater electrodermal activity (EDA) than novice drivers [20, 21].

Several stressors have been identified and studied while driving: a recent work highlighted that speed limits, presence or absence of intersections, traffic, pedestrians, and cyclists are variables that can influence the level of stress [22]. Other environmental stressors concern atmospheric conditions, driving visibility [23], or the behavior of other drivers [24]. Measures of heart rate variability (HRV) have been widely used to measure stress.

Given this evidence, a preliminary experiment has been conducted to assess EDA and HRV during the video interaction with real scenes related to risk and dangerous situations while driving and displayed on a laptop [25]. The measurements were taken with a wrist-worn sensor (E4, Empatica) and gold standard electrodes (passive electrodes placed in the second lead for heart rate measurements and active sensors on two phalanges for EDA). The following metrics were collected with both systems: inter-beat interval (IBI), heart rate (HR), root mean square of successive differences between normal heartbeats (RMSSD), ratio of low to high frequency (LF/HF ratio), mean phasic and tonic EDA signals. Preliminary results on 8 subjects showed a strong correlation between wrist-worn and gold standard sensors for mean IBI and mean HR (Spearman's r of 0.86 and 0.96, respectively), a medium correlation for RMSSD (r between 0.43 and 0.89), and LF/HF ratio (r between 0.25 and 0.79), a weak correlation for mean phasic and tonic EDA signals (r between 0,78 and −0,35).

5 Conclusion and Future Work

This work presents the design of a car simulator aimed at assisting the decisions of INAIL operators when assessing the driving abilities of people with disability and suggesting them potential assistive devices to be mounted on their vehicles.

In the next months, the design phase will be completed making decisions about the motion platform rotations and the screen placement and dimensions, which must allow visualizing the virtual environment throughout the driving experience (see Fig. 1). Indeed, it will be essential not to lose sight of part of the screen due to the car's inclination while braking or turning. Further, preliminary tests on simplified environments will enable us to define more precisely which are the most critical situations (e.g., to elicit high CW and stress) and to tune the measurements of all the physiological parameters of interest. Subjective data relating to the driving experience will also be collected, such as level of immersion, sense of presence, and cybersickness, to understand how the Human Factor intervenes in this complex task and how it correlates with performance and physiological data.

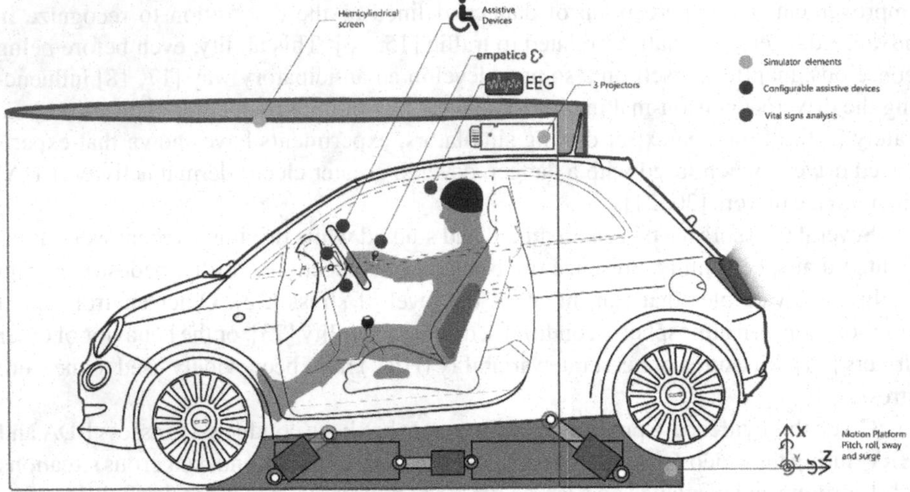

Fig. 1. Graphical representation of Rip@rto simulator setup.

References

1. International Transport Forum: Disabled Motoring: Travel Opportunities for Motorists with a Disability - ITALY. https://disabledmotoring.fia.com/country/italy
2. Fiat Chrysler Automobiles S.p.A.: Centri di mobilità - i simulatori di guida. https://www.fcaautonomy.com/centri-mobilita/#simulatori
3. Riley Garrott, W.: Simulator motion base sizing using simulation. SAE Tech. Pap. (1994). https://doi.org/10.4271/940227
4. Murgovski, N.: Vehicle modelling and washout filter tuning for the Chalmers vehicle simulator. M.sc. thesis, Chalmers, vol. 1, no. 4, pp. 1–4 (2007)
5. Reid, L., Nahon, M.A.: Flight simulation motion-base drive algorithms: part 1. In: Developing and testing equations. Technical Report (1985)
6. Nahon, M.A., Reid, L.D.: Simulator motion-drive algorithms - a designer's perspective. J. Guid. Control. Dyn. **13**(2), 356–362 (1990). https://doi.org/10.2514/3.20557
7. Wynne, R.A., Beanland, V., Salmon, P.M.: Systematic review of driving simulator validation studies. Saf. Sci. **117**(Dec), 138–151 (2019). https://doi.org/10.1016/j.ssci.2019.04.004
8. Gopher, D., Donchin, E.: Workload. An examination of the concept. In: Handbook of Perception and Human Performance: Volume 2, Cognitive Processes and Performance, pp. 41/41\r–41/49 (1986)
9. Babiloni, F.: Mental workload monitoring: new perspectives from neuroscience. In: Longo, L., Leva, M.C. (eds.) H-WORKLOAD 2019. CCIS, vol. 1107, pp. 3–19. Springer, Cham (2019). https://doi.org/10.1007/978-3-030-32423-0_1
10. Di Flumeri, G., et al.: EEG-based mental workload neurometric to evaluate the impact of different traffic and road conditions in real driving settings. Front. Hum. Neurosci. **12**, 509 (2018). https://doi.org/10.3389/fnhum.2018.00509
11. McDonnell, A.S., Simmons, T.G., Erickson, G.G., Lohani, M., Cooper, J.M., Strayer, D.L.: This is your brain on autopilot: neural indices of driver workload and engagement during partial vehicle automation. Hum. Factors (2021). https://doi.org/10.1177/00187208211039091

12. Hart, S.G., Staveland, L.E.: Development of NASA-TLX. Hum. Ment. Workload. Adv. Psychol. **52**, 139–183 (1988)
13. Dias, R.D., Ngo-Howard, M.C., Boskovski, M.T., Zenati, M.A., Yule, S.J.: Systematic review of measurement tools to assess surgeons' intraoperative cognitive workload. Br. J. Surg. **105**(5), 491–501 (2018). https://doi.org/10.1002/bjs.10795
14. Hart, S.G.: NASA-task load index (NASA-TLX); 20 years later. In: Proceedings of the Human Factors and Ergonomics Society Annual Meeting, pp. 904–908 (2006). https://doi.org/10.1177/154193120605000909
15. Horswill, M., McKenna, F.: Drivers' hazard perception ability: situation awareness on the road. In: A Cognitive Approach to Situation Awareness: Theory and Application (2004)
16. Preece, M.H.W., Horswill, M.S., Geffen, G.M.: Assessment of drivers' ability to anticipate traffic hazards after traumatic brain injury. J. Neurol. Neurosurg. Psychiatry **82**(4), 447–451 (2011). https://doi.org/10.1136/jnnp.2010.215228
17. Tagliabue, M., Sarlo, M., Gianfranchi, E.: How can on-road hazard perception and anticipation be improved? Evidence from the body. Front. Psychol. **10**(Feb), 167 (2019). https://doi.org/10.3389/fpsyg.2019.00167
18. Tagliabue, M., Sarlo, M.: Affective components in training to ride safely using a moped simulator. Transp. Res. Part F Traffic Psychol. Behav. **35**, 132–138 (2015). https://doi.org/10.1016/j.trf.2015.10.018
19. Gianfranchi, E.: A tool for training hazard perception and for assessing driving behaviors in adolescents and inexperienced drivers: a simulation study. Università degli Studi di Padova (2019)
20. Crundall, D., Chapman, P., Phelps, N., Underwood, G.: Eye movements and hazard perception in police pursuit and emergency response driving. J. Exp. Psychol. Appl. **9**(3), 163–174 (2003). https://doi.org/10.1037/1076-898X.9.3.163
21. Kinnear, N., Kelly, S.W., Stradling, S., Thomson, J.: Understanding how drivers learn to anticipate risk on the road: a laboratory experiment of affective anticipation of road hazards. Accid. Anal. Prev. **50**, 1025–1033 (2013). https://doi.org/10.1016/j.aap.2012.08.008
22. Ringhand, M., Vollrath, M.: Effect of complex traffic situations on route choice behaviour and driver stress in residential areas. Transp. Res. Part F Traffic Psychol. Behav. **60**, 274–287 (2019). https://doi.org/10.1016/j.trf.2018.10.023
23. Hill, J.D., Boyle, L.N.: Driver stress as influenced by driving maneuvers and roadway conditions. Transp. Res. Part F **10**(3), 177–186 (2007)
24. Paschalidis, E., Choudhury, C.F., Hess, S.: Combining driving simulator and physiological sensor data in a latent variable model to incorporate the effect of stress in car-following behaviour. Anal. Methods Accid. Res. **22**, 100089 (2019). https://doi.org/10.1016/j.amar.2019.02.001
25. Maffei, A., Angrilli, A.: E-MOVIE - experimental MOVies for induction of emotions in neuroscience: an innovative film database with normative data and sex differences. PLoS ONE **14**(10), e0223124 (2019). https://doi.org/10.1371/journal.pone.0223124

Mixed Reality as Assistive Technology: Guidelines Based on an Assessment of Residual Functional Vision in Persons with Low Vision

Florian Lang[1(✉)], Albrecht Schmidt[1], and Tonja Machulla[2]

[1] LMU Munich, Frauenlobstr. 7a, 80337 Munich, Germany
{florian.lang,albrecht.schmidt}@ifi.lmu.de
[2] TU Dortmund University, Emil-Figge-Straße 50, 44227 Dortmund, Germany
tonja.machulla@tu-dortmund.de

Abstract. Residual visual capabilities and the associated phenomenological experience can differ significantly between persons with similar visual acuity and similar diagnosis. There is a substantial variance in situations and tasks that persons with low vision find challenging. Smartglasses provide the opportunity of presenting individualized visual feedback targeted to each user's requirements. Here, we interviewed nine persons with low vision to obtain insight into their subjective perceptual experience associated with factors such as illumination, color, contrast, and movement, as well as context factors. Further, we contribute a collection of everyday activities that rely on visual perception as well as strategies participants employ in their everyday lives. We find that our participants rely on their residual vision as the dominant sense in many different everyday activities. They prefer vision to other modalities if they can perceive the information visually, which highlights the need for assistive devices with visual feedback.

Keywords: Low vision · Visual perception · Assistive technology

1 Introduction

In 2019 the World Health Organization estimated 82.5 million persons worldwide to have a cataract, glaucoma, or age-related macular degeneration [1]. More than 40 million others have been diagnosed with less common eye diseases. For persons with such a visual impairment, prescription glasses or contact lenses cannot fully restore the visual acuity. However, many have substantial residual visual capabilities. Even people classified as "blind" according to the WHO classification [1], can have a visual acuity of up to 0.05 (or 1/20). Only a very small portion of individuals with a vision impairment has no light perception whatsoever. In our work, all participants, except for P9, are "blind" according to the WHO classification. Such a classification aids the common misconception that a blind person cannot see at all [12]. This misconception together with the limited

K. Miesenberger et al. (Eds.): ICCHP-AATE 2022, LNCS 13342, pp. 484–493, 2022.
https://doi.org/10.1007/978-3-031-08645-8_57

technology available in the past may have hindered the development of visual assistive technology and led to assistive devices often using other modalities like audio [8] or haptic [9] feedback.

Leveraging residual vision when designing an assistive device is challenging due to interindividual differences and visual acuity not being a good indicator to describe visual perception [2]. Even persons with the same diagnosis and visual acuity may have vastly different subjective experiences. Nevertheless, visual feedback does not rely on the user's hearing or a well-developed sense of touch, which benefits especially elderly users.

Assistive technology with visual feedback is often designed as general-purpose devices; it disregards all context and shows an enhanced and enlarged image to the user. This can range from optical magnifiers over electronic magnifiers to magnifying software on computers or smartphones. Most of these solutions are either stationary or need to be held in the user's hand. Novel devices such as smartglasses (SG) offer a hands-free solution for visual support. There are companies that bring electronic magnifiers to the user's head [7] or research into other magnification approaches [11], but SG offer more than magnification; they offer context. This allows to carefully select task-specific information needed by the user and display it in a way the user can perceive [4,14,15].

We interviewed nine people with very low vision and a range of visual impairments to obtain information about their subjective perceptual experience as well as everyday activities in which they use their visual sense or would like to use it. We find that the visual sense is used frequently and preferentially wherever possible, rather than as a supporting sense, and that participants expressed a desire for visual adjustments to the environment, such as made possible by SG. As the reported subjective experience and visual strategies differ substantially, we conclude that vision aids should offer options to customize the visual presentation of the feedback.

2 Related Work

Assistive Technology and Smartglasses. Assistive technology ranges from non-electronic devices like a white cane to advanced technology and machine learning like the OrCam [8]. The Orcam provides audio feedback and can read text, recognize colors, and identify people. Other research combines audio with tactile feedback for navigation [9]. Both mentioned devices have one advantage-they are hands-free. Another emerging technology to provide hands-free visual feedback are smartglasses like the Microsoft HoloLens [6]. Augmented reality (AR) applications can assist users by visually highlighting the desired product during a shopping task [10] or by augmenting stairs for safer navigation [14]. Visual augmentations can support users during interactions with touchscreens [4] and provide information in the context of reading clock faces or the facial expression of a conversational partner [5].

Visual Perception and Preferences. There are different parameters that can be measured, such as visual acuity, visual field measurements, and contrast sensitivity to characterize visual perception [3]. However, these measures only provide a hint on how the person perceives a visual stimulus. Zhao et al. evaluated how visual stimuli in SG are perceived by persons with low vision [13] and found that colors, shapes and text displayed in the SG can be perceived by users with visual impairment. Sandnes asked three people with low vision about challenges out of their control in their everyday lives and where SG could assist them [10]. They find recognizing of facial expressions and reading text as the biggest challenges where a solution through assistive technology is desired.

3 Methodology

We conducted semi-structured interviews with nine participants with low vision over the phone due to restrictions caused by an ongoing global pandemic. The duration of the interviews averaged around 1.5 h and the participants were reimbursed with around 13.5 USD equivalent per hour. We sent participants a consent form and information regarding their data privacy and rights via email in advance. The participants could abort or interrupt the interview at any point; however, no participant made use of this option. Afterwards, the interview recordings were transcribed and analyzed for themes.

Participants. We recruited participants with severe visual impairment and with residual vision by contacting local support organizations. The group of participants consists of five female, four male, and zero diverse participants with a mean age of 54 (SD: 22.6) years. Five participants have central vision loss (P2 age-related macular degeneration, P4 and P9 Stargardt's disease, P6 and P7 cone dystrophy), P8 has peripheral vision loss since birth, P3 has a strong Myopia due to albinism, P1 a retinal detachment, and P5 Nystagmus. Except P9, all participants are "blind" according to the WHO classification [1]. A detailed overview of the participants and their visual acuity is shown in Table 1.

Table 1. A detailed list of all nine participants.

ID	Age	Gender	Visual acuity	Diagnosis
P1	68	m	0.02	Retinal detachment
P2	84	f	0.05	Age-related macular degeneration
P3	68	m	0.05	Albinism
P4	66	f	0.05	Stargardt's disease
P5	29	f	0.02–0.06	Nystagmus
P6	78	m	<0.05	Cone dystrophy
P7	22	f	0.01–0.03	Cone dystrophy
P8	47	m	0.02	Peripheral vision loss
P9	24	f	0.15	Stargardt's disease

Questions. In addition to demographic and medical information, we had structured the questions in two categories. First, we focused on the subjective visual perception. We asked participants to describe their perception of color and contrast, the influence of flicker, movement and motion, how their perception changes with distance, their preferred lighting as well as the occurrence of glare, reading, recognizable object sizes and shapes, and unpleasant visual stimuli in general. In the second part, we inquired about everyday activities, strategies, and assistive devices. Specifically, we asked the participant about assistive devices they use and about everyday situations where they use mainly their visual sense, their sense of hearing, or their sense of touch and whether they were to prefer using their visual sense given visual adaptations of the environment. If not mentioned by the participant, we specifically asked about using stairs, cooking, doing laundry, computer and smartphone usage, shopping, social interaction, and traveling with public transport. In the following three sections, we report the results and supplement them with suggestions for the design of visual assistive technology.

4 Subjective Visual Perception

Reported individual capabilities and subjective experiences differed widely. However, some aspects were similar for most participants. For instance, color vision and prior knowledge play a crucial part in the processing of visual information.

Top-down Processing. Our brain takes prior knowledge about where things are located and what is happening in the environment and uses this information to structure and interpret the inputs provided by our sensory system. This is termed top-down processing. All but one participant mentioned profiting from top-down processing when they impose strict order onto their environment, e.g., in the fridge (P1, P4, P7), storage space (P4, P7) or working space (P3, P2, P6, P7, P9). This effect is not merely a memory effect, but directly influences visual perception, as P2 describes, "I cannot find it because I cannot see it. [...] If I know it lies there [...] then, I can see it." Suppose one knows the location, shape or color of an object or expects certain persons in a situation. In that case, picking the right object or identifying a person (P4) is possible based on visual features. However, structuring the environment increases cognitive load, "[...], then you need to remember everything. I could not be on the phone while cooking" - P7. Therefore, visual aids could be particularly useful if they expose structure in the environment, e.g., alert the user when they disrupt an existing order, i.e., misplace an object, or directly display the correct position where the user should place an object to reduce cognitive load.

Colors and Contrast. All participants reported seeing colors and using them in their everyday lives. Three participants can distinguish colors easily; the others need high contrasts or strong colors. P6 only uses the brightness contrast of colors in his central visual field but sees colors in the peripheral field of view. Shades of grey are often challenging to perceive (P2, P5, P8). For example, P5 reported traffic light poles to be hardly visible due to their grey color, "but I can see the yellow [button to indicate pedestrians want to cross] then I know that is a traffic light". Participants also use color to mark objects, e.g., a colorful post-it on P3s phone ("I am famous for this, I mark everything with colors"), or structure their environment (P4, P7, P1). P1 even notes, "This is important. Seeing colors complements the missing vision." The color perception also depends on contrasts, as P4 and P6 only recognize a coin if it lies on a contrasting surface. Visual feedback should be designed colorful and in contrast to other visual elements and the background, i.e., the real world.

Object Size and Shape. All participants agree that contrast is more important to them than shape and, to some extent, the size of objects. Within the same color, perceptibility is better for larger objects, but a small contrast-rich object can be perceived more easily than a large object with little contrast. However, small objects disappear in central vision loss and require peripheral fixation to be perceived (P6). Only three participants expressed a preference regarding shape. Rectangles are easier to recognize (P8), or it is clearer where and how to grab them (P7). P3 prefers objects with characteristic and unusual outlines. Despite the minor role of the shape and size of an object compared to its color and contrast, a developer of a visual aid should keep these in mind and offer customization.

Movement, Motion, and Distance. One participant cannot perceive distance at all; the others recognize a moving car from two meters (P7) up to 30m to 50m (P4, P9). For larger distances, movement (P2, P3, P6, P9), especially movement through the visual field (e.g., left to right) (P4, P7), is reported as a crucial cue. Only P1 prefers still objects over movement. P2 stated, "If it does not move, I do not detect it.", but also clarified that for perceiving details, a still object is required. In contrary to movement, motion-in the sense of movement at a constant position of the visual field, e.g., a person waving-compared to a still object is only favorable for half of the participants and seen as little helpful (P2, P4, P7) or only useful in extreme cases (P1) by the others. Therefore, movement can serve as a cue to get the user's attention but is probably not particularly useful to convey detailed information.

Illumination and Glaring Lights. Most participants prefer daylight or bright white light (P1, P2, P4, P5, P7, P8, P9); P3 prefers uniform lighting independent of the brightness, and P6 prefers warm light at a low brightness level. However, except P4 all participants indicated to be bedazzled easily, e.g., by white walls or white furniture in well-lit rooms. Many use sunglasses or cut-off filter glasses when outside. Flickering or blinking lights are often perceived as noticeable but irritating, especially if multiple are present (P1). P3 states that if a police car drives by, "I just stand still because I notice that my perception is disturbed [by the police lights]," and P5 finds not only flickering lights but also lights moving through her visual field hard to perceive and irritating. P2, P4, and P8 are not disturbed by blinking lights, but P4 and P8 additionally do not notice blinking lights in well-lit situations. Therefore, visual feedback needs to be adjustable and SG should support wearing sunglasses or cut-off filter glasses underneath. Flicker and blinking should only be used sparsely, e.g., for emergency warnings.

5 Everyday Activities

In the following, we present the results regarding everyday activities, in which participants use their visual perception or employ strategies to compensate for the visual impairment. From few situations to daily usage, all participants have situations where they rely on their vision. As P4 puts it, "I see really little [...], but I am used to doing a lot visually with that little. Through years of training."

Navigation and Stairs. Navigation is a crucial element in everyday life. Multiple participants reported using their visual perception to "recognize the border between the grass [and the sidewalk]" (P8) or navigate through crowded areas "thanks to my peripheral vision" (P6). Participants also read the destination boards for public transport, although this is not always possible (P1, P4). For recognizing other traffic participants, especially cars when crossing a street, P5 does not rely on her senses and uses vision to follow other pedestrians. Others use their hearing (P4, P7, P8), vision (P3) or a combination (P9). P1 and P2 adjust according to the situation "if they have lights on, I can see them; otherwise I do not" -P2, "if it is quiet, then a quick look left and right is sufficient. When there is a lot of noise then [...] I have to trust my vision more" -P1. For obstacles, especially stairs, participants use a combination of their vision and touch through a white cane or their foot. If unknown stairs cannot be visually perceived, touch is used. Three participants mentioned contrast-rich stairs as visually accessible for them and four more agreed when asked that such markings reduce the need for using touch. Therefore, assistive devices can already provide a benefit with little augmentations to increase the contrast of objects. Designers should be careful not to occlude visual cues from the real world.

Food Preparation. All participants reported cooking or baking themselves. Four mentioned strong counter-top lighting as a necessity. Four participants use their hearing (talking kitchen scale) and all use their sense of touch at least as supporting information, e.g., when peeling carrots. On the other hand, three participants mention peeling potatoes as a mainly visual task. Others adjust their surroundings to use their visual sense: P7 uses bowls with strong colors and contrast to the kitchen counter and one participant uses a thermal imaging camera to fry steak. Thus, even a manual task like cooking is supported by the users' vision and some participants already use visual "assistive" devices.

Household Appliances. All participants base their interactions with household appliances on training and knowledge ("I looked at the scale with my electronic magnifier and said 'if the pointer is at 9 o'clock, then it is 180 °C"' -P1). Some combine it with visual or tactile markings. For example, P2 uses visual markers for her iron and stove, but tactile markers for the washing machine. P9 uses the sense of touch when she is certain about her interaction, otherwise she visually confirms her input. An assistive device should generally focus on unknown devices, but support the user for known devices by checking and confirming the user's action.

Reading. None of the participants can read the newspaper. However, six participants (P1, P3, P4, P5, P6, P8) frequently read text with a large font size or use magnifiers. For long texts, these six use text to speech or screen readers, as do the others for all text. While text in a sufficient font size is useful for many participants, it should only be used as visual feedback if necessary.

Computer and Smartphone. All participants reported to frequently use smartphones and computers. P7 sorted her desktop so that she can use the PC only with magnification and P4 uses vision for all tasks but reading long texts. P6 reads news only on the smartphone because the PC websites are too overloaded. One participant (P3) even reported working for eight hours at a time on his PC, including reading text. Further, the smartphone was frequently mentioned as a magnifying assistive device (taking a photo) for other tasks highlighting the usage of visual assistive devices.

Social Interactions. All participants mentioned that they cannot recognize other persons unless they are spoken to. Then most can use the voice to identify the speaker. P4 and P6 can recognize well-known persons if they expect them to appear in a certain situation by visually recognizing the shape and stride of the persons. Facial expressions are not recognizable, but eight participants recognize body language. Together with the voice, this is enough to tell the coarse emotions of a conversational partner, but not enough to tell if they are bored or distracted (P3, P4), or hold eye contact (P6, P9). A device providing the status of the conversational partner's attention, eye contact and facial expression would provide a great benefit for persons with visual impairment.

6 Personal Strategies and Adjustments to the World

All participants noted that they prefer their visual sense wherever possible and have regular activities where their visual sense is crucial for their perception. Accordingly, they often use visual aids and only P8 does not use magnifiers at all. Three participants reported carrying a flashlight to illuminate dark scenes or spotlight objects in front of them to perceive details. One uses a thermal imaging camera during cooking. A similar focus on the visual sense is apparent in the adjustments participants make. P1, P2, P3 use visual markers and large-text labels in their home and others rely on differently colored objects to file documents. When asked for any changes in the environment, six participants requested visual adjustments, such as contrast-rich markings for stairs or white lines on the sidewalk as orientation in cities. P9 indicated that although she can accomplish a task without vision in many cases, it is usually just barely within the threshold of being possible and "it just takes way longer".

7 Guidelines and Challenges

Our results show that persons with low vision can profit from assistive technology using visual feedback. Here, we condense our findings into guidelines for developers of mixed-reality assistive technology. Specifically, the following properties are desirable in a visual aid: it should be adjustable by the user, automatically adapt to the user and the environment, carefully select the information the user needs at the moment, and automatically infer the user's intention.

Adjustability. It should be possible for the user to adjust the device for their subjective perception. The most important properties for this are color and brightness. However, the form and level of detail of the presented information, and the tasks, for which aid is desired, are important factors, as well. The physical and software-based user interface should be accessible to allow the user quick changes without asking other persons for help.

Context-Sensitivity. The system should automatically adapt to the user and the environment. For example, the brightness can be changed temporarily based on the illumination in the environment and the visual complexity of the displayed information can be adapted to the user's day to day condition. If the user's actions indicate that the presented information is not correctly processed, permanent adjustments can be made, e.g., reduce the level of detail. Additionally, the system can successively introduce other modalities, e.g., sound, if the user is gradually losing their remaining visual capabilities due to a progessive medical condition.

Selectivity. Participants expressed the concern that the visual feedback may be too much, e.g., if stimuli for multiple tasks are presented simultaneously, or if they occlude the real world. Therefore, the user should be able to clearly specify tasks they need assistance with as well as an order of priority, in which aid for simultaneous tasks should be presented.

Intention Recognition. The system should recognize the users' intention and provide aid only for such tasks the user is currently doing or attempting to do. For example, other traffic participants on the road should only be highlighted, if the user actually wants to cross the street and not while they are walking down the sidewalk.

Challenges. At present, building such an application poses a challenge to designers. Current hardware provides a limited field of view for visual augmentations, often paired with further disadvantages such as a considerable size and weight

of the headset as well as a short battery life. While this challenge is likely to be solved with time other issues are not. To perfectly adapt to the user, the device requires medical information and permanent monitoring of the user's actions and the environment. When taking data privacy of the user and of by-standers into account, some features may become difficult to implement from an ethical point of view.
Personalized assistive technology that uses machine learning and artificial intelligence to learn the user's preferences and subjective perception can provide optimal task and user dependent visual feedback.

8 Conclusion and Outlook

We contribute an overview of the functional vision of persons with low vision and a summary of their everyday activities, which does not focus on what the participants cannot see, cannot do or find challenging but covers an extensive range of capabilities and learned strategies of the participants. We further show that there are specific situations and activities for all individuals, in which the visual sense is dominant and crucial for the task and give some generalized guidelines for designers and developers. These insights can raise the awareness of the impact novel visual solutions can have for "blind" individuals as well as provide some guidance with regard to the design of vision aids.

Acknowledgments. This research was supported by the German Federal Ministry of Education and Research as part of the project IDeA (grant no. 16SV8102) and Hive (grant no. 16SV8183). We would also like to thank the reviewers and ACs for their work and valuable feedback.

References

1. Blindness and vision impairment. World Health Organization (2021). https://www.who.int/news-room/fact-sheets/detail/blindness-and-visual-impairment
2. Colenbrander, A.: Vision rehabilitation is part of AMD care. Vision **2**(1), 4 (2018). https://doi.org/10.3390/vision2010004, https://www.mdpi.com/2411-5150/2/1/4
3. Hyvärinen, L.: Visual perception in 'low vision'. Perception **28**(12), 1533–1537 (1999). https://doi.org/10.1068/p2856, https://doi.org/10.1068/p2856, pMID: 10793885
4. Lang, F., Machulla, T.: Pressing a button you cannot see: evaluating visual designs to assist persons with low vision through augmented reality. In: Proceedings of the 27th ACM Symposium on Virtual Reality Software and Technology, VRST 2021. Association for Computing Machinery, New York, NY, USA (2021). https://doi.org/10.1145/3489849.3489873
5. Lang, F., Schmidt, A., Machulla, T.: Augmented reality for people with low vision: symbolic and alphanumeric representation of information. In: Miesenberger, K., Manduchi, R., Covarrubias Rodriguez, M., Peňáz, P. (eds.) Computers Helping People with Special Needs, pp. 146–156. Springer, Cham (2020)
6. Microsoft (2022). https://www.microsoft.com/hololens

7. NuEyes (2022). https://nueyes.com/
8. OrCam (2022). https://www.orcam.com
9. Patil, K., Jawadwala, Q., Shu, F.C.: Design and construction of electronic aid for visually impaired people. IEEE Trans. Hum. Mach. Syst. **48**(2), 172–182 (2018). https://doi.org/10.1109/THMS.2018.2799588
10. Sandnes, F.E.: What do low-vision users really want from smart glasses? Faces, text and perhaps no glasses at all. In: Miesenberger, K., Bühler, C., Penaz, P. (eds.) Computers Helping People with Special Needs, pp. 187–194. Springer, Cham (2016)
11. Stearns, L., Findlater, L., Froehlich, J.E.: Design of an augmented reality magnification aid for low vision users. In: Proceedings of the 20th International ACM SIGACCESS Conference on Computers and Accessibility, pp. 28–39. ASSETS 2018. Association for Computing Machinery, New York, NY, USA (2018). https://doi.org/10.1145/3234695.3236361
12. Thevin, L., Machulla, T.: Three common misconceptions about visual impairments. In: 2020 IEEE Conference on Virtual Reality and 3D User Interfaces Abstracts and Workshops (VRW), pp. 523–524 (2020). https://doi.org/10.1109/VRW50115.2020.00113
13. Zhao, Y., Hu, M., Hashash, S., Azenkot, S.: Understanding low vision people's visual perception on commercial augmented reality glasses. In: CHI 2017, pp. 4170–4181. Association for Computing Machinery, New York, NY, USA (2017). https://doi.org/10.1145/3025453.3025949
14. Zhao, Y., Kupferstein, E., Castro, B.V., Feiner, S., Azenkot, S.: Designing AR visualizations to facilitate stair navigation for people with low vision. In: Proceedings of the 32nd Annual ACM Symposium on User Interface Software and Technology, UIST 2019, pp. 387–402. Association for Computing Machinery, New York, NY, USA (2019). https://doi.org/10.1145/3332165.3347906
15. Zhao, Y., Szpiro, S., Knighten, J., Azenkot, S.: CueSee: exploring visual cues for people with low vision to facilitate a visual search task, pp. 73–84, September 2016. https://doi.org/10.1145/2971648.2971730

Characterization of the Response of Fiber Bragg Grating Sensors Embedded in 3D Printed Continuous Fiberglass Reinforced Composite for Biomedical Applications

Giada Luppino[1(✉)], Davide Paloschi[1], Paola Saccomandi[1], Marco Tarabini[1], Luca M. Martulli[1], Andrea Bernasconi[1], Milutin Kostovic[2], Gennaro Rollo[2], Andrea Sorrentino[2], Marino Lavorgna[2], and Emanuele Gruppioni[3]

[1] Department of Mechanical Engineering, Politecnico di Milano, Via La Masa 1, 20156 Milano, Italy
giada.luppino@polimi.it
[2] CNR-IPCB Lecco, Lecco, Italy
[3] INAIL, Centro Protesi, Vigorso di Budrio, Bologna, Italy

Abstract. Nowadays, additive manufacturing play an increasing role in the design of assistive technology. In particular, 3D printed prosthetic devices, such as artificial limbs, still lack a comprehensive characterization of the materials and biomechanical properties, especially during the daily use. This technology can therefore benefit from advanced materials, such as smart composites, that combine high strength and lightweight properties with sensing capability. They exploit different kind of sensors embedded in the composite matrix to detect stress, strain, temperature or pressure depending on the design and the application considered. These sensors are miniaturized not to modify the mechanical behaviour of the embedding material and not to compromise its structural resistance. This study focuses on the characterization of 3D printed composites with embedded Fiber Bragg Grating (FBG) optical sensors for strain measurements, with future application in the prosthetic technology. The adhesion between the optical fiber containing the FBG and composite matrix was studied through pull-out tests, as the mechanical integrity of the whole smart material and its performance is investigated with quasi-static tensile tests. Results and discussion are provided considering polyamide and acrylate coated optical fibers embedded in specifically designed 3D printed samples.

Keywords: Fiber Bragg Grating · Optical sensors · Pull-out tests

1 Introduction

3D printed thermoplastic fiber-reinforced composites are increasing in importance as high-strength and lightweight structural materials in several industries. With proper design and reinforcements these composites can potentially replace traditional materials such as steel and aluminum, offering significant advantages over thermoset composites

K. Miesenberger et al. (Eds.): ICCHP-AAATE 2022, LNCS 13342, pp. 494–501, 2022.
https://doi.org/10.1007/978-3-031-08645-8_58

due to shorter production cycle times and improved recyclability. Additive manufacturing (AM) makes thermoplastic fiber-reinforced composites suitable for the fabrication of highly customizable products such as those in interaction with the human body. Given the diversity of every human being, having a quickly produced and easily adjustable product can be fundamental in the development of high comfort assistive devices [1], and for this reason AM technologies has already been widely studied for the application in biomedical field, creating products such as prosthetic limbs [2] or dental prostheses [3]. Under this prospective, the fabrication of composites by AM represents an interesting and still not completely explored opportunity for the realization of rehabilitation devices. The still developing nature of this technology justifies the lack of data available from tests and validations to define both material and prototypes' properties. The investigation on mechanical behavior of AM fiber-reinforced composites is therefore the first step to allow their spreading in medicine and bioengineering areas.

The integration of sensors in newly developed materials allows both their characterization and the possibility of employing them in so called smart structures. These structures are able to perform autonomous data collection exploiting different kinds of sensors; further data analysis allows the health monitoring of the structure and the identification of symptoms reflecting possible anomalies. For what concerns composite materials, Fiber Bragg Grating (FBG) are widely employed as monitoring sensors in bioengineering [4], aeronautics [5], aerospace [6], wind energy generation [7] and many more industries [8]. Indeed, they can be embedded in printed or laminated structures without affecting their mechanical properties [9, 10], thus providing a high accuracy measure of the internal strain and temperature field. In addition to that, they offer the property of lightweight, immunity to magnetic field and corrosion, flexibility and easy multiplexing.

These characteristics are particularly important for the design and fabrication of smart tools usable in the field of assistive technology, including prosthetics, where inclusive design strongly benefit from sensors and 3D printed fiberglass objects [11]. The monitoring of prostheses as a form of Assistive Technology results vital for overcoming the challenges that amputated patients face in their everyday life, such as pain, discomfort and motion difficulty, that often bring to premature prosthesis abandonment [12], and can lead to the development of new solutions aimed to meet users requirements, for a life quality increase of patients with disabilities.

In this work, a feasibility study for the integration of FBGs in 3D printed composite materials is conducted through a series of tailor-made experiments carried out by IPCB and Politecnico di Milano. The aim of the study is that to understand whether this smart material could be employed in the development of future prosthetic 3D printed devices. In particular, the experimental campaigns focused on the requisites to have the optical fiber sensors effectively embedded in the in the composite material during its manufacturing and on the choice of the appropriate fiber coating between polyimide and acrylate. Sensors' performances are evaluated in terms of both mechanical resistance and efficient signal transmission when subjected to external loads. In addition to that, the capability of the fiber in following the deformation of the samples without slippage is considered and the strain transmission effectiveness was evaluated. Note that the first paragraph of a section or subsection is not indented. The first paragraphs that follows a table, figure, equation etc. does not have an indent, either.

2 Materials and Methods

3D printed samples reinforced with continuous fiberglass were employed (Fig. 2). The fiberglass filament and the thermoplastic matrix named "Onyx" were both supplied by Markforged®, USA. The base matrix (Onyx) is a Polyamide 66 filled with micro carbon fibers. A dual extruder nozzle (Mark One from Markforged, USA) was used for the fabrication of composite samples. The print parameters were set in the Eiger Markforged software. Both pull-out and tensile tests were performed with different samples shapes.

Interfacial properties play an important role in analysing the mechanical behaviour of composites and fibers [13]. The pull-out tests evaluate the interfacial interaction between fiber and composite under various bonding situations [14]. Generally speaking, results depend on each fibre-matrix combination as well as the applied fiber coating and sizing, surface roughness and temperature regimes. In this study, the effect of the presence of adhesive between fiber and sample was evaluated at fixed speed of 2 mm/min [15], using an Instron 5526 test machine. Pull-out tests were carried out by making pure Onyx samples in which the optical fibers were immersed to a known depth during the printing process (Fig. 1). The size of the printed samples was 30 × 8 × 3 mm, the fiber's location was in the middle of the sample, with a diameter of 0.5 mm. Regarding the printing parameters, the extrusion temperature was set to 275 °C and the number of layers was 30. The fiber was with polyimide coating.

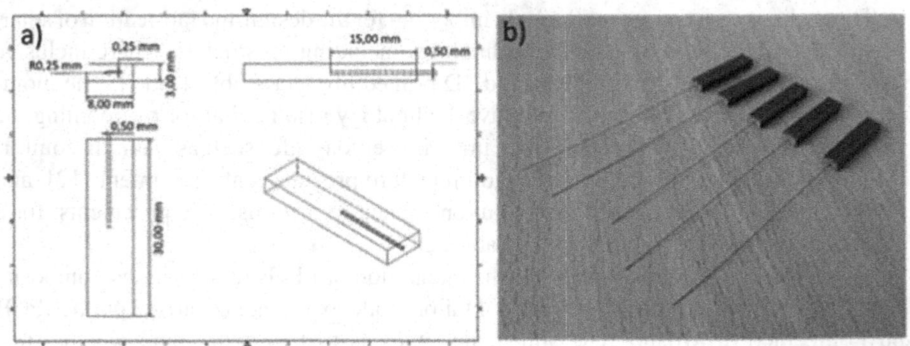

Fig. 1. Drawing of the sample for the pull-out test (a) and 3D printed samples with FBG (b).

For what concerns the tensile test, two fiberglass reinforced samples were specifically printed by adding FBGs coated with acrylate and polyamide. Figure 2a shows the sample design with a groove located at its middle to insert the FBG. The groove was realised by stopping the print at the predefined layer, inserting the FBG and continuing the print above it. Figure 2b shows one of the 3D printed samples with a polyimide coated FBG inside (Fig. 2b inset), and a cross-section showing the disposition of the continuous fiberglass. The print layer height was set to 0,1 mm and the number of reinforcing layers was set to 8. The number of layers was then determined to a total of 21. These specimens were tested as shown in Fig. 3.

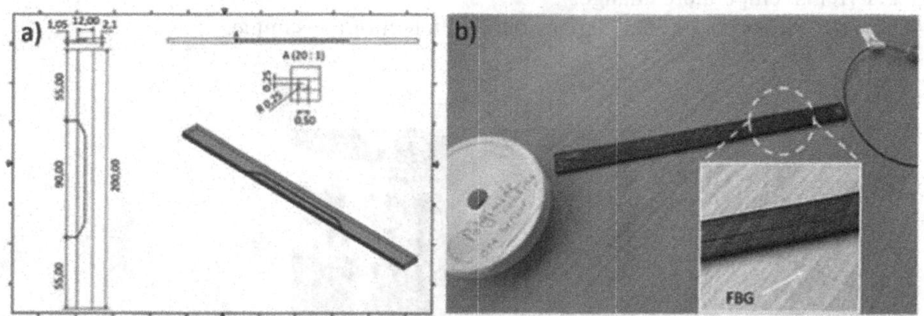

Fig. 2. Drawing of the sample for tensile test (a) and 3D printed specimen with FBG inside (b).

The FBG is a periodic modulation of the refractive index of the core of an optical fiber. When broadband light is incident on it, it reflects a specific wavelength. This wavelength changes when strain or temperature variations are applied to the grating, therefore allowing strain or temperature point measurements. In order to perform the measurements, the spectrum of the light reflected by the FBG is measured with an optical interrogator, and the peak wavelength in the spectrum (i.e., the Bragg wavelength) is acquired. The position of the peak wavelength in the spectrum is then related to the fiber deformation.

FBG Bragg wavelengths were chosen in the typical range of 1550 nm, for a sensing length of 10 mm. Testing procedure was repeated for the two samples with the same methodology: a tensile test machine MTS Alliance RT 100, with maximum load of 100 kN was employed at Politecnico di Milano for the quasi-static traction of the samples. Each sample was gradually tensioned with a deformation-control strategy, imposing a displacement corresponding to 0,1% incremental strain variations, up to the maximum value of 1%. The corresponding strain was acquired using a 50 mm extensometer, and it was compared with the one theoretically derived from the wavelength shift of the FBG as in Eq. (1) [16]. Isothermal condition was supposed, reducing calculations to Eq. (2). Reflective spectra of FBGs were acquired with the optical interrogator Micron Optics Si255 at the sampling frequency of 1 kHz (Table 1).

$$\varepsilon_m = \frac{1}{k} * \frac{\Delta\lambda}{\lambda_0} - \left(\alpha_{sp} + \frac{\alpha_\delta}{k}\right) * \Delta T \tag{1}$$

$$\varepsilon_m = \frac{1}{k} * \frac{\Delta\lambda}{\lambda_0} \tag{2}$$

where:

- $\Delta\lambda$ [nm] is the FBG wavelength variation;
- λ_0 [nm] is the FBG wavelength at test start;

- α_δ [10^{-6}/K] is the optical fiber refraction index;
- k is the gage factor, expressed as k = (1 − p), being p the photo-elastic coefficient (p = 0,22);
- ΔT [K] is temperature change;
- α_{sp} [10^{-6}/K] is the thermal expansion coefficient of the sample.

Fig. 3. Tensile test setup, Onyx and fiberglass sample with 50 mm extensometer applied.

Table 1. Sample characteristics.

Characteristic	Fiberglass	Onyx
Layer orientation [°]	0	45
Layer thickness [mm]	0,1	0,1
Number of layers	8	2 + 9 + 2
Sample length [mm]	200	200
Sample width [mm]	12	12
Sample thickness [mm]	2,1	2,1
Layer disposition	[2O, 4F, 9O, 4F, 2O]	[2O, 4F, 9O, 4F, 2O]
Fiberglass filament disposition	Isotropic	Isotropic
Volume fraction (fiberglass)	30,1%	30,1%

3 Results

The pull-out tests investigated the necessity of adding adhesive layer to ensure a stable and resistant embedding of the FBG in the printed sample. Samples with fibers are loaded in the testing machine and the fiber is pulled at a fixed speed. The fiber is gradually pulled outside the sample as its displacement and the load applied by the machine were registered. The load applied to the fiber end is recorded as a function of the displacement of this end with respect to the grips holding the matrix. Figure 4 shows the load and displacement curves registered by the machine in order to unthread the fiber from the sample. The red curve refers to the sample with adhesive between fiber and substrate, the black curve refers to samples created without adhesive. It can be seen how peak load values in the two tests differ of an order of magnitude. Similarly, with adhesive, the fiber displacement before failure is four times greater. Given these results, an acrylic adhesive was used for the subsequent 3D printed samples for the tensile tests.

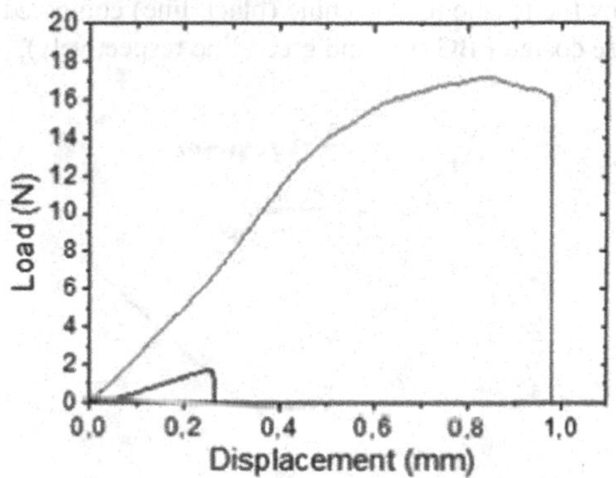

Fig. 4. Pull-out results of specimen without adhesive (black line) and with adhesive (red line). (Color figure online)

Tensile test results are reported in Fig. 5, in which each sample deformation acquired with the extensometer is plotted (black line) along with the deformation measured by FBGs with Eq. (2), both with respect to the testing time. For the acrylate coating (red line), a fiber slippage due to adhesive failure is visible at approximately 0,4% strain. The maximum strain measured by the acrylate fiber is approximately 0,8%, which corresponds to a strain transfer loss of 20% with respect to the imposed 1% strain measured by the extensometer. Higher performance is observed with the polyamide coated fiber (green line), for which no slippage is detected and almost no transfer loss is recorded. The response of this fiber suggests the possibility of applications for strains higher than 1%.

Further performance comparison can be done with respect to Fig. 6, in which acrylate and polyamide coated FBG strains are plotted with respect to the imposed deformation measured by the extensometer. The measured and the imposed strains, in order to have an ideal sensor, are supposed to be perfectly matching. This condition is well represented by the polyamide curve (black line). On the contrary, for the acrylate coating fiber (red line), a strain transmission loss is detected (line offset) with variable gain depending on the imposed strain (line slope). This effect can be traced back to the ineffective bonding between acrylate, adhesive and substrate, which can lead to fiber slippage.

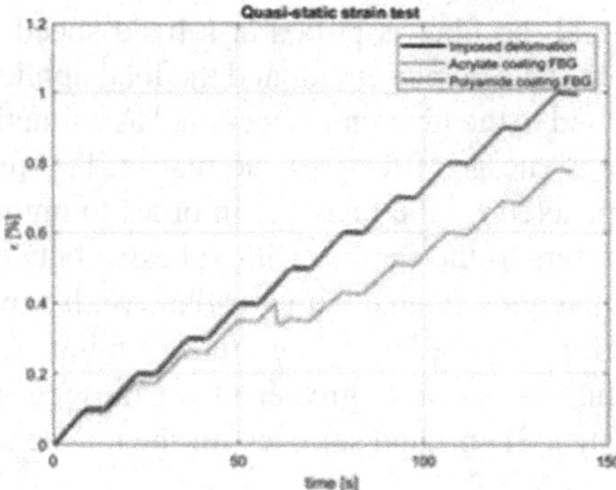

Fig. 5. Imposed strain by the tensile test machine (black line) compared to the one acquired by the acrylate ad polyamide coated FBG (red and green line respectively). (Color figure online)

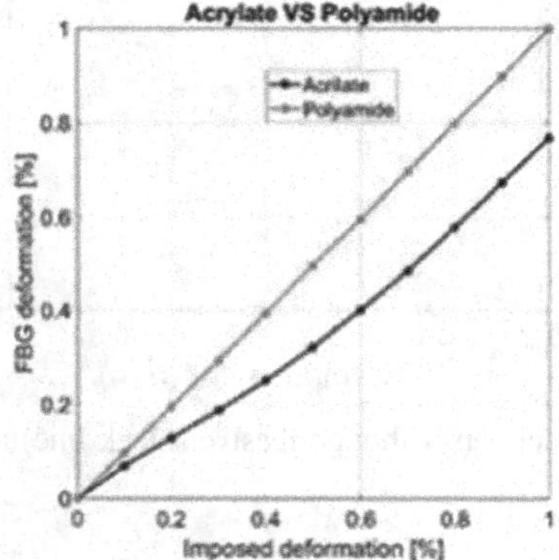

Fig. 6. Sensitivity comparison between FBG with polyamide and acrylate coating. (Color figure online)

4 Discussion and Conclusions

A feasibility study for the embedding of Fiber Bragg Grating sensors into 3D printed composite materials was conducted. Both acrylate and polyamide coated fibers were considered. The characterization of the mechanical resistance of the fiber and the substrate adhesive layer was studied via ad-hoc experiments involving pull-out and tensile tests. The pull-out tests confirmed the need of an adhesive layer between composite and sensor in order to ensure an effective bond between the two. The strain transmission efficiency was quantified with the tensile test, where the polyamide coating outperformed the acrylate coating (20% gain loss). Almost zero strain loss was detected for the polyamide coated fiber, with unitary gain in all the tested strain range. These preliminary results show the possibility of effectively embedding optical fibers in composite materials for the realization of smart devices, for applications such as rehabilitation and assistive technology in general.

Acknowledgements. The authors are grateful to Centro Protesi INAIL for supporting this study through the PROFIL Project (FILamenti multimateriali per la realizzazione di PROtesi personalizzate ad alte prestazioni con focus su adaptive sport).

References

1. Yao, Y., Saccomandi, P., Tarabini, M.: User-driven design and monitoring systems of limb prostheses: overview on the technology and on the gender-related aspects. In: IEEE International Workshop on Metrology for Industry 4.0 and IoT, MetroInd 4.0 and IoT 2021 - Proceedings, pp. 313–318 (2021)
2. Jin, Y.A., Plott, J., Chen, R., Wensman, J., Shih, A.: Additive manufacturing of custom Orthoses and Prostheses – a review. Procedia CIRP **36**, 199–204 (2015)
3. Li, H., Song, L., Sun, J., Ma, J., Shen, Z.: Dental ceramic prostheses by stereolithography-based additive manufacturing: potentials and challenges. Adv. Appl. Ceram. **118**(1–2), 30–36 (2018). https://doi.org/10.1080/17436753.2018.1447834
4. Mitrogiannis, C., Tsiokos, D., Nianios, G., Papaioannou, G., Kanellos, G.T., Pleros, N.: Two dimensional polymer-embedded quasi-distributed FBG pressure sensor for biomedical applications. Opt. Express **18**(1), 179–186 (2010)
5. Ramly, R., Kuntjoro, W., Rahman, M.K.A.: Using embedded Fiber Bragg Grating (FBG) sensors in smart aircraft structure materials. Procedia Eng. **41**, 600–606 (2012)
6. Kabashima, S., Ozaki, T., Takeda, N.: Structural health monitoring using FBG sensor in space environment. In: Proceedings of SPIE, vol. 4332 (2001). https://doi.org/10.1117/12.429644
7. Park, S., Park, T., Han, K.: Real-time monitoring of composite wind turbine blades using Fiber Bragg Grating sensors. Adv. Compos. Mater. **20**(1), 39–51 (2012). https://doi.org/10.1163/092430410X504198
8. Paloschi, D., Bronnikov, K.A., Korganbayev, S., Wolf, A.A., Dostovalov, A., Saccomandi, P.: 3D shape sensing with multicore optical fibers: transformation matrices versus Frenet-Serret equations for real-time application. IEEE Sens. J. **21**(4), 4599–4609 (2021)
9. Kim, D., Kim, H., Song, M., Sampath, U.: Polymer-coated FBG sensor for simultaneous temperature and strain monitoring in composite materials under cryogenic conditions. Appl. Opt. **57**(3), 492–497 (2018)
10. Lau, K.-T., Lau, K.-T.: Structural health monitoring for smart composites using embedded FBG sensor technology. Mater. Sci. Technol. **30**(13), 1642–1654 (2014). https://doi.org/10.1179/1743284714Y.0000000608
11. Lenoe, E.M., Radicic, W.N., Knapp, M.S.: Implications of smart materials in advanced prosthetics. Smart Struct. Mater. **2189**, 84–104 (1994). https://doi.org/10.1117/12.174087
12. Biddiss, E., Chau, T.: Upper limb prosthesis use and abandonment: a survey of the last 25 years. Prosthet. Orthot. Int. **31**(3), 236–257 (2007). https://doi.org/10.1080/03093640600994581
13. Zhandarov, S., Mäder, E.: Characterization of fiber/matrix interface strength: applicability of different tests, approaches and parameters. Compos. Sci. Technol. **65**(1), 149–160 (2005). https://doi.org/10.1016/J.COMPSCITECH.2004.07.003
14. Yang, Q.S., Qin, Q.H., Peng, X.R.: Size effects in the fiber pullout test. Compos. Struct. **61**(3), 193–198 (2003). https://doi.org/10.1016/S0263-8223(03)00066-7
15. DiFrancia, C., Ward, T.C., Claus, R.O.: The single-fibre pull-out test. 1: review and interpretation. Compos. Part A Appl. Sci. Manuf. **27**(8), 597–612 (1996). https://doi.org/10.1016/1359-835X(95)00069-E

Assistive Technologies and Inclusion for Older People

Assistive Technologies and Inclusion for Older People
Introduction to the Special Thematic Session

Özge Subaşı[1], Paul Panek[2], and Jean D. Hallewell Haslwanter[3](✉)

[1] Media and Visual Arts, Koç University, Istanbul, Turkey
ozsubasi@ku.edu.tr

[2] TU Wien (Vienna University of Technology), Vienna, Austria
paul.panek@tuwien.ac.at

[3] University of Applied Sciences Upper Austria, Wels, Austria
jean.hallewell@fh-ooe.at

Abstract. This special thematic session aims to continue the discussions around Active Assisted Living (AAL) by looking into how AAL systems and technologies are related to older people's lives. Almost all countries are challenged by the aging demographics and issues that people face in the course of aging. A great diversity of technologies have been developed and implemented. However, there are many challenges involved in developing and deploying systems that truly fit the needs and wishes of older people. The papers included in this session look at various topics, including ageism, addressing privacy with sensors, and evaluations of systems.

Keywords: Older people · Assistive technologies · Active Assisted Living (AAL)

1 Motivation for the Session

Digital ecosystems for the inclusion of older people into society have long been popular agenda items for many stakeholders, from technology developers to governments, city councils, hospitals, and academics, as the aging demographics is a challenge almost everywhere. These technologies are often developed to ease or remove the burdens of changes such as changing homes, living with a new health condition, adapting to a new living environment, transitioning from working to retirement, and so on. These digital systems, also called Active Assisted Living (AAL) systems, are very diverse and include smart homes, robotic systems, telehealth, telecare monitoring, self-care technologies, and even technology enhanced community services and environments. However, there are many challenges involved in developing these types of systems. Developing and deploying innovative multi-stakeholder systems for an emerging, not yet fully explored social change is a significant challenge.

K. Miesenberger et al. (Eds.): ICCHP-AAATE 2022, LNCS 13342, pp. 505–510, 2022.
https://doi.org/10.1007/978-3-031-08645-8_59

Growing older, being old, and belonging to a demographic group can mean different things at different times. Previous work showed and criticized that older people frequently presented with some stereotypical assumptions, such as being a socially isolated group in need of bolstering connections with family [3]. These stereotypical assumptions need to change. We suggest that AAL ecosystems include both the technologies and all the decision-makers and people affected by the technologies equally. The new and emerging AAL systems are pushing boundaries to answer the needs of an aging population in their diverse wishes such as to stay connected, social, independent, and age with more dignity and enjoyment.

Older people's abilities, life experience, and cultural and social infrastructures surrounding them are all diverse. It is essential to design ecosystems by focusing on how older people themselves approach their relationships with families and friends [3], rather than top-down definitions. There is a need to question common assumptions about older adults and their use of new and emerging technologies [2]. For instance, it is important to re-position older users as active agents [7].

Furthermore, older people may face physical, sensory, or cognitive limitations associated with the biological aging process. However, this should not create assumptions about how and when to assist older people. As an example, the assumptions on older people's will to be monitored by family members are proven contradictory, as the older people are more likely to enjoy observing their younger generations, but not that much to be monitored by them [3]. The AAL systems and technologies market is not yet able to deal with all of these complexities. A discourse analysis study [7] showed that previous interaction design work focused on the limitations to the cognitive and physical abilities and health-related problems, thus rendering aging as a 'problem' that technologies can manage. One idea for shifting this view is moving beyond what a person can do, focusing instead on the collective care that makes those capacities possible (i.e. how people work together to bring about attentive relationships) [1].

The Special Thematic Session (STS) follows our previous calls (AAL Forum 2018, ICCHP 2018). It aims to continue the discussions related to assistive and inclusive technologies for older people and the ecosystems in which they are created. We aim to define the changing role of the technologies within the changing context and perceptions of aging.

2 AAL Ecosystems: An Inclusive Perspective on Assistive Technologies in Later Life

For furthering the discussions in the placement of AAL and older people, we find the following topics relevant:

AAL for Individuals and Communities aims to point to the unique potentials of how people interact with each other and the role of AAL in supporting those interactions. For example, how are emerging social needs reflected in the AAL products? How do we design for the new norms after Covid-19 (independence vs. interdependence)? Are there emerging digital artifacts, environments, and technologies? How does AAL change shape in a fast-changing world and contribute to better health, finance, education, etc.? In defining those assets, it is essential to remember that many of the older people are autonomous, do not define themselves as old, and have a similar approach towards the notion of family friendship as younger people [3]. Recent work showed that during Covid-19, a group of older people actively used an ecosystem of communication tools to maintain multimodal connectedness [6].

AAL at Scale: Cities, Governmental Services aim to point to AAL ecosystems' growth and scale potentials. Public services, smart cities, and citizen-centric digital systems are all exciting areas of research and development. Almost endless possibilities are available to support older people from automotive interactions and restaurants to hospitals, care homes, daycare, and therapy centers.

In Social Challenges and Opportunities for AAL Systems, we see ageism, sexism, and race issues in AAL, as no environment is free of social bias. More broadly, getting it right on ethics, legal aspects, security, and privacy are crucial when assessing impact, deploying and evaluating assistive technologies for older people. Thus, this extends to the broader societal implications and business models for inclusive assistive technologies for older people. The complexity of the designs can easily lead to technology being developed for older people by non older populations. Systematically belittling, disregarding, ignoring and dehumanizing a group contributes to an epistemic exclusion [8]. It is essential that AAL systems do not treat the older people in these ways.

Lastly, we put a focus on *AAL across borders.* How do geographical differences, e.g. rural vs. urban, affect the assistive technologies for older people? What are the significant issues of cross-cultural experiences and mobility (migration, relocation)? Are there potentials for a low-cost AAL rethinking business models for geographies marked by low-income per person?

3 Papers in the Session

In the following, we describe the papers from the session. We have divided these into two parts, those about *Impressions about older people*, and those about *privacy considerations* and *outcome assessment.* In addition, we introduce the papers from this session that are included in the open access compendium for the conference.

3.1 Impressions About Older People

Related to the topic *social challenges*, at a previous ICCHP conference, Helen Petrie investigated ageism and sexism amongst young computer scientists in the United Kingdom [4]. Participants were shown a picture of either an old or young woman or man and asked to assess the likelihood that this person would use different computer systems, and their level of expertise with these technologies. The results found both ageism and sexism.

In this conference, Yao Chen and Helen Petrie build on this work in their paper "Ageism and sexism amongst young technicians and older people in China" and look *across borders* to investigate attitudes in China. This study investigated not only the attitudes of young computer scientists there, but also compared these to the attitudes of older people. It is interesting to compare the results to those of the previous study, and see that many issues transcend not only continents, but also generations.

In their paper "Ageism in Design: Accessibility without User Experience?", Jean Hallewell Haslwanter and Christiane Takacs also build on this work to explore how the prejudices against older people affect the designs considered for them, i.e. those aspects they are thought to want and need. Based on an image of either a younger or older person, participants were asked to suggest design aspects for that person. The aspects recommended for each age group were grouped into the elements of user experience, and compared. Furthermore, the study looks at the aspects young computer scientists recommend to support the accessibility of technologies for older people.

These attitudes are important, as it may affect whether the technologies produced are adopted by older people, so that they can profit from them.

3.2 Privacy Considerations and Outcome Assessment

In the topic *AAL at scale* we look at the high growth potential of the AAL ecosystems, which not only brings many opportunities, but also requires a serious consideration of many aspects related to it.

In their paper "Addressing Privacy Concerns in Depth Sensors", Wiktor Mucha et al. describe a study on privacy concerns related to depth sensors. Compared to the RGB camera sensors, the depth sensors are widely considered to be much less obtrusive as these types of sensors do not provide texture detail. Due to privacy considerations, depth sensors are commonly used in modern AAL systems to monitor user behaviour and detect emergency situations such as falls. In their study, the authors show that although depth sensors generally protect privacy better, this does not mean that they guarantee privacy under all circumstances.

Advances in sensor resolution, and particularly in deep learning technology, have significantly improved the level of detail that can be seen in depth sensor data. The authors have demonstrated this effect using test data and conclude that depth data is more confidential than RGB data, but that when using depth sensors in AAL systems, it is of great importance to analyse a possible disclosure of user identity in individual cases and prevent it. This is particularly important in the case of a small number of users and in the case of high-resolution depth sensor data.

Both AAL and AT can have a high impact on the user's day to day life. However, there still is a lack of reliable data regarding the user's actual needs and the real ability of AT and AAL products to reduce the impact of disability, disease or age-induced limitations. In "Assessing the Outcome of Mobility Assistive Technology (OMAT) in daily living: preliminary results in an Italian sample" Francesca Borgnis et al. report about an ongoing research study where preliminary results showed positive impact of the provided AT products on the quality of life not only for the patients (primary users) but also for the caregivers (secondary users).

Scientific evidence for the impact and outcome of AT and AAL use is of high importance for the future growth of the ecosystem.

3.3 Additional Papers in the Session

In addition to the papers in this volume, further papers presented in the session are available in the open access compendium for the conference [5].
These include papers evaluating specific technologies and problems users have with them in practice:

- "Long term impact of using Smart Speakers in accessing literary works by people with vision loss - usability study of BLVNZ Alexa Skill" by Jarek Beksa and Sara Chin.
- "SmartGlass implementation: Lessons learned in long-term elderly care" by Monique Lexis et al.
- "Technical support needs of older users of digital health technologies to support self-management of multimorbidity" by Suzanne Smith.

One looks at the state of the art in community-based services and points out some of the current limitations:

- "Smart Community-Based Services for older persons with disability: A desk review and analysis of design projects" by Mabel Giraldo et al.

Others look at the needs with respect to these technologies:

- "Ageing, Technology, and Experiences of Home" by Jeffrey W. Jutai.
- "Needs assessment regarding ICT for elderly people and their carers: The PROADAS study" by Maria Prodromou.

The final paper from the compendium links into the topic of ageism:

- "Narratives of digital technology use: Understanding the role of ageism in the digital inclusion of Older Adults" by Cora van Leeuwen.

We encourage readers to look at these in [5].

Finally, there was an entry in the inclusion forum, a format intended to provide an opportunity for discussion and participation: "Elderly people living in the Information society supported by *intelligence*" by Laura Burzagli and Pier Luigi Emiliani, which describes the limitations of AI with respect to two specific apps that address difficulties preparing complex meals and loneliness.

In sum, the papers in this session provide interesting insights about aspects to be aware of (e.g. ageism and privacy), but also show there are a variety of technologies, some of which can reduce the impact of disability, disease or age-induced limitations and improve the lives of people. For this, it is essential not to think only of the technology or the carer point of view, but take a holistic view of the AAL ecosystem and be sensitive to the views and needs of older people, who are in end the primary users.

Acknowledgements. We thank Klaus Miesenberger for encouraging us to do the session and Geraldine Fitzpatrick, who fostered collaboration between different research groups at her institute at TU Wien. This session is partially funded by INCA Intergenerational New-Crafts Associations project at Koç University.

References

1. Bennett, C.L., Rosner, D.K., Taylor, A.S.: The care work of access, pp. 1–15. Association for Computing Machinery, New York, NY, USA (2020). https://doi.org/10.1145/3313831.3376568
2. Durick, J., Robertson, T., Brereton, M., Vetere, F., Nansen, B.: Dispelling ageing myths in technology design. In: Proceedings of the 25th Australian Computer-Human Interaction Conference: Augmentation, Application, Innovation, Collaboration, OzCHI 2013, pp. 467–476. Association for Computing Machinery, New York, NY, USA (2013). https://doi.org/10.1145/2541016.2541040
3. Lindley, S.E., Harper, R., Sellen, A.: Designing for elders: exploring the complexity of relationships in later life. In: Proceedings of the 22nd British HCI Group Annual Conference on People and Computers: Culture, Creativity, Interaction, BCS-HCI 2008, vol. 1, pp. 77–86. BCS Learning & Development Ltd., Swindon, GBR (2008)
4. Petrie, H.: Ageism and sexism amongst young computer scientists. In: Miesenberger, K., Kouroupetroglou, G. (eds.) ICCHP 2018. LNCS, vol. 10897, pp. 421–425. Springer, Cham (2018). https://doi.org/10.1007/978-3-319-94274-2_60
5. Petz, A., Hoogerwerf, E.J., Mavrou, K. (eds.): Assistive Technology, Accessibility and (e)Inclusion, ICCHP-AAATE 2022 Open Access Compendium. Johannes Kepler University, Linz, Austria (2022). https://www.icchp-aaate.org
6. Richards, O.K., Marcu, G., Brewer, R.N.: Hugs, bible study, and speakeasies: designing for older adults' multimodal connectedness. In: Designing Interactive Systems Conference 2021, DIS 2021, pp. 815–831. Association for Computing Machinery, New York, NY, USA (2021). https://doi.org/10.1145/3461778.3462075
7. Vines, J., Pritchard, G., Wright, P., Olivier, P., Brittain, K.: An age-old problem: examining the discourses of ageing in HCI and strategies for future research. ACM Trans. Comput.-Hum. Interact. **22**(1), 1–27 (2015). https://doi.org/10.1145/2696867
8. Ymous, A., et al.: "I am just terrified of my future" - epistemic violence in disability related technology research. In: Extended Abstracts of the 2020 CHI Conference on Human Factors in Computing Systems, CHI EA 2020, pp. 1–16. Association for Computing Machinery, New York, NY, USA (2020). https://doi.org/10.1145/3334480.3381828

Ageism and Sexism Amongst Young Technicians and Older People in China

Yao Chen and Helen Petrie(✉)

University of York, York YO10 5GH, UK
{yc2046,helen.petrie}@york.ac.uk

Abstract. A study was undertaken with 85 young Chinese people involved with technology design and development (either as students or workers) and 101 older Chinese people. The main aim was to investigate whether the young people, as current and future designers and developers of technologies for older people, have ageist and sexist attitudes about older people as users of technology. A second aim was to investigate whether their attitudes differ from those of older people. Participants were shown a picture of either a young or old Chinese woman or man and asked to assess the likelihood that this person would use a desktop computer, laptop computer and a smartphone, and their level of expertise in each of these technologies. Both young and older Chinese people showed negative attitudes towards older adults compared to young ones as both users of and experts in technology, and negative attitudes towards women compared to men. However, there was only slight evidence of "double discrimination" towards older women, this was on use of the technologies rather than expertise with the technologies. These results show that young Chinese workers in technology need education in the characteristics and needs of their older potential audiences.

Keywords: Perceptions of older Chinese people · Ageism · Perceptions of older Chinese women · Sexism · Perceptions of technology use · Perceptions of technology expertise

1 Introduction

Older people increasingly need and want to use technologies to assist them in living more independent and productive lives. But it is largely younger people who design and develop these technologies, so it is important that they are able to understand and empathise with the needs and wishes of older people. Yet it is well-known that young people in European countries tend to have negative attitudes and beliefs about older people [1], although there is a much stronger tradition of respect for older people in China [7, 8]. There is also a tendency to believe that women are less likely to use and less expert about technology [6]. Finally, there is often a "double standard" in attitudes and beliefs, with older women being more negatively viewed than older men [3].

Researching this topic with young British computer science students (who were very predominantly male), Petrie [5] found that they thought that older people were less

K. Miesenberger et al. (Eds.): ICCHP-AAATE 2022, LNCS 13342, pp. 511–516, 2022.
https://doi.org/10.1007/978-3-031-08645-8_60

likely to use a range of digital technologies (desktop computers, laptop computers and smartphones) and less likely to be expert in using them. While she found no difference in beliefs that women would use these technologies less than men, there was a difference in beliefs about expertise, with women perceived as being less expert than men. However, she found no evidence of a "double discrimination" against older women being seen as less likely to use these technologies or less expert with them than the other groups.

2 Method

This study investigated the perceptions of young Chinese university students studying technology related subjects and young Chinese people working in technology related industries of younger and older men and women as users and experts of computers and smartphones. It then compared these perceptions with the perceptions of older Chinese people.

85 young Chinese people participated, 42 university students (studying computer science and other technology related subjects) and 43 professional technology developers (working in software development, UI and UX design, product management, and other related jobs). 43 (50.6%) were men, 41 (48.2%) were women and 1 (1.2%) preferred not to give a gender. Their ages ranged from 20 to 33 years, with a median age of 26 years. 101 older Chinese people participated, 38 (37.6%) were men, 63 (62.4%) were women. Their ages ranged from 60 to 85 years, with a median age of 63 years.

The young participants were recruited using a number of different channels, including personal contacts and messages on the WeChat social media site. The older participants were recruited through personal contacts and by publicity at an activity centre for older Chinese people in Hefei in the Province of Anhui.

The survey comprised a photograph of either an old or young man or woman (see Fig. 1). Eight different versions of the survey were created, each with a different photograph. Four of the photographs were of older people, four were of younger people. Photographs were chosen carefully so that the person looked to be in their 70s for the older people, and in their late 20s/early 30s for the younger people (so a little older than the target respondents for the survey, but people they would still consider young). Within each group two images were of women and two were of men. All the photographs were chosen to be close up shots of a person reading a book. All the photographs were copyright free images from the Internet.

The survey asked the following nine questions about the person in the photograph. Firstly, three questions about the age of the person and old age in general:

How old do you think the person is?
Would you call this person old?
What is the minimum age you would think of someone as old?

Three questions about the person's use of technology:

How likely do you think it is that this person uses a desktop computer regularly (rated on a scale from 1 = not at all likely to 7 = very likely)?

Fig. 1. Photographs of younger and older Chinese women and men used in the study.

How likely do you think it is that this person uses a laptop computer regularly (same rating)?
How likely do you think it is that this person uses a smartphone regularly (same rating)?

Three questions about the person's expertise with technology:

How expert do you think this person would be with a desktop computer (rated on a scale from 1 = not at all expert to 7 = very expert)?
How expert do you think this person would be with a laptop computer (same rating)?
How expert do you think this person would be with a smartphone (same rating)?

Finally, participants were asked their age and gender.

3 Results

Preliminary analyses showed there were very few differences between the answers from young students and young professionals, so all the young respondents were treated as one group for the analyses.

For the question on when old age begins, young respondents gave a mean estimate that old age begins at 61.33 years (SD: 5.20), with a range of answers, from 50 to 70 years. However, the majority of young respondents (73, 85.8%) thought that old age begins after 60 years of age. The older respondents gave a mean estimate that old age begins at 65.42 years (SD: 5.43) with a range from 50 to 85 years. Again, the majority of older respondents (93 out of 96, 96.8%, 5 older respondents did not answer this question) thought that old age begins after 60 years of age. The difference between young and older respondents was significant ($F = 25.70$, $df = 1, 176$, $p < .001$, $\eta p^2 = 0.13$), although the magnitude of the difference is not great (only a mean difference of just over 4 years). There was no significant difference between men and women respondents in their view on this and no significant interaction between age and gender.

For the ratings of the likelihood that the people in the photos would use a desktop computer/laptop computer/smartphone regularly, a five way multivariate analysis of variance was conducted: Device (desktop/laptop/smartphone) × Photo Age (Young or Old) × Photo Gender (woman or man) × Respondent Age (Young or Old) × Respondent Gender (Young or Old).

There was a significant main effect for Device with a large effect size ($F (2, 322) = 49.12$, $p < 0.001$), $\eta p^2 = 0.23$) with smartphone being rated as the most likely to be used, (mean rating: 5.02, SD: 2.28) followed by laptop, (mean: 4.26, SD: 2.41) with desktop the least likely to be used (mean: 4.00, SD: 2.28).

In terms of how the characteristics of the photo affected ratings, there was a main effect for Photo Age with a large effect size ($F (1, 161) = 150.936$ $p < 0.001$, $\eta p^2 = 0.48$) with photos of young people rated significantly more likely to use all the devices than photos of old people (mean young: 6.03, SD: 1.02; mean old: 3.05, SD: 1.86). There was also a significant main effect for Photo Gender but with a small effect size ($F (1, 161) = 5.85$, $p < 0.05$, $\eta p^2 = 0.04$), with photos of men rated as significantly more likely to use all the devices than photos of women (mean men: 4.78, SD: 2.11; mean women: 4.08, SD: 2.11).

There was also a very nearly significant interaction between Photo Age and Photo Gender but again with a small effect size ($F (1, 161) = 3.57$, $p = 0.06$, $\eta p^2 = 0.02$), illustrated in Fig. 2. It shows there is some slight evidence of the "double discrimination" against women – the difference between the ratings of young and old women is considerably greater than the difference between young and old men, nearly one increment on the 7 point rating scale).

In terms of how the characteristics of the respondents affected ratings, there were no main effects for respondent age or gender. There were some significant interactions with other variables, but none of particular interest for this research.

For the ratings of people's expertise with the technologies, another multivariate analysis of variance was also conducted. There was a significant main effect for Device with a large effect size ($F (2, 318) = 41.85$, $p < 0.001$, $\eta p^2 = 0.21$) with people's expertise with smartphones being rated as the highest, (mean rating: 4.73, SD: 2.29) followed by laptop computers, (mean: 4.18, SD: 2.35) and desktop computers the lowest (mean: 4.18, SD: 2.29).

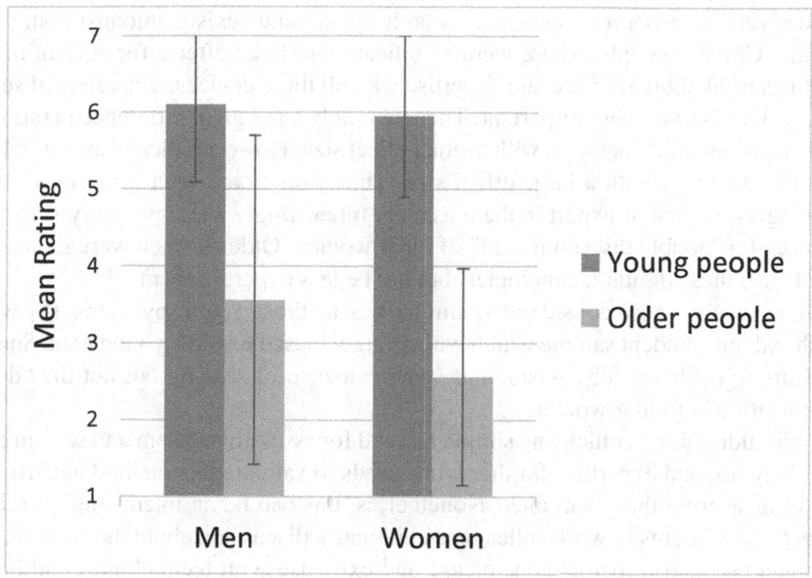

Fig. 2. Ratings of likelihood of use for Photo Age and Photo Gender

There was a main effect for Photo Age with a large effect size (F (1, 159) = 189.27 p < 0.001, ηp2 = 0.54) with young people rated as having significantly a higher level of expertise with all the devices than old people (mean young: 6.13, SD: 2.29; mean old: 2.84, SD: 1.82). There was also a significant main effect for Photo Gender with a large effect size (F (1, 159) = 4.63, p < 0.05, $\eta p^2 = 0.28$) with men rating as having a significantly higher level of expertise than women (mean men: 4.67, SD: 2.17; mean women: 4.06, SD: 2.27).

There was no significant interaction between Photo Age and Photo Gender for the expertise ratings, so no suggestion of a "double discrimination" against older women on expertise.

In terms of how the characteristics of the respondents affected ratings, there were no main effects for respondent age or gender. There were some significant interactions with other variables, but none of particular interest.

4 Discussion

This paper reported on an investigation into the attitudes of young and older Chinese people into whether they have ageist and sexist attitudes about older people as users of technology.

The most interesting finding is that the attitudes of both young and older Chinese people were very similar, in that there were no main effects for participant age or gender and no important interactions of these variables with other variables.

However, there is strong evidence of both ageism and sexism amongst both young and older Chinese people. There were significant and large effects for ageism in both the ratings of likelihood of use and expertise with all three devices. The effect of sexism was less clear, but still very important. There was only a marginal difference in ratings of likelihood of use of all devices, with a small effect size. However, there was a significant effect for expertise, with a large effect size. Thus women are seen as users of digital technologies, but not as expert in them as men. Interestingly, there was only very slight evidence of a "double discrimination" of older women. Older women were seen as less likely to use these digital technologies, but not be less expert in them.

These results show considerable similarities to those found by Petrie [5] with a British and only student sample which was strongly biased towards young men. She also found strong evidence for ageism, and some evidence of sexism, but not the "double discrimination" of older women.

Both studies used a quick and simple method for assessing ageism and sexism about technology use and expertise. Further work needs to validate this method against other ways of measuring these variables. Nonetheless, this can be an interesting exercise to conduct with students or work colleagues to initiate a discussion about the issues around ageism and sexism in perceptions of use and expertise with technologies and how to address these issues.

It is particularly important that young Chinese people involved in technology development do not have negative attitudes towards older people and women using technology products. Therefore, positive education is needed to address these issue in both Europe (building on Petrie's results) and China.

References

1. Ayalon, L.: Perceived age, gender, and racial/ethnic discrimination in Europe: results from the European social survey. Educ. Gerontol. **40**, 499–517 (2014)
2. Chen, K., Chan, A.H.: The ageing population of China and a review of gerontechnology. Gerontechnology **10**(2), 63–71 (2011)
3. Lin, X., Bryant, C., Boldero, J.: Measures for assessing student attitudes towards older people. Educ. Gerontol. **37**(1), 12–26 (2011)
4. National Bureau of Statistics (2020). Annual data 2020. https://data.stats.gov.cn/easyquery.htm?cn=C01&zb=A0301&sj=2020
5. Petrie, H.: Ageism and sexism amongst young computer scientists. In: Miesenberger, K., Kouroupetroglou, G. (eds.) ICCHP 2018. LNCS, vol. 10897, pp. 421–425. Springer, Cham (2018). https://doi.org/10.1007/978-3-319-94274-2_60
6. Reilly, E.D., Rackley, K.R., Awad, G.H.: Perceptions of male and female STEM aptitutde: the moderating effect of benevolent and hostile sexism. J. Career Dev. **44**(2), 159–173 (2017)
7. Sung, K.-T.: Elder respect: exploration of ideals and forms in East Asia. J. Aging Stud. **15**, 13–26 (2001)
8. Vauclair, C.-M., Hanke, K., Huang, L.-L., Abrams, D.: Are Asian cultures really less ageist than Western ones? It depends on the questions asked. Int. J. Psychol. **52**(2), 136–144 (2017)

Ageism in Design: Accessibility Without User Experience?

Jean D. Hallewell Haslwanter(✉) and Christiane Takacs

University of Applied Sciences Upper Austria, Wels, Austria
jean.hallewell@fh-ooe.at

Abstract. We investigated the perceptions of young computing science students about older people with regard to computer-based systems. Participants were shown a picture of either an old or young woman or man and asked to assess that persons computer literacy and suggest appropriate design aspects for them. The goal of this study was to see if the biases against older people and their perceived computer literacy extend to the design of systems for them.

The results draw on 216 questionnaires from students in the first year of their Information and Communications Technology (ICT) studies at an Austrian university of applied sciences. Mixed methods were used to explore the differences between the perceived design needs for older and younger people, and how those relate to the components of user experience and accessibility.

The results show that the design aspects mentioned for older people differ greatly from those mentioned for younger. Whereas for younger people many aspects that could be considered valuable and desirable are mentioned, for older people the focus is on accessibility and usability, almost to the exclusion of aspects that are valuable and desirable. Regarding accessibility, despite the perceived lack of expertise, the focus was on aspects like large fonts. This is concerning, as future systems will be designed by the students of today. These biases may influence whether future systems are acceptable to older people, and hence whether older people will benefit from them.

Keywords: Active Assisted Living (AAL) · Older people · User interface design · Ageism · Usability · User experience (UX) · Accessibility

1 Introduction

Ageism is still a problem today. Older people are often thought to have little expertise with computers [7]. This is compounded by the fact that many older people have some sort of limitations, which can include perceptual, physical and cognitive abilities [13]. However, with age there is increasing variability between people [3], so that some older people may have few or no limitations and considerable computer experience. It has been found that developers' hidden

K. Miesenberger et al. (Eds.): ICCHP-AAATE 2022, LNCS 13342, pp. 517–525, 2022.
https://doi.org/10.1007/978-3-031-08645-8_61

stereotypes about older people can lead to the priority being given to the needs of other groups, e.g. carers [4]. This may lead to older people not using systems, as with older users it is particularly important that systems be useful and not stigmatizing [11]. Of course, products must be physically accessible for the users. But focusing on all aspects of User Experience (UX) "increases the chances of a project's success when it finally comes to market" [9, p. 8].

This study was inspired the work of Petrie [7], which gathered impressions of young computer scientists about women and older people with regard to their computer literacy. Her study, which was presented at *ICCHP 2018*, found a bias against older people with regard to computer literacy. We repeated the study in Austria and extended the questionnaire to explore which design aspects would be considered suitable for each cohort. Here we look at the results for the additional questions regarding design aspects to see if there are differences here, i.e. if the bias towards older people extends to the design ideas suggested, and to analyze in which way the design aspects suggested for younger and older people differ.

The research questions (RQ) guiding this study are:

RQ1 Do the participants think an adaptation of the design is needed for older persons and is this greater than for young people?
RQ2 How does the number of participants mentioning design aspects compare for the cohorts? Which types design aspects are mentioned for each? Are these different? Is more weight put on basic aspects, e.g. those related to accessibility and usability, and less on those related to added value?
RQ3 Which factors of User Experience are mentioned for each cohort?
RQ4 Which factors of accessibility are mentioned for older people? Is more weight put on one of the main factors?

2 Methods

Each questionnaire depicted one person reading a book. There were eight different images: two of younger men, two of older men, two of younger women and two of older women (see Fig. 1). The older people were approximately in their seventies. Based on these images, participants were asked to first assess the computer literacy of the person depicted and then asked about appropriate design aspects for them. The questions were the same for all images. Thus, we could explore the preconceptions or stereotypes participants had about each group and what impact these may have on the design of systems. For this study, only the answers for the questions related to design aspects were used:

1. In your opinion, which design aspects would be particularly important for this person with regard to use? (open question with three boxes for answers)
2. In your opinion, should adapted technology be developed for this person? (yes/no/don't know)

The questionnaires were piloted and then distributed to 216 first year students of an Austrian university selected to be representative of computer science

Fig. 1. Some of the images used (taken from [7]), pictured from left to right: an older man, an older woman, a younger man, a younger woman

students in Austria. 16 were incomplete or invalid. Thus, there were 200 in the final sample, of which 100 depicted younger people and 100 depicted older people. A mixed method approach with both qualitative and quantitative methods was used to improve the validity of the findings [8].

The analyses regarding **UX** were based on Morvilles's Honeycomb, which describes the factors *useful, usable, desirable, valuable, findable, credible* and *accessible* [9]. Based on this, we see that UX goes beyond usability, which is defined by effectiveness, efficiency and user satisfaction [5], e.g. by also looking at how desirable the system is.

The analyses regarding **accessibility** were based on information about how the Web Content Accessibility Guidelines (WCAG) apply for older people [10]. This splits it into factors *perceivable, operable, understandable* and *robust*, the same as in the current WCAG 2.1 version. A number of sub-points are included for each. This is an appropriate complement to the guidelines for UX, as both come from website design. Note that these aspects have some overlap with the UX factors usable, findable and accessible.

For RQ1, a quantitative analysis was done. Pearson's chi-squared test was used to determine if there was a significant difference concerning the perceived need for adaptation of the design needed between questionnaires with younger and older people depicted.

For RQ2, a mixed analysis was done. First, a quantitative analysis was done to analyze if design aspects were mentioned more often for the older cohort. The answers were then categorized to analyze how many people mentioned basic attributes, value added attributes, both or none, to see whether this differed significantly between cohorts. Basic aspects were those related to whether a system *could* be used, e.g. findable; value-added aspects included aspects that were not absolutely necessary, e.g. useful features. To reduce potential bias, the categorization was done by mixing the questionnaires and hiding the information about what cohort the answers were for.

For the final analysis for RQ2, the answers were *coded* to unify the terminology used, much like is done in thematic analysis [2]. Since the answers were short, the analysis was done inductively, i.e. the codes were taken from the data, and at the semantic level, i.e. we did interpret beyond what was written [2]. As an example, answers such as "usable", "usability" and "user-friendly" were all coded as *usability*, a separate code was used for *ease of use*. The most commonly mentioned unified terms were then identified, i.e. those mentioned by at least 5% of the participants answering for that cohort, i.e. those with the greatest extensiveness [6, p. 147]. Since fewer participants included design aspects for the younger cohort, those that were mentioned by at least 5% of those with answers for the cohort were also considered in an extended analysis.

RQ3 followed up on RQ2 with a more detailed qualitative analysis of the seven factors of UX. The original answers from each questionnaire were examined to see if they related to the categories, akin to a theoretical coding of thematic analysis [2]. This was repeated for each cohort.

RQ4 repeated the analysis for RQ3 for the factors of accessibility. For each of the four factors, the sub-points were considered, which includes between 1 and 7 for each [10]. In addition, it was considered if the responses related to the factor, even if they didn't specifically mention one of the recommendations. The analysis was repeated for each factor. Afterwards we analyzed the differences between the four factors. Since the sub-points are specifically aimed at older people, an analysis for younger people does not make sense here.

3 Results

The unified terms mentioned in one of the three blanks for design aspects on questionnaires are shown in Fig. 2.

Fig. 2. Weighted design aspects for the younger (left) and older (right) cohorts

3.1 Adaptation Needed?

The perceived need for adaptation was found to be dependent on the age of the cohort, i.e. older are thought to need adaptation by more participants (see Table 1 left, p–value 1.4×10^{-17} from a chi-squared test).

Table 1. In numbers: perceived need for adaptation and categories for design aspects

Need for adapt	Yes	No	Don't know	Σ
Older	59	16	25	100
Younger	4	64	32	100
Σ	63	80	57	200

Design aspects	Basic	Value	Both	Σ
Older	81	1	8	90
Younger	20	31	17	68
Σ	101	32	25	158

3.2 Design Aspects

The first analysis looks at whether design aspects were significantly more likely to be mentioned for the older cohort. This was the case, with 90 participants mentioning when older people were depicted and 68 when younger were (p−value 1.3×10^{-4} from a chi-squared test).

A further analysis categorized the original answers to see whether the aspects mentioned by a participant were basic, value added or included both. Pearson's chi-squared test shows significant differences based on the cohort (p−value 3.8×10^{-15}). For the older cohort *basic* aspects were mentioned most often, and *valued added* aspects were mentioned most for the younger cohort (see Table 1 right).

For each cohort, over 90 unique unified terms were identified. The terms mentioned by at least 5% for each cohort helps to illustrate these differences. The most extensive terms in decreasing order (with results from the extended analysis based on percentage of those with answers in parentheses):

- For younger: *aesthetic design, simple, easy to use, modern, small size, sleek design, colors, efficient to use (usability, intuitive design, easy to transport, easy to get an overview).*
- For older: *large fonts, simple, easy to use, large buttons, large symbols, easy to read, easy to get an overview, reduce functions, easy to understand, usability.*

Although *usability* and *easy to get an overview* are mentioned for both, for the younger cohort desirable things, such as *aesthetic design* are included, where for the older many are related to accessibility, e.g. being perceivable and operable.

3.3 User Experience - Young vs. Old

Since the previous analysis does not rule out that there is a larger number of different terms that relate to one of the factors, here the original answers from each participant were categorized for the UX factors. The factors mentioned most differs greatly between the cohorts, as is shown in Fig. 3. The order shows some differences to the analysis of only the most common terms. For the younger cohort aspects related *usable* were mentioned by most participants most followed by *desirable* and *valuable*; for the older, *accessible* was most extensive, closely followed by *usable.*

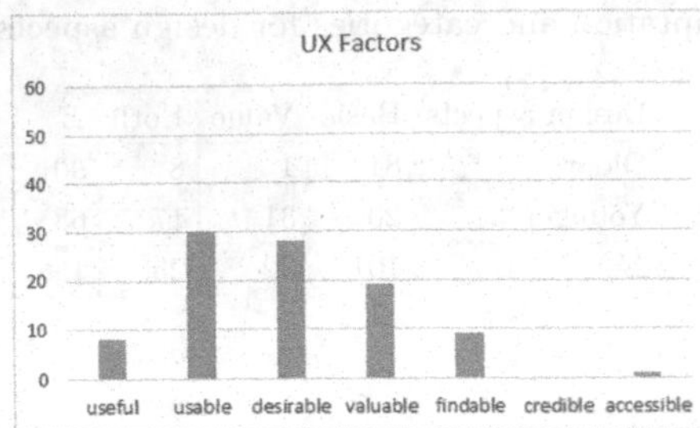

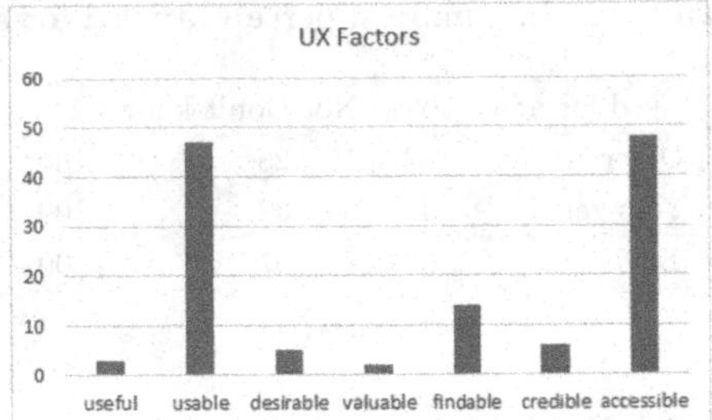

Fig. 3. UX factors identified for younger (left) and older (right) cohorts

3.4 Factors of Accessibility

Answers on 87 questionnaires with older people depicted could be linked to some aspect of accessibility. The design aspects mentioned relate primarily to being *perceivable*, followed by *understandable* and *operable* (see Fig. 4). *Robustness* is mentioned by only 4 participants, but also has fewer sub-points. There is relatively little diversity among the specific aspects mentioned: 89% of *perceivable* specifically mention large font, 38% of *understandable* relate to being clearly structured and 35% of *operable* specifically mention large buttons. With both *understandable* and *operable* some sub-points are not mentioned by any participants, including the recommendations for mouse use, distraction, sufficient time and pop-up windows.

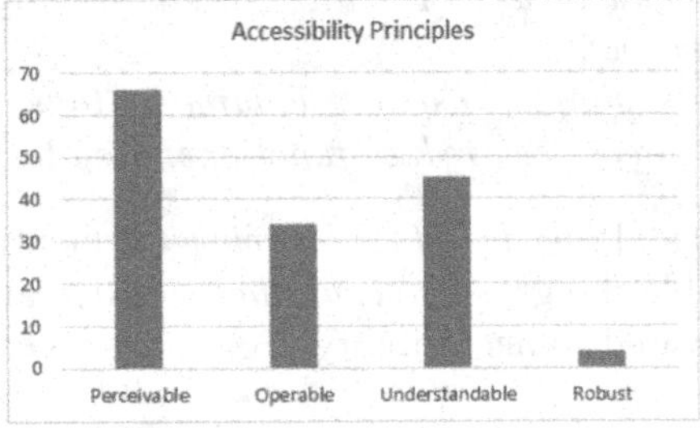

Fig. 4. Accessibility factors identified for older cohort

4 Discussion

The results show that not only do young computer scientists have preconceptions about the likelihood that older people to use computer systems and their expertise with these, but that in consequence they also suggest different aspects when considering designs for them.

The design of the study whereby we first ask about perceived computer literacy and then design aspects was designed to ensure this was considered for the design aspects. This seems to have succeeded. The results show how the preconceptions about older people bias design ideas for them, i.e. specifically what they suggest. That all images included a book may, however, have increased the focus on the large font.

It is encouraging that being simple and easy to use was considered important for all age groups. Although all main factors of accessibility are mentioned, most suggestions relate to a few aspects and some important points are neglected.

As described in the introduction, usefulness, something that was included also with *valuable*, is important to older people [11]. With respect to *desirable*, it is uncertain whether the aspects thought to be desirable to young people, such as a sleek design, are also desirable to older people. This highlights the importance of including older users early in projects, to help to build empathy and help understand their true needs and preferences. It also shows the tension between universal design, i.e. one design for all, and special designs to fit the needs of certain groups. Certainly universal design can reduce the bias and stigmatization.

Of course, the participants are students. Thus, it shows natural biases and so topics computer science educators need to address. As further study, it would also be interesting to evaluate how these views change, i.e. to repeat the study with students just before they graduate and start to develop systems.

5 Conclusion

We investigated the preconceptions of young computer scientists with regard to the design needs of older people. The young computer scientists of today will be the designers of future products. Depending on whether an older or younger person was depicted, there were very significant differences both in the perceived need to adapt a system and number that mentioned specific design aspects. This indicates that systems are generally thought to be designed for younger people. So even if systems are designed to be aesthetically pleasing, the aspects chosen may be stilted to younger tastes.

Detailed analysis showed whereas for older people the focus was on basic attributes, for younger it was on on value-added attributes. While for both cohorts *usable* was mentioned often, for younger *desirable* and *valuable* aspects were mentioned often and for older *accessible* ones were most extensive. Although it is not new that people often put focus on the limitations of older people [1], this analysis allows us to see which aspects are thought to be important. With regard to accessibility, for older people, despite the perceived lack of expertise with computers [7], the focus was on being perceivable (specifically *large fonts*).

While it is encouraging that these young developers are aware, since many older people do have limitations. But as described in marketing models such as Kano [12], customer satisfaction is low if only basic needs are fulfilled, such as accessibility for older people, and features that contribute to the performance of the system or excitement, represented here by usefulness and aesthetic design, are not given enough weight. This supports the importance of involving end users at eye level in the design of systems, as with older people, a lack of usefulness may even prevent the adoption of systems that provide benefits [11].

The results show the importance of teaching students about getting to know the users and their true needs and wishes, particularly when designing for older people and those with disabilities. Furthermore, it may be beneficial for educators to broach the biases against these groups to increase awareness.

Acknowledgements. We thank Martina Gaisch who distributed the questionnaire, Helen Petrie for sharing the questionnaire and images, Jana Zaladova for the data entry, the reviewers for their suggestions, and all those who participated in the pilot and final study.

References

1. Blythe, M.A., Monk, A.F., Doughty, K.: Socially dependable design: the challenge of ageing populations for HCI. Interact. Comput. **17**(6), 672–689 (2005). https://doi.org/10.1016/j.intcom.2005.09.005
2. Braun, V., Clarke, V.: Successful Qualitative Research. Sage, London (2013)
3. Gregor, P., Newell, A.F., Zajicek, M.: Designing for dynamic diversity: interfaces for older people. In: Proceedings of the Fifth International ACM Conference on Assistive Technologies, ASSETS 2002, pp. 151–156. ACM (2002). https://doi.org/10.1145/638249.638277
4. Hallewell Haslwanter, J.D., Fitzpatrick, G.: The development of a sensor-based system for older people: a case study. In: Proceedings of the 27th Intl BCS Human Computer Interaction Conference, pp. 11:1–11:10. British Computer Society (2013). https://doi.org/10.14236/ewic/HCI2013.10
5. ISO: 9241: Ergonomics of human-system interaction: Part 210 Human-centred design for interactive systems (2019)
6. Krueger, R.A., Casey, M.A.: Focus Groups: A Practical Guide for Applied Research. Sage Publications, Inc., Thousand Oaks (2014)
7. Petrie, H.: Ageism and sexism amongst young computer scientists. In: Miesenberger, K., Kouroupetroglou, G. (eds.) ICCHP 2018. LNCS, vol. 10897, pp. 421–425. Springer, Cham (2018). https://doi.org/10.1007/978-3-319-94274-2_60
8. Plano Clark, V.L., Creswell, J.W.: The Mixed Methods Reader. Sage, Thousand Oaks (2008)
9. Soergaard, M. (ed.): The Basics of User Interaction Design. Interaction Design Foundation (2018)
10. W3C: Developing websites for older people: how web content accessibility guidelines (WCAG) 2.0 applies (2010). https://www.w3.org/WAI/older-users/developing.html. Accessed 11 2021
11. Wandke, H., Sengpiel, M., Sönksen, M.: Myths about older people's use of information and communication technology. Gerontology **58**, 564–570 (2012). https://doi.org/10.1159/000339104
12. Wikipedia: Kano model (2021). https://en.wikipedia.org/wiki/Kano_model. Accessed 1 2022
13. Wildenbos, G., Peute, L., Jaspers, M.: Aging barriers influencing mobile health usability for older adults: a literature based framework (MOLD-US). Int. J. Med. Inform. **114**, 66–75 (2018). https://doi.org/10.1016/j.ijmedinf.2018.03.012

Addressing Privacy Concerns in Depth Sensors

Wiktor Mucha(✉) and Martin Kampel

Computer Vision Lab, TU Wien, Vienna, Austria
{wiktor.mucha,martin.kampel}@tuwien.ac.at

Abstract. Image-based assistive solutions raise concerns about the privacy of the individuals being monitored. The issue involves the situation when such technology is used in medical institutions to protect patients' health and support the personnel. These devices are installed in facilities and process images that include personal and behavioral data during the day. Other types of images than RGB are used to maintain privacy in this type of application, like depth images. Usage of depth cameras in the majority of publications is considered private protective. This paper discusses the issue of privacy in vision-based applications using depth modality. The factors affecting privacy in depth images are presented. The main problem that makes an image non-private is that the subjects' faces allow identification. This paper compares the Face Recognition (FR) technique between RGB and depth images. In the experimental part, a state-of-the-art model for FR in depth images is developed, which is used to establish boundary conditions when a person is recognized. The performance of FR between these two modalities is compared on two existing datasets containing images in both versions, including the training process. The study aims to determine under which conditions depth cameras preserve privacy and how much privacy they reveal.

Keywords: Privacy · Depth sensors · Multimodal vision · Face recognition · AAL

1 Introduction

Camera-based systems are used in assistive devices such as Active Assisted Living (AAL) solutions. They are installed in all kinds of medical facilities and by observing patients, reveal their private data which is questionable and may be unacceptable. It creates a demand for privacy-preserving solutions. A recurring method to face this is to replace the RGB camera with a depth sensor. This work is motivated by conflicting assumptions about privacy in depth-based applications. Some papers consider depth imaging to be privacy-preserving [2], and some do not [7]. Biometric features available in depth image are studied to determine how private it is. Various situations of revealing privacy are discussed. The main focus is put on Face Recognition (FR) from depth data which allows automatic recognition of subjects. In related work, the FR task is dominated by Deep

K. Miesenberger et al. (Eds.): ICCHP-AAATE 2022, LNCS 13342, pp. 526–533, 2022.
https://doi.org/10.1007/978-3-031-08645-8_62

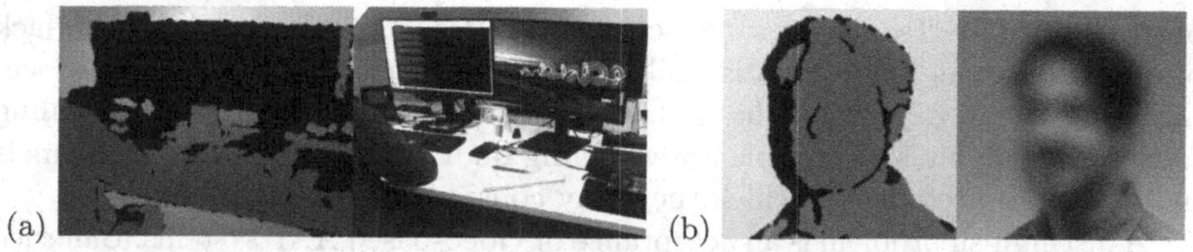

Fig. 1. Example of same scenes visible in RGB and depth modality.

Learning (DL) algorithms that replace traditional feature extraction methods. Their accuracy reaches almost 100% and depends on the image resolution. This study answers whether depth camera-based systems preserve subjects' privacy, under what circumstances, and what are the performance differences between RGB and depth FR. The experimental part aims to find the border conditions of correct identification by seeking minimal face resolution that allows this process. Further, it compares FR performance between these two modalities. The depth FR is less robust than RGB, and the learning process is slower. However, identification from depth data is correct under specific factors, showing that this modality does not fully preserve a person's identity. FR is correct even when faces are downsized to 40% of the original dimensions.

This paper is organized as follows. Section 2 describes privacy concerns in depth images, conditions for subjects recognition, facial features which permit FR in depth images, legal aspects of FR and personal privacy, and related work in FR from depth data. Section 3 introduces our experiment with results. Section 4 highlights key parts of this paper and its message.

2 Privacy in Depth Images

There is no single definition of privacy existing. This work takes deeper dive into this topic from a legal aspect. We consider data private when it does not reveal a person's identity or sensitive information. This statement is expanded more in Sect. 2.3. In contrast to RGB-based techniques in which subjects are monitored, depth sensors have an opinion of being privacy-protecting devices [2]. In this publication, the authors choose depth images to create a privacy-preserving fall detection system, and the sensor's privacy is taken for granted. Fall detection system [22] considers depth data as private but to additionally ensure, the system does not store any depth data during monitoring. On the contrary, Chou et al. [7] who design an Activity Recognition (AR) system for healthcare usage, address depth sensors as not privacy-preserving due to existing works performing FR form depth images. They employ their system for hand hygiene analysis where sensor captures faces. The image resolution is downsized to remove privacy-relevant information, and the activity recognition utility is retained. There are more such contradictory examples of publications.

Depth sensors do not preserve texture information, which protects against disclosing information related to colors. Only shapes are preserved in this type of image. Figure 1(a) depict same scene in RGB and depth modality. The lack of available colors hides what is visible on a computer screen. In a real-life scenario, depth image protects the AAL device users' privacy, e.g., by not revealing information about what people are watching on TV. Certain shows or channels indicate their preferences, which they may consider private.

A distinguish problem is an acceptance of video-based AAL systems. Banerjee et al. [4] acknowledge this problem and present depth imaging technologies to their patients with an explanation. During the test of fall detection application in a hospital environment, depth data is presented to hospital staff and patients who consider it more private and acceptable than RGB. Ballester et al. [3] introduce a toileting assistance system for people with dementia. The concept is discussed with healthcare professionals from a facility for dementia patients. The outcome shows acceptance and trust for privacy in depth sensors, even in such an intimate environment as a toilet. The monitoring with depth image is fully accepted by 8 out of 13 people, where all participants reject RGB based system.

2.1 Recognition Scenarios in Depth Images

Privacy of depth data differs between circumstances, and each application should be judged differently based on the environment. In health facilities, the personal identity is revealed from a human perspective when people vary in geometry. In the case of a group of 30 people, one of them is recognizable when it is a disabled person in a wheelchair, is taller or shorter than the others, or is using a walking support device like a walking frame. Viewing a situation when there are only images or videos available without any additional data, what allows automatically recognize people are biometric features, e.g., face, height, gait, skin color, tattoos, and scars [19]. Depth images do not contain the last three of them, enhancing privacy by reducing the number of information allowing identification. In the literature, there are publications presenting gait recognition. Dubois et al. [10] use depth images to extract gait pattern using Hidden Markov Model (HMM) to recognize people inside the house. In their experiment, they detect correctly 17 individuals out of 20. However, such tests are too narrow to compare with real-world conditions. Publications referenced in Sect. 2.4 show FR allows correct identification in available depth datasets. However, most test data has a low number of subjects (around 20). Complete FR pipeline for identification from a depth camera includes face detection at an early stage. These detectors tend to perform with lower accuracy than RGB, directly impacting FR systems' performance which favors RGB-based models at the very first step [18].

2.2 Face Features for Depth FR

FR is based on facial features which DL models extract. Abudarham et al. [1] shows that the most impactful features for FR are landmarks, e.g., eye shape, eyebrows, and lips. They hypothesize that Convolutional Neural Networks (CNN) employ similar features for FR as human beings. Looking at the depth image, there are fewer features visible from a human perspective than in the RGB modality. However, their visibility is linked with the resolution of the sensor. What can be seen by humans are basic shapes of hair, nose, lips, or eyes, but it lacks texture information (Fig. 1(b)). In studies of Kendrick et al. [15] authors detect shapes of mouth, nose tip, nostrils, eyes, and forehead using DL networks in depth images. Nevertheless, depth modality performs worse than RGB by achieving the largest error in their position estimation, and models are tested in laboratory conditions, which does not answer how accurate it works in the wild.

2.3 Legal Aspects of Privacy and FR

The concept of privacy is not explicitly normalized. The right to it is centrally standardized in Art. 8 (1) European Convention on Human Rights (ECHR), according to which everyone has the right to respect for his private and family life, his home, and his correspondence. Further standards are in Art. 7 of the Charter of Fundamental Rights of the European Union (CFR), which regulates violations of privacy and certain professional secrets. The right to data protection is also understood as a facet of privacy. Art. 8 of the CFR standardizes the right to the protection of personal data for every person. Art. 1 of the General Data Protection Regulation (GDPR) specifies the protection when personal data is processed. The GDPR can be understood as a substantive concretization of Art. 8 of the CFR and as a formulation of it in Union law.

Except reviling personal information, identity identification invades privacy. Regarding the study [14], forensic FR becomes a ubiquitous tool to guide court investigations. Automatic FR systems lack methodological standardization and empirical validation, placing FR below fingerprints or DNA in terms of trust. In continental Europe, there is no legal limit on the admissibility of scientific evidence. Judges evaluate the relevance of the evidence on their own according to the state of available scientific knowledge. In the USA, according to the Federal Rule of Evidence 702, the evidence has to be accepted by the scientific community, and the employed method has to have known error rates and be available for peer review and publication.

2.4 Face Recognition in Depth Images

Face recognition is the task of identifying people by their faces. First, the face has to be detected and cropped. Further image is processed to extract features describing the face. RGB is not employed in depth recognition, and features are extracted from 3d data. In the literature, there are works performing FR from depth data using feature extractors like Soon-kak Kwon [16] who starts the framework with a face detector based on depth data only. Further, features are extracted by applying the 3D-LBP descriptor. DL models overtake traditional descriptors. Feng et al. [12] presents a system with an additional DL network for normalizing facial images into the frontal pose and neutral expression, reducing noise and reconstructing missing regions. A second CNN performs feature extraction and recognition task. Another DL approach is presented by Hu et al. [13] who boost recognition from low-quality data employing high-quality samples. This method is restricted by the low availability of datasets, including

Table 1. Comparison of FR top results on depth datasets, which differ in image quality and a number of subjects.

Databases	No. of subjects	Sensor	Resolution	Sensor precision [mm]	Accuracy [%]
BU-3DFE	100	3dMD	8K	0.2	99.3 [20]
Lock3DFace	509	Kinect II	20K	≥2	86 [12]
IIIT-D	106	Kinect I	13K	2–4	26.8 [8]
CurtinFaces	52	Kinect I	13K	2–4	89.9 [5]

low and high-resolution images. In [21] normalization impact is studied for FR task. Models are validated with different variants of pre-processing. According to this study, these techniques combined with CNN decrease recognition accuracy because applying them reduces the 3D content available for the model.

Table 1 lists examples of datasets with a different number of subjects, captured with various sensors distinct in resolution and precision. Higher accuracy is achieved in works using higher precision sensors and datasets with fewer subjects, which does not answer how accurate FR is in the wild.

3 The Experiment

In this study, the DL model [23] is implemented and trained for depth FR to achieve state-of-the-art performance. Such architectures are proved by literature in Sect. 2.4 to perform robustly on depth images for FR. The learning process is performed on combined *BIWI* [11], *Pandora* [6], and *UMBDB* [9] datasets. They all include depth images of people's faces taken in laboratory conditions. The resulting model of our process is compared with existing works by tests on a separate set of data. The test subset of *HRRFaceD Database* [17] is taken to perform cross-dataset validation. Every image in test data has a predicted vector of embeddings. From predictions, image pairs are composed, and the distance is calculated between their vectors. The predicted label of input images is the class of the image with which the minimum pair is obtained. Our model is placing second in accuracy with 97.95% after Borghi et al. [5] who achieve 98.90%.

In real-world conditions, the correctness of FR depends on the distance between the subject and the sensor, which comes down to the face size in pixels. When the subject's face is near, its size is close to sensor maximum resolution. With the distance increasing, the face dimension reduces. A larger resolution of the face provides higher quality descriptions of facial landmarks, which results in better performance. Analysis of Table 1 confirms this thesis. To find the border conditions of correct identification, minimal resolution of the face allowing this process is searched. Faces from *HRRFaceD* are scaled-down, and the FR accuracy is calculated for each subset created.

A decrease occurs when the face is smaller than 40% of the original size (Fig. 2(a)). Since the test faces vary in dimensions, their average values are computed. The original size is 118×153 pixels, and for 40% it is 47×61 pixels. The worst FR results are seen below 10% (11×14 pixels).

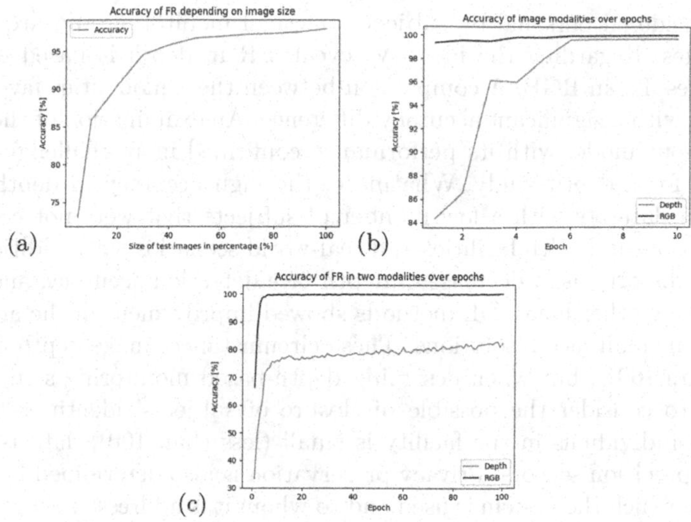

Fig. 2. Accuracy of depth FR depending on image size (a) and on epochs with RGB and depth FR trained form scratch on *Pandora*(b) and *BIWI*(c).

The second part of our experiment compares RGB and depth modalities. Firstly, the best possible models are viewed. The training is performed on *Pandora*, *UMBDB* and *HRRFaceD* and test data is randomly chosen 2000 images from *BIWI* where every depth image has a corresponding RGB frame. For RGB modality *vggface2* model is fine-tuned on *Pandora*. The accuracy is calculated five times, every iteration on a different subset, and the average value is given to reduce a random factor. The result is 98.79% accuracy for RGB and 80.50% for depth modality. A similar process is performed with tests on *Pandora*. This scenario gives a better overview of potential FR accuracy in real-world conditions due to the various occlusions in images, where previously tested *BIWI* does not include any. Learning is done on *UMBDB*, *HRRFaceD* and *BIWI*. RGB performs with 85.15% accuracy and depth scores 53.23%. Secondly, both models are trained from scratch on the same data with similar parameters. The experiment is carried out twice. *Pandora* used for training and *BIWI* as a test results in 98.39% (RGB) and 79.38% (depth). Replacement of subsets with tests on *Pandora* gives 84.60% (RGB) and 48.74% (depth) accuracy. For depth images, the learning process is observed to be longer (Fig. 2(b)). When trained on *BIWI*, the validation of RGB reaches ≈100% before the 10th epoch. In depth modality, 100 epochs are not enough to get close to RGB performance (Fig. 2(c)).

4 Conclusion

Under the law, everyone has a right to privacy. The available publications are not consistent with the privacy of depth images which is problematic with respect to legal regulations. The main advantage of them is the protection of data that can be considered personal by subjects of visual monitoring and are visible in RGB images. Regarding the identity reveal, FR in depth is based on similar face features like in RGB. A comparison between these modalities favored RGB over depth with a significant accuracy difference. An examination of the learning process of our model with its performance confirmed more challenging feature extraction for a depth study. Whatmore, the high accuracy in depth FR was achieved in datasets with a low number of subjects that were not comparable with conditions in health facilities and real-world scenarios with additional environmental distortions, a decrease of depth face detection accuracy, and sensor's range. On the other hand, DL methods showed improvement in the accuracy of FR, even on small face resolutions. These circumstances make depth data more private than RGB, but when designing depth-based monitoring solutions, it is necessary to consider the possible disclosure of subjects' identities, when the number of individuals in the facility is small (less than 100), data is gathered with high precision sensors. Privacy preservation is also determined by the environment in which the system is used and to whom it is addressed, what activities are monitored, and what data can be recognized.

Acknowledgements. This work was partly supported by VisuAAL ITN H2020 (grant agreement No. 861091) and the Austrian Research Promotion Agency (FFG) under the Grant Agreement No. 879744.

References

1. Abudarham, N., Shkiller, L., Yovel, G.: Critical features for face recognition. Cognition **182**, 73–83 (2019). https://doi.org/10.1016/j.cognition.2018.09.002
2. Arulselvi, G., Poornima, D., Anand, S.J.: Privacy preserving elderly fall detection using Kinect depth images based on deep convolutional neural networks. Eur. J. Mol. Clin. Med. **7**(3), 5492–5510 (2020)
3. Ballester, I., Mujirishvili, T., Kampel, M.: RITA: a privacy-aware toileting assistance designed for people with dementia. In: Pervasive Computing Technologies for Healthcare, pp. 318–330. Springer, Cham (2022). https://doi.org/10.1007/978-3-030-99194-4_20
4. Banerjee, T., et al.: Monitoring Hospital Rooms for Safety Using Depth Images. AI for Gerontechnology, Arlington (2012)
5. Borghi, G., Pini, S., Vezzani, R., Cucchiara, R.: Driver face verification with depth maps. Sensors **19**(15), 3361 (2019). https://doi.org/10.3390/s19153361
6. Borghi, G., Venturelli, M., Vezzani, R., Cucchiara, R.: POSEidon: face-from-depth for driver pose estimation. In: 2017 IEEE Conference on Computer Vision and Pattern Recognition (CVPR), pp. 5494–5503. IEEE (2017). https://doi.org/10.1109/CVPR.2017.583
7. Chou, E., et al.: Privacy-preserving action recognition for smart hospitals using low-resolution depth images. arXiv preprint arXiv:1811.09950 (2018)
8. Chowdhury, A., Ghosh, S., Singh, R., Vatsa, M.: RGB-D face recognition via learning-based reconstruction. In: 2016 IEEE 8th International Conference on Biometrics Theory, Applications and Systems (BTAS), pp. 1–7. IEEE (2016). https://doi.org/10.1109/BTAS.2016.7791199

9. Colombo, A., Cusano, C., Schettini, R.: UMB-DB: a database of partially occluded 3D faces. In: 2011 IEEE International Conference on Computer Vision Workshops (ICCV Workshops), pp. 2113–2119. IEEE (2011). https://doi.org/10.1109/ICCVW.2011.6130509
10. Dubois, A., Bresciani, J.P.: Person identification from gait analysis with a depth camera at home. In: 2015 37th Annual International Conference of the IEEE Engineering in Medicine and Biology Society (EMBC), pp. 4999–5002. IEEE (2015). https://doi.org/10.1109/EMBC.2015.7319514
11. Fanelli, G., Dantone, M., Gall, J., Fossati, A., Van Gool, L.: Random forests for real time 3D face analysis. Int. J. Comput. Vision **101**(3), 437–458 (2013). https://doi.org/10.1007/s11263-012-0549-0
12. Feng, Z., Zhao, Q.: Robust face recognition with deeply normalized depth images. In: Zhou, J., et al. (eds.) CCBR 2018. LNCS, vol. 10996, pp. 418–427. Springer, Cham (2018). https://doi.org/10.1007/978-3-319-97909-0_45
13. Hu, Z., et al.: Boosting depth-based face recognition from a quality perspective. Sensors **19**(19), 4124 (2019). https://doi.org/10.3390/s19194124
14. Jacquet, M., Champod, C.: Automated face recognition in forensic science: review and perspectives. Forensic Sci. Int. **307**, 110124 (2020). https://doi.org/10.1016/j.forsciint.2019.110124
15. Kendrick, C., Tan, K., Walker, K., Yap, M.H.: Towards real-time facial landmark detection in depth data using auxiliary information. Symmetry **10**(6), 230 (2018). https://doi.org/10.3390/sym10060230
16. Kwon, S.K.: Face recognition using depth and infrared pictures. Nonlinear Theory Appl. IEICE **10**, 2–15 (2019). https://doi.org/10.1587/nolta.10.2
17. Mantecón, T., del Blanco, C.R., Jaureguizar, F., García, N.: Visual face recognition using bag of dense derivative depth patterns. IEEE Signal Process. Lett. **23**(6), 771–775 (2016). https://doi.org/10.1109/LSP.2016.2553784
18. Mucha, W., Kampel, M.: Depth and thermal images in face detection - a detailed comparison between image modalities. In: 2022 the 5th International Conference on Machine Vision and Applications (ICMVA) (ICMVA 2022). ACM (2022). https://doi.org/10.1145/3523111.3523114
19. North-Samardzic, A.: Biometric technology and ethics: beyond security applications. J. Bus. Ethics **167**(3), 433–450 (2020)
20. Ocegueda, O., Passalis, G., Theoharis, T., Shah, S.K., Kakadiaris, I.A.: UR3D-C: linear dimensionality reduction for efficient 3D face recognition. In: 2011 International Joint Conference on Biometrics (IJCB), pp. 1–6. IEEE (2011). https://doi.org/10.1109/IJCB.2011.6117521
21. Pini, S., Borghi, G., Vezzani, R., Maltoni, D., Cucchiara, R.: A systematic comparison of depth map representations for face recognition. Sensors **21**(3), 944 (2021). https://doi.org/10.3390/s21030944
22. Planinc, R., Kampel, M.: Introducing the use of depth data for fall detection. Pers. Ubiquitous Comput. **17**(6), 1063–1072 (2013). https://doi.org/10.1007/s00779-012-0552-z
23. Schroff, F., Kalenichenko, D., Philbin, J.: FaceNet: a unified embedding for face recognition and clustering. In: Proceedings of the IEEE Conference on Computer Vision and Pattern Recognition, pp. 815–823 (2015)

Assessing the Outcome of Mobility Assistive Technology (OMAT) in Daily Living: Preliminary Results in an Italian Sample

Francesca Borgnis, Lucia Pigini(✉), Marina Ramella, Claudia Salatino, Maurizio Saruggia, Chiara Folini, and Rosa Maria Converti

IRCCS Fondazione Don Carlo Gnocchi ONLUS, Milano, Italy
{lpigini,mramella}@dongnocchi.it

Abstract. The World Health Organization has defined assistive technologies (AT) as the fourth pillar of global health and supported identifying AT outcomes among the five top priorities in AT research. In this framework, the research study OMAT (Outcomes of Mobility Assistive Technology in rehabilitation pathways) was developed by Fondazione Don Carlo Gnocchi. The OMAT study aims to develop and test the applicability of a model of rehabilitation pathway related to prosthetic interventions in the field of mobility: a multidisciplinary assessment of patients' needs and expectations was made at baseline and after an adequate period of use of the prescribed assistive devices in everyday settings. To date, the study is ongoing. The present work aims to show the preliminary results of the OMAT research study, in particular its primary outcomes. Specifically, OMAT AT outcome assessment consists of 1) perceived effectiveness of assistive mobility products, 2) satisfaction of the intervention and 3) possible changes in quality of life. Among the recruited subjects (N = 32), most patients (87.5%) received only one mobility assistive product, especially bimanual self-propelled wheelchairs. Patients used the received mobility assistive products for 3–6 months, with a good frequency (few-days/ week) and moderate support. Preliminary results showed a positive impact of assistive mobility products in terms of perceived effectiveness, intervention satisfaction, and quality of life. Interestingly, patients showed improved quality of life, showing a significant decrease of the severity degree in problems identified at baseline evaluation. Further studies will be conducted to replicate these promising results in a larger sample.

Keywords: Mobility assistive technologies · AT assessment · AT service delivery · AT outcome measurement · Rehabilitation pathways

1 Introduction

The World Health Organization (WHO) has defined assistive technologies (AT) as the fourth pillar of global health (launch of the GATE initiative "Global Cooperation on Assistive Health Technology", "Priority Assistive Products list", 2016), along with drugs, vaccines, and medical devices. Specifically, the assistive products must be considered a

The original version of this chapter was revised: Acknowledgment section with funding was added. The correction to this chapter is available at https://doi.org/10.1007/978-3-031-08645-8_64

K. Miesenberger et al. (Eds.): ICCHP-AAATE 2022, LNCS 13342, pp. 534–541, 2022.
https://doi.org/10.1007/978-3-031-08645-8_63

necessary component to maintain or improve the person's functioning. However, only a minority of countries in the WHO European Region have comprehensive monitoring mechanisms for assistive technology in terms of evaluating needs for assistive technology and assessing the impact on disease in the patient's life (World Health Organization 2021). For this reason, AT outcome evaluation has been indicated by the World Health Organization as among the five top priorities in AT research (Gutenbrunner et al. 2015).

Within the Italian National Health Service, the AT service delivery process is already structured in steps: assessment, prescription, authorisation, delivery, while inspection and follow-up are still not regulated and left to the initiative of service providers.

Over the years, several works have focused on the high rate of abandonment of received AT due to changes in health conditions (Lenker and Paquet 2004) or failure of AT to meet patients' needs and expectations (Federici et al. 2016). These observations led to think that the assessment of the prosthetic intervention's effects must be carried out "on the field" after a reasonable time of use of the assistive products (APs) by the users in their real living environment (Salatino et al. 2016).

In this framework, the research study OMAT (Outcomes of Mobility Assistive Technology in rehabilitation pathways) was developed by the Italian research rehabilitation institute "Fondazione Don Carlo Gnocchi" (FDG), funded by the Ministry of Health (2020–2022). The OMAT project aims to develop and test the applicability of a new model of rehabilitation path related to assistive technology interventions in the field of mobility that, after an initial multidisciplinary evaluation of patients' needs and expectations, also includes inspection and follow up phases with outcome assessment after an adequate period of use of the prescribed AP in everyday settings. This research study is ongoing; the present work aims to show its preliminary results.

2 Methods

To date, seventy-five patients that needed mobility assistive devices were recruited at two centres of Fondazione Don Carlo Gnocchi ONLUS: "IRCCS Santa Maria Nascente" in Milan and "Spalenza" in Rovato (Brescia). The recruited patients were classified by the International Classification of Disease (ICD-9).

The research protocol includes two sessions at a distance of 3/6 months:

1) baseline standard clinical evaluation and prescription of the mobility APs (T1)
2) experimental follow-up session in which patients are re-contacted after 3–6 months of use of received AT in the real living environment (T2).

Overall, the research protocol involved a standard clinical evaluation with the addiction of validated AT outcome assessments instruments selected on the basis of a previous literature review (Salatino et al. 2018).

In detail, all participants underwent a baseline evaluation (T1) of the state of health/disability, made by a clinician, consisting of Barthel index 20, to evaluate autonomy degree in daily life activities (Mahoney 1965), Mini-Mental State Examination (MMSE) (Folstein et al. 1975; Measso et al. 1993), to assess the global cognitive functioning and Modified Cumulative Illness Rating Scale, to measure any comorbidities

(CIRS) (Linn et al. 1968). According to the clinical interview and cognitive screening, the health practitioner decided whether the patient would be able to provide responsive answers to the self-reported questionnaires; on the contrary, the caregiver was involved. Therefore, the questionnaires "36-item Short Form Health Survey" (SF-36) (Ware et al. 1992) or "Adult Career Quality of Life Questionnaire" (AC-QoL) (Elwick et al. 2010) were administered to evaluate the quality of life involving patients or caregivers. Moreover, the subjects completed the IPPA (Individual Prioritised Problems Assessment) (Wessels et al. 2004) first questionnaire (IPPA1) to assess the severity of the problems they expected to solve by the prescribed assistive solutions. After that, patients received different mobility APs (e.g., manual or powered wheelchairs, seating systems, walkers, hoists). Conventionally, we have used the International Standard ISO 9999:2016 as reference classification systems for assistive devices.

The study is ongoing. Currently, thirty-two patients have been evaluated at follow-up (T2) after 3–6 months of using products in the real living environment. At follow up, participants performed the same quality of life scales and IPPA second questionnaire (IPPA2) to detect how the user's expectations had been met with assistive solution received. Moreover, participants evaluated the received assistive solutions in terms of satisfaction through the QUEST questionnaire (Quebec User Evaluation of Satisfaction with Assistive Technologies) (Demers et al. 2000). In this work, we report the preliminary data on these 32 patients. Outcome assessment instruments involved: 1) perceived effectiveness of assistive mobility products evaluated by IPPA (IPPA = IPPA1-IPPA2); 2) satisfaction of the intervention by QUEST and 3) possible changes in quality of life.

3 Statistical Analysis

All statistical analyses were conducted using Jamovi software 1.6.23. Descriptive statistics included frequencies, Median and Interquartile Range (IR) for categorical variables and Mean and Standard Deviation (SD) for continuous measures. Moreover, T-tests for paired samples were calculated to investigate longitudinal changes in the primary outcome measures. Pearson correlation was used to evaluate any relationship between the outcome assessment instruments' results. A statistical threshold of $p < 0.05$ was considered statistically significant.

4 Results

The recruited subjects (N = 75) are predominantly female (M:F = 32:43) with a mean age of 74.3 years (SD = 16.7, min = 18, max = 94). At the baseline evaluation, patients showed an average score on the Barthel scale of 8.63 (SD = 4.18) and 0.78 (SD = 0.36) on the severity index of CIRS. 48% of patients (n = 36) received a bimanual self-propelled wheelchair (ISO:122203). Only ten patients have received two mobility APs.

Thirty-two patients completed the research protocol (follow-up-T2). Table 1 reports the main demographic and clinical characteristics of these patients. The subjects are predominantly females (M:F = 9:23) with a mean age of 71.7 years (SD = 19.1, min = 18, max = 94) and education near to 4 (9–13 years). The patients were classified by the International Classification of Disease (ICD-9): most of the patients (53.1% - N = 17) belonged to "Diseases of the nervous system and sense organs" (320–389) followed by 18.8% in "Musculoskeletal and Connective Tissue Diseases" (710–739), and 9.4% in "Diseases of the circulatory system" (390–459). Regarding the evaluation of health/disability status, patients showed an average score on the Barthel scale of 8.63 (SD = 3.78 – range 0–19), with one patient that showed an absence of autonomy in carrying out all everyday activities, such as bathing, transfers, mobility, stairs (Barthel score = 0) and two patients with independence in the most of daily life activities (Barthel score ≥ 15). Moreover, 28 patients (87.5%) presented at least one comorbidity, particularly hypertension (50%) and disorders in the sense organs (40.6%), musculoskeletal-skin system (93.7%) and nervous system (62.5%). However, patients exhibited a low average score of 0.78 (SD = 0.33 – range 0.23–1.46) on the severity index of CIRS.

Table 1. Clinical and demographic characteristics of the sample. N = Number, SD = Standard Deviation, M = Males, F = Female, IR = Interquartile Range, CIRS = Cumulative Illness Rating Scale, SI = Severity Index.

		Patients [N = 32]
Age (years)	Mean (SD)	71.7 (19.1)
Sex (M:F)		9:23
Education (years)	Median (IR)	4 (3–4)
Barthel total score (/20)	Mean (SD)	8.63 (3.78)
CIRS_SI	Mean (SD)	0.78 (0.33)

Most of the patients (87.5%) needed only one mobility assistive device. Specifically, 46.9% of patients (n = 15) received a bimanual self-propelled wheelchair (ISO: 122203). The other products included rollators and walking chairs (ISO: 120606 and 120609 respectively) (15.6%), motorized mobile stair climbers (ISO: 121703) (9.4%), propulsion unit for manual wheelchairs (ISO: 121809) (6.3%) and other wheelchairs (18.8%, e.g., power wheelchairs (ISO: 122306)). Patients used the prescribed mobility assistive products for 3–6 months, with a good frequency (median = 4 - a few days a week) and moderate support (median = 2 - assistance required for certain operations). Specifically, only two patients did not use the prescribed mobility assistive devices, while 37.5% used them everyday. Among the most used APs (frequency ≥ 4), the bimanual self-propelled wheelchair appeared the most utilized (47.4%), followed by rollators and walking chairs (15.8%). After the clinical interview and cognitive screening, 19 patients and 13 caregivers completed the self-evaluated questionnaires.

Interestingly, a comparison between patients that completed or not the self-evaluation questionnaires has shown the absence of significant differences in terms of number ($X^2(1) = 2.24$, $p = 0.135$) or type ($X^2(9) = 8.92$, $p = 0.445$) of prescribed APs. On the contrary, a significant difference emerges in the frequency of use and need for assistance with the first group that used more often the received APs ($p = .003$: median 5, everyday vs 3, a few days a month) and with less support ($p = .045$: median = 2, moderate vs 3, high).

As regards the quality of life, patients obtained a significant improvement ($t(18) = -2.650$, $p < .05$) in the "health change" domain of SF-36 after using assistive products. On the contrary, an aggravation appeared in "physical function" and "general health", two domains strongly influenced by numerous factors (e.g., environmental stressors). However, patients showed no significant worsening in the "role emotional", "social function", "pain", "role limitation", "energy", and "emotional" domains. In evaluating their quality of life, caregivers showed the absence of significant worsening in AC_QoL total score and domains, except for "money matter". Specifically, they obtained at T2 a mean total score of 76.31, confirming a mid-range reported quality of life. Moreover, they confirmed a mid-range reported quality of life in all domains, except "caregiving stress," in which they obtained a better result (mean = 11 ± 3.98 – the high-reported quality of life).

Figure 1 shows scores obtained by patients or caregivers in the pre-post evaluation of the perceived effectiveness of assistive mobility products evaluated by IPPA1 and IPPA2.

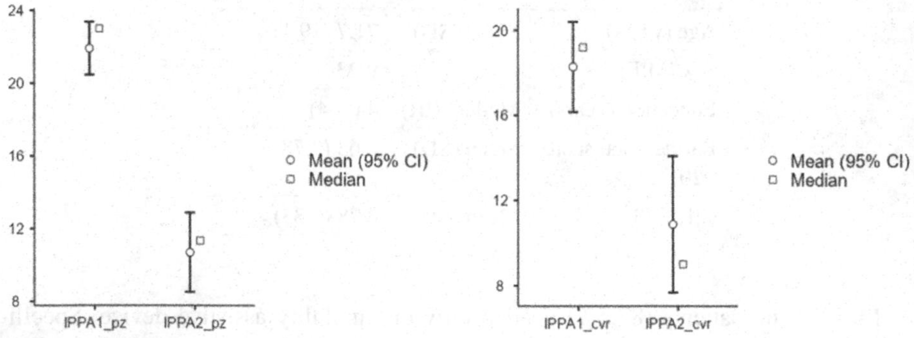

Fig. 1. Scores obtained by patients or caregivers in the IPPA scale first interview (IPPA1) and IPPA scale second interview at follow up (IPPA2). IPPA = Individual Prioritised Problems Assessment; pz = patient; cvr = caregiver

Results showed a significant difference between the IPPA first questionnaire (IPPA1) and IPPA second questionnaire (IPPA2) both for patients ($t(18) = 10.88$, $p < .001$) and caregivers ($t(12) = 4.71$, $p < .001$), underlying a good perceived effectiveness of assistive mobility products. Participants provided, in mean, lower scores for IPPA at T2 evaluation (IPPA_pz = 11.2 ± 4.5; IPPA_cvr = 7.4 ± 5.67). Interestingly, all patients underlined good perceived effectiveness of assistive mobility products, with a significant decrease of the degree of severity in problems identified at baseline evaluation. Furthermore, only one caregiver supported the presence of a slight worsening (IPPA_crv = −3).

Furthermore, all participants (patients and caregivers) evaluated the satisfaction of the intervention by QUEST, showing high scores in total score (respectively, mean = 4.61 ± 0.41 and 4.34 ± 0.60) and the evaluation of product (respectively, mean = 4.55 ± 0.47 and 4.28 ± 0.83) and service (respectively, mean = 4.75 ± 0.48 and 4.44 ±

0.53). Patients provided a high satisfaction (>4) of the intervention due to all products. Caregivers provided good scores to all products (total score ≥ 3.50), particularly bimanual self-propelled wheelchairs (mean = 4.52) and rollators and walking chairs (mean = 4.70/4.92).

Finally, no significant correlations ($p > .05$) appeared between IPPA scores, QUEST scores and frequency of use both for patients and caregivers.

5 Conclusions

The research study OMAT (Outcomes of Mobility Assistive Technology in rehabilitation pathways) developed by Fondazione Don Carlo Gnocchi fits perfectly with WHO guidelines that inserted the AT outcome among the five top priorities in AT research (Gutenbrunner et al. 2015). Over the years, several researches focused on the high rate of abandonment of the received AP due to patients' health condition improvement or worsening (Lenker et al. 2004) or failure of the assistive device to meet the patient's expectations (Federici et al. 2016). Therefore, it is clear that measuring the prosthetic intervention's effects must be carried out "on the field" after a reasonable time of use of the APs by the users in their real living environment (Salatino et al. 2016). This work proposes the preliminary results of the assessment of the impact of assistive mobility products using a model of rehabilitation path related to assistive technology interventions that includes clinical and outcome assessment instruments in addition to the standard delivery process of AT currently envisaged by the Italian national health system. In particular, the project proposes to add, after an initial multidisciplinary evaluation of patients' needs and expectations, an outcome assessment phase (follow-up phase) after an adequate period of use of the prescribed APs.

Therefore, thirty-two patients underwent a multifaceted evaluation at baseline, and after 3–6 months of use of mobility assistive devices in the real living environment to evaluate: 1) perceived effectiveness of assistive mobility products evaluated by IPPA; 2) satisfaction of the intervention by QUEST and 3) possible changes in quality of life. Our sample is heterogeneous in terms of demographic (i.e., age, sex and education) and clinical characteristics (i.e., cognitive, functional and clinical health/disability status), allowing us to evaluate outcomes, including different possible clinical conditions that could need assistive mobility intervention. Most of the patients (87.5%) only required one mobility assistive device, particularly bimanual self-propelled wheelchair (46.9%), rollators and walking chairs, motorized mobile stair climbers, propulsion unit for manual wheelchairs and other wheelchairs. Overall, patients used the prescribed mobility assistive products for 3–6 months, with a good frequency and moderate support. Preliminary results of the OMAT research study showed the positive impact of assistive mobility products in all primary outcome aspects. Most of the participants (96.88%) supported the good perceived effectiveness of assistive mobility products evaluated by IPPA, showing a lower degree of severity in problems identified at baseline evaluation. Only one caregiver supported the presence of a slight worsening. Moreover, patients and caregivers showed an improved quality of life as evaluated by self-questionnaires. Specifically, patients obtained a significant improvement in the "health change" domain of SF-36 after using assistive products, and caregivers obtained a better result in the "caregiving stress" domain. Furthermore, the absence of significant worsening appeared in other quality of life domains (e.g., social functions, pain, energy), except for "physical function" and "general health", two domains strongly influenced by numerous factors (e.g., environmental stressors). In light of these results, it will be important to evaluate the functional and clinical status of the patient also at the follow-up to investigate any other conditions that may occur in everyday life. These promising results in improving quality of life and significant change in problems identified at baseline evaluation supported the need to consider the APs a primary component to maintain or enhance the person's functioning (launch of the GATE initiative "Global Cooperation on Assistive Health). Finally, the preliminary data showed that all participants evaluated the overall intervention as highly satisfactory, both in terms of product and service. Interestingly, patients provided a high satisfaction (>4) of the intervention due to all products.

Overall, the preliminary results of the OMAT research study showed the applicability of selected outcome assessment instruments in the clinical context and a positive impact of assistive mobility products in terms of perceived effectiveness, satisfaction of the intervention and quality of life both for patients and caregivers.

In conclusion, the model of rehabilitation path in the field of mobility, which includes an initial evaluation of patients' needs and expectations and an outcome assessment after a period of use of prescribed APs in everyday settings, could allow to overcome the lack of comprehensive monitoring mechanisms for assistive technology in the WHO European Region (World Health Organization 2021), also going beyond the standard delivery process of AT currently envisaged by Italian National Health Service.

Further studies will be conducted to replicate these promising results in a larger sample.

Acknowledgement. This work was supported and funded by the Italian Ministry of Health - Ricerca Corrente.

References

Demers, L., Weiss-Lambrou, R., Ska, B.: Item analysis of the Quebec user evaluation of satisfaction with assistive technology (QUEST). Assist. Technol. **12**(2), 96–105 (2000)

Elwick, H., Joseph, S., Becker, S., Becker, F.: Manual for the Adult Carer Quality of life Questionnaire (AC-QoL). The Princess Royal Trust for Carers, London (2010)

Federici, S., Meloni, F., Borsci, S.: The abandonment of assistive technology in Italy: a survey of users of the national health service. Eur. J. Phys. Rehabil. Med. **52**(4), 516–526 (2016)

Folstein, M.F., Folstein, S.E., McHugh, P.R.: "Mini-mental state": a practical method for grading the cognitive state of patients for the clinician. J. Psychiatr. Res. **12**(3), 189–198 (1975)

Gutenbrunner, C., Negrini, S., Kiekens, C., Zampolini, M., Nugraha, B.: The Global Disability Action Plan 2014–2021 of the World Health Organisation (WHO): a major step towards better health for all people with disabilities. Chance and challenge for Physical and Rehabilitation Medicine (PRM). Eur. J. Phys. Rehabil. Med. **51**(1), 1–4 (2015)

Lenker, J.A., Paquet, V.L.: A new conceptual model for assistive technology outcomes research and practice. Assist. Technol. **16**(1), 1–10 (2004)

Linn, B.S., Linn, M.W., Gurel, L.E.E.: Cumulative illness rating scale. J. Am. Geriatr. Soc. **16**(5), 622–626 (1968)

Mahoney, F.I.: Functional evaluation: the Barthel index. Md. State Med. J. **14**(2), 61–65 (1965)

Measso, G., et al.: The mini-mental state examination: normative study of an Italian random sample. Dev. Neuropsychol. **9**(2), 77–85 (1993)

National Center for Health Statistics (US), & Council on Clinical Classifications: The International classification of diseases, 9th revision, clinical modification: ICD-9-CM (Vol. 2). US Department of Health and Human Services, Public Health Service, Health Care Financing Administration (1980)

Salatino, C., Andrich, R., Converti, R.M., Saruggia, M.: An observational study of powered wheelchair provision in Italy. Assist. Technol. **28**(1), 41–52 (2016)

Salatino, C., Pigini, L., Andrich, R.: How to measure the impact of assistive technology solutions on the person's quality of life? In: ACM International Conference Proceeding Series, pp. 238–242 (2018)

Ware Jr., J.E., Sherbourne, C.D.: The MOS 36-item short-form health survey (SF-36): I. Conceptual framework and item selection. Med. Care, 473–483 (1992)

Wessels, R., et al.: IPPA: individually prioritised problem assessment. Technol. Disabil. **14**(3), 141–145 (2002)

World Health Organization: Consultation on assistive technology in the WHO European Region: meeting report: virtual meeting hosted by the WHO Regional Office for Europe, 12 October 2021 (No. WHO/EURO: 2021-4207-43966-61970). World Health Organization. Regional Office for Europe (2021)

Correction to: Computers Helping People with Special Needs

Klaus Miesenberger, Georgios Kouroupetroglou,
Katerina Mavrou, Roberto Manduchi,
Mario Covarrubias Rodriguez, and Petr Penáz

Correction to:
K. Miesenberger et al. (Eds.): *Computers Helping People with Special Needs*, LNCS 13342, https://doi.org/10.1007/978-3-031-08645-8

Chapter 35
In an older version of this paper, Acknowledgment section with funding was not given by author. This has been added.

Chapter 39
The chapter "Gauging Awareness of Accessibility in Open Educational Resources" was previously published non-open access. It has now been changed to open access under a CC BY 4.0 license and the copyright holder updated to 'The Author(s)'. The book has also been updated with this change.

Chapter 41
In the originally published version of this paper, some of the author names did not include special characters, in addition there were typing errors in two of the names. This has been corrected.

Chapter 63
In an older version of this paper, Acknowledgment section with funding was not given by author. This has been added.

The updated original version of these chapters can be found at
https://doi.org/10.1007/978-3-031-08645-8_35
https://doi.org/10.1007/978-3-031-08645-8_39
https://doi.org/10.1007/978-3-031-08645-8_41
https://doi.org/10.1007/978-3-031-08645-8_63

K. Miesenberger et al. (Eds.): ICCHP-AAATE 2022, LNCS 13342, p. C1, 2022.
https://doi.org/10.1007/978-3-031-08645-8_64

Author Index

Printed in the United States
by Baker & Taylor Publisher Services

Printed in the United States
by Baker & Taylor Publisher Services